BLACK ATHENA REVISITED

BLACK ATHENA
REVISITED

EDITED BY

Mary R. Lefkowitz

&

Guy MacLean Rogers

THE UNIVERSITY OF NORTH CAROLINA PRESS

Chapel Hill & London

© 1996
The University of North Carolina Press
All rights reserved
Manufactured in the United States of America

The paper in this book meets the guidelines
for permanence and durability of the Committee on
Production Guidelines for Book Longevity of the
Council on Library Resources.

Library of Congress Cataloging-in-Publication Data
Black Athena revisited / edited by Mary R. Lefkowitz
and Guy MacLean Rogers.
p.   cm.
Includes bibliographical references and index.
ISBN 0–8078–2246–9 (alk. paper). —
ISBN 0–8078–4555–8 (pbk.: alk. paper)
1. Greece — Civilization — Egyptian influences.
2. Greece — Civilization — Phoenician influences.
3. Greece — Civilization — To 146 B.C.
I. Lefkowitz, Mary R., 1935– .
II. Rogers, Guy MacLean.
DF78.B54   1996
938—dc20   95-8903
CIP

00   99   98   97   96   5   4   3   2   1

In Memoriam

ARNALDO MOMIGLIANO

CONTENTS

MAPS

PREFACE

In 1885 the professor of Greek at University College, Dublin, wrote to a colleague in Oxford asking him to supply information about possible prehistoric connections between Egypt and Greece. The professor was not an archaeologist specializing in early history; his field was Greek literature, and the texts he studied were written long after the remote period he had now become interested in. Couldn't myth and etymology provide a key to lines of influence otherwise unknown?

> . . . the enquiry that ought to be made is when did this Egyptian colonisation of Crete etc. take place. It seems to be mixed with the Phoenician, not altogether opposed to it. This wd. then seem to be at the Hyksos period. (I remark also that the legend of Isis connects her with Phoenicia).
>
> I find Nefert in a female proper name and now suggest Aphrodite = Nefrat-isi.

According to the professor's biographer, these "wild linguistic surmises" and "observations on obscure etymological instances" were a means of releasing "some pent-up poetic, assertive side of himself" (White 1992, 413–14). It is in fact for his poetry, and not for his scholarly investigations, that this professor is still remembered: his name was Gerard Manley Hopkins. Hopkins's theories and speculations have long since been forgotten, and justifiably so. But their existence offers proof of how tantalizing such inquiries can be to amateurs who have some knowledge of and interest in ancient Greek civilization. Hopkins bombarded his Oxford friend for months with questions about Egyptian myth and language, but apparently he never received any confirmation of the conjectures that so tantalized him.

Few professional classicists in the 1980s would have imagined that the English-speaking world would take such wide interest in another amateur attempt—this time much more systematic and extensive—to discover the true extent of Greece's debt to Egypt and the civilizations of the Near East. Nonetheless Martin Bernal's *Black Athena I: the Fabrication of Ancient Greece* has enjoyed considerable popular success, and has been widely discussed and reviewed in scholarly literature as well. More people have heard of *Black Athena* than of books like Walter Burkert's *The Orientalizing Revolution: Near Eastern Influence on Greek Culture in the Early Archaic Age* (1992). But then Burkert is a professional who draws carefully limited conclusions and deliberately concentrates on a particular set of evidence. Bernal's field of inquiry is more extensive, and he is much more willing to speculate and to make imaginative leaps.

Such passion and daring accounts for some of Bernal's remarkable impact. Like Hopkins's, his speculations about Egypt and Greece convey a determination at once poetic and assertive. He is the armchair archaeologist par excellence, the dauntless explorer who travels backward in time to uncover what the experts with all their learning and prejudices could never find. In an academic world where few scholars are willing to move outside their areas of concentration, Bernal appears to be familiar with the major issues in a wide number of highly specialized and complex fields.

But there is a more fundamental reason why Bernal's project has won so many adherents, and that is the appeal of iconoclasm in an age where everything traditional has been questioned and found wanting. It is not at all coincidental that Bernal's first volume appeared at the same time that academics were beginning to demand major changes in the "canon" of works and cultures studied in universities in the United States. In humanities disciplines, much that is written by Europeans, and especially European males, is regarded with suspicion. If it is true (and many people seem not to doubt it) that scholars and writers consciously and unconsciously promote in their works the values of their societies, all literature and history written before the present may be regarded with suspicion and even with hostility for its limited and noninclusive picture of the world.

In the process of an investigation with such high motives, it is only natural that the work of ancient historians and of classicists should come under special scrutiny. The study of Greek and Latin language and literature is considered to be the most traditional of disciplines, as a legacy from the European past when the study of the "classics" was synonymous with education. Although these subjects occupy only a tiny portion of today's university curriculum, they are also professed almost exclusively by men and women of European background, and the majority of these, particularly in the past, have been at least nominally Christians. What discipline would it be more natural to suspect, if not of overly racist motives, of the kind of racism and elitism that is perhaps unconsciously practiced even by educated people?

Ideally the person best qualified to undertake such an investigation would need to come from outside the field, so that she would not feel obliged to defend her teachers, or her colleagues, or indeed anything she had learned or currently was teaching. Similarly, if we accept the notion that all scholarship is culturally determined, it would be more effective if she came from an ethnic group not well represented in the field. Martin Bernal perhaps does not have all of these "ideal" qualifications, but in addition to great energy and enthusiasm for his work, he has the very real advantage of being able to look at the ancient Mediterranean world with the fresh perspective of someone who has studied in depth a non-European culture, a knowledge shared by few if any of the classicists and historians whose values he is investigating.

It is this outsider's stance of moral superiority that gives the *Black Athena* project its particular appeal in today's academic world, and it is this sense of mission that is primarily responsible for the generally favorable reception it has had from scholars and writers outside the fields Bernal discusses. His work has also been taken up enthusiastically by certain Afrocentrist historians, who argue that European scholars have drastically underestimated the extent of Greece's debt to Egypt. In this way the influence of Bernal's work has affected the school as well as the university curriculum. For example, in the new social sciences section of the African Puerto-Rican Centric Curriculum Guide of the Camden (N.J.) school system, Professor Molefi Kete Asante states: "A recent book by Martin Bernal, *Black Athena*, establishes the fact that the name of the greatest Greek city, Athens, is also from Africa" (Asante 1993b, 119).

In this volume several of us will show why Bernal's etymology of Athens is highly uncertain and improbable, intrinsically no more persuasive than Hopkins's attempt to derive Aphrodite from Nefertiti. Rather, as we shall see, none of Bernal's other etymologies can offer a real challenge to what linguists have long since documented and maintained: that Greek is basically an Indo-European language, incorporating some loan words from its neighbors, primarily in the Near East. Several of us demonstrate why Bernal has not shown, and in fact no one can show, that European scholars of antiquity and of linguistics have participated, even unwittingly, in an attempt to make the Greek language into something that it is not. We show why it is a mistake to want to revive (in revised form) the "Ancient Model" of ancient history, because ancient notions of Egyptian origins were based on surmise and misinformation. We suggest why Bernal's term "Aryan Model" is misleading, and perhaps deliberately chosen to imply racial or religious prejudice where none in fact exists. Those of us who have studied Bernal's claims about European scholarship in the eighteenth and nineteenth centuries believe that he has considerably overstated his case. Although there were and are some scholars who bring to their research an explicitly political agenda, European scholars in both centuries characteristically display such a diversity of opinion and disagreement with one another that one cannot accurately speak of models or schools of scholarship (Turner 1989, 108–9).

We also take issue with other major contentions made in *Black Athena*, and in Bernal's other writings on antiquity. We discuss why ancient myths cannot be understood as history, and why even the writing of history in antiquity was affected by unstated beliefs and preconceptions. We do not believe that the influence of Egypt on Greece was nearly so profound as Bernal suggests. There is no reason to think that modern scholars have sought to minimize the importance of such cultural contact and correspondences as there were. We examine the archaeological data, and the surviving evidence for Egyptian elements in Greek philosophy and science, and express the wish that Bernal had sought instead to describe some of the important lines of influence on Greece from the Near East. In addition, we suggest why the notion of a "Black Athena" is at best misleading. On the basis of the available evidence, we believe that it can be shown that the ancient Egyptians regarded themselves as ethnically distinct from other African peoples, as well as from the peoples of the Near East and of Europe: that although they are "people of color" by modern definition, in their own minds and in the minds of the ancient Greeks they were a different nation from the Ethiopians.

The authors of the essays in this book are young and old, black and white, male and female, European and American, and, within the United States, from all parts of the country. Together or separately we present no homogeneous point of view. We are united only in our respect for the significance of the questions Bernal raises in *Black Athena*, and in our conviction that our criticisms of it are offered in spirit of scholarly endeavor, which must always be to get at the truth, no matter how painful our discoveries may be to any or all of us. Even though most ancient historians and classicists have been critical of many aspects of Bernal's work, all of us have been stimulated to think creatively and seriously about the questions Bernal has raised, and we are grateful to him for raising them. To have refused to reexamine these issues would have been a sign that we were as Eurocentric and elitist as our critics imagine us to be.

The Editors have chosen the essays in this book from a large and interesting literature about *Black Athena*. Our first aim has been to cover as many different aspects of Bernal's large project as possible, including especially some topics that have not yet been covered in sufficient detail, such as science and linguistics. We were also eager to offer several different perspectives on the vexed question of "race." Several essays specifically consider the evidence for cultural diffusion, and/or invasion, especially from Egypt and the Near East. Others deal with the question whether scholars of antiquity, past and present, have suppressed evidence about the non-European elements of Greek culture. Virtually every essay in the book has something to say about how to read the scattered and difficult cultural data that have come down to us, whether in literary, linguistic, or archaeological format. In short, we have tried to provide the information our readers will need if they wish to get a full and accurate impression of the complex web of cultural influences during the period when Greek civilization developed.

The organization of the book is roughly chronological and geographical. After an introduction that attempts to describe the cultural significance of Bernal's work, we begin with Egypt, the earliest civilization to have had an important influence on Greece, and then move to the question of ethnic identity: Who were the Egyptians? Who did *they* think they were? After Egypt, we turn to the Near East. To suggest the complexity of the general question of cultural "debt" within the context of the ancient Mediterranean world, we look at "borrowing" in two general areas, language and science. We then turn to Greece itself, and finally to the historiographical questions that Bernal raises in his first volume, and which underlie his whole discussion: To what extent does myth represent history? How far did European scholars in the eighteenth and nineteenth centuries misrepresent the extent of Greece's cultural links to the older civilizations in her neighborhood? In a general conclusion, we try to suggest some of the reasons why our assessment is so often different from Bernal's.

Because not all the contributions in this book were written expressly for this collection, we cannot pretend to offer our readers the seamless presentation that they would expect from a volume that was specially commissioned for the purpose, or from the papers of a particular conference. Some of the essays were originally written for the general public; these have been revised and edited for this volume, and wherever possible we have placed these at the head of a subdivision (Lefkowitz, Bard, Vermeule, Coleman). Most of the other contributions were originally intended for more specialized audiences (Brace, Palter, Tritle, Hall), but all have been revised and updated for this volume. There are practical reasons for the considerable differences in length and density that remain. In a topic so highly charged as race, we think it important to offer our readers all the particulars of the evidence. We also have sought to offer a detailed discussion of the claims made about ancient science by Bernal and other writers, because of the importance of that subject in the school curriculum. We have included a detailed discussion of Bernal's treatment of the eighteenth century, because his claims about European scholarship have been eagerly believed by writers who seek to find reasons to be critical of traditional scholarship (e.g., Rabinowitz 1993, 5; Davidson 1994b, 332–33).

The Editors thank the many friends and colleagues who have helped us in the process of collecting these essays and preparing them for publication. In particular we thank the authors themselves, some for taking the time and trouble to rework previously printed essays, others for writing completely new articles dealing with issues that had not yet been explored in the earlier literature about *Black Athena*. We received valuable help and encouragement from several scholars who had hoped to contribute to this volume but who could not in the end manage to meet our rather stringent deadline.

We are indebted to Lewis Bateman of the University of North Carolina Press for suggesting that we put this collection together, and for his help in choosing what was to go in it. Laura Oaks improved the volume by her thoughtful reading and attention to detail. We thank Molly Levine of Howard University for generously allowing us to use the bibliography she had assembled, and the Ford Foundation and Wellesley College for grants to support editorial assistance. We are particularly grateful to Beatrice Cody and Stephanie O'Hara; their good sense and hard work have improved every aspect of the book. Our thanks also to Richard Cody, Kelly King, Hugh Lloyd Jones, Barbara Nathanson, and Mark Rogers for their advice, encouragement, and technical support.

M.R.L.

G.M.R.

September 1995

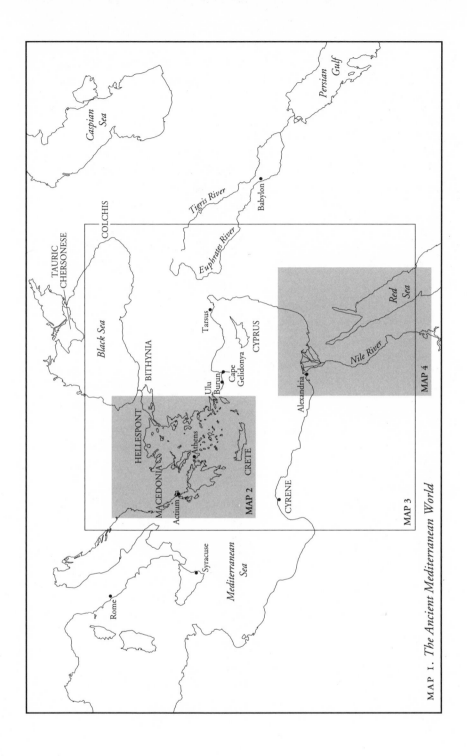

MAP 1. *The Ancient Mediterranean World*

MAP 2. *The Aegean*

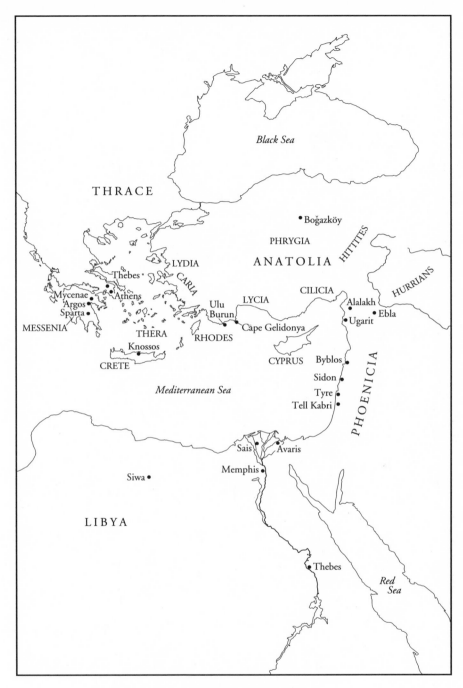

Black Sea

THRACE

• Boğazköy

PHRYGIA

ANATOLIA

HITTITES

HURRIANS

LYDIA

CARIA

Thebes •

Mycenae •
Argos •
Sparta •

Athens •

CILICIA

LYCIA

Ulu
Burun

Alalakh
•

Ebla
•

Ugarit
•

MESSENIA

THERA

RHODES

Cape Gelidonya

Knossos
•

CRETE

CYPRUS

Byblos
•

Sidon
•

Tyre •

Tell Kabri •

PHOENICIA

Mediterranean Sea

Sais •

• Avaris

Memphis •

Siwa •

LIBYA

Thebes
•

Red
Sea

MAP 3. *The Eastern Mediterranean*

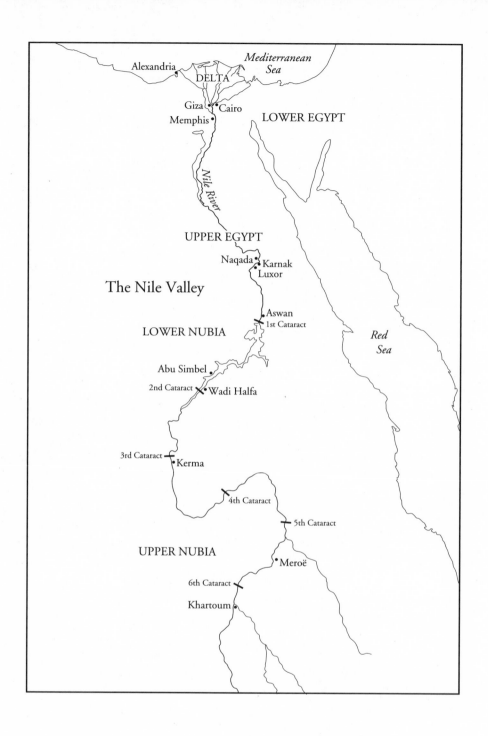

Alexandria
Mediterranean Sea
DELTA
Giza• •Cairo
Memphis•
LOWER EGYPT
Nile River
UPPER EGYPT
Naqada• •Karnak
Luxor
The Nile Valley
•Aswan
1st Cataract
LOWER NUBIA
Red Sea
Abu Simbel•
2nd Cataract ✕•Wadi Halfa
3rd Cataract ✕•Kerma
4th Cataract
5th Cataract
UPPER NUBIA
•Meroë
6th Cataract
Khartoum•

ANCIENT EGYPTIAN CHRONOLOGY
Frank J. Yurco

(All dates are B.C.E.)

PREDYNASTIC (PREHISTORIC) ERA (CA. 5500–3100)

Nubia

ca. 3800–3100	A-Group
3100–2680	Terminal A-Group

Upper Egypt

ca. 5500–4500	Badarian
ca. 4500–3800	Naqada I
ca. 3800–3300	Naqada II
3300–3100	Naqada III (Protoliterate Period, earliest kings)

Lower Egypt

ca. 5500–4500	Fayyum A–B
ca. 5500–4000	Merimde
ca. 4000–3500	El-Omari A–B
3500–3100	Maadi, Buto, Sais

DYNASTIC EGYPT (3100–30)

Archaic Period–Old Kingdom (3100–2234)

3100–2750	Dynasties I–II, Archaic Era
2750–2234	Old Kingdom, Dynasties III–VIII

First Intermediate Period (2234–2040)

2235–2040	Dynasties I–X (Heracleopolis)
2134–1991	Dynasties XI (Thebes)

Middle Kingdom (2040–1674)

2040–1991	Dynasty XI
1991–1786	Dynasty XII
1786–1674	Dynasty XIII

Second Intermediate Period (1674–1566)

1674–1566	Hyksos Dominion
1674–1566	Dynasty XV (Hyksos overlords)

Dynasties XIV and XVI (minor rulers, Hyksos and Egyptians, subject to Hyksos)
Dynasty XVII (Thebes, vassal to Hyksos)

New Kingdom (1566–1080)

1574–1293	Dynasty XVIII [alt. 1574–1321]
1293–1184	Dynasty XIX [alt. 1321–1184]
1184–1080	Dynasty XX

Renaissance Era (1080–1070)

Third Intermediate Period (1070–663)

1070–945	Dynasty XXI (Tanis; high priests of Amun rule Thebes)
945–712	Dynasty XXII (Tanis)
805–712	Dynasty XXIII (Leontopolis)
718–712	Dynasty XXIV (Memphis)
712–663	Kushite Dominion
712–663	Dynasty XXV
671–663	Assyrian Invasion

Late Period (663–30)

663–525	Dynasty XXVI (Saite)
525–405	Persian Occupation, Dynasty XXVII

Egyptian Independence (405–343)

405–399	Dynasty XXVIII
399–380	Dynasty XXIX
380–343	Dynasty XXX
343–332	Persian Reconquest
332	Macedonian Conquest
332–323	Alexander the Great
323–30	Dynasty XXXI (Ptolemies)

Sources: Royal Annals, Dynasties I–V; Turin Canon, Dynasties I–XIX; Demotic Chronicle, Dynasties XXVIII–XXX; Manetho, Chronology, Dynasties I–XXXI; Dynasty XI and later, based upon Parker's Sothic Date calculations. First Intermediate Period, based upon Klaus Baer, unpublished notes. Volcanic eruptions of Thera (1628) and Hekla III (1159) provide additional anchors, as do cross-dates to Mesopotamian cultures and later Western Asian cultures.

(All dates are B.C.E.)

3000	Minoan culture on Crete begins
1600	Mycenaean palace culture in Greece
1450	Mycenaeans take over palaces on Crete
1200	Destruction of the Mycenaean sites in Greece
1184	Destruction of Troy, according to later Greek writers
1100	Dorian invasions begin
1050	Ionian migration to Aegean islands and coast of Asia Minor begins
776	First Olympic Games
683	Athenian archon list begins
594	Reforms of Solon at Athens
508	Reforms of Cleisthenes at Athens; popular government begins
490	First Persian invasion of mainland Greece
480	Second Persian invasion of mainland Greece; battles of Thermopylae and Salamis
431–404	Second Peloponnesian War; defeat of Athens
399	Trial and execution of Socrates at Athens
371–362	Hegemony of Thebes in Greece
338	Philip II of Macedon defeats Athens and Thebes at Battle of Chaeronea
323	Death of Alexander the Great

INTRODUCTION

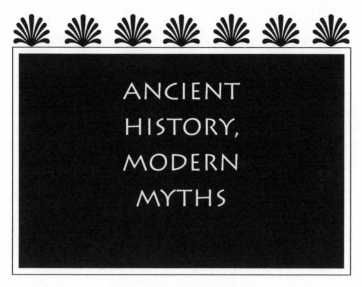

ANCIENT HISTORY, MODERN MYTHS

Mary R. Lefkowitz

ARE ANCIENT HISTORIANS RACIST?

As the principal text in our second-year Greek course I prefer to use Plato's *Apology*, his account of the trial of Socrates. I stick with this traditional text, even though it is hard for students who have had time to learn only the bare essentials of Greek grammar, because it deals with so many matters that are central to our civilization. Should a man be condemned for his beliefs, if they differ from the majority's? Why did the majority make a judgment that is now universally regarded as unfair? How could Socrates think that no man would willingly commit an evil act? Important questions, all; but several years ago I had a student who seemed to regard virtually everything I said about Socrates with hostility. Before she graduated she explained why she had been suspicious of me and my classes: her instructor in another course had told her that Socrates (as suggested by the flat nose in some portrait sculptures) was black. The instructor had also taught that classicists universally refuse to mention the African origins of Socrates because they do not want their students to know that the so-called legacy of ancient Greece had been stolen from Egypt.

Further study persuaded this student that most of what she had heard in this other course could not have been strictly accurate. Because Socrates was an Athenian citizen, he must have had Athenian parents; and since foreigners couldn't become naturalized Athenian citizens, he must have come from the same ethnic background as every other Athenian. Even though Greeks in Socrates' day did not pay much attention to skin color or more generally to physical appearance, they did care about nationality. If Socrates had been a foreigner, from Africa or any other place, he would not have been an Athenian citizen. It was as simple as that.[1]

Meanwhile another student wrote to complain that we had sponsored, as part of our Bad Ancient History Film series, a screening of the film *Cleopatra*, starring Elizabeth Taylor. The student had grounds for complaint; Taylor's sexpot Cleopatra certainly had little in common with the charming, manipulative queen whom Plutarch describes, the woman who spoke many languages and captivated everyone she knew with her conversation. But no, this student was indignant for a different reason: Elizabeth Taylor is, after all, a white woman, whereas Cleopatra was black. We did our best to persuade this student, on the basis of Cleopatra's ancestry (and her name), that Cleopatra was a member of the Macedonian Greek dynasty that had imposed itself on Egypt, and that despite her fluency in the Egyptian language, the style of her dress, and the luxury of her court, she was in origin a Greek.[2]

Classicists in the late modern world have more than enough grounds for paranoia. We are reminded daily that our subject is useless, irrelevant, and boring—all the things that, in our opinion, it is not. But now a new set of charges has been added. Not only students, but also the many academic acolytes of Martin Bernal's influential theories about "the Afroasiatic roots of Western civilization," and Bernal himself, ask us to acknowledge that we have been racists and liars, the perpetrators of a vast intellectual and cultural cover-up, or at the very least the suppressors of an African past that, until our students and our colleagues began to mention it, we had ourselves known nothing about. Had our teachers deceived us, and their teachers deceived them?

Classicists should be perfectly willing to ask themselves these questions, because we know, at least as well as our critics, that much of our so-called knowledge of the past is based on educated guesswork and sensible conjectures. In my own lifetime I have seen many histories and many textbooks rewritten to take account of new finds. Before the Mycenaean Linear B syllabary was deciphered in 1952, many scholars believed that people who lived in Greece and Crete between the sixteenth and twelfth centuries B.C.E. spoke a language other than Greek. When the tablets written in Linear B script were deciphered, however, it became clear that Greek had been spoken in settlements such as Mycenae and Knossos. That is, the world described by Homer was in some respects real.

If we had once thought that Homer's world was imaginary, it is conceivable that our notions of the origins of the Greeks might also be based on uncertain premises. Before it was known that in the second millennium the inhabitants of Mycenae and other settlements spoke Greek, students of the ancient world imagined that there was a kernel of truth in the Greek myths about the invasion of Greek-speaking tribes, known as the Dorians, after the twelfth century. Some textbooks still follow the outline of the Greek myth of the "races" of man, which tells of a distinct separation between the Bronze (Mycenaean) Age and the Iron (Dorian) Age, whereas in actual fact there seems to have been considerable cultural and linguistic continuity from the twelfth century to the eighth century B.C.E. And until our own century, relatively little importance was attributed to the influence of Semitic peoples, such as the Phoenicians, on the civilization in mainland Greece. Until very recently, moreover, the Greek alphabet was regarded as a relatively late invention, coming into general use only after the beginning of the eighth century B.C.E. Now Semiticists insist that the shape of the letters shows that the Greek alphabet was modeled on the characters of a much earlier version of the Phoenician syllabary, perhaps from the tenth century, perhaps even earlier (Lloyd-Jones 1992, 55–56).

If classicists managed to get all these things wrong, isn't it possible that they have ignored Egyptian and African elements in Greek culture? It is possible. Still, there is the slightly touchy matter of the intention behind this alleged ignorance. The students who believed that Socrates and Cleopatra were black assumed that we had deliberately tried to deny them the truth, that we had used (or misused) history as yet another means of enforcing European political domination on Africa. In their view, classicists are propagandists from the White European Ministry of Classical Culture. In our view, classicists are historians who try to look at the past critically, without prejudice of any kind, so far as humanly possible. If classicists have indeed misinterpreted the facts about the Greeks' past, they certainly have not done so willingly. I know that I run the risk, in the aftermath of Foucault and poststructuralism, of seeming naive in my belief that some kind of objectivity is possible, but it is my view that classicists and ancient historians would have been only too delighted to discover the true answer, whatever it was, *if it were possible to know it.*

No responsible historian of antiquity would deny that it is possible to misinterpret the facts, either through ignorance or malice; but the open discussion of scholarly research has made it rather difficult to conceal or to manufacture facts without arousing the skepticism or the scorn of colleagues. There are, after all, canons of evidence and standards of argument. For the student of ancient history, moreover, it is often the case that certainty is impossible. The classicist frequently deals with sources that are partial and scattershot and essentially obscure. To speak with complete confidence, without any tincture of doubt, about some of the great controversies is to betray a misunderstanding of what classicists do.

Still, the absence of certainty does not mean that one interpretation is as valid as any other. Probabilities and plausibilities matter; and when the evidence is less precise or less tangible than we would like it to be, some explanations are still more likely than others. Thus, if Socrates and his parents had had dark skin and other African racial features, some of his contemporaries would have been likely to mention it, because this, and not just his eccentric ideas about the gods, and the voice that spoke to him alone, would have distinguished him from the rest of the Athenians. Unless, of course, all the rest of the Athenians also had African origins; but then why are they not depicted as Africans in their art? (Snowden 1970, 1–99).

This distinction appears to have been lost in the din of the great Afrocentrism debate. For this reason, it cannot be too much emphasized: to show influence is not to show origin. One people or culture may introduce its ideas or its symbols or its artifacts to another people or culture, but the difference between the peoples and the cultures may remain. Borrowings, even when they can be demonstrated, are only borrowings. They do not, in most cases, amount to a transformation of identity. And even when borrowings do overwhelm a people or a culture sufficiently to transform it, they still shed little light on the actual historical beginnings of the borrowers.

The evidence of Egyptian *influence* on certain aspects of Greek culture is plain and undeniable, though surely it must be pointed out that other Mediterranean civilizations also had important influences on Greek (and Egyptian) culture, so that the picture of who came first, and who took from or loaned what to whom, is anything but clear. But the evidence of Egyptian *origins* for Greek culture is another thing entirely. The principal reason that students of antiquity have not given the Africans or the Egyptians primary credit for the achievements of Greek civilization is that Greek culture was separate and different from Egyptian or African culture. It was divided from them by language and by genealogy.

AFROCENTRIC ANCIENT "HISTORY"

Given the nature of the evidence, or rather the lack of it, it is not at all surprising that modern scholars hold many conflicting opinions about the true origins of the Greeks and their civilization. But the situation is further complicated by the tendency of all modern cultures to make the Greeks like themselves, or at least to give priority to the aspects of Greek culture that they themselves most admire. In grade school we were taught about Athenian democracy, but not about the widespread slavery that supported it, or the other governmental systems in Greece that coexisted alongside it, including some fairly brutal tyrannies. Democracy and the other accomplishments of Greek civilization, however real or imaginary, remain so precious to us that virtually every modern civilization has wanted to claim them for itself.

It was inevitable, therefore, that black peoples in the English-speaking countries of this continent, as they developed a sense of their own identity, would want to show that they had a stake in the cultural legacy of ancient Greece. Marcus Garvey (1887–1940), the founder of the Universal Negro Improvement Association, began to study history while he was a teenager in Jamaica, and he used his knowledge of Egyptian and African history to help promote racial emancipation. As Tony Martin writes in *Race First*, his biography of Garvey: "History, like everything else for Garvey, was a subject to be used for the furtherance of racial emancipation. He used history first to establish a grievance—to show that the black man had been wronged" (1986, 83). Garvey thought of history as a means of instilling self-confidence in a people who had lost faith in themselves and had been compelled to lose touch with their past. In his essay "Who and What Is a Negro?" (1923), Garvey wrote:

> The white world has always tried to rob and discredit us of our history. . . . Every student of history, of impartial mind, knows that the Negro once ruled the world, when white men were savages and barbarians living in caves; that thousands of Negro professors at that time taught in the universities in Alexandria, then the seat of learning; that ancient Egypt gave the world civilization and that Greece and Rome have robbed Egypt of her arts and letters, and taken all the credit to themselves. (Garvey 1986, 2:19; T. Martin 1986, 84)

Garvey's claims are not supported by the citation of any archaeological or linguistic data. It was not his purpose to assess the evidence objectively. He was not a historian; he had a use for the past. He needed the past to show that it was not the fault of black people that they had no great historical achievements to look back on, because European whites had conspired to steal the credit for all the great achievements of past civilizations:

> Out of cold old Europe these white men came,
> From caves, dens and holes, without any fame,
> Eating their dead's flesh and sucking their blood,
> Relics of the Mediterranean flood;
> Literature, science and art they stole,
> After Africa had measured each pole,
> Asia taught them what great learning was,
> Now they frown on what the Coolie does.
> (Garvey, as quoted by Martin 1986, 81–82)

Contemporaries like W. E. B. Du Bois objected to Garvey's methods (Martin 1986, 273–74); but the theory of white conspiracy survived him, and it was explored by other writers, particularly in recent years. By now it has developed into what amounts to a new philosophy of black history. The post-Garvey school of historians objects to the way that Europeans have discredited the

African contribution, and more generally to the European methods of distinguishing fact from fiction. According to Molefi Kete Asante, the chair of the African American Studies Department at Temple University and the author of *Kemet, Afrocentricity and Knowledge*, black historians finally have been freed from dependence on "Eurocentric frames of reference." In Asante's opinion, the scholar who has done most to release Afrocentric historians from this dependency is the Senegalese historian Cheikh Anta Diop (Asante 1990, v–vii, 5).

In *The African Origin of Civilization*, an English translation of a work published in French in 1967, Diop claimed that Europeans have consistently falsified evidence that suggests that the Egyptians were black-skinned. He traces Egyptian influence on Greece back to prehistoric times, claiming that Cecrops (a half-snake/half-man whom Athenians themselves regarded as indigenous) came to Attica from Egypt and that Danaus (who, according to the Greeks, was of Greek descent) taught the Greeks agriculture and metallurgy. According to Diop, Greek mythology reflects the resentment of the Indo-Europeans against this cultural domination. Cadmus was driven out of Thebes; Orestes' murder of his mother Clytemnestra celebrates the triumph of patriarchy over matriarchy; Aeneas rejects and abandons Dido. The white world rejected the ideas of other cultures as soon as it could—and "this is the meaning of the *Aeneid*."[3]

Another influential Afrocentric work appeared in the 1950s: George G. M. James's *Stolen Legacy* (1954). This book offers a detailed account of how Greek philosophers derived most of their doctrines from the secret Egyptian mysteries said to be preserved in Masonic cult: "the term Greek philosophy, to begin with, is a misnomer, for there is no such philosophy in existence" (1). James claims that the basic doctrines in Aristotle's *De Anima* were based on the Egyptian *Book of the Dead*.[4] On the basis of anecdotes related by the gossipy ancient biographer Diogenes Laertius, James concludes (107, 109) that Plato stole the ideas for his *Republic* and *Timaeus* from other Greek philosophers. Thus Plato is doubly unreliable: he stole his ideas from Greeks who in turn stole them from the Egyptians.

James suggests various ways in which the knowledge of the Egyptian mysteries could have been brought to Greece from Egypt. Certain Greek wise men studied there, such as Solon and Pythagoras. Because Aristotle had been his tutor, Alexander the Great gave the philosopher the money that he needed to buy books for his Academy in Athens. Other Afrocentric scholars have gone farther, implicating Aristotle in the takeover of Egyptian knowledge; not content with the notion that the Greeks simply failed to acknowledge the Egyptian sources of their wisdom, Yosef ben-Jochannan, in *Africa, Mother of Western Civilization*, states that Aristotle began to write his philosophy only after "he totally sacked the temples and lodges of the African Mysteries in

Egypt upon his arrival in 332 B.C.E. with Alexander the Great" ([1971] 1988, 395–96; cf. 379, 399, 423, 492).

Not a single one of these assertions about cultural expropriation and scholarly dishonesty can be directly substantiated from ancient sources (see also Snowden, this volume). Not one responsible ancient author (certainly not Aristotle) doubted that Plato wrote the *Republic* and *Timaeus*. And there is no reason to believe that Aristotle had much contact with Alexander after he ceased to be his tutor, before 338 B.C.E. It is simply untrue, to the best of my knowledge, to claim that Greek philosophy was stolen from Egyptian sources. There is no evidence whatever for James's claim that Alexander took books from the library at Alexandria (which was founded after his death) to give to Aristotle, or for ben-Jochannan's assertion that Aristotle came to Egypt with Alexander and sacked the temples of ideas and books (Lefkowitz 1992a, A52; 1994).

Corrections and criticisms such as these, however, do not seem to matter: they are based, after all, on European sources, which are by nature suspect. It is axiomatic for Afrocentric authors that there has been, since antiquity, a European conspiracy to suppress evidence of African origins, and therefore any argument that a European makes against their ideas, especially on the basis of European writings, ancient or modern, can be regarded ipso facto as invalid.

The Afrocentric description of ancient history has been circulating in print for at least seventy years, but it is only since the late 1960s that Afrocentric ideas have begun to be included in the curricula of the most prominent universities in this country, and it is only in the last several years that, as a result of the "canon wars," they have begun to be taken seriously by historians who might themselves have been otherwise regarded as Eurocentric. The debate has significant consequences for the teaching of Greco-Roman antiquity. For if the Greeks and Romans and the people who teach about their civilization have suppressed the truth, why should the classics (and the European literatures that drew inspiration from them) occupy a privileged place in the curriculum, or any place at all? I myself would agree that they should be eliminated, if these charges could be shown by any objective standard to be true. If . . .

ANCIENT MYTHS OF GREEK ORIGINS

Where did the Greeks themselves think that they came from? No surviving Greek author, not even Herodotus, attempts to provide anything like a systematic historical account. Presumably the question did not interest them: they seem not even to have imagined that as a population they were anything but indigenous. The Athenians believed that they were *autochthonous*, that is, sprung from the ground (*chthon*) itself. The Myrmidons, the soldiers who came with Achilles to Troy, would have said that their ancestors were ants, or *myrmēkes*, turned by Zeus into men to be companions for Achilles' grandfather Aeacus. Some Thebans spoke of themselves as the descendants of the "sown men" who sprang up from the teeth of the dragon killed by Cadmus, the founder of their city. According to another story, the Titan god Prometheus made mortal beings from clay and breathed life into them, and taught them letters and craftsmanship, though another myth said that the alphabet and numbers were invented by Palamedes, a mortal. Or mankind derived from the sticks and stones thrown by Prometheus' mortal son Deucalion and his wife Pyrrha after the great flood sent by Zeus to put an end to human wrongdoing.

Whoever the Greeks may have been, and whatever stories they preferred to tell about their origins, they believed that their ancestors were born in the land that their descendants inhabited, that the language they spoke was their own, and that one of their own gods or people invented their system of writing. They called all foreign peoples, whatever their origin or language, barbarians, *barbaroi*, that is, people who, instead of speaking Greek, spoke nonsense, *barbar*. (They did not seem to know or to care that the word barbarian is itself a loan word, from the Babylonian-Sumerian *barbaru*, "foreigner" (Hall 1989, 4).

Cadmus himself was said to have come to Thebes from Phoenicia, bringing some of his own people with him. Pelops, the founder of the Olympian Games, was said to have been a Lydian. Io, daughter of the king of Argos, was exiled to Egypt by the jealous goddess Hera, and later her descendants the Danaids sought asylum in her homeland. The Corinthian hero Bellerophon was exiled to Asia Minor carrying a letter with "baneful signs" that the king of Lycia was able to interpret; Bellerophon's descendants settled in Lycia and later fought with the Trojans against the Greeks (Homer *Iliad* 6.150–211).

How "true" are these myths? We must, as always, proceed with caution (see Coleman, Hall, this volume). The myths appear to represent history only in the most general way. They mention the names of real places, but they do not attempt to give an accurate picture of who their inhabitants were or how they lived. Myths are resolutely anachronistic, and tend to give only a vague impression of actual time. For historians, they can serve at best as a general guide to the existence of a particular place or its inhabitants. Although Mycenae, for example, was only a small town in the fifth century, according to the myth of the Trojan War there was an important settlement at Mycenae toward the end of the second millennium B.C.E. The general truth of the myth has since been confirmed by archaeological excavation.

The myths that mention foreign places seem also to be "true" in this same general way. They confirm that in the second millennium B.C.E. civilizations large enough to trade with and to visit existed in Egypt, Phoenicia, Mesopotamia, and parts of Asia Minor. But they can tell us nothing more specific about the movements of peoples, the languages that they spoke, or the particular wars that they fought. That Danaus came to Greece from Egypt, that Cadmus came from Phoenicia, or that Pelops came from Lydia, tells us no less but no more than that the Greeks had contact with those places. If the myths of their arrival in Greece represent anything more substantial than a trade mission or a piratical raid, archaeology has not confirmed it.

Before the Persians invaded the Greek cities of Asia Minor and then the mainland itself in the early fifth century B.C.E., the Greeks themselves did not acknowledge any debts to neighboring cultures. Nor did they make much show of their own uniqueness. Instead they tended to imagine that everyone was like themselves. In the *Iliad* the Trojans speak the same language, worship the same gods, wear the same clothes, and have the same laws and customs as their Greek enemies, even though in reality the Trojans may have spoken a different Indo-European language, Luvian, or some derivative of Hittite.

It was only as a result of the Persian Wars in the early fifth century B.C.E., in which they were almost defeated, that the Greeks became aware of, and began to celebrate, the unique features of their own civilization. But even when they became interested in the differences between themselves and other peoples, like the Persians or the Egyptians, they seem never to have asked in any systematic way whether or not they might at some much earlier time have been influenced by the civilizations of their neighbors or derived from the same origins. We know that Greeks visited Egypt in the seventh century; but the only explicit description of Egypt that has come down to us dates from around the 430s B.C.E. Its author was Herodotus.

Herodotus, a Greek from Halicarnassus on the coast of Asia Minor, claims that he traveled around Egypt and writes with admiration and appreciation of the antiquity and the achievements of Egyptian civilization. He records the names of some of their kings, and he describes the pyramids. But curiously (at least from a modern point of view) he says nothing about the Egyptian features in archaic Greek art, and nothing about language, with one apparent exception: the names of the gods. About these names he says that he "learned by inquiry" that "the names of almost all of the gods came from Egypt to Greece," with the exception of the gods whose names the Egyptians did not know. Those gods, Herodotus claims, were named by the Pelasgians, the first people to settle in the Greek mainland, with the exception of Poseidon, who was Libyan (2.50.1–3). And after talking with priests at a temple near the mouth of the Nile, he discovered that the tragic poet Aeschylus had "snatched" from local stories the myth that the goddess Demeter (rather than Leto) was the mother of the goddess Artemis (2.156.6).

Modern historians are understandably frustrated when they try to use

Herodotus to discover "what really happened," or even what most of his contemporaries might have believed. He is a famously slippery historical source. What did the priests really tell him? What did he ask them? Did he even go to Egypt? Should we take Herodotus literally, or try instead to reconstruct, on the limited basis of what he tells us, what the purpose of his inquiry was, and what he meant his readers to learn about themselves? (Pritchett 1993, 1–9). Perhaps all we can say with confidence is that he meant his audience (who probably heard rather than read what he wrote) to respect the "barbarians" and their customs, and not to regard them as culturally and morally inferior.

It appears to have been the similarities between certain Egyptian and Greek myths, and the impressions that they gave of the character of particular gods, that suggested to Herodotus that the Greek gods derived from the Egyptian. He does not speak about representations in the visual arts, or discuss the architectural style of sacred buildings in the two countries. Certainly he does not consider the etymology of the gods' names, since he gives both their Egyptian and Greek names. His general practice is to call the gods of all cultures by Greek names, and to describe their cults in all foreign settings; thus he also discusses how the Phoenicians worshiped Heracles (2.44).

Herodotus also points out that (because of their climate) the Egyptians were different from the Greeks in many respects: "their habits and customs are different from those of the rest of humankind; their women go to market and conduct trade; their men sit at home and do the weaving"; Egyptian men were circumcised; the Egyptians ate different food, and buried their dead and offered their sacrifices with different rituals, and wrote from right to left, and so on (2.35.2–36.4). At the end of the fifth century the Athenian dramatist Sophocles could offer his audience a similar account of the contrariness of Egyptian behavior (*Oedipus at Colonus* 337–41). From the Greek point of view, in sum, Egypt was a strange and foreign culture.

BERNAL'S RECONSTRUCTION OF THE PAST

The question of Greek origins recently has been broached again, and become a subject of passionate popular discussion, with the publication of the first two volumes of Martin Bernal's *Black Athena: the Afroasiatic Roots of Classical Civilization* in 1987 and 1991. Unlike most of his Afrocentric admirers, Bernal can read hieroglyphics and Greek, and he claims he knows other ancient languages; and though his field is political science, he seems at home in the chronological and geographical complexities of the ancient Mediterranean. Moreover, he insists that he reached Afrocentric conclusions about Greek origins independently of the Afrocentrists. "I had been studying these issues for eight years," he writes in his first volume, "before I became aware of this literature" (401–2).

As Bernal's discussion, notes, and bibliography testify, he has read widely and thought strenuously about the Mediterranean as a whole, if not exactly with an open mind, at least without giving priority to the Greeks, as classically trained scholars tend to do. Still, his assessment of the evidence for the Egyptian contribution starts from the premise that European scholars have distorted the evidence, documentary and archaeological. His first volume, subtitled *The Fabrication of Ancient Greece*, is a kind of historiographical prelude to the subject, in which he attacks the nineteenth-century notion that the Greeks were Aryans from the North. Bernal proposes to return from the "Aryan Model" to the "Ancient Model," that is, to Herodotus' notion that the Greeks derived their religion and possibly other important customs from the East, and from Egypt in particular.

To speak of "fabrication," and thereby to suggest some conspiracy theory about European scholars who wished to give priority to the contribution of northern peoples like themselves, is to exaggerate wildly. But Bernal has ample justification for calling into question many widely accepted hypotheses, such as the traditional date of the Greeks' adaptation of the Phoenician syllabary into their own alphabet. (In *Cadmean Letters* [1990a], he suggests that the Greek alphabet came into use much earlier, in the middle of the second millennium.) Bernal is right to point out, often amusingly, that scholars are apt to treat hypotheses as orthodoxies, and so have been incapable of giving proper weight to new and important data.

Bernal shows how Egypt and its culture were misrepresented or simply ignored by European writers. He argues that widely influential books, such as Flaubert's *Salammbô* (1862), promoted the notion that African cultures were more depraved and uncivilized than those of the Greeks or the Romans. He describes how Flaubert had originally meant to write a historical novel about Egypt but fixed on ancient Carthage as his subject because the Egyptians were not sufficiently depraved for his purposes. The Carthaginians, particularly because they sacrificed young children, provided him with an almost ideal opportunity to criticize non-Christian and non-European values, and to condemn the Carthaginians' Phoenician background and culture, and by association Jewish culture as well (*BA* 1:355-59).

Bernal regards Flaubert's description of Carthaginian life as a typical illustration of Eurocentric hypocrisy: "Flaubert implied that Europeans—with the possible exception of the English—were incapable of such things. In fact, the Romans outdid the Carthaginians in virtually every luxury and outrage while the Macedonians [i.e., Greeks] were not far behind" (*BA* 1:357). He proceeds to note a few specific examples of the cruelty shown by the Romans to some of their war victims, and mentions some of the horrors of the treatment of colonial populations in Flaubert's own lifetime, and many more examples of Greco-Roman (and European) atrocities might be mentioned. Both the Greeks and Romans "exposed" unwanted children. But Bernal might have noted that in Carthage firstborn children were often sacrificed to protect the lives of younger ones, and a civic crisis could elicit a mass slaughter; more than two hundred children were said to have been sacrificed in 310 B.C.E. because the Carthaginians thought the gods were angry at them (Diodorus 20.14.5; Stager and Wolff 1984, 43–44, 49).

Surely there is something rather simple about these comparisons. Which civilization, ancient or modern, has *not* been guilty of unspeakable atrocity? And is Bernal being fair even to Flaubert? For in *Salammbô* Flaubert attempted, like Homer and the Greek tragic poets, to portray rather than to condemn or to expose. It is true that Flaubert treats his characters, no matter how horrific their actions, with a certain sympathy, but that is so that we can imagine what it was like to see vast armies marching to their death, or to prepare to sacrifice one's own child. Bernal reads the novel as if it were a political pamphlet.

The problem for this critic of other historians and historical writers is that his own "Revised Ancient Model" betrays considerable historiographical naiveté. Bernal relies too much on Herodotus' treatment of Egypt. And he painstakingly describes how Egyptian scientific notions were preserved in certain Christian legends and in Masonic ritual, claiming that "no one before 1600 seriously questioned either the belief that Greek civilization and philosophy derived from Egypt, or that the chief ways in which they had been transmitted were through Egyptian colonizations of Greece and later Greek study in Egypt" (*BA* 1:121).

It is perfectly correct that nobody before 1600 questioned these historical propositions, but that is because nobody before 1600 (or thereabouts) knew much about Egyptian history. Hieroglyphics were not deciphered until 1824; before that historians relied primarily on Greek sources that were more or less fictional. Among the most influential of these Greek writings were the so-called *Hermetica*, which are purported to have been written at the beginning of time by Hermes Trismegistus, grandson of the god. Until the early part of this century these writings were believed to have been earlier than any other Greek philosophical works. But now it is clear that they were composed only in the second century C.E., centuries after Plato and Aristotle. In fact the vocabulary in which they are written was created by those philosophers (Copenhaver 1992, xlv–lix; Lefkowitz 1994, 31).

Another influential fiction is the notion that Masonic rituals are based on the "Egyptian Mysteries," which were an integral part of an elaborate system for the education of Egyptian priests. But in reality the earliest descriptions of these mysteries, along with academies for Egyptian priests, with large libraries and art galleries, first occur not in any ancient text but in an eighteenth-century French work of historical fiction, the novel *Séthos* by the

Abbé Jean Terrasson, first published in 1731. Terrasson's novel was widely read; it had a profound influence on portrayals of Egyptian religion in later literature, such as Mozart's *Magic Flute* (Lefkowitz 1994, 30). Bernal owes it to his readers to remind them that the "Ancient Model" was largely based on these misconceptions. But instead, as in the case of his treatment of myth, he adduces historical superstition as if it were historical fact.[5] He does not point out that these ancient and medieval beliefs about cultural relations in antiquity were based on the acceptance of mythology as history, and on taking Herodotus and ancient anecdotal biographers at their literal word.

Again, myth is a tricky object of historical inquiry. If the myth of Danaus coming to Argos has been interpreted as an example of Egyptian penetration of Greece, it can also be understood, as the Greeks themselves tended to understand it, as the return to Greece of a native after many generations. Similarly, the myth of the journey of Danaus' ancestor Io to the Nile Delta can be understood to suggest that a civilization from the North, perhaps even a Greek civilization, penetrated Egypt at some early time. But as the Egyptologist Donald Redford has recently argued (1992, 122), the story of Io may be based instead on a Canaanite myth that reflects the conquest of Egypt in the second millennium by the people known as the Hyksos. Or, one wonders, did Greeks visit Egypt and simply identify cow-headed images of the goddess Isis with Io, a character from their own mythology?

Bernal cites Herodotus on the Egyptian origin of Greek religion and ritual, but he does not show how the Greeks came to borrow their "philosophy" as well. He does not discuss the implications of Herodotus' very explicit statement that Egyptian habits and customs in his own time were totally different from those of the Greeks. He suggests that the Eleusinian Mysteries were derived from Egyptian rites (Herodotus 2.171; *BA* 1:119), but he does not point out that such a claim cannot be proved or disproved: ancient mysteries were (as their name suggests) kept secret, and no one now knows much about their origins.

Bernal tries to support his discussion of the "Ancient Model" etymologically—with etymologies of Greek names such as Danaus, Aegyptus, and Io. These examples appear to be plausible, because the Greek names and the Egyptian (or Semitic) counterparts that Bernal produces certainly look alike, and usually have some connection in meaning. It is worth noting that lookalike etymologies also feature in other Afrocentric discussions of African origins of European societies: John G. Jackson, for example, in his *Introduction to African Civilizations* (1990, 150) lists a few examples of Egypto-English words, such as *cow/kaui*, without noting that there are also other more plausible etymologies. (In fact, the word *cow* is Indo-European, cognate to Greek *bous* and Latin *bos*.)[6]

Bernal chooses a more sophisticated range of words to investigate, but the results of his research still cannot be taken as positive proof of an Egyptian presence in Greece. Consider, for example, his ingenious explanation of the name of the people who invaded Egypt in the second millennium. To the Greeks they were known as Hyksos (see Vermeule, Coleman, this volume). According to Bernal, *Hyksos* may be related to the Greek *hiketides*, the term used to describe the daughters of Danaus, who came with him to Argos as "suppliants." If so—and it is very unlikely (see Jasanoff and Nussbaum, this volume)—the etymology would help establish that the story of Danaus represented the Hyksos invasion of Greece (*BA* 1:96–97). It is, perhaps, not impossible. But there is a much more likely interpretation of the invaders' name: that *Hyksos* is a Greek garbling of the Egyptian word for "ruler of foreign peoples," which designated the regime, rather than the nationality, of the invaders (Redford 1992, 100).

Bernal also proposes that the city of Athens' name derives from the Egyptian *Ḥt Nt* (vocalized), "house of Nēit," who was identified by the Greeks with their goddess Athena. This derivation would provide a striking confirmation of Herodotus' claim, better than any that Herodotus himself was prepared to offer, as the Greeks had only the most rudimentary "sound-alike" understanding of the history of words. But even though it sounds plausible to us, it is no more likely than his farfetched suggestion that *Hyksos* is cognate to *hiketis* (Ray 1990, 80; see Jasanoff and Nussbaum, and Coleman, this volume).

But even if common etymologies could be found, they would not in themselves confirm that the Greeks borrowed their religion from the Egyptians. For place names and proper names, and even the occasional ordinary noun, easily make their way into foreign cultures as loan words. That is to say, they reveal patterns of influence and little else. A linguistic proof of origins requires more than a similarity in names and nouns. The derivation of one culture from another is almost invariably reflected in other aspects of the language, such as its grammar and its working vocabulary. That is why we would have discovered that French-speaking peoples occupied the island of Britain after the eleventh century C.E., even if we did not know it from history.

Bernal's account of the origins of Greek knowledge is presented in an equally unsatisfactory way. He does not point out at the beginning of his discussion, although it would be reasonable to expect him to do so (see also Baines, this volume), that the Hermetic Corpus that preserves many of the details of Egyptian wisdom is not at all as ancient as it claims to be, but rather was written in Greek writing in the second century C.E. (This was one of the earliest and the most important discoveries of modern critical history.) That is, he refrains from stating explicitly that what the authors of Masonic ritual and other Europeans considered to be "Egyptian" knowledge was in fact thoroughly Hellenized. Certainly elements of ancient Egyptian religion were retained, but within a Neoplatonic framework (Fowden 1986, 31–44). What Bernal represents as Egyptian is essentially Greco-Egyptian.

In his treatment of the transmission of Egyptian knowledge Bernal seems to have reproduced the Afrocentric analysis. According to Bernal, G. G. M. James's "fascinating little book *Stolen Legacy* also makes a plausible case for Greek science and philosophy having borrowed massively from Egypt" (*BA* 1:38). He speaks of James as a pioneer in the effort to promote awareness of the "Afroasiatic formative elements in Greek civilization" (1:435). But like James and other Afrocentrics, Bernal tends to ignore possible influences *not* from Africa. He overlooks eastern Semitic cultures in favor of the Egyptian. And he does not speak of Egyptian influences so much as of Greek borrowings.

Bernal's tendentious treatment of Flaubert, his eager credulity about Herodotus, his selective etymologies, and his neglect of the distinctively Greek element in Egyptian "science," all suggest that his own discussion of European historiography is rather less free of historiographical bias than he would have his readers believe. Why, instead of cataloguing mistakes made by nineteenth-century writers, did he not begin his discussion of the problem with an attempt to describe the general identifying characteristics of the societies in question at the times when they could have been thought to have had some influence on each other? Why exactly is it likely that we should think that Egyptian culture was absorbed in greater or lesser degree by the Greeks? Why not attempt to survey some of the more tangible evidence that can be provided by art and architecture, before going on to discuss any similarities that might be found in language and customs?

To this task Bernal turns in his second volume, and finally concentrates on trying to demonstrate the truth of his account (which he now calls the "Revised Ancient Model") by assessing the ancient archaeological and documentary evidence for the origins of Greece. That volume surveys the varied information that can be gleaned from disparate and often fragmentary sources about the movements of Mediterranean peoples in the second millennium. It is difficult and exhausting to read, though not because Bernal fails to state his case clearly, or to arm the reader with maps, dates, a glossary, and excellent indices. Unfortunately for Bernal, unfortunately for all of us, the second millennium B.C.E. so far has dealt us only a partial hand of cards. Occasionally new evidence is found, but we have little hope of ever recovering the complete deck. Bernal plays his cards with confidence, however, and with an exuberance that is more characteristic of the amateur than the professional; but they are in the end cards from the same old incomplete and incompletable pack.

Bernal (to press the metaphor a little further) clearly believes that certain suits are luckier than others, those suits being mythology and etymology. But to capture the reader's imagination, and to move his theory closer to the evidence that exists, he should have provided illustrations of the visual evidence, not least as reminders of why these varied cultures may be thought to have had some influence on one another. What of the frescoes depicting bull-leaping from the palaces at Knossos and Thera? The archaic Greek statues that try to replicate the stance of Egyptian figures? The imaginary compound animals on sixth-century Greek vases that seem to have been inspired by Near Eastern archetypes? They are not in Bernal's book. He is clearly more comfortable at some distance from such evidence, more comfortable with theory and speculation than with the archaeologist's potsherds and leafmold.

Instead he returns again to Herodotus' statement about the Egyptian and Greek gods, discussing the many rough but intriguing parallels that can be drawn between Egyptian and Greek myth and cult. Again, none of these seem in themselves conclusive; and again, Bernal seems somewhat reluctant to investigate all possible explanations. The Greeks, for example, devised an elaborate irrigation system in Boeotia (the region of which Thebes was the principal town). Where did they learn how to control water? The question puts Bernal in mind of the Nile. But how much weight should be given to the fact that in Greek myth the hero Heracles is depicted as controlling large bodies of water, and do references to the hero's control of water necessarily suggest that Heracles originated in Egypt? (*BA* 2:116–19). The Nile is perhaps the most famous body of water in the Mediterranean world that causes problems, but it is certainly not the only one. The behavior of the Euphrates has hardly been without consequence.

Such correspondences are not exact parallels, and at most they suggest only influences. But then there remains the question of how such influences might have been transmitted, and here, too, Bernal is on less than solid ground, again relying heavily on Herodotus. Herodotus talks about invasions by an Egyptian king whom he calls Sesostris, whose armies penetrated as far north as the Black Sea, and conquered the Scythians and the Thracians. This Sesostris, Bernal believes, should be identified with the twelfth-dynasty pharaoh Senwosret I (1959–1914 B.C.E.), although this involves some rearrangement of generally accepted chronology (*BA* 2:195–235). And (later in the millennium) the myth of Danaus could be understood to suggest that influences were imposed by immigration, invasion, or even a peaceful takeover.

On the infirm basis of this myth Bernal seems to assume that Egyptians or some bearers of their culture occupied the Greek mainland during the second millennium. The Hyksos invaders are the logical candidate for this role.[7] In order to let them play it, however, Bernal argues that they came to Greece two centuries earlier than the ancients thought they did, and he insists that they managed to transmit, along with elements of their own Semitic language and culture, aspects of Egyptian culture as well. It does not trouble him that Herodotus fails to state that Sesostris' armies conquered or even penetrated mainland Greece.

And the Hyksos invasion, even if it happened as Bernal supposes, is very different in character from the Egyptian cultural domination described by Diop, or from James's notion of the wholesale plundering of Egyptian ideas by Greeks in the first millennium B.C.E. It is both more gradual and more passive: it allows for two-way exchange—Egyptian and Semitic influence on Greece, and Greek influence on Egypt and the Eastern Mediterranean. That is, it suggests that cultures and words can be transmitted peacefully, by trade or by physical coexistence. A useful analogy may be found in the conquest of Greece by Rome in the second century B.C.E.: according to the Roman poet Horace (first century B.C.E.), it was the culture of the conquered that dominated the culture of the conquerors.

This analogy has an important implication. For it seems that Bernal, as he leaves the world of nineteenth-century speculation and confronts the new evidence brought to bear on the problem by the archaeological and linguistic discoveries of the twentieth, edges ever closer to precisely the complex multicultural "model" of Greek origins championed by most modern classical scholars. Indeed, Bernal himself now admits, "with some surprise and distress," that the "Aryan Model" may in some respects be valid (as in the case of the Hyksos invaders; *BA* 2:525).

Bernal is right to insist that all scholars, and particularly archaeologists and anyone who seeks to understand incomplete and fragmentary data, must start from assumptions of some sort. But why test only the Aryan and the African assumptions, when others are also tenable? Why not a "Semitic Model" or a "Hebrew Model" or a "Mesopotamian Model"? In both the Greek and Hebrew accounts, heaven and earth are created from a formless void and then separated, man's behavior becomes offensive, so that he is compelled to lead a hard life, and the human race is almost destroyed by a flood. And why not a "Hittite Model"? In both Hittite myth and Greek there is strife among the generations of gods, and fathers are violently overthrown by sons. And why not a "Multicultural Model," to take account of the various elements that seem to have been incorporated into Greek mythology and culture?

Perhaps that is what Bernal himself is intending for his subsequent volumes. He seems to have found himself trapped in a Procrustean model of his own making. Thus he has revised the "Ancient Model" (really the "African Model") not only to put the Hyksos' invasion of Greece earlier than the time of their departure from Egypt, but also to allow that Greek speech, since it must have come to the Greek peninsula in some way from the North, is undeniably Indo-European. If he can admit that the Hyksos invaders may have included speakers of Hurrian (a non-Semitic, non-Aryan agglutinative language) and even speakers of Indo-European languages (*BA* 2:323), is he prepared to admit that linguistic and other cultural transmission is really too complex to be accurately portrayed in a single model, or as a myth of invasion or even immigration?

Bernal has forcefully reminded us of what may have been the principal reason that contact with Egypt was essential for the Greeks and other Mediterranean peoples, including, in the second half of the first millennium, the Romans: Egypt provided an abundant source of grain. In this way, and with the data that he has assembled, he may have sharpened the quality of the debate about the origins of Greek culture. But I do not think that he has brought about any dramatic change in the way the evidence about Greek origins should be interpreted. The slim and difficult evidence shows, at most, the ways in which elements of foreign cultures could have been transmitted, whether by trade or by conquest, but it does not establish that the Greeks stole anything, or that they were not people who came from the North, speaking an Indo-European language, whose culture was influenced over many centuries by their neighbors, through invasion, trade, and importation. The basic picture remains unchanged.

Nobody would deny that the Egyptians had a notable influence on Greek religion and art. On the basis of the most scrupulous scholarly evaluation of the present evidence, however, nobody should claim that the Greeks stole their best or their most significant ideas from the Egyptians, or from anyone else. Certainly, and fortunately, they did not copy their system of government from the Egyptians. We need only to look at the remains of public buildings. The pharaohs built the pyramids for themselves and their families; the citizens of Athens voted to build the Parthenon for the use of all the city's inhabitants.

CONCLUSION

To the extent that Bernal has contributed to the provision of an apparently respectable underpinning for Afrocentric fantasies, he must be held culpable, even if his intentions are honorable and his motives are sincere. But not even he has dealt with the racial issue squarely. One hopes that in his forthcoming volumes he will finally assess how much of the Afro-Asiatic legacy to the Greeks involved *black* Africans, or as the Greeks called them, "Ethiopians." So far Bernal has simply ducked the issue. Or rather, he has tried to have it both ways, allowing the Egyptians to stand for the rest of Africa, whatever their racial type or types. In a colloquium about *Black Athena* at the American Philological Association in 1989, he admitted that he would have preferred to have called the book *African Athena*, but his publisher insisted on its present title because the combination of blacks and women would "sell."[8]

Bernal would prefer to emphasize that Egypt is a part of Africa, rather than try to determine the exact proportion of darker-skinned central Africans in the population. For to speak of the ancient (or modern) Egyptians as "black" is misleading in the extreme. Not that it would have mattered from the Greek point of view, since the Greeks classified people by nationality rather than skin color, as Frank Snowden pointed out a quarter-century ago (Snowden 1970). But Herodotus, the earliest Greek source, refers just once to the skin color of the Egyptians, and then only to prove that the Egyptians under Sesostris managed to penetrate as far as the northeast end of the Black Sea; he says that the Colchians, the people who lived there, could be classified as Egyptians both because they had dark skin and woolly hair and because they spoke the same language, practiced circumcision, and worked their linen in the unique Egyptian manner. Bernal takes this passage as evidence that the Egyptians were "black" in the modern sense of Negroid. But if that had been what Herodotus meant, he would have referred to them as Ethiopians, who spoke a different language from the Egyptians and had different customs (see Snowden, this volume; Snowden 1989, 88–89; Snowden 1993).

Will believers in the Athenian conspiracy be persuaded by these and other historical arguments? Some will perhaps continue to believe that the Greeks stole African culture, without wishing to inquire what exactly they mean by African culture or Egyptian culture or Greek culture. That would be a pity, because in the process of claiming Greek history as their own, they will miss an opportunity to learn about real Africa and its own achievements and civilizations.

When Marcus Garvey first spoke about the Greeks' stealing from the Africans, he was not creating a new historiography, he was creating a new mythology. The reasons are not far to seek. For black Americans (many of whom now prefer to be known as African-Americans), the African origins of ancient Greek civilization promise a myth of self-identification and self-ennoblement, the kind of "noble lie" that Socrates suggests is needed for the utopian state he describes in Plato's *Republic* (3.414b). It is the Afrocentric view that is, to use Bernal's term, the fabrication; but such fabrications may build confidence and may encourage marginalized groups to quit the margins and participate in the common culture. In that sense, they may be useful and even "noble."

But hope is not enough of a reason for illusion. What constructive purpose will the myth of African origins really serve? If it causes us to ignore or even to subvert the truth about the past, it damages our ability, the ability of all of us, no matter what our ethnic origins, to judge fairly and accurately, which is the best purpose of education. And even if a myth helps people to gain confidence, it will teach them simultaneously that facts can be manufactured or misreported to serve a political purpose; that origins are the only measure of value; that difference is either a glory or a danger, when in fact it is a common, challenging fact of life; that the true knowledge of customs, language, and literature is unimportant for understanding the nature of a culture.

The Greeks, least of all peoples, deserve the fate to which the Afrocentrists have subjected them. The great historian Arnaldo Momigliano observed that "what I think is typically Greek is the critical attitude toward the recording of events, that is, the development of critical methods enabling us to distinguish between facts and fancies. To the best of my knowledge no historiography earlier than the Greek or independent of it developed these critical methods; and we have inherited the Greek methods" (1990, 30). Momigliano was not a Greek. He was an Italian Jew, and a refugee from one of the most terrible political myths of all time, the not very noble lie of Jewish inferiority that provided the justification for the Holocaust. But the rational legacy of Greece belonged to him, too, exactly as it belongs to people of African descent, whatever their skin color or their exact place of origin. Like everyone in both the African and the European diasporas, and like everyone in the American melting pot, they should take pride in the Egyptians, in the Phoenicians, and in the ancient Greeks, and give them each their due for their actual achievements, as well as for their contributions to other civilizations. For all these civilizations, like everything else in the past, belong equally to all of us.

NOTES

Reprinted by permission from *The New Republic*, 10 February 1992. I am grateful to Leon Wieseltier and Ann Hulbert for many improvements in the original version of this article.

1. I do not believe that Socrates could have been black just because it is conceivably possible that Socrates (or any other Greek) *might have had* an African ancestor; cf. Lefkowitz 1993b, 13–14. But here is how Asante interprets this incident: "Lefkowitz's response to the student and use of the student's alleged statements demonstrates one of the major issues involved in the attacks on Afrocentricity: white racism. Most whites cannot believe that a person with the reputation of Socrates or his teachers could have been black because of the institutional disregard for Africans. Of course there is no indication that he was black, and for me, it is not a question of interest, but for whites it strikes right at their souls" (Asante 1993a, 39).

2. The student wrote: "Cleopatra's father was not a full blooded Greek. Generations after Ptolemy I and many interracial marriages the Greek ancestry was no longer pure. By the time Cleopatra was born she was almost, if not all Egyptian" (as quoted in T. Martin 1993, 59). Similar "information" may be found in J. H. Clarke 1984. According to the known facts, Cleopatra VII was the daughter of Ptolemy XII

and his sister Cleopatra V. Ptolemy XII was the son of Ptolemy IX and a mistress. Who was the mistress? Since none of our sources tells us otherwise, the natural presumption is that she was a Greek, like the Ptolemies. That of course does not prove she was not African, but there is no evidence at all that she was African. See Snowden, this volume.

3. Diop 1974, 100–112. The text of the *Aeneid* does not support Diop's interpretation: Aeneas vows to honor Dido wherever his travels take him (1.607–10), and remember her so long as he lives (4.335–36). Virgil expresses such sympathy for her in order to convey the enormous personal and moral cost of founding an empire.

4. James 1954, 123–26; curiously, Bernal finds it "in many ways useful" to look at the *Odyssey* as a "Greek version of the Egyptian *Book of the Dead*" (*BA* 1:87). But only one book of the twenty-four books of the *Odyssey* describes the world of the dead, and the description of souls there bears virtually no resemblance to anything in the Egyptian *Book of the Dead*.

5. For example, "In this case, then, the Masonic claim of drawing their traditions from Ancient Egypt has a basis in fact" (*BA* 1:176).

6. Eng. *cow* and Greek *bous* derive from the Indo-European root *$g^w ou$- (ox, bull, cow). The sound represented by *g^w* (known as a labiovelar) was treated differently in different Indo-European languages. Sometimes the velar (the *w*-like element) was lost, leaving just *g* or *k*, as in Sanskrit *gaus*. In other languages the labial element was strengthened at the expense of the velar articulation, leaving the labials *b* and *p*, as in Greek *bous*. Another example of the same kind of shift in sound is Indo-European *$k^w o$-, which comes out as *what* in English, but *quod* in Latin.

7. *BA* 2:405–6 compares the Hyksos "conquest" of Greece to the Norman invasion of England; but the comparison is absurd, because there is no archaeological record of a Hyksos invasion, or linguistic changes that can be traced to such an event.

8. Muhly (1990b, 105) observes that the title was not forced on Bernal, as he uses it for a course at Cornell (cf. also Snowden 1993, 321).

EGYPT

ON THE AIMS
AND METHODS OF
BLACK ATHENA

John Baines

Because only half of *Black Athena* is available so far, it is not possible to give any full evaluation of Martin Bernal's work. Yet his ideas have aroused such interest and such strong reactions that some response from people working in fields upon which he draws is desirable even now; nor have discussions of the first volume of *Black Athena* been lacking (Levine and Peradotto 1989; Muhly 1990c). In this essay I consider questions of method and theory that *Black Athena* poses insistently in various ways. No doubt later volumes will raise complementary issues.

Many classicists welcomed the first volume of *Black Athena* for its treatment of the history and biases of classical scholarship. Near Eastern specialists and Egyptologists may react similarly, because they too are aware of the isolationism often seen in traditional classics—or more precisely in studies of Greek civilization—with its emphasis on the events of a relatively short period, primarily in a particular exemplar of a single group of cultures. Studies that appear to see fifth-century B.C.E. Athens as the defining experience of all civilization puzzle those whose interests lie in other areas of Mediterranean antiquity, and still more those concerned with other regions of the world. Two examples chosen almost at random are Anthony Andrewes's explanation that he restricted coverage in his *The Greeks* to the pre-Hellenistic period because the book was "about the original Greek contribution" (1967, xxv–xxvi; cf. xix), and Karl Popper's study of the origins of democracy and pluralism in *The Open Society and Its Enemies* (1966; cf. Ray 1991a). In the latter, the argument was directed against totalitarianism with its perceived mentor, Plato, and was cast in a broad context of social evolution, but it was not addressed to the Near East. In tracing the history of this focus on Greece, Bernal seems to neglect the fact that the emergence of Greece as an ideal was part of the incipient secularization of the Enlightenment and of Romanticism, so that it had its own legitimation and agendas which led its proponents to distance themselves from the focus on the Roman world prevalent in their time (e.g., *BA* 1:212–22). This motivation is not coextensive with the racist biases he sees in the work of scholars before the present generation.

There has been less general reaction to Bernal's work from Near Eastern specialists. One reason for this is that the first volume of *Black Athena* discusses the Near East itself relatively little. In the end, it may transpire that the later volumes do not change this position and the involvement of Near Eastern specialists very much, because Bernal's principal purpose is to elaborate a perspective on Greece and the Aegean through the ancient Near East, rather than to focus on the Near East itself. Whereas the first volume is concerned with earlier scholarship and its biases against entertaining the idea of Near Eastern influence on Greece, the second volume of *Black Athena* moves to the actual historical setting and puts forward a number of interpretations, some new, and some known from the existing literature but presented within a new picture.

Like many who come into an area of study from outside, Bernal is adept at spotting anomalies and inconsistencies in established opinions and interpretations in ancient Near Eastern studies. His work on the alphabet is an example (*BA* 1; 1990a). Here he covers evidence, also explored by others, that does not well fit the normal explanation that the alphabet was transmitted to the Aegean in about the eighth century B.C.E. (There are, however, also problems with his proposal that it arrived in the Aegean in the mid second millennium.) At the end of the second volume of *Black Athena* (522–27) he notes that many of his interpretations take up those of the early years of this century, whose conclusions he ultimately follows while abjuring what he perceives as having been the motivations and politics of those who proposed them (see also *BA* 2:48).

Because the second volume has been less a focus of discussion than the first, I present its principal contents very briefly, and then discuss Bernal's approach and methods, issues that lie in the background to both volumes, which belong together for the purpose of this study. I can address only a few issues of method; in particular, I omit his treatment of linguistic questions—to be detailed in later volumes—and say little about his discussion of Egyptian deities.

In what follows, I often include Egypt under the term "ancient Near East"; instances where this does not apply should be clear. It is not possible to present full documentation here, particularly in the summary in the next section.

THE ARGUMENT OF **BLACK ATHENA** 2

The second volume of *Black Athena* is subtitled *The Archaeological and Documentary Evidence*, but it covers more than that description implies. The third volume is to be concerned with language, and Bernal has not yet described the focus of the fourth. The essential historical conclusions of the "series" (as Bernal terms it, *BA* 1:1) seem thus to be presented in the second volume. They are usefully summarized in the introductory chapter (2:1–61) and resumed in the conclusion (2:522–27).

Four principal episodes of Egyptian influence or influence from Egypt in the Aegean are identified: the later third millennium B.C.E., mainly in Boeotia; the early second millennium, centering on the Middle Minoan culture; the Hyksos period, which is related to the period of the Shaft Graves at Mycenae; and the Eighteenth Dynasty.

After an introductory chapter reviewing the position of Crete in the third millennium, Bernal discusses other third-millennium connections between Egypt and the Aegean, which he proposes mainly on the bases of irrigation works around lakes in Boeotia, of the "Tomb of Amphion and Zethos" in the same region, and of mythological parallels with the Near East and Egypt. Bernal then returns to Crete to discuss the early palace period, whose genesis he ascribes largely to Egyptian influence in the early Middle Kingdom, when he believes that the bull cult was introduced from Egypt in association with the Theban god Montu, after whom the reunifier of Egypt, Nebhepetre Mentuhotep, was named. The word for the Labyrinth in Greek is given an Egyptian derivation, as are the names Minos and Rhadamanthys. For the following century, Egyptian domination in Palestine is assumed, partly on the basis of fictional descriptions such as that in the *Story of Sinuhe*. Bernal proposes, notably through using the Twelfth Dynasty Mit Rahina inscription to support traditions in classical authors, that Senwosret I launched a raid which went through much of Anatolia to Colchis, and possibly to Scythia. He suggests that this raid produced destructions known to have occurred in the region during the early second millennium, such as that of Kültepe, and that Senwosret left victory reliefs or stelae which influenced local artistic styles (see O'Connor, this volume).

Egyptian dating is then surveyed; Bernal follows in outline the high chronology proposed by James Mellaart (1979). He then discusses evidence for the date of the eruption of Thera, for which he accepts the figure 1628; the myth of Atlantis is discussed in relation to that eruption and there is an excursus on

Chinese history in relation to the Late Bronze Age eruptions in Europe. The following chapter reviews the identity of the Hyksos and proposes that as well as conquering Egypt, Hyksos people spread to the Aegean, where they were responsible for the destruction of the Middle Minoan palaces and formed the elite buried in the shaft graves at Mycenae. The culture of pre-eruption Thera and the Cyclades is also discussed.

The next chapter deals principally with the period of the Egyptian New Kingdom, starting with textual material and possible Egyptian and Near Eastern etymologies for Cretan and Aegean place names. Bernal proposes that Thutmose III mounted naval expeditions to the Aegean and sees the later Eighteenth Dynasty as a high point of a *pax aegyptiaca* when Egypt exercised hegemony throughout the Aegean and the eastern Mediterranean, there was active trade through the region, and Egyptian temples were dedicated at Mycenae. In the last main chapter he ascribes the fall of the Mycenaean world to a variety of factors, including the decline of eastern Mediterranean trade (he suggests that the Aegean had until then been sustained by imports of grain), invasions from the north, and climatic deterioration caused by the eruption of the volcano Hekla III in Iceland.

Essentially, the second volume of *Black Athena* fleshes out interpretations proposed in outline or in asides in the first volume. As the first volume referred back to ancient material in its discussions of modern scholars, so the second continues the ideological debate in frequent digressions from the immediate matter at hand. The argument proceeds at two levels, in terms of the ancient evidence and of the motivations and attitudes of previous interpreters of that evidence (so far as these two can be separated). In contrast to general practice, Bernal introduces modern scholars with their ethnicity and often a sort of academic genealogy, and he frequently mobilizes these factors—explicitly or implicitly—as well as the tone of people's writings, in explaining, approving, or dismissing what they say. This quirk is in keeping with his view of what one might term the embedded and committed character of scholarly discourse.

METHODS AND THEORIES

The Point of Departure

Bernal's methodological point of departure in the first volume of *Black Athena* is that Western classical scholarship has been dominated by agendas for maintaining the uniqueness and originality of European culture and race. He holds that this scholarship is Eurocentric and in important respects racist. In general, a racist mode of explanation is to be expected from periods when such forms of argument were widespread—that is, until around the middle of the twentieth century. Bernal's argument is thus about the specific effects of a normal style of reasoning, which he sees as being the minimizing or ignoring of the contribution of the Near East, and especially of Egypt, to the development of ancient Greece and the Aegean. He never quite states whether he thinks that today's classicists continue to be racists, but by stopping his dates at 1985 he may seek to imply that they are not.

In a broader perspective, such a turning away from the past and from cultural forebears is one of two basic strategies people use in approaching predecessors or ancestors and applies both to scholars and to a society's response to its past and cultural environment.[1] Either predecessors and ancestors legitimize by providing the source and value of who one is and what one can do; or one emphasizes one's own uniqueness and innovative character. These strategies need not be mutually exclusive, and innovation is very frequently legitimized as a return to the past; but over the world the first of these strategies is altogether more frequent than the second. In the Western case, which may owe some of its particular character to Western culture's untypical emphasis on innovation, Bernal sees racism in the denial by classical scholarship that the Aegean was strongly influenced by black—or, more broadly, African—and Semitic cultures. Western scholars will have had a racist agenda for adhering to the second approach, while the ancient Greek approach will be an instance of the much more widespread first strategy, and thus be unremarkable so far as this aspect is concerned. Critics of Bernal (see Hall, this volume) have cited such examples as the use of Trojan ancestry by aristocrats in medieval and modern Europe as showing that the first approach has a general value in legitimizing a culture whose members feel "provincial" in relation to a dominant or more ancient tradition, and that such a value has little to do with any truth content which these conventional or invented cultural genealogies may possess.

In using ancient narratives of the past directly in his work, Bernal himself belongs to the first of these tendencies, but he wishes, unlike the authors just alluded to, to move toward or to establish the truth, rather than to mobilize a myth. He defends the "competitive plausibility" of his position, which, he maintains, both approximates more fully to the truth and generates "hundreds of testable hypotheses" (*BA* 1:73). His political agenda is to give due credit to the contribution of black and Semitic peoples to European and Western civilization and "to lessen European cultural arrogance." In pursuing the contribution of black peoples to history, he at times uses arguments—including the title of his work—that he admits are overstated (Bernal 1989a, 31; 1990b, 133). One example is the statement that "black" kings of the Eleventh Dynasty reunited Egypt in the Middle Kingdom and inaugurated a new age of expansion (e.g., *BA* 2:22). Starting from the premise that Western scholarship has suppressed black and Semitic involvement in Mediterranean history, he wishes to mobilize anything possible that may be claimed to be "black" in support of this aim.

The point about "blackness" involves arguments about the paternity and maternity of specific individuals in ancient Egypt and their particular regional origins, as well as detailed and unknown nuances of their skin color, and seems inappropriate to any society that does not have an overriding obsession with race; it appears thus to suffer in reverse from the defects Bernal sees in classical scholarship. If this aspect of his presentation is left aside, as being addressed to a particular audience and rather extraneous to the work's main intellectual focus, there remeans nevertheless a remarkable omission, in that Bernal hardly treats Egypt's broader relations with the rest of Africa to its south and west, and still less the widespread evidence in other parts of the continent for the independent evolution of civilizations, or the appearance of distinctive advanced cultures under stimulus from outside, from times before European contact (Connah 1987) down to the Merina kingdom in late precolonial Madagascar (Bloch 1986, 12). If the African contribution to world cultures is to be evaluated, these societies deserve attention as much as Egypt or still more so, while the interaction of Egypt and the rest of Africa and their relations with the Near East can hardly be studied without reference to Egyptian relations with Nubia and Sudan. Egypt's direct contribution in Africa outside Nubia seems relatively small (e.g., Shinnie 1971). This does not imply inferiority on the part of the other African cultures, but rather that they were well able to develop on their own, and that certain of them achieved levels of creativity comparable with civilizations that evolved separately elsewhere in the world. The existence of a number of traditions of civilization in Africa is thus a major factor which Bernal largely leaves aside.

To insist on the significance of Egypt in these developments is to side with the classicists Bernal attacks and, intentionally or not, to present the role of Europe, and especially Greece, as being dominant in more general cultural evolution. Such a focus is surprising in a scholar whose original field of research was China and who appears to espouse cultural plurality and diversity. The only method that can avoid such a narrow view of cultural evolution is one that uses typological rather than unilinear models and adheres to theoretical and not simply narrative paradigms. This approach can give civilizations a proper position without positing an unrealistic level of diffusion among them. Although Bernal's concern is not with the theories which implicitly see the West as the goal of social evolution, but rather with the "teleology" of less theoretical Western scholarship, he seems to fall prey to assumptions similar to those of the theorists.

In relation to the Near East and the Aegean, Bernal has in one sense little to prove. Egypt and the Near East formed much of the wider cultural and economic region in which the Aegean was sited and provided its most complex civilizations with the most widespread high-cultural traditions. Insofar as they influenced the Aegean, which few will deny, their contribution is evident and only the precise extent of their involvement is at issue. Much of this is not known or understood, and the amount of identified Egyptian and ancient Near Eastern influence continues to grow. Beatrice Teissier (in press) has shown the great extent of Egyptian influence on the glyptic art of Syria-Palestine in the early second millennium, and the discovery of "Minoan" wall paintings in a palace of the Hyksos period at Tell el-Dab'a (Bietak 1992; Davies and Schofield 1995)[2] and at other sites in Syria-Palestine (Niemeier 1991) could point to cultural influence from the Aegean to Egypt, to the presence of Aegean craftsmen in the eastern Mediterranean, or perhaps to a cultural *koinē* in the late Middle Bronze Age which influenced the Aegean. The finds of Late Bronze Age shipwrecks off southern Turkey have produced notable surprises (Bass et al. 1988), documenting the intensity of trade in luxury goods in the whole region. All of these discoveries and studies serve to enrich the picture of Egyptian–Near Eastern relations in the second millennium, but they do not radically reorient it. The seal material is indicative of Egyptian artistic supremacy and points to the existence in antiquity of Egyptian exports of artistic materials in the form of small and perishable objects that hardly survive in the archaeological record (apart from such exported commodities as grain and papyrus). It may also relate to the considerable importance of Byblos as a port through which the trade passed. The role of Byblos, however, implies something else. That city's special relationship with Egypt and Egyptianizing culture would hardly make sense in a region where Egypt was generally dominant. Byblos used Egypt to set itself apart from its peers and neighbors.

For both the Middle and the New Kingdoms, the archaeological evidence, supported by texts from the New Kingdom, cannot easily be reconciled with the idea of an Egyptian colonial empire in the Syria-Palestine, as against cultural dominance in the Middle Kingdom,[3] followed by political hegemony in a context of local political and cultural autonomy in the New Kingdom.[4]

Yet while these relatively modest interpretations, which nevertheless present Egypt in a more prominent role than would have been envisaged a generation ago, may seem reasonable from the perspective of specialists in ancient Near Eastern studies, for Bernal they are inadequate. He wishes to rewrite much of the history of the Near East in the third and second millennia, giving Egypt a much greater role in events, cultural influences, and movements of peoples while also emphasizing the significance of the Phoenicians for the end of the period.

There is a problem with Bernal's focus on Egypt as the immediate or mediate source for influences on the Aegean. Egyptian culture was monolithic and highly interconnected and inward-looking in its organization and style.

Egyptian society appears to have been more homogeneous than that of its Near Eastern contemporaries. Perhaps in part for this reason, many Egyptian cultural traits did not travel well.[5] In contrast, Mesopotamian culture was plural in all periods. The Mesopotamian cultural area had no well-delimited boundaries, and its societies incorporated a range of ethnicities, diffusing vital cultural elements (such as the cuneiform writing system) in a number of directions. In these respects Mesopotamia was far more like a cultural area such as the Aegean—also a grouping of numerous polities and ethnicities (see Hall, this volume)—than was Egypt. Egypt offered a dominant model of a large-scale society that confronted the outside world in relative isolation while also interacting with it. Since Egypt was both nearer to the Levant and the Aegean than Mesopotamia and, for outsiders, had the perceived virtues of size and stability, its significance as a model is easily understood, and has been appreciated at least since the time of Herodotus. But Mesopotamia, which Bernal cites relatively little, was much more generally influential in the ancient Near East, and there were many routes by which its influence traveled. In giving a greater role to Egypt, Bernal bypasses these characteristic differences between the civilizations of the region and their impact outside themselves.

Agendas and Methods in Ancient Near Eastern Studies

How can Bernal's explicit agenda, as against his historical interpretations, be compared with the largely implicit agendas of most ancient Near East specialist studies? These scholars tend to see their own work as lacking agendas beyond those of the topic at hand: they wish perhaps to look for the truth, or to interpret their material in relation to particular theoretical approaches. Mostly they are drawn to their subjects by what they see as their intrinsic fascination, by their promise to provide rewarding evidence for specific problems, or by the unexploited material they offer, more than by what the cultures they study contributed to other parts of the world. But although these scholars may see their work in this way, they cannot avoid maintaining agendas, and their aspirations toward objectivity may suffer from their seldom bringing those agendas into the open. One purpose of using theoretical approaches and interpretive models is to control such biases by making them explicit, but theories come and go, and these methods can do no more than combat subjectivity. Theories are also a focus of research, and thus provide scholars with an agenda—to contribute broadly to the disciplines involved in the regional study of the Near East, such as linguistics, literature, art history, history of religions, cultural anthropology, theoretical archaeology, and so forth. In the academy as a whole, such agendas are vital to the standing of regional studies. In this context there is little in these agendas that would disqualify specialists in ancient Near Eastern studies from perceiving the significance of their cultures for the Aegean. If they are blinded in this way, it should be by something else.

The best-known critique of the implicit and political agendas of a discipline connected to ancient Near Eastern studies has been Edward Said's *Orientalism* (1978), but similar discussions, many of them related in some way to deconstructionism, are widespread in the humanities and social sciences and are linked in turn with the broad politicization of academic discourse and the politics of gender. Scholarship on the ancient Near East has seen rather little work in this area, and such of it as exists is not always of high quality (Horn 1972). These studies, including Said's, tend to suffer from not adopting rules of interpretation that would normally apply to the study of alien periods or cultural contexts: that the interpreter should seek to comprehend evidence in context and to identify positive aspects of what the material under study was designed to achieve. Instead these works are often exercises in putting people from contexts other than those of today in the dock and judging them by anachronistic criteria. The constant drift in interpretive values makes this danger hard to avoid, even in the evaluation of works quite close in time and context to a critic. If research is to advance, it is necessary for scholars to distance themselves from their predecessors; a balanced understanding of them also requires an act of empathy, even with a position the later interpreter may find objectionable.

Another danger is that of seeing an author's interpretation as being determined by social and intellectual context to a degree that almost excludes both the specific subject matter of the work and any personal independence of mind the author may possess (Ray 1990). Such determinism may become apparent either where a topic is ideologically relevant to the interpreter's position or where interpreter and object of interpretation are less clearly linked. An instance of the former possibility is the tendency of many scholars to identify with the societies they study, for example in their imperialism, and to write in partisan fashion of the needs to which the imperialism of "their" civilization responded. Such attitudes, as Said and Bernal well appreciate, are typical of imperialist epochs. They are also a natural part of classical studies, which they probably affect most strongly for Hellenistic times. Bernal makes an opposite case when he suggests that Colin Renfrew's support for the separate evolution of civilizations from small-scale beginnings relates to the latter's engagement in politics for the Conservative party (Bernal 1990b, 128). The reverse is as likely: British Conservatism was the partner of imperialism and large-scale capitalism, so that a Conservative might support diffusion. Bernal's reading looks unlikely, because the party's emphasis on small business belongs to the 1980s rather than the time of Renfrew's *Emergence of Civilisation* (1972). Renfrew should be allowed his own intellectual agenda.

Within an academic context, Bernal suggests (e.g., *BA* 2:523) that scholars

of the ancient Near East labor under a sense of inferiority, one manifestation of which is a desire to appear objective and "scientific," often at the
expense of the truth or of an unbiased approach, while nonetheless resisting
the conclusions of natural scientists. This pseudo-scientific approach, he suggests, tends to belittle the civilization under study. Effects include the down-
dating of historical periods from the higher figures proposed by scholars at
the beginning of this century. Bernal sees this tendency as a specific motivation for Egyptologists' failure to appreciate or propound the dominant role
of Egypt in the eastern Mediterranean. Moreover, he rather puzzlingly states
that unlike those who work on the ancient Near East in the humanities and
social sciences, the natural scientists have a "naive open-mindedness" and no
"axe to grind" in their approach to datings and other questions (e.g., *BA* 2:27,
29). There is no obvious reason why natural scientists studying the ancient
Near East should be exempt from the biases of other specialists or should
have a methodological neutrality which has repeatedly been demonstrated to
be a fiction in relation to their work within their more traditional fields.[6]

In the case of datings, one difficulty in Bernal's treatment is that whether
or not scholars were and are motivated as he suggests, an argument for a
higher date can hardly proceed by appeal to other scholars—of an imperialist
epoch—who proposed higher dates or by citing the work of Mellaart (1979),
which Bernal himself states was shown to be seriously flawed soon after it
appeared (Kemp 1980; Weinstein 1980). Bernal concludes (*BA* 2:210–11) that
James Henry Breasted's chronology of the early 1900s is "more trustworthy"
than later ones, not on the basis of detailed arguments and evidence for its
dates—Breasted was not a specialist in chronology—but "because of later
pressures to down-date." Bernal sets techniques from the natural sciences,
whose conclusions are also not definitive and which in this case he himself
modifies, against the dates of Egyptologists and Near Eastern archaeologists, and he reviews discussions over dating among the latter, but he does
not present a consistent critique.

Thus the reduction of about thirty years in Middle Kingdom dates proposed by Rolf Krauss (1985) is based on new readings in documents, new
calculations of lunar dates, statistical arguments, and revisions in the lengths
of reign of Twelfth Dynasty kings. Krauss's dates, later built on by Detlef
Franke (1988),[7] supersede those of Richard A. Parker (1950), which can no
longer be reconciled with the evidence. Krauss and Franke may well wish
their work to be thought "scientific," but their standards of comparison are
relatively recent work in Egyptology and, at least in Krauss's case, involve
astronomical methods and data, rather than a more generalized desire to assert the rigor of Egyptology against its denigrators. If higher dates are to be
used, they must be shown to be compatible with the evidence used by Krauss
and Franke, as against being in consonance with the standing of an academic

discipline, so far as Egyptology or ancient Near Eastern Studies are disciplines (see below), or of an ancient civilization—both of which are matters of indifference for the dates themselves. (The only thing one can confidently predict about proposed ancient dates is that they will be superseded.) Bernal cites the work of Krauss but inclines toward Parker's chronology without noting the problems of consistency inherent in doing so. In this instance the adjustment is slight and little is at stake, but Bernal's case for a larger change in third-millennium dates is weakened in that he does not engage with the specific evidence used to establish the dates he attacks (see also Yurco, this volume).

A difficulty that Bernal identifies correctly is the tendency of scholars to adopt an excessively evolutionary attitude to their material—this is my formulation rather than his—in a teleological as against a classificatory sense (see *BA* 2:33). Such an approach implies that because the ancient Near East was earlier than classical civilizations, it could not have exhibited features characteristic of later times, and its achievements are important more for how they pointed the way toward more "advanced" cultures than for their own sake. In a discussion of religion in the first volume of *Black Athena* (257–66) Bernal cites the example of literature (esp. 1:484 n. 146): the dominance in Western tradition of the Hebrew Bible and classical Greek literature has tended to blind scholars to the artistic complexity of ancient Near Eastern works, and relatively few have used analytical techniques appropriate to what they are studying or assimilated wider developments in the study of literature. A narrow evolutionism would imply that there is only one trajectory toward literary achievement and that earlier developments are of interest for how they contributed to later achievements rather than for their own sakes.

In this case Bernal may be unaware of more recent work. Although few studies of Egyptian literature from before about 1950 used productive strategies—this applies to favorable and perceptive evaluations such as Gardiner's (1941, 72), as well as to unfavorable ones—much later work addresses the material in terms that are far more appropriate to its character as literature and evaluates it positively, naturally identifying somewhat different categories and types from those of the Occident.[8] Counterexamples can of course be found (Caminos 1977, 76); these relate in part to the necessary plurality of scholarship and to the coexistence of several generations of practitioners. It is thus incorrect to assume that analyses of Egyptian literature belittle their object of study. The difficulties there have been in identifying suitable approaches are due partly to the need to develop basic skills of reading and comprehension before undertaking elaborate analyses and partly to a lack of theoretical sophistication in older studies in the field. And if these earlier works also in some respects partake in the evolutionism to which Bernal may be objecting, this is hardly their principal deficiency.

Aside from the case of literature, there are general ways in which methods in ancient Near Eastern studies have lagged behind those of many disciplines. An important reason for this gap is the dearth of adequate models of the ancient societies they address. If it is asked what group of people produced the evidence under discussion, how that group related to the society as a whole, and what the general character of the society was, it may be possible to improve approaches. At the same time, it is necessary to use methods and styles of argument that are applicable in as wide a range of contexts as possible, in order to avoid introducing implausible special modes of explanation for societies that belong to types recognizable in other periods, contexts, and regions of the world.[9]

Advances in method are important especially for archaeology. Perhaps in part because of the spell cast by Greece, its archaeology is relatively well known, and it is possible to construct trajectories of social evolution from a wide range of evidence (I. Morris 1987). Influences from other cultures must be seen in the context of the receiving society and whether it assimilated innovations or would have been in a position to exploit them. For the third millennium and early Iron Age Aegean, complex societies that would have assimilated more than stray items of high-cultural foreign influence are not apparent. A full colonial Egyptian presence, which might be an alternative model for influence, should have left much more substantial evidence than has been found, and might be expected to parallel in character the well-known finds of Nubia. Early Iron Age Greece would have had no use for writing and the alphabet, which Bernal (1990a) proposes were disseminated there by Late Bronze Age times and survived into the eighth century, when writing reappears in the archaeological record. Here and elsewhere, Bernal requires Aegean societies to have assimilated and retained influences from abroad across changes that would have left those influences without meaning for the actors. He does not take into account archaeological studies of societal collapse (cf. esp. Yoffee and Cowgill 1988), which have demonstrated the phenomenon's reality and variety and documented that collapses occurred in archaeologically attested societies without massive outside intervention. The Aegean world experienced more than one such collapse, as Bernal acknowledges at least for the end of the Mycenaean period (*BA* 2:495–521), yet he does not accept the potential cultural significance of such an episode. There is no need to seek a *deus ex machina* to explain these events, but they are likely to have affected the continuity of cultural traditions severely and adversely. After the end of the Bronze Age, several centuries elapsed before the Aegean achieved its previous level of population and prosperity.

Thus in the widely separate fields of literature and archaeology the use of theoretical models and of methods common over a whole field is directly relevant to interpretation, which will be the poorer without such procedures. Bernal seldom takes advantage of the possibilities offered by these approaches, and so restricts the potential of his work.

Is there nonetheless some crucial flaw in the approaches of specialists engaged with the ancient Near East, who are not often self-critical in their examination of their own political or other agendas, that renders their work unsuited to studying Aegean–Near Eastern relations? This question is far from the research interests of many scholars, but that point is not relevant here. To establish his case that their understanding of historical events is fatally compromised, Bernal would need to show either that they were so thoroughly subjugated intellectually by classicists that they could not use their evidence properly, or that their methods enacted the supremacist agendas of others and hence (in this case unintentionally) misinterpreted that evidence irretrievably—or both.

Very roughly, the first volume of *Black Athena* sets out to demonstrate the former possibility, and the second volume the latter. The former looks like a conspiracy theory and credits an often wayward group of people with little independence of mind; although it is impossible to prove such a point one way or other, I find the hypothesis unlikely. The latter possibility is superficially implausible, because essentially similar methods are used throughout the humanities and social sciences: ancient Near Eastern studies do not exist in an intellectual vacuum. Ultimately Bernal would need either to show, on the same evidence that specialists in that field use, that their interpretations are wrong according to commonly agreed criteria, or to propose a theoretical framework that would subsume their interpretations into a more cogent general understanding. So far, he has not adopted the first of these approaches, and for the second he would need to address theoretical issues comparable to those of the scholars he attacks. His principal strategy, however, is to bypass such arguments and attempt something that is in one sense completely different, although in another it returns to older interpretive strategies (see *BA* 2:48).

Implications of Bernal's Methods

Bernal's approach involves its own methodological difficulties. Apart from a generally positive evaluation of ancient Egypt, he says little of the nature of the Egyptian state or of its principal values. In respect to styles of argument, he uses ancient texts somewhat as if they aimed to record the truth, and he largely ignores the genre of a composition and the bias it might contain. In this he disregards a style of analysis that has been developed for all Near Eastern texts;[10] he also does not use the method he applies to Western texts in the first volume of *Black Athena*. Whereas studies such as those of Mario Liverani (1990) have advanced enormously our understanding of the ancient ideologies embodied in "historical" sources, progress in reconstructing actual events in ancient history is far less spectacular, and the nature of the material available is such that rapid improvement is not to be expected. As for the classical world, so for the ancient Near East: only a tiny proportion of "what happened" can be known, yet there is rich evidence for how events or nonevents were presented to contemporaries and to posterity, that is, for political and literary discourse and rhetoric. However strong the temptation may be, it is not possible to approach the sources without taking into account discourse and rhetoric, because the validity of modern arguments depends upon how the ancient sources on which they are based are handled.

Bernal does not exploit the methodological gains which have come with these improved approaches to ancient texts and archaeological materials. The most striking examples of his overconfident use of sources are in his treatment of Greek myths and legends. He gives these credence to an extent hardly found in other modern writing on such subjects, whatever the culture from which the material may derive. An analogue would be the view among earlier Egyptologists that the Egyptian state was formed by a King Menes who united the two lands of Upper and Lower Egypt. That reconstruction was assembled from a range of sources rather than read from a narrative, but the sources were from within a single cultural tradition and not superficially propagandistic, and so might reasonably have been accorded credence. Although the revision of our understanding of early Egypt over the last generation, due primarily to Werner Kaiser (1959–64), used similar sources as a point of departure, the essential demonstration of the new, more complex model came from archaeology—a model that fundamentally contradicts both the older Egyptological view and the dominant ancient model.[11] Despite the continuity of their civilization, the Egyptians appear to have had no more privileged access to their own early history than do we. Yet Bernal maintains that Greek traditions from the Classical and Hellenistic periods which would relate to times as early as the third millennium and, in part, to a different civilization are basically reliable. There is no clear reason why the Greeks' access to their past should have been superior to that of other peoples. Here he would seem, no doubt unintentionally, to follow older classicists in assuming that the Greeks were a people with quite special qualities; this is not something that even culturally partisan classicists now propose for this material.

In terms of general approach, Bernal can be characterized as a diffusionist; in fact he calls himself a "modified diffusionist" and dedicates the second volume of *Black Athena* to the memory of Gordon Childe. He seems to have little time for the evolutionary autonomy of any but a few societies, and he associates antidiffusionist interpretations with political conservatism. This last point is perplexing, because ideas of cultural autonomy have generally been associated with radical movements, whereas diffusionists have been the political conservatives (see above). However this may be, diffusionism is a mode of explanation that often circumvents questions concerning the constitution of societies, which allow cultural developments to be placed in a proper social context and theoretical framework. The diffusion of single traits is notoriously hard to prove, whereas large-scale cultural influence, such as can be demonstrated between Egypt and the Kerma and Kushite states (O'Connor 1984, 1994; Török 1989), typically affects societies that are tending toward comparable complexity and becomes evident over a wide range of features. Bernal does not use these well-established examples. The degree of Egyptian influence he posits for the Aegean is comparable to that attested between Egypt and Kush, yet the evidence from Kush is overwhelmingly greater than that from the Aegean. The identification of single traits would in any case not support Bernal's position strongly, as it would imply a lower level of diffusion and an absence of generalized and systemic influence.

This argument from Egypt's nearest African neighbors could be thought to be special pleading because of close contiguity, but similar points apply to Egyptian relations with Syria-Palestine. Egypt is known to have dominated this region up to the Euphrates for parts of the New Kingdom, and to have exerted major cultural influence at Byblos from the early third millennium, and in a broader region during in the Middle Kingdom. Archaeological finds commensurate with Egypt's role, including buildings more or less clearly identifiable as Egyptian, have been found from around the beginning of the First Dynasty (Gophna 1990; Ben-Tor 1991; Ward 1991; Na'aman 1991, 44) and from the New Kingdom (Kokhavi 1990), and by the late New Kingdom Egypt had long exerted a pervasive artistic influence that led into the Syrian styles of the first millennium, known principally from ivories, which virtually constitute an offshoot of Egyptian art outside Egypt (I. J. Winter 1973; Barnett 1982). This style was disseminated, especially on scarabs, throughout the Mediterranean in the first half of the first millennium (Vercoutter 1945). These developments show far more evidence of Egyptian presence and influence than material from the Aegean, and the spread of scarabs illustrates how a secondhand cultural influence can be diffused during a period of relative weakness in the culture which was the style's ultimate origin. This does not seem to me to offer a good parallel for the kind of political rather than cultural influence from a dominant state which Bernal believes Egypt exerted on the Aegean.

Even though Bernal hardly exploits current models and styles of interpretation, he repeatedly states that it is in these theoretical areas that he wishes to make his ultimate contribution. The model of classical civilization he attacks is what he terms the "Aryan Model." He would replace this with the "Revised

Ancient Model," incorporating the major role he propounds for Near Eastern—primarily Egyptian—influence in the constitution of Greek culture and civilization.

Since the publication of the first volume of *Black Athena* Bernal has termed his revision of current views of Near Eastern–Egyptian relations a "paradigm," in Thomas S. Kuhn's sense (1970; see Bernal 1989a, 17). Whether he is right to see the numerous meetings discussing his views as evidence that a paradigm shift is in progress—and he says that Kuhn himself does not view the matter in that way—neither the current state of ancient Near Eastern Studies nor Bernal's proposed replacement of parts of it necessarily constitutes a Kuhnian "paradigm." Those paradigms are coherent theories, formulated in relation to specific observations of natural phenomena, that have a normative force for a whole area or discipline in natural science. (Later studies have shown that Kuhn used the term in several senses; I believe this is an adequate characterization.) Despite the extended applications of Kuhn's term that have appeared since the publication of his book, ancient Near Eastern studies are not a "science" or a discipline in the Kuhnian sense. Rather, they are the sum of a range of methods and approaches applied to a great variety of materials from a particular geographical region and period; even definitions of the area and period are open to revision. So far as the ancient Near East relates to "paradigms," these are, for example, theories of social complexity and change, or in other cases theories of literary form and discourse.

This point is where Bernal's aims depart farthest from those of many specialists in ancient Near Eastern studies. In the second volume of *Black Athena* he commits himself to constructing a narrative for relations between the ancient Near East and the Aegean, rather than to creating a "model" or paradigm. Narratives are what the evidence supports least effectively, so that he builds his edifice on the most difficult ground. His narrative spans well over a millennium—probably both more than a narrative can effectively span and more than the actors can perceive as a coherent entity. Over that vast timespan, the character of Egypt, the civilization which forms the point of departure, changed slowly, but the Bronze Age and Iron Age Aegean underwent transformations so far-reaching that one would not expect much continuity in the ideologies of the successor societies or much accurate recall of earlier periods. I therefore doubt whether it is an appropriate strategy to seek to identify a single narrative thread running through such a span of time and space. If it is not, the separate phases of the reconstruction should not be seen as supporting one another, and the actors in the latest phases will not have been in a privileged position in relation to earlier phases. Thus, rather than a paradigm or an overintegrated narrative, Bernal's reconstruction in the second volume of *Black Athena* should, if possible, be evaluated as a set of readings of particular groups of evidence. I say "if possible" because the vast scale of his project renders such an undertaking difficult, and certainly outside the scope of this essay. His work is also so wide-ranging and touches on so many disciplines and categories of evidence that few have the competence to evaluate more than individual elements in it.

Thus, despite its temporal sweep, Bernal's approach is methodologically atomistic and does not exploit recent developments in theory or in analysis of contexts. There would be a positive value in ignoring such developments or in going back upon them if they were vitiated by their underlying ideology, but this is hardly a plausible reason for Bernal's abstention. Rather, his view of ancient history is of a "Romantic" character, somewhat different from that of the old-style classical scholarship he attacks but still presenting a world of grand events and individuals more familiar from such figures as Alexander the Great than from the ancient Near East in general. It is doubtful whether we should admire a civilization that would instigate events of this sort any more than we need admire the humanity of Alexander. If the contribution of Africa and Egypt in the evolution of Occidental civilization is to be revalued, the role of Bernal's Senwosret I, who is proposed to have conquered as far afield as Anatolia, Colchis, and possibly Scythia, leaving a trail of destruction and abandonment in his wake, will be morally uncomfortable. This Senwosret remains for me a figure of myth, not history. (Among the Egyptian and Hyksos conquests of the Aegean which Bernal proposes, he suggests only that Senwosret I's is demonstrated by a trail of destruction; the others would be among the most benign colonizations in history.)

THE EGYPTIAN SOCIAL AND INTELLECTUAL CONTEXT

Another aspect of the intellectual world Bernal posits should be reviewed here. In his first two volumes he is not principally concerned with exploring such areas as religion, although he draws freely upon the names of deities and other scattered material. He does not address Egyptian cosmology, which is relevant to his position because it may be the only accessible aspect of Egyptian thought that encompasses regions as remote from Egypt as those which concern him. As do many peoples, the Egyptians saw their country as the true cosmos and regions around it as peripheral.

The most detailed presentation of Egyptian views of the cosmos comes in astronomical texts, which mention the watery edge to the world in the north, from which migratory birds are said to come (Edel 1964, 105). Migratory birds are also mentioned in the *Story of Wenamun* (ca. eleventh century B.C.E.), whose protagonist stands on the seashore in Byblos and observes the migratory birds flying past to or from Egypt for the second time since he set out on his travels.[12] The astronomical texts do not incorporate "realistic" conceptions of the north coast of the Mediterranean, and their vision remains restricted to Egypt itself. Similarly, the huge numbers of offering-bearers personifying geographical areas include few instances of figures from north of Egypt, in contrast with relatively frequent instances from districts and countries to the south (there is no convenient collection of this material). The persistence of such a limited cosmological vision in face of the vast northern conquests and territorial interests that Bernal proposes would suggest a striking discord in Egyptian ideological presentation.

This point has a more specific ideological dimension. Egyptian kings, like many others, claimed dominion over the entire world, but there is little in their claims that relates clearly to a specific reality.[13] Where the claims are given in detail, they tend to refer about as far upstream as the region of the Fifth Nile Cataract in the south (O'Connor 1987a), or to Syria-Palestine in the north. This contrast between grandiose claims and more sober statements suggests that most of the rhetoric was not taken literally, any more than the imperialist motifs stamped on British coins until quite recently reveal underlying expectations. This distinction between rhetoric and other perceptions is in keeping with a relatively modest level of expansionism in Egyptian culture. Egypt's most dynamic achievements, such as the construction of the great pyramids or the temples of later times, were internal and unwarlike; its greatest extent of well-documented cultural contact, during the later New Kingdom, the Late Period, and the Ptolemaic period, was achieved as much by diplomacy and economic strength as by force of arms. In relation to its large size as a state in its own region, Egypt may not have been strongly oriented toward the outside world. Its rise was in no way as meteoric as that of Persia, nor its culture so readily exported as Mesopotamia's.

Bernal might respond that such an image results from a present-day failure of nerve among Egyptologists and Near Eastern scholars, induced by racism and by the dominance of Western classical studies. But if the character of the culture is to be evaluated on internal criteria, it may be better to see Egypt as basically nonexpansionary, rather as many African cultures have been throughout history. In the West, the predatory activities of states in recent centuries have given an unwarranted prestige to conquest—which is not to say that human beings are naturally pacific—and the ground on which Bernal has chosen to argue his case is rendered problematic by his own use of notions of conquest and diffusion. These may do no credit either to the epochs in which they originated or to the character of ancient Egypt.

Similarly, in the first volume of *Black Athena* (121–88) Bernal reviews evidence for the significance of Egypt for Western culture in terms of the Hermetic tradition and related phenomena that have been extensively studied during the twentieth century. He reviews some of the controversy over the extent of Egyptian ideas present in the Hermetic texts,[14] arguing that Egypt contributed much to the religious movements of which the texts are in part a product, both through the earlier diffusion which is his principal concern and through the environment of "late antiquity," which he dates, following W. M. F. Petrie, between the sixth century B.C.E. and the second century C.E. He cites with approval (*BA* 1:140) James Henry Breasted's suggestion that the "Memphite Theology" contains concepts comparable with Greek *nous* and *logos*. Unlike his revival of Petrie's datings, Bernal's view that there is a substantial element of Egyptian ideas in the Hermetic Corpus is conventional. Yet in this discussion there is no suggestion that Egyptian modes of religious and philosophical expression might differ importantly from Greek or Iranian ones, and that they might have their own systematic character that should be examined. He does not cite discussions and editions of crucial Egyptian religious texts like the solar hymns and underworld books, by such authors as Jan Assmann (1983) and Erik Hornung (1984). He also scarcely mentions Egypt's much-discussed artistic influence on the West, which is in many ways more potent than its influence through ideas and texts.

Here as in other respects, Bernal's basic strategy (1990b, 111), of treating Egyptian and Levantine civilizations through their influence on the Aegean and classical world, has the opposite of its intended effect. He gives Egypt stature only in relation to a later and different culture and thus succumbs to the Eurocentrism he wishes to combat. Civilizations vary in character and achievement. If a past civilization is to be comprehended and given a fit stature, as Bernal wishes, it should not be seen through the medium of a different and later past civilization. In this respect Egyptologists and other specialists in ancient Near Eastern studies pay their subject the due of making it the center of their concern. Africa and the ancient Near East will prosper more in a truly pluralistic scholarship, which encompasses civilizations of the whole world without seeking a single line of evolution, than in one that focuses on a single tradition and cultural style.

More narrowly, Bernal's reluctance to engage with ancient Near Eastern civilizations on their own terms leads to bizarre interpretations. Thus for the late third millennium he ascribes a major role in diffusion abroad to the second-rank Egyptian deity Montu, whose name he sees underlying the Greek Rhadamanthys (*BA* 2:178–82), and derives the name of the Greek goddess Rhea from the Egyptian Raet(-tawy), *r*'*wt-(t3wj)*, who is known almost exclusively from the Theban area and relatively late times (Gutbub 1984). Such readings look like solutions to problems in crossword puzzles, where context is unimportant or self-referential (see Jasanoff and Nussbaum, this volume), rather than interpretations integrated into considered models of the societies and complexes of beliefs that may have diffused and received cultural transmission. Thus, although Bernal is correct to insist that the sociology of knowledge illuminates the interpretations of Western scholars, he does not seem to apply the same principles to ancient peoples.

CONCLUSION

Bernal ends the second volume of *Black Athena* on two paradoxes (522–27). The first of these is a rhetorical listing of his "outrages" against what he sees as academic orthodoxy; he promises to provoke greater outrages in the third volume, which is to be about language. Yet outrages are hardly likely to win over those who are unconvinced by his approach, and one wonders whether they are really intended to do so—or whether they are presented at least partly with the aim of producing outraged reactions. However this may be, Bernal does not seem to consider the possibility that specialists in the Near East might in any case have an interest in promoting "their" civilizations— whether or not that is the best basis for disinterested study—or that he and they may have a very different feel for the nature of their data and of the society or societies which produced it.

The second paradox rests in a more general comment Bernal makes on his historical reconstruction, where he remarks that he has returned to many interpretations of the early years of the twentieth century, but in a different framework and in a different spirit. He notes that these interpretations were offered by people who may have held the racist and colonialist beliefs he abhors along with most of the rest of the academic profession. Elsewhere, he discusses the ethnic composition of the Hyksos, whom he sees, against his own "ideological reluctance," as including Hurrians and Indo-Europeans as well as Semitic groups (*BA* 2:346–48); one would hope rather that he might be personally neutral, rather than racially committed in some way, when considering which ethnic groups may have been present among the Hyksos. He does not, however, comment on the methodological implications of his preference for views formulated before source-critical methods had developed significantly in Near Eastern studies, even though the company he finally keeps might have alerted him to difficulties there.

Despite his professed radicalism, Bernal's methods and conclusions are in the end deeply conservative. His world of great events and broad historical sweeps seems remote from the mainly small-scale, slowly changing societies described by archaeologists and students of texts. He does not completely address the complexity of societies, whether small communities or large states. As both his discussion of the Hyksos and his treatment of "black" Egyptian kings cited earlier (*BA* 2:32) exemplify, his concern with race also leads him to adopt models of ancient ethnicity that are both inappropriate to the materials studied and ethically somewhat distasteful.[15]

In this essay I have explored implications of Bernal's methods rather than the question of whether he has established a secure, or in his words "competitively plausible," interpretation of the evidence he uses. In Egyptological terms, which are my principal concern here, his interpretations appear implausible for a number of reasons. Among these are that they give a thin sense of an ancient society, focusing on its principal protagonists to the exclusion of a broader picture either of the people as a whole or of the possible beliefs and motivations of those central protagonists. His readings do not confront the subject matter or the secondary literature to its full extent, ignoring, for example, the well-established parallels for Egyptian expansion in Nubia and Kush and in Syria-Palestine. Often, when an author's conclusions do not suit Bernal's position, he argues against them by associating them with that author's beliefs or academic school rather than by confronting the specifics of a case (e.g., *BA* 1:138, on Walter Scott, the editor of the *Hermetica*, against Petrie, who was certainly not an expert in the area). As this tone and interpretive style pervade his work, I suspect that this stricture applies also to parts I am not competent to evaluate.

Bernal, however, sees his methodological challenge and rewriting of the historical outline of a millennium as more significant than his Egyptology. That subject may of course seem more central to its practitioners than to others, and he need not commit himself to it, but Egyptological materials are so vital for his reconstruction that so limited a use of them may endanger his position. As I have indicated, the Egyptological argument is not finally in terms of "Egyptological method," which does not exist as such, but in terms of the range of general methods and approaches that are brought to bear upon materials from ancient Egypt. The same applies to ancient Near Eastern scholarship as a whole: the field is not governed by a single, close-knit approach and method, but by the evidence and periods it studies.

Although Bernal has assembled fascinating material from many different fields and has identified a number of weaknesses in the understanding of Egyptian relations with the Near East, the implications of these discrepancies may not be as profound as he suggests. Like most scholars, he is more successful in demolishing interpretations than in creating new ones; and, at least in my perception, the parts of his construction visible so far have altogether less interpretive power than the framework he wishes to discard. It seems unwise to abandon the methodological gains in analyzing complex societies and categories of evidence, as well as the moral caution, of recent decades in favor of his new old world of vastly extended social memory, grand events and coincidences, unambiguous values, and heroes and villains.

NOTES

This essay reworks some material in Baines 1991. Some of the discussion relates also to Baines 1990, 1–6. I am grateful to Antonio Loprieno for inviting me to write it, but I must also apologize to Martin Bernal for flouting the convention that one does not review a book twice. I hope, however, that I have managed usefully to cover rather different ground here. I thank Norman Yoffee in particular for criticizing drafts both of the review and of this essay, and Susan Sherratt for references.

1. For Egypt, Baines 1989; more generally, Assmann 1992.

2. Bietak's subsequent finds are as yet unpublished.

3. Raphael Giveon's (1974) view that there was lasting Middle Kingdom control in Palestine has not gained acceptance; see also O'Connor, this volume.

4. For the character of Egypt's Near Eastern "empire" see Kemp 1978; Frandsen 1979; Weinstein 1981 (problematic in some areas); for analyses of the texts see Liverani 1990.

5. The great exception of the alphabet (treated in Bernal 1987b, 1990a) is generally agreed to be a mediated transmission through Syria-Palestine.

6. See Kuhn 1970, which Bernal cites with approval elsewhere; and *BA* 2:51.

7. See now also Luft 1992, with another proposal. No consensus has emerged in this area.

8. Among earlier examples are Fecht 1965; Assmann 1969; despite its influence, Posener 1956 is rather problematic here; for a valuable survey including recent work see Loprieno, in press.

9. For a possible approach see Baines and Yoffee, in press.

10. For a summation see Liverani 1990, not available to Bernal in time for *BA* 2.

11. Günter Dreyer's recent work (e.g., 1992) further enriches and complicates the picture.

12. Lichtheim 1976, 228; for interpretation see Egberts 1991.

13. Liverani (1990) analyzes this general ancient Near Eastern phenomenon.

14. Without citing discussions by Egyptologists (e.g., Derchain 1962).

15. Contrast the illuminating discussion of Mesopotamian ethnicity by Kamp and Yoffee 1980.

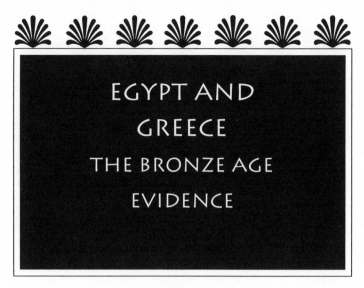

EGYPT AND GREECE
THE BRONZE AGE
EVIDENCE

David O'Connor

Martin Bernal has published in part, and continues to work on a major re-evaluation of the interrelationships between Greece and the Aegean, on the one hand, and Egypt and the Levant on the other. His basic thesis is stated with great clarity, that "there is a real basis to the stories of Egyptian and Phoenician colonization of Greece" which were current among Greeks of the Classical and Hellenistic ages. This colonization began in the first half of the second millennium B.C.E., and "Greek civilization is the result of the cultural mixtures created by these colonizations and later borrowings from across the East Mediterranean." In addition, Indo-European speakers who invaded or infiltrated Greece from the north were also an important element (*BA* 1:2).

Elsewhere Bernal restates his thesis in a slightly different way, namely, that there is a real "possibility of a massive Semitic component in the Greek vocabulary"; that there were "possible Egyptian colonizations of Greece"; and that it is an arguable hypothesis "that Egyptian language and culture played an equal or even more central role" (as Semitic languages and cultures) "in the formation of Greek civilization" (*BA* 1:37).

This thesis is put forward in the context of an elaborate and fascinating analysis of the changing scholarly and public ideas about the origins of Greek civilization during the sixteenth, seventeenth, eighteenth, nineteenth, and twentieth centuries of the present era. These changes led to the rejection of the idea that the Levant and Egypt had contributed in any significant way to the development of Greek civilization. Bernal, however, has force-fully restated the earlier proposition, which he terms the "Ancient Model," as the "Revised Ancient Model." The results, as he points out, are that "many interesting new questions" are raised, "hundreds of testable hypotheses" generated, and the interest of specialized scholars aroused in the issue; and that "European cultural arrogance" is lessened.

Proposed revisions of accepted scholarly theory must be taken seriously and approached sympathetically. In a general way, such revisions go on all the time, albeit often on a small scale; but sometimes they can be quite substantial in impact. Egyptology itself is replete with examples. For instance, generations of scholars had accepted virtually as fact the theory that many marriages between pharaonic Egyptians were consanguineous, indeed incestuous—until Jaroslav Černý (1954) carefully analyzed the abundant data available and demonstrated that the theory was wrong.

In particular, as students of Egyptology or other disciplines relating to Africa and the Near East in ancient times, we need to be constantly aware of a debilitating tendency. It would, I think, be too strong to describe this tendency, in Bernal's words, as "European cultural arrogance," although one could more legitimately have done so some thirty or fifty years ago. But certainly we must all struggle to overcome an inevitable ethnocentrism, particularly as this is often abetted by the attitudes of the ancient Egyptians themselves. In the area of foreign relations (one very relevant to Bernal's thesis), for example, ancient Egyptian sources reveal a dismissive attitude to foreigners which makes it difficult for us to work out the real nature of the relations between Egypt and other regions at specific moments in time.

However, as Bernal repeatedly emphasizes, the point of hypotheses is to test them; the hypothesis challenges accepted theory, but has no advantage over it unless it can survive tests that at least establish its *probability*, and perhaps—even better—show reasonably surely that the hypothesis is true. It is my purpose here to take some of the hypotheses—not so much the grand ones, but the smaller ones upon which the grand ones depend—raised by Bernal about Bronze Age Egypt and the Aegean, and to test their probability, or near certainty, in terms of what we currently know.

I also focus on certain historical and archaeological data. Much of Bernal's discussion in the first volume of *Black Athena* (and that proposed for subsequent volumes) concerns linguistic and etymological arguments that extend well beyond my competence and well beyond the Bronze Age as well (but see Yurco, and Jasanoff and Nussbaum, this volume). But I think it would be true to say that these arguments gain much of their strength for Bernal from his belief that an Egyptian "colonization" of the Aegean region was a historical reality throughout most of the second millennium B.C.E. The material I discuss is very germane to this last issue. To the extent that Bernal has already changed his mind on some points that I have presented here as being his, I apologize. My concerns are the data discussed and the issues raised in the first volume of *Black Athena*, published in 1987.

BERNAL'S HYPOTHESES

Bernal advances several specific hypotheses, the validity of which can be examined here.

1. During the later Eleventh Dynasty, Egypt had a substantial impact on the Aegean world. This impact manifested itself in "widespread destructions" (*BA* 1:17), in the establishment of a Cretan bull cult modeled on that of the Egyptian god Montu, a god to whom the Eleventh Dynasty showed special devotion, and in the establishment of palaces on the island of Crete (1:63). The impact may have been "direct or indirect" (1:18), and the mechanisms may have been Egyptian "raids and colonies" in the Aegean (1:17) or, at least, the wide-ranging contacts Egypt had at this time, contacts "certainly including Crete and possibly the Mainland [of Greece]" (1:18). The most suggestive support for this theory is provided by the known expansiveness of later Eleventh Dynasty, during which the Levant was attacked (1:18, 63), and there is "archaeological evidence of contacts between Egypt and the Aegean at this time" (1:63).

2. Herodotus and later authors describe the widespread conquests of a pharaoh Sesostris, who could represent one or more of the Twelfth Dynasty pharaohs of that name; ancient legends also describe the wide-ranging expeditions of an Ethiopian or Egyptian prince called Memnon, possibly representing one or more of the Twelfth Dynasty pharaohs called Amenemhet. These accounts have been given little credence; but "both legendary cycles" may have been "vindicated" by a text discovered at Mit Rahina, describing the "conquests, by land and sea," of Senwosret I and Amenemhet II (*BA* 1:19), later described by Bernal as "wide-ranging Egyptian land expeditions and marine voyages in the 20th century B.C.E." (1:39–40, 64). To the impact of this Egyptian activity on the Aegean Bernal attributes a "destruction at the end of Early Helladic III" in the Aegean (1:17) and "most of the ram-cults found around the Aegean," derived from the Twelfth Dynasty's devotion to the god Amun and the ram associated with him (1:19, 64).

3. The Hyksos who conquered Egypt soon after invaded the Aegean; more specifically, this was a "Hyksos-Egypto-Canaanite conquest of Crete," with the establishment of "colonies" further north (*BA* 1:44–45, 19–21). As a result, all the Cretan palaces were destroyed, then rebuilt; Levantine swords, shaft graves and royal motifs became important in the Mycenaean world; and Aegean influence was visible in objects found in Egypt in the Hyksos period and the early Eighteenth Dynasty (1:44–45, 19–21).

4. Another "high tide of Egyptian influence" in the Aegean is to be dated to the Eighteenth Dynasty. The specific evidences are that Ahmose, founder of the dynasty, claimed "some kind of suzerainty over *Ḥꜣw Nbw*" ("a region plausibly identified with the Aegean") and his mother, Aḥḥotep, came from the *Ḥꜣw Nbw*; that there was "some interchanging of population" between Egypt and the Aegean, evidenced by a contemporary list of names; that from Tuthmosis III onwards Eighteenth Dynasty pharaohs exercised "some form of suzerainty over Crete and beyond"; and that the Egyptians were aware of the conquest of Crete by the Mycenaeans, and list (under Amenhotep III) places in Ta-na-yu (almost certainly the Danaans and Greece, according to Bernal), "several of which have been plausibly identified with toponyms in Crete and Greece." Finally, because Egyptian plaques of a type placed in temple foundation deposits (here, of Amenhotep III) were found at Mycenae, it is likely that the Eleusinian cult of Archaic Greece "was the descendent of an Egyptian foundation made there 700 years earlier" (*BA* 1:2, 40, 69).

The evidence referred to is both textual and archaeological, and some (depictions of Aegean tribute-bearers in Eighteenth Dynasty officials' tombs) is iconographic. The textual evidence is the most significant, because of its capacity for being precise and explicit, and I address that first. The archaeological evidence is inherently more ambiguous, and I turn to it thereafter.

THE TEXTUAL EVIDENCE: TWELFTH DYNASTY

The earliest textual datum is the Mit Rahina inscription, a long, incomplete text of which a hand copy has been published (Farag 1980), as well as a brief commentary (Posener 1982). In the circumstances, my observations are necessarily quite tentative; but they are based on an analysis of the text itself.

The text recorded a flow of items, their provenances, and their destinations. The destinations are mainly cults associated with Senwosret I and Amenemhet II respectively—and perhaps of Amenemhet I as well (cf. the Petrie fragment mentioned by Posener). One might reasonably conclude that the gifts recorded were allotted by Amenemhet II (his full titulary is given at one point, hinting at his authorship) to cults of his grandfather (Amenemhet I), father (Senwosret I), and himself. It follows, then, that the expeditions abroad, and the visits to Egypt by tributaries, which generated some of these gifts, all date to the reign of Amenemhet II, and not in part to Senwosret I's, as Bernal has suggested. Alternatively, the text's "author" may be an even later pharaoh, in which case the expeditions and tributaries in question would date to *his* reign, not that of Amenemhet II.

There is no doubt that this is a Twelfth Dynasty text of considerable historical importance. But does it describe "wide-ranging Egyptian land expeditions and marine voyages" likely to have reached as far as the Aegean, and having upon that region the effects Bernal assumes, namely, "destruction" and the establishment of ram cults?

The expeditions and voyages in question (and there may have been others; the text is incomplete) are several. First is an expedition, probably peaceful and seaborne, to Lebanon (*ḥnty-š*). Such an expedition is, in fact, referred to twice (in lines 7 and 18), but it is perhaps the same expedition in both cases. Obviously, if *two* cult establishments received gifts from the same expedition, the expedition would then be referred to twice, for the text is organized in terms of the recipient cult places, not in terms of the expeditions. Another, apparently pacific expedition, was dispatched to Setjet, a generalized term for Syria-Palestine, or parts thereof (line 8). Yet a third expedition, also pacific, was sent to Sinai to recover turquoise (line 13). Only one clearly hostile expedition (or, better, campaign) is referred to in the surviving text, in line 16 and perhaps again (the text is damaged) in line 26, perhaps for the same organizational reasons that the abovementioned expedition to Lebanon was referred to twice. This hostile expedition was sent to "hack up" two lands, which are named and were inhabited by Aamu, or Syro-Palestinians, and many prisoners were brought back as a result.

These expeditions deserve several comments. First, only one (of the four surviving) is a hostile one, whereas the other three are peaceful, and for either trading or mining purposes. There is also no reason to think that the hostile expedition was anything other than a serious raid (such as the Egyptians periodically launched against Upper Nubia in the Twelfth Dynasty), without any permanent Egyptian occupation following. The expeditions, then, should not be described as "conquest, by land and sea," as Bernal states.

Second, none of the expeditions went beyond the rather limited range of foreign contact documented textually elsewhere for the Twelfth Dynasty. Sinai and Lebanon were traditional areas of contact, and the hostile attack probably occurred in Palestine, a favorite Egyptian raiding ground during the Twelfth Dynasty. There is no indication here of aggression, or even trading contacts, further north than Lebanon along the Levantine coast, and certainly no hint of contact with the Aegean.

Bernal does not mention the tributaries who delivered products to Egypt, but they are of course relevant. Insofar as the text survives, these tributaries came from the Aamu (Syro-Palestinians) of Setjet (line 12); from Tjempaw, a land yielding lead and probably, therefore, also Levantine (Posener 1982, line 15); and from Kush (Upper Nubia) and Webetsepet, a desert region east of Upper Nubia (Posener 1982, 7–8 line 11). Given the ideological distortion typical of Egyptian monumental texts, it need not be assumed that *any* of the tributaries came from regions occupied by Egypt. They could be from contiguous regions, anxious to placate Egypt, and also to trade (very likely the case with Kush and Webetsepet, both independent of but raided by Egypt in the Twelfth Dynasty), or from relatively remote regions, purely interested in trade. So these passages are not evidence for a far-spread Egyptian "empire" at the time. Moreover, these places all were certainly or possibly within Egypt's rather limited range of contact at the time and do not indicate contact with the Aegean or with regions far from Egypt.

Neither this text, nor any other datum, changes the current impression that Twelfth Dynasty Egypt was relatively restricted in terms of campaigning and direct trading contacts. To the south, only Lower Nubia was colonized; Kush and the desert kingdoms remained independent, although they endured aggressive Egyptian campaigns, and the former indeed had become a substantial state (cf. O'Connor 1987b). To the northeast, Sinai was held by Egypt, and Byblos, a small coastal state, functioned to some degree as a vassal state. Palestine, however, was independent. (The claims for Egyptian "empire" in this region are weakly based.) Like Kush, it periodically endured Egyptian attack; but it housed a complex of city-states from which was to rise the impressive power of the Hyksos invaders of Egypt after the Middle Kingdom (Weinstein 1981, 5–10). The Egyptians may well have sent trading expeditions to coastal Syria, but the available evidence is ambiguous, since many of the Middle Kingdom objects found here may have reached Syria in post–Middle Kingdom times (Weinstein 1975).

Were the Egyptians capable of sailing as far as the Aegean? Technically yes, for during the Middle Kingdom they dispatched seaborne voyages to Punt on the Red Sea coast, involving a round trip of about 1,700 kilometers. The direct distance between the Egyptian coast and Crete is actually less than that between Egypt and Punt. However, as in the Red Sea, the Egyptians would probably have sailed along coasts, not out in open waters; to do so along the hostile Libyan coast with its poor water supplies would be difficult (and still involve a long open-sea voyage in the end), whereas any effort to do so along the Levantine and southern Anatolian coasts would have been discouraged by the many maritime powers distributed along such a route.

On the basis of textual evidence, then, a significant Twelfth Dynasty impact on the Aegean seems unlikely.

THE TEXTUAL EVIDENCE: EIGHTEENTH DYNASTY

The other textual data concern the Eighteenth Dynasty; and it should be said at the outset that iconographic evidence indicates that at least in the mid–Eighteenth Dynasty, people from the Aegean were indeed visiting Egypt, probably as traders whose activity was reinterpreted as that of "tributaries" in the officials' tombs in which they are depicted (Vercoutter 1956; cf. also Wachsmann 1987; Cline 1987, 1–23; Cline 1990, 210, n. 46). Even later Mycenaean material continued to reach Egypt, again suggesting possibly direct contact, although the intermediary role of the Levant must also be taken into account (Cline 1987, 13–17). So there is no doubt that the Eighteenth Dynasty and the Aegean were in contact; but could Egypt claim any kind of "suzerainty" over the Aegean, and influence its culture in the way Bernal suggests? Indeed, did Egyptians even get to the Aegean at all? Or was it only a question of Aegean navigators' reaching Egypt?

Turning to the textual data cited by Bernal, one notes first the claim that at the opening of the Eighteenth Dynasty, Ahmose claimed suzerainty over the Aegean, and his mother Aḥhotep actually came from that region. The first suggestion is based on a panegyric of Ahmose, which includes the statement that the "Haunebut in (their) entirety say: that which we serve, is in him" (*Urk.* 4.17.12–13) and the second on a panegyric of his mother and regent Aḥhotep, who is praised as the "mistress of the world (*t3*), the mistress of the shores of the Haunebut, whose name is elevated over all foreign lands" (*Urk.* 4.21.3–5). First, it should be noted that being a "mistress" of the Haunebut does not imply one is *from* there, as Bernal suggests; Egyptian pharaohs (and Aḥhotep here is conceived of in the role of a pharaoh) are often said to be "lords" of different foreign lands, yet they are all indisputably Egyptian. Second, it must be remembered that—in monumental texts such as these—pharaohs often claimed control over regions that in reality were quite independent.

Moreover, it is by no means certain that *Haunebut* refers to the Aegean. Two sustained analyses of the use of the term (Vercoutter 1956, 15ff.; Vandersleyen 1971, 139ff.) both reached the conclusion that in the Late Bronze Age and earlier it did not refer to the Aegean but rather to areas generally located within Syria-Palestine. As yet, no compelling case has been put forward that would lead to a different conclusion. A more probable candidate as a description of the Aegean islands is the phrase translated "the islands in the midst of the sea," although even this has been disputed (Vandersleyen 1985, 44–46).

As to the idea that there was an interchange of population between Egypt and the Aegean at about this time, the relevant datum is a scribal palette bearing a text that begins: "Making the names of the country of Kefty [Crete]," followed by a list of personal names. The rubric indicates that each person should be from Kefty (assuming the list itself to be homogeneous), but six of the names are Egyptian, two possibly so, four apparently Keftiu, and two of uncertain ethnic significance. On the face of it, this circumstance might appear to mean that Egyptians could be considered inhabitants of Crete (reflective of the "colonization" envisaged by Bernal) or that native Cretans bore Egyptian names in Crete, indicative at least of substantial Egyptian influence. However, the alternative explanation, that we have here a list of Cretans settled in Egypt (forcibly or otherwise), some of whom have been assigned Egyptian names, fits in well with a custom known elsewhere in

Late Bronze Age Egypt. In this case, a population interchange, or strong Egyptian influence on Crete, need not be involved (Vercoutter 1956, 45–50).

Finally, we come to the famous list of Cretan and Aegean place names found on a statue base of Amenhotep III, referred to by Bernal as providing a list of places under the control of the Greek mainland, dominated by the Mycenaeans. This document relates to Bernal's idea that Egypt at this time exercised "some kind of suzerainty over Crete and beyond." The statue base in question was one of five, lined up along the western side of a court in the funerary temple of Amenhotep III, north of the temple axis; the meaning of the base in question can only be understood in relationship to the other four (Edel 1966; Cline 1987, 26–30; Osing 1992, 25–36).

The statue bases ran south to north along a line at right angles to the temple axis. Analysis shows that they were laid out according to the map of the ancient world, north of Egypt, as it was known to educated Egyptians of the day. Edel had already observed that the bases A_N and E_N respectively represented the northeast and northwest extremities of Egypt's geographical knowledge; but he does not carry this insight as far as I do here. I would argue that the statue bases represent a map that, from "bottom" (southernmost) to "top" (northernmost) moves from south to north (quite literally) but also, if less obviously, from east to west.

The toponyms distributed over the five bases can be envisaged as a single list, a probability indicated by the traditional list of the "Nine Bows" covering all the world known to Egypt: this list is found on the left side of the statue base A_N, immediately adjacent to the temple axis, and indicates the coverage of the following, more specific list, distributed over the five statue bases. This distribution, as Edel observed, was not random; rather, it shows that the designers had a mental "map of the world" according to which specific toponyms were allotted to specific statue bases (see figures 1 and 2).

Thus base A_N records the world northeast of Egypt, a northeast zone of reference beyond Egypt's area of domination. Once the Nine Bows are recorded, the lefthand list moves from the [Hittites] through Arzawa to Assyria (and contiguous regions?), and is thus an itinerary (Redford 1982) running from the northwest to the north center of this sphere of reference. The righthand list moves from Babylonia to Mittani, thence through Syria, and on to the Hittites (and contiguous regions?), and is thus an itinerary running from the southeast to the northwest of the northeast zone of reference.

B_N focuses on toponyms in Egyptian-held or -dominated territory in Palestine, Lebanon, and southern Syria (Edel 1966, 8–9); no particular itinerary-like structure is evident. The lists of toponyms on C_N and D_N are (like the others) incomplete and also include many new names, hitherto unknown; the relevance to subsections of Egypt's "world map" is therefore not known. However, they clearly belong to the northeast sphere of reference.

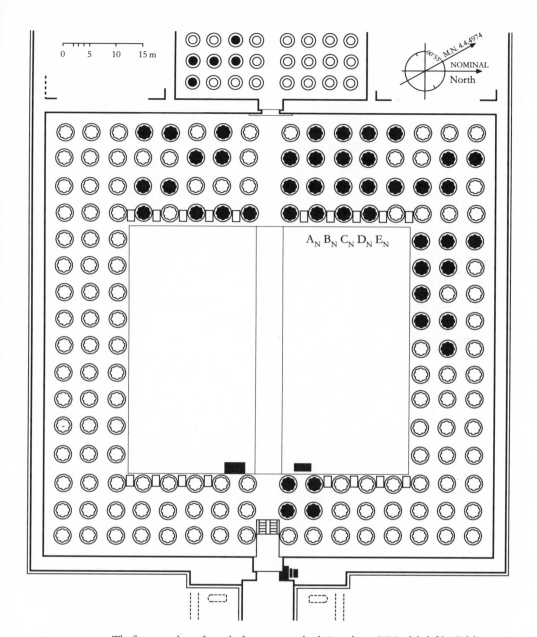

$A_N \; B_N \; C_N \; D_N \; E_N$

FIGURE 1. *The five statue bases from the funerary temple of Amenhotep III (as labeled by Edel):*
actual sequence (from south to north, A_N to E_N) has been reversed so the bases correspond
in location to the areas on the map in figure 2.

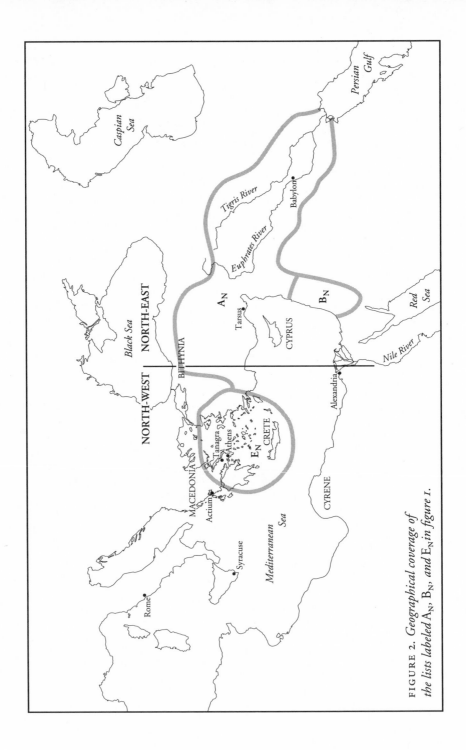

FIGURE 2. *Geographical coverage of the lists labeled A_N, B_N, and E_N in figure 1.*

Possibly they relate to particular kinds of relationships between Egypt and certain places or identify particular categories of peoples and places whose unusual status excluded them from the A_N and B_N lists. Thus in D_N one group of names is a series of nomadic tribes, beginning with the Aramaeans (Edel 1966, 33). Finally, E_N is restricted to the northwest zone of reference, covering, insofar as preserved, Rhodes (possibly), Crete, Kythera, and the Greek mainland (cf. Cline 1987, 2–6 with table 2).

The significance of this interpretation, I think, is clear. Pharaoh claims ideological dominance or suzerainty over *all* the places mentioned; but in reality he had suzerainty over only *some* of them, and the layout of the toponyms reflects sensitivity to this reality. Clearly Arzawa, the Hittites, Mittani, North Syria, Assyria, and Babylonia were *not* in reality subject to pharaoh; and by the same token, the Aegean islands and lands were not either, unless some *other* evidence should show that they were—and no such conclusive evidence exists.

The E_N base calls for additional comment. First, it must have been intended for this statue base to have had two lists, one lefthand, the other righthand (cf. the general demand for symmetry, and the specific example of the other four bases); in actuality, only the first two names of the righthand list were inscribed. Edel argued (1966, 34–35) that these two names are shown by the superscription above them actually to belong to the lefthand list; but the superscription can more reasonably be interpreted as *independent* of the lefthand superscription, and the righthand list as independent of the lefthand list. Moreover, as noted above, symmetry and analogy demand that the two righthand names began a (never inscribed) righthand list. Incidentally, the superscriptions do *not* correlate geographically with the list below them; in the superscription on the lefthand side, the "Fenkhu" (of the Levant) and "Nubia" are placed above toponyms of Crete!

Third, on the analogy of A_N especially (the closest complement to E_N), one might suggest that the lefthand and righthand lists respectively defined different "itineraries" and were largely different in composition, although with some overlaps (as in the possible two occurrences of the Hittites in A_N; for the general dissimilarity between righthand and lefthand list, see *all* the bases). Thus (if we deny that "Troy" is recognizable; cf. Cline 1987, 3–4; Osing 1992, 35) the lefthand list moves from central to western Crete, and thence to the mainland (a southeast to northwest "itinerary"); then it moves, via Kythera, back to central Crete, a northwest to southeast "itinerary" (its separate character indicated by the repetition of Amnisos; cf. Wachsmann 1987, 96). The righthand list begins with "Crete" as a totality, thence moves to *Tny*; although some prefer to see this as a reference to the mainland (Cline 1987, 3), geographical necessity (the eastern Aegean, to this point, being unrecognized) suggests that Edel's suggestion of Rhodes is preferable. The righthand list may then have been (if it had been completed) an itinerary running from southeast (Crete) to Rhodes, and from thence to the north or northwest (that is, to the central Aegean islands) and perhaps back to Crete. This is a possibility not apparently envisaged before (cf. Wachsmann 1987, 97–98). E_N would then represent the total northwest sphere of reference (as known to Egypt, and beyond Egyptian domination) just as A_N represented the comparably independent lands of the northeastern sphere of reference, as far as Egypt was concerned.

The preceding remarks are not intended to gainsay the theory—well supported by data—that Eighteenth Dynasty Egypt and the Aegean were in close contact at certain levels. Indeed, an Egyptian embassy *may* have visited Crete and the mainland under Amenophis III (Cline 1987, 19–22), although whether a temple was founded as a result and a prototypical Eleusinian Mysteries established seems much less likely. But such contacts are not equivalent to "suzerainty" and do not imply the substantial cultural impact of Egypt upon the Aegean required by Bernal's theory.

SOME ARCHAEOLOGICAL OBSERVATIONS

Now for the archaeological data: these consist of Egyptian objects (or objects reflecting Egyptian styles) found in the Aegean, and Aegean objects found in Egypt. The archaeological data are supposed to reflect Eleventh Dynasty activity in the Aegean; Hyksos "Egypt-Canaanite" conquest of the Aegean; and relatively intense relations, based on Egyptian "suzerainty," in the Eighteenth Dynasty. As there is not sufficient space here to take up the archaeological material in detail, I must merely make a few observations.

First, the cultural and political implications of archaeological material are notoriously difficult to elicit; for most of the material cited explicitly or implicitly—by Bernal, I should say—the similarities suggested are strained (as in the supposed "Hyksos" character of the shaft grave burials at Mycenae), or the material is of types that could easily have reached Egypt or the Aegean via trade, and possibly indirect trade mediated by middlemen. Trading contacts are, on the whole, not good mechanisms for transmitting cultural modes likely to affect substantially the political and religious ethos and structure of either trading partner.

Second, what *does* have a major impact on a people's culture is the colonization of their homeland by another, dominant people; and the archaeological manifestation of that process, so far as Egypt is concerned, is well known. During the Middle Kingdom, Lower Nubia and, during the New Kingdom, Lower and Upper Nubia were colonized by the Egyptians; the impact on the indigenes was clear: gradually they acculturated to Egyptian norms in material culture, and presumably in political and religious life. The colonizing process evidences itself throughout the material culture as a whole; and more specifically in the form of typically Egyptian temples, towns, and cemeteries (cf., e.g., Trigger 1976). Thanks especially to the work of Eliezer Oren and others, we can see that Palestine underwent a comparable although not identical process in Ramesside times, manifested through similar kinds of archaeological data (cf. Weinstein 1981, 17–23). Archaeological evidence of this kind, evidence of a colonizing process by the Egyptians, is totally absent from the Aegean, despite many years of field work.

In conclusion, I find Bernal's theses about Egypt's impact on the Aegean in the Middle and Late Bronze Ages unpersuasive, so far as the Egyptian evidence (which is crucial to his argument) is concerned. But I salute his sustained and thoughtful effort to understand the roots of Greek civilization and his sensitivity to the potential complexity of the processes involved. Serious challenges, such as this, to accepted orthodoxy always stimulate productive rethinking of the evidence and the issues and can indeed lead to a changed understanding of important processes in the past.

BLACK ATHENA
AN EGYPTOLOGICAL
REVIEW

Frank J. Yurco

Volumes 1 and 2 of Martin Bernal's *Black Athena* have issued a broad challenge to established Egyptological and classical scholarship. His position is that from the late eighteenth century onward the "Ancient Model" of Mediterranean history was displaced by an "Aryan Model." Briefly summarized, the Ancient Model was a reflection of the views of Greek and Roman writers, who in Bernal's opinion were far more willing than their modern counterparts to admit the influence of Egypt on the development of Greek civilization, as well as influence from the Mesopotamian and Levantine civilizations of antiquity. The Ancient Model, he claims, was later displaced, in the eighteenth and nineteenth centuries, by an Aryan Model championed by European scholars who by contrast saw the ancient Greeks as Aryans, ethnically, and also as the earliest ancestors of Western civilization as a whole. Advocates of the Aryan Model thus downplayed or denied outright any substantial formative influence on ancient Greece from Egyptian, Mesopotamian, or Levantine cultures. Bernal further posits that European–American racial attitudes that evolved in the slaveholding era of the eighteenth and early nineteenth centuries sustained the Aryan Model and encouraged its further development. Thus the Egyptians, being Africans, the Mesopotamians and Levantines, including Jews, Phoenicians, and Arab peoples, all speakers of Semitic languages, faced not only the desire of the Aryan Model to view ancient Greece as the real originator of Western culture, but also the growing European racism and anti-Semitism that peaked in the colonial era. How could the peoples of Egypt, Mesopotamia, and the Levant have contributed anything significant to the Aryans, who, in their own view must have originated their own "high" civilizations?

History seemingly supported this view. In ancient India, Aryan peoples had conquered an earlier, indigenous Harappan culture. (The Harappan people are now known to have originated an advanced Indus Valley civilization that evolved many traits characteristic of all later Indian civilizations.) Farther west, the Greeks, considered to be Aryans, had likewise come down from the north and conquered an indigenous Mediterranean people. In the same way, the ancient Kassites and Mitanni, discovered later, as well as the Hittites, were all thought to be Aryan peoples who had descended from the north and conquered indigenous Levantine peoples.

The Aryan Model was based upon the Indo-European language family and the cultures represented by speakers of those languages. This included most languages spoken in Europe, as well as other languages that spread eastward across Iran and India among its Aryan peoples. The ancient Greek and Latin languages were Indo-European, and so too was ancient Hittite. Many consider the ancient Mitanni and Kassites as Indo-European in origin, and those peoples had invaded Mesopotamia and Syria from the north and had imposed their rule over indigenous Hattian and Semitic peoples of Anatolia and the Levant.

Thus advocates of the Aryan Model came to view their Aryan ancestors as a superior human stock, who dominated supposedly inferior Semitic and Mediterranean peoples through their use of horse-drawn chariots and superior weaponry. Egypt had also been invaded and dominated for a little more than a century by the Hyksos, a group that possessed horse-drawn chariots and superior weapons, though ethnically they have been considered by many to have been a blend of Indo-European Mitanni and Semitic peoples.

Otherwise Egypt posed a special problem to this Aryan Model, as indisputably it lay in Africa. How could Africans have raised so superior a civilization as pharaonic Egypt, and one of such profound antiquity? The solution lay in analysis of the Egyptian people. Though swarthy and sometimes very brown-complexioned, Egyptians had in many instances straight or wavy hair and, in some instances, non–Sub-Saharan craniofacial features. From these observations arose the theory that the pharaonic Egyptians of the Dynastic Era must originally have been of non-African and possibly Aryan origin, and that these people early had migrated into Egypt, where they conquered and subdued the indigenous people, bringing in their train kingship, writing, and all the trappings of advanced civilization. This so-called dynastic race, Bernal supposes, was conceived by Aryan scholars in order to deny Egypt its African roots and to bring it under the Aryan Model.

How well does current Egyptology agree with this supposition?

The history of ancient Egypt was first recovered scientifically through the efforts of savants who had accompanied Napoleon on his Nile campaign of 1798–1801. They elucidated evidence of the high Egyptian civilization that the Greeks of the Ancient Model had rather dimly and imperfectly recalled. The Rosetta Stone was found during this campaign, and scholars who had earlier been groping toward decipherment of the pharaonic Egyptian hieroglyphic script received a fresh impetus. In 1822 Jean-François Champollion finally announced that he had discovered the secret of translating hieroglyphics by using the parallel Greek, Demotic Egyptian, and Hieroglyphic Egyptian texts found on the famous stone. (Napoleon's Egyptian campaign ended in 1801 with British and Ottoman victory over his forces there; as a result the Rosetta Stone, though originally found by French engineers, passed into British control and has since resided in the British Museum in London, rather than in the Louvre in Paris.)

For scholars, ancient Egyptian culture offered a special allure, for it featured in the traditions and memories of late antiquity, of the Renaissance era, and of later times. Even before Napoleon's campaign, scholars had been studying Coptic, the script adopted by Christian Egyptians during the third century C.E. Renaissance-era churchmen and scholars had learned Coptic from the few Egyptian Copts who still spoke it in the sixteenth century. This proved a fortunate link, for the Copts, who adopted Christianity in the first few centuries C.E., had rendered their pharaonic language into the Greek alphabet, supplemented by seven signs taken from Demotic (Gardiner 1957, 5–6). Thus it was that Champollion, who was well versed in Coptic, was able to decipher the Rosetta Stone texts.

During the nineteenth century research and excavations in the Near East in turn revealed the Sumero-Babylonian civilizations. Again, a lucky find provided a key to decipherment of the cuneiform script of these societies: at Behistun in Persia, a rock cliff bore a bilingual text with a scene and inscriptions in Old Persian and in cuneiform Akkadian-Babylonian. With the finding of the Assyrian king Asshurbanipal's library came a trove of documents, including tablets that contained materials of myth and legend: the story of a hero named Gilgamesh, who closely matched the Greek hero Heracles in deeds and exploits; fascinating accounts of the Babylonian Creation epic; and, especially alluring, an amazing parallel to the biblical Flood story. Because of such biblically linked findings, funds for further excavation and collecting streamed in from European sources. Egypt too received additional study by biblical scholars, for ancient Israelite traditions linked Egypt to Abraham's sojourn and to Moses and the Exodus tradition. Further interest was spurred by the vast numbers of papyrus fragments and inscriptions excavated from the ruins of Greco-Roman–era sites in Egypt. Many of these contained references to Greek literary and other texts, some were Demotic Egyptian, and some even contained biblical texts and extracts of New Testament writings. These in turn prompted further research and excavation.

Amid the newly collected and excavated evidence of Egypt from the Predynastic and Early Dynastic ages there emerged a few cylinder seals, a knife handle with Mesopotamian-style decoration on one side, and niched-brick architecture loosely resembling Mesopotamian models: the "dynastic race" theory of the foreign origin of Egyptian civilization gained a new lease on life. Sir Flinders Petrie, the founder of modern Egyptology, who himself subscribed to that theory, thus inferred several invasions of Egypt, on the basis of cultural changes seen in the shift from Predynastic Naqada I to II, and again from late Naqada III to Dynastic Egypt.[1] Certain skeletal finds and naturally preserved bodies from Predynastic cemeteries seemed to support this view. In addition, the apparently sudden flowering of already well-developed hieroglyphs on First Dynasty monuments indicated that Egypt's writing system also must have been brought from abroad, probably by the selfsame dynastic race.

Supporters of the Aryan Model could now detach Egyptian pharaonic civilization from any supposed African origin. Egypt's high civilization was proclaimed the work of the "dynastic race." This race was variously said to have come from somewhere to the north, from Mesopotamia, from Elam, or even possibly from India. By the early decades of the twentieth century the dynastic race theory seemed unassailable. Thus far, Bernal's account of Aryan supremacy accords with the early study of Egyptian antiquity as it is generally recognized.

THE DYNASTIC RACE THEORY AND ITS PROBLEMS

Egyptological reaction to the dynastic race theory set in by the second quarter of the present century. Analysis of Predynastic skeletal material showed tropical African elements in the population of the earliest Badarian culture (Morant 1935, 1937; Strouhal 1971). Not much later, two seminal studies of Egyptian skeletal material reported continuity from the ancient down to the modern population (Batrawi 1945, 1946). Certainly there was some foreign admixture, but basically a homogeneous African population had lived in the Nile Valley from ancient to modern times. (It simply happened that North African Nilotic peoples showed a wide variety of skin complexions, hair types, and craniofacial structures; see Trigger 1978; Keita 1990.) Continuity in Upper Egyptian cultures from Predynastic to Dynastic times was also demonstrated (Kantor 1944). High-quality archaeological work (by Gertrude Caton-Thompson) that disclosed a stratified site from Badarian to Naqada II produced the first evidence that ancient Egypt's earliest connections were indeed to prehistoric Saharan African peoples. The excavations revealed that the Badarians were poorly acquainted with the Nile Valley's limestone cliffs and rich flint deposits, for they fashioned their stone tools and weapons from surface-collected flints. By the time of Naqada I, people had begun quarrying flint from the limestone cliffs. Thus the Badarians had most probably come from outside the Nile Valley; their hollow-base arrow points and rippled and punched pottery decoration suggested origins in the Sahara.[2]

The Saharan peoples were first identified through research in the deserts west of Egypt (by members of the Egyptian royal family, using automobiles) and also (by French scholars) in Algeria. They discovered impressive rock paintings and also evidence of settlements and the beginnings of cattle pastoralism in Africa (Hoffman 1991, 53–77, 215–48, esp. 229, 239; Lhote 1959). A systematic survey of the desert high country outside the Nile Valley disclosed a rich prehistoric lithic cultural sequence dated back to the Middle Paleolithic (Sandford and Arkell 1928, 1929, 1933, 1939). Reanalysis of the Predynastic Egyptian sequence documented its continuity by introducing the terms "Naqada I–II" for Petrie's "Amratian" and "Gerzean," and "Naqada III" for the transition from Terminal Predynastic to the First Dynasty (Kaiser 1957). U.S. archaeologists and prehistorians who resumed research in Egypt's western desert (the eastern stretch of the Sahara) demonstrated the extreme antiquity and independent domestication of cattle by the Saharan peoples of North Africa.[3]

All this earlier research has been brilliantly summarized in Michael Hoffman's *Egypt before the Pharaohs* (1991). Hoffman's work on long-term climate change revealed a fluctuating climatic situation over the Sahara, with alternating wet and dry cycles that corresponded generally to climate shifts caused by the advances and retreats of Pleistocene glacial sheets over the continents in the Northern Hemisphere (1991, 25, fig. 5; 53–77). This alternation of climatic cycles featured strongly in the evolution of humans from hominids, especially as *Homo erectus* moved from tropical Africa to cooler northern lands. Climatic cycles acted as a pump, alternately attracting African peoples onto the Sahara, then expelling them as the aridity returned (Keita 1990). Specialists in Predynastic archaeology have recently proposed that the last climate-driven expulsion impelled the Saharans—with their cattle pastoralism, wheat, barley, and flax crops, sheep and goats, and pottery and lithic traditions—into the Nile Valley ca. 5000–4500 B.C.E., where they intermingled with indigenous hunter-fisher-gatherer people already there (Hassan 1989; Wetterstrom 1993).

Such was the origin of the distinct Egyptian populace, with its mix of agriculture/pastoralism and hunting/fishing. The resulting Badarian people, who developed the earliest Predynastic Egyptian culture, already exhibited the mix of North African and Sub-Saharan physical traits that have typified

Egyptians ever since (Hassan 1985; Yurco 1989; Trigger 1978; Keita 1990; Brace et al., this volume). The drying climate also impelled other peoples into the Upper Nile Valley. In the Sudan the distinctive Khartoum Neolithic culture had emerged by ca. 7000 B.C.E., quite different from Egypt but (even early on) nevertheless using the distinctive Saharan-style pottery, as did Egypt's Badarians. These people, cattle pastoralists as well as agriculturalists, inter-mingled with earlier Nilotic societies based on aquatic and hunting resources (Haaland 1992, esp. 58–61; Wetterstrom 1993). The peoples of Egypt, the Sudan, and much of East African Ethiopia and Somalia are now generally regarded as a Nilotic continuity, with widely ranging physical features (complexions light to dark, various hair and craniofacial types) but with powerful common cultural traits, including cattle pastoralist traditions (Trigger 1978; Bard, Snowden, this volume).

Language research indicates that this Saharan-Nilotic population became speakers of the Afro-Asiatic languages, including Cushitic and Omotic, Egypto-Coptic, Berber, Tuareg, and several Chadic language; latest findings suggest that they spread out from the Sahara as the climate deteriorated (Fulco 1981; Hodge 1971; Haaland 1992, 58–61). Alternatively, the Afro-Asiatic languages originated in the Upper Nubian Nile Valley (Blench 1993, 134–37 and fig. 2). Another branch of the Afro-Asiatic language family, Semitic, was evidently spoken by Saharans who crossed the Red Sea into Arabia and became ancestors of the Semitic speakers there, possibly around 7000 B.C.E. Of the Nilotic peoples, only the Nubians of later times are distinct, speak-ing Nilo-Saharan (rather than Afro-Asiatic) languages; but those presently living in the Nuba Hills are still very close to Nilotic peoples in their cultural traditions.

In summary we may say that Egypt was a distinct North African culture rooted in the Nile Valley and on the Sahara. The dynastic race theory has been shown to be an outdated myth generated by the "Aryan Model."[4]

Most recently, excavations in the Nile Delta have demonstrated that a limited amount of Mesopotamian cultural influence reached Egypt during Naqada II–III as luxury trade developed; Egyptian gold was exchanged for lapis lazuli and cedar wood, among other products.[5] This contact occurred via the Amuq region of northern Syria, perhaps based at Ebla and Byblos. Egypt's contacts with Byblos were very ancient: imports of cedar wood and oils are documented from late Predynastic times (Hoffman 1991, 272, 283, 317, 338–39). Excavations have shown that Ebla was an outpost of Sume-rian culture; it also served as a redistribution center for lapis lazuli, derived from what is now Afghanistan, through long-distance trade (Pettinato 1981, 168–69, 202).

Vestigial traces of the dynastic race theory still linger in the writings of some scholars, who hint at a "Mesopotamian stimulus" to Egyptian culture, through writing or other cultural aspects.[6] But it has now been definitively shown that Mesopotamian writing arose from clay tokens used in early invoices for livestock transshipments (Schmandt-Besserat 1992, 1–13, 93–128, 130–65, 184–99). Later, indeed, scribes in Mesopotamia predominated in the temple and palace economies; but kings and royalty were rarely literate. In Egypt, by contrast, writing arose from the desire of early chieftains and kings to commemorate their deeds and accomplishments (Arnett 1982; Hassan 1983, 1, 7–8; Williams and Logan 1987, 245–85). Its roots lay in the painted buffware of Naqada II, whose totemic emblems for divinities show forms recognizable in later hieroglyphic script (Hoffman 1991, 31, fig. 7; Arnett 1982). Thus Egyptian and Mesopotamian writing systems have totally disparate origins. In later Egyptian Dynastic times literacy extended from the top of society downward. Egyptian kings and royalty had to be literate—in sharp contrast to those in Mesopotamia—and the bureaucracy that arose around the early Dynastic rulers encouraged the spread of writing, as did the religious needs of lower-ranked Egyptians (Baines 1983; Ray 1986). A scribal class evolved from the Archaic Period to the Old Kingdom, basically as account keepers for the elite and as bureaucrats for the government's taxing and documentary functions. During all periods the means of social advancement to the elite classes was through literacy (Baines 1983).

The ancient Egyptian writing system was therefore a distinctly African development, and the evidence for this does indeed contradict some of the diffusionist reasoning that grew out of the Aryan Model, as well as the prominent position ascribed to Mesopotamian influence.

DETERMINING CHRONOLOGY

The first problem with Bernal's reasoning arises from his decision to follow Mellaart's Egyptian chronology, which sets the start of the First Dynasty at 3400 B.C.E. (Mellaart 1979). This chronology was based upon faulty radiocarbon readings (Weinstein 1992, 382; cf. Baines, this volume). Carbon 14 is a valuable dating device, especially where written archives are lacking. But as any beginning archaeology student knows, it falls prey to inherent problems: (1) variable atmospheric deposition rates over time, and (2) contamination of samples taken from archaeological sites, either through improper on-site handling or through decades of storage in museums in industrial cities. Another problem is (3) the type of sample taken. Samples from charcoal, or from an ancient hearth, or from perishable crop or weed plants are far superior to samples from logs of wood or large wooden pieces, as the age of the tree from which the wood originated, and its long survival time in arid conditions, may mean that a sample is hundreds of years older than the material discovered around it in archaeological contexts (Weinstein 1993). Cedar wood of the late fourth millennium, for instance, came from virgin-growth Lebanese forests never previously harvested. The trees might have been many centuries old when first cut.

Carbon 14 readings can be calibrated through dendrochronology—tree ring analysis (Shaw 1985)—but the margin of error in such readings may be up to ±200 years. This is far inferior to the precision attainable through Egyptian historic dating based on the Sothic Calendar and on king lists like the Turin Canon, or on the Royal Annals of the Old Kingdom (Yurco 1993). For example, the Sothic date recorded in the seventh regnal year of Senwosret III fixes the Middle Kingdom at 2134–1998 B.C.E. for the Eleventh Dynasty; then seven kingless years; then 1991–1786 for the Twelfth (R. A. Parker 1976, 177–84; 1971). Recent efforts to downdate the Twelfth Dynasty were based upon shortening the reigns of Senwosret II and III (Simpson 1972, 50–54; 1984, 900, 903 and nn. 6–7, 906).

Another recent proposal, at best speculative, has been that observation of the reappearance of the Sothic star was sited at Elephantine (Krauss 1981, 1985; Wells 1985; Barta 1981)—rather than at It-T3wy (near Memphis), the political center during the Middle Kingdom. In the area of It-T3wy lay the pyramid towns of the Middle Kingdom pharaohs, from one of which (Kahun) was recovered the text recording the Sothic date of Senwosret III (Luft 1992, 156–57, 230–34; 1982, 153). Thus the very same site was most probably the place from which the reappearance of the Sothic star was observed. Another possible sighting area might be Thebes, in Upper Egypt, for Thebes was Egypt's religious capital. Elephantine, by contrast, had no inherent association with central government administration in the Middle Kingdom, save as a regional capital for Egypt's Nubian activity.[7] It is least likely as an observation point for the Sothic phenomenon. That being the case, it is preferable to retain R. A. Parker's (1976, 1971) Middle Kingdom chronology, or the twelve-regnal-year (or so) reduction proposed by Simpson (1972).

Both those proposals for reducing the duration of the Twelfth Dynasty have inherent problems of their own. Both disagree with the totals for that dynasty as given in the Royal Canon of Turin.[8] Also, limiting Senwosret II to just six regnal years is not without difficulties. That pharaoh built a complete pyramid at Kahun, with a solid granite funerary temple and complex of buildings. Such projects optimally took fifteen to twenty years to complete, even with the mudbrick cores used in Middle Kingdom pyramids (I. Edwards 1985, 98, 292; Grimal 1992, 166, 391). As for Senwosret III, the nineteen regnal years assigned to him by the revised figures are a bare minimum from his highest attested regnal dates.

The reign of this pharaoh had two distinct phases: a well-documented military phase, regnal years 1–19, and a period of administrative reform, presumably later. Senwosret III's administrative deeds included abolition of the provincial nomarchs (district governors) and the creation of a strong central government based upon three *warets* (governmental departments), all based on a very powerful vizierate.[9] He faced determined opposition from dissident nomarchs, as Khakheperre-seneb's complaints attest (Kadish 1973; Lichtheim 1973, 145–49; Ockinga 1983, 88–95). Yet loyalists from the newly created bureaucratic middle class of scribes and officials wrote supportive hymns and tracts for the king (Lichtheim 1973, 198–201; Simpson 1973, 279–84). Is it logical to assume that he would promulgate such controversial governmental reforms while absent from Egypt on campaigns against powerful Kush? Perhaps it is worth recalling here, as a historical parallel, the experience of Richard I of England (the Lion-Hearted) while absent on a crusade: his throne was seized by his brother John, with the complicity of the nobles, who then took the opportunity to exact reforms from John—at the signing of the Magna Carta in 1215. Senwosret III's reforms and centralization of power involved abolition of power among provincial nobles whose relation to pharaohs during the Ninth through Twelfth Dynasties had been somewhat like the medieval barons' to their king. Khakheperre-seneb's text shows that the nomarchs did not accept this abolition without protest.

Furthermore, the Twelfth Dynasty was replete with political intrigue and occasional strife. Amenemhet I, the founder, had been assassinated, and Senwosret I, his son and successor, had used literature as propaganda to swing elite opinion to support the dynasty (Posener 1956, 87–115, 145–57, 127–30; 1971, 231–32). Senwosret III in his turn also used political propaganda, as the loyalist tracts and hymns demonstrate. His opposition was the entrenched and resisting nomarchs, and they too had their literary spokesman in Khakheperre-seneb. It seems likelier that Senwosret III pushed his governmental reforms while continually resident in Egypt—that is, after regnal year 19. One tantalizing hint of the controversy he faced is that most surviving statues of him have suffered mutilation or breakage; only a small sphinx (Metropolitan Museum of Art, New York) is relatively free of damage.[10] Most other rulers from the Twelfth Dynasty are represented by at least a few undamaged statues, though many were later usurped. Recent excavations at Dahshur have found both a year 30 controller's inscription and a first *Heb-sed* inscription of Senwosret III (F. Arnold 1992; D. Arnold and A. Oppenheim 1995, 47–48, fig. 5 and n. 5). Further, this pharaoh's statues show him at various ages, from youth (Aldred 1970, figs. 21–22) to extreme old age (Hayes 1953b, 198, fig. 120; A. Page 1976, 28, no. 30), and such aging hardly concurs with only a nineteen-year reign.

At any rate, for working purposes, my observations here retain Parker's date of 2134 B.C.E. for the start of the Eleventh Dynasty.

In a study that never reached publication owing to his untimely death, Klaus Baer assessed the length of the First Intermediate Period at roughly one hundred years. This conclusion was based upon his analysis of dated quarrying expeditions sent out in the Sixth Dynasty, and again in the Eleventh and Twelfth, recorded in terms of the Sothic Calendar by regnal date. Because the Sothic Calendar as kept by the Egyptians lost one day every four years (from the loss of an extra quarter-day each year), the quarrying dates of the Middle Kingdom shifted forward in the calendar. The Egyptians tended to send out quarrying expeditions during the cooler part of the year with considerable consistency. By taking the number of days that the dates had shifted forward by the Eleventh and Twelfth Dynasties, and multiplying by four, Baer determined that about a century had elapsed between the end of the Sixth through Eighth Dynasties (2250–2234 B.C.E. and the beginning of the Eleventh (2134 B.C.E.).[11]

To gauge the combined length of the Archaic Period and Old Kingdom one can choose either the Royal Canon of Turin, with its total of 955 years, 10 + x days that elapsed from the start of the reign of Menes, at the outset of the First Dynasty, to the end of the Eighth Dynasty, which concludes the Old Kingdom, or else, as Baer chose, figure the duration of the Old Kingdom by dead reckoning, utilizing highest attested dates of kings and other data. Baer preferred the latter method because certain of the regnal lengths given in the Royal Canon of Turin disagree with data from Old Kingdom documents. Using this method he arrived at a date of 3100 B.C.E. for the beginning of the First Dynasty. If one adds the Turin Canon's figures for the Archaic Period through the Old Kingdom (955 years and 10 + x days) to the date 2234 B.C.E. (the end of the Old Kingdom, in Baer's reckoning), the start of the First Dynasty would be 3189 B.C.E. — remarkably close to Baer's dead reckoning date and far closer than the ±200 years that a carbon 14 date of this antiquity would permit. Simpson's shortening of the Twelfth Dynasty by twelve years would be a negligible change for the inception of the First Dynasty, all but used up in an uncertainty factor that must be allowed for dates of such remote time.

This dual approach, and its remarkably close agreement, is a powerful argument against Mellaart's (and Bernal's) option that the First Dynasty began at 3400 B.C.E. — which would lengthen the First Intermediate Period to three hundred years! Baer's hundred-year estimate is governed by calendar shift, something that is not elastic. His data allot 214 years to the Ninth and Tenth Dynasties: these immediately followed the collapse of the Eighth, in 2234, and would end with the reunification of Egypt under Mentuhotep II in 2020. There was in fact some overlap between the end of the Heracleopolitan dynasties and the Eleventh Dynasty in Thebes. For the relatively few rulers attested from the Heracleopolitan era, the activities of Ankhtify of Mo'alla in Upper Egypt, and the few other details of data surviving for the First Intermediate Period, this time frame is quite adequate. Thus Bernal's reliance on Mellaart's outdated and absurdly high dates is mistaken and indefensible. The super-low chronology proposed by Krauss, which would lop the First Intermediate Period to fifty years or less, is likewise contradicted by Baer's calendar-based data, and so cannot be accurate. As outlined above, the proposition that Sothic dates were taken at Elephantine is equally unlikely.

THE LEGEND OF SESOSTRIS: FACTS AND FICTION

Another issue that also relates to the Twelfth Dynasty is Bernal's claim that Senwosret I essentially served as the model for classical legends about Sesostris (*BA* 2:186–235; Herodotus 2.102–11; see also O'Connor, this volume). Bernal uses an inscribed stone, recently recovered from beneath a Ramesside-era (New Kingdom) statue at Mit Rahinah as evidence that Senwosret I and Amenemhet II conquered a vast Asiatic empire extending into Anatolia, on to the Colchis area east of the Black Sea, and into ancient Scythia.[12] For this interpretation he again cites the classical legend of Sesostris, which was much elaborated during the first millennium b.c.e. to provide the Egyptians with a rational counter to the claims of kings, like Darius I and Alexander the Great, who saw themselves as world conquerors exceeding all earlier monarchs. For example, in his *History* (2.102–11, esp. 110) Herodotus reports that an Egyptian priest who told him the legend had already previously used it to refute the Persian ruler Darius I, who had wished to erect a statue of himself before that of Sesostris. (The statue of Sesostris was probably a colossus of Ramesses II [1279–1212 b.c.e.]; see A. B. Lloyd 1975–88, 3:36–37; 1982, 38 and n. 13.) The Asiatic, European, and Scythian conquests the legend accords to Sesostris are precisely the elements that would outshine Darius I and Alexander the Great, especially as neither succeeded in subduing either the Scythians or Kush, as it was claimed Sesostris had done.

According to the legend, Sesostris and his army reached such distant realms through protracted absence from Egypt. Both the Achaemaenid Persians and Alexander the Great did indeed make such long campaigns, spanning several years, but no pharaoh of the Middle Kingdom, or even of the New Kingdom, ever made such a multiyear excursion. All attested early campaigns mounted by the Egyptians lasted one season, within a single year. These were essentially annual campaigns, each closing with a return to Egypt. Even the great Thutmose III conquered Syria and Palestine in a series of seventeen annual campaigns, structured into a program (Gardiner 1961, 189–95; Grimal 1992, 213–17). And even so, none of the early pharaohs came anywhere near Anatolia, let alone Scythia! These fictitious campaigns are first-millennium accretions to the Sesostris legend, aimed at outdoing the recorded achievements of foreign conquerors of Egypt (A. B. Lloyd 1975–88, 3:16–37, 2:1–98; 1982, 37–40; Obsomer 1989).

The Sesostris legend does have a basis in Egyptian history, as Bernal and others affirm. But just what is that historical basis, and what king figured into the legend? The Middle Kingdom inscription from Mit Rahinah, for all its problems, does attest an Egyptian-ruled Asiatic empire, in at least part of the Twelfth Dynasty. *Stt* is a generic Egyptian word for Asia, but it does not imply any particular territories (Gardiner 1947, 1:77). Thus Bernal's guesses about locating other names listed in the text are just that, guesses. The text does record the reception of prisoners and tribute from Asiatic realms, but the text dates from Amenemhet II (mid–Twelfth Dynasty), after Senwosret I is considered to have died (Redford 1992, 78–80).

Asiatic campaigns by Amenemhet II might make some sense historically. His predecessor Amenemhet I's policy regarding Asia, as enunciated in the *Prophecy of Neferti* and confirmed by the *Story of Sinuhe*, had been entirely defensive: he built the Wall of the Ruler, cited by both texts, to prevent infiltration of the eastern Delta by Asiatics (see Lichtheim 1973, 139–45, 222–35, esp. 224; Redford 1992, 80). Early in his reign he was occupied with consolidating his rule over Egypt; but toward the end, he did initiate operations in Lower Nubia and also a campaign to Libya. Senwosret I, as co-regent, led those military operations. The assassination of Amenemhet I shocked the kingdom, but Senwosret I came through the crisis, as the *Teaching of Amenemhet* demonstrates (Simpson 1973, 193–97; Foster 1981). Sinuhe thought success far less certain and, indeed, feared civil strife when he set out on his journey of self-exile—not without good cause, for he was the crown princess Noferu's minister (Lichtheim, 223). Once settled in Syria, Sinuhe hewed a pro-Egyptian line. He counseled his hosts: "Be loyal to him [Senwosret], and he will reward you richly, be disloyal and you'll risk his implacable wrath" (225–26). Such words of advice do not amount to the bellicose policy toward Syria that Bernal would assume (*BA* 2:189–92).

Senwosret I, the next pharaoh, for his part, occupied himself with Nubia. He attacked Kush, now known to have been a powerful Upper Nubian state, based at Kerma (Bonnet 1986b, 1987a, 1987b), and built a series of fortresses along the Lower Nubian Nile, to protect his southern frontier adjoining Kush and also to support mineral exploitation of Lower Nubia (W. Y. Adams 1984, 188–89; Trigger 1976, 64–67). Gold, amethysts, and other gems had been discovered there by prospectors sent out by Senwosret I early in his reign. The nomarch of Elephantine was made responsible for coordinating Nubian-Kushite policy and supervising operations. Senwosret I also embarked on a very ambitious building program for the duration of his lengthy reign (Grimal 1992, 164; W. S. Smith 1981, 168–75). Sinuhe's career in Syria paralleled Senwosret's in Egypt; and the comings and goings of Egyptians to the Syro-Palestinian chieftain's residence where Sinuhe lived indicate that Senwosret I maintained a zone of interest in Syria-Palestine. But this shows nothing about conquest, right down to the point where Sinuhe, in old age, departed for Egypt (Lichtheim 1973, 228–33; Redford 1992, 80). As Amenemhet I related in reference to palaces (in the *Prophecy of Neferti*), cedar wood was back in vogue, and that meant a resumption of sea voyages to Byblos, as well as Red Sea voyages to Punt (Lichtheim, 157, 211–15). In all this, no overt hostility toward Asia is evident.

It was his successor, Amenemhet II, who most likely initiated campaigns into Asia. Relations with Nubia and Kush were now stable and secure, thanks to his father's operations. As Bernal and others note, it was under Amenemhet II that the silver trove was deposited in the temple at Tod in Upper Egypt, including silver now attested to be from the famed mine at Laurion, near Athens; perhaps it originated as some of the booty mentioned in the Mit Rahinah inscription.[13] Yet this does not amount to an Egyptian expedition against Greece, nor to widespread campaigning in Anatolia and Scythia, as Bernal proposes for Senwosret I/Sesostris. The silver from Tod is decorated in Aegean and North Syrian style; this suggests it might well be an import from Greece, worked in Syria and then paid to Egypt as tribute.

Senwosret II in his turn might have continued Asiatic campaigning, particularly if he reigned more than the six years some allot to him. But again, neither he nor Amenemhet II campaigned in Nubia, and Senwosret II did not add to the system of fortifications. The mineral exploitation of Nubia proceeded apace during both reigns. There is also good evidence of quite rich trade between Egypt, Syria, Crete, and perhaps Mycenae as well (W. S. Smith 1981, 208; Kantor 1965).

Senwosret III resumed the offensive drive against Kush (Trigger 1976, 67–77, 73, fig. 20; W. Y. Adams 1984, 1975–83). He drove south to the Dal stretch of the Second Cataract, secured Semna with three powerful fortresses, and linked them to Mirgissa (ancient Iken) with a series of brilliantly designed island forts. Each of these had protected access to river water, and all stood within signaling distance of one another; and, via observation posts on high eminences, they could transmit signals right back to Buhen. Senwosret III transformed Iken into a huge trade *entrepôt*. Like the legendary Sesostris, he erected a stela at the fortress of Uronarti, marking Semna as his frontier. The Kushites were to be allowed past Semna northward only for trade at Iken, or on diplomatic assignments. At Iken, besides the vast storage facilities for trade, Senwosret III built a remarkable slipway, some five miles in length, around Batn el-Hagar, the worst rapids of the Second Cataract (Trigger 1976, 67–88, fig. 21, plates 20, 25–26). All of this is the sort of material from which legends arise.

Further, Senwosret III utilized magic against his foes. We know that he at least used "execration texts," employed by writing the names of foes on clay figures and then smashing them in rituals (Vila 1963). The enemies named on these include Syro-Palestinians but, significantly, also Kushites (Vila 1963;

Redford 1992, 87–93; Pritchard 1969b, no. 593; Trigger 1976, 75). Senwosret III may thus have controlled part of Syria-Palestine, but his main concern certainly was Kush. He may be called something of a prophet too, for in his boundary stela he warns his successors not to yield Semna to the Kushites, whom he scorned. Still, he saw Kush as a powerful foe—with good cause, as is now known from excavations at Kerma, which have revealed a sophisticated bronze-working factory and paintings showing that Kush also possessed a powerful riverine fleet (Bonnet 1982, 34–39; 1986b, 1987a). Suddenly those Egyptian forts, with their formidable defenses and signaling capability, make eminently good sense and are far from being the material hypertrophy that Adams termed them.[14] No wonder that during the New Kingdom, Senwosret III was described as a deity in Nubia—a deification that could well have come to figure in the legend of Sesostris. And yes, this pharaoh even fought a minor skirmish in Canaan (Gardiner 1961, 132).

In summary, Amenemhet II and, especially, Senwosret III are the most likely candidates for the pharaoh who figures in the Sesostris legend. By the first millennium B.C.E. Amenemhet II's deeds may have been conflated with Senwosret III's to incorporate both the Kushite and the Asiatic elements. Clearly, though, the multiyear campaigning, plus details about Thrace, Anatolia, and Scythia, were accreted to the legend in the first millennium.

Amenemhet III (as Lamares) also made the transition into legend. His two pyramids, a vast funerary temple famed as "the labyrinth," and his hydraulic works in the Fayum and along Bahr Yusuf feeding into it, all stand out as significant deeds, but his reign was free of wars, so far as is known. The centralized government and the *waret* system that had been inaugurated by Senwosret III now functioned smoothly in the interior, and the Kushite frontier was firmly held, though Kush waxed ever stronger. The vizierate and strong central government would also uphold Amenemhet IV's reign and that of his sister Sobek-noferu. She, the first female ruler of Egypt known to have assumed the full fivefold titulary of pharaoh—the Turin Royal Canon acknowledges her as fully legitimate ruler (Gardiner 1959, plate III, Turin VI.2; 1961, 141, 439)—ended the Twelfth Dynasty, in all respects a remarkable royal line.

Her successors, the kings of the Thirteenth Dynasty, were by comparison shadows. A powerful family of viziers ran the centralized bureaucracy and the *warets* and successfully held the Nubian realm right up to Semna (Von Beckerath 1958; Hayes 1953a, 1955; Cruz-Uribe 1987). It was a highly efficient bureaucracy, as the Brooklyn Prison Papyrus demonstrates (Hayes 1955): begun under Amenemhet III as a ledger of fugitives from prison labor battalions, this document was kept open until seventy-four of the seventy-six fugitives were retaken. The Thirteenth Dynasty progressed untroubled by the transitory reigns of its monarchs. The viziers retained a tight grip on the regime. Semna was still held fast, and documents mention even a campaign against Kush (Trigger 1976, 84; Grimal 1992, 184). Nubia continued to supply gold and mineral wealth, and the Kushite trade continued, though Kush had now reached the pinnacle of its power (Gratien 1978, 181–221; Bonnet 1986b, 1987a, 1987b). Around 1700 B.C.E. some traces of disintegration appeared in Egypt, as Xois, in the western Delta, split off from the regime.

Large numbers of Asiatics are attested in late Middle Kingdom Egypt, mostly as servants. Are these now explicable as captives and descendants of captives brought by Amenemhet II, Senwosret II, and perhaps Senwosret III? If so, then infiltration, or sale of foreigners into Egyptian servitude, need not loom so large as in previous assessments. That these Asiatics helped weaken the regime of the viziers seems unlikely; its downfall came about suddenly and abruptly.

THE ARRIVAL OF THE HYKSOS

Around 1674 B.C.E. a foreign group of Asiatics violently attacked the Egyptian frontier town of Hwt-Wᶜrt, better known as Avaris (Redford 1970; 1992, 111–22). Seizing it, they overwhelmed the Egyptian defenders with new and vastly improved weaponry (compound bows and a new style of battle axe) and horse-drawn chariots, seen for the first time in Egypt. Next they marched on It-T3wy, the capital, and seized it too, sending the viziers and their puppet monarchs reeling. Known as Hyksos, these people may have included an upper element of Mitanni–Indo-European origin, as the Mitanni were particularly known, all over the ancient Levant, as expert handlers and trainers of horses. (Bernal is wrong, by the way, in claiming that it was the Hyksos who introduced donkeys to Egypt. Donkeys had been quite common there since at least Naqada II times and are frequently depicted in Old Kingdom *mastaba* scenes.)[15]

The Turin Royal Canon lists 108 years of Hyksos rule of Egypt, in a dynasty of six great rulers (Gardiner 1959, plate 3, Turin X.21 + 15; 1961, 159, 442). Bernal raises the question of the *extent* of their rule and domination. He sees the Hyksos as colonizing Greece (Boeotia in particular) and initiating irrigation works around Lake Kopais (*BA* 2:78–153). Earlier scholars too had theorized a widespread dominion as far as Crete, and Baghdad in Mesopotamia, all on the basis of a few scattered artifactual finds. These scant objects are hardly sufficient evidence for a widespread kingdom, as they may simply represent diplomatic gifts sent abroad, or goods sold later by Egyptians or by Hyksos masters of Egypt, even sometimes looted from tombs. This explanation could account for the reported find of goldwork from the pharaoh Sahure's time (Fifth Dynasty) in Anatolia at Dorak (*BA* 2:148–49; also W. J. Young 1972). That Egypt's Old Kingdom pyramids were looted during the

First Intermediate Period is widely accepted; the lack of documentation or adequate description of the Dorak find renders it at least less valuable historically and possibly suspect, as most scholars have judged it (e.g., Trigger et al. 1983, 148).

For the Hyksos themselves there is some slight evidence of a wider empire. Kamose's second stela mentions some Hyksos ships that he captured in the waters near Avaris. They were filled with weaponry and other goods, including much wood from Syria and perhaps elsewhere. Aegean-style paintings have also recently been found at Avaris, the Hyksos capital.[16] That indicates considerable Hyksos seapower, and at least widespread trade.

Yet that the Hyksos moved as far north as Boeotia and inaugurated ruling dynasties that controlled part of Greece, as Bernal believes, is unlikely, given the thus far slender evidence available for the Hyksos era in general. Bernal's claim that the irrigation works at the Kopais could only be Egyptian is not proven. Sumero-Babylonian civilization was also heavily involved in irrigation projects (e.g., Oppenheim 1977, 40–45, 84). Indeed many societies worldwide independently developed extensive irrigation works, such as the Harappans of the Indus Valley and the Maya and Incas of the Americas. Were these too all inspired by Egypt? Only extreme diffusionists would claim so, for each society's irrigation systems show unique features, adapted to particular, localized situations—a recognized characteristic of independent invention.

Many advanced civilizations arose around 5000 B.C.E., in the Americas, in China, in India, and (in the Near East) in Egypt and in Mesopotamia: all riverine civilizations. Their environments encouraged irrigation and flood control, and many learned independently how to control floods or conduct irrigation. Each river system had unique features. In Egypt the annual flood of the Nile created distinct basins. These, plus manmade canals, brought the flood as far inland as feasible and held the water on the land as long as possible. Such were the main flood control and management systems developed in Egypt (Butzer 1976, 12–56). In Boeotia, however, the main problems were draining marshes and controlling floods by keeping open the *katavothres*, natural drainage channels (*BA* 2:133–35)—clearly different concerns than Egypt's river control problems.

The existence of a large pyramidal structure in the Kopais Valley (*BA* 2:128–33, 152) is a very risky proposition on which to base arguments for elaborate Egyptian or Hyksos colonization schemes. The pyramid form is one of nature's basic and most stable shapes, and many natural forms suggest it, including conical mountains and other landforms (Feder 1990, 126–29), as do many human constructions where mound-like features are desired. Few indeed would venture to suggest that the pyramidal structure at Silbury in Britain, or the pyramidal temples of Central America, were inspired by

Egypt. Thus accrediting the Kopais Valley pyramidal hill to Egyptians seems overly diffusionist in reasoning.

LINGUISTIC PROBLEMS

The remainder of Bernal's thesis about Boeotia is focused on some proposed linguistic cognates. He would, for instance, derive Greek *Kekrops* from the prenomens of Senwosret I, II, or III: respectively, Kheper-ka-Re, Kha-kheper-Re, and Kha-kau-Re (*BA* 2:120). But voiced and unvoiced Egypto-Coptic *kh* were two distinct phonemes (*ḫ* and *ẖ*). When the Greeks adopted a *kh* from Egyptian, or from Semitic, where it also occurs, it was rendered *ch*. Thus Semitic *ḫrs* becomes Greek Chrysos, and Egyptian *ẖ3rt* became Greek *chera* (Rendsburg 1989, 71–72). This distinction in voiced/unvoiced sounds persisted even into Coptic Egyptian; when the Greek alphabet was adopted for writing Coptic, a distinct Demotic Egyptian letter was retained for *kh*, for the Greek alphabet lacked this distinctive Afro-Asiatic phoneme (Gardiner 1957, 27). Thus Egyptian *kh* to Greek kappa, the first letter of Kekrops, is not a valid transmission, especially as early as the second millennium B.C.E. Furthermore, to derive the element *-krops* from *ka-Re*, *kau-Re*, or *per-ka-Re* involves not a straight transmission but rather the loss of several semivowel letters; a transmission from *kheper-Re* again confronts the difficulty of assimilating Egyptian *kh* to Greek kappa. Thus some of the proposed etymologies are not so facile a transmission as Bernal assumes.

His attempt to derive Greek *Alkmēnē* from Egyptian *Rḫt-Imn* (*BA* 2:79–81, 105–6) in fact requires rather vivid imagination. Not only does a prothetic letter alpha have to be invented, but Egyptian *r* must become Greek lambda; this latter is certainly possible, as *r* and *l* in Egyptian were merged and not distinct phonemes. But then Greek *-mēnē* has to be derived from Egyptian *Imn*. As Bernal notes (*BA* 2:80) *Imn* was pronounced *amāna* in the Amarna letters: but that only worsens the match, for the strong initial letter aleph from Egyptian would have to drop out.

So too with Greek *Athēna* from Egyptian *Ḥwt-Nt* (House of Neith) (*BA* 2:87–88, 99–106): there are complications. *Ḥ* is a strongly voiced phoneme in Egypto-Coptic, also found in Hebrew and Arabic (Rendsburg 1989, 71–72). Greek, in instances where it adopted Egyptian *ḥ*, gave it zero value—as in *ophis*, from Egyptian *ḥf3w*; and Amen*ophis*, from Amen*ḥotep*. For Greek *Athēna* the Egyptian *ḥ* would have to become alpha, a strong initial vowel—again, a transmission that does not work. Greek theta does not exist in Egypto-Coptic, but it would have to derive from the final *t* in Egyptian *Ḥwt*. Moreover, the final *t* in Egyptian *Nt* (Neith) has a strong final letter, not the feminine ending that could drop away in Middle to Late Egyptian (Rendsburg 1989, 72; see Jasanoff and Nussbaum, this volume).

More seriously, had Hyksos-Egyptian-Semitic influences on Boeotia been as intensive as Bernal proposes, early Greek would reveal much more intensive traces of Egyptian and Semitic. Such linguistic influences would include not only vocabulary cognates, of which Bernal has produced some that may be valid, but also second-level phonetic influences in the alphabet, and tertiary influences in grammatical forms.[17] But although the Greek alphabet of the first millennium B.C.E. derived from Phoenician Semitic, the language remained phonetically Indo-European and thus lacks distinct phonemes found in Egypto-Coptic and in the Semitic languages. There is virtually nothing of Egypto-Coptic or Semitic grammar in Greek. Moreover, Rendsburg's analysis (1989, 71–79) notes Greek borrowings from Semitic and Egyptian over an extended period of time, especially the first millennium, when (most scholars agree) the Phoenicians and the Egyptians did have stronger influence on Greece. Thus much of Bernal's proposed massive linguistic influence vanishes. As a support for his colonization theory, what remains is not sufficient.

Had the Hyksos indeed established a dynasty in Greece, Semitic and Egypto-Coptic would have been heavily imposed on Greek, in phonetic structure and even in grammar. Evidence of this level of influence is lacking, and hence Bernal's thesis of Hyksos colonization of Greece remains unproven (see Vermeule, Coleman, this volume).

Nor is the linguistic analysis projected above arbitrary. It is of the same order that linguists have employed in striving to find other Afro-Asiatic languages in northwestern Africa (see Hodge 1971; Fulco 1981). A well-documented example of strong linguistic influence in an ancient context is found in the development of Coptic Egyptian, the final form of the Egypto-Coptic language, which evolved in Christian Egypt in the third and fourth centuries C.E. Because of the change of religion in post-pharaonic Egypt and the demand for Greek literacy in administration of Roman Egypt (Gardiner 1957, 10–11; Bagnall 1993, 235–46), hieroglyphs were abandoned, as was Demotic, and the Greek alphabet plus seven Demotic letters were thenceforth used to write Egypto-Coptic. Greek influence in Greco-Roman Egypt was very strong, owing both to Greeks who settled in Egypt and to administrative pressures to use Greek language. Despite all this the Egyptians of the period clung to their language. As the Christian church encouraged literacy among its clergy, the newly adopted alphabetic script made the replacement of hieroglyphs and Demotic easier. Yet it was the loss of pharaonic religion that delivered the hardest blow to the old hieroglyphic script. As expected under such massive influences, Coptic shows good evidence of Greek grammar, and the Coptic alphabet is a compromise phonetically. It is precisely such grammatical and phonetic borrowings that are lacking in the second- and first-millennium Phoenician and Egyptian influences that Bernal has attributed to Greek.

The manner of external contact that *is* documented for the New Kingdom, and could be envisioned for the Hyksos period and even the Middle Kingdom, was trade. There is indeed strong evidence of trade between pharaonic Egypt and Mycenaean Greece, and between the Semitic Levant and Mycenaean Greece.[18] And substantial trade can indeed introduce strong influences, as other cultural parallels demonstrate. For instance, the well-attested early Mesopotamian trade with the Indus Valley Harappan culture involved not only exchange of goods but also the posting of Harappan merchants in Sumerian cities, where their distinctive seals have been excavated and even (in one instance) a street was named for them.[19]

That sort of contact can be envisioned, for the Hyksos period and Late Bronze Age, between the Levant, Egypt, and Mycenaean Greece. As Bernal and others posit, it does appear that *Kadmos* in Greek derives from Semitic *Kedem* (*BA* 2:58–59, 501–4; Rendsburg 1989, 76–77); Greek traditions call him a Phoenician, further supporting the idea. Kadmos might well be the echo of a Phoenician merchant who had settled, centuries before, in Mycenaean Greece.

From the Middle Kingdom we have the instructive example of Sinuhe, who fled from Egypt and was adopted by a Syro-Palestinian chieftain. He took up residence in Syria, married the chieftain's daughter, and had an Egypto-Syrian family. He largely adopted the dress and manners of the Syrians, something that caused much wonder and bemusement in the queen (his former employer) and her royal children when in old age he returned to Egypt (Lichtheim 1973, 226–33). Sinuhe also mentions other Egyptian exiles living abroad. The New Kingdom story *The Doomed Prince* offers another example of an Egyptian living abroad and marrying a foreign princess (Simpson 1973, 85–91). Such individual personalities could similarly account for legendary Greeks of foreign origin, whether Kadmos or others. Egyptian documentation also records many foreigners who took up residence in Egypt and even married Egyptians. Normal trade and other cross-cultural relations such as military contacts led to a certain degree of linguistic borrowing, as is found in the New Kingdom in Egypt (Wente 1990, 106; Redford 1992, 214–15). Analogous contacts are documented toward the south, between Egypt and Nubia-Kush.[20]

Ancient Crete certainly shows influences both from Egypt and from the Levant. Bernal mentions, for example, Early Dynastic stone bowls from Egypt found on Crete (*BA* 2:71–72), but their implications must be carefully considered (see Vermeule, Coleman, this volume). Stone bowls of the First and Second Dynasties were circulating in Egypt as late as Djoser's reign in the

Third Dynasty, for he buried vast numbers of them under his step pyramid in Saqqara (Lauer 1976, 100, 133–34, plates 103–9). Thus the bowls on Crete could represent either routine exports or special diplomatic gifts. Old Kingdom reliefs of Sahure's reign do indeed depict seagoing ships, and the Byblos sea trade was even more ancient (Hoffman 1991, 272, 338–39; Redford 1992, 37–43, 54, fig. 4). Egyptian trade contact with Crete may thus have originated as early as in the Old Kingdom. Alabaster vases of Pepy I–II were found at Kerma, in the Sudan, the site of ancient Yam, with which Harkhuf traded in the Sixth Dynasty (Trigger 1976, 56–57). So too, alabaster vases inscribed with the pharaoh's cartouches were sent to Byblos during the Twenty-second Dynasty (Kitchen 1986, 292, 308, 324–25).

The prudence necessary in interpreting the significance of stone vases and other goods is further exemplified by the finds at Kerma. After excavating statues there of Hepdjefa, governor at Asyut, and of his wife, Sennuwy, and a trove of other Middle Kingdom materials, Reisner theorized (in the 1920s) that Hepdjefa had been posted to Kerma as a sort of colonial governor and that (to judge from the tumulus style of burial in which the statues were found) he had "gone native."[21] But later excavations and research revealed Hyksos period seals and pottery in the selfsame tumulus! Thus it emerged that the tomb was actually that of a powerful Kushite king, buried on a bed in good Kushite style and accompanied by hundreds of sacrificed retainers.[22] The Middle Kingdom statues and other materials had either been acquired during a Kushite raid into Egypt, or were sold by the Hyksos to the Kushites (O'Connor 1971, 7; Helck 1976). The Second Kamose Stela verifies that the Hyksos rulers and the ruler of Kush were allies (Habachi 1972, 39–40). Far from being an Egyptian colony, with an Egyptian governor, Kush was a powerful Sudanese state, controlling a vast territory and—as recent excavations have shown—possessing a strong riverine fleet (Bonnet 1986a, 1986b, 1987a, 1987b; O'Connor 1993, 12–13; 1994). This drastic reinterpretation from emerging evidence at Kerma should serve as a healthy caution against reading too much into such disparate finds as the Dorak gold of Sahure, the Early Dynastic stone bowls on Crete, isolated Middle Kingdom statues of personages known to have lived in Egypt, and other objects found on widely scattered sites.

Cretan culture does show other evidence of Egyptian influence. The Thera paintings, sealed by the volcanic eruption in 1628 B.C.E., show ships with Middle Kingdom Egyptian-style construction, sail rigging, and side-mounted steering oars. They also follow the Egyptian color convention for depicting human figures: the men are reddish-brown, the women yellowish-white. (This convention, widespread in Egypt during the Old Kingdom, is also found occasionally in paintings from the Middle Kingdom.) The Egyptian convention for depicting human posture, in profile and partly head-on, is also evident in the paintings on Thera. All this detail in the rendering of daily life seems quite clearly the result of Egyptian influence.

Evidence is less clear that the Cretan bull cult of the Minotaur can be ascribed (as Bernal does, *BA* 1:165–84), to Egyptian influences from the Eleventh and Twelfth Dynasties. Bull cults occurred all through the ancient Near East, from very early in prehistory onward. The cult as practiced on Crete has distinctions not attested in Egypt, including the bull-leaping ritual and human sacrifices to the Minotaur. Cretan palaces seem closer, in construction and decoration, to examples from Mari in northern Syria than to Egyptian styles, as Bernal himself acknowledges. Yet he then proceeds to ascribe them to Egyptian influence (*BA* 2:157–58, 160–62).

This tendency is observable throughout Bernal's writing. In assessing a cultural factor, word, or toponym, he often discounts quite plausible Indo-European or Semitic analysis and, after much discussion, finally ascribes the influence to Egypt, even when this involves tortuous reasoning. His discussion of the Colchians described by Herodotus (2.104–5) is a case in point. Herodotus says that the Colchians, who lived east of the Black Sea, claimed a relationship to the Egyptians. He notes that they were dark-complexioned, had frizzy hair, and practiced circumcision of males, traits that indeed pointed to Egypt. Herodotus hastens to add, however, that dark-complexioned people are found in other cultures as well. To account for the Colchians' particular claims of affinity he proposes that they derived from the army of Sesostris, as recounted in the Sesostris legend. Bernal takes this to mean that Middle Kingdom pharaohs had campaigned in the Black Sea area.

He neglects to consider that dark, Egypto-Kushite people in that region might much likelier have arrived through some more recent operation, such as the Assyrian deportation of Kushites and Egyptians captured during their attacks on Egypt in 671–633 B.C.E. (Kitchen 1986, 392–93). Esarhaddon had fought with Taharqa in 671 and had captured a number of Kushites, including members of the royal family (Kitchen 1986, 392; Pritchard 1969b, no. 447). Assyrians had a policy of deporting rebellious foes to the opposite end of their empire. Such was the fate of the Ten Lost Tribes of Israel, deported under Shalmanesar V and Sargon II (722–720 B.C.E.) and replaced with a population deported from various parts of Babylonia (Saggs 1984, 263–64; Cogan 1974, 100–102). Hence the Colchians described by Herodotus might well have originated in Kush and Egypt and been deported by one of the Neo-Assyrian kings who invaded Egypt. By the Twenty-fifth Dynasty, Kushites had adopted many Egyptian customs; but the frizzy hair described by Herodotus would better suit them. It is also far likelier that a population deported during the first millennium would retain vivid memories of their land of origin than one left behind by a Middle Kingdom pharaoh some fifteen hundred years before.

Herodotus' further observation, that Egyptians he encountered during his visit to Egypt (448 B.C.E.) did not in turn recall the Colchians, can be explained in the context of the Kushite-Saite era. Psamtik II's campaign against Napata in 593 had resulted in vilification of the Kushite kings and the erasure of their monuments and memorials in Egypt (Kitchen 1986, 406). This *damnatio memoriae* could account for Egyptians' having forgotten the Neo-Assyrian deportation by Herodotus' time, 150 years later, particularly if some of the deportees were Kushites. Besides, foreign invasions and deportations cause painful memories: another reason why the Egyptians of Herodotus' day may have forgotten.

But suppose an earlier cause is truly needed to explain the presence of Egyptians and Kushites in Colchis. Shuppiluliumas II took Egyptian prisoners from Amka in Syria, in the late fourteenth century B.C.E. (Pritchard 1969a, 394–96). During the New Kingdom the Egyptian army had a Kushite battalion, and the regular army also numbered many Kushites both in the ranks and as officers (Wente 1990, 106; Trigger 1976, 138–39). The Hittites may have deported some of these as prisoners of war back to the area east of the Black Sea. All this would, incidentally, validate the allusions in other early legends, such as the story of Jason and the Argonauts, to a dark-complexioned people that dwelt in the environs of the Black Sea (*BA* 2:245–57). But as Bernal himself has noted (2:253–56), the Dravidian population of Elam (to the southeast of Colchis) may also have been dark-complexioned.

If a historical model is required to explain Herodotus' report of the Colchians, Egyptian and Kushite captives taken by Esarhaddon or Asshurbanipal and deported to that area make the most sense. Such exiles would probably prefer to trace their origins to a legendary conqueror than to Assyrian deportees; the well-circulated first-millennium legend of Sesostris, with all its late accretions, would suit their needs perfectly. The least attractive possibility is that a Middle Kingdom pharaoh left those ancestral settlers behind in Colchis when he returned with his army to Egypt. Yet Bernal has made this his chosen explanation.

VOLCANIC EVIDENCE: HEKLA III AND THERA

When Bernal discusses the volcanic eruptions at Hekla III and Thera (*BA* 2, chapter 7), his arguments are by and large more convincing. Certainly dendrochronologists and physical geologists have cogently demonstrated the impact of enormous volcanic events, both in recent history, as with Tambora (1815) and Krakatoa (1883), and in the more remote past, as with

Hekla III (1159 B.C.E.), Thera (1628 B.C.E.), and Kuwae, in Vanuatu (1453 C.E.). Such megaeruptions caused significant environmental and climatic disruption worldwide, which remains as evidence in shrunken tree rings, ash in ice cores—and economic and political upheaval in societies most strongly affected. Environmental effects included a drop in global temperatures such that frosts and snowfall occurred in normally warm areas, and killing summer frosts in temperate climates, leading to loss of a year's crops.[23] Tambora, which erupted in 1815 in the East Indies, caused just such problems in 1816–17 as far away as Europe and North America. Shrunken tree rings for the years 1159 B.C.E. and 1628 B.C.E. and parallel evidence in cores from polar ice caps and in radiocarbon readings from plant material on Thera all attest the eruptions of Hekla III in Iceland and Thera in the Aegean Sea (*BA* 2:285–88).[24]

Egyptian societies have generally survived such climatic disasters, partly because of the region's unique river system, which draws water from deep in Africa and from monsoon rainfall over the Ethiopian highlands. Indeed Egypt has often provided other regions with grain during such episodes, for instance in the "year without a summer" (1816–17), when it shipped grain to Scandinavian countries.[25] Whether Egypt felt effects of the Thera eruption in 1628 B.C.E. is unknown, because of the sparse documentation from the Hyksos era, but ash from Thera has been found in sediments from the Delta lakes. Though not connected to the reign of Ahmose I, as some have supposed,[26] the eruption's effects might have weakened the Hyksos sufficiently to enable Seqenenre Taʿaa II to attempt to revolt, albeit unsuccessfully, against them.

Hekla III, dated 1159 B.C.E., may account for some hitherto inexplicable troubles in Egypt during the mid–Twentieth Dynasty. That eruption would have occurred toward the end of the reign of Ramesses III (1182–1151) (Wente and Van Siclen 1976, 218; *BA* 2:305–7). In his last few regnal years Ramesses III had difficulties in paying the monthly grain wages to the workers who carved the royal tombs at Deir el-Medinah (Edgerton 1951). Was this the result of a diminished grain harvest, perhaps caused by disturbances in the Nile flood attendant upon the eruption? Interestingly, later in the Twentieth Dynasty, under Ramesses VI–VIII, wheat and barley prices rose sharply in Egypt while livestock and other commodities remained stable; grain prices had returned to normal levels by the time of Ramesses IX.[27]

This was also an age of great disruptions in Mycenaean Greece. Even in normal times Greece experienced marginal harvests and food supply. During the first millennium B.C.E. it imported grain, often from Egypt, and perhaps it had done so at times in the second millennium as well. If the eruption of Hekla III perceptibly damaged Egypt's agriculture, the effects could only have been worse in Greece and Anatolia. The demise of Hittite Bronze Age civilization and the fierce Aramaean invasions from the desert into the Assyrian homeland may be further echoes of Hekla III, though other factors will have played a role as well (Sandars 1987, 179–91; Drews 1993, 97–157). Other such disruptions may have occurred earlier: Merneptah (1212–1202 B.C.E.) mentions in his great Karnak inscription that grain had to be sent to the Hittites, who were in need (Wainwright 1960; Kitchen 1982, 215). Bernal cites similar disturbances in China: crop failures, atmospheric phenomena caused by ash-filled wind belts, and accompanying upheavals in government, including the collapse of one dynasty and the rise of another, all ascribable to Hekla III (*BA* 2:305–9). In Mesopotamia the Kassite Dynasty expired during the same century (Roux 1964, 217, 229).

Documentary evidence of the dramatic effects of megavolcanic eruptions has only recently been compiled and assessed, yet it may with considerable confidence be added to the list of factors that have contributed to some of the "dark ages" in history. The ancient world was less well able than the modern to cope with worldwide disruptions, as long-distance trade routes were not as widespread. Usually Egypt was able to assist other nations, except (as in the mid–Twentieth Dynasty) when its own grain production was disrupted.

The megaeruption of Thera in 1628 B.C.E., centered in the Mediterranean, must have had some major impacts in Egypt; but as noted above, it occurred during the exceptionally poorly documented Hyksos era. Many scholars agree that Thera's eruption caused major havoc in Greece and especially on Crete. The extent of Thera's ash cloud has been debated, but evidence of it from the Egyptian Delta lake sediments indicates a widespread effect (Watkins et al. 1978). Bernal and others have considered that the biblical Exodus story has traces of volcanic effects, including darkness by day, a pillar of fire, and parting of the seas. Still, as Bernal notes, the Thera eruption would have been hidden from view in the eastern Mediterranean owing to the earth's curvature.

Tsunamis from the Thera eruption, which have also been discussed extensively, seem to account for certain dislocations on Crete and in Greece and the Levant. The low-lying Egyptian Delta must likewise have felt some of these effects. If the Hyksos were a naval power, that region may have suffered the greatest damage. But the parting of the sea in Exodus refers to one of the brackish lakes of the eastern Delta, not to the Mediterranean (Kitchen 1977, 78–79; 1992). The Suez Isthmus would have sheltered those lakes and the Red Sea from tsunamis. Given the total absence of Hyksos documentation of such events, they can only be inferred from geological interpretation of the impact of Thera.

As for other biblical phenomena, darkness by day in Egypt is also produced by severe sandstorms that often strike in the spring months; the darkness thus cannot conclusively tie the Exodus to the eruption of Thera. Local weather disturbances can dramatically shift the waters in the shallow northeastern Delta lakes (Kitchen 1977, 78–79). Sudden shifts in wind direction can cause sudden surges of the lake water. Here again there is no need to invoke the effects of Thera. But if some of the Hebrews had indeed been in Egypt since the Hyksos era, and they dwelled in the northeastern Delta (as tradition has it), might they not retain dim ancestral memories of the eruption and its effects? If, as Bernal thinks (along with others), Plato had some such knowledge of Thera as late as the mid–first millennium, might not the Hebrews also have retained something similar, from 1628 B.C.E. to the time of the Exodus dated to the reign of Ramesses II (ca. 1249 B.C.E.)—a mere few centuries after the event? (See Kitchen 1977, 75–79, 146; 1982, 70–71.)

Bernal and others also associate with Thera myths that describe the flood of Deucalion. Bernal further thinks that Thera is echoed in Near Eastern Creation epics (*BA* 2:291–304, 317–18); but this is very speculative. Most of the great myths were already well fixed in the various traditions by 1628 B.C.E.— for example, the Egyptian Creation stories, and the myths of Gilgamesh and Enuma Elish in Mesopotamia. There are strong parallels between the biblical and Egyptian Creation myths (Currid 1991); thus it may well be that the biblical tradition, too, predates 1628 B.C.E. The biblical Flood story quite closely matches the Flood story in *Gilgamesh*, which may trace its conceptual origins to the severe floods that sometimes occurred on the Tigris and Euphrates (Oppenheim 1977, 262–63; Roux 1964, 97–101).

CHRONOLOGY AND THE HYKSOS ERA

Bernal's account of the Hyksos era is particularly contradictory. He seems all too willing to cast away the one solid bit of data for the period: the 108 years and six great kings recorded in the Turin Royal Canon. Throughout, he prefers absurdly high chronology and would date the Hyksos' rise in Egypt as early as 1775–1750 B.C.E. (*BA* 2:206–16, esp. 212). When combined with Simpson's date for the end of the Twelfth Dynasty (1801 B.C.E.) or Parker's traditional date (1786 B.C.E.), this would leave almost no space for the Thirteenth Dynasty, which Bernal assesses as degenerate and unstable (2:323–26, 334–36). He fails utterly to mention the studies of Hayes (1953a) and von Beckerath (1958) regarding the Thirteenth Dynasty and its strong line of viziers, who are attested for a much longer time. Nor does he seem to take into account recent Nubian excavations and their evidence from the Kushite era, or the long span of post–Twelfth Dynasty settlement in Lower Nubia (Trigger 1976, 82–84; Gratien 1978, 133–221; Bonnet 1986b, 1987a, 1987b).

As Hayes and von Beckerath demonstrate, the strong vizierate that Senwosret III had created took power and ruled through shadow kings with ephemeral reigns. Six viziers, in hereditary succession, governed Egypt from It-Tꜣwy. Reckoning about twenty years in office for each, on average, this would denote some 110 to 120 years between the end of the Twelfth Dynasty and the advent of Hyksos dominion in Egypt. Using Parker's date, 1786, for the end of the Twelfth Dynasty, that would mean that Hyksos rule began ca. 1676–1666 B.C.E. This date can be double-checked by a backward projection from a Sothic date found on Papyrus Ebers, dated to Pharaoh Amenhotep I of the Eighteenth Dynasty. The calculation also uses the 108 years of Hyksos rule mentioned in the Turin Royal Canon. As Bernal notes, there are (in addition to Krauss's speculative theory) two prevailing opinions about the Papyrus Ebers date. One view, which posits that the Sothic observation was made at Memphis, would date Amenhotep I to 1551–1524; the other, which sets the Sothic observation at Thebes, would date him at 1527–1506.[28]

Amenhotep I's immediate predecessor Ahmose I, who had twenty-two regnal years at minimum, would thus date to 1573–1551 (Memphis observation) or 1548–1527 (Thebes). Thutmose III has been dated to 1504–1450, on the basis of Egyptian sightings of the new moon, or—a lesser probability—to 1490–1436 (Wente 1975; Wente and Van Siclen 1976, 218). Reckoned by the Memphis Sothic date, the expulsion of the Hyksos would be dated about 1565; from the Theban Sothic date, about 1540. (Krauss's Elephantine Sothic observation would yield an even later date for the expulsion of the Hyksos, but that would conflict with the lunar dates for Thutmose III.) Adding the 108 years of Hyksos dominion to the two dates considered here, the higher sets the advent of Hyksos rule at 1673, the lower at 1648. With these data clearly the better match is between Parker's date of 1786 for the end of the Twelfth Dynasty, plus 110 or 120 years for the Thirteenth, and the Memphite Sothic observation from the Papyrus Ebers data. Simpson's proposed closure for the Twelfth Dynasty, 1801, is also conformable with this dating, by adding a few extra years to the Thirteenth Dynasty. This is not impossible, as the tenure of the six viziers is an estimate. The end of Hyksos dominion would date to Ahmose I, around his tenth or eleventh regnal year, something most scholars can agree with (e.g., Goedicke 1985; Vandersleyen 1971, 34–40).

Thus the dates for the Twelfth Dynasty (established by a Sothic dating, the Turin Royal Canon, and the 108 years of Hyksos dominion) and the rough calculation of the duration of the Thirteenth Dynasty (based upon six hereditary viziers and the Papyrus Ebers Sothic date) together produce at least a broad chronological framework for the Second Intermediate Period. This likewise provides adequate time for the Thirteenth Dynasty, which, though not a glorious period, did provide stable rule for more than a century. It also matches the lengthy post–Twelfth Dynasty Egyptian occupation of Lower Nubia and allows adequately for the now emerging chronology of the Kushite rulers (Gratien 1978, 133–223). The shrunken Thirteenth Dynasty that Bernal proposes does not fit at all well with this broad chronological outline, nor with the emerging Kushite chronology, and those are major difficulties. There are several better-documented pharaohs in the Thirteenth Dynasty (one Neferhotep and several Sobekhoteps); most Egyptologists date them to 1730–1700 (Trigger et al. 1983; Grimal 1992, 184–85). This framework also allows us to fit in the other attested kings of that dynasty—which both Bernal's compressed Thirteenth Dynasty and Krauss's trim chronology would render nearly impossible, unless that dynasty was agreed to have overlapped extensively into the period of Hyksos rule.

Bernal also appears not to have considered Redford's (1970) article that returns to a traditional view that a violent Hyksos takeover overthrew the Thirteenth Dynasty (see also Redford 1992, 105–6). This position has received strong support from Austrian excavations of Avaris (Bietak 1979), which demonstrate a violent end and a burning of the Middle Kingdom town and palace complex at the old Ḥwt-Wʿrt. After that incursion the Hyksos moved rapidly to see It-T3wy–Memphis, which led to the downfall of the regime of the viziers and their shadow kings (Trigger 1976, 85; Trigger et al. 1983, 158–59; Redford 1970).

And if, as Bernal implies, the Hyksos did *not* terminate the Thirteenth Dynasty, there would be an anomaly in the direct emergence of the Seventeenth Dynasty in Thebes after that collapse. Further, the now-emerging Kushite chronology, which shows cross-links to both Egypt and the Hyksos rulers, suggests that the Thirteenth Dynasty existed for a considerable time. Nor has Bernal taken into account all the recent excavations of the Nubian-Kushite kingdom of Kerma (Bonnet 1986b, 1987a; Gratien 1978, 160–233), which demonstrate a substantial duration of time parallel to the Thirteenth Dynasty, for which Egyptian records suggest perhaps 110 to 120 years. This dating firmly contradicts Bernal's high dates for the advent of the Hyksos and his extreme truncation of the Thirteenth Dynasty.

Many scholars agree that the Hyksos were basically an Asiatic Semitic group that contained a Hurrian elite with special proficiency in horse training and chariot technology (*BA* 2:228–30, 232–68). The Hyksos' victory over the Thirteenth Dynasty is understandable through their superiority in weaponry: the horse-drawn chariot, an improved compound bow, and an improved battle axe. Previously it was believed that the Hyksos and other invaders of the Near East in the same era brought the domesticated horse to the area for the first time. Though the Oriental Institute in Chicago recently announced the discovery of a horse sculpture in northern Syria, dating to the third millennium B.C.E.,[29] there is still no evidence of horse-drawn chariotry before the Hyksos age. Sumerian carts were drawn by onagers and donkeys; in Egypt the Old Kingdom caravans of Harkhuf were comprised of donkeys. The horse found at Buhen, which Bernal cites, might well date to the Hyksos era, for Buhen continued as an active fortress during the later Second

Intermediate Period, first under Egyptian control and later under Kushite control (Trigger 1976, 85, 96–98). Evidence from the fortress indicates an extended Egyptian occupation during the Thirteenth Dynasty; it was captured by the Kushites at the same time that the dynasty collapsed under the Hyksos onslaught (Trigger 1976, 82–85; Trigger et al. 1983, 154–55).

The contemporaneity of Hyksos domination with the outbreak of the rebellion of the Theban Seventeenth Dynasty is attested in *The Story of Seqenenre and Apophis* and in two stelae of Kamose. These show that the Hyksos had diplomatic contact with the Kushite kingdom in Kerma and the Sudan, which had now reached a peak of power (Bonnet 1986a, 1987a, 1988b; Gratien 1978, 279–81, 181–221). The Theban Seventeenth Dynasty was vassal to the Hyksos ruler and directly ruled only between Aswan and Coptos in Upper Egypt (Trigger et al. 1983, 159–60).

The Hyksos were a land-based power, but on evidence from the Second Stela of Kamose—his capture of Hyksos ships laden with weaponry and trade goods from all over the Levant—it seems they were also a substantial sea power. Nevertheless the widely dispersed Hyksos objects recovered archaeologically from Crete to Baghdad should not be taken at face value as evidence of Hyksos *rule*, as some (including Bernal) would suppose. Aegean-influenced paintings have been found at the Hyksos' capital, Avaris (Bietak 1992); thus they assuredly had some contact with the Aegean. But it is doubtful that they colonized Greece, as Bernal and others argue. The chariot that appears in Mycenaean Greek art does not exhibit the technical quality of the Levantine and Egyptian models of the early New Kingdom. This suggests independent discovery and development of the chariot, among the forebears of the Hurrians and Mitanni on the one hand, and those of the Mycenaeans on the other. Mycenae may have continued to use its earlier-style models, but in the competitive Near East the more sophisticated chariots evolved rapidly.

EGYPT AND GREECE DURING THE NEW KINGDOM

In chapter 11 of the second volume of *Black Athena* Bernal takes an approach that more scholars can agree with: that Egyptian and Levantine impact on Greece was strongest during the Mycenaean age, approximately the fifteenth through twelfth centuries B.C.E., known also as the Late Bronze Age. There truly is strong evidence of contacts in that era. At the outset, perhaps one reason that Ahmose I (who liberated Egypt from the Hyksos) and his mother, Queen Ahhotep, claimed the inhabitants of Ḥ3w-nbwt, considered by many to be Aegean lands, as followers of the king with Queen Ahhotep as their mistress—even though there is no evidence that they actually campaigned there—could be that, having defeated the Hyksos, they were taking title to places that had previously acknowledged Hyksos suzerainty. This might provide a bit of further evidence concerning Hyksos relations with Ḥꜣw-nbwt (Vercoutter 1948, 1956; T. James 1973, 303) and lend a measure of support to Bernal's position.

Bernal probably is correct in viewing the change from Minoan to Mycenaean costumes in paintings in the tomb of the vizier Rekhmire as evidence of Mycenaeans' eclipse of the Minoans. Against the thesis that Egyptian tomb paintings of such scenes are entirely stereotypical stands the fact that tombs of specific officials contain distinct scenes from their careers (like Rekhmire's as vizier), just as other tombs show details of their owners' careers as generals, treasurers, or astronomers. Standard religious scenes and others of traditional genre certainly might be reproduced from copybooks and pattern scenes; but unique, career-specific scenes, by their very nature, could not have been copied. The duties of the vizier encompassed receiving ambassadors and envoys from foreign lands, and a vizier would be expected to be kept up to date on political changes abroad (Lichtheim 1976, 21–25; T. James 1984, 51–71, esp. 69–70). Thus the alteration of Minoans into Mycenaeans in the tomb of Rekhmire may be viewed as reflecting political reality, as Bernal proposes (*BA* 2:429, 432).

Granted the extended suzerainty of Thutmose III, it would not be unusual that the Minoans and Mycenaeans sent him diplomatic gifts. After his Eighth Campaign, deep into Mitanni territory along the Euphrates, Hittite potentates and Kassite rulers from Babylonia did indeed convey such gifts (Drower 1973, 457; Redford 1992, 160). This generosity was simply acknowledgment of his notable achievements and the arrival of Egypt as a great power. Egyptians termed all such presentations "tribute," regardless of whether these were tribute owing to the suzerainty of Egypt or were simply gifts (Trigger et al. 1983, 226; Redford 1992, 209–13, 227). No one seriously considers Thutmose III to have been suzerain over Babylonia or Hittite realms merely because he received tribute from those lands; similarly, receipt of what Egyptians called "tribute" is not evidence of Egyptian control of Crete or Mycenaean Greece. In the absence of evidence of actual Egyptian campaigns or rule, it is still preferable to consider closer contacts with the Aegean world as intensified trade.

There is very solid evidence of Mycenaean trade to Egypt during the New Kingdom, in the wide distribution of Mycenaean pottery and sherds (Redford 1992, 227–28, 241–43; Helck 1979), and Egyptian products certainly went to Crete and Mycenae in return. Bernal's proposal of Egyptian grain exports is reasonable, given the common shortages of grain in Greece due to inadequate harvests (*BA* 2:250; J. Winter 1972; Redford 1992, 242). Other Egyptian products sought widely in the ancient world included papyrus, gold, and linen. Merchants from nations that participated in such trade certainly would have been present abroad, in reciprocating countries. Names such as

Pa-Keftyw ("the Cretan/Mycenaean") or Pa-Neḥsy ("the Kushite"), found frequently in Egyptian documents from the New Kingdom, would denote persons from those nations present in Egypt; although such names eventually were even taken by native Egyptians, and even by other foreigners — e.g., Phineas (P3-neḥsy) in Hebrew — individual Egyptians in Mycenaean lands, or on Crete acting as merchants, could also be presumed. Such merchants and traders could exert profound influence, as now is known from the Mesopotamian–Indus Valley contact mentioned above, or from later, historical Indian Ocean–Swahili African trade.[30] The Ptolemies, the Romans, and Arabs in the Indian Ocean trade all had commercial posts in India and lands farther east. The spread of Islam along this route, and along the East African Swahili route, attests the power of trade and mercantile activity as a purveyor of cultural or religious ideas and values. Thus it is not at all a surprise to find strong Egyptian influence in Mycenaean Greece and Crete, an influence that it is reasonable to assign to trade rather than suzerainty or colonization.

Egyptian geographical lists of Amenhotep III (Cline 1987; Redford 1992, 242 and n. 5) and a find of foundation-deposit-type ceramic plaques at Mycenae bearing his cartouches may indicate that royally sponsored trade expeditions sailed to the Aegean. The foundation plaques do denote an Egyptian shrine, but we must not forget a parallel situation that existed at Byblos on the Syrian coast, where a shrine to the Egyptian goddess Hathor had stood since at least Old Kingdom times. This is noteworthy because although no city in the Levant had closer ties to Egypt, Byblos came under direct Egyptian suzerainty only during the New Kingdom (so far as is documented).

Egyptologists would generally agree with Bernal in these matters, but they part company with him on the subject of Egyptian colonies and rule in Aegean lands. Greek legends such as those in which Danaos and his daughters are said to originate from Egypt might well have arisen from accounts of individuals like Sinuhe in the Middle Kingdom, or the Doomed Prince in the New Kingdom — both of whom went abroad, married foreign wives, and started a new life. Most such sojourners would be traders, but political refugees are also attested, and economic refugees may be considered. Urhi-Teshub, the expelled Hittite king, sought refuge in Egypt in the reign of Ramesses II, as did a Hittite general, Urhiya, who ended up serving in that pharaoh's armies (Kitchen 1982, 30, 70, 73, 139–40). In the later Bronze Age, the Mycenaeans established commercial colonies along the eastern Mediterranean seaboard, in Ionian Greece, on Rhodes, and on Cyprus (Sandars 1987, 38–39). Thus trade contacts went both ways, and many Aegean artistic motifs were adopted in Egypt and in the Levant. Syria had been absorbing Egyptian influences for an even longer time (Helck 1971; Redford 1992, 33–43), and through trade and political contact some of those influences were secondarily transmitted to Crete and Mycenae.

Many scholars acknowledge the cosmopolitan nature of the Late Bronze Age. New Kingdom Egypt too absorbed much influence from Syria and the Mitanni, and even adopted foreign deities (Redford 1992, 231–32). Here again, a similar cultural interchange is quite possible between Egypt, Crete, and Mycenaean Greece. Thus the Aegean world might have received a double dose of Egyptian influence—one directly from contacts with Egypt, or through Egyptians residing in Mycenae and Crete; another secondarily, through Syria-Palestine, in addition to Levantine influences. Bernal is quite correct that *some* classicists have been slow to accept this evidence, or have even sought to deny it. Given the very cosmopolitan nature of the Late Bronze Age, of which the Aegean world was part, such a stance is unreasonable—the more so, considering the evidence for Mesopotamian–Indus Valley trade, and later Indian Ocean–East African trade and influence on other cultures.

Even such close cultural parallels as common measuring systems, as in Egyptian, Levantine, and Mycenaean examples, can be the outcome of trade, as weights and measures figure most heavily in trade relations. That measures utilized in Linear B are closer to Mesopotamian/Levantine systems, whereas those in Linear A are closer to Egyptian systems (*BA* 2:442) suggests a shift toward more Mycenaean connections with the Levant in the Late Bronze Age. Additional support for this reasoning comes from Late Bronze Age shipwrecks such as those recently discovered at Ulu Burun and Cape Gelidonya, which appear to have been Levantine merchant vessels operating between Egypt, Cyprus, Levantine ports, and ultimately Mycenae (Bass 1967, 1986; Redford 1992, 242).

The depiction of Aegean peoples in Egyptian tomb paintings indicates that some individuals from the Aegean world voyaged directly to Egypt during the earlier New Kingdom. The reduction in trade and political contacts attested for Ramesside Egypt can be ascribed partly to loss of Egyptian naval supremacy in the eastern Mediterranean attendant upon Akhenaten's misrule (Redford 1984, 185–203). This was further complicated by the onset of raids by the Sherden Sea Peoples, documented as early as a stela from regnal year 2 of Ramesses II (Kitchen 1982, 40–41). Yet the presence of Mycenaean pottery in Egypt during the Ramesside era, and such indicators as Merneptah's shipments of grain to the Hittites (Wainwright 1960), would suggest that contacts with the Aegean and the Levant did not completely cease. Bernal's association of the Ahhiyawa (from Hittite documents) with the Achaeans in Homeric texts, as an Ionian-Mycenaean population that had left Anatolia to raid the Near East, follows positions taken by other scholars. Similarly, his discussion of the Danuna/Denyen as being the Homeric Danaoi is reasonable and in accord with other specialists' assessments (Redford 1992, 242–52). And his idea that environmental problems, such as drought, encouraged such population movements and the raids of these and other Sea Peoples (*BA* 2:519–21) may be partially correct.[31]

However, the Sherden raids documented for the early Nineteenth Dynasty were also partly the result of loss of Egyptian naval supremacy in the eastern Mediterranean, further complicated by the capture of Crete by the Mycenaeans, which effectively removed the Minoan navy from action and replaced it with Mycenaeans—who were as apt to trade as to raid. From later eras we may observe a clear pattern whereby decline in major naval powers in the Mediterranean is matched by an increase in piracy and freebooting by certain coastal peoples (Redford 1992, 244–45; Sandars 1987, 37–38). Sherden raids in the early to mid–thirteenth century B.C.E. may be regarded as piratical activity and may partly account for the reduced trade between Egypt and the Aegean and the Levant in Ramesside times. They may likewise account for Ramesses II's construction of a line of coastal fortresses from Rosetta to Marsah-Matruh (Kitchen 1982, 71–72).

Other evidence of decline in Egyptian naval power can be adduced from changes in Egyptian military strategy toward Syria-Palestine during the Ramesside era. Unlike pharaohs of the Eighteenth Dynasty from Thutmose III to Amenhotep III, who had used the navy to ferry the army (Säve-Söderbergh 1946, 30–59, 62–70), Ramesside pharaohs conducted strictly land-based campaigns in the Levant (Kitchen 1982, 20–24, 50–60, 68–70). This shift in strategy is also reflected in Horemheb's decision to begin rebuilding the old Hyksos capital Avaris (see Morris, Vermeule, this volume), a project later brought to its fullest by Sety I and particularly Ramesses II. The latter shifted his capital to the new site, calling it Per-Ramesses, and built other military store cities throughout the Delta; Per-Ramesses itself became a major military staging area (Kitchen 1982, 43, 70–71; Redford 1992, 204). The change in strategy, together with Egypt's loss of naval supremacy, explains how most Mediterranean trade now passed into the hands of Levantine merchants; it also explains why Ugarit and other Levantine ports flourished so richly in the mid– to late thirteenth century B.C.E. Because Ugarit was a Hittite vassal state at the time, the Hittites were at last getting a share of the trade (Redford 1992, 176; Sandars 1987, 37–39). Ramesses II and Hattusilis III ended the Egyptian-Hittite struggle over Syria with a great peace treaty in 1258, thus inaugurating a brief period of peace in the Levant (Kitchen 1982, 74–83; Redford 1992, 189–92). This may have brought Egypt back into the Levantine–Mycenaean trade, for a brief spell. But it was the lull before the storm that burst upon Egypt in the reign of Merneptah, in 1207, his fifth regnal year (Kitchen 1982, 215–16; Sandars 1987, 105–15).

Like the northern European vikings of a later age, the Mycenaeans could be both raiders and merchant traders (Redford 1992, 241–43; Drews 1993, 91–92). As climatic conditions deteriorated after 1210 (as partly indicated by

Merneptah's grain shipments to the Hittites, mentioned above), Aegean and coastal Anatolian peoples turned more to raiding and piracy. One group landed in Libya, probably in Cyrenaica, past the westernmost Egyptian coastal fortress of Ramesses II, and made common cause with the Libyans to attack Egypt. These Sea Peoples also armed the Libyans, as is evident from a list of captives and booty seized during Merneptah's fifth year (1207), when the king utterly defeated their attempt to penetrate Egypt. The Sea peoples comprised only about 3,000 of the 9,376 enemy casualties (the rest being Libyans), yet the Egyptians captured more than 9,000 pieces of bronze weaponry and armor (Kitchen 1982, 215–16; 1968, 4:8–9). As Libyans traditionally went lightly armed and without body armor, the conclusion must be that the Sea Peoples had equipped them. Merneptah expressly mentions that the raids had disrupted his grain shipments to the Hittites. He also sent weapons to Ugarit and perhaps elsewhere, in an effort to help stave off Sea Peoples' raids in other quarters (Kitchen 1968, 4:24, no. 7; Schaeffer 1953, 141–42 and fig. 15).

Perhaps the Mycenaean expeditions against Thebes and Troy, recorded in Homeric epics, should be viewed as more such raids by Sea Peoples. Egypt was powerful enough to fight them off and inflict severe casualties, but the isolated and semi-independent city-states of the Aegean world succumbed one after another. Just as the Homeric sagas possibly preserve the memory of such expeditions against Thebes and Troy, another Greek legend—that Odysseus raided Egypt—may encapsulate a memory of some failed raid by the Sea Peoples. That captives taken by the Egyptians during such raids were impressed into the pharaohs' armies, where they received pay and benefits like regular Egyptian veterans, also makes sense of this same legend, which tells that Odysseus served in Egypt for twenty years and came away wealthy.[32] Some of the same Sherden who raided the Delta in regnal year 2 of Ramesses II later fought bravely on the Egyptian side at the Battle of Kadesh in regnal year 5, as the many battle reliefs of Ramesses II show. Ramesses III also conscripted Sea Peoples who raided Egypt, and the Shasu forces depicted in his battle reliefs may originate from captives taken by Merneptah during his Canaanite war.[33] It was standard practice in Ramesside Egypt to recruit such militarily capable captives, and a papyrus dated to Ramesses II indicates just how commonly foreigners were found in the Egyptian armed forces of that era.[34] This is yet another indication of the cosmopolitan diversity of the Late Bronze Age.

If other states experienced as many foreign influences during this era as New Kingdom Egypt did, we should indeed have a picture of the sort of Egyptian and Levantine influences that Bernal perceives in Mycenaean Greece, and earlier on Crete. Many foreign words became incorporated into Late Egyptian, the dialect of the period, which might by analogy explain some of the Egyptian and Levantine vocabulary Bernal postulates in

Mycenaean Greek. Culturally, Egypt was strong enough to absorb these influences and turn them to its own advantage, just as the pharaohs had an effective policy for coopting foreigners into Egyptian society.

Yet how the other Levantine and Aegean states coped with such influences is less well documented. What glimmers of evidence we have from cities like Ugarit and Byblos indicate that these too were Egyptianized to an extent; but they also showed Mesopotamian and Aegean influences. That some Levantine cities were cognizant of such influences is indicated by a sarcastic passage in the *Story of Wenamun* (Simpson 1973; Nims 1968, 163–64). Yet none of the deep influences discussed here resulted from extensive foreign colonization, for neither Egypt nor the Hittites, who controlled those cities for a time, tried to impose their cultures on others. Accordingly, Bernal's thesis that Egyptian and Hyksos colonies existed on Crete and in Mycenaean Greece remains highly speculative and is not convincingly demonstrated. But his claims of substantial influence from Egypt and from the Levant upon the Aegean world, albeit mostly through the agency and trade and political diplomatic contacts, are in essence reasonable.

CONCLUSION: THE PUZZLE OF THE PAST

Despite the recognized effects of the "Aryan Model" proposed by Bernal, was it the only factor that influenced the early scholars of ancient Near Eastern cultures? It remains also to consider whether classicists' unwillingness to accept evidence of Egyptian and Levantine influence on the Aegean world is an effect of what Bernal calls the "Aryan Model," or of some other factors. While some nineteenth- and mid-twentieth-century scholars were almost certainly influenced by political developments in expressing Aryan views, it is equally clear that in all fields involving ancient civilizations, the amount of documentation and archaeological evidence has increased enormously over the past century. Some of the earlier misinterpretations of the past might have thus resulted as much from a lack of sufficient evidence as from racial-theoretical models. As the case of Egypt demonstrates, "Aryanist" theories did arise, to the effect that since Egypt lay geographically in Africa, it could not have evolved a great civilization independently—hence the various "dynastic race" theories proposing that the Egyptians and even the Nubians were non-African. Indeed, incomplete early evidence did sometimes seem to support such theories.

One such instance concerns the matter of Mesopotamian influence on Egypt, which was once seen as all-pervasive, leading to Egyptian kingship, architecture, writing, and all higher civilization. Research during the past three-quarters of a century, however, not only has reversed this interpretation but has also demonstrated that not one, but two, great civilizations arose in northeastern Africa. Egypt was one, arising directly from the Saharan and Badarian descendants of earliest African prehistory. The other was ancient Kush, in Nubia and the Sudan. Recent excavations that have investigated the Kushite and Saharan cultures attest just how powerful a state Kush was and confirm its derivation from the Yam mentioned in Old Kingdom Egyptian records, back to Qustul in Lower Nubia.[35] The establishment of an independent Nubian tradition, the Khartoum Neolithic, is now traced back to 7000 B.C.E.; it is thus as old as the earliest settlements in Egypt and perhaps a bit older. The cattle pastoral tradition found today in the Sudan and East Africa has likewise been traced directly back through both ancient Egyptian and Kushite civilizations to the Saharan cultures, who independently domesticated cattle and started the African cattle pastoral tradition—and who now are also considered to have been the earliest speakers of Afro-Asiatic languages.

Fresh evidence has also flowed in from Mesopotamia. Recent analysis of Mesopotamian writing and its origins (Schmandt-Besserat 1992) has demonstrated how it arose from tokens used in early invoicing systems, and how these led to the creation of the tablet and cuneiform writing, and how cuneiform writing and literacy spread in Mesopotamia, mainly among the business scribal classes—and leaving most of the rulers and kings illiterate. By contrast, in Egypt writing developed from Naqada II buffware decoration and later from the desire of chieftains and proto-kings to commemorate their great deeds and victories (Arnett 1982; Hassan 1983; Williams and Logan 1987). From these arose the Royal Annals of the First Dynasty, and writing later spread down the social hierarchy to bureaucrats and scribes. Literacy in Egypt was a prerequisite to belonging to the elite class, and the scribal school was the road to literacy and social advancement (Baines 1983). Egyptian royalty were all literate, male and female alike. This very recently recognized distinction between these two major writing systems shows that they are totally disparate and developed independently. There was not even so much as a Mesopotamian stimulus in the development of Egyptian writing.

Mesopotamian influences are now correctly viewed as having arrived in the Nile Delta through Buto, transmitted through trade from the Amuq region of northern Syria. Remarkable finds there, in excavations at the site of ancient Ebla, have rewritten the early history of Syria and demonstrated the strong penetration of Mesopotamian-Sumerian culture into that area. In Egypt, development of elites led to a desire for certain luxury goods, such as cedar and lapis lazuli, which Syria possessed or could obtain; Byblos became the conduit whence such materials flowed. In turn, the discovery of gold in the eastern desert of Egypt enriched the elite and drew the interest of foreigners. The very name of ancient Naqada (Nubt, in Egyptian) meant Gold Town—a sign of the early importance of gold in Egypt.[36]

Once demolished, the dynastic race theory gave diffusionism a very bad reputation among most modern Egyptologists, for it was part of the effort to extend what Bernal would term the Aryan Model. The same problem clouded the history of the state of Kush, and Nubian studies had a much later start historically than Egyptology because of political events in the Sudan during the late nineteenth century. Now the latest evidence shows that the early exploitation of desert resources and the rise of elites in the proto-Dynastic eras of both Egypt and and Mesopotamia led to the desire for foreign luxuries. Egypt also needed timber, and this led it to Byblos and the famed cedars of Lebanon. The *Gilgamesh* epic shows that Mesopotamia too needed timber. Both societies developed a desire for lapis lazuli, supplied by a mine in what today is Afghanistan. Enterprising "middleman states" like Ebla in Syria and Maadi in Egypt arose to transship the commodities.

Desire for foreign goods also led these early societies to venture from their river valleys onto neighboring seas, where the Mesopotamians eventually encountered the Indus Valley Harappan civilization, while Egyptians traveled to Byblos and, down the Red Sea coast, to Punt. The very early pharaohs preferred sea trade in the eastern Mediterranean, and they eliminated Maadi; in Lower Nubia they also eliminated Qustul and the A-Group Nubians. Very recent research has also resolved the long-standing mystery of where the early Egyptians, Levantines, and Mesopotamians obtained their tin, to manufacture bronze: a tin mine has been located in southern Anatolia.[37] This resolution to a knotty problem obviates the need to postulate very early sea voyages as far as Iberia, or to what is now Cornwall in Britain.

Metallurgical analysis has now revealed that the silver mine at Laurion, near Athens, was in operation by Egyptian Middle Kingdom times. Recent studies in volcanology, which show how megavolcanic eruptions have had profound effects on natural and human history, have likewise brought modern science to bear on ancient evidence. Radiocarbon analysis and subsequent refinements in dendrochronology have revolutionized the study of chronology, and even ice core data have come into play in dating volcanic eruptions. In many instances these fresh approaches have breathed new life into old legends and annalistic sources, and they have helped to resolve some puzzling "blips" in the ancient record, such as the remarkable inflation in grain prices in mid–Twentieth Dynasty Egypt that can now perhaps be attributed to the megaeruption of Hekla III in Iceland in 1159 B.C.E. No less impressive is the accumulating evidence that Egypt has long been the breadbasket of the Mediterranean world. Already known for feeding Rome and Constantinople and, previously, in the first millennium B.C.E., for its aid to Greece, Egypt in the second millennium B.C.E. can now also be recognized for aiding the Hittites and, possibly, earlier Mycenaean civilization as well.

By collecting and elucidating such evidence Bernal has indeed contributed to scholarship. So too have his data from Chinese history contributed fresh evidence. But elsewhere, in his own proposed, uncritical Egyptocentric diffusionism, as with the Sesostris legend and theories of Egyptian and Hyksos colonies in Greece and on Crete, he has gone far beyond reasonable interpretation. In his overanalysis of cognates and his proposed pharaonic origins for certain names in Greek legend and other instances, he has again gone beyond the reasonable, failing to follow regular linguistic three-step analysis involving phonetic systems and grammar. Such unevenness and unreliability make the *Black Athena* volumes difficult to use. Certainly, knowledgeable scholars will find useful data in them, but their misuse by Afrocentrists (see Phillip 1995, 16–17; Lefkowitz, Snowden, this volume) demonstrates the danger of encouraging undocumented and unhistorical pan-African claims.

Bernal's speculations have lent support to the doubtful claim that ancient Egyptian people were like the peoples of Sub-Saharan or West Africa, and to the notion that African colonists expanded worldwide in antiquity. As a result, many who make Afrocentric diffusionist claims cite his work uncritically and are further unwilling to consider contemporary anthropological analysis and the findings of prehistorians and archaeologists; they have now written off Egyptologists as tools of Eurocentrism. Diffusion, even the modified diffusion that Bernal proclaims, cannot be applied indiscriminately as a developmental model onto every ancient society. It has some validity where ancient cultures lay geographically close to one another, as with China, Korea, and Japan, and indeed Egypt, the Levant, Mesopotamia, and the Indus Valley. But it has none in the evolution of cultures separated by oceans, such as those of the Americas and the Pacific islands. Ancient epidemiological data and data on exchange of crops and domestic animals are our strongest evidence against any pre-Columbian American contacts with Africa—but that is a topic for another essay.

NOTES

1. Petrie 1920, 47–50; 1931, esp. 79–80; 1937; 1939, 65–79; Engelbach 1943.
2. See Brunton and Thompson 1928, 75; Mond and Mond 1937, 267–68; Hoffman 1991, 136–44.
3. See Wendorf and Schild 1976; Wendorf, Schild, and Close 1984; Close 1980.
4. The last firm support for the dynastic race theory (see Derry 1956; Emery 1961, 31–31, 38–42) had appeared by mid–century. See also Rice 1990, though much tempered in scope.
5. For a well–balanced view see von der Way 1988; Moorey 1990; Redford 1992, 17–24.
6. See Trigger et al. 1983, 36–37; Aldred 1984, 77; Rice 1990, 45–67; Ray 1986, 309–11.

7. Trigger 1976, 65; E. F. Wente, personal communication.

8. See Gardiner 1959, plate III Turin VI.3; 1961, 125, 439; Yurco 1993, 9, 12, n. 13.

9. See the cautions mentioned by Simpson (1972, 52, 54) regarding Senwosret III and the length of his reign; also Cruz-Uribe 1987; Hayes 1953a.

10. Hayes 1953b, 97–98, fig. 119. Broken examples are very numerous: e.g., Hayes fig. 120, also Bourriau 1988, 41–44, nos. 28–30.

11. Baer, unpublished notes (Oriental Institute, Chicago). See Yurco 1993, esp. 12 n. 13.

12. *BA* 2:188–96; Farag 1980, esp. plates 1–3. See now Redford 1992, 78–80, for an updated translation.

13. *BA* 2:224–26. See Redford 1992, 76–82, for operations in the Levant.

14. W. Y. Adams 1984, 187. See, however, Trigger 1976, 72–77, 85–98; Bonnet 1978, 1980, 1982, 1986a, 1986b, 1987a, 1987b; Gratien 1978; Yurco, forthcoming.

15. Zeuner 1969, 374–82; Lauer 1976, plate 4; Hoffman 1991, 201, 205, 243–44.

16. See Habachi 1972, 37 (Kamose stela); Bietak 1992.

17. An example of how dangerous analysis from cognates alone can be, appears in *Pygmy Kitabu* (Hallet and Pelle 1973), an outrageous work whose authors sought to relate Twa–Pygmy languages to Scandinavian Indo-European languages, entirely on the basis of a few cognates in vocabulary (123–42)!

18. See Hankey 1970; Astour 1973; Sandars 1987, 47–49, 72–77.

19. Oppenheim 1954; 1977, 63–64; During-Caspars 1965, 1970–71, 1971; Ratnagar 1981.

20. Trigger 1976, 54–65, 77–81, 85–102, 114–31; Yurco, forthcoming.

21. Reisner 1923a, 61–121; 1923b, 3–21; Trigger 1976, 90–91; Bonnet 1986b, 1987a.

22. Trigger 1976, 91–94; Säve-Söderbergh 1941, 110–14; Haynes 1992, 20–22.

23. Rampino and Self 1982; Simpkin and Fiske 1983, 423; Stommel and Stommel 1979.

24. See also Sigurdsson, Carey, and Devine 1990, esp. 107–10.

25. Stommel and Stommel 1979; Marsot 1988, 144, 167.

26. *Contra* Goedicke (1985), the date of 1628 B.C.E. for the eruption at Thera disassociates the event from year 11 of Ahmose I. See Watkins et al. 1978 for the distribution and extent of the Thera ash cloud.

27. See Janssen 1975, 112–16, 119–22; Trigger et al. 1983, 228–29. Note that livestock prices also remained stable in New England in 1816–17 C.E., because of selling off of herds; see Stommel and Stommel 1979, 182. It is thus quite likely that the crisis in Egypt was caused by the eruption of Hekla III.

28. See R. A. Parker 1976, 185–86; Edgerton 1937; and, in general, discussion of chronology earlier in this essay, with references there.

29. *University of Chicago Magazine* 1993, 37; BARlines 1993, 16. See also Zeuner 1969, 299–365, for other possible examples of the horse in the ancient Near East.

30. See Redford 1992, 242; Toussaint 1966, 32–41, 50–52; Horton 1957.

31. See Sandars 1987, 179–96. Drews (1993, 77–84) downplays the role of drought in this period, but Merneptah's sending grain to Hatti suggests a food crisis; Herodotus (1.94) also mentions drought in Lydia severe enough to set part of the population to emigrating. Thus there seems to be enough ancient evidence to postulate that

drought played a role in the disintegration of the Late Bronze Age civilizations of Anatolia and Mycenae.

32. See Dothan and Dothan 1992, 219; Kitchen 1982, 40–41; Homer *Odyssey* 14.284–86.

33. See Yurco 1986, 209–10, figs. 6, 8, 9; Epigraphic Survey 1930, plates 17–18, 35; 1932, plate 62).

34. See Wente 1990, 106, on a text that reports foreigners comprising 62 percent of the division–sized unit!

35. See Williams 1986, 163–85, for the possibility that the Qustul monarchy paralleled and influenced later Nubian developments. See also Gratien 1978, 38, 256–60, for development of the Kerma monarchy; and Trigger 1975, 82–102. And now see Bonnet 1986b, 1987a, 1989, showing that Kerma's earliest beginnings date back to 3000 B.C.E., with clear affinities to the A-group.

36. Redford 1992, 19; but see Hoffman 1991, 121, 260, 272–73. Despite Redford's doubts, enough gold has been found in Predynastic burials to indicate that the Naqada II Egyptians had begun mining it. Moreover, what else enriched and elevated the elites of Nubt and Nekhen too (both with easy access to the eastern desert) and prompted their presence there? (See Hoffman, 243–48).

37. See Yener and Vandiver 1993a. Muhly (1993) doubts that discovery; but see now Yener and Vandiver 1993b, where their case seems quite convincing.

RACE

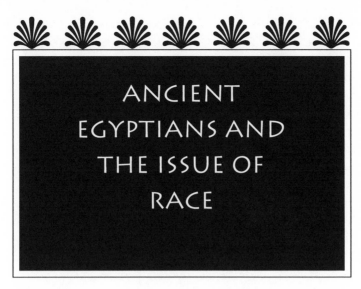

ANCIENT EGYPTIANS AND THE ISSUE OF RACE

Kathryn A. Bard

Egypt straddles two major geographical regions: the continent of Africa and the Middle East. Because it was located on the African continent, ancient Egypt was an African civilization, though perhaps its African identity has been subtly minimized within the discipline of Near Eastern studies, which has its roots in European Orientalism of the nineteenth century. Many earlier European scholars working in Egypt, particularly during the days of the British empire, assumed that ancient history began with Egypt and Mesopotamia—in other words, that the earliest civilizations were Near Eastern ones, and ancient Egypt could be understood as such (and not as an African civilization). Some scholars, such as Sir Flinders Petrie (1899, 10) and Walter Emery (Emery 1967, 39), assumed that civilization was introduced into Egypt by an invading dynastic race from southwestern Asia, who replaced the prehistoric hunters and gatherers and early farmers living along the Nile—peoples much too primitive to "invent" civilization.

It is now known that as the land bridge between Asia and Africa, Egypt was the recipient of earlier technological developments in southwestern Asia, especially agriculture. The major cereal cultigens, emmer wheat and barley, as well as the domestic sheep/goat, are species not known in their wild form in Africa; they were domesticated much earlier, in southwestern Asia, and only later introduced into Egypt (Wetterstrom 1993, 200). There is no archaeological evidence, however, to suggest that a large-scale migration of peoples from southwestern Asia brought farming into Egypt, and the mechanisms by which domesticated cereals and perhaps the technology of farming were introduced into Egypt remain unclear. But recent research on the Predynastic period in Egypt (ca. 4000–3000 B.C.E.), including my excavations near Nag Hammadi in Upper Egypt, has shown that the cultural roots of Egyptian civilization are indeed indigenous (Hoffman 1988, 47).

Less clear, however, has been the issue of race in ancient Egypt. The modern concept of race was unknown to the ancient Egyptians. Non-Egyptians were identified by their ethnic/tribal affiliations or by the region/country from which they came. Most physical anthropologists in the second half of this century do not believe that pure races ever existed, and they view the concept of "race" as a misleading one for their studies (Trigger 1978, 27). But a number of Afrocentrists have claimed that black civilization began with ancient Egypt. The very title of Martin Bernal's *Black Athena* alludes to the putative roots of Greek—and therefore Western civilization—as a black African civilization in Egypt.

Ancient Egyptians were Mediterranean peoples, neither Sub-Saharan blacks nor Caucasian whites but peoples whose skin was adapted for life in a subtropical desert environment. Ancient Egypt was a melting pot; peoples of different ethnic identities migrated into the Nile Valley at different times in its prehistory and history. The question of whether ancient Egyptians were black or white obscures their own identity as agricultural peoples of *Kmt*, as opposed to *dšrt*, the barren "Red Land" of the desert. *Kmt* means "Black Land," the fertile floodplain of the lower Nile Valley, where cereal crops grew in such abundance. It does not mean "Land of Blacks."

Egyptians were Egyptians, the people of *Kmt*. The name points to the importance of the Nile in their lives. Unlike that of other early riverine civilizations, the Egyptian floodplain required no fallow time, nor was salinization of soils a problem with irrigation agriculture (Butzer 1976, 90). The economic base of pharaonic civilization was provided by the incredibly rich potential of cereal agriculture in the Egyptian Nile Valley. Egyptians were the indigenous farmers of the Lower Nile Valley, neither black nor white as races are conceived of today.

Just who the ancient Egyptians were can be addressed by several types of evidence: language, historical records, the material culture, and physical remains (usually skeletons from burials). Evidence may be used to study cultural and biological relationships between different groups as well as within groups. For the most part, analyses of the different types of evidence have to be pursued independently, using different data because of the very different variables of such data; only after that can relationships between the different data be studied—within a specific cultural context.

Looking first at the linguistic evidence, there is nothing that links Egypt to other areas in Africa except very generally. Egyptian, the language spoken by the ancient Egyptians and written on monuments in hieroglyphs, evolved over more than four thousand years, to be finally replaced by Arabic following the Arab invasion in the seventh century C.E. Egyptian is classified by linguists as one of the five main groups of what is called the Afro-Asiatic language family. The other languages in this family include the Semitic languages spoken in southwestern Asia (including modern Arabic and Hebrew); Berber, spoken by Berbers in North Africa to the west of the Nile; the Chadic languages, spoken in northern Central Africa in the vicinity of Lake Chad; and the Cushitic languages spoken in the Horn of Africa, such as Galla in eastern Ethiopia (and probably covering Omotic; cf. Greenberg 1955, 43). Egyptian is so distinctly different from these languages in its structure and vocabulary as to be classified by itself. But it is more closely related to other languages in the Afro-Asiatic family than to any Indo-European languages or to the Bantu languages spoken today in Sub-Saharan Africa. In the New Kingdom (ca. 1558–1085 B.C.E.), when Egypt had an empire in southwest Asia, more Semitic words appeared in what is called Late Egyptian, but this can be explained by increased interaction with Semitic-speaking peoples, and not with other Africans (although that too certainly occurred). The linguistic evidence, then, points to the relative isolation of speakers of Egyptian in relation to other languages spoken in Africa.

Another important type of evidence for the study of ancient populations is from the physical remains that have been preserved in Egyptian burials. D. E. Derry, who studied the physical remains of Old Kingdom elites buried at Giza (excavated in the first decade of this century by George Reisner of Harvard University), took skull measurements and concluded, like Petrie and Emery, that the pyramid builders were a dynastic race of invaders, probably from the East, "who were far removed from any negroid element" (1956, 81).

As practiced by Derry, however, craniometry is no longer considered a valid statistical means for evaluating genetic relationships of ancient populations. A more recent analysis of nonmetrical variations in skulls (Berry and Berry 1973) suggests that the Egyptian samples show genetic continuity from Predynastic times through the Old and Middle Kingdoms — over two thousand years — with a shift in the New Kingdom, when there were considerable infiltrations of new peoples into the Nile Valley. In this same study the Egyptian skulls were then analyzed with samples from the northern Sudan (the Neolithic site of Jebel Moya), West Africa (Ashanti), Palestine (the site of Lachish), and Turkey (Byzantine period). Not surprisingly, the Egyptian skulls were not very distinct from the Jebel Moya skulls but were much more distinct from all others, including those from West Africa. Such a study suggests closer genetic affinity between peoples in Egypt and the northern Sudan, which were close geographically and are known to have had considerable cultural contact throughout prehistory and pharaonic history. But the Egyptian and the Jebel Moya samples also seemed no more related to the samples from southwestern Asia in Palestine and Turkey than to modern (black) populations of West Africa (Berry and Berry 1973, 206).

Clearly more analyses of the physical remains of ancient Egyptians need to be done using current techniques, such as those Nancy Lovell at the University of Alberta is using in her work (see A. L. Johnson and N. Lovell 1994). Two problems, however, hinder such studies. First, graves in Egypt have been robbed since prehistoric times. Intact tombs, such as Tutankhamen's, are the great exception, and even his tomb had been penetrated twice in antiquity by robbers. Second, many skeletons excavated by earlier archaeologists working in Egypt were either not kept, or have been stored so poorly that today they are in very bad condition. The prehistoric burials that I excavated in 1978 at Naqada in Upper Egypt were sent off to storage in the basement of the Cairo Museum, never to be seen again. Even for the same age/sex group within a burial sample representing one small village community (in which there probably was some or even considerable intermarriage), there can be significant skeletal variability, and large samples need to be analyzed so that statistical findings will be valid. But nonskeletal features, which are the ones most frequently used to distinguish race today, have long since disappeared in the physical remains of burials—even when they have been mummified as in pharaonic Egypt (Trigger 1968, 11).

It is disturbing to me as an archaeologist that archaeological evidence—the artifacts, art and architecture of ancient Egypt—has been identified with race and racial issues. Racial issues, which in all fairness have arisen because of racial inequalities in the United States and elsewhere, have been imposed on the material remains of a culture even though these remains do not in themselves denote race. I am reminded of the excavation report of the Wellcome expedition at the site of Jebel Moya (Addison 1949). The English archaeologists who worked there in 1911–12 were certain that the advanced stone tools they excavated had to have been made by a prehistoric people who were white. This seems like a ridiculous conclusion today: stone tools thousands of years old cannot tell us the race of their makers any more than they can tell us what language their makers spoke.

The conventions of Egyptian art, as established by the beginning of the First Dynasty (ca. 3050 B.C.E.) do not represent humans as seen in perspective by the eye, but represent them in an analytical manner that transforms reality. The head, arms, and legs are drawn in profile; the torso is depicted frontally. Art may sometimes be grossly mannered and exaggerated, as it was during the reign of Akhenaten (ca. 1363–1347 B.C.E.) because of religious and cultural reforms conceptualized by that pharaoh. The conventions of Egyptian art were those of the crown and elites associated with the crown, and what is characteristic of Egyptian style in art for the most part represents a very small segment of the population.

Who and what were depicted on the walls of temples and tombs depended on Egyptian beliefs and ideology. Art was functional, and much of what is seen today in museums was created for the mortuary cult. Ancient Egypt was a class-stratified society, and age and sex in art were differentiated by scale of figures, style of dress, and symbols of status or office, as well as by skin tone. Statues and reliefs of women were painted in lighter tones of yellow ochre-based paint; men were painted in darker tones of red ochre-based paint. This is not to suggest that all Egyptian men were darker than all Egyptian women, but rather that established artistic conventions served to convey such ideas as sex differentiation. Such conventions, however, were not hard and fast rules, and there are many known exceptions. For example, in the tomb of Queen Nefertari, Rameses II's chief wife, the queen's skin is painted a brown (red ochre) color in a scene where she is playing a board game, as a contrast to the solid background of yellow ochre paint.

Non-Egyptian Africans, as well as Asiatics, were usually depicted in representational art as distinctly different from Egyptians, especially in their clothing and hairstyles. In the well-known scenes from the Eighteenth Dynasty tomb of Rekmire, Asiatics, Cretans, and Nubians are painted in registers bringing tribute to the court of Tuthmoses III. The Nubians, from the Nile Valley south of the First Cataract at Aswan, are painted in darker skin tones than the Asiatics, and are depicted with more prognathous jaws than the Egyptians. Bringing exotic goods and pets that originated in regions south of Nubia, the Nubians also carry gold ingots shaped into large rings. Nubia had little agricultural potential compared to Egypt, but rich gold mines were located there in *wadis* to the east of the Nile. That in part explains why Egypt occupied Nubia and built forts and temple towns there in the Middle and New Kingdoms.

Nubians bearing gold ingots and exotic tribute in paintings from the tomb of Huy (Thebes, no. 40), dating to the time of Tutankhamen, wear long, pleated Egyptian robes, but their hairstyles and large earrings are distinctly non-Egyptian. They have neck markings that may represent scarification, a practice unknown in ancient Egypt, and their facial features may possibly be interpreted as prognathous. In one scene an elite Nubian woman is depicted standing in a cart drawn by oxen, something in which Egyptian women would never have ridden. The Nubian tribute-bearers are painted in two skin tones, black and dark brown. These tones do not necessarily represent actual skin tones in real life but may serve to distinguish each tribute-bearer from the next in a row in which the figures overlap. Alternatively, the brown-skinned people may be of Nubian origin, and the black-skinned ones may be from farther south (Trigger 1978, 33). The shading of skin tones in Egyptian tomb paintings, which varies considerably, may not be a certain criterion for distinguishing race. Specific symbols of ethnic identity can also vary.

Nor are black Africans depicted by standardized conventions. The scenes of Queen Hatshepsut's expedition to the land of Punt, from her Eighteenth Dynasty mortuary temple at Deir el-Bahri, show a land very different from Egypt. Punt is thought to have been located along and to the west of the Sudanese/Eritrean coast (Kitchen 1993). The houses of the Punt peoples were hemispherical and built on elevated posts, unlike the rectangular mudbrick houses of Egyptians. Punt was the source of incense, ivory, and ebony, and tribute-bearers are seen carrying these goods to the seafaring Egyptians. A grossly obese "queen" of Punt is very unlike the lithe Egyptian upper-class women shown in tombs of this period. The "king" of Punt, whom she follows, is depicted in an Egyptian loincloth, but with a long and very un-Egyptian beard.

Though some Egyptian details appear, the ethnographic details in the Punt expedition scenes portray a culture that is distinctly non-Egyptian. But what race the Punt peoples were cannot really be determined from these scenes. Egyptian artists or scribes who accompanied this expedition recorded very distinctive ethnographic details, but the Puntites' facial features look more Egyptian than "black." Identifying race in Egyptian representational art, again, is difficult to do—probably because race (as opposed to ethnic affiliation, that is, Egyptians versus all non-Egyptians) was not a criterion for differentiation used by the ancient Egyptians.

As enemies of Egypt—peoples who threatened the boundaries of Egypt's kingdom—Nubians and Asiatics were depicted generically on the walls of Egyptian temples in the New Kingdom. The enemies of Egypt were shown as bound captives, being vanquished by pharaoh. On Egyptian temples in Nubia, reliefs showing such scenes must have had as one of their purposes the intimidation of local people. It was the duty of the king to destroy Egypt's enemies, and this is what is symbolized on the handle of a cane and on a footstool from Tutankhamen's tomb, both carved with generic Asiatic and Nubian captives. The Nubians carved on these two artifacts have very different facial features from those of the bearded Asiatics, but the facial features of both types of foreigners differ from the sculpture of Tutankhamen in the tomb.

Given that conventions for differentiating ethnic identity varied, as did artistic conventions for skin tones, anomalies in Egyptian art cannot be used with any certainty for drawing inferences about the race of ancient Egyptians. A limestone female head found in Giza tomb 4440, dating to the Fourth Dynasty (ca. 2613–2494 B.C.E.), is described in the catalogue of the Museum of Fine Arts in Boston as "of negroid type with thick lips, wide nostrils, and full cheeks" (W. S. Smith 1960, 35). A limestone head representing the woman's husband, also from tomb 4440, is distinctly different in its facial features: "the aquiline type of face so characteristic of some of the members of the

Cheops family" (Smith, 35). Neither of these heads is painted, so their skin tones are unknown. The genre (called "reserve heads"), known only from the Fourth Dynasty, suggests more individualistic portraits than are usual in Egyptian art, and this female head "of negroid type" is different from other known reserve heads. As the identity of the person represented is unknown, her place in Egyptian society cannot be ascertained—though she certainly was a woman of high position.

A sandstone statue of Mentuhotep II, the king who unified Egypt and founded the Middle Kingdom in the twenty-first century B.C.E., was found in a pit to the east of the king's mortuary complex at Deir el-Bahri. The king is shown wearing a white robe and the red crown of Lower Egypt—and his skin is painted black. But as with analogous cases noted above, paint applied to a statue offers no real indication of his actual skin color. Black-painted skin could be symbolic of something of which we are unaware four thousand years later.

Perhaps better known than the painted statue of Mentuhotep II are the two New Kingdom figures of Tutankhamen that Howard Carter found guarding the entrance to that king's burial chamber. The black, resin-covered skin on these two wooden figures is contrasted by their gold skirts, sandals, headdresses, and jewelry (Reeves 1990, 128). These two black renditions of the king contrast the lighter-toned paintings of him on the walls of the burial chamber, and with the colored inlay on the back of the famous golden throne. Other art in this tomb likewise depicts a young man with brown skin, in keeping with Egyptian artistic conventions. Far from suggesting that the king had black skin, the two guardian figures of Tutankhamen may appear black simply because resin was applied to the skin areas. It is possible, too, that the resin was originally lighter and became dark over time. Resin, a costly and exotic import in ancient Egypt, was a material befitting a king who was to go to the afterlife displaying all forms of worldly wealth.

The people who lived south of Egypt are also known from archaeological evidence excavated in Nubia. From the fourth millennium B.C.E., when complex society evolved in Egypt, there is evidence in Lower Nubia of what archaeologists call the A-Group culture: people who traded with the Egyptians for Egyptian craft goods found in their burials. But with the founding of the First Dynasty in Egypt, ca. 3050 B.C.E., the newly unified Egyptian state penetrated into Lower Nubia, probably by military campaigns, and the A-Group disappeared there. Who the A-Group were in terms of race cannot be ascertained from the artifacts in their graves, but their locally made grave goods demonstrate a different material culture from that of the Predynastic Egyptians (Trigger 1976, 33).

From the Old Kingdom (ca. 2686–2181 B.C.E.) there is some archaeological evidence of small-scale Egyptian settlements in Lower Nubia, but by the late

Old Kingdom a group of indigenous peoples, known to archaeologists as the C-Group, moved into Nubia as Egyptian occupation ended. After Egypt was reunified during the Middle Kingdom (ca. 2040–1786 B.C.E.), large mudbrick forts were built along the Nile in the region of the Second Cataract (near the modern-day border of Egypt and the Sudan). But evidence of the C-Group in Lower Nubia is also known to date to the Middle Kingdom, and the C-Group culture actually survived the Egyptian withdrawal from Nubia at the collapse of the Middle Kingdom.

During the Middle Kingdom a powerful African polity arose whose capital was at Kerma near the Third Cataract in the Nile, in the northern Sudan. In Egyptian texts this culture is called "Kush." The eastern cemetery at Kerma was excavated by George Reisner, and artifacts from eight very large round tumuli are now in the Museum of Fine Arts in Boston (Reisner 1923a). These tumuli are of a different architecture than Egyptian tombs. Some of them, moreover, contained human sacrifices, not found in Egyptian burials (with the possible exception of the First Dynasty royal tombs at Abydos). A Swiss archaeologist currently excavating the town and cemetery at Kerma estimates that there are 30,000 to 40,000 burials (Bonnet 1992, 613). The sway of Kerma extended into Lower Nubia until the reunification of Egypt at the beginning of the New Kingdom.

With Egyptian control in the New Kingdom extending as far south as Gebel Barkal near the Fourth Cataract, where a temple to the god Amen was built, the Kerma kingdom came to an end. Egyptians restored the Middle Kingdom forts in Lower Nubia and built temple towns farther south. But after the collapse of the New Kingdom, ca. 1085 B.C.E., a new Kushite power eventually arose at Gebel Barkal, where the cult of Amen continued to be practiced. The earliest burials in the royal cemetery at el-Kurru near Gebel Barkal (see Dunham 1950), also excavated by George Reisner, date to around 850 B.C.E. A hundred years later the first Kushite garrisons were established in southern Egypt during the reign of the Kushite king Piye, who later established his rule over all of Egypt (Trigger 1976, 140, 145). The Twenty-fifth Dynasty (ca. 760–656 B.C.E.), whose kings were all Kushites, ruled in Egypt for about sixty years. The later kings of this dynasty were frequently at battle with the Assyrian army, which finally succeeded in ending Kushite control in Egypt. Piye built the first pyramid tomb at el-Kurru, whereas in Egypt pyramids as royal burial monuments had not been built for a thousand years. Later Kushite kings were mummified, according to Egyptian custom, and spread the cult of Amen throughout Nubia.

The archaeological evidence of African kingdoms south of Egypt, at Kerma and Gebel Barkal, suggests distinctly different cultures that came into contact with Egypt. During the Twenty-fifth Dynasty the polity centered at

Gebel Barkal actually controlled Egypt for a period. Cultural connections, if any, between the earlier Kerma kingdom and the later kingdom centered farther up the Nile at Gebel Barkal are uncertain, but the well-preserved burials recently excavated at Kerma by Bonnet (1992) provide a new source of information about Nubian populations.

Presumably the Kushites buried at Kerma and later at el-Kurru were related to the Nubians depicted in New Kingdom tomb paintings, as opposed to blacks living farther south in Africa, but once again the evidence seems ambiguous. Skin color, which is considered a criterion for race, cannot be determined from skeletal remains, and the evidence of representational art is problematic. The archaeological evidence at Kerma and el-Kurru points to African cultures that were different from Egyptian culture but that were responsible nonetheless for major cultural achievements. The Kushite peoples were considered non-Egyptians by Egyptians—in other words, ethnically different—but how physically different they were has yet to be determined by physical anthropologists. In any event, they are certainly better candidates for "black" African kingdoms than is ancient Egypt (see Vermeule, this volume).

Culturally and linguistically the ancient Egyptians were different from other peoples living outside the Nile Valley, as well as those farther south and east. From textual and representational evidence it may be shown that ancient Egyptians had a sense of ethnic identity—of being Egyptian, as opposed to non-Egyptian. Today in Africa there are many different ethnic groups speaking many different languages. With the exception of South Africa, identity in Africa today is not by race or, for the most part, by nation, but by ethnic or tribal affiliation, which often has a close association with a spoken language or dialect. Ancient Egypt was definitely the earliest African civilization and as such certainly had an influence not only on the other cultures that arose in the Near East, but also on the states that arose farther south in Africa—at Kerma, Gebel Barkal, and later at Meroë. The evidence cited here strongly suggests that the ancient Egyptians were North African peoples, distinct from Sub-Saharan blacks. But to state categorically that ancient Egypt was either a black—or a white—civilization is to promote a misconception with racist undertones that appeals to those who would like to increase rather than decrease the racial tensions that exist in modern society.

NOTE

Reprinted by permission from *Bostonia* magazine, Summer 1992.

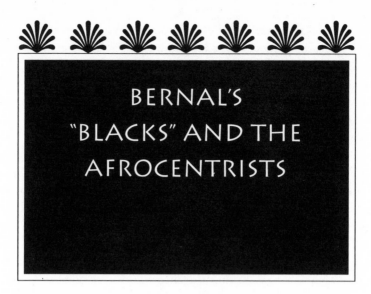

BERNAL'S "BLACKS" AND THE AFROCENTRISTS

Frank M. Snowden, Jr.

TERMINOLOGY

The question of who in the ancient world were and who were not African blacks in the modern sense of blacks or Negroes has given rise to considerable debate. What does the ancient written and iconographical evidence reveal about the physical characteristics of the Egyptians and of their southern neighbors? What physical types in ancient iconographic and written documents most closely resemble Africans and peoples of African descent in the modern world who have been designated in anthropological, historical, and common usage as Negroes or blacks? A summary of the highlights of the ancient evidence pertaining to these questions is an appropriate introduction to this discussion of the "blacks" of Martin Bernal's *Black Athena* (volume 1) and of the Afrocentrists.

Egyptians, Greeks, and Romans were all far from unclear on the question of the color and other physical characteristics of Egypt's southern neighbors—the Kushites of Egyptian documents, and the Ethiopians and Nubians of classical texts. Our earliest evidence comes from Egyptian craftsmen, who in countless paintings, sculptures, mosaics, and other pieces from their workshops realistically portrayed the physical features of the southerners. And on this point David O'Connor (1971, 2) has observed: "Thousands of sculpted and painted representations from Egypt as well as hundreds of well preserved bodies from its cemeteries show that the typical physical type was neither Negroid nor Negro." Particularly valuable, however, is the often overlooked evidence from the Greeks and Romans, who, as the first Europeans to encounter Nubians, left a more detailed description of the observable physical traits of the Nubians than that of any other ancient account.[1]

Ironically, the clarity of classical authors in their descriptions of the blackest and most woolly-haired peoples in their experience provides a model for emulation by those Afrocentrists who so loosely apply the terms "black," "Egyptian," "African," "Africoid," and "Negro" to several ancient populations, and use them interchangeably. Both Bernal and the Afrocentrists are mistaken in assuming that the term *Afri* (Africans) and various color adjectives for dark pigmentation as used by Greeks and Romans are always the classical equivalents of Negroes or blacks in modern usage. Only by taking words out of context and by ignoring the total evidence is it possible to conclude, as some have, that "black" should be applied (in the modern sense) to a wide range of peoples not included in the classical context. I share the hope that a "restatement of the evidence against identifying Egyptians as 'black' might . . . do something to eliminate a misconception that has brought the book [*BA* 1] into contemporary racial politics" (J. F. Gardner 1991).

Greeks and Romans differentiated clearly between the various gradations in the color of dark-skinned Mediterraneans and used several adjectives — e.g., *melas* and *niger* (black and dark), *fuscus* (dark but lighter than *niger*) — to describe peoples darker than themselves. Not all peoples described by such color terms were blacks or Negroes in the modern sense, but *only* the inhabitants of the Nile Valley south of Egypt and of the southern fringes of northwestern Africa. These Africans, the blackest people known to the Greeks and Romans, were characterized by various combinations of dark or black skin, woolly or tightly coiled hair, flat or broad noses, and thick lips. The inhabitants of southern Nubia possessed these characteristics in a more pronounced form than those in the northern part of the country — differences attributable to environmental variations in the region.

The color of these Africans, their most characteristic feature, was highlighted in the name Greeks and Romans invented for them: *Aithiopes* or *Aethiopes* (Ethiopians), literally "burnt-faced peoples." That Ethiopians were the blackest peoples known to Greeks and Romans is illustrated by a familiar "color-scheme," succinctly stated in the first century C.E. by Manilius (4.722–30), who classified dark- and black-skinned peoples as follows: Ethiopians, the blackest; Indians, less sunburned; Egyptians, mildly dark; and Moors, the lightest. Several classical authors specifically emphasized that Ethiopians were darker than Egyptians. Inhabitants of the area near the Ethiopian–Nubian boundary were said by Flavius Philostratus (*Life of Apollonius* 6.2) to be not fully black, not as black as Ethiopians, but blacker than Egyptians. That the pigmentation of Egyptians was seen as lighter than that of Ethiopians is also attested by the adjective *subfusculi* ("somewhat dark") which

Ammianus Marcellinus (22.16.23) chose to describe Egyptians. The people inhabiting the regions around Meroë, on the other hand, were deeply black in color and were pure Ethiopians (Ptolemy *Geography* 1.9).

Ethiopians differed from other dark-skinned peoples (e.g., Egyptians, Moors, and Indians) not only in that they were the blackest of all populations known to Greeks and Romans but also in that their hair was the woolliest or most tightly curled. Herodotus clearly located Ethiopians in the Nile Valley to the south of Egypt (e.g. 2.28–30) and in northwestern Africa to the south of the Libyans (4.197) and described some of the former as the most woolly-haired of all mankind (7.70). The classical practice of using Ethiopians as the yardstick for comparing both the color and hair texture of colored peoples is further illustrated by an emphasis on the contrast often made between the woolly and the "nonwoolly" hair of Egyptians and Indians. Arrian's observation (*Indike* 6.9) emphasized the differences between Ethiopians, Egyptians, and Indians: southern Indians resemble Ethiopians in that they are black, but they are not so flat-nosed or so woolly-haired; whereas northern Indians are physically more like Egyptians. Southern Indians resembled Ethiopians in color; northern Indians, the Egyptians—but Strabo adds (15.1.13) that although southern Indians resembled Ethiopians in color, they were similar to the rest of the Indians in countenance and hair, with the explanation that their hair does not curl or become woolly in the climate of India. The pseudo-Aristotelian *Physiognomonica* (812a, b) describes both Egyptians and Ethiopians as *melanes*, but mentions only Ethiopians, *not* Egyptians, as having exceedingly woolly hair. In short, Ethiopians whose skin was the blackest and whose hair was the woolliest or most tightly curled of all mankind were the only people in classical texts who correspond roughly to the concept of blacks or Negroes as generally understood in modern usage.

"Ethiopian," the word of crucial import as to the full significance of the ethnic identification of peoples darker than Greeks and Romans, was applied, with a few poetical exceptions, neither to Egyptians nor to inhabitants of northwestern Africa, such as Carthaginians, Numidians, or Moors. In other words, *all* Ethiopians were black or dark, but with hair, noses, and lips differing from these features in other peoples described as black or dark. And *Afri* (Africans) generally referred to the lighter-skinned populations of countries west of Egypt along the northern coast of Africa—peoples whose physical characteristics Greeks and Romans distinguished from those of the dark-skinned inhabitants of the interior of northwestern Africa.[2]

"Ethiopian," a color word emphasizing the blackness of peoples so designated, it should be added, carried no stigma of inferiority similar to that associated with color terms in postclassical societies which have subjected black-skinned peoples to discrimination on the basis of the color of their skin.

Long before Greek and Roman writers had described in accurate detail the physical characteristics of Ethiopians, and classical artists had called attention to the ethnic differences between Egyptians and Ethiopians, important iconographic documents from Egypt depicted clearly the black skin and woolly or tightly curled hair of Kushites, which differed from these features as portrayed in Egyptians. There was also a mixed Egyptian-Nubian element in the population of Egypt at least as early as the middle of the third millennium B.C.E., and interracial intermingling continued as black soldiers increasingly served in the Egyptian army, married Egyptian women, and sired racially mixed children. Amenemhet I (1991–1962 B.C.E.) was reported to have been the son of a woman from Nubia and an Upper Egyptian father. The harems of the pharaohs included Nubian women; and the Twenty-fifth Dynasty was a period which would have witnessed an increase in Nubian admixture. There is, however, insufficient evidence to estimate precisely either the size of the Nubian element in the population of ancient Egypt or the extent of Nubian-Egyptian racial mixture. On this point the modern experience of the United States is illuminating. Even on the basis of the substantial documentation relevant to the size of the black population in the United States and to the existence of racial mixture from slavery onward, it would be inaccurate to describe the United States as either a black or a predominantly black nation. It would be equally inaccurate to describe ancient Egypt as either black or predominantly black when much less is known about the Nubian element in the population.

Three important points relevant to the blackness of Africans in the ancient world emerge from an examination of the copious ancient iconographic and written evidence. First, Egyptians and their southern neighbors were perceived as distinctly different physical types. Second, it was the inhabitants of Nubia, not the Egyptians, whose physical type most closely resembled that of Africans and peoples of African descent referred to in the modern world as blacks or Negroes. Third, the Bernal-Afrocentrist practice of describing Egyptians as blacks overlooks crucial distinctions made in antiquity between the physical characteristics of Egyptians and Nubians, and actually equates the two physical types—an equivalence not supported by the ancient evidence.

MODERN MISUSE OF ANCIENT EVIDENCE

Bernal's view of "blacks" and the similar Afrocentric outlook appear with increasing frequency in current discussions of university curricula, proposals for the revision of courses of study for elementary and secondary schools, and the popular press. I have space here to illustrate only a few of the consequences resulting from the Bernal-Afrocentrist approach to blacks in the ancient Mediterranean world. Not the least of these outcomes has been a failure of many Afrocentrists to give proper attention to Nubians and their experience in Egypt, Greece, and Italy, although Nubians were the only Africans whose physical characteristics, according to the ancient evidence, most closely resembled those of peoples described as blacks or Negroes in modern usage.

Among statements relating to "blacks" in the first volume of *Black Athena* are these: Egyptians, according to Herodotus, were black; "many of the most powerful Egyptian dynasties . . . were made up of *pharaohs whom one can usefully call black*" (emphasis mine); "Egyptian civilization was fundamentally African"; Herodotus' portrayal of Egyptians as black was the inspiration of the title *Black Athena*; there is no doubt that most blacks will be unable to accept the research of black scholars who conform to white scholarship (*BA* 1:52–53, 242, 436). These statements, together with Bernal's warm approval of two frequently cited Afrocentrists, C. A. Diop and G. G. M. James, have provided important ammunition for the armory of Afrocentric political and ideological warfare. Why? Bernal had demonstrated in the first volume of *Black Athena* that, *mirabile dictu*, at least one white man had finally adopted two major Afrocentric theses: (1) white racists had robbed blacks of an important part of their heritage by denying that Egypt was a black civilization; and (2) black scholars who disagree with Afrocentric views have been duped by white scholarship.

A more recent statement of Bernal's has given added impetus to the Afrocentric gravamen that white racists have designedly distorted the role of blacks in history. Writing as recently as 1993, six years after the publication of the first volume of *Black Athena*, he argued: "my emphasis on the African nature of Egyptian civilization and the presence of *'people whom one might usefully call black'* (emphasis mine) among its rulers are [*sic*] important to contemporary readers" on social and political levels. Such an emphasis is needed "to counter the cultural debilitation to peoples of African descent brought about by implicit assumptions or explicit statements that there has never been a great 'African' culture which has contributed to world civilization as a whole and that 'Blacks' have always been servile" (Bernal 1993a, 316).

Like many Afrocentrists before and after him, Bernal in this passage, as in the first volume of *Black Athena*, uses "black," "Egyptian," and "African" interchangeably as equivalents despite copious ancient evidence to the contrary. As a result he has been hailed as "the great white hope." For example, in a reply to an editorial in *Archaeology* describing the view that Egyptians were black as "a serious misreading of the historical and archaeological record" (P. A. Young 1992, 2), a teacher identifying himself as a black historian wrote that despite all the evidence pointing to Egyptians as a black people, the editor was unable to admit the truth about Egypt, and extolled Bernal as "the only white historian today with the guts to tell the truth about history and not the white supremacists' version" (Merritt 1993).

Bernal's emphasis on "whom one might usefully call black" in the two contexts cited calls into question his sincerity in disclaiming responsibility for Afrocentric excesses, as several scholars have noted. J. Griffin, for example, points out that Bernal's notion of "fundamentally African" is a "puzzling phrase" and that his choice of "useful" suggests a value judgment rather than a statement of fact (1989, 27). Bernal's label "fundamentally African" has been questioned as "misleadingly simplistic" because evidence from the classical world shows that there were several Africas: "the northern face of Africa" along the Mediterranean coast; "Black Africa" to the south; and "almost a third Africa" formed by the connection via the Nile through Nubia to the Sudan (Brace et al., this volume). In discussing Bernal's disclaimers of responsibility for Afrocentric misuse of *Black Athena*, M. Levine has observed that Bernal has temporized in condemning the excesses of some Afrocentrists and that he should "be as outspoken in condemning the racism of some Afrocentrists as he is in condemning white racists" (1992b, 459). After commenting on Bernal's "black" Egyptians and C. A. Diop's falsification of history by portraying Egyptians as black, J. Ray writes that Bernal is "flirting dangerously" in not distancing himself from the proponents of "black Egyptians" (1991b). And in the opinion of J. D. Muhly, Bernal "has chosen to throw in his lot with the group centered around the *Journal of African Civilizations*," a publication that has emphasized studies of pharaonic Egypt as a black civilization. Analysis of several issues of this journal has convinced Muhly that the writing is "well-intentioned but quite unconvincing and lacking in the basic techniques of critical scholarship" (1990b, 103, 105).

Afrocentrists have long maintained that the history of blacks has been distorted or neglected in traditional curricula. Many historians and educators have agreed that this has often been the case, and specialists have pointed to "omissions and errors which have passed for the truth" (Connor 1970a, 3). Many Afrocentrists, however, continue to reject valid criticisms of their inaccuracies and denounce their critics as Eurocentric racists if they are white, and as dupes of white scholarship and traitors to their race if they are black. It is neither racist nor traitorous, however, to insist upon truth, scholarly rigor, and objectivity in the treatment of the history of blacks.

The methodological shortcomings and inaccuracies of those Afrocentrists who have misread the evidence have been properly noted. More than twenty years ago, the sociologist O. Patterson wrote that the school of black history which he describes as the "three P's approach — Black history as the discovery of princes, pyramids, and pageantry," seeks to "prove that white history has been a big lie" and heads for "the civilizational big-time . . . the 'great' civilizations" of the ancient world. Such an approach, Patterson argued, "does violence to the facts . . . is ideologically bankrupt and is methodologically and theoretically deficient" (1971, 305, 307). Patterson's criticisms are equally applicable to several recent Afrocentric approaches to blacks in Mediterranean antiquity. In their statements about blacks in the ancient world these Afrocentrists demonstrate that they have not approached the ancient evidence with the relevant scholarly methodology. The resulting shortcomings include the following: unfamiliarity with the pertinent primary sources; reliance on the undocumented opinions of fellow Afrocentrists (always the same few); a tendency to generalize on the basis of a few lines from a single author or a few texts without considering the whole context; the use of language charged with political rhetoric; and a determination to read a "white conspiracy" into their critics' interpretations of the ancient evidence.

Like many Afrocentrists before and after him, Bernal cites only one passage from Herodotus (2.104) on which he relies heavily to support his interpretation that Herodotus portrayed Egyptians as blacks. Although the ancient historian in this passage describes both Egyptians and Colchians as *melanchroes* (dark- or black-skinned) and *oulotriches* (woolly- or curly-haired), he emphasizes in the very next sentence that this fact certainly amounts to nothing, since other peoples shared the same features. In referring to the dark color of Egyptians and Colchians, Herodotus was merely following a standard Greco-Roman practice in describing peoples darker than themselves — a practice which did not mean that peoples so described were Ethiopians, that is, Negroes. After rejecting the criteria of hair[3] and skin color as a valid basis for his belief in the Egyptian origin of Colchians, Herodotus argues that similarities of customs, language, and general mode of life point to the kinship of Egyptians and Colchians. And it is clear that in defense of the validity of cultural criteria Herodotus is comparing Colchians and Egyptians — *not* Ethiopians, whose language and customs, like their physical characteristics, he emphasizes, differ from those of Egyptians (2.30, 42; cf. 3.19). In brief, Herodotus bases his belief that Colchians were of Egyptian origin on the similarity of *cultural*, not physical, criteria.

Afrocentrists have welcomed Bernal's observation that C. A. Diop, one of their favorite sources and models, had used Herodotus for the same purpose. And in this connection Bernal wrote: "What most concerned him [Diop] was the great achievements of Egyptian civilization; the systematic denigration of them by European scholars, and his faith that the Egyptians were, as Herodotus had specified, black" (*BA* 1:435). Diop, however, in his use of Herodotus included details not mentioned in *Black Athena*, which Afrocentrists, encouraged by Bernal's observation, have often echoed. Citing as his sources Greek and Latin writers contemporary with the ancient Egyptians, Diop stated that Egyptians "were Negroes, thick-lipped, kinky-haired and thin-legged" and argued that "the unanimity of the authors' evidence on a physical fact as salient as a people's race will be difficult to minimize or pass over" (1981, 36). But both Bernal and Diop themselves, however, have minimized and passed over what Diop referred to as salient contemporary evidence.

Diop not only distorts his classical sources but also omits reference to Greek and Latin authors who specifically call attention to the physical differences between Egyptians and Ethiopians. Furthermore, most of the passages which Diop cites do not support his statement that "Egyptians were Negroes, thick-lipped, kinky-haired and thin-legged." Indeed, most of these passages do not even mention lips or hair but demonstrate only that adjectives denoting color in classical texts, though used to describe several peoples darker than Greeks and Romans, by no means indicate that persons so described were Ethiopians, that is, blacks or Negroes in the modern usage of such terms. Five of the passages cited describe Egyptians as black or dark in color but mention no other physical characteristic.[4] In addition, Diop cites one source describing Egyptians only as black in color but omits another reference in the same source which mentions only Ethiopians but not Egyptians as having extremely woolly hair (pseudo-Aristotelian *Physiognomonica* 6.812a, b).

Bernal has referred to a need "to counter the cultural debilitation to peoples of African descent" resulting from the distortion of the role of blacks in world civilization (Bernal 1993a, 316). Afrocentrists have argued along similar lines that a "white conspiracy" has been responsible for this cultural debilitation, which has deprived blacks of their proper role in world history brought about, according to Bernal, by implicit and explicit negative statements about blacks. A frequently quoted Afrocentrist, Chancellor Williams, for example, ignoring extensive evidence to the contrary, has stated: "In ancient times 'African' and 'Ethiopian' were used interchangeably because both meant the same thing: A Black." He adds that the equivalence of these words "was before the Caucasians began to reorder the earth to suit themselves and found it necessary to stake their birthright over the Land of the Blacks also" (1971, 30–31).

Afrocentrists have gone beyond Bernal in invoking "white conspiracy" to illustrate how Eurocentric racists have "whitened" important historical figures such as Cleopatra, Eratosthenes, Septimius Severus, and Hannibal, all of whom, they claim, were actually blacks. A recent revival of the "black" Cleopatra theory, proclaimed earlier by J. A. Rogers (1946, 66), appears in a chapter entitled "African Warrior Queens" in *Black Women in Antiquity*, in the *Journal of African Civilizations* series. The author, who draws heavily on Rogers, presents the case as follows:

> More nonsense has been written about Cleopatra than about any other African queen, mainly because it has been the desire of many writers to

paint her white. She was not a white woman. Until the emergence of the doctrine of white superiority, Cleopatra was generally pictured as a distinctly African woman, dark in complexion. Shakespeare in the opening lines of *Antony and Cleopatra* called her "tawny." In his day mulattos were called "tawny Moors." In the *Book of Acts* Cleopatra described herself as "black." (Clarke 1984, 126–27)

In the first place, it cannot be demonstrated that Shakespeare intended to suggest a "black" by his use of the word "tawny"; he would more likely have used the word "Ethiope," which in other plays was applied to a Negroid type.[5] Further information advanced as proof of Cleopatra's "blackness" is a reference to the queen as "fat and black" in *Believe It or Not* by Ripley, who, Clarke adds with a final flourish, checks all his facts! If so, Clarke would do well to follow Ripley's example, for there is no reference to Cleopatra in the Book of Acts. Clarke's final "evidence" adduced is a *modern* painting of a Negroid Cleopatra. It is unfortunate that he makes no reference at all to the Macedonian lineage of the entire Ptolemaic dynasty, and the clearly non-Negroid features of the Ptolemies and of Cleopatra herself depicted on the queen's own coinage, including those commemorating her union with Mark Antony.

For northwestern Africa, as for Egypt, some Afrocentrists with the gift of Midas have created "blacks" out of "nonblacks" and have invoked the great "white conspiracy." G. G. M. James, for example, using "African" and "black" as equivalents, referred to the geographer Eratosthenes from the Greek colony of Cyrene, head of the Alexandrian Library, as a black because Cyrene was in northwestern Africa (1954, 50). Similarly, the Roman emperor Septimius Severus has been claimed by the Afrocentrists as black because he hailed from Leptis Magna in North Africa. For example:

History has been so whitewashed that the peoples of the world, including Africans, believe that Africa is inhabited by Europeans, and any time a person achieved fame or became outstanding in ancient or medieval history, it was taken for granted that they were white. A large number of Black African Emperors of Rome and other African leaders are usually portrayed in statues of *white limestone* instead of black marble, or at least bronze. You know what this means? We Africans who have visited the different museums of the world passed by our soul brothers without receiving one vibration. Such a cruel hoax has been played on the African people—but they are awakening now and will never get caught sleeping again. (E. L. Jones 1972, xv–xvi)

In this statement, however, Jones has underestimated the skill of ancient artists in portraying Negroid traits realistically even in white marble and limestone. And, despite Jones's emotionally charged rhetoric, none of the numerous portraits of Septimius Severus provides any evidence whatever of Negroid characteristics (cf. McCann 1968).

Hannibal has also been frequently described by some Afrocentrists as a black. According to J. A. Rogers, the Carthaginians were a Negroid people, and Hannibal, a full-blooded Negro with woolly hair, was traditionally known until the rise of the doctrine of white supremacy as black (1946, 50; 1967, 88). I. Van Sertima (1985a, 138–39) refers to Carthaginians as Africoid peoples, although, like Rogers, he cites no ancient source indicating that the Carthaginians were Ethiopians, that is, Negroes or blacks as the term then applied. According to Van Sertima, the Negroes depicted on the obverse of some third-century B.C.E. coins (with elephants on the reverse) indicate the Africoid ancestry of the Carthaginians, although he provides no supporting facts and omits evidence noted by scholars who have suggested that the Negroes on the coinage depicted black mahouts recruited for their well-known skill in handling elephants (Snowden 1983, 31–32, 121 n. 55).

A final example of a major thesis often proclaimed by Afrocentrists is the claim that Aristotle and his pupils stole important philosophical ideas from the great library at Alexandria. This thesis is proposed by G. G. M. James (1976, 17, 47), whom Bernal describes as a pioneer among scholars sensitively aware of the racism in nineteenth- and twentieth-century European and North American culture (*BA* 1:435). But Aristotle was not guilty as charged. There is no ancient evidence attesting that he ever went to Egypt. Furthermore, according to some ancient sources, the library was founded by Ptolemy Philadelphus (283–246 B.C.E.)—long after the death of Aristotle (in 322). Even if the library had been founded by Ptolemy I (323–283) at the very beginning of his reign and before Aristotle's death, it is doubtful that it would have been much of a bibliographic center at such an early date.[6]

NUBIANS IN THE ANCIENT MEDITERRANEAN WORLD

One of the great ironies of the Afrocentrists' position is their emphasis on ancient Egypt, "a rather distorted and myopic view of history" that has led them to neglect the significance of ancient Nubia, "which really was a black African culture of enormous influence and power" (Kendall 1991b, C1 and C10). The experience of Nubians in various parts of the Mediterranean world, in itself a fascinating chapter in the history of blacks, also sheds light on some of the reasons for the absence of intense color prejudice in antiquity—and for its development in the modern world. Kushites, Ethiopians, and Nubians, the blackest, most woolly-haired people known to the Greeks and Romans, unlike blacks in later societies, were not subjected to economic, political, and social discrimination on the basis of their color. Yet the highlights of ancient

Nubian civilization and the experience of Nubians in Egypt, Greece, and Italy have not received the attention they deserve in Afrocentrist publications and in revisions of courses of study designed to present an accurate picture of blacks in the ancient Mediterranean world. The need for revisions of courses in black studies has been noted in a recent observation by H. L. Gates, Jr.: "Some of the work being done in more than 200 Afro-American studies programs around the country is intellectually 'bogus' because they are essentially inventing a past that never was" (quoted in Butterfield 1992, B7).

What are some of the highlights of this important chapter neglected or omitted entirely in many Afrocentric programs? In the first place, Nubia itself was perceived by Egyptians, Greeks, and Romans as an independent country, rich in coveted resources, inhabited by the blackest people in their experience. The ability of Nubia, a nation of skilled archers, to defend itself from foreign exploitation gained the respect of its enemies. About 750 B.C.E., after almost five hundred years of Egyptian occupation, the Nubians centered around Napata came north, turned the tables on their former conquerors, and ruled Egypt until they were driven out in 663 by the powerful Assyrian war machine—the only time in history that a state from deep in the interior of Africa played an important role in Mediterranean politics. Nubia also laid the foundation of a state—"a major landmark of ancient Africa" (Shinnie 1967, 169)—which, with its later capital at Meroë, survived for more than a thousand years (ca. 300 B.C.E.–350 C.E.), a span longer than any single period of Egyptian unification.

Nubian military power also won the respect of the Ptolemies and later of the Romans, who decided that the most effective way to prevent attacks upon their southern boundary in Egypt was by diplomacy, not by arms. In fact, according to Strabo (17.1.54), the emperor Augustus granted the ambassadors of the Ethiopian queen everything they pleaded for, including the remission of the tribute he had imposed. Nubians of the Twenty-fifth Dynasty were looked to by some Delta chieftains for leadership in their efforts to cast off the yoke of Assyrian dominion. Taharqa, the fifth pharaoh of the Dynasty, was still regarded as a great military leader six hundred years after his death; Strabo (1.3.21, 15.1.6) included him in an account of famed monarchs.

Egyptians, Greeks, and Romans attached no special stigma to the color of the skin and developed no hierarchical notions of race whereby highest and lowest positions in the social pyramid were based on color. Underlying this view of blacks was an objective approach to human diversity. Despite Egypt's centuries-old conflicts with black southern neighbors, the *Great Hymn to the Aten* looked impartially at diversity in skin color, speech, and character, and viewed all peoples, whether Egyptian, Syrian, or Nubian, as creations of the Aten, the sun disk, and made no claim to Egyptian superiority (Pritchard 1969a, 370).

The unknown author of the hymn, sometimes identified as Akhenaten, antedated by many years the Greco-Roman environment theory, which became a keystone of the classical view of other peoples. Setting forth the effects of environment on the physical characteristics of peoples and their mode of life, this explanation of their differences was applied in a uniform manner to all peoples. For Egyptians, the people of Nubia and Syria had been "the Others," *ethnic* types differing from themselves; among Greeks and Romans, the black, woolly-haired Ethiopians of the far South and the fair, straight-haired Scythians of the far North were cited again and again as favorite illustrations of "the Other" in the *environment* theory. In view of the vast climatic differences between Scythia and Ethiopia, Diodorus stated that "It is not at all surprising that the fare and manner of life as well as the bodies of the inhabitants of both regions should be very different from those that prevail among us" (3.34.8). In short, regardless of their color, peoples who lived at the outer regions of the earth followed customs that differed from those of more temperate climes. But blacks were not stereotyped in Greco-Roman records as "primitives." In fact, according to Strabo (4.5.4) it was *whites*, not *blacks*, who were the most "savage": even more savage than Britons were the inhabitants of ancient Ireland, who considered it honorable to devour their fathers when they died and to have intercourse with their mothers.

The relevance of the environment theory to the unbiased view of blacks is seen in the fact that North–South, Ethiopian–Scythian contrasts were deliberately chosen by later Greek and Roman advocates of the view that color is of no consequence in evaluating people, as well as by early Christians in their pronouncements that all whom God created, He created equal and alike. Menander (fragment 612 Koerte), for example, stated that it matters not whether one is as different from a Greek as an Ethiopian or a Scythian: it is merit, not color, that counts. And in his reflections on the traditional criterion of birth, Menander purposely chose the environment theory's familiar Ethiopian–Scythian contrast because its unbiased view provided an effective framework for his own view of what was important in judging the worth of an individual.

The color of Nubians presented no obstacles that excluded them from opportunities available to other newcomers of alien extraction living in Egypt, Greece, or Italy. Ancient slavery was color-blind. Both whites and blacks were slaves, and the ancient world never developed a concept of the equivalence of slave and black; nor did it create theories to prove that blacks were more suited to slavery than others. Blacks were in a no more disadvantageous position than anyone else unfortunate enough to be captured as a prisoner of war or to be enslaved for whatever reason. Enslaved prisoners of war undoubtedly accounted for a substantial number of blacks, but not all blacks were slaves. The advantages of cosmopolitan centers like Alexandria and

Rome were as attractive to enterprising blacks as to others—Greek, Jew, or Syrian—who migrated for many reasons, educational, occupational, or personal. H. Frankfort's observation on the *carrière ouverte aux talents* in Egypt was also true of blacks in the Greco-Roman world: "The talented and industrious were not frustrated by a . . . colour bar" (1951, 90).

Like other slaves and freedmen, blacks often engaged in occupations at the lower end of the economic scale, but blacks with special qualifications found a place for their talent and skill. In Egypt blacks had for centuries found a career in the military a means of achieving positions of security and prestige. Pinehas, who was perhaps of Nubian extraction, attained high rank in the pharaoh's army: he was one of the last viceroys of Kush and remained in Kush, probably as its independent ruler after Egyptian withdrawal ca. 1085 B.C.E. (Frankfort 1951, 90; O'Connor 1971, 9). The large basalt head of a Negro, found in Egypt and now in the Greco-Roman Museum in Alexandria, was probably that of an officer in the Ptolemaic army ca. 80–50 B.C.E. (Snowden 1970, fig. 71). Cleopatra's ships were filled with pitch-black warriors (Sidonius *Carmina* 5.460). Roman imperial armies included Ethiopians like those in the *numerus Maurorum* of Septimius Severus' troops in Britain (*Historia Augusta, Septimius Severus* 22.4.5). It is not unlikely that the emperor also recruited other blacks from northwestern Africa, like the black soldier depicted in a scene on a third-century sarcophagus, apparently a member of the emperor's elite bodyguard (Salerno 1965, 214 and fig. 281).

In the Roman world, some blacks were popular in the theater and the arena. Glycon, a tall, dark man with a hanging lower lip, attained great popularity as a tragic actor and was manumitted by Nero, who paid one of his owners 300,000 sesterces for his share in the actor (*Scholia ad Persium* 5.9). Olympius, a famous black animal-fighter, winner of innumerable victories and a favorite of the people, received a tribute from the poet Luxorius, whose epitaph to the *venator* concluded with these words: "The fame of your renown will live long after you and Carthage will always remember your name" (*Anthologia Latina* nos. 353–54).

Egyptians distinguished between themselves and outsiders, yet once a foreigner came to live in Egypt, learned the language, and adopted Egyptian dress, he was accepted as one of "the people" (J. A. Wilson 1950, 33–34). Greeks called foreign cultures barbarian; yet the name "Hellenes," according to Isocrates, should be applied to persons sharing in the culture, rather than the ancestry of the Greeks (*Panegyricus* 50). Greek was taught at Meroë, and the Ethiopian king Ergamenes, according to Diodorus (3.6.3), had a Greek education and studied Greek philosophy. Reported among the disciples of Aristippus, a Cyrenaic philosopher, was a certain Aethiops, and included in a list of distinguished followers of Epicurus were two from Alexandria named Ptolemaeus, one black, the other white (Diogenes Laertius 2.86, 10.25). The dark-skinned Terence, who may have been of Negroid extraction, was born in Carthage, arrived in Rome as a slave, received a liberal education and his freedom from his owner (a Roman senator), became a member of the learned Scipionic circle, and achieved distinction as a comic playwright. A black known only as Memnon was one of the most talented disciples of Herodes Atticus, the celebrated sophist and patron of the arts (Philostratus *Life of Apollonius* 3.11; Graindor 1930, 114–16; Vercoutter et al. 1976, figs. 336–38).

Racial mixture between blacks and nonblacks gave rise to nothing resembling modern strictures against miscegenation. Intermarriage between Nubians and Egyptians was not uncommon and dated back at least to the Fourth Dynasty (about 2600 B.C.E.), as attested by the limestone "reserve heads" of a prince from the court of Memphis and his black wife (Snowden 1983, figs. 1–2). Black mercenaries in the Egyptian army, like those stationed at Gebelein (Fischer 1961, 56–80), found wives in Egypt. In language reminiscent of the Nubian-Syrian phraseology of the *Hymn to the Aten*, a vizier commenting on a Twentieth Dynasty marriage settlement, proposed by a man for his second wife, observed: "Even if it had not been his wife but a Syrian or a Nubian whom he loved and to whom he gave property of his, [who] should make void what he did?" (Černý and Peet 1927).

Like other peoples white and black, in their expressions of aesthetic preferences the Greeks and Romans used their own physical traits as a yardstick — what H. Hoetink (1967, 120) has called a "somatic norm image." There is nothing pejorative in the fact that lovers in classical poetry often stated a preference for their own complexion to that of the extremely fair Germans or of dark-hued Africans. Some scholars have read a nonexistent anti-black sentiment into what was merely an expression of a prevailing Greco-Roman somatic norm image, ignoring the fact that there were those who extolled the beauty of blackness, and still others with a preference for blackness who had no hesitation in saying so. Asclepiades praised the beauty of one Didyme: "Gazing at her beauty, I melt like wax before the fire. And if she is black, what difference to me? So are coals, but when we light them they shine like rosebuds" (*Anthologia Palatina* 5.210; Snowden 1991). And Martial (1.115) wrote of a preference for a woman who was blacker than pitch, an ant, a jackdaw, and a cicada. Realistic portrayals of racially mixed types from the workshops of ancient artists from Egyptian to Roman times confirm in a most striking manner textual evidence of interracial mixture and provide dramatic evidence that the Greco-Roman norm image was not always observed. In short, Greeks and Romans were no more "racist" than blacks or Scandinavians in using their own physical traits as a norm. And there is no doubt that many blacks were physically assimilated into the population of a world in which there were no institutional barriers or social pressures against miscegenation.

Religion knew no color bar, and swept racial and social distinctions aside.

Blacks and whites worshiped Isis at the same shrines, and blacks played an influential role in the spread of Isiac ritual, not only in Egypt at Philae, but also in Greece and Italy. The expert ritualistic knowledge and authentic dances and music of blacks were welcomed for their contribution to the genuineness of Isiac ceremonials (Snowden 1983, 97–99). The strong bond that had united blacks and whites in the common worship of Isis was reinforced by the early Christian church. In no Afrocentric study have I found any mention of the prominence given to blacks in the ecumenical creed, which welcomed blacks into the Christian brotherhood on the same terms as others. The exegetical interpretation of the Scriptures, much broader in scope than the limited demonological references, provides important insights into fundamental beliefs of the early Christians (Snowden 1983, 99–105). By deliberately choosing and adapting familiar patterns of black-white imagery, early Christian writers were able to interpret scriptural passages more meaningfully and to explicate their message more convincingly for audiences acquainted with classical associations of blackness.

The pioneer in the adaptation of black-white and Ethiopian symbolism was Origen, who in his explication of the "black and beautiful" bride of the Song of Songs (1:5–6), showed his awareness that the classical somatic norm image had not been accepted by all Greeks and Romans. The bride of the Song of Songs, according to Origen, illustrated the applicability of black-white symbolism to all men: "We ask in what way is she black and in what way fair without whiteness. She has repented of her sins; conversion has bestowed beauty upon her and she is sung as 'beautiful.' If you repent, your soul will be 'black' because of your former sins, but because of your penitence your soul will have something of what I may call an Ethiopian beauty" (*Homiliae in Canticum Canticorum* 1.6, *GCS* Origen 8:36). The marriage of Moses to a black Ethiopian woman Origen interpreted as a symbolic union of the spiritual law (Moses) and the Church (the Ethiopian woman)—a foreshadowing of the Universal Church (Numbers 12:1–16; *Commentarium in Canticum Canticorum* 2.362, 2.366–67, *GCS* Origen 8:115, 117–18). And by making the traditional Ethiopian-Scythian formula more inclusive, Origen expressed a basic Christian tenet. It makes no difference, he declared, whether one is born among the Hebrews, Greeks, Ethiopians, Scythians, or Taurians: all whom God created, He created equal and alike (*De Principiis* 2.9.5–6, *GCS* Origen 5:164–70).

By baptizing an Ethiopian, a high official of the Ethiopian queen (Acts 8:26–40), Philip the Evangelist proclaimed that color was to be of no importance in determining membership in the Church. And Christianity, Augustine wrote, was to embrace the Ethiopians who lived at the ends of the earth (*Enarrationes in Psalmos* 71.12, *CCL* 39:980). One of these Ethiopians was a young slave from the most distant part of a region where men are darkened by the rays of the sun. The spiritual welfare of this black catechumen, not yet whitened by the shining grace of Christ, was the subject of concern in a correspondence between Fulgentius, Bishop of Ruspe in North Africa, and a deacon (Fulgentius *Epistulae* 11–12, *Patrologiae Latinae* 65:378–92). St. Menas, sometimes portrayed as a Negro on *ampullae* (pottery flasks) bearing his name and effigy, was a national saint of Egypt, and pilgrims from Asia and Europe as well as from Africa came to worship at his shrine west of Alexandria. And one of the most outstanding Fathers of the Egyptian desert was a tall, black man, Abba Moses, who was known as a model of humility and the monastic life, an excellent teacher, and a Father's Father, who reportedly left some seventy disciples when he died at the end of the fourth or early fifth century (Snowden 1983, 106–8). In short, in the early church blacks found equality in both creed and practice.

In the entire corpus of evidence relating to blacks in the Egyptian, Greco-Roman, and early Christian worlds, only a few concepts or notions (such as the classical somatic norm image and black-white symbolism) have been pointed to as so-called evidence of anti-black sentiment. These misinterpretations and similar misreadings of the ancient evidence, however, are examples of modern, *not* ancient, prejudices: "In treating a subject which is so alive today, nothing is easier than to read back twentieth-century ideas into documents which in reality have quite another meaning" (Baldry 1965, 6). And this is precisely what some modern scholars have done: misled by modern sentiments, they have seen color prejudice where none existed.

SUMMATION

In summary, despite abundant textual and iconographic evidence to the contrary, Bernal and many Afrocentrists have used "black," "Egyptian," and "African" interchangeably as the equivalents of blacks/Negroes in modern usage. According to this misinterpretation, ancient Egyptians were blacks, and their civilization, an important part of the heritage of blacks of African descent, has been "covered up" by white racists. Focusing on "black" Egypt, Afrocentrists have given insufficient attention to the Nubians, the black southern neighbors of Egypt, and their experience in various parts of the Mediterranean world. It is unfortunate that Afrocentrists fail to realize the serious consequences of their distortions, inaccuracies, and omissions, and the extent to which the Afrocentrist approach to ancient Egypt has motivated many blacks to stir up anti-white hostility. Substituting fiction for fact is a disservice to blacks. The twentieth century has already seen sufficient proof of the dangers of inventing history. What will be the effect on future generations, black and white alike, if the present "mythologizing" Afrocentrist trend continues, and if the historical record is not rectified? The time has come for scholars and educators to insist upon truth, scholarly rigor, and accuracy in the reconstruction of the history of blacks in the ancient Mediterranean world.

NOTES

1. Kluckhohn (1961, 27) has commented on the importance of Greek descriptive anthropology, which, he points out, "was carried further and carried out more systematically than that of any other people whose records have survived." Physical anthropologists have called attention to the importance of ancient iconography and the reports of Herodotus for information on the color of the inhabitants of the Nile Valley (see Brace et al., this volume, on clines and clusters versus "race"). Classical authors did not employ modern anthropological terms such as *phenotypes*, *natural selection*, and *clines*. But they did describe in detail the physical characteristics of many peoples in Europe, Asia, and Africa and attributed the variations in the characteristics to the direct action of the environment (Snowden 1970, 172; 1983, 85; 1993, 322, 325) and did not believe, as Keita (1993a, 199) has implied, that "an 'intermediate' phenotype must be the result of intermarriage, and cannot be a 'natural' occurrence."

2. On the meaning of *Libyes* and *Afri* see Gsell 1921, 2:99; 1927, 5:102; 1930, 7:2.

3. *Oulos* was used of the woolly hair of some Ethiopians and the tightly curled hair of others; also of plants like parsley, "twisted, curly, wrinkled" (cf. Philaenion, a short, dark woman with hair curlier than parsley, *Anthologia Palatina* 5.121); and of the hair (*oulas komas*) of a Greek when curled (Homer *Odyssey* 6.231, 23.158). Hence *oulotriches* at Herodotus 2.104 (cf. [Aristotle] *Problemata* 14.4.909a) could refer to the curly, "less than straight hair" of Egyptians, which has been described, on the evidence of Egyptian mummies, as "curly, wavy, or almost straight" (Baker 1974, 518).

4. Herodotus 2.57; Aeschylus, *Supplices* 719; Diogenes Laertius 7.1; Achilles Tatius 3.9; Ammianus Marcellinus 22.16.23.

5. E.g., *Much Ado about Nothing* 5.4.38; *Romeo and Juliet* 1.4.162; *The Two Gentlemen of Verona* 2.6.26; *Love's Labour's Lost* 3.26.7.

6. Lefkowitz (1994) has analyzed in detail the methodological shortcomings of James's efforts to substantiate his thesis, which appears as the subtitle of his book, *Stolen Legacy: The Greeks Were Not the Authors of Greek Philosophy, but the People of North Africa, Commonly Called the Egyptians* (James 1976; see also p. 158).

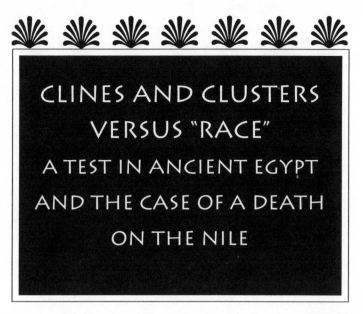

CLINES AND CLUSTERS VERSUS "RACE"
A TEST IN ANCIENT EGYPT AND THE CASE OF A DEATH ON THE NILE

C. Loring Brace, with David P. Tracer, Lucia Allen Yaroch,
John Robb, Kari Brandt, and A. Russell Nelson

A sense of one's biological heritage can easily transcend the familial and spill over into feelings of "racial" identity. These in turn lead all too quickly to attempts to bolster feelings of individual worth by invoking the collective reinforcement of "racial" pride. This was a favorite ploy of advocates of differential "racial" rank in the recent past. One of the clearest statements attributing merit not to individual achievement but to group membership was made by a former chairman of the Department of Psychology at Columbia University, who admonished that "no matter how low (in a socioeconomic sense) an American white may be, his ancestors built the civilizations of Europe; and no matter how high (again in a socioeconomic sense) a Negro may be, his ancestors were (and his kinsmen still are) savages in an African jungle" (Garrett 1962, 984).

He was wrong on both counts. Most American "whites" are descendants of European farmers—peasants—and most American "blacks" are descendants of African farmers. The main differences in the nature of the selective forces that influenced their chances for survival were related to the different conditions associated with farming in the tropics as opposed to farming in the temperate zone. Actually, despite claims that populations are adapted to the "civilizations" with which they are associated (Jensen 1969), none of the world's cultures has endured unchanged for as much as 10,000 years, and that is not sufficient time to have allowed for the accumulation of enough biological change to be statistically distinguishable from error in measurement.[1] The denigration of people of African or any other ancestry by tying individual worth to collective accomplishment is just as indefensible as the assumption that "civilization" has anything whatsoever to do with the biological differences of its creators. On the other hand, it is no more justifiable, however understandable it might be, for the positions to be reversed and for people of Black African origins to lay claims to status by virtue of a putative relationship with the creators of the ancient cultural achievements in the Valley of the Nile.[2] Despite his explicit denial, the most outspoken supporter of the claim that "ancient Egypt was a part of the Negro world" (Diop 1968, 24) cannot allay the suspicion that this stance may well be a case of "inverted racism" (23).[3]

The questions of who the ancient Egyptians were, who was related to them, and to what degree, constitute an interesting issue in and of itself, but it has absolutely no relevance to the matter of the generation and flourishing of the phenomenon of Egyptian civilization. Our concern here is with the completely unrelated question of the biological relationships of the inhabitants of the Nile Valley who, just incidentally, created that remarkable civilization. Even more important, it is our intent to show how the treatment of this issue demonstrates that a successful resolution can only be accomplished by dispensing with the concept of race altogether.

The most enduring symbols of ancient Egypt are the great pyramids built for the Old Kingdom rulers along the west bank of the Nile from Giza south for more than 100 km. Those gigantic monuments to the dead are tombs marking the last resting places of people who were buried well over 4,000 years ago. From written records we know who some of those people were said to be. This applies to the pharaohs, their consorts ("great wives"), and other high officials, but in addition to these, thousands of other associated burials are attested (Leca 1981; Spencer 1982). Who were these people, not just in name, but in terms of their relationships to their contemporaries and successors there and in other parts of the world?

The ancient Egyptians' quest for eternal life led them to develop elaborate practices for the preservation of the dead. The deciphering of Egyptian hieroglyphic writing with the help of the Rosetta Stone (see Andrews 1981) and subsequent intensive archaeological investigations in the later nineteenth century produced an impressive volume of evidence concerning the practical mortuary techniques designed to prepare the mortal remains of the recently deceased for continuation in an afterlife.[4]

A major part of the documentation of those beliefs and practices is the quantity of human skeletons unearthed in the course of that archaeological work. One of the most tireless of those excavators was Sir W. M. Flinders

Petrie (1853–1942), who began his work in 1880 at Giza, across the Nile from Cairo (see Drower 1985). The human remains that were recovered as a result of his efforts have served as the basis for measurement and analysis by several succeeding generations of physical anthropologists.[5] A goodly number of those specimens now repose in the collections of the Duckworth Laboratory of Physical Anthropology at Cambridge University.

Despite a century of such research efforts, little in the way of memorable results comes to mind in retrospect. This is clearly reflected in Colin Renfrew's reproof that "craniometry, the study and measurement of human skulls, has in recent years enjoyed about as much prestige in scientific circles as phrenology" (1987, 4). He goes on, however, to blame this failure on methodological flaws: "It would be wrong . . . to place much weight upon conclusions drawn from physical anthropology until the methodology is better developed" (93).

The failures of physical anthropology are very real, but a better case can be made that they have been the result of flaws in theoretical expectations rather than methodological inadequacies.[6] It was an item of faith in the physical anthropology of yesteryear that the conformation of each individual human being was an approximation to an underlying "racial" essence that constituted true reality. In wondrously Platonic fashion (see *Republic* 7.517b–c), anthropological practitioners assumed that each individual specimen was an imperfect shadow of that "real but directly unattainable thing," the supposed underlying "racial" reality whose elucidation was the ultimate goal of their aspirations.[7]

This assumption sails on undisturbed in the convictions of those who, like the "modern" racialist J. Philippe Rushton (1989), claim that the intellectual capacity of an individual or a group can be directly determined by the crude expedient of running a tape measure around the skull and reading off the numbers. Inevitably, individuals whose cranial circumference is below a group average by virtue of its association with smaller body size would necessarily be stigmatized as of lower than average intelligence. Such a stance ultimately leads to the conclusion that women are less intellectually endowed than men, and that large men are smarter than small men.

If this epitomizes the theoretical poverty of the old physical anthropology, it does not automatically follow that there is absolutely nothing to be learned from the measurement and study of crania in skeletal collections. It is rather a matter of adjusting our theoretical expectations, asking the right questions, and then applying the increasingly powerful arsenal of methods that are at our disposal.

We have taken the present opportunity to demonstrate how the study of cranial material can be used to deal with an issue that has recently been elevated to the realm of what could well be called "racial politics." The collections that are the focus of our attention include the Egyptian specimens assembled by Sir W. M. Flinders Petrie as a result of his work at Naqada in Upper Egypt in 1895–96 (Petrie and Quibell 1896) and at Giza in Lower Egypt in 1906–7 (Petrie 1907), now housed in the Duckworth Laboratory at Cambridge University. Unlike the classic mystery story *Death on the Nile* (Christie 1937), where the main issue is to identify the agent of the death under investigation, our concern is mainly with the identity of the dead. Who in fact were the ancient Egyptians, and to whom were they most closely related? And what kind of data and what sort of theoretical framework do we need to use in order to deal with problems of this nature? We attempt to answer these questions in the sections that follow.

MATERIALS AND METHODS

The Measurement Battery

Representative samples of all the major population blocks of the world have been measured in a standardized fashion to serve as a background against which comparisons can be made. This information is stored in a data bank at the University of Michigan Museum of Anthropology, and it can be used to test the relationships of other populations, or even of individuals, to these and to each other as the occasion arises.

The measurements in our battery are listed in table 1. They were originally chosen because of their utility in sorting out the relationships between the prehistoric and modern inhabitants of the Japanese Archipelago. Subsequently it became clear that they could also serve to elucidate the relationships of all the other populations in the world, although perhaps with somewhat less precision than is the case in the groups for which they were originally designed.[8]

If we could start all over again and expand the list to include again as many measurements of adaptively insignificant features, we suspect that we could provide an even better test of relationships. Those who have pioneered the use of larger batteries of variables that are relatively meaningless in and of themselves have been notably successful.[9] The reasons why this works are related to the reasons why DNA sequence comparisons can sort out such relationships. That is, measurable divergence in the details of inherited but adaptively trivial features between populations that ultimately stem from the same source will be strictly proportional to the time that has elapsed since they shared a common ancestor (Brace and Hunt 1990). The one advantage that the use of craniofacial measurements has over nucleic acids is that the former can be used on prehistoric and other specimens in which no unmodified cellular residue is preserved. For this reason, among others, we suggest

TABLE I. *Craniofacial Measurements Used in This Study*

Variable Number	Measurement Name
I.	Nasal height (Martin no. 55) [1]
2.	Nasal bone height (Martin no. 56[2])
3.	Piriform aperture height (Martin no. 55[1])
4.	Nasion prosthion length (Martin no. 48)
5.	Nasion basion (Martin no. 5)
6.	Basion prosthion (Martin no. 40)
7.	Superior nasal bone width (Martin no. 57[2])
8.	Simotic width
9.	Inferior nasal bone width (Martin no. 57[3])
10.	Nasal breadth (Martin no. 54)
11.	Simotic subtense [2]
12.	Inferior simotic subtense
13.	FOW subtense at nasion
14.	MOW subtense at rhinion [3]
15.	Bizygomatic breadth (Martin no. 54)
16.	Glabella opisthocranion (Martin no. 1)
17.	Maximum cranial breadth (Martin no. 8)
18.	Basion bregma (Martin no. 17)
19.	Basion rhinion
20.	Width at 13 (fmt–fmt)
21.	Width at 14
22.	IOW subtense at nasion [3]
23.	Width at 22 (fmo–fmo)
24.	Minimum nasal tip elevation [4]

1. Martin numbers are from Martin 1928.
2. Howells 1973.
3. Woo and Morant 1934.
4. Brace and Hunt 1990.

that the late Allan Wilson overstated things when he said, "You can dispense with the bones" (quoted in Marshall 1990, 800).

Samples Used

Whether our assessments are based on biochemical or on fossil evidence,[10] it is clear that all "modern" human populations can trace their ultimate roots to Africa. There is considerable disagreement on just how long ago they may have diverged from that common African source,[11] but that need not concern us here. Although our data do present a quantitative picture of the diversity visible in modern human populations, and those differences had to have arisen since their departure from Africa at whatever date back in the Pleistocene, we do not yet have a scale of calibration that will allow us to say how long it took for such a picture of diversity to have arisen (Brace and Tracer 1992; Brace 1993a, 1994).

Samples representing the human inhabitants from all the major regions of the world have been shown to assort themselves into eight major regionally identifiable clusters: African, Amerind, Asian-Mainland, Australo-Melanesian, Eskimo-Siberian, European, Jōmon-Pacific, and South Asian.[12] These regional clusters are not simply an attempt to resuscitate the old-fashioned "race" concept under another name (Brace 1993a). We address in a later section (see "Discussion") the fundamental differences between a reflection of the shared trivial traits by which our cluster diagrams are produced, and the idea of approximation to an underlying "essence" assumed by any concept of "race."

These major clusters and the summed numbers from their constituent samples are listed in table 2. Also noted there are two samples from ancient Egypt—a Predynastic group excavated by Petrie in 1894–95 at Naqada on the west bank of the Nile, 30 miles downstream from Luxor (Thebes) in Upper Egypt; and a Late Dynastic collection from Giza in Lower Egypt also excavated by Petrie in 1906–7—as well as a lumped group of prehistoric and recent Nubians; a sample of modern Somalis; an amalgamated assortment of North Africans; and a Mesolithic sample from Wadi Halfa in the Sudan. When the various Nubian and North African subgroups were treated as separate twigs, the Nubians invariably clustered with each other and the North Africans clustered with North Africans before either showed roots with any other group. This was why they were lumped in the fashion displayed in table 2. The locations of the Nile Valley sources for these samples are shown in map 4 (Maps and Charts section, following the Preface, this volume).

The Wadi Halfa material was the result of two research expeditions to the Sudan some thirty years ago by teams from the University of Colorado at Boulder and Southern Methodist University in Dallas, Texas (J. E. Anderson 1968; D. L. Greene and Armelagos 1972). The Predynastic Egyptian sample was collected by Petrie at the specific request of his London colleague Karl Pearson (Fawcett and Lee 1901, 411), and it dates from before 3,000 B.C.E., before the pyramids were built, and prior to a knowledge of writing (Petrie and Quibell 1896). The Predynastic skeletons, then, can be regarded as belonging to the final stages of the Egyptian Neolithic and just after (cf. the treatment in Wenke 1989). The Late Dynastic specimens date from between 664 and 341 B.C.E., when first Persia and then Greece asserted military and political control as the glories of the long era of Egyptian cultural achievement were beginning to fade toward oblivion (Bowman 1986; T. G. H. James 1988). In effect, the people in this last sample date well into the Early Iron Age.

TABLE 2. *Samples Used in Constructing Figure 1*

	Range of n for Mean z Scores		n for Dendrogram	
Population	Female n	Male n	F	M
Africa [1,2,3,4]	58–59	59	57	59
Amerind [1,3,5,6,7]	83–95	108–121	83	100
Asia [2,8,9,10,11,12,13,14,15,16,17]	282–456	384–807	218	321
Australo-Melanesia [1,3,5,18]	69–89	97–121	62	86
Eskimo [1,19]	68–71	80–83	68	78
Europe [1,2,3,19,20,21,22,23,24]	121–135	214–251	108	196
Central	64–70	120–136	56	113
Northwest	39–49	61–91	38	60
India [1,25,26]	45	68	45	68
Jōmon-Pacific [1,3,12,15,16,27]	104–170	119–185	76	82
Late Dynastic Egypt [2]	25	27	25	27
Predynastic Egypt [2]	26	27	26	27
North Africa [3]	24	40	24	40
Nubia [28]	31–32	34	31	34
Somali [2]	4	25	4	25
Wadi Halfa [28,29]	3–4	2–4	3	2

Note: The ranges of *n* used to generate the *z* scores and the *n* used for the dendrograms are indicated (Brace and Hunt 1990, 346–48).

1. American Museum of Natural History, New York
2. Duckworth Laboratory of Physical Anthropology, Cambridge University
3. Musée de l'Homme, Paris
4. Instituto di Antropologia, Universidade do Porto
5. Lowie Museum, University of California, Berkeley
6. Museum of Anthropology, University of Michigan, Ann Arbor
7. U.S. National Museum of Natural History, Smithsonian Institution, Washington, D.C.
8. Institute of Vertebrate Paleontology and Paleoanthropology, Beijing
9. Department of Anatomy, Chengdu College of Traditional Chinese Medicine
10. Institute of Anthropology, Fudan University, Shanghai
11. Prince Philip Dental Hospital, Hong Kong
12. Laboratory of Physical Anthropology, Kyoto University
13. Department of Anatomy, Kyushu University Medical School
14. Department of Anatomy, Nagasaki University Medical School
15. Department of Anatomy II, Sapporo Medical College
16. University Museum, University of Tokyo
17. Department of Anatomy, Sriraj Hospital, Bangkok
18. Department of Anatomy, Edinburgh University Medical School
19. Department of Anthropology, University of Zürich Irchel
20. Département d'Anthropologie, Université de Genève
21. Antropologisk Laboratorium, Panum Instituttet, Copenhagen
22. Institute of Anatomy, University of Oslo
23. British Museum (Natural History), London
24. Peabody Museum, Harvard University, Cambridge, Massachusetts
25. Naturhistorisches Museum, Basel
26. Département d'Anthropologie, Université de Montréal
27. B. P. Bishop Museum, Honolulu, Hawaii
28. Department of Anthropology, University of Colorado, Boulder
29. Department of Anthropology, Southern Methodist University, Dallas, Texas

TABLE 3. *Numbers for the Samples Used to Generate Figure 2*

Population	Range for Mean z Scores		n for Dendrogram	
	Female *n*	Male *n*	F	M
Algeria	9	16	9	16
Bengal	10	18	10	18
Berber	4	11	4	11
Calcutta	10	12	10	12
Dahomey	16	17	16	17
Late Dynastic Egypt	25	28	25	28
Predynastic Egypt	26	27	26	27
Europe	121–135	214–251	108	196
Gabon	18–19	19	17	19
Greek Neolithic	3	4	3	4
Haya, Tanzania	18	18	18	18
Jericho Bronze	1–2	3–5	1	3
Morocco	11	13	11	13
Natufian	1	2	1	2
Nubia Christian Era	31–32	33	31	33
Nubia Bronze	5	10	5	10
Singhalese	5	12	5	12
Somali	4	25	4	25
Tamil	7	10	7	10
Vedda	13	15	13	15
Wadi Halfa	3–4	2–4	3	2
Zanzibar	2	2	2	2

Note: These are subdivisions of the groups listed in table 2.

To test the relationships between the ancient Egyptians and their nearest neighbors in greater detail, we have broken down the adjacent major clusters — Africa, Europe, and India — into the constituent samples for which we have metric data. These, along with indications of sample size, are recorded in table 3. The representatives of Africa and India are from the extant populations only, but (as is further shown in table 4) we were able to add prehistoric samples from Europe, North Africa, and Israel that were approximate contemporaries of the Predynastic burials from Naqada in Egypt. We have also included data on samples from North Africa, Nubia from the upper reaches of the Nile to the south of Egypt, and the Horn of East Africa. These, like the Egyptians themselves, are not core members of our major regional clusters. As indicated in tables 3 and 4, they include Epipaleolithic, Bronze Age, and Medieval Nubians and modern Somalis. The locations of the groups on which our attention is focused are shown in map 4 (Maps and Charts, following Preface, this volume).

TABLE 4. ns *for the Added Samples Used in Constructing Figure 3*

Population	Range of *n* for Mean z Scores		*n* for Dendrogram	
	Female *n*	Male *n*	F	M
England Neolithic [1,2]	4–7	8–13	4	8
Denmark Neolithic [3]	11–15	15–17	8	9
France Neolithic [4,5]	19–22	25–28	19	25
Germany Neolithic [6]	6	3–4	6	3
Iran [5]	4	6	4	6
Portugal Neolithic [7]	9–10	9–11	9	9
Russia (Caucasus) Neolithic [5]	14–15	17–18	14	16
Switzerland Neolithic [8]	13	12	12	12

1. Duckworth Laboratory of Physical Anthropology, Cambridge University
2. British Museum (Natural History), London
3. Antropologisk Laboratorium, Panum Instituttet, Copenhagen
4. Institut de Paléontologie Humaine, Paris
5. Musée de l'Homme, Paris
6. Landesdenkmalamt Baden Würtemberg, Tübingen
7. Instituto di Antropologia, Universidade do Porto
8. Département d'Anthropologie, Université de Genève

Actually, we defend the position that Medieval samples make as good a basis for assessing the "modern" form of populations in continuously settled areas as do more recent samples. Population movements of considerable significance occurred during Medieval times; but these, for all the historically recorded social disruptions they created, had a barely discernible effect on the picture of in situ genetic continuity in comparison to the changes that occurred at both the eastern and western edges of the Old World as a result of the post-Pleistocene Neolithic spread (Brace and Tracer 1992). If the maximum recorded rate of metric change in human populations is 1 percent per thousand years (Brace, Rosenberg, and Hunt 1987), the changes that have occurred in any group that has continuously inhabited a given area will not be distinguishable from errors in measurement for a span of 2,000 years at the very least.

In addition to the major impetus that led us to undertake this work, an interesting tangent emerged. This derives from the striking impression made by the morphology of one particular specimen in the "Egyptian E Series" of crania from the Twenty-sixth through Thirtieth Dynasties (664–341 B.C.E.). When our senior author (Brace) encountered specimen E597 while working through material in the Duckworth Laboratory in the autumn of 1988, he was immediately suspicious that a mistake had been made and a patently non-Egyptian skull had been inadvertently incorporated into the collection. So strong was the impression that it did not belong that he wrote at the bottom of the data sheet, "But this one walked straight out of the German Neolithic!"

The heavy, double-arched brow ridges, the shelflike horizontal ridge at inion, and the massive mastoid processes flaring laterally at the bottom were utterly unlike anything else in "E" series or in the earlier Predynastic Egyptian material. And yet there was clear evidence that the brain had been extracted via the nasal aperture after death in the manner described by Herodotus (2.86), and the individual had been embalmed with the full mortuary treatment usually reserved for socially prominent and wealthy Egyptians.[13] What was such an obvious intruder doing in a collection of Late Dynastic Egyptians?

This situation provided the opportunity to engage in an interesting methodological exercise. Because craniofacial measurements for a battery of two dozen variables on samples representing all the major geographic provinces of the world were available to us, it was a simple matter to test E597 against that spectrum to see who he could or could not be. Naturally, that first required that we be able to place the Egyptians themselves in the perspective of that worldwide context—the reason behind our project in the first place. The issue of who E597 actually could have been was only a minor if interesting sideline; but as we shall see, he does cast light on the larger issues involved.

Analytical Procedure

In the past, physical anthropology attempted to compensate for manifestly subjective judgments as to how much a particular population exhibited some "racial element" or another by adopting measurements that permitted comparisons of a more objective nature to be made. Unidimensional treatment, however, did not provide a very satisfactory appraisal of what are clearly multifaceted objects. Even the combination of two such dimensions into a proportion or index led to simplistic abuses—the cephalic index and its associated racist nonsense being a classic example.[14]

In more recent decades, computer-assisted multivariate analysis has offered some promise of solving the impasse of performing a simultaneous treatment of multiple dimensions from which a simple solution would emerge. The favorite such multivariate technique among many practitioners has been the assessment of common variance produced by the generation of principal components or canonical variates, but the solutions that it has provided are less than unanimously acclaimed.[15] The problem is that this technique is particularly appropriate for use in assessing the loadings of separate variables on an assumed underlying dimension. But if there is no such underlying entity to which the objects measured can be approximated, the factor loadings may be (at best) hard to interpret and (at worst) idiosyncratic to meaningless. If human beings really were approximations to one or another underlying "race," this should have been demonstrated by factor analysis long ago. At a sheerly methodological level, the fact that this has not even come close to happening is a fine demonstration that there simply are no "races" out there waiting to be discovered.

This does not mean, however, that multivariate approaches to the analysis of population relationships are futile. It simply means that we need to choose the kind of multivariate technique that is appropriate to answer the questions we really should be asking. One of these is the question of the morphological proximity of a given individual or population to a series of others; for this, the statistics of clustering and discrimination work quite well. To produce a picture of the relationships and distinctions between populations for whom we have measurements on the same set of variables, several cluster-generating techniques are now available that can produce quite satisfying results. The one we have followed here is the calculation of Euclidean Distances that are then used in the unweighted mean pair-group method to produce branching diagrams — dendrograms — in which the named twigs provide a graphic display of how near and how far each group is with respect to every other group entered (Romesburg 1984).

At the moment, we have no theoretical reason to favor the use of this procedure over other possible cluster-producing algorithms beyond the fact that this avoids the problem of covariance generated by size alone and that the results it has produced are compatible with analyses that have used different algorithms (Pardoe 1991; Pietrusewsky et al. 1992). The quantification of group differences is based on the information from the nonoverlapping contributions of the measurements used, which can be considered to have "counterbalanced" the extent of "redundancy" from the correlated portions (Sneath and Sokal 1973). We did make trial dendrograms based on D^2 values. The resulting patterns were very similar to those based on Euclidean Distance values, but the twigs generally showed a much greater degree of separation. From the perspective of pragmatic simplicity, the Euclidean Distance dendrograms are easier to interpret.

CLUSTERS AND RELATIONSHIPS

For each of the samples to be compared, we converted the raw measurements (see table 1) into sex-specific C scores in the fashion pioneered by Howells (1986). We then used mid-sex C scores as the data for generating Euclidean Distance dendrograms.[16] To test our various samples, we tried a maneuver that had been successful in sorting out population relationships in eastern Asia.[17] We used transformations involving the C scores of nine of the variables: nos. 6, 13, 16, 17, 18, 19, 21, 22 and 23 in table 1. These transformations created the six new variables: nos. 6/19, 13/21, 16/17, 16/18, 17/18, and 22/23.

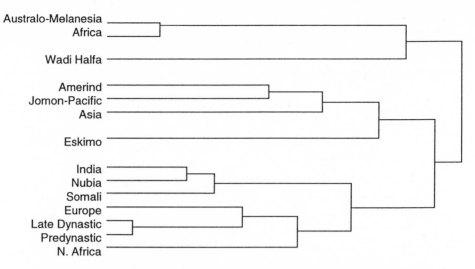

FIGURE I. *Euclidean Distance dendrogram, based on C scores, depicting the relationships between samples ranging from the Nile Delta southward through Nubia to Somalia and samples representing the eight major regional clusters of the world.*
(Storage location and n for each sample is shown in table 2.)

The nine untransformed variables were dropped from the battery to avoid redundancy; this left us with a set of 21 variables. The intent was to test for relative cranial height, for relative nasal projection, and for Woo and Morant's (1934) assessment of "facial flatness." Figure 1 shows the results when the samples listed in table 2 are compared with each other in this manner. It is obvious that both the Predynastic and the Late Dynastic Egyptians are more closely related to the European cluster than they are to any of the other major regional clusters in the world. If South Asia—India—is discounted for the moment, the Somalis at the southernmost extent of this series show that there is a continuum of related groups which, given the Norwegians and Lapps in our European sample, runs all the way from the equator to the Arctic Circle. When South Asia is separated into its available constituents (as in figure 2), the Somalis change to show a tie with the Egypt–Europe spectrum.

The prehistoric sample from Naqada is also closely related to the more recent Egyptians, as the first systematic study of their crania demonstrated (Fawcett and Lee 1901), and this tie remains when we break the various groups down into their constituents and test the possibilities of finer local relationships. This contradicts Petrie's initial impression that his Naqada burials represented a "New Race" of "invaders" who were "entirely different to any known among native Egyptians" (Petrie and Quibell 1896, vii). At first, Petrie did not know that the site was Predynastic; his initial assessment was from his impression of the associated cultural material, not from an appraisal of

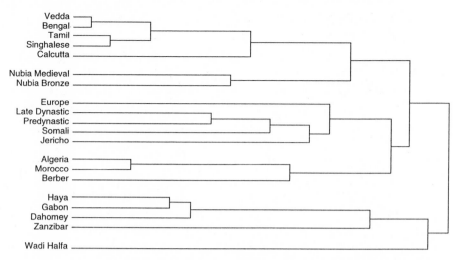

FIGURE 2. *Euclidean Distance dendrogram, based on* C *scores, for the constituent subsamples of the African and Indian (South Asian) regional clusters compared with samples from Bronze Age Jericho and up the Nile Valley to Somalia. The Nubian sample in figure 1 is here broken down into constituent Bronze and Christian-era (Early and Medieval) subsamples. (The* n *for each group used is shown in table 3.)*

the form of the skeletons themselves. Even his subsequent work, devoted to an appraisal of their "race," was based more on a perusal of the portraiture of ancient Egypt than on an examination of the actual crania (Petrie 1901, 1911).[18]

Returning to the assessment of relationships based on actual data as presented in figure 1, it is interesting to see that the mainland of eastern Asia ties more closely with the derived clusters in Oceania and the Western Hemisphere than with any other clusters (see also Brace et al. 1990; Brace and Tracer. 1992). The tie between Africa and Australo-Melanesia, however, is more likely to be the result of what, in cladistic terms, would be a sharing of plesiomorphic—that is, "primitive" or undifferentiated—features that go back to the original dispersion of the genus *Homo* early in the Pleistocene. The attainment of modern levels of cranial size, we would argue, could be an instance of parallel evolution (Brace 1993c). The lack of subsequent significant nasofacial differentiation may well be because both the eastern (Australo-Melanesian) and western (African) representatives have continued to pursue similar subsistence strategies in similar tropical environments (Cavalli-Sforza, Menozzi, and Piazza 1993; Li et al., 1991). Samples from Wadi Halfa tie to Africans and Australo-Melanesians only one step before the populations of the eastern and western edges of the temperate parts of the Old World are joined. Insofar as India has metric ties with any other populations, it combines with Nubia and then the Somalis to join Europe and the

Egyptians as a last link before that set of branches ties in with the rest of the world.

Figure 2 shows what happens when we run the two Egyptian groups against two of the major adjacent regional clusters—Africa and India—broken down into their constituent samples. We also added a Neolithic sample from Algeria (Gambetta); a Bronze Age sample from Jericho; Bronze Age and Medieval Nubians; Berber, Algerian, and Moroccan samples from North Africa; the Somalis; and an undifferentiated all-European group. As can be seen, the samples from the Indian subcontinent—South Asia from from Bangladesh down to Sri Lanka—all tie with each other before they make a common connection with any other group. Likewise, samples from Wadi Halfa and from West Africa southwards also tie with each other before a connection is made with any other group. This remains true however much we expand the numbers of populations tested and however much we adjust and transform the variables used. We have tried dozens of combinations, and small sample sizes notwithstanding, the African and South Asian clusters invariably retain their cohesion.

The Wadi Halfa connection with the rest of Sub-Saharan Africa, on the other hand, is always very weak and occurs as a last possible step. The Somalis, on their part, never tie in with any of the other populations of Sub-Saharan Africa. In figure 2 they are aligned with Egyptians and modern Northwest Europeans one step before a common rooting with Bronze Age Jericho. The Bronze Age and Medieval Nubians cluster together and show a more remote tie with South Asia.

When we ran the major continental clusters as single branches but subdivided Europe (as Continental and Northwest Fringe) and tested a whole series of European Neolithic samples, we generated the pattern seen in figure 3. What this did was to separate the Egyptian samples from each other. The Predynastic sample from Naqada then fell into a tie with South Asia, the Somalis, and, at another remove, the Nubian groups; the Late Dynastic sample from Giza clustered with a series of European Neolithic groups and with North Africa. Northwest Europe (England, the Faeroe Islands, Norway), which had been separated from central and eastern Europe (France, Germany, Switzerland, Czechoslovakia) in previous studies (Brace and Hunt 1990; Brace and Tracer 1992), was brought back to form a loose tie with the rest of modern Europe. At this point, however, their connections with the European Neolithic and Egypt become more remote.

Discriminant Function: Who Was That Masked Man?

Before discussion of the relationships displayed in figures 1–3, let us return to our little subproblem and find out just where specimen E597 in the Late Dynastic Giza series fits when tested against the rest of the samples at our

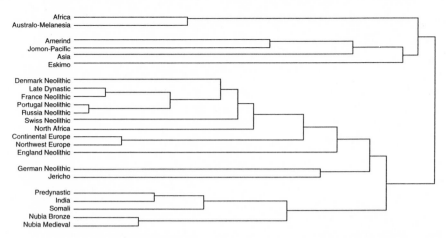

FIGURE 3. *Euclidean Distance dendrogram, based on C scores, showing the relationships between seven of the undivided major regional clusters and a series of Neolithic and Bronze Age sites ranging from Nubia to Israel to western Europe. Recent Europe is divided into Northwest (England, Faeroe Islands, Norway) and Central (France, Germany, Switzerland, Czechoslovakia) constituents. (The n for each group used is shown in table 4.)*

disposal. Because he is just one individual, we could not create C scores and run him in our cluster program. We could, however, use a Discriminatory Analysis procedure (Rao 1973) to see whether that combination of measurements could occur in any of the populations considered. This procedure uses Fisher's linear discriminant function (Rao 1973, 575). The probability figures for these data were generated using the Michigan Interactive Data Analysis System (Fox and Guire 1976) and are recorded in table 5.

When we did this, we discovered that the configuration of measurements found in E597 was significantly different from that observable in almost all of the samples against which we tested it, except for one: the Neolithic specimens from Mühlhausen between Stuttgart and Tübingen in southwestern Germany. E597 cannot be statistically distinguished from the Mühlhausen sample ($p = 0.743$). Moreover, the probability that such an individual was an indigenous member of the Late Dynastic Giza population in which it was found is 0.065, which is tenuous at best. It is most unlikely that E597 was a native Egyptian, and the specimen is similarly distinct from most of the other groups against which it was tested. The only other groups from which its separation could not be conclusively demonstrated were Predynastic Naqada (.063) and modern European (0.116), but these figures do not approach the level of similarity found when E597 is compared with the German Neolithic group.

The other columns in table 5 each show (instead of statistics based on a single actual individual) discriminant function probabilities based on a

TABLE 5. *Probability That the Name in the Column Heading Can Be Accommodated in the Groups Named in the Row Designations*

Group	Giza	Predy.	Nubia	X Grp.	Wadi	Som.	Jer.	Afal.	Alg. N.	Eng. N.	Ger. N.	E597
Africa	.000	.001	**.069**	.009	**.784**	.002	.000	.000	.001	.000	.000	.000
Europe	**.837**	**.390**	**.109**	**.163**	.011	**.452**	**.603**	**.627**	**.406**	**.686**	**.168**	**.116**
India	.011	**.145**	**.514**	**.210**	.001	**.096**	.018	.012	.043	.004	.032	.004
Giza	—	**.218**	.028	.027	.001	**.167**	**.177**	.034	.021	**.089**	**.065**	**.065**
Predyn.	**.110**	—	**.229**	**.168**	.018	**.172**	**.151**	**.080**	**.110**	**.172**	**.381**	**.053**
Nubia	.009	**.162**	—	**.406**	**.164**	**.087**	.009	**.112**	**.184**	.009	**.077**	.002
Wadi Halfa	.000	.000	.000	.000	—	.000	.000	.000	.000	.000	.000	.000
Somali	.026	**.069**	.048	.014	.000	—	.036	.005	.023	.012	**.246**	.004
Jericho	.007	.010	.003	.002	.000	.009	—	.019	.015	.017	.021	.011
Afal.-Taf.[1]	.000	.000	.000	.000	.010	.000	.000	—	**.055**	.000	.000	.000
Alg. Neo.[2]	.000	.000	.000	.000	.009	.000	.000	**.070**	—	.006	.001	.000
Eng. Neo.	.001	.002	.000	.000	.001	.002	.002	.037	**.133**	—	.009	.001
Ger. Neo.	.000	.003	.001	.000	.000	.012	.003	.003	.011	.005	—	**.743**

1. Institut de Paléontologie Humaine, $n = 10$.
2. Institut de Paléontologie Humaine, $n = 3$.

mid-sex C score for the given population—that is, a score derived by condensing data for the whole population into a representative androgynous "individual." These permit comparison of each population with each, in terms of the probability of excluding each from the other. Higher probability scores (toward 1.0) indicate that the group named in a column heading cannot be distinguished from (is similar to) the group named in each row.

It should be emphasized, however, that the discriminant function technique we have used here is better at indicating grounds for exclusion than for inclusion (see Brace and Tracer 1992). The algorithm demands that the probability figures add up to a sum of 1.00. This means we can believe it when the *p* value says that there is virtually no chance of membership in a given group; but when it says that membership cannot be excluded, we have to be somewhat more careful. For example, we could enter the measurements from the cranium of a chimpanzee or a sea lion, and the program would generate figures indicating the degree of discrimination, but their sum would have to add up to 1.0. If we compare these or others with any two modern human cranial series and they are equally unlikely to be included, the *p* value in each cell will be 0.5, which is not sufficient to exclude the possibility of membership. Yet obviously we know that a chimpanzee or a sea lion cranial configuration will never be found in a modern human series.

The groups compared in table 5 are all Late or post-Pleistocene *Homo sapiens* from adjacent parts of the Old World: Late Paleolithic Afalou and Taforalt specimens from Algeria and the Wadi Halfa material from the Sudan; Neolithic specimens from Naqada, Algeria, England and Germany; Bronze Age specimens from Nubia and Jericho; Somalis, and Late Dynastic Egyptians; and modern lumped clusters from Africa, North Africa, Europe, and South Asia. There is no chance, then, of creating the absurdity of the example we have just mentioned, but the theoretical possibility remains that we have more reason to trust loadings indicating *exclusion* from a comparison group—that is, who a given androgynous individual *is not*—than we can have confidence in figures showing that it cannot be eliminated from consideration for inclusion. The latter point may in part be a product of the nature of the algorithm rather than a reliable indicator of group membership.

That being said, let us look again at the exclusions indicated in table 5. First we should note that the averaged figure represented in each column heading was run separately against the groups represented in the labels for the rows; thus the results are not comparable to a picture of common variance, and this is not a symmetrical matrix. For example, when the Late Dynastic sample from Giza was treated as a single individual and tested against the roster named, it proved significantly different ($p < 0.01$) from nine of the twelve other groups represented. The groups from which it was least likely to be excluded were the lumped Europeans ($p = 0.837$) and the Predynastic population from Upper Egypt (0.110). When the Predynastic group was tested against the other twelve, the probability that it could be excluded from modern Europeans was 0.390, and from the Late Dynastic sample it was 0.218, neither of which is significant. (Here again, this is *not at all* the same thing as saying that the Late Dynastic people of Lower Egypt had an 84 percent chance of being Europeans, or that the Naqada sample had a 39 percent chance of being Europeans or a 22 percent chance of being from Giza.)

The indications of exclusion, however, are much easier to interpret. For example, the likelihood that either the Giza or Naqada configuration could occur in West Africa, the Congo, or points south is vanishingly small, around 0.000 and 0.001. Whatever else one can or cannot say about the Egyptians, it is clear that their craniofacial morphology has nothing whatsoever in common with Sub-Saharan Africans'. Our data, then, provide no support for the claim that there was a "strong negroid element" in Predynastic Egypt.[19]

Nubia, on its part, is significantly different from six of the twelve groups with which it is compared. It comes close to being excluded from the Late Dynastic sample from Giza in Lower Egypt, and it comes only a few percentage points from being excluded from Sub-Saharan Africa as well. Nubians cannot be excluded from modern Europeans or from their northern neighbors at Predynastic Naqada, and barely from modern Somalis. Perhaps somewhat more surprisingly, they also cannot be excluded from South Asia (the Indian subcontinent). This simply reaffirms what can be seen in figures 1–3.

The discriminant function procedure allows us to test single specimens against whatever groups we choose. In table 5 we have included the results of comparisons of a series of Epipaleolithic, Neolithic, Bronze Age, and more recent specimens and groups with the three major adjacent geographic areas—Africa, Europe, and South Asia—and our samples from the Nile Delta south to the equator. The terminal Pleistocene material from Afalou and Taforalt in Algeria (Arambourg, Boule, and Verneau 1934; Vallois and Movius 1953, 200) and Wadi Halfa in Nubia (Greene and Armelagos 1972) are roughly contemporary (Wendorf 1968) but obviously very different.

Of all the groups and specimens tested, Wadi Halfa differed at a high level of significance in more comparisons than any other. There were only two groups from which it could not be convincingly excluded: the recent Nubians and the roster of Sub-Saharan Africans. Remembering our cautions about the nature of the discriminant function algorithm, it still seems reasonable to suspect that there was something of a mixture of Sub-Saharan Africa as well as Nubia in that prehistoric group at Wadi Halfa.

The Late Pleistocene material from Afalou and Taforalt in North Africa, on the other hand, showed no similarity to material from Sub-Saharan Africa. Instead, the groups from which it cannot be distinguished range from the Neolithic of Algeria and Egypt, to modern Nubia, and especially modern Europe. The pattern of affiliations of the Algerian Neolithic is remarkably similar to that of the Algerian Late Pleistocene at Afalou and Taforalt and suggests long-term population continuity in situ.

Table 5 also includes a column representing measurements we collected for for a single specimen from what was called the Nubian X Group in Reisner's (1909) terminology. This was a population that immediately preceded the Early Christian Nubians of 550 C.E. (Carlson and Van Gerven 1979) and, in the subjective treatment of a generation gone by, had been regarded as evidence for a "Negroid incursion" (Batrawi 1935; G. E. Smith 1909; Seligman 1915). The probability of finding our representative specimen in a Sub-Saharan population is 0.009, that is, highly unlikely. Its column loadings are generally similar to the loadings in the column for the Predynastic Naqada sample, and (except that it is only marginally unlikely that it can be excluded from the Giza sample) it cannot be denied membership in the Naqada, European, or South Asian samples. In all, however, it is least likely to differ from its successors right there in Nubia (.406) than from any of the other groups against which it is compared.

DISCUSSION

The first volume of *Black Athena* (1987) quickly generated a great deal of interest and publicity (e.g., Barringer 1990; Levine 1989). The author's main theme is a demonstration that rising currents of racism and anti-Semitism starting in the late eighteenth century led to the depreciation or denial of Phoenician and Egyptian contributions to the genesis of classical civilization in Greece. With this we are in complete sympathy, but some have taken its message to mean that the Egyptian strain of that unappreciated or even denigrated contribution was derived from "Black Africa" (Barringer 1990). Bernal has steadfastly defended his claims that traditional classical scholarship has been dominated by the "Aryan Model" and that Egyptian culture is "African." In his first exposition on "Black Athena" (Bernal 1985), he said nothing whatsoever about "race" beyond the article's obviously suggestive title. Later, in his major presentation, he does record his conviction that "African, South-West Asian and Mediterranean types" have been present in Egypt for the last 7,000 years and that a number of the most powerful dynasties "were made up of pharaohs whom one can usefully call black" (*BA* 1:242). Subsequently he has been cautiously noncommittal about the "racial" nature of the ancient Egyptians themselves (Bernal 1989a).

Others, however, have taken the symbolic import of the words "Black Athena" and the designation of Egyptian civilization as "African" to mean that the ancient Egyptians must have looked like West Africans and their modern "black" descendants in America and elsewhere (Associated Press 1989; Barringer 1990). Our data and treatment obviously have a bearing on these matters, and we use them here to take issue with the provocative implications in Bernal's title. None of this is dealt with in the material presented in his book, nor does it even have much bearing on his principal thesis, and we want to make it clear that we have no quarrel with the substance of the major issues he has raised in his actual text.

As many have noted, there is a gradient of skin color in the Nile Valley from north to south. Pigmentation becomes more intense upstream as one goes south into Nubia and toward the equator, as was recognized in the descriptions and portrayals of ancient Egypt.[20] The standard explanation has attributed this to a mixing of "black" equatorial African elements into the lighter Mediterranean population of the Nile delta in the north.[21]

This "Egypt as a zone of mixture" hypothesis, however, assumes the prior existence of discrete parent populations of different appearance—in this case, a light-skinned one in the north and a dark-skinned one in the south.[22] Whether that hypothetical southern, dark-skinned population is called "Ethiopian,"[23] "*nègre*" (Diop 1955, 1981), "Bantu," "Black," "Kaffir," "Negro," or whatever, the universal assumption is that the increase in skin pigmentation is accompanied by everted lips, low-bridged noses, projecting jaws and teeth, attenuated lower legs, and a variety of other physical attributes. Recent assessments of ancient Egyptian art invariably focus on the portrayal of this configuration.[24] Whatever name is used, the underlying mindset is the same—the old-fashioned typological essentialism of the "race" concept.

The category in the minds of the users of those various names is the same as the "true Negro" of traditional "racial" anthropology (Morton 1844; Seligman 1930, 1957). We do not deny that such a configuration exists and is identifiable, and that people who exemplify it can be found in known areas of Sub-Saharan Africa. The problem lies in the assumption that those separate elements are invariably linked together so that the presence of one can inevitably be taken to indicate the presence of the others.

Traits under the Control of Selective Force

The most immediately obvious and visible of that set of traits is skin color, and it is the one that most traditionally has been used as a designation of "race." The very term "Negro," for example (the Spanish word for *black*) was intended to indicate a person with a visible concentration of the pigment melanin in the skin. But melanin serves as protection against the potentially damaging effects of solar radiation,[25] and selection can lead to similar degrees of melanin concentration in the skin of people in different parts of the world who, because of geographic separation, do not share the quantity of adaptively trivial genetic features usually held in common by relatives and neighbors.

The elongation of the distal segments of the limbs is also clearly related to the dissipation of metabolically generated heat. Because heat stress and latitude are clearly related, one would expect to find a correlation between the two sets of traits that are associated with adaptation to survival in areas of great ambient temperature, namely, skin color and limb proportions. This is clearly the case in such areas as Equatorial Africa, the tropical portions of South Asia, and northern Australia, although there is little covariation with other sets of inherited traits. In this regard it is interesting to note that the limb proportions of the Predynastic Naqada people in Upper Egypt are reported to be "super-Negroid," meaning that the distal segments are elongated in the fashion of tropical Africans (G. Robins and Shute 1986). It would be just as accurate to call them "super-Veddoid" or "super-Carpentarian," because skin color intensification and distal limb elongation are apparent wherever people have been long-term residents of the tropics. The term "super-tropical" would be better, as it implies the results of selection associated with a given latitude rather than the more "racially loaded" term "Negroid."

Nasal bridge elevation and elongation are also traits influenced by the forces of selection. These are related to a relative lack of moisture in inspired air (Glanville 1969). That in turn is only very tenuously determined by the intensity of solar radiation. Air in tropical deserts, of course, is obviously arid, but cold air in the less insolated parts of the world also has a notably reduced moisture carrying capacity, and one would expect to find a discernible development of the anatomical features associated with the moistening of inspired air in those people whose ancestors were long-time residents in the colder parts of the world. This is indeed the case, as is shown by the examples of the members of the European and Amerind clusters (Brace and Hunt 1990). We would not expect this kind of adaptation to be selected for in the moist tropics such as West Africa and the Congo Basin, and there, as anticipated, we can note the absence of nasal elevation and elongation.

The East Horn of Africa, however, is another situation entirely. Like much of the Arabian Peninsula and the Sahara itself, it is very dry. Solar radiation is intense, and we would expect to find an increased amount of melanin in the skin of the long-term residents of the equatorial portion of that area. We would also expect them to display a degree of nasal elevation and elongation unlike that of long-term residents at the same latitude but in the moist tropics to the west. This in fact is the case, as we can demonstrate with with our own measurements. When the nonadaptive aspects of craniofacial configuration are the basis for assessment, the Somalis cluster with Europeans before showing a tie with the people of West Africa or the Congo Basin.

An earlier generation of anthropologists tried to explain face form in the Horn of Africa as the result of admixture from hypothetical "wandering Caucasoids,"[26] but that explanation founders on the paradox of why that supposedly potent "Caucasoid" people contributed a dominant quantity of genes for nose and face form but none for skin color or limb proportions. It makes far better sense to regard the adaptively significant features seen in the Horn of Africa as solely an in situ response on the part of separate adaptive traits to the selective forces present in the hot, dry tropics of eastern Africa. From the observation that 12,000 years was not a long enough interval to produce any noticeable variation in pigment by latitude in the New World and that 50,000 years has been barely long enough to produce the beginnings of a gradation in Australia (Brace 1993a), one would have to argue that the inhabitants of the Upper Nile and the East Horn of Africa have been equatorial for many tens of thousands of years. On the other hand, the residual similarity of craniofacial configurations between the Somalis and people farther north suggests that genetic exchange has been more continuous along that axis than with peoples farther west in Sub-Saharan Africa.

Jaw and tooth size are also under selective force control and have a separate evolutionary trajectory that has nothing whatsoever to do with either solar radiation or ambient humidity. One would expect their distribution in the world to be independent of the distribution of skin color and nose form, and this is in fact the case (Brace 1993a, 1993d). It has been shown that dental reduction since the end of the Middle Pleistocene is proportional to the antiquity of the technology associated with the preparation of food (Brace 1979; Brace, Rosenberg, and Hunt 1987) and that the time depth of this is different in different parts of the world, which is why there is a spectrum of tooth-size difference among modern human populations (Brace 1993c; Brace, Smith, and Hunt 1991). Most of our Sub-Saharan African samples fall into the "megadont" category used by Flower to indicate relative tooth size (Brace and Hunt 1990; Brace, Smith, and Hunt 1991; Flower 1885), but the Somalis from the Horn of East Africa sit right on the dividing line between "mesodont" and "microdont." Evidently the ancestors of the Somalis had long been associated with food preparation practices that reduced the selective force intensity maintaining tooth size. This is consistent with the possibility that the Ethiopian highlands were the locale of one of the ancient and semi-independent centers of plant domestication.[27]

Adaptively Trivial Traits and Regional Clusters

It is essential, at this point, to emphasize the distinction between traits whose manifestation and distribution are principally determined by natural selection and those which are simply indicators of genes that are shared because of regional proximity (Brace 1993a). Of the various traits assumed to be present in the "true Negro," skin color, lower limb attenuation, nose form, and tooth and jaw size are certainly under selective force control. The first two, skin color and limb elongation, are adaptations to the intensity of solar radiation—the first directly so, and the second indirectly. Because this is so clearly the case, we should expect those two traits to covary, as indeed they tend to do, throughout the world.

Evidently, traits that are distributed in conjunction with the graded intensity of their controlling selective forces will be poor indicators of population relationships (Darwin 1859). This is the logic behind Livingstone's classic phrase, "There are no races, there are only clines" (Livingstone 1962, 279). Using a characterization of a single trait that is under selective force control to generalize about any particular human population can only create confusion. This, then, will be the inevitable consequence of using a description of skin color to say anything about the general nature of human biological variation—the designation "black" in America today, to specify a person of African ancestry, being the most flagrant example. In the first place, although human skin color may be very dark, it is never black. Furthermore, "black" Americans almost always have a non-African genetic component and are rarely as dark as their African ancestors. Finally, skin color in such places as southern India, Melanesia, and the northern part of Australia is every bit as dark as it is in "Black Africa," and yet the time depth of the separation of those various "black" populations may well be greater than the time of the divergence of the ancestors of Europeans from African forebears.

It can also be misleading to use an ethnic or linguistic designation to characterize human biological form. Elsewhere it has been shown that the Mongols proper are metrically peripheral to the mainland cluster in East Asia, and the use of their name to refer to the bulk of Asians would be just as misleading as the use of "Eskimoid" to encompass the bulk of the original inhabitants of the Western Hemisphere (Brace 1993a; Li et al. 1991). The use of the term "Ethiopian" to stand for all the heavily pigmented people in Africa—as was done in classical antiquity, and from the Bible to Kipling—is equally confusing.[28] As our data show, the people of the Horn of Africa are craniofacially less distinct from a spectrum of samples marginally including South Asia and running all the way from the Middle East to northwestern Europe than they are to any group in Sub-Saharan Africa. Likewise, the use of a term such as "Hamitic" to indicate biological relationships among people who speak Afro-Asiatic languages (Seligman 1913, 1915, 1934) runs into trouble when the tie can be shown between Somalis, Egyptians, and various other groups such as Bronze Age Jericho and Neolithic and modern Europe.

It has long been a matter of common observation, however, that people who come from the same part of the world bear a recognizable resemblance to each other. Traditionally that resemblance was the basis for assigning "racial" labels. These in turn were thought to reflect differences in origin, and it was further assumed that the configuration of traits by which a "race" was recognized had some kind of rankable adaptive value. But as we have seen, traits with adaptive value are clinally distributed according to the distribution of the relevant selective forces. What is not clinally distributed, then, must be what remains after the distribution of adaptive traits is accounted for (Brace 1993a).

Traits that show associations with each other only within the context of a given region thus inevitably have no adaptive significance. When a large number of features occur together in a given geographic area, the principal agent controlling their occurrence is the sharing of genes between neighboring groups that are by definition relatives. Traits that combine to produce a picture of delimited regional occurrence will then (of necessity) be nonadaptive or trivial traits. Because of their trivial nature, they will not easily suggest labels by which their possessors can be denoted.

The pragmatic solution to the problem of designation is best dealt with by the use of simple geographic terms. This is graphically demonstrated in figure 1. Not only is there no invidious "loading" involved, but the focus can be expanded or contracted in simple and efficient fashion—as, for example, by specifying directions such as Northwest Europe, Central Europe, West Africa, Southeast Asia, and the like.

A full-scale biological assessment of the ancient Egyptians, as of any other people, must include both consideration of their genetic relationships and evaluation of the status of those traits that have responded to the forces of selection (Brace and Hunt 1990). Our own battery of craniofacial measurements, however, deals with traits that for the most part have little demonstrable relationship to specific selective forces. For this reason, the similarities and differences that emerge from their use are largely indicators of the genetic relationships of the groups compared.

Figure 1 might be construed as providing support for the hoary folk belief that modern *Homo sapiens* can be sorted into three convenient "races": "Caucasoid," "Mongoloid," and "Negroid." When the number of separate regional representatives is increased, however, it becomes clear that the ties between adjacent twigs on the dendrograms are simply indications of the extent to which geographically adjacent people are genetically related to each other rather than the extent to which they reflect anything that could be called a "racial" essence. Large geographic regions obviously will have many resident and related populations, and an assessment of their trivial traits will automatically produce adjacent twigs on a dendrogram which by definition constitute a cluster.

Because the traits by which these genetic relationships are demonstrated have little if any adaptive value, there is no way to assert that any given configuration is, in any determinably adaptive sense, "better" or "worse" than any other. The picture of regional clusters simply reflects that genetic exchange between people in a given area is more frequent than genetic exchange between people of differing areas. What we get, in essence, is exactly the same as what we would get if we could compare the nucleotide sequences of either nuclear or mitochondrial DNA. Gene flow between adjacent areas does occur, however, and the characteristics of one region will grade insensibly into those of another where they adjoin. For that reason, people who live in between major geographical areas will share aspects of the trivial configurations of each.

The Skin Color Cline in the Nile Valley

Traits that *are* determined by the forces of selection and *are* of adaptive value, however, are not simply a reflection of the frequency of genetic exchange. In these instances, the gene flow between one region and another is sufficient to offer the genetic potential for selection to operate and to produce the gradients in adaptive traits that pass from one geographic region to another without any break. The best studied example of this phenomenon is the distribution of hemoglobin S in conjunction with the distribution of *falciparum* malaria (Livingstone 1958; Bernal 1989a, 1989b). The covariation of skin color and the intensity of the ultraviolet component of solar radiation is another such example. The distribution of malaria, however, is not determined by the intensity of ultraviolet radiation. Consequently the distribution of hemoglobin S is completely unrelated to the distribution of melanin in the skin.

For these reasons, we agree with Bernal when he speaks of the "dubious" utility of the concept of "race" and that it is based more on human mental constructs than on biological reality (*BA* 1:241; Bernal 1989a). However, we can use our data to take issue with his claim that "it is impossible to achieve any anatomical precision on the subject" of the biological relationships of the ancient Egyptians. Because we had too few Neolithic Greek specimens and no recent samples from Greece or the adjacent Balkan countries, we are not in a position to test Bernal's suggestion (*BA* 1:2, 29) that the emergent Greek cultural phenomenon owed an important debt to the actual movement of people from Egypt to the Aegean—although there is no reason why our procedures cannot be applied to provide a direct test of this question when the relevant samples are measured and assessed. In fact, that so many European Neolithic groups in figure 3 tie more closely to the Late Dynastic Egyptians near the Mediterranean coast than they do with modern Europeans provides suggestive support for an eastern Mediterranean source for the people of the European Neolithic at an even earlier time level than Bernal proposes for the Egyptian-Phoenician colonization and influence on Greece early in the second millennium B.C.E.[29]

Because our data are exclusively measurements on skulls, we can say nothing concerning the skin color of their owners when they were alive. Our information on that score comes from the reports of Herodotus and from inscriptions and pictures of the ancient Egyptians themselves.[30] From what we can learn from these various sources, and taking account of the shades assigned by Egyptian artistic conventions to depict male and female appearance (Yurco 1989, 29), it would appear that skin color in ancient Egypt was essentially the same as it is today (see also Bard, Yurco, this volume).

Dark skin color is an indicator of long-term residence in areas of intense solar radiation, but it cannot help distinguish one tropical population from another. There is a very real possibility, for example, that the darker skin pigmentation visible in the people of the Upper Nile is not caused by mixing with a population that came from somewhere else. Instead it could just be the result of selection operating on the people who were already there, as has been suggested by those who have argued for the continuity of human biological form through time in Nubia.[31] With the relatively tentative exception of the Epipaleolithic at Wadi Halfa, our own data are comfortably compatible with a picture of long-term local regional continuity. That would make the skin color gradient running from Cairo via Khartoum 1,600 km to the south and deep into the tropics an example of a true cline (J. S. Huxley 1938).

This would lead us to agree with Trigger that the attempt to assign the people of the Nile Valley to "Caucasoid" and "Negroid" categories is "an act that is arbitrary and wholly devoid of historical or biological significance" (1978, 27).

Who Were the Ancient Egyptians?

Because adaptive features are inadequate indicators of population relationships, the latter are best demonstrated by the use of dimensions that are not significantly related to the action of specific selective forces (Darwin 1859, 427). As we have already noted, most of the measurements that contribute to the construction of our dendrograms record dimensions that have little obvious adaptive value. Nasal elongation and elevation clearly does respond to selective force constraints, and insofar as our measurements actually reflect this kind of variation, there may be some cases in which the picture of relationships derived from our analyses is blurred by similar adaptive responses in otherwise unrelated populations. The one instance where we suspect that this may have occurred is treated elsewhere (Brace and Hunt 1990; Brace and Tracer 1992). In the present analysis, however, we have no reason to anticipate that this could have created a problem or produced a spurious picture of relationships. The dendrograms in figures 1–3, then, depict degrees of proximity that are based more on actual kinship than on similarities in adaptive response.

By the use of the discriminant function procedure, we reinforce the conclusions drawn from an examination of our dendrograms. The Predynastic sample from Upper Egypt differs less from the Somali to the south than do the Late Dynastic people from Lower Egypt. The latter in turn show ties with the inhabitants of the circum–Mediterranean Basin past and present. Geographic proximity alone would lead us to expect such a result. Furthermore, it is fully consistent with what we know from late dynastic Egyptian history (MacIver 1900). The very fact that Herodotus himself visited Egypt around 450 B.C.E. illustrates this contact (Sayce 1896), as does the presence of E597 (our mystery man with Neolithic German traits) in the Late Dynastic cemetery at Giza.

Assyrian political domination in Egypt was followed by Persian control; Egyptian independence ultimately ended with the invasion of Alexander the Great in 332 B.C.E. (Bowman 1986). Before he set off on his career of conquest, however, Alexander made a foray up the Danube to enforce the domination of Greece over its neighbors to the north (Plutarch *Alexander* 11.5). In the course of this exercise he accepted gifts from representatives of people still farther to the north and west (Arrian *Anabasis* 1.4.6–1.5.4; Strabo 7.3.8; Chinnock 1884, 14–18), and he concluded alliances with a Germanic group that appears to have borne a close physical resemblance to our sample of the German Neolithic. Of course that Neolithic was several thousand years earlier, but it is just possible that their descendants were still living there in what is now southwestern Germany, and that their kinsmen were among those who concluded that alliance with Alexander. And, given his use of troop contingents from tributary states, it is just possible that one of them accompanied Alexander to the Nile Delta in 332, where he was left with the occupying forces while Alexander himself went back for his final confrontation with Darius and his foray into India.[32]

A scenario such as this could account for E597 in Egypt prior to 300 B.C.E. Whether it was this exactly or another story, the presence of the mummy of a palpable early German in a Late Dynastic Egyptian cemetery exemplifies the contact that the Delta region had with the world to the north and west. The contribution that such individuals surely made to the Lower Egyptian gene pool (Bowman 1986) could well explain why both our dendrograms and our discriminant function analysis suggest that the people of Lower Egypt at the end of Dynastic times had more in common with members of our European regional cluster than was true for the inhabitants of Upper Egypt 3,000 years earlier. In turn, the Nubians still farther up the Nile are more closely tied to their neighbors in Upper Egypt than they are to the Late Dynastic Egyptians farther off to the north, and they are even less close to the European cluster farther yet to the north and west.

The growing record of written history that has accumulated in an unbroken stream since Herodotus in the fifth century B.C.E. shows us that contact between one region and another was a continuous phenomenon in the form of military excursions and trading expeditions. However, there is every reason to believe that the same thing had been going on back in the Bronze Age and earlier. The three millennia of pictorial and written accounts extant from the Bronze Age in the Nile Valley provide ample evidence of contact between the Egyptians and people of the Middle East as well as with people farther south into "Black Africa."

The very plants and animals whose tending constituted the agricultural basis for Egyptian civilization were imported from the Middle East, where they had been domesticated in the first place (Wenke 1989; but cf. Yurco, this volume). The subsequent development of hieroglyphic writing may well have been influenced by the earlier Sumerian model (Gregersen 1977). Anatomist-anthropologists from an earlier generation (e.g., G. E. Smith [1923] 1970), despite the blatant racism of interpretation, concluded (rightly) from the study of Egyptian and Nubian burials that genetic contact with Africa to the south was also a continuing matter (G. E. Smith 1910; G. E. Smith and Derry 1910).

Despite all this, the genetic continuity in situ maintained a predominantly Egyptian configuration in those trivial biological features that have no differential survival value. Like China, which has managed to absorb its various

Manchu and Mongol conquerors and yet remain recognizably Chinese since the Neolithic, Egypt, also from the Neolithic on, absorbed its various Assyrian, Persian, and Greek ruling elites with barely detectable effects on its basically Egyptian identity.[33]

The argument over the "racial" identity of the ancient Egyptians appears to have been fueled more by "racial" pride than by any kind of objective assessment. Early in the nineteenth century Cuvier declared that the Egyptians were "caucasiques" (1817), and this was repeated with self-satisfied pride by others subsequently (Colfax 1833; Morton 1844; Nott 1844). Recently there have been attempts to claim Egypt as a support for pride in a "black" heritage, as, for example, in the statement that "Egyptians belong among the black races" (Diop 1981, 35), emphasized by the identification of "une origine nègre de la race et de la civilisation égyptienne" (Diop 1955, 161, clearly followed in Asante 1990). The pride in "racial" accomplishment evident in claims that the Egyptian "pyramid-builders" and even the Harappans of the Indus Valley in present-day Pakistan were "Africoids" (Finch 1985) received a boost in Bernal's use of the term "Black Athena" to promote his emphasis on the "Afroasiatic" background to the development of classical Greek language and culture.

Consistent with the position we have developed above, we would have to argue that these statements are hopelessly simplistic, misleading, and basically wrong. Even the categorical labeling of the civilization of ancient Egypt as "fundamentally African" (BA 1:242; Bernal 1989a) is misleadingly simplistic. To the classical world, there were several Africas: the "north face of Africa" along the Mediterranean coast, the "Black Africa" to the south, and especially the connection via the Nile through Nubia to the Sudan (W. Y. Adams 1979) that formed "almost a 'third Africa'" (Brilliant 1979, 55). When the debt of Greece and later Rome to that "third Africa" is stressed by the label "Black Athena," it is misrepresented. Even the use of the term "Afroasiatic," however justified, should be accompanied by the note that this implies no more than the identification of the language family that includes ancient Egyptian and modern Arabic, Hebrew and Somali (Greenberg 1955; Gregersen 1977).

Remarkably, Blumenbach's consideration of Egyptian form in the perspective of what he knew (at the end of the eighteenth century) about the worldwide spectrum of human biological variation was more sophisticated than the crude, categorical "either/or" treatment of his nineteenth- and twentieth-century successors. He identified three "varieties in the national physiognomy of the ancient Egyptians": an "Æthiopian cast," "one approaching to the Hindoo," and "*mixed*, partaking in a manner of both the former" (1794, 191). His use of the term "mixed," however, did not refer to the actual mixing of separate populations. Instead it was a purely descriptive expression. He concluded that "the Egyptians will find their place between the Caucasian and the Ethiopian" (193)—using the term "Ethiopian" to refer to all of Sub-Saharan Africa.

All nineteenth-century treatments dealing with the biological relationships of the ancient Egyptians made respectful reference to Blumenbach's observations and duly considered a possible tie with the people of the Indian subcontinent/South Asia. Lawrence (1819), Morton (1844), and Nott (1844) all echoed Blumenbach. In the same vein, Prichard remarked on the "resemblance between the Egyptians and the Hindoos" and wondered whether it derived from a "partial colonization of one country from another" or had instead ensued from a "close relation in the first ages of the world" (1851, 218). Pruner-Bey (1863) also followed Blumenbach's lead but (though impressed by the physical resemblances) rejected the idea of actual relationship because of the lack of any linguistic connection; he concluded that the visible similarities were just a case of parallelism.

The possibility of a connection between South Asia and Egypt reemerged in the twentieth century as a result of metric exercises conducted by some of Karl Pearson's protégés in London. Although there was a continuing effort to see something "Negroid" in the Predynastic Egyptians (Morant 1935, 1937), the use of the Coefficient of Racial Likeness (CRL) managed to provide a quantitative dimension to Blumenbach's assessment. Cranial similarities were shown between Predynastic Egyptians and "the primitive Indian, the Dravidian and the Veddah," at the same time that a clear-cut separation from the "Negro type" was noted (Stoessiger 1927, 147). The Predynastic Egyptians were also claimed to show some resemblance to the Sardinians west of the Italian Peninsula (Morant 1935).

Although the Coefficient of Racial Likeness was abandoned after its statistical flaws were pointed out (Fisher 1936a), it is interesting to note that, flaws or not, the patterns shown in our figure 3 and in our table 5 also indicate similarities between the Predynastic Egyptians and India. In separate tests that we removed from the already cluttered figures presented here, we were able to show that Sardinians and, somewhat less obviously, Etruscans in the western Mediterranean are about equidistant between Late Dynastic Egyptians and modern Europeans.

Both discriminant function (Fisher 1936b, 1938) and D^2 (Mahalanobis 1930, 1936, 1949) have been accepted as useful approaches to population comparisons that are not plagued by the problems of the CRL (Howells 1973), and we have used discriminant functions to produce the values shown in table 5. Just to make doubly sure, however, we also tried Mahalanobis's D^2 statistic as well. Instead of the C scores for the individuals used to generate figure 3, we used raw measurements to produce D^2 values for all of the groups represented. These were then used to generate a dendrogram, whose results were strikingly similar to our figure 3. The only difference is not one of pattern, but rather a tendency to show a greater degree of group separation as a result of using D^2 figures to produce the dendrogram. Because this dendrogram was so similar to our figure 3, we did not deem it necessary to include it here; but we do list its D^2 values in table 6, for readers interested in using them to generate their own dendrograms and test our assertions.

The tie between the Nubians and South Asia is even more obvious than that between Predynastic Egypt and South Asia, but this merely adds another dimension to what Blumenbach first recognized two centuries ago. On the map, the Nile Valley is physically located between the main bulk of the African continent (to the west) and South Asia (to the east). That its population should show aspects of people both to the east and to the west was to be expected in the way that Blumenbach looked at the nature of human variation.

His successors (except Prichard) adopted an increasingly categorical and essentialist view of the nature of human biological variation, whereby a population was either one thing or another—or a literal mixture between them. But Blumenbach himself in his doctoral dissertation saw human form as grading without break from one region to another (see Blumenbach 1865, 264 [written in 1795]). The continuum could be cut however one might choose to suit one's convenience. The Egyptians who displayed a mixture of "Hindoo" and "Æthiopian" characteristics were not therefore a mixture of separate "primordial" elements but just what would be expected to occur between one region and another.

These expectations are precisely what we are defending in our present treatment, although we are not making an attempt to resuscitate Blumenbach's view that human origins are to be sought in the Caucasus (Blumenbach 1865, 269 [written 1795]; see also Stoessiger 1927). If this is at odds with the way that most physical anthropologists have dealt with the matter, that is because of the categorical and "polygenist" concept of "race" that grew and flourished in America and France during the nineteenth century and after, and which subsequently has been the model adopted by much of the rest of the world (see Brace 1982, 1990, 1993a).

CONCLUSIONS

Attempts to force the Egyptians into either a "black" or a "white" category have no biological justification. Our data show not only that Egypt clearly had biological ties both to the north and to the south, but that it was intermediate between populations to the east and the west, and that Egypt was basically Egyptian from the Neolithic right on up to historic times. In this, our analysis simply reinforces the findings of other recent studies.[34] Although it was cast in a somewhat patronizingly "sociobiologistic" fashion, this was clearly the message of the English Egyptologist Sir E. A. Wallis Budge when he noted that although the "physical and mental characteristics of the original Egyptians were modified temporarily as a result of intermarriage with their conquerors, . . . no amount of alien blood has so far succeeded in destroying the fundamental characteristics . . . of the 'dweller of the Nile mud,' i.e., the fellâh, or tiller of the ground, who is today what he has ever been" (1925, 11).

If this conclusion is close to the one that we have reached after wrestling with the best data available at present and with nearly two centuries of scholarly pronouncements, it has been most directly stated recently by Abdel-Latif Aboul-Ela, director of the Cultural Office in the Egyptian Embassy in Washington D.C. In 1989 the Dallas Museum of Natural History sponsored an exhibit at the Texas State Fair Grounds depicting Egyptian culture at the time of Ramses the Great. When the Blacology Speaking Committee in Dallas threatened to boycott the exhibit unless Ramses II was represented as "black," Mr. Aboul-Ela justifiably complained that the point of the exhibit was being distorted by what we might call a peculiarly American form of "racial politics." As he put it,

> Ramses II was neither black nor white but Egyptian. . . . [Referring to the scope of the exhibit:] This is an Egyptian heritage and an Egyptian civilization 100 percent. Egypt of course is a country in Africa, but this doesn't mean it belongs to Africa at large. . . . We cannot say by any means we are black or white. We are Egyptians.

The press release (Associated Press 1989) that carried these words was entitled "Egypt Says Ramses II Wasn't Black." It could just as well have read "Egypt Says Ramses II Wasn't White," but either version misses the point. Egyptians are Egyptians, and in a society where the perception of human biological identity is distorted to the point where it can only be rendered in black and white, any rational denial that an Egyptian is one thing must also be accompanied by denial that an Egyptian is the other—just as Mr. Aboul-Ela did.

Where human traits have adaptive significance, their distributions are determined by the distribution of the controlling selective forces, and "there are no races, there are only clines" (Livingstone, cited above). Where traits have no adaptive significance, neighbors will share traits with neighbors, and analysis of adjacent samples will show that they cluster together. Both situations occur in the Nile Valley. The quantity of melanin in the skin increases from the Delta southward up the Nile into the tropics, reaching a maximum at the equator. Neighboring populations share trivial traits with each other to the extent that they form clusters based on relationships and strictly in proportion to breeding distance.

TABLE 6. *Matrix of Mahalanobis' D^2 Values for the 25 Samples Represented in Figure 3*

	1	2	3	4	5	6	7	8	9	10	11	12	13	14	15	16	17	18	19	20	21	22	23	24	25
1	—																								
2	23.6	—																							
3	13.8	8.2	—																						
4	11.4	19.0	5.5	—																					
5	2.3	16.7	8.9	9.0	—																				
6	20.1	3.4	3.6	15.4	14.0	—																			
7	20.8	3.1	7.2	17.4	15.6	4.4	—																		
8	13.8	3.9	6.9	15.5	9.3	4.9	1.9	—																	
9	19.5	5.8	6.2	16.6	12.4	3.3	4.5	3.7	—																
10	22.9	24.6	9.2	7.3	16.1	18.0	25.1	22.5	16.3	—															
11	20.7	4.7	5.5	14.1	14.9	3.9	1.8	4.5	4.1	20.0	—														
12	26.2	6.0	5.6	14.5	20.4	4.7	3.4	7.9	7.5	21.7	1.7	—													
13	21.7	3.1	5.4	16.8	16.4	1.8	1.6	3.7	4.2	24.0	2.1	2.2	—												

	1	2	3	4	5	6	7	8	9	10	11	12	13	14	15	16	17	18	19	20	21	22	23	24	25
14	21.3	3.8	6.6	15.2	15.0	4.7	6.1	4.3	6.3	18.5	9.2	9.9	6.3	—											
15	18.5	6.8	11.0	23.1	14.2	6.4	6.0	4.7	9.2	33.4	10.1	12.6	5.7	7.1	—										
16	12.6	4.4	9.6	18.6	8.2	6.4	4.5	1.9	5.9	26.2	6.3	10.7	6.0	8.0	6.6	—									
17	28.1	7.6	4.9	13.8	22.6	4.5	7.1	11.2	10.7	20.8	5.8	2.9	4.3	8.4	13.1	14.4	—								
18	23.3	5.8	7.4	17.2	16.6	5.4	2.8	3.5	4.6	21.2	4.8	5.6	4.3	4.3	8.7	7.4	8.1	—							
19	11.4	15.4	3.6	3.9	7.0	10.1	15.7	12.5	11.3	4.8	13.6	15.0	14.4	10.9	17.7	14.6	13.6	13.6	—						
20	5.0	9.7	8.0	10.2	3.7	9.9	8.3	5.1	9.1	21.0	8.8	12.9	9.5	10.6	4.9	15.3	11.7	10.2		—					
21	6.5	9.4	9.3	13.2	4.3	9.8	6.8	3.2	7.7	23.4	7.6	13.2	8.8	11.4	2.8	17.1	10.8	12.7	1.8		—				
22	15.5	2.6	4.6	14.2	10.3	2.1	2.2	1.5	2.2	19.3	3.5	5.4	1.9	3.1	4.5	7.6	3.3	10.8	5.7	5.7		—			
23	15.5	3.2	2.3	9.3	10.8	2.1	2.5	2.8	4.0	16.1	2.9	3.2	1.6	3.2	6.2	5.5	4.0	8.1	6.1	6.7	1.2		—		
24	9.6	5.8	11.6	6.8	7.1	3.9	2.1	5.2	18.9	5.0	9.0	6.2	7.1	7.9	2.8	12.9	6.1	9.8	3.0	2.9	3.1	3.8		—	
25	17.6	5.5	8.2	20.1	14.0	4.4	2.4	2.6	5.2	28.5	4.7	6.9	2.6	7.0	3.5	10.0	5.5	17.5	7.7	6.7	2.0	3.8	5.5		—

1. Africa
2. Africa, Northern
3. Amerind
4. Asia
5. Australo-Melanesia
6. Denmark, Neolithic
7. Egypt, Late Dynastic
8. Egypt, Predynastic
9. England, Neolithic
10. Eskimo
11. Europe, Central
12. Europe, Northwest
13. France, Neolithic
14. Germany, Neolithic
15. Greece, Neolithic
16. India
17. Iran
18. Jericho, Bronze Age
19. Jōmon-Pacific
20. Nubia, Bronze Age
21. Nubia, Christian
22. Portugal, Neolithic
23. Russia, Neolithic
24. Somalia
25. Switzerland, Neolithic

The old-fashioned chimerical concept of "race" is hopelessly inadequate to deal with the human biological reality of Egypt, ancient or modern. The study of clines or clusters alone cannot present a complete account, either. An assessment of *both* is necessary before we can begin to understand the biological nature of the people of the Nile Valley. Because the ancient Egyptians lived with this knowledge of themselves, they "did not think in terms of race" (Yurco 1989, 24). For our own part, we should recognize how "presumptuous" it is "to assign our own primitive racial labels" (Yurco, 58) to them or to anyone else. These not only prevent us from dealing with human biological variation in an adequate fashion, but they also lend themselves to the perpetuation of social injustice. The "race" concept did not exist in Egypt, and it is not mentioned in Herodotus, the Bible, or any of the other writings of classical antiquity (Brace 1990). Because it has neither biological nor social justification, we should strive to see that it is eliminated from both public and private usage. Its absence will be missed by no one, and we shall all be better off without it. R.I.P.

NOTES

Reprinted, with revisions, by permission from *Yearbook of Physical Anthropology* 36 (1993).

For access to the collections mentioned in tables 2, 3, and 5 we are in debt to a large number of curators, collection managers, technicians, and others associated with their care. Most of these have been previously acknowledged (Brace, Rosenberg and Hunt 1987; Brace, Brace and Leonard 1989; Brace and Hunt 1990; Brace, Smith and Hunt 1991; Brace and Tracer 1992). For additional material used in the present study, we are especially thankful for the help rendered by C. Duhig and G. Man at the Duckworth Laboratory, Cambridge University; D. L. Greene and D. P. Van Gerven of the Department of Anthropology, University of Colorado, Boulder; A. E. Marks, F. Wendorf, and R. K. Wetherington of the Department of Anthropology, Southern Methodist University, Dallas; P. Bennike, Panum Instituttet, Copenhagen; B. Kaufmann, Naturhistorisches Museum, Basel; O. da Veiga Ferreira and G. Zbyszewski, Serviços Geológicos de Portugal; J. M. Cruz, Instituto di Antropologia, Universidade do Porto; C. Simon, Département d'Anthropologie, Université de Genève; J. Wahl, Landesdenkmalamt, and A. Czarnetzki, Institut für Anthropologie und Humangenetik, Tübingen; W. Scheffrahn, Anthropologisches Institut, Universität Zürich, Irchel; A. Langaney and J.-L. Heim, Musée de l'Homme, Paris; J. Papadopoulos, Verroia, Greece; and R. J. Rodden, Saffron Walden, Essex, England. Valuable suggestions were provided by M. Bernal, Department of Government, Cornell University, Ithaca. Partial support was provided by the Committee on Scholarly Communication with the People's Republic of China (1980, 1985), by the University of Michigan Museum of Anthropology Research Fund (1984, 1985, 1986, 1992), by the L. S. B. Leakey Foundation (1986), by Diana Blaban Holt (1987), by the National Science Foundation (BNS-8616298, 1987, 1988), by the Irene Levi Sala CARE Archaeological Foundation (1992), and by the generosity of the late G. W. and H. L. Brace. Essential help was also provided by C. L. Brace V, M. G. Brace, M. L. Brace, R. C. Brace, K. Clahassey, and K. E. Guire. Critical advice was offered by R. V. McCleary and H. T. Wright. The final responsibility for this treatment, however, is ours alone.

1. Brace, Rosenberg, and Hunt 1987; Brace, Smith, and Hunt 1991; Brace 1993a.

2. See, e.g., Asante 1990; Barringer 1990; Diop 1955, 1981; Finch 1985.

3. See also Ortiz de Montellano 1991, 1992.

4. See B. Adams 1984; Andrews 1984; Budge 1925; T. G. H. James 1988; G. E. Smith and Dawson 1924; Spencer 1982.

5. See, e.g., Berry, Berry, and Ucko 1967; Castillos 1981; Crewdson-Benington 1911; Crichton 1966; Fawcett and Lee 1901; Keita 1990; Morant 1925, 1935; Myers 1905; Pearson 1896; Pearson and Davin 1924; Petrie 1901; Warren 1898.

6. For critiques see Brace 1981, 1982, 1988, 1993b; esp. on theoretical flaws, Brace 1989; Brace and Hunt 1990.

7. Quotation attributed to Topinard in Ripley 1899, 111–12; Vallois 1953, 15.

8. Japanese data: Brace, Brace, and Leonard 1989; Brace et al. 1990. Broader applications: Brace 1990; Brace and Hunt 1990; Brace and Tracer 1992; Brace, Tracer, and Hunt 1992; Li et al. 1991.

9. Howells 1973, 1989; Pietrusewsky 1984, 1990; Pietrusewsky et al. 1992.

10. Biochemical evidence: Cann 1988; Cann, Stoneking, and Wilson 1987; Wilson and Cann 1992. Fossils: Brace 1967, 1991, 1993c.

11. Spuhler 1988, 1989; Stringer and Andrews 1988; Templeton 1992, 1993.

12. Brace 1990; Brace and Hunt 1990; Brace and Tracer 1992; Li et al. 1991.

13. R. V. McCleary, personal communication; G. E. Smith and Dawson 1924.

14. See, e.g., Brigham 1923; Grant 1918.

15. Techniques: Howells 1966, 1973, 1986, 1989; Keita 1990. Critiques: Birdsell 1966; Sternberg 1985.

16. See Brace, Brace, and Leonard 1989; Brace, Tracer, and Hunt 1992; Brace and Hunt 1990, 346–47; Brace and Tracer 1992; Li et al. 1991.

17. Brace 1993a; Brace and Tracer 1992; Brace, Tracer, and Hunt 1992; Li et al. 1991.

18. This methodology was a continuation of an old tradition in which the "race" of the ancient Egyptians was assessed not on any direct examination but on artistic depictions and repetitions of offhand verbal accounts. An eighteenth-century French traveler, the comte de Volney, is frequently cited as justification for identifying the ancient Egyptians as "black" (Diop 1981; G. E. Smith [1923] 1970), although, as both Blumenbach (1794) and Lawrence (1819) noted, the basic "evidence" offered was citation of a passage from Herodotus (2.104) referring to black skin and "frizzy" hair and de Volney's own assertion that the head of the Sphinx was characteristically "*Nègre dans tous ses traits*" (Volney 1792, 49, original emphasis; 1823, 33).

19. Asante 1990. This is a persistent topic: see also Morant 1937; Randall-MacIver and Woolley 1909; Strouhal 1971.

20. Modern observations: see *BA* 1, passim; Bernal 1989a; Prichard 1851; Seligman 1957; Trigger 1978; Yurco 1989. Ancient descriptions and portrayals: see T. G. H. James 1988; Vercoutter 1976.

21. Mokhtar and Vercoutter 1981; Morton 1844; G. E. Smith and Derry 1910; Snowden 1989; Yurco 1989.

22. Batrawi 1935; Burnor and Harris 1968; Lawrence 1819; Morant 1925, 1935; Morton 1844; G. E. Smith 1909; Strouhal 1971.

23. Blumenbach 1794; Prichard 1851; Snowden 1970, 1976, 1983, 1989.

24. Breasted 1909; Diop 1955; T. G. H. James 1988; Van Sertima 1985b; Vercoutter 1976.

25. Parrish et al. 1978; A. H. Robins 1991; and see the papers collected in Urbach 1969.

26. W. Y. Adams 1967, 1977; MacGaffey 1966; Seligman 1913, 1915, 1934.

27. Harlan 1969, 1971; Harlan, De Wet, and Stemler 1976; Stemler 1980; Vavilov 1951.

28. See, e.g., Blumenbach 1794; Jeremiah 13:23; Kipling 1912; Snowden 1970, 1989.

29. Ammerman and Cavalli-Sforza 1973, 1979; *BA* 1:241–42; Cavalli-Sforza, Menozzi, and Piazza 1993; Sokal, Oden, and Wilson 1991.

30. Herodotus 2.104; Snowden, this volume, and 1970, 1976, 1983; Vercoutter 1976.

31. W. Y. Adams 1979; Batrawi 1946 (in marked contrast to 1935); Berry, Berry, and Ucko 1967; Carlson and Van Gerven 1977, 1979; D. L. Greene 1966, 1972; Van Gerven 1982; Van Gerven, Carlson, and Armelagos 1973.

32. Budge 1925; Malik 1974; Quintus Curtius in McCrindle 1896.

33. China: Brace and Tracer 1992; Li et al. 1991. Egypt: Berry, Berry, and Ucko 1967, 566.

34. W. Y. Adams 1967, 1979; Berry, Berry, and Ucko 1967; Carlson and Van Gerven 1977, 1979; D. L. Greene 1966; Keita 1990; Van Gerven 1982.

THE NEAR EAST

THE LEGACY OF
BLACK ATHENA

Sarah P. Morris

Revisiting *Black Athena* means, for me, addressing for the first time Bernal's second installment in his multi-volume series, still promised when I discussed *BA* I at a public panel in 1989 and in an invited debate published in 1990. At the time, my own work on the relationship between Greece and the East was also still in press. Thus I admitted: "A full discussion of the archaeological aspects of Bernal's theories would be premature without these two volumes" (Morris 1990, 57). In the meantime, the second volume of *Black Athena* not only appeared, in 1991, but has been extensively reviewed by Hellenists, Egyptologists, and Near Eastern specialists, most of whom have deplored its unscholarly methods and untenable conclusions.[1] I find myself obliged to agree with them, and would echo scholars who found it "a whirling confusion of half-digested reading, bold linguistic supposition, and preconceived dogma" (Vermeule, this volume), or just plain "bad scholarship" (Weinstein 1992, 382).

Bernal's unlikely scenarios of Egyptian punitive expeditions to the Aegean, occupations of Troy and Thera, conquests by Sesostris I, and Hyksos invasions are so stubbornly linked to controversial adjustments in chronology that it is difficult to treat them separately as the wrongheaded agendas they are. In fact I simply find it difficult to tackle the second volume of *Black Athena*, so unwieldy are its cumbersome detours to Atlantis or Iceland and its labored misunderstandings of Greek mythology as historical event. The appearance of my own study of similar problems (Morris 1992) takes the place of a lengthier discussion here of my differences with Bernal. In that book I have tried to suggest some more plausible scenarios in reconstructing Aegean relations with the Eastern Mediterranean in the Bronze Age; I am in the unusual position of being thanked by Bernal in his preface to the second volume of *Black Athena* for assistance in writing the volume, yet being praised for admiring Bernal's theories at a "sanitary distance" in my work (Sherratt 1993, 916).

Perhaps our primary differences lie in subtleties of method: we are both convinced of the same historical phenomenon, the influence of the Near East on the cultures of the Aegean. Moreover, we have both used the same bodies of evidence, combining archaeology, linguistics, and mythology to demonstrate Eastern connections. Although the subtitle of Bernal's second volume promises "archaeological evidence," the one section ostensibly devoted to such evidence (chapter 11) forms but fifty pages in a total of more than five hundred and deals primarily with legends (Pelops) and foreign texts (from Egypt and Hittite Anatolia), while summarizing some basic realia of Mycenaean pottery abroad and Oriental imports in the Aegean. My treatment of the same period (the Late Bronze Age) and some of the same evidence (the Kaş wreck, Egyptian finds in the Aegean, Mycenaean pottery in the East) imagines not conquest or colonization, those military encounters exaggerated by ancient rulers and overestimated by modern historians, but regular and mutually profitable transactions. But Bernal begins with "texts" without questioning their nature as historical tools, and seeks confirmation in discoveries, rather than treating "texts" such as legends and images as reflections, even transformations, of experience. Thus in chapter 5 he accepts Herodotus' account of the conquests of Sesostris I, ignoring its dubious veracity, compares it to an actual Egyptian text of the Middle Kingdom (which does not mention Greece), and applies it to an unlikely spectrum of landscapes "conquered" by the Egyptian pharaoh (see O'Connor, Yurco, this volume). In an equivalent chapter of my book (also chapter 5) I depart from the importance of resources in international relations to test different landscapes where minerals and mythology overlapped with the evidence of material culture. As an archaeologist, I seek to draw attention to activities that are invisible to philologists and historians who rely on texts and "events," to the more normative processes of daily life.

In other words, I am interested in human experiences more common than invasion or conquest—not only commerce but kidnapping, slavery, and marriage—which form the background to our only written sources on the period, primarily in myth and poetry. For a successful example of this technique I continue to recommend Walter Burkert's *Orientalizing Revolution* ([1984] 1992), which demonstrates how the evidence of linguistics and mythology can be deployed against the historical and archaeological background to reveal Semitic connections, without the fantastic scenarios invented by Bernal. The existence and the eloquence of treatments like Burkert's, including his frank exposition of the virulent anti-Semitism of giants of *Altertumswissenschaft* like Wilamowitz-Moellendorff, serve as more effective criticism of Bernal than any detailed review. In our different ways, all three of us pursue the reconstruction of the past through visual as well as verbal testimony, a pursuit fraught with perils as well as success.[2]

My own, archaeological version of this method leads away from the inexorable axis with Egypt and hence, I hope, deflects welcome attention away from the vexed non-issue of whether Egyptians were "black" or not. It is worth reiterating my earlier argument (Morris 1990, 60–62) that the mirage of Egypt has distorted views (both ancient and modern) of the Western relationship with the Near East. Just as Herodotus was dazzled by the monuments and antiquity of the civilization of the Nile, so Greek and Roman rulers of Egypt, its European colonizers, and, most recently, Afrocentrists who would reclaim their "stolen legacy" are all determined on possession, through occupation or heritage, of that magic land and culture. Many of these interested parties, particularly the latter, would learn much by exploring such neglected issues as Egypt's own treatment of foreigners, and the developed ideology and imagery with which Egypt portrayed foreigners and even inspired those foreigners to represent themselves as Egyptians (see Loprieno 1988). Bernal seems just as naive as the most radical Afrocentrists in insisting that Egypt dominate the hierarchy of ancient cultures and their interrelations. This emphasis is partly a function of reliance on texts, which in the case of Egypt tend to be self-promoting more often than they are critical or historically useful.

Other ancient relations, outside direct contact with Egyptian pharaonic society, were more critical to long-term developments. My own conclusions and recent discoveries increase the weight of evidence in favor of such a direction and point to the northern Levant as a primary source of Near Eastern influence, culminating in the adoption of the Northwest Semitic alphabet. Burkert ([1984] 1992, 21–33) makes an eloquent case for the lost evidence of epigraphy and literature from the Phoenician, Syrian, and Aramaean spheres in later centuries; here is where archaeology convinces us of those connections. The most spectacular additions to these connections are more recent than Bernal's second volume and my book but have not been lost on our reviewers.[3] The Hyksos settlement at Tell el-Dabʿa (Avaris) in the Nile Delta has now produced frescoes of Minoan bull-leapers, and perhaps even a labyrinth. At the other end of the Via Maris, at Tell Kabri in northern Israel, polychrome frescoes equally Aegean in flavor have been found in fallen plaster fragments. In the excitement over these unmistakably Aegean images, attention to their context should not be neglected.

The archaeological context of the Avaris fragments is uncertain, as they were not found in direct contact with buildings but were disturbed from their ancient setting. At both sites the dominant culture is Canaanite (the "foreign kings" of the Hyksos dynasty in the Nile Delta were not Egyptian), and both show the closest affinity, in terms of the material culture from the excavations, with the Levant. In other words, these two sets of pictorial fragments in Aegean style clearly reveal the strong connections between Minoan Crete (Keftiu, Kaphtor) and the northern Levant, rather than directly between Crete and Egypt. This leaves Egypt at best as the indirect partner of Aegean merchants and artists, with the fulcrum of commercial activity still shared by Cyprus and Syria. Remains at Egyptian trading posts, such as Marsa Matruh (Bates' Island) on the Libyan coast, corroborate this picture, as does the latest evidence from the Kaş (Ulu Burun) wreck, which is looking more and more like a Syrian vessel (Morris 1992, 101–24; M. H. Gates 1994, 259–60). Although this makes Cyprus and the Levant primarily transmitters rather than originators of cultural traditions which they passed on to the Aegean, it does downplay the direct and active role of Egyptian and Aegean dynasts in international relations with each other.

Often revived recently in understanding this triadic relationship in the eastern Mediterranean is a poetic phrase from Ugaritic epic describing Kothar-wa-Hasis, the Canaanite craftsman-god, as being located in the other spheres: "His seat is at Memphis (Egypt), his throne is at Kaphtor (Crete, or the Aegean)" (Morris 1992, 93). The city-based states of the northern Levant, in both the Late Bronze Age and the Early Iron Age, more closely resemble the independent polities of Greece, especially those that evolved into Greek *poleis*, than they do Egyptian rulers and their domains. Thus Sinuhe, Wenamun, and the hero(es) of the *Odyssey* experienced Bronze Age life in similar ways; we have submerged their more modest but familiar tales in grander scenarios that link dynasts of Amarna and Mycenae, instead.

The situation I imagine can be compared to the medieval transmission of ancient knowledge from the eastern Mediterranean to Europe: to trace this route in history and philology follows Syriac and Arabic translations of Greek literature, the migration of such texts and learning to Moorish Spain, the role of Sephardic Jews in translating and understanding these texts in Arabic, Hebrew, and Latin, and the further migration of scholars and learning to northern Europe. Bernal's view of the ancient equivalent of such a route leapfrogs from Egypt to Greece, disregarding more critical connections via the land of the alphabet, as someone might bypass the role of Islamic and Jewish scholars to transplant Greek learning directly to Europe. If Solomon's Temple had survived in Jerusalem, and the pyramids had not, we might entertain more ancient scenarios which embraced the Levant. The cover of my book (Morris 1992) presents the very "Black Athena" which Bernal and others have long sought to illustrate their ideas: an early Greek vision of the birth of Athena from the head of Zeus, inspired by an Orientalizing transformation of an Egyptian ruler image applied to a sealing found, if not made, at Byblos. I believe that this image epitomizes the ancient migration of ideas from Egypt to Greece, via the Levant.

What I hope this adjustment of scenario can do, by reducing the dominance of Egypt on our imaginations, is to dispel the mirage that Egypt has cast over modern claims on the past. Why does African America need Egypt, more than it does the magnificent cultures of the West African coast, to legitimize its past and its present? Why does Greece have to be "invaded" or conquered by Egypt to learn its lessons and absorb its culture, instead of being "captured" in cultural terms, as it in turn (in the immortal phrase of Horace) captivated Rome? In other words, ancient Egypt need no longer be a bone of contention between Afrocentrists and classicists, if we recognize its unique position, acknowledge its close and fruitful connections with adjacent cultures, but do not contest it as an exclusive ancestor. Cannot one bolster the claims of the Levant, without dividing more deeply those of African heritage from modern Jews and appearing "partisan" to the latter cause?

Other perspectives have been submerged in the polarization of Africa and Europe. Unvoiced in the modern debate, which is focused in America, is the reaction of modern Greeks, who stand to be just as much interested as modern African-Americans in the implications of *Black Athena*.[4] Bernal himself has remarked that he found only partial receptivity to his ideas among Greek audiences: the Egyptian connection pleased them, the Levantine less so. This divided reaction surely has modern causes. Modern Greek enthusiasm for Egypt reflects both the "mirage" of that country and their own historical involvement there, where Greeks were resident, even rulers at times, from Alexander the Great—if not earlier, if one includes Naukratis, Amarna, and now Tell el-Dab'a!—until modern Egyptian nationalism expelled them. But the Orient is a different matter: "Anatoli" (*Anatole*, the Greek equivalent of Latin *Oriens*) sounds too much like Anatolia, the land lost to the Turks and a reminder of five hundred years of Islamic and Turkish dominance. This attitude toward the Levant is also not unaffected by more recent relationships, including Greece's poor historical record in the treatment of Jews since independence[5] and its reluctance to support the cause of Israel (until recently, there was not even an Israeli mission in Greece). Many of these factors may play a role in individual and national reactions to Bernal's arguments.

This brings me to the second direction for self-criticism which Bernal's books have opened up. If their emphasis on Egypt is misguided, my discussion of their reception in Greece brings us back to their modern, rather than ancient, implications. The first volume of *Black Athena* unquestionably opened the discipline of classics to a period of self-criticism which has reshaped research and the teaching of classics, at least in the United States.

Details of Bernal's dissection of recent (modern European) intellectual history have been rightly criticized: for example, his blaming anti-Semitism for all scholarly neglect of the ancient Near East obscures much more profound and important intellectual revolutions of the nineteenth century, such as the liberation of philology from theology and of science from religion, and the quest for pagan paradigms to demonstrate independence from the Bible (see F. M. Turner 1989). How modern prejudices reorder ancient events is now a fundamental principle of research on antiquity, whether it results in extremes of Afrocentrisms or elaborate disclaimers of revisionist histories. Unfortunately, current events have substantiated Bernal's claims in ever more painful demonstrations of the power of political persuasion over historical fact. His championship of Egypt has now bolstered the claims of irrational Afrocentrism; his emphasis on nationalism in scholarship has been corroborated in the most extreme manner.

What makes revisiting *Black Athena* so painful is the resurgence of virulent nationalism and interethnic violence on an international scale. Since the publication of the first volume of *Black Athena*, the Soviet Union has dissolved into republics quick to revive long-dormant ethnic resentments; Germany has reunited itself only to witness outbreaks of racism and violent attacks on such long-suffering minorities as Turks and Gypsies and on Jewish cemeteries; what was Yugoslavia has become a nightmare of Serbian aggression against Catholic Croats, Muslims in Bosnia, and other ethnic targets, with no end in sight. In short, the nineteenth century has caught up with us, and ugly scenarios that had to be imagined to understand the background to the first volume of *Black Athena* are now broadcast live on the news. With those resurgences have come political appropriations of cultural traditions: one central to the classical world is the belabored phenomenon of Macedonia. What was a distinctive culture in northern Greece and eventually the dominant power of the Hellenic world now lies divided between the former Yugoslavic Republic of Macedonia (or Skopje), the former Yugoslav province misnamed "Macedonia," and the northern part of the Republic of Greece. The dispute over the political status, name, and flag of this territory, and the propaganda generated on both sides of the border, have paralyzed relations not only between the two neighbors but throughout the Balkans and between Greece and its allies in Europe and America.[6] On the Greek side, the campaign has engulfed nearly every political party, absorbed Greek public relations abroad, and dominated the public stance of several governments over the past few years. The cultural remains of ancient Macedonia have been turned into arguments for ethnicity — for Hellenism — and for political identity.

In the current century, vehicles other than scholarly texts have enriched the arsenals of cultural nationalism; more effectively, museum exhibitions and popular literature deliver the message. As an archaeologist I find myself uncomfortable about the way antiquities have been exploited by embassies and ministries. To pick a case squarely in my own field, it was curious to witness a recent exhibition at the National Gallery of Art in Washington, D.C., devoted to early Greek art, which included no reference—in either the choice of objects and their discussion and presentation, or the symposium of invited lecturers which accompanied its opening—to the role of the Orient in forming such images.[7] That this exhibition was initiated by the Greek Embassy in Washington and was inspired by (to compete with?) an earlier exhibition in the same venue (the National Gallery of Art) which celebrated the antiquities of Ottoman Turkey, only makes more conspicuous the neglected role of the Orient in this cultural event. Meanwhile, a conference organized by academic archaeologists in New York in 1990 described the same period as "Greece between East and West"; the papers were published in 1992 with a frontispiece illustrating a famous Greek Geometric amphora (National Museum 804, by the Dipylon Master) but identifying it in the caption simply as "Phoenicianizing."[8] An exhibition of Greek Geometric objects in the United States, subtitled "Art in the Age of Homer," dedicated an entire section (one quarter of the thematic issues) and an entire chapter of the catalogue to the role of Orient; the organizer of the exhibition and conference has explored intriguing Near Eastern connections for early Greek art in a number of scholarly articles, some of them treating the same types of figures in the Washington exhibit.[9] In other words, there is a noticeable gap between the scholarly fruits of *Black Athena* and popular perceptions of antiquity which continue to serve the self-portrayal of nations.

This highlights a fundamental difference not only between foreign policy and academic research, but between Europe and America, as I stressed in the public forum on the first volume of *Black Athena*, hosted by the American Philological Assocation (Morris 1989, 51). As academics in America, we can indulge in a certain distance from ethnic disputes in Europe because our neighbors are not threatening our borders or making territorial claims by using names which manipulate ancient evidence. Yet it is in America that the most tragic divide, for example between blacks and Jews, now dominates public and academic discourse. The gap reflects a failure to communicate across the Atlantic as well as between the academy and the outside world.

Where does this leave us? What hath *Black Athena* wrought? On the one hand, it has inspired a healthy phase of self-examination among professional classicists, comparable to the drive to incorporate perspectives sensitive to differences in class, gender, and sexual orientation into the teaching of classical antiquity. On the other hand, it has bolstered, in ways not anticipated by the author, an Afrocentrist agenda which returns many debates to ground zero and demolishes decades of scrupulous research by eminent scholars such as Frank Snowden. An ugly cauldron of racism, recrimination, and verbal abuse has boiled up in different departments and disciplines; it has become impossible for professional Egyptologists to address the truth without abuse, and Bernal's arguments have only contributed to an avalanche of radical propaganda without basis in fact. (So far, his only response has been to admit the existence of black racism, but to pronounce it preferable to white racism; see *BA* 2:xxii). The drama of these public debates has terrorized teachers and campuses, but the determined lessons of Afrocentrism have bypassed some curricula of higher learning and landed squarely in many public schools. For classicists and university professionals the "challenge of *Black Athena*" is no longer an internal debate but a public forum, and demands a dialogue between professors and teachers, researchers and the public. The debate over *Black Athena* has moved beyond its eponymous volumes, whose details have failed to satisfy scholarly scrutiny, to the wider implications of what the academic profession owes its students and its community.

NOTES

1. Hellenists: Vermeule 1992; Pounder 1992; Lefkowitz 1992b. Egyptologists: Baines 1991; Ray 1991a; Burstein 1993; Weinstein 1992. Near Eastern specialists: Muhly 1991a.

2. For fascinating discussions of such historical method see Ginzburg 1989 and F. Haskell 1993. For Bernal's review of my book see now Bernal 1995.

3. See Vermeule, Coleman, this volume; Burstein 1993, 162; Sherratt 1993, 917.

4. For an interesting discussion of various aspects of the modern legacy of ancient Greece see the special issue of *Arkhaiologia* (June 1988), "Greece and Europe: Antiquity after Antiquity," which includes articles by Bernal and by Greek scholars on such topics as classicism in Nazi Germany.

5. On Jews in Greece see Stavroulakis 1990, 49–55; Dalven 1990, 29–47.

6. Silberman (1990) devotes a chapter to Macedonia, before the republic's claim to independent status launched a wave of hysterical nationalism in Greece in response to unreasonable and inaccurate cultural propaganda north of the border. See Brown 1994.

7. Buitron-Oliver 1988 and 1991. In a recent review of the latter volume of essays Stieber notes this absence (1994, 169) without further comment on the phenomenon.

8. Kopcke and Tokumaru 1992; I drew attention to this in a paper delivered at the exhibition "From Pasture to Polis" in Columbia, Missouri, 22 October 1993 (see Langdon 1993).

9. See Langdon 1993, and the forthcoming proceedings of the conference held in October 1993; also Langdon 1989 and 1990, for her studies of Geometric art.

LINGUISTICS

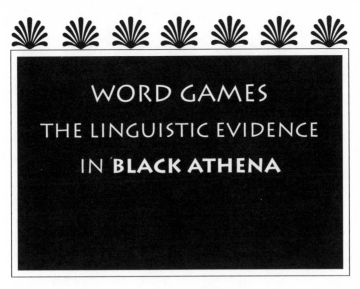

WORD GAMES
THE LINGUISTIC EVIDENCE
IN BLACK ATHENA

Jay H. Jasanoff & Alan Nussbaum

The first volume of *Black Athena*, whatever one thinks of it in other respects, was a considerable success from a public relations point of view. In it Martin Bernal argued, deftly enough to impress many reviewers who should have known better, that the overthrow of the "Ancient Model" in the nineteenth century owed more to Northern European racism and anti-Semitism than to any actual improvement in our knowledge of Greece, the Levant, and Egypt since classical antiquity. In Bernal's telling, the decipherment of Egyptian hieroglyphic writing, Babylonian cuneiform, and other early scripts were only minor incidents in the racially motivated "fall of Egypt" and "final solution of the Phoenician problem." The fact that neither Herodotus nor Plutarch could read a word of Egyptian, Phoenician, Akkadian, or Mycenaean Greek was no reason, in Bernal's eyes, not to trust them as authorities on the Eastern Mediterranean Bronze Age. Above all, these and other ancient writers passed the *Black Athena* age test: none had the misfortune to be born after 1750 of the present era.

It is not our purpose here to review Bernal's version of Western intellectual history. It is undeniably true that many nineteenth- and early twentieth-century scholars held views on race and ethnicity that are now generally and quite properly condemned. It is also true that the Greeks, as the supposed "founders" of Western civilization, have repeatedly been idealized, not to say caricatured, by modern scholars with cultural axes of their own to grind. To the extent that Bernal's work has fostered a greater public awareness of these familiar facts, it can be said to have played a useful role. But social enlightenment is not the main purpose of *Black Athena*. Bernal's object in attacking what he terms, with characteristic innuendo, the "Aryan Model" is to argue for a revisionist version of Greek prehistory that better conforms to his own preferences. His "Revised Ancient Model" is an exercise in politically up-to-the-minute wishful thinking — a farrago of hypotheses, ancient and modern, all tending to support his vision of Hellas as a second Gift of the Nile.

The evidence on which Bernal bases his case is of three kinds — archaeological, documentary, and linguistic. The purported archaeological and documentary evidence, which includes both historical records proper and literary sources such as Homer, Hesiod, and Aeschylus, is presented in the second volume of *Black Athena*. This material is discussed by specialists elsewhere in this volume; here we simply note that archaeologists and historians have not rushed to embrace the Revised Ancient Model, despite Bernal's apparent confidence that a Kuhnian "paradigm shift" is in full swing. Our focus in the following pages will be entirely on the words, place names, and personal names that make up Bernal's linguistic evidence. The philology in *Black Athena* has never, to the best of our knowledge, been reviewed by a competent historian of the Greek language.[1] It is easy to see why. The material is nowhere systematically presented; although over a hundred etymological proposals are scattered through the pages of the two volumes of *Black Athena* published so far, they are neither discussed coherently as a group nor supported with detailed linguistic arguments. A more orderly examination of the facts will presumably be supplied in the long-promised linguistics (third) volume, which we will be interested to see when it appears. But Bernal has already revealed enough of his claims and methods for it to be clear to any trained historical linguist that his evidence for "massive" Egyptian and Semitic borrowing in Greek is a mirage.

Before we proceed further, a few disclaimers are in order. As linguists, we have no professional interest in the politically charged issues that most exercise Bernal. It is immaterial to us, for example, whether the Egyptians — or the Greeks, for that matter — were black, white, or brown. We have no deeply held convictions on the extent of Sesostris' conquests, the ethnic composition of the Hyksos, or the accomplishments of the historical Kadmos. If we are thoroughly skeptical of what Bernal has to say on these matters, it is because his misuse of linguistic data leads us to question his ability to deal fairly with evidence from other sources. We emphasize, however, that we have nothing *in principle* against the Revised Ancient Model. We reject it not because it challenges our cultural convictions but because it seems, on the basis of the facts that we control, to be wrong.

Greek, as Bernal admits, is an Indo-European language. The implications of this statement are worth spelling out in detail. Languages are said to belong to a family, or to be *genetically related*, if they are descended from a common parent. The modern Romance languages—French, Spanish, Italian, etc.—are a case in point. If we could examine the forms of the Romance languages spoken a century ago, two centuries ago, three centuries ago, and so on backward in time, we would find them gradually approximating each other until they merged as a single form of speech around the beginning of the Christian Era. By a fortunate chance, this language happens to be preserved in documents that have come down to us; we call it Latin. But it is more typical for the parent language of a family not to be directly attested. Thus the Germanic languages (e.g., English, German, Dutch, Swedish), the Semitic languages (Hebrew, Arabic, Akkadian, etc.) and the ancient Greek dialects (Attic, Ionic, Doric, etc., which may be thought of as nascent languages) are just as clearly related to one another as the Romance languages, but their respective parent languages—we speak of "Proto-Germanic," "Proto-Semitic," and "Proto-Greek"—were never written down. The characteristics of these unattested "protolanguages" must be inferred from the characteristics of their descendants, a process about which we will have more to say presently.

Families such as these may themselves be related in higher-order groupings. Thus Latin is closely related to the long-extinct Italian languages Oscan, Umbrian, and Venetic, with which it constitutes the so-called Italic family; Romance, properly speaking, is thus a subfamily of Italic. Less obvious to the untutored eye, but firmly established since the end of the eighteenth century, is the fact that Italic, Germanic, and Greek belong to a larger family, the protolanguage of which was probably spoken around six millennia ago. This superfamily, generally called Indo-European (IE), also includes, inter alia, the Celtic languages (Gaulish, Old and Modern Irish, etc.), the Slavic languages (Old Church Slavonic, Russian, Polish, etc.), and the groups known as Anatolian (Hittite, Luvian, Lydian, etc.; all extinct) and Indo-Iranian (Sanskrit, Hindi, Old and Modern Persian, etc.). The structure of the IE family as a whole can be represented in a branching diagram, or *Stammbaum*, of the type shown in the second volume of *Black Athena* (2:532).[2] The IE languages are in no way unique. The Semitic languages, for example, are clearly not IE but can be shown to be related to Egyptian, the Berber languages, and a number of other African families. Taken together, Semitic and its relatives make up the vast Afro-Asiatic superfamily, with a time depth even greater than is usually assumed for IE. The possibility of a distant genetic link between IE and Afro-Asiatic—that is, of a single "Indo–Afro-Asiatic" protolanguage going back ten or more millennia—has been discussed for more than a century but remains, despite Bernal's confident pronouncement on the subject (*BA* 1:11), a largely unsubstantiated conjecture.

The existence of a protolanguage, of course, implies a population speaking it. In the case of Proto-Indo-European (PIE), this population is thought by many archaeologists to have inhabited the steppes of southeastern Russia in the early fourth millennium B.C.E.; a dispassionate account of the evidence is given by Mallory (1989). But it does not follow, as some nineteenth-century scholars wished to believe, that the earliest documented *linguistic* descendants of the Proto-Indo-Europeans—the Greeks, the Romans, the Teutons, the Vedic Aryans, etc.—were also their racially identifiable *genetic* descendants. Languages are cultural artifacts, transmissible in the same way as religions, social conventions, or political institutions. English is a Germanic language, the earliest speakers of which, the Angles and the Saxons, were northern Europeans of "Nordic" physical type. Anglo-Saxon genes, however, are no prerequisite for membership in the present-day community of English speakers, which includes representatives of virtually every non-European ethnic heritage in the world. In general, linguistic and racial boundaries rarely coincide, and it is a mischievous fantasy to suppose that the situation was essentially different in the third, second, or first millennium B.C.E. The Greeks were not "Indo-Europeans" but simply speakers of an IE language.

Related languages show resemblances in vocabulary and grammar that reflect their common ancestry. Greek, Latin, and Sanskrit, for example, have similar words for the numerals from one to ten, for kinship terms like "mother" and "father," and for a host of other common lexical items. They also show similar endings in the inflection of nouns and verbs. One of the major achievements of nineteenth-century linguistic scholarship was the development of the *comparative method*, a set of techniques for using such resemblances to reconstruct actual words and forms in long-extinct protolanguages.

Let us consider an example. The masculine nominative form of the word for "three" in Greek is *treîs* (phonetically [trēs]), contracted from an earlier two-syllable *trées*, a variant still found in the conservative Cretan dialect. The corresponding words in Latin and Sanskrit are *trēs* and *tráyas*, respectively; taken together, the evidence of these three forms clearly points to a common origin in the parent language. Let us try to determine what the PIE word for "three" actually was. To begin with the obvious, the initial *tr-* and final *-s* found in Greek, Latin, and Sanskrit must already have been present in the protolanguage; to deny this would be to claim, in effect, that *tr-* and *-s* evolved in each daughter language independently. We can likewise assume that Gk. disyllabic *trées* and Skt. *tráyas*, with two short vowels, represent a more original state of affairs than Lat. *trēs*. This conclusion is motivated by typological considerations: it is known from a vast body of accumulated evidence that contractions of two short vowels into a single long vowel are a very common kind of linguistic change, whereas "distractions" of a long vowel into sequences of two shorts are extremely rare. By the same reasoning, it can be inferred that Gk. *trées*, with its two vowels in hiatus, is less archaic than Skt. *tráyas*, with its two vowels separated by the consonant -*y*-. The masculine nominative of the word for "three" in PIE must therefore have been a form of the type $*trx_1yx_2s$, where the identity of the vowels $*x_1$ and $*x_2$ remains to be determined.

How to advance beyond this point is not at first glance obvious. The vowels $*x_1$ and $*x_2$ are represented by *a* in Sanskrit but by *e* in Greek. Lat. *trēs*, with *ē* contracted from $*x_1$ and $*x_2$, tends to argue for the priority of the Greek treatment; it cannot, however, settle the question of the PIE vocalism definitively. The natural candidates for the common preform are *tráyas*, the form suggested by Sanskrit; *tréyes*, the form suggested by Greek; and the hybrids *tréyas* and *tráyes*. The problem is to find a principled way of making the correct choice.

The required principle has in fact been available for more than a century. In the 1870s a number of Indo-Europeanists made the surprising and important empirical discovery that the process of sound change is phonetically conditioned and "regular." What this means, in everyday parlance, is that if over a given period in the history of a language a sound *A* develops into a sound *A'* in a particular phonetic environment, then *A always* develops into *A'* in this environment. Examples of language-specific "sound laws" of this kind are innumerable. Thus, for example, PIE $*s$ always gives Gk. *h* at the beginning of a word (cf. Gk. *heptá* "seven," *héx* "six," *hérpō* "I creep" beside Lat. *septem, sex, serpō*); Latin *ē* always gives French *oi* ([wa]) in accented open syllables (cf. Lat. *rēgem* "king," *lēgem* "law," *mē* "me" > Fr. *roi, loi, moi*); Middle English accented *e* always gives Modern English *a* when followed by *r* in the same syllable (cf. ME *derk, lerk, person* > Eng. *dark, lark, parson*). In the case of the PIE word for "three" the crucial fact is that Skt. *a* routinely corresponds to three different vowels in Greek, namely, (1) *e*, as in *tráyas* : *trées* or 3 sg. Skt. *ásti* : Gk. *estí* "is"; (2) *a*, as in Skt. *ájra-* : Gk. *agrós* "field" or *ápa* : Gk. *apó* "away (from)"; and (3) *o*, as in Skt. *ávi-* : Gk. *oîs* "sheep" or Skt. *páti-* : Gk. *pósis* "lord, husband." If we took the position that the PIE vowel in all these forms was $*a$, there would be no discoverable phonetic condition for the change of $*a$ to *e* or *o* in Greek: we would simply have to state that PIE $*a$ yielded Gk. *e* in some cases, *o* in others and *a* in yet others. "Sporadic" changes of this kind are precisely what the regularity principle disallows. We thus have no choice but to assume that the three-way distinction of *a*, *e*, and *o* in Greek goes back to the parent language, and that the change of PIE *a, *e and *o to a was a regular sound law of Sanskrit. The common prototype of Gk. trées, Lat. trēs, and Skt. tráyas is uniquely reconstructible as *tréyes.

It will be seen from this example that comparative reconstruction in PIE—or, *mutatis mutandis*, in Proto-Germanic or Proto-Semitic—is anything but a guessing game. Every decision to set up a particular sound in a reconstructed word entails a set of hypotheses which can be tested against the evidence of other forms. Thus, for example, our decision to reconstruct a medial *y in "three" is equivalent to the assertion that *y was regularly lost between vowels in Greek and Latin; we can support this claim by finding additional instances of the -aya- : -ee- : -ē- correspondence pattern (there are many), and refute it by finding counterexamples (there are none). The cumulative effect of such hypothesizing and cross-checking, applied to a large number of individual examples, is an internally consistent and remarkably detailed phonetic history of the languages under comparison. Time and again the results of the comparative method have been independently confirmed by fresh discoveries. The decipherment of Mycenaean in 1952, for example, revealed an archaic and conservative Greek dialect which retained intervocalic y in precisely the forms where its existence had been predicted on linguistic grounds. The Mycenaean dialect was also found to preserve the "labiovelar" consonants k^w, g^w and k^{w}h—sounds which had been posited for Proto-Greek in the nineteenth century, but which were no longer distinguished from the labials (p, b, ph) and dentals (t, d, th) in the dialects of the classical period. We shall see more of these phonemes below.

The viability of a proposed etymology within a family of related languages, then, depends not on whether the forms being compared "look alike" in an impressionistic sense, but whether they can be referred back to a common prototype via independently motivated sound laws. No one casting a casual eye on Gk. dúō "two" or its cognates Skt. dvá(u) and Lat. duo would suppose that these forms had anything to do with erku, the corresponding word in Classical Armenian. Yet dúō, dvá(u) and duo go back to a preform of the type *dwō, with a PIE dw- cluster which is *always* represented by erk- in Armenian (compare Arm. erkar "long," cognate with Gk. dērós < *dwārós; also Arm. erki- "fear," cognate with Gk. 1 pl. perf. deídimen "we fear" < *de-dwi-). Noteworthy too is the Armenian word for "three," erek', which despite its superficial strangeness can be traced via well-established sound changes to PIE *tréyes. Examples like these illustrate the elementary principle that a good etymology depends not on phonetic similarity, but on phonetically regular patterns of correspondence.

We cannot tell whether Bernal is unaware of these facts or whether—to adopt one of his favorite locutions—he simply finds it "useful" to ignore them. What is certain is that he repeatedly advances etymologies that rely on superficially suggestive but demonstrably secondary phonetic resemblances between Greek and Egyptian or Semitic words. Thus he casually remarks that Gk. *érebos* "darkness" "almost certainly comes from the Akkadian *erebu* (sunset)" (*BA* 2:93). The intent of this formulation is to impress the reader with the external similarity of the two forms; no mention is made of the difficulties. He does not explain, for example, why the Greeks should have borrowed *érebos* from Akkadian, a language of distant Mesopotamia, rather than from the source of Semitic loan words that he usually prefers—the Canaanite of the Levant proper. In fact, the reason for the choice of Akkadian will be obvious to any Semitic philologist: the Canaanite counterpart of *erebu* in the second millennium B.C.E. would have been **ʿaribu*, with a preserved initial consonant ("ayin") and an archaic vowel pattern distinctly unhelpful to the comparison with *érebos*. Nor is that all. Only the reader who sifts through Bernal's footnotes will discover that "the Indo-Europeanists prefer to derive *erebos* from a root **regʷos* (dark) found in Sanskrit and Armenian" (2:557 n. 87). This bland concession to scholarly honesty utterly fails to convey the real import of the comparative evidence. Skt. *rájas-* "dark region of the sky," Arm. *erek* "evening," and Gothic *riqis* "darkness" (a form apparently unknown to Bernal) point not to a root meaning "dark," but to a neuter abstract noun **h₁régʷ-os* (genitive **h₁régʷ-es-os*) meaning "darkness."[3] Such a noun, had it come down into Greek, would have been treated according to the regular sound laws: initial **h₁r-* would have yielded *er-*, **gʷ-* would have given *-b-* before *a* or *o*, and intervocalic **-s-*, after developing to **-h-*, would have disappeared entirely. In effect, the Sanskrit, Armenian and Gothic forms make a prediction: they tell us that a search of the Greek lexicon might be expected to reveal an "*s*-stem" neuter *érebos* "darkness," with genitive *erébeos* < **-ehos* < **-esos*. And that is exactly what we find. Significantly, *érebos* is *not* a masculine *o*-stem with genitive in *-ou*—the class to which the vast majority of Greek nouns in *-os*, including almost all loan words, belong. The gender and inflection of this word are unexplained under Bernal's borrowing theory; the standard theory not only explains but predicts them. To say that linguists "prefer" to compare *érebos* with its IE cognates is, in its way, a bit like saying that geographers prefer to believe that the earth is round.

This example brings us to the subject of loan words in general. There is no human language which has not occasionally borrowed words, names, or other meaningful elements from its neighbors. In the most typical instances, new words are introduced into a language along with new articles of material culture, as, for example, in the case of Eng. *coffee* (from Arabic via Turkish), *chocolate* (from Nahuatl via Spanish), and *vodka* (from Russian). But sometimes, particularly when one speech community has been subject to the political or cultural domination of another, the effects of linguistic contact are more far-reaching. Medieval England, in the centuries following the Norman Conquest, was ruled and administered by a French-speaking aristocracy. Although French virtually disappeared as a spoken language in England in the course of the fourteenth century, English emerged from the Middle Ages with literally thousands of French borrowings, the majority of them relating to upper-class interests, tastes, and pursuits (e.g., *art, beauty, beef, chamber, curious, defy, envy, feast, fool, forest, jelly, judge, loyal, marry, noble, ointment, paint, peace, prison, royal*; the list could be extended for pages). Many comparable instances of large-scale borrowing are known. The vocabulary of Armenian is so rich in Middle Iranian loan words—a legacy of the period when Armenia was ruled by a dynasty of Parthian origin—that Armenian was for many years mistakenly believed to be an Iranian language. Similarly, the lexicon of Modern Persian has been heavily Arabized since the Muslim conquest of Iran in the seventh century C.E. In East Asia, Japanese, Korean, and Vietnamese have acquired thousands of words from Chinese, the dominant language of the region. Cases like these are important because they furnish an independent standard for assessing Bernal's claims about the Egyptian and Semitic elements in Greek.

Names—of people, gods, and places—can be borrowed as well. The pan-European distribution of originally Semitic personal names like *John, Joseph,* and *Mary* (Fr. *Jean, Joseph, Marie*; Ital. *Giovanni, Giuseppe, Maria*; Ger. *Johann(es), Joseph, Maria*; Russ. *Ivan, Osip, Marya*) is due, of course, to the influence of the Bible; Muslim names like *Mohammed, Omar,* and *Fatima* are comparably widespread in the Islamic world, even among non-Arabic-speaking peoples. In societies with polytheistic religions, the names and cults of the gods themselves may be of foreign origin. Thus, for example, the Roman legionaries who popularized the worship of Cybele, originally an Anatolian fertility goddess, and Mithras, originally an Indo-Iranian god of contracts, never thought it necessary to provide these divinities with native Latin names. Toponyms (place names) exhibit a great deal of variety. A map of the eastern United States gives a good overview of the possibilities: here we find, inter alia, recent English coinages, such as *New Haven* and *Fairlawn*; older names of English origin, such as *Hartford* and *Cambridge*; names introduced by immigrants from other European countries, such as *Brooklyn* (< Holland) and *Bala Cynwyd* (< Wales); and Native American names retained by the early settlers, such as *Passaic* (< Algonquian) and *Oswego* (< Iroquoian). Such indigenous toponyms are also surprisingly well attested in Western Europe, where many towns in England (e.g., London) and France (e.g., Nîmes, Arles) still bear names of Celtic origin.

Because two languages rarely share the same sound system, words commonly undergo a certain amount of phonetic "naturalization" in the course of the borrowing process. The sounds of the source language are replaced by their closest equivalents in the target language; thus we find, e.g., that the Arabic distinction between plain and "emphatic" (velarized) consonants is ignored in Persian, and that the nasalized vowels of Old French are represented by sequences of vowel plus nasal consonant in Middle and Modern English (cf. Eng. *chant, chamber* < OF *chant* [čãt], *chambre* [čãbrə]). In situations where borrowing is heavy and bilingualism can be assumed to have been widespread, sound substitutions of this kind are carried out with a high degree of consistency. Our knowledge of the pronunciation of Ancient Chinese depends in large part on the systematic way in which Chinese words were rendered into Japanese and Korean in the third century C.E. Closer to home, the vowel sounds of Old French were reproduced in Middle English with such accuracy that word pairs which rhymed in Old French were preserved as rhymes in Middle English; a few such pairs, modified by later English sound changes, remain in the modern language (cf. OF *loyal, royal; beste, feste* > ME *loyal, royal; bęste, fęste* > Eng. *loyal, royal; beast, feast*).

Let us now turn to the facts of Greek. It is perfectly true, as Bernal says, that a large number of Greek words, such as *thríx* "hair," *thálassa* "sea," *ámpelos* "vine," *glaukós* "gray," and *árkhō* "I rule," lack good IE etymologies. What is *not* true is that this situation is unusual for an IE language, or that the existence of such words in Greek constitutes a mystery which threatens to turn our picture of the ancient world on its head. In fact, every branch of the IE family, and every individual IE language, has lexical items of unknown—or at least undetermined—origin. To take a prosaic example, the Proto-Germanic words corresponding to Eng. *hand* (= German *Hand*), *finger* (= Ger. *Finger*), *wife* (= Ger. *Weib*), *sheep* (= Ger. *Schaf*), and *good* (= Ger. *gut*) have no etymological connections outside Germanic. Words like Eng. *boy, girl, dog, bad,* and *kidney* are even more isolated, with no known cognates at all, Germanic or otherwise. The "problem" of the Greek vocabulary must be seen in perspective: while the percentage of demonstrably inherited IE words in Greek is lower than in the highly conservative Sanskrit of the Rig-Veda, it is probably about the same as in Latin, and vastly higher than in the earliest attested IE language, Hittite.[4]

In principle, there are two possible reasons why a given Greek word or name may appear to lack a IE etymology. On the one hand, the form may be a genuine inheritance whose cognates have been lost or obscured. This possibility is actually a probability in the case of morphologically archaic words like *athér* "ear (of grain)," *pélōr* "monster," or *dipsáō* "I am thirsty," which are too isolated ("irregular") from a synchronic point of view to be explicable as recent additions to the language.[5] Alternatively, the form in question may be a loan word. No competent scholar has ever denied that the Greek lexicon, like that of most other IE and non-IE languages, is full of borrowings. The question on which competent scholars and Bernal part company is the one that inevitably arises next: borrowings from where?

The people who introduced the Greek language into its historical home were not the first to live there. The linguistic ancestors of the Greeks, as even Bernal admits, were immigrants from the north; most reputable archaeologists place the date of their arrival toward the end of the third millennium B.C.E. We are very poorly informed about the ethnic affiliations of the pre-Hellenic population that lived in Greece at that time. Nevertheless a few basic facts are clear from the archaeological record and from general considerations. We can be sure, for example, that the pre-Hellenic inhabitants were acquainted with local plant and animal species unfamiliar to the newcomers; we can likewise be sure that they possessed a relatively sophisticated material culture and that, like other members of the human race, they spoke a fully developed language. The actual character of the pre-Hellenic language (or languages) can only be gathered from indirect evidence. It has often been noted that the map of Greece abounds in foreign-looking place names in *-nthos* (e.g., *Amárunthos*, *Erúmanthos*, *Zákunthos*, *Kórinthos*, *Périnthos*, *Ólunthos*) and *-(s)sos* (e.g., *Dírphōssos*, *Ilisós*, *Kēphis(s)ós*, *Kerēssós*, *Parnassós*, *Pḗdasos*). Significantly, the same two suffix-like elements also appear in ordinary Greek vocabulary items—mainly non-IE words denoting Mediterranean plants and plant products (cf. *erébinthos* "chickpea," *ólunthos* "wild fig," *términthos* (*terébinthos*) "terebinth," *huákinthos* "bluebell"; *kupárissos* "cypress," *kérasos* "cornel cherry," *písos* "pea," etc.) but also sometimes animals and articles of material culture (cf. *bólinthos* "European bison," *asáminthos* "bathtub"; *pétasos* "broad-brimmed hat," *támisos* "rennet," etc.). The natural inference is that *Amárunthos*, etc., are place names of the *Passaic*/*Oswego* type that have been retained from a vanished aboriginal language and that words like *erébinthos* and *ólunthos* (note the agreement in form with the city name *Ólunthos*) are borrowings from the same unknown source.

The elements *-(s)sos* and *-nthos* are also associated with the island of Crete—the former through place names (e.g., *Amnis(s)ós*, *Knōs(s)ós*, *Tulis(s)ós*), the latter through personal names and the apparently Cretan word *labúrinthos* "labyrinth." Many scholars have accordingly sought to identify the pre-Hellenic language of the Greek mainland with the language of the Cretan Linear A tablets, which cannot be read, and/or with the fragmentarily attested "Eteocretan" language, which can be read but not understood. Whether or not this is correct, there can be no doubt that Crete, like mainland Greece, was once the home of a language that was not IE or Semitic or Egyptian.[6] The almost universally held view that Greek borrowed heavily from one or more such languages is not a racist fantasy concocted to suppress the European debt to the Near East and Egypt. It is the commonsense position, the null hypothesis.

This line of argument, of course, is highly uncongenial to Bernal, who uses every rhetorical device at his disposal to suggest that any Greek word or name which lacks an IE etymology is a priori likely to be a borrowing from Semitic or Egyptian. His own discussion of the place names in -*nthos* and -*(s)sos* (*BA* 1:48–49, 392) is a model of tendentious confusion. The only reason these forms are considered important, he hints, is that they were used by the "Aryanist" scholars Haley and Blegen to bolster their 1927 theory of Bronze Age settlement patterns. This is nonsense: the evidence for a pre-Hellenic language or languages is utterly independent of the Haley-Blegen theory or any other particular reconstruction of Aegean prehistory. Bernal disparages the testimony of -*nthos* and -*(s)sos* on the grounds that these elements "have never been given any meaning" by their traditional defenders. In fact, however, his practice belies his principles, for he freely admits that, meaning notwithstanding, "-*(i)ssos* would seem to be a characteristic Aegean ending." His objection to conceding the same point for -*nthos* is motivated not by semantic scruples but by an etymology of his own: he wishes to derive *labúrinthos* from the Egyptian phrase *Ny-mꜣꜥ t-Rꜥ ntr*, apparently meaning "holy *Ny-mꜣꜥ t-Rꜥ* [= Amenemḥe III]" (*BA* 2:175). We confess to finding this derivation wildly far-fetched even by Bernal's standards. But Eg. *ntr*, variously glossed as "pure," "holy," and "divine [in a pantheistic sense] growth," enjoys a specially favored position in the Revised Ancient Model, being used to supply etymologies for *ánthos* "flower," *kántharos* "kind of beetle," *nítron* "nitre" (see below), *sáturos* "satyr," and *Satrai* (a Thracian tribe), as well as "some cases" of the suffix -*nthos*. The single word *ntr* thus had, according to Bernal, five distinct phonetic treatments in Greek! As for the remaining cases of -*nthos*—those which do *not* contain *ntr*—Bernal attributes the bulk to "simple nasalization before a dental," as if this were the name of a linguistic development well enough known to be invoked without further explanation. There is a fine Greek word for all this: chaos.

Contrary to what Bernal implies, it is universally recognized that there are both Semitic and Egyptian loan words in Greek. Readers of *Black Athena* may be surprised to learn that the most recent "Aryanist" survey of the Semitic material (Masson 1967) lists no fewer than twenty-seven secure, fully naturalized Greek words of Semitic origin or transmission and cites many others as probable or possible. These are not, however, randomly distributed through the lexicon. The great majority fall into a small number of semantic groups, namely, (1) fabrics and items of clothing, e.g., *bússos* "fine linen; silk, cotton" (cf. Hebr. *būṣ*, Phoen. *bṣ*),[7] *khitón* "(man's) tunic" (cf. Hebr. *kətonet*, Phoen. *ktn*), *sák(k)os* "coarse hair cloth, bag of coarse hair cloth" (cf. Hebr. *śaq* "shaggy fabric," Akk. *śaqqu*); (2) commercial terms, e.g., *arrabón* "(nonrefundable) deposit" (cf. Hebr. *ꜥērābōn*, Ugar. *ꜥrbn*), *khrūsós* "gold" (cf. Hebr. *ḥaruṣ*, Ugar. *ḥrṣ*); (3) vessels, e.g., *kádos* "(wine) jar" (cf. Hebr. *kad* "jar," Ugar. *kd*)); and (4) plants and plant products, e.g., *kúminon* "cumin" (cf. Hebr. *kammon*, Phoen. *kmn*), *kúpros* "henna" (cf. Hebr. *koper*), *múrra* "myrrh" (cf. Hebr. *mor*,

Ugar. *mr*). Such words, several of which are already found in Mycenaean, suggest lively Greek–Phoenician commercial relations going back to the second millennium B.C.E. But unlike the Norman French loan words in English or the Chinese loan words in Japanese, these do not suggest the kind of prolonged, transformative cultural contact that the Revised Ancient Model presupposes.

The Egyptian words in Greek are on the whole fewer and later than the Semitic words.[8] A high percentage are confined to the Greek spoken in Egypt in Hellenistic and Roman times; others are merely quoted as foreign words by late Greek authors. Of those that remain, the overwhelming majority refer specifically to objects of Egyptian origin. Representative examples are *pápuros* "papyrus" < Eg. *pз-pr* (with the definite article *pз-*); *íbis* "ibis" < Eg. *hby*; *érpis* "type of wine" < Eg. *ỉrp* (Coptic *ērp*); *bâris* "boat" < Eg. *br* (Coptic *bari*); *ébenos, ebénē* "ebony" < Eg. *hbn(y)*; *pságdan, pságdas, ságdas* "unguent" < Eg. *p(з)-sgnn, sgnn* (with and without the definite article); *kullêstis* "kind of Egyptian bread" < Eg. *kršt*; *kíki* "castor oil" < Eg. *kyky* (also *kзkз*); *kómmi* "gum" < Eg. *kmy(.t)* (Coptic *komi*). Note too the long-standard derivation, which Bernal repeats, of Gk. *nítron* "nitre" (used as a mummy preservative) from Eg. *ntr* in the sense "pure." None of these words is found as early as Homer, and most are Hellenistic or later. Under any reasonable standard of philological rigor, the only genuinely old Egyptian borrowing in Greek is the name of Egypt itself, which appears in Mycenaean in the adjectival form *ai-ku-pi-ti-jo* (= *Aigúptios*) "Egyptian."

It may be useful to reflect for a moment on why the above examples are as convincing as they are. First of all, the semantic match between the Greek words and their Semitic and Egyptian counterparts is exact: Hebr. *hārus̱*, and Ugar. *hrs̱*, e.g., mean precisely "gold" (Gk. *khrūsós*), and not merely "bright" or "yellow"; Eg. *hby* means "ibis" (Gk. *íbis*), and not simply "bird" or "long legs." Critically, the identity of meaning is correlated with a striking similarity of form. The phonetic agreement is not, of course, perfect; as we have already seen, some loss of phonetic detail is an inevitable consequence of linguistic borrowing, even in cases of prolonged and intimate contact. But within fairly narrow limits, the resemblances between the Greek words cited above and their Semitic and Egyptian prototypes are obvious and persistent. The voiced stops of Semitic and Egyptian (*b, d, g*), for example, are quite systematically represented by voiced stops in Greek; the same holds true, *mutatis mutandis*, for the voiceless stops (*p, t, k*, etc.),[9] liquids (*r, l*), and nasals (*m, n*). It is also significant—and deserving of emphasis—that the hypothesis of borrowing is fully compatible with the morphological and derivational evidence at our disposal. All the above examples belong to one or another of the common Greek declensional types: most are *o*-stems and *i*-stems, and the rest are *ā*-stems and *n*-stems. By contrast, rare and/or archaic stem types, such as the "r/n-stems" (e.g., *húdōr*, gen. *húdatos* "water") and *s*-stems (e.g., *génos*, gen. *géneos* "race"), are entirely absent from the list of assured Semitic and Egyptian borrowings in Greek—a fact already noted in connection with Bernal's misguided discussion of the *s*-stem *érebos*. Genuine loan words in Greek are for the most part completely isolated, not only in the sense that they lack convincing IE etymologies but also in the sense that they are not visibly derived from other, simpler Greek words or roots. It is characteristic that there is no verb **khrúsō* "I shine" beside the borrowed word for "gold," or a verb **íbomai* "I catch fish" or "I stride" beside the borrowed word for "ibis."

BERNAL'S ETYMOLOGIES

The new etymologies in *BA* are intended to bolster Bernal's claim that the number of Semitic and Egyptian borrowings in Greek is vastly greater than traditionally assumed. The claim is a crucial one, given Bernal's agenda, for it is utterly inconceivable that the Egyptians or their variable-race surrogates, the Hyksos, could have had the cultural effects attributed to them without having an impact on the Greek language similar to that of, say, the Normans on English. The linguistic evidence, in short, is no mere accessory to the archaeological and historical evidence but an integral and indispensible part of Bernal's case. If the attempt to establish a "massive" presence of Semitic and Egyptian elements in early Greek is successful, then the Revised Ancient Model will have received external support of the most powerful kind. By the same token, if the effort fails, the Revised Ancient Model will itself have failed—regardless of the date of the Thera eruption, the chronology of the Eighteenth Dynasty, or any other nonlinguistic issues. With this in mind, let us take a closer look at what Bernal has to offer.

Names

Not even the most inattentive reader of the Egyptian and Semitic etymologies in *Black Athena* can fail to notice how high a percentage of them are of names—names of places, names of people, and names of mythological figures. This is no accident, for a name, functionally speaking, is merely a label; its etymological meaning, if discoverable at all, need not stand in any detectable relation to the person or thing named. A man may be called "God is Gracious" (John) or "Elf Counsel" (Alfred) or "Horse Lover" (Philip); a city name may be derived from a topographical feature, a characteristic form of local vegetation, or the self-designation of a tribe that once lived there. Because names normally furnish so few clues to their original meaning, methodologically sophisticated etymologists usually treat them with special caution. Bernal does the opposite: the semantic opacity of names becomes, in his hands, a license for etymological speculations of the most extravagant kind. Any geographical feature can be used to support the derivation of a Greek place name from an Egyptian or Semitic original—either another place name or a generic word for "river," "mountain," or the like. Any fragment of legend connected with a Greek personal or divine name can be taken out of context and used to establish a "link" between the Greek form and a similarly disembodied word or phrase in Egyptian or Semitic. The undisciplined character of Bernal's method can be seen from some typical examples:[10]

Télphoûsa, the name of a Boeotian spring, and *Thelpoûsa*, the name of an Arcadian town, are said by Bernal to represent Eg. *t3lbyw*, a "rarely attested variant of Rb or Libu Libyans" (*BA* 2:92–93, 98). His bases for the connection are that "most of this area [i.e., Libya] was made up of desert and oases" and that "the Boeotian Telphousa included the steep cliff and the 'oasis'-like spring below," from which "—as in Libya—flowed a river Tritōn, connected to a marshy lake."

Methônē, a city name in Macedonia and Thessaly with variants *Mothônē* (Messenia) and *Méthana* (Argolid), is said to go back to Eg. *mtwn* "bull fight, bull arena" (*BA* 1:50). Cited in support is the fact that the four Greek towns "are all set on bays that could well be described as theatrical."

Láris(s)a, a city name with variants found in many parts of Greece, is taken to be from the Egyptian toponym *R-3ḫt*, "Entry into the Fertile Lands," which "was probably used for the Hyksos capital Avaris, in the rich soils of the Eastern Nile Delta" (*BA* 1:76). From the fact that the town of Larisa in Thessaly is located in the middle of a fertile plain, Bernal concludes that "the semantic fit between Laris(s)a and R-3ht is excellent."

Rhadámanthus, the name of a legendary king of Crete, can be "fruitfully" derived, according to Bernal, from Eg. **Rdỉ Mntw* ("Mntw or Mont gives" or "whom Mntw or Mont has given") (*BA* 2:180ff.). Both Rhadamanthys and Mntw "were warlike and in some way father to a wandering hero/pharaoh." Both, in addition, "were closely connected to Amon/Zeus and were more or less connected to bulls."

Thêbai "Thebes" is said to come from Canaanite *têbâh* "ark, chest," itself allegedly a borrowing from Eg. *tbỉ* or *dbt* "box" and connected to Eg. *db3* "wicker float, ark of bulrushes" and *db3t* "coffin, shrine," whence "palace" (*BA* 1:51). According to Bernal, this etymology, which tacitly assumes the identity of the name "Thebes" with the barely attested Greek noun *thîbis* "basket," was "generally accepted" before the advent of the Aryan Model.

Kōpaḯs, a term applied to a lake in Boeotia, is traced by Bernal to Eg. *kbḥ* "purify," which is said to have had the subsidiary meaning "lake with wild fowl" (*BA* 1:49). The lake had "many Egyptian connections in Greek tradition" and was fed by a river *Kēphisós*, for which a related etymology is proposed.

Because names, in principle, can mean almost anything, it would be inaccurate to say that any of these suggestions is *impossible* on semantic grounds alone. None of them, however, is in any way compelling, and most are wholly arbitrary. Even granting Bernal's hypothesis of an early Egyptian or Hyksos presence in Greece, it is hard to believe that a visitor from the Nile Delta, beholding the spring of Telphousa for the first time, would have been moved to name it "Libya" or "Libyans," rather than "Cataract," "Traveler's Rest," or any of a thousand other possibilities. The same applies to *Methōnē*: when all is said and done, a "theatrical"-looking harbor is very different from a bull arena, and it is simply not credible that four Greek towns should have taken their name from this not-too-compelling metaphor. With the name "Laris(s)a" there is a further problem. The "fertile" Larisa mentioned by Bernal was not the only town to bear this name in antiquity. Another Larisa, likewise in Thessaly, was located high on a mountainside—a fact which accords with the explicit statement of a Byzantine scholiast that *Láris(s)a* originally meant "citadel." As for Rhadamanthys, the parallels between the figure of the Cretan king, best known as a judge and lawgiver, and the Egyptian solar god Mntw are far too nebulous to support any connection between the two at all—much less Bernal's specific derivation of the name "Rhadamanthys" from an Egyptian phrase of his own invention. The city of Thebes has no discoverable link in Greek tradition to baskets or chests, which figure in Bernal's etymology only because a late compiler, writing at a time when the sound $\bar{e}$ had become $\bar{i}$ by regular sound change, mistakenly substituted the letter eta for iota in the unfamiliar word *thîbis*.[11] This leaves only the equation of *Kōpaḯs* with an Egyptian word said to mean "lake with wild fowl." Here Bernal has simply misread the facts: *Kōpaḯs* in Greek is not, properly speaking, the name of a body of water at all, but an adjective derived from the name of a city on its shores (see below).

Hand in hand with Bernal's lack of semantic rigor goes an almost complete disregard for phonetic consistency. Even in the short list above, Egyptian *b* is supposed to have yielded Greek *b* in *Thêbai*, *p* in *Kōpaḯs*, and *ph* in *Telphoûsa* and *Kēphisós*. Egyptian *r* gives both Greek *r(h)* in *Rhadámanthus* and *l* in *Láris(s)a*; the latter name shows that Greek *r* can also, in Bernal's scheme of things, go back to Egyptian *ȝ*, which elsewhere is said to give *l* (cf., e.g., *Kólkhis* "Colchis" < *Kȝš* "Upper Nubia"[!], *BA* 2:253) or to disappear, usually leaving a vowel in its place (cf. the "common river or lake name Pheneos or Pēneios" < *pȝ nw(y)* "the flood," 2:19; *Aigúptos* "Egypt" < *ḥt kȝ Ptḥ* "temple of the spirit of Ptah," 2:443; etc.). Another protean Egyptian sound is *ḥ*, which is alleged to give a vowel (cf. *Kōpaḯs, Aigúptos*), to become *s* (cf. *Láris(s)a*), or to become *h* (cf. below). Multiple reflexes are claimed for the non-Greek sounds transcribed *ỉ, ḥ, š, s,* and *ʿ,* as well as for virtually every other consonant in the Egyptian and Semitic alphabets.[12] With such an abundance of potential "Afroasiatic" sources available for every sound in Greek, and with the vowels of Semitic and Egyptian effectively ignored, the task of etymologizing a Greek name reduces to a parlor game that anyone can play with the help of a few good dictionaries. Bernal, as an advanced student of the game, naturally plays it with facility, sometimes finding two or more mutually incompatible etymologies for the same item. Thus, the name *Ió* is said to be "firstly from the Egyptian *i'ḥ* 'moon,'" but at the same time "basic[ally]" from two different Egyptian words for "cow," *iḥt* and *iw3* (*BA* 1:95). Competing explanations are likewise offered for *Pán* (2:171) and *Mínōs* (2:172). In the same vein, the first part of the transparent compound *Hēraklês* ("whose fame is of/from/for Hera") is said to rest on "a sacred paranomasia [*sic passim*] or combination of three West Semitic roots all based on the consonants ḥrr" (2:108). Nowhere does the essentially frivolous character of Bernal's linguistic argumentation emerge more clearly than in examples like these.[13]

Etymologies of this kind are too capricious and unsystematic to be of any value. Most of them, as we have said, are not individually refutable; they are unacceptable because they rest on impressionistic resemblances which, in the absence of semantic and phonological constraints, can be found between lists of names and words in any two languages. In a certain number of cases, however, Bernal's derivations run directly contrary to established Greek sound laws. Thus, for instance, the supposed connection of "Thebes" with Canaanite *tēbâh* and Eg. *tḥi/dbt* is not only semantically arbitrary; it is also inconsistent with the Mycenaean forms *te-qa-de* "to Thebes, *Thêbasde*" and *te-qa-ja* "Theban, *Thēbaíā*," which show that the -*b*- of *Thêbai* goes back not to an original **b*, but to a Proto-Greek "labiovelar" **gʷ* (cf. further below, s.v. *basileús*). Even the superficially attractive — and inherently far more plausible — comparison of the Cretan and Elean river name *Iárdanos* with Canaanite *Yardēn* "Jordan" (*BA* 1:49) is of doubtful value as evidence for Greek-Semitic linguistic contact in the Bronze Age. Since **y* was still a distinct phoneme in Mycenaean Greek, the name *Yardēn*, if borrowed from Semitic before ca. 1300 B.C.E., would almost certainly have been rendered in early Greek as **Yárdēnos* or **Yárdanos*, with initial **y*-. With the late Mycenaean change of **y*- to *h*- (cf. *hós* "who, which" < **yós*), **Yárdanos* would in turn have given **Hárdanos* in the dialects of the classical period. That we find the form *Iárdanos*, with four syllables, shows either that the similarity of *Iárdanos* and *Yardēn* is illusory or that the name was borrowed after ca. 1300 B.C.E., when the vowel *i* was the closest Greek equivalent to the Semitic consonant *y*.[14]

In other cases Bernal's etymologies fly in the face of obvious morphological facts. *Kōpaïs* (gen. *Kōpaïdos*), as remarked above, is basically an adjective: its proper meaning is "Copaean," that is, "of or belonging to the town of Copae (*Kôpai*)." The phrase *Kōpaïs límnē*, conventionally glossed "Lake Copais," is literally the "Copaean lake, lake near Copae," completely parallel to the attested phrase *Kōpaídes enkheleîs* "Copaean eels, eels from the waters off Copae."

Bernal's effort to trace the name of the lake to an Egyptian word for "lake" is thus misconceived: the real problem, thus far unsolved, would be to find the origin of the city name *Kôpai*, in form the plural of an unknown *ā*-stem noun. Other unexplained names for which structure-defying etymologies are offered in the pages of *Black Athena* include *Lakedaímōn* "Lacedaemon, Sparta" and *Mukênai* (also *-ênê*) "Mycenae." *Lakedaímōn*, according to Bernal, "can be plausibly explained as the 'Howling/Gnawing Spirit'" and is "an exact calque for Kanōbos/Kanōpos < k₃ inpw 'spirit of Anubis'" (*BA* 1:53). This pronouncement shows that he imagines a segmentation *Lake-daímōn*, with *Lake-* understood to be either a form of the verb *lélāka* "I cry out" or of the completely different verb *lakízō* "I rend." Neither interpretation is possible. The first reading is simply out of the question: *verb* + *noun* compounds of this type are adjectives with a transitive first member (cf., e.g., *pheré-oikos* "bearing a house," whence "snail"). The second reading, if it were formally in order, would have to mean "rending a (minor) divine power," with *daímōn* as the understood object of *Lake-* "rending." This too, however, is extremely unlikely. The Mycenaean personal name *ra-ke-da-no* (dat. *ra-ke-da-no-re*) is almost surely to be read as *Laked-ānōr* (cf. Myc. *Ant-ānōr*, *Ekh-ānōr*, etc.), showing that the correct segmentation of *Lakedaímōn* is not *Lake-daímōn* but *Laked-aímōn*—however we choose to interpret that sequence.[15]

In the case of "Mycenae," Bernal favors Levin's derivation from Semitic **maḥaneh* "camp" (cf. Hebr. *maḥăneh*), or, more particularly, from the corresponding dual form **maḥanayim* "two camps" (*BA* 1:51). There is, of course, no independent reason to believe that the name of Agamemnon's capital originally meant anything of the kind. But more to the point is Bernal's failure—or refusal—to notice that the ending *-ēnai/-ēnē* (< older *-ānai/-ānā*) is a recurring element in Greek place names. No credence can be attached to an analysis of "Mycenae" which separates the termination *-ēnai/-ēnē* from the corresponding *-ānai/-ānā* of names like *Messánā* "Messene" and *Kuránā* "Cyrene"—to say nothing of *Athênai* "Athens," which in view of its symbolic status in Bernal's narrative requires a discussion of its own.

Bernal's derivation of "Athens" and "Athena" (*Athênē* < *Athánā*; Myc. *a-ta-na*) from Eg. *Ht Nt* "Temple of (the goddess) Nēit" (*BA* 1:51ff.) is the showcase exhibit of the Revised Ancient Model, the etymology that gives meaning to the title *Black Athena*. It is also an excellent example with which to end our survey of Bernal's "name" etymologies, as it perfectly illustrates the deficiencies of his method. Morphologically, the derivation of "Athens" from *Ht Nt* is suspect for the same reason that the above explanation of "Mycenae" is suspect: it forces us to find separate ad hoc explanations for a recurring sequence (*-ānai/-ānā*) that is better explained as a unitary suffix. Phonetically, the only feature that the names *Athánā* and *Ht Nt* have in common is an *n* preceded by a *t(h)*. Even this agreement is deceptive, for while in Egyptian the *t* and the *n* are (Bernal's claims notwithstanding) in direct contact, in Greek the corresponding consonants are separated by an accented long vowel which is neither predicted nor explained.[16] On the semantic side, the *Athánā* : *Ḥt Nt* equation shows the customary lack of rigor. The simple fact is that the original meaning of "Athens" and "Athena" is unknown; "temple of Nēit" is no more likely, a priori, than "olive grove," "rocky crag," or countless other possible glosses. The most that Bernal can say in favor of comparing the two goddesses is that "in Antiquity, Athena was consistently identified with . . . Nēit" and that "both were virgin divinities of warfare, weaving and wisdom." The latter description is a highly misleading characterization of Nēit, whose association with weaving and wisdom was less conspicuous, as far as we can judge, than her role as patroness of the hunt and mother of the crocodile god Sobek (cf. Schott 1982, Bonnet 1952, 512ff).

This is not the place for a lengthy rebuttal of Bernal's case. The all-important fact is that under the rules of the game as laid down in *Black Athena*, any eye-catching or merely convenient etymological proposal is as good as any other. No principle is given for why we should take *Athánā* from *Ḥt Nt* rather than, say, from the Anatolian city name *Adana*, which is attested in exactly this form from the middle of the second millennium B.C.E. Nor—if goddesses are at a premium—is it obvious why we should not prefer to compare Athena with the Carthaginian (i.e., "Canaanite") deity Tanit, whose name, preceded by the Greek feminine article *hā* (< *sā*; later Attic *hē̦*), could easily (by Bernal's standards, at least) have given first Gk. **Hāthānā* and then, with the regular loss of *h-* before an aspirate, *Athánā*. The phonetic development **sā Thānā* > **Hāthāna* > *Athánā* suggests a still more lurid possibility. Augustine, as good a representative of "the Ancients" as Jerome (cf. *BA* 2:253), tells us that the pagan gods and goddesses of the Greeks and Romans were demons whose worship was dispelled with the adoption of Christianity. Under Bernal's logic, it would seem perfectly legitimate to contemplate a direct borrowing of "Athena" from a feminized variant of Hebr. *śāṭān* "Satan" (older spelling *Sathan*), via the phonetic stages **Sāt(h)ānā* > **Hāthānā* > *Athánā*. Responsible scholars will not be convinced by such linguistic sleight of hand, but the Great Deceiver would surely be amused.

Ordinary Words

The Egyptian and Semitic etymologies that Bernal proposes for ordinary Greek words are no more convincing than his etymologies of names. The fact that words, unlike names, have known meanings clearly cramps Bernal's style; it is harder for him—as it would be for anyone—to argue that a word which palpably means "sword" or "team of horses" originally meant "Mntw gives" or "moon" or "cottage cheese" than to make such arguments for names like *Rhadámanthus* or *Ió*. Nevertheless his quest for regular vocabulary items with "Afroasiatic" etymologies is pressed forward with unflagging energy. What his suggestions lack in semantic inventiveness they make up for in their complete disregard for established sound laws and patterns of word formation.

Some representative examples:

hárma "chariot," to which Bernal adds the inexplicable gloss "tackle," is stated to come from "the Semitic root √*ḥrm* (net)" (*BA* 1:60). There is nothing to be said for this proposal. Phonetically, it is falsified by the fact that the corresponding form, in the meaning "chariot wheel," is spelled *a-mo* in Mycenaean, pointing to a synchronic reading *árhmo*. The *h-* of Attic *hárma* is thus not original, as Bernal implicitly claims, but the result of a secondary "anticipation" of the *-h-* in a preform reconstructible as *árhma. Mycenaean *árhmo* and pre-Attic *árhma in turn go back to pre-Greek **ár-smn̥*, a well-formed action noun consisting of the root *ar-* "fit, join (together)" (cf. *ararískō* "I fit") and the common nominal suffix *-(s)m(e)n-*. Semantically, there is every reason to prefer this analysis to Bernal's: a Greek word meaning "chariot" or "chariot wheel" is far more easily referred a PIE form meaning "thing fitted together" than to a Semitic root meaning "net." Here as elsewhere, Bernal has attempted to impose a Semitic or Egyptian etymology on a Greek word whose form, inflection, and meaning are utterly unproblematic in IE terms.

deilós "pitiable, vile, cowardly" and *doûlos* "(born) slave"—Bernal's gloss "client" is simply wrong—are traced to a Canaanite *dāl* or *dal*, said to mean "dependent, reduced" or "poor" (*BA* 1:60). The internal Greek evidence, however, shows *deilós* and *doûlos* to be unrelated. *doûlos* appears in Mycenaean as *do-e-ro*, representing trisyllabic **do(h)elos* (< *doselos?)—a reading hard to reconcile with Bernal's alleged Semitic source, which presupposes a biliteral root *dl*. As for *deilós*, Bernal omits to mention the critical fact that the *d-* of this word "makes position" in Homer—that is, it behaves metrically not as a single consonant, but as a cluster **dw-*. The underlying stem was thus probably **dwey-lo-* or **dwey-elo-*, an adjectival derivative of the well-known PIE root **dwey-* "fear" (cf. Gk. *déos* "fright, dread" < *dwey-os). The original meaning of *deilós* must have been "fearful, cowering," from which the attested sense evolved.

kḗr (also *kár*), said to mean "soul," is compared with Eg. *k₃* "spirit, soul" (*BA* 2:262ff.). Despite Bernal's special pleading, however, the meaning of *kḗr* is not "soul" but "fate, doom, (violent) death, ruin," sometimes divinized as Doom in the singular and (the) Fates in the plural.[17] From a phonetic point of view the equation is hopeless: neither here nor elsewhere is there a shred of evidence to support Bernal's oft repeated claim that Eg. *₃* was sometimes borrowed as *r* in Greek. He is likewise unable to explain, and does not discuss, the relationship of the variants *kḗr* and *kár*, the dialectal distribution of which demonstrates that *kḗr* is *not* simply a phonetic variant of *kár* showing the normal Attic-Ionic change of -*ā*- to -*ē*-. Both vocalisms are easily accounted for under the standard assumption of a PIE "root noun" *$*kér$ (nom. sg.), *$*kr̥r-és$ (gen. sg.), literally "a cutting (off), a termination" (cf. *keírō* < *$*ker-yō$ "I cut"). Such a verbal noun—perfectly regular in PIE terms—would have yielded an early Greek paradigm *$*kér$, *$*kar-ós$, the "weak" stem of which (*$*kar-$) was taken as the point of departure for the creation of a new nom. sg. *kár* in some dialects.

basileús "king," a word with no good IE etymology, is derived by Bernal from an Egyptian phrase *pꜣ sr*, meaning "the official" (*BA* 1:62, 2:504ff.). This is a priori unlikely, as Eg. *p* is never represented by Gk. *b* in uncontroversial loan words, and the Egyptian article *pꜣ* combines with a following *s*- to give Gk. *ps*- in authentic Egyptian borrowings like *pságdān* "unguent" (< Eg. *pꜣ sgnn*; cf. above) and *pskhént* "royal headdress" (< Eg. *pꜣ shmty*). But the decisive objection to Bernal's etymology comes from the Mycenaean spelling *qa-si-re-u* (i.e., [gʷasiléus]), which shows that the *b*- of this word, like the -*b*- of *érebos* "darkness" and *Thêbai* "Thebes," goes back to a second-millennium labiovelar *gʷ*. In the first volume of *Black Athena* Bernal seems unaware of the existence of labiovelars; he finds "no phonetic difficulty" with the derivation of *basileús* from *pꜣ sr*. In the second volume, however, he takes up the case again, this time adding a lengthy excursus on the use of the signs *qa* and *qo* in Myceanaean (2:504ff.). There is no empirical support for his assertion that the PIE labiovelars had already "broken down" in Linear B, leaving *qa* and *qo* free to serve as specialized writings for the sounds *p*, *b*, and *ph* in foreign words. On the contrary, not a single instance is known in which the labiovelar signs are used to write a demonstrably old labial, or in which the labial signs are used to write a demonstrably old labiovelar.[18]

kûdos, which Bernal glosses as "divine glory," is said to come from the Semitic root *qdš* "sacred" (*BA* 1:60). But here again the deck has been stacked: there is nothing essentially "sacred" or "holy" about the Greek word, which simply means "renown." Morphological considerations make *kûdos* a very poor candidate for a loan word. In the first place, it is a neuter *s*-stem, and hence representative of a formal type to which very few borrowings belong. The final -*os*, moreover, is merely a formative suffix; the root proper is *kūd*-, which also appears, with no change of meaning, in the adjective *kūdrós* "glorious" and the compositional combining form *kūdi*- (cf. *kūdi-áneira* "in which men have glory"). Comparison with Sanskrit and other languages shows that the synchronically irregular alternation pattern *kûd-os* : *kūd-ró*- : *kūd-i*- results from the archaic set of PIE derivational rules known collectively as Caland's Law. Alternations of this type became obsolete so early in the history of Greek that word families which exhibit Caland behavior are virtually always direct inheritances from the parent language. Not surprisingly, *kûdos* has a perfectly good IE etymology: it is cognate with Old Church Slavonic *čudo* (gen. *čudese*) "wonder, marvel," also a neuter *s*-stem.

bōmós "altar" is referred by Bernal (*BA* 1:59), modifying Cuny (1910:161), to a Semitic form akin to Hebr. *bāmāh* "high place, (raised) altar." The semantic agreement between the Greek and Semitic forms, however, is misleading, for *bōmós* may also denote a base or platform, even a low one—anything, in fact, upon which something else stands. As such, it comes very close in meaning to *básis* "base" and *bêma* "platform," both of which are regularly formed action nouns ("a step") built to the verb *(é)bē* "went, walked, stepped." A parallel explanation is clearly indicated for *bōmós*, which transparently consists of the regular "*o*-grade" form of the root *bē-* (< *bā-*) followed by the well-established PIE nominalizing suffix **-mo-*. A comparable formation is seen in the noun *thōmós* "pile," a derivative of *thē-* "put, deposit." The Proto-Greek root was **gʷā-*, corresponding to Sanskrit *gā-* "go."

eteós "true, genuine," according to Bernal, comes from "*it m it* in Middle and Late Egyptian, literally 'barley in barley' . . . [or] 'really barley'" (*BA* 1:453 n. 16). It is not clear to us how he thinks the meaning "true" could conceivably have developed from "true barley," or why he believes that Greek *eteó-krīthos* "genuine, good barley" sheds any light on the question. What *is* clear is that *eteós* was originally **etewós* (cf. Mycenaean *e-te-wo-ke-re-we-i-jo* = later Gk. *Eteokleíos*), an adjective in *-o-* which presupposes an underlying "*u*-stem" **etu-/*etew-*. Related to *ete(w)ós* is the nearly synonymous *étumos* (i.e., **étu-mo-*) "genuine." The connection between the two words is significant because it shows that the stem **etu-/*etew-* must have existed in Greek at a time when the suffixes **-mo-* and **-o-* were still living and productive morphemes—that is, very early indeed, perhaps as early as late PIE itself. Bernal's statement that *eteós* "has no etymology" is thus extremely misleading; the morphological structure of the word virtually excludes the possibility of borrowing.[19]

Karuátides, properly a name secondarily used to refer to standing female statuary figures ("caryatids"), is said to mean "daughters of the city" and to go back to a "stem Kary(at)," which according to Bernal can be "plausibly explained in terms of the standard West Semitic word for town—*qrt* . . ." (*BA* 1:50). But this arbitrary assertion ignores the other Greek items with which *Karuátides* makes up a morphological class; cf., e.g., *Pulátides* "women of *Púlai*," *Spartátides* "women of *Spártā*," and more generally *aguiátides* "women of the neighborhood" (cf. *águia* "street"). In this light *Karuátides* can only mean "women of *Káruai*." A town by this name ("Caryae") is known to have existed in Laconia; it was a center of the worship of Artemis, whose priest-esses were called *Karuátides*. Note that the name *Káruai* itself has nothing to do with Bernal's "stem Kary(at)"; it means "nut trees," standing in the same relationship to *káruon* "nut" as, e.g., *elaía* "olive (tree)" to *élaion* "olive oil."

óphis "snake," for which Bernal favors the old pre-scientific derivation from Demotic Egyptian *ḥf*, has been known for more than a century to be an IE word with unimpeachable cognates in Indo-Iranian (Skt. *áhi-* "snake," Avestan *aži-*) and Armenian (*iž*). Morphological considerations—in this case the existence of the closely related word *ékhis* "viper"—again rule out the possibility of a loan word. The relationship between *óphis* and *ékhis* can only be explained on the assumption of a PIE "acrostatic" declensional pattern, in which a "strong" stem with *o*-grade of the root (*$h_1óg^wh$-i-*) was proper to some case forms (e.g., the nominative singular), whereas a "weak" stem with *e*-grade of the root (*$h_1ég^wh$-i-*) was proper to others (e.g., the genitive singular). Typical pre-Greek forms would thus have included the nom. sg. *$ók^wh$-i-s* and the gen. sg. *$ék^wh$-y-os*, in the latter of which the labiovelar *-k^wh-* would regularly have become delabialized to *-kh-* before *-y-*. The result was a paradigm with both *$ók^wh$-* (> later *oph-*) and *ekh-*; the inconvenient synchronic alternation was eliminated by the well-known process of "paradigm split," in which each variant was provided with a complete set of case forms and reconstituted as an independent word (cf. Eng. *shade* and *shadow*, both from Old English *sceadu*, gen. *sceadwes*). Bernal's crude "juxtaposition" of *óphis* and *ḥf* leaves *ékhis* entirely unaccounted for.

xénos/xeînos "foreign(er)" is said to derive from West Semitic *śn'* "hate, enemy" (*BA* 1:60, 2:369). This is semantically unsatisfactory, because a *xénos*, far from being an object of hatred, is fundamentally a "guest-friend"—a person from another city or country with whom one enjoys a warm and often generations-long family relationship in which the roles of guest and host are regularly exchanged. The later and more general uses of the word are likewise free of hostile connotations. On the phonological side, Bernal's etymology is inconsistent with the fact that the Proto-Greek form of *xénos* was **xénwos*, which is implicit in Ionic *xeînos* and directly attested in Mycenaean (e.g., *ke-se-nu-wo* = *Xénwōn* [personal name]) and in inscriptions from Corinth and Corcyra. The Mycenaean *"ke-se-ne"* quoted by Bernal in the meaning "stranger" does not exist. Nor is there any reason to believe that a Semitic *ś* would have been rendered into Greek as the cluster spelled by the letter *x* ([ks]); Bernal's talk of a "velarized sibilant" in this connection is unintelligible as it stands and seems to rest on a misunderstanding of what the phonetic term "velarization" really means.[20]

tīmá̄, tīmḗ "honor," according to Bernal, "probably comes from an Egyptian **dỉ m₃ʿ* attested in Demotic as *tym₃ʿ*, meaning (render true, justify)" (*BA* 1:61). As usual, there are both semantic and formal difficulties with the proposed equation. *tīmḗ* has no essential or demonstrable connection with either "truth" or "justification" anywhere in its range of values—especially not in Homer, where its meanings are "honor(s) accorded to gods and kings, perquisite held by virtue of royal status; reward, compensation." From a morphological point of view, Bernal's derivation ignores the fact that *tīmē* "honor" is patently connected with the verb *tíō* "I honor." To a disinterested observer this would seem merely to confirm the standard interpretation of **tīmā* as an action noun built to the root **tī-*, parallel, e.g., to *kōlúmē* "prevention" beside *kōlúō* "I prevent" (cf. Chantraine 1961, 148). Bernal implicitly rejects this analysis; we are not sure whether he would follow the logic of his own position and derive *tíō* directly from the Egyptian verb *dî* (older *rdî*), which outside the (purely hypothetical) phrase **dî mꜣꜥ* means simply "give." In any case, it should be noted that Gk. *tī-* can plausibly be compared, via the preform **kʷī-*, with the Sanskrit root *ci-/cāy-* "note, observe, respect."

xíphos "sword" is thought by Bernal to be a borrowing from Eg. *sft* (> Coptic *sēfe*) "sword" (*BA* 2:369ff.; cf. 1:61). The idea is an old one, and it is not impossible that *xíphos* is has indeed been borrowed into Greek from some other language. But the phonetic fit between the Greek and the Egyptian forms is very poor. On the Egyptian side, as pointed out by R. H. Pierce (1971:96 ff.), the *-ē-* of Coptic *sēfe* points to a Middle Egyptian stressed long vowel, whereas the *-i-* of *xíphos* is short. Bernal, who seems to have no use for such niceties when they fail to serve his purposes, decries Pierce's "extraordinary faith in the reconstruction of Ancient Egyptian vowels from Coptic" and tendentiously quotes an irrelevant passage from Gardiner (1957) as "the more usual view." He fails, however, to report Gardiner's true position on the reconstruction of Egyptian vocalism, namely, that "scholars have succeeded in determining from the Coptic the position and the *quantity* [italics ours] of the original vowels in a large number of words; but the quality is far less easily ascertainable" (1957, 28). On the Greek side, it is clear from the Mycenaean spelling *qi-si-pe-e* "two swords" that the Proto-Greek form of *xíphos* began with the cluster **kʷs-*, which is utterly incomprehensible as a reflex of Eg. *s-*. Bernal's solution is to sweep the Mycenaean form under the rug; to infer anything from the labiovelar, he says, is "a case of misplaced precision."

khílioi (dialectal *kheílioi, khéllioi*) "thousand" is said to be a borrowing from Eg. *ḫꜣ* (*BA* 2:484). The semantics, for once, are unexceptionable. The Greek dialect forms, however, point unequivocally to Proto-Greek **khéhliyo-* < **khésliyo-*, with nothing but an initial consonant in common—and that only after a fashion—with Bernal's Egyptian comparandum.[21] On the other hand, the correspondence is exact with Skt. *sa-hasríya-* "thousandfold" (*sa-* means "one"), which taken together with the prototype of the Greek forms establishes a PIE adjective **ǵheslíyo-*, itself a derivative of the noun **ǵheslo-* "thousand" (cf. Skt. *sa-hásram*, Avestan *ha-zaŋrəm*). The derivation of *khílioi*, etc., from PIE is absolutely straightforward—a point that requires emphasis in light of Bernal's report that P. Chantraine, the principal author of one of the standard Greek etymological dictionaries (see note 4), finds "many formal difficulties with this derivation." This is a misrepresentation. The discussion to which Bernal alludes (Chantraine, p. 1260), which was actually authored by J.-L. Perpillou, merely suggests—wrongly, in our opinion—that more than one analysis is available for this word *in IE terms*.

neós (dialectal *nēós*, *nāós*, *nāwós*, *naûos*) "temple" is connected by Bernal—correctly, as it happens—with the verb *naíō* "I dwell" (*BA* 1:60). He takes both from the Semitic root *nwh*, for which he provides no gloss; we presume he has in mind Hebr. *nåwåh* "dwell." This is phonologically impossible. The aorist of *naíō* is built on the stem *nas-sa-*, which shows that the present *naíō* itself must go back to pre-Gk. **nás-yō*, with a root **nas-* followed by the common present-forming suffix **-yo-*. *neós* is based on the same root **nas-*; here, however, the preform is reconstructible as a suffixed stem **nas-wó-* "habitation," which became the source, via independently motivated sound changes proper to the individual Greek dialects, of *nēós*, *nāwós* and the other attested forms. All that the Greek and Semitic words have in common is an initial **n-*; once again, an impressionistic resemblance vanishes when all the relevant facts and forms are taken into consideration. It should be emphasized that the objections to Bernal's etymology are in no way vitiated by the fact that *neós* and *naíō* happen to lack problem-free cognates in the other IE languages.

We end our list here. The examples just cited, for which dozens of others could easily be substituted, are in no way exceptional or atypical. There is a certain sameness to all of Bernal's etymologies. In each case, a Greek word is said to "come from" an Egyptian or Semitic expression to which it bears some real or fancied similarity of meaning and a vague, often extremely tenuous, phonetic resemblance. No effort is made to go beyond the realm of appearances; known and inferable facts about the history of individual forms are systematically ignored, misrepresented, or suppressed. Above all, there is a thoroughgoing contempt for phonetic consistency: vowels materialize and disappear on command, consonants mutate beyond recognition, and "exotic" phonemes like Eg. *ꜣ* become almost anything that Bernal finds "useful" (contrast the fortunes of Eg. *kꜣ* and *ḥꜣ*, said to give Gk. *kḗr* and *khílioi*, respectively). To be sure, an excuse is offered for the confusion; the inconsistencies that we observe in the treatment of foreign sounds, Bernal tells us, are due to differences in the date at which individual words were borrowed. But he makes no effort to substantiate this claim by arguing, for example, that Greek words which exhibit the "early" treatment of Eg. *ꜣ* also consistently show the "early," and never the "late" or "middle" treatment of the similarly variable sounds *ḥ*, *ꞽ* and *ṯ*. In fact, it is quite clear that no such regularities exist; the hypothesis of relatively early versus relatively late borrowing is simply another wild card, an untestable assumption whose only function is to generate a limitless supply of unsystematic and unverifiable etymologies.

We are reminded in this connection of a passage near the beginning of the first volume of *Black Athena*, where Bernal discusses the differences between a "constructive outside radical innovator," such as Michael Ventris, the decipherer of Linear B, and a "crank," such as Immanuel Velikovsky, the author of an earlier and very different "Revised Ancient Model" of Eastern Mediterranean history. Cranks, unlike constructive innovators, Bernal says, tend to "add new unknown and unknowable factors into their theories: lost continents, men from outer space, planetary collisions, etc." (*BA* 1:6). We agree, noting merely that what others do with lost continents Bernal accomplishes just as successfully—or unsuccessfully—with lost consonants.

CONCLUSION

Our judgment, then, is that Bernal's claim to have uncovered "hundreds" of viable Greek-Egyptian and Greek-Semitic etymologies is simply false. We doubt that he has discovered even one such etymology that is wholly new. Certainly there are Semitic and Egyptian borrowings in Greek, but they are, as standardly believed, relatively few in number and—with some conspicuous exceptions on the Semitic side—late in date. Indeed, if there is any positive linguistic result that can be said to follow from *Black Athena*, it is that most of the identifiable Semitic and Egyptian loan words in Greek have already been found, as Bernal's unremitting search for further examples has been so notably unproductive. All this amounts to a very strong argument against the Revised Ancient Model, which posits intimate and prolonged contacts of precisely the kind that ought to have been reflected in a large and transparent body of second-millennium loan words. In relation to Bernal's overall project, the linguistic evidence is worse than unhelpful.

Some readers will find this evaluation surprising. Is it really possible that a writer so obviously well-read as Bernal, so apparently proficient in a variety of difficult languages, and so clearly "on the right side" of a gamut of cultural issues can be as wrong as we say he is? The answer, unfortunately, is that where linguistic evidence is concerned it is possible to be very wrong indeed. Most educated nonspecialists—including classicists, archaeologists, and historians—are at best only dimly aware of how language can be used as a tool for investigating the past. For the general reader of a work like *Black Athena*, it is all too easy to fall into the trap of confusing the study of particular *languages* with the study of *linguistics*—of supposing that knowledge of an arcane language is the only prerequisite to speaking with authority on its history, or to making meaningful discoveries about its prehistoric contacts with other languages. This was the general view in the sixteenth, seventeenth, and eighteenth centuries—the Golden Age of the Ancient Model, in Bernal's telling—when scholars of leisure, well-versed in a variety of Western and Oriental languages, filled learned tomes with erudite nonsense deriving Chinese from Hebrew and Huron from Latin. It was the age, too, when Voltaire could with justice deliver his famous quip labeling etymology as a science in which the consonants counted for little and the vowels for nothing at all.

The reality is, however, that the development of comparative philology in the nineteenth century marked a genuine step forward in the fitful progress of human knowledge. The early Indo-Europeanists may have shared some of the prejudices of their time—so does Bernal, and so do we—but they were also great scholars, who with immense learning and prodigious energy created the discipline of historical linguistics. Thanks to their work and the work of their successors, we are now in possession of a vast store of information about the history of particular languages and about the principles governing language change in general. Much of this information is technical in character and of little interest to the general reader. But the methods of historical linguistics are easily accessible to any college student,[22] and specialized etymological dictionaries and historical grammars are available for most of the world's major language families. The days of word-association games are happily past.

It is only fitting, given Bernal's passion for "contextualizing" the scholarship of others, that we close with a few remarks in the same spirit. Etymologists à la Voltaire did not disappear with the advent of the comparative method, any more than would-be circle-squarers and angle-trisectors disappeared with the development of higher mathematics. Obscure volumes deriving (for example) Hungarian from Sumerian, or Classical Mayan from Greek, can be found in the bowels of any well-stocked university library. Often such works simply reflect the casual linguistic experiences of their authors, as in the case of a book entitled (in French) *Annamite* [= Vietnamese], *the Mother Tongue: the Common Origin of the Celtic, Semitic, Sudanese and Indochinese Races* (1892), by the French army general Henri Nicolas Frey. Frey went further; by 1905 his researches had progressed to the point where he was able to bring out a sequel: *The Prehistoric Egyptians Identified with the Annamites on the Evidence of the Hieroglyphic Inscriptions.* There is no methodological difference between works like these, written a century ago, and contemporary efforts like *America—Land of the Rising Sun* (D. R. Smithana 1990), which claims a Japanese origin for such indigenous American names as *Ontario, Alaska,* and *Eskimo* (the last said to be from Jap. *ashi kimo* "sea lion livers," i.e., eaters of fresh livers of seals). An especially conspicuous role in the crank linguistic literature is played by the Celts, whose popular reputation for "mystery" accounts for their pivotal position in the fantastic speculations of Barry Fell in *America, B.C.* (1976). The author, a former professor of marine biology at Harvard, finds pre-Christian "Celtic" texts from a variety of New World locations, the language of which combines an anachronistic mixture of Irish,

Scots Gaelic, and Welsh with a confused potpourri of Semitic and Egyptian.[23] Another work pervaded by an ill-informed Celtomania is *The White Goddess* (1948), subtitled "a historical grammar of poetic myth," by the well-known English poet Robert Graves. Unlike Bernal, Graves is only marginally interested in attacking the received view of the Greeks, but in his talent for generating unsound etymologies in support of bizarre hypotheses he is nearly Bernal's equal. It is among authors like these that we believe Bernal has earned his place in the history of scholarship. As far as "the linguistic evidence" goes, Black Athena is nothing more than a White Goddess with a different axe to grind.

NOTES

We would like to thank Anna Morpurgo Davies, Gérard Diffloth, Ives Goddard, Sheila Jasanoff, and James Weinstein for valuable help in the preparation of this article. All errors, unless specifically credited to others, are our own.

We follow the standard practice of using square brackets to represent phonetic transcriptions. The asterisk denotes a reconstructed form.

1. Rendsburg 1989, by a Semitist and avowed "dear friend" of Bernal, is at best a very partial exception to this statement.

2. Scholars who believe that the Anatolian languages split off from the rest of the family before Italic, Germanic, Greek, etc., began to diverge from each other often prefer the term "Indo-Hittite" to "Indo-European." Bernal follows this usage; we will retain the traditional "Indo-European" here.

3. The symbol $*h_1$ represents a PIE consonant—one of the so-called "laryngeals"—whose phonetic value is uncertain. There is reason to believe that it may have been [h].

4. Readers interested in verifying this for themselves may wish to compare Ernout-Meillet 1985 for Latin and Puhvel 1984- for Hittite. The standard Greek etymological dictionaries are Chantraine 1968–75 and Frisk 1955–72. Bernal seems not to know the latter work.

5. *athḗr*, like *patḗr* "father," but unlike most other nouns in *-ēr*, shows inner-paradigmatic stem variation ("ablaut"), with short *-ĕ-* in case forms like the acc. sg. (*athéra*). *pélōr*, like *húdōr* "water," belongs to the restricted class of nouns in *-ōr* that are neuter rather than masculine. *dipsáō* is one of the very few contract verbs in which the 3 sg. ends in *-êi* rather than *-âi*, *-eî*, or *-oî*—showing that the *-a-* of the precontracted forms was originally long.

6. C. H. Gordon's decipherments of Eteocretan and Linear A as Semitic (1962b, 1966) have found almost no acceptance outside his immediate circle; the same applies to his efforts to find Semitic inscriptions at various locations in the New World (see, e.g., C. H. Gordon 1982). Note that place names in *-(s)sos* (e.g., *Halikarnassós*, *Telmēssós*) are also found in Anatolia.

7. Where possible, Semitic forms are cited from the closely related Northwest

Semitic languages Hebrew, Phoenician, and Ugaritic. The vowels of Phoenician and Ugaritic are not normally expressed but can often be surmised from comparative and other evidence.

8. See Fournet 1989, on which the following discussion is based. Egyptian writing, like Phoenician and Ugaritic writing, is purely consonantal. Some information about the vowels of Middle and Late Egyptian can be inferred from the vowels of Coptic and from foreign transcriptions of Egyptian names; cf., e.g., Osing 1976.

9. The frequent use of the Greek voiceless aspirates (*ph*, *th*, *kh*) to represent the Semitic and Egyptian voiceless stops (*p*, *t*, *k*) suggests that the Semitic and Egyptian sounds may have had a slightly aspirated pronunciation.

10. Readers should be warned that in the discussion that follows we have not, in general, been able to check the accuracy of Bernal's glosses and transcriptions of Egyptian and Semitic forms. If the reliability of his Greek glosses is any guide (cf. especially note 15 below), such checking is badly needed.

11. It is thus the connection of *Thêbai* and *thîbis* that has no adequate basis in fact; *thîbis* itself could well be an Egyptian or Semitic word.

12. Useful light on the phonetics of Semitic and Egyptian is shed by the treatment of the numerous Semitic words and names that appear in Egyptian texts; cf. Hoch 1994.

13. Despite Bernal's handwaving, the lack of consistency in his Egyptian–Greek and Semitic–Greek phonetic correspondences cannot be explained away by invoking different dates of borrowing; cf. below.

14. The "late" treatment of Semitic **y-* is illustrated by the word *íaspis* "jasper," from an immediate source akin to Hebr. *yåšpēh*.

15. The second term is perhaps more likely to be connected with *haimós* "hedge" and/or *haimasiá* "wall" than with anything else, but the origin of this name is essentially unknown. If *Lakedaímōn* furnishes a good example of Bernal's opportunistic glossing practices, a still more egregious case can be seen in his discussion of the city name *Árgos*. "Strabo maintained," Bernal says, ". . . that *argos* in Greek meant 'flat land' . . . However, *argos* also signified 'speed' and 'dog' or 'wolf' . . . The core meaning of the word was 'brilliant' or 'silver'" (*BA* 1:76). Most of this is quite fanciful. The passage in Strabo to which Bernal refers (8.6.9) is ambiguous and uninformative. The underlying sense of the adjective *argós* was indeed "bright, flashing" (cf. *árguros* "silver")—a meaning which evolved into "swift" (not "speed") via the same figure of speech as in English *quick as a flash* and *Twinkletoes*. Bernal's gloss "dog" is presumably based on the fact that Odysseus had a hound Argos, whose name must originally have meant "Swiftie" or the like. The basis for the gloss "wolf" escapes us completely.

16. Bernal's arguments for reading the Egyptian name as **Anait*, with an initial vowel, are completely ad hoc. It is curious too that the final *-t* of the goddess's name, which was evidently perfectly audible in classical times, has left no trace in *Athánā/Athếnē*.

17. Cf. Lee 1960, 191 ff. It should be noted that the term *kērostasíā*, which plays an important part in Bernal's elaborate attempt to justify the gloss "soul," is a word of his own invention.

18. The (non-)exception that proves this rule is that when—and only when—an

early Greek word contained *two* labiovelars, one of them could be dissimilated to a labial which was then spelled with a labial-initial sign in Mycenaean. This has no bearing on the words treated by Bernal, which all had only one labiovelar. In any case, he seems not to take his own statement about the use of *qa* and *qo* in foreign words very seriously, for he disregards it in examples like *phásganon* "sword," allegedly from Semitic **píg* (*BA* 2:372) but spelled with *pa-* in Mycenaean, and *Poseidôn* "Poseidon," allegedly from mixed Egyptian/Semitic *p3(w) Sidôn* "he of Sidon" (*BA* 1:67) but spelled with *po-* in Mycenaean.

19. A possible IE etymology is given in Peters 1980, 185 n. 140.

20. "Velarization" refers to a retraction and raising of the back of the tongue, such as that which accompanies the "emphatic" consonants of Arabic (*s̱*, *t̠*, etc.).

21. The representation of Eg. *ḫ* by Gk. *kh* is independently documented in *pskhént* < *p3 shmty* (cf. above). Note, however, that Bernal's derivation of Gk. *l* from Eg. *3*—like his parallel claim for Gk. *r*—is unsupported by any reliable examples.

22. Probably the most widely used textbook of historical linguistics in the United States at the present time is Hock 1991. More elementary, but still serviceable as an introduction to the comparative method, is Arlotto 1971. Pedersen 1931 gives a dated but valuable and informative history of Indo-European studies in the nineteenth century; his account of the period is a useful corrective to Bernal's.

23. Purported ancient inscriptions in unknown or hard-to-read scripts—sometimes genuine, sometimes not—have long served as a lightning rod for fringe scholarship. For every good decipherment there are innumerable bad ones, many of which can be dismissed on linguistic grounds alone.

SCIENCE

BLACK ATHENA, AFROCENTRISM, AND THE HISTORY OF SCIENCE

Robert Palter

Martin Bernal's *Black Athena* and Afrocentrism have been much in the news in recent years. Out of scores of possible items which could be cited, consider just the following. The *New York Times*, which did not bother to review the first volume of *Black Athena*, featured a lead review of the second volume by an Oxford Egyptologist (Baines 1991). It was reported that Professor Leonard Jeffries, the controversial chairman of the Black Studies Department at the City University of New York, left a copy of *Black Athena* with former New York City mayor Edward Koch, after a debate between the two men on alleged Jewish complicity in the early slave trade (see Noel 1991). A leading news weekly featured a lengthy cover story on Afrocentrism including a two-page summary of *Black Athena* (*Newsweek*, "African Dreams," 23 September 1991). The American Anthropological Association held a symposium on *Black Athena* at its annual meeting in October 1991 in Chicago. A video film entitled *Black Athena: Did Europe Start in Africa?* was released in Great Britain and the United States (see *Black Athena* 1991 [Bandung File, Channel 4]).

In the spate of critical writings on the two published volumes of Bernal's *Black Athena* (two more are promised),[1] I have discovered almost nothing on the history of science. It is true that Bernal makes only scattered comments concerning science (all in the first volume), but the general drift of his views is clear enough, and, besides, he tells us in no uncertain terms just which historians of science he trusts (many of them self-styled Afrocentrists) and which ones he suspects of bias. More recently, in his contribution to a symposium on ancient science, Bernal has spelled out his claims concerning Egyptian science and its relation to Greek science.[2] There are really two claims, which can be—and are best—kept apart. First, he maintains that there were scientific elements in Egyptian medicine, mathematics, and astronomy long before there was any Greek science at all; second, he maintains that Egyptian medicine, mathematics, and astronomy critically influenced the corresponding Greek disciplines. (He also believes that Mesopotamian science influenced Greek science but takes this to be noncontroversial; in fact, as we shall see, some Afrocentrist scholars whom he enthusiastically cites seem to deny the very existence of significant Mesopotamian science.) It is these claims that I examine here.

A few remarks about method. Methodologically speaking, I engage Bernal and the Afrocentrists on their own ground, which is mostly that of old-fashioned intellectual history (or history of ideas), with its primary technique the explication of texts. Of newer historiographical approaches (e.g., G. E. R. Lloyd 1992; von Staden 1992) little will appear here, and I forbear speculating as to what such approaches might do for—or to—the interpretations of ancient science offered by Bernal and the Afrocentrists.

The texts to be explicated have several features worth noting. First of all, it is not always obvious just what constitutes a "scientific" text or a text containing "scientific" elements, but instead of attempting to decide in advance on a general answer to the question, it will be more helpful to take up the issue as it arises in connection with specific texts. It is also helpful to distinguish two different groups of scientific texts: the *primary* ones, which are those written in antiquity in Egyptian, Greek, Latin, Sumerian, or Akkadian (the two latter among the various languages of the ancient Mesopotamians); and the *secondary* ones, which are those referring to or commenting on the primary texts and written in Greek, Latin, Sanskrit, Persian, Arabic, Hebrew, and a long list of other languages, including prominently the European vernaculars. The especially important Greek, Latin, and Arabic scientific texts have, of course, been more or less continuously available and comprehensible since they were written, with some interruptions at particular times and places (as in the early Middle Ages in Western Europe, when Greek was not widely understood) and, of course, with all too frequent attrition and textual corruption. Egyptian, Sumerian, and Akkadian scientific texts, on the other hand, only became available and comprehensible to modern scholars in the late nineteenth century (and in some cases not until well into the twentieth).

The primary texts for ancient Greek science are relatively easy to come by, both in the original language and in modern translations; one need only recall the volumes of the Loeb Classical Library and, for English-speaking readers, Cohen and Drabkin's (1958) valuable collection of key texts in English. The situation is not nearly so favorable in ancient Egyptian science.

But help is perhaps soon on the way in the form of a set of source books edited by Marshall Clagett.[3]

It is sometimes necessary—and frequently tempting—to rely on secondary texts instead of primary ones, especially when, on some topic of interest, the primary texts are only sporadically extant or are difficult to interpret. (One might, for example, rely on textbooks, digests, or popularizations instead of direct reports of original scientific results.) This practice can have its dangers, for it sometimes happens that, as Otto Neugebauer explains, "ancient authors whom we constantly consult . . . can concur in statements which are demonstrably wrong" (1975, 2:609). Consider the following case, cited by Neugebauer himself. In 1888 a German scholar concluded that the Babylonian day began at sunrise and the Egyptian at sunset, on the basis of his thorough canvassing of all the Greek and Latin sources he could find (some eight or nine) (see Bilfinger 1888, 10–16). It was only after cuneiform tablets and Egyptian papyri were eventually deciphered that it was discovered that all the classical authors had it backwards! That a consensus in error among classical authors can be obtained on such a straightforward factual matter suggests we should exercise extreme caution when we rely solely on secondary texts.

Fortunately, scientific texts are in certain respects easier to interpret than literary, philosophical, or political texts, and for two reasons: scientific requirements of meaningfulness (such as the prevalence of literal over metaphorical meanings) and logical consistency tend to reduce ambiguities; and the occurrence in scientific texts of key numerical parameters (such as the length of the solar year or the value of π) and of distinctive technical procedures (whether mathematical or empirical) often make it relatively easy to trace the influence of earlier on later ones. Thus, the influence of Babylonian lunar theory on Hipparchus' lunar theory can be demonstrated beyond any doubt by the presence in the Greek theory of the characteristic Babylonian value for the length of the lunar month: in Neugebauer's words, "a mean synodic month of 29;31,50,8,20d[ays]"—where, by convention, the semicolon denotes the sexagesimal point and the commas separate sexagesimal places—"a value frequently attested in ancient and medieval astronomy and famous since Kugler's *Mondrechnung* [1900] as evidence for Babylonian influence on Greek astronomy" (in Leichty et al. 1988, 301).[4]

But influence-tracing also requires care. For example, consider an illustration from the history of medicine: an Egyptian medical papyrus and a much later Hippocratic treatise give much the same description of a procedure for treating a dislocated jaw (the Greek text is more detailed). The great Egyptologist J. H. Breasted concluded that the Greek medical text had clearly been influenced by the Egyptian medical text. But Henry Sigerist, the eminent medical historian, had his doubts; as there is really only one anatomically possible way to correct a dislocated jaw—the physician's thumbs inside the patient's mouth and the rest of his fingers under the patient's chin—all descriptions of a successful procedure will necessarily sound alike. Egyptians and Greeks may well have independently discovered the procedure (which is still used today).[5]

Let us now consider ancient Egyptian and ancient Greek astronomy, mathematics, and medicine. I believe the comparison between the respective Egyptian and Greek disciplines is rather straightforward for astronomy, more complex for mathematics, and distinctly difficult for medicine. I choose to begin with the easier cases.

ANCIENT ASTRONOMY

It is convenient to begin the study of ancient astronomy with the surviving text which is most complete and most detailed: Ptolemy's *Mathematical Composition*, more usually referred to by its Arabic name, *Almagest* (The Greatest).[6] This treatise, dating from approximately 150 C.E., is both the culmination of earlier developments in astronomy and the foundation on which rest all subsequent developments in the Greek-Indian-Syrian-Islamic-Jewish-Latin astronomical tradition. This tradition survived until at least 1609—the date of Kepler's *New Astronomy*, perhaps the last major astronomical treatise to be composed with no regard for the radically new source of astronomical data provided by the telescope, and the first such treatise to alter radically the physical assumptions and mathematical methods of traditional astronomy. Prolonged and careful analysis of this long astronomical tradition by scholars using modern historical methods has been under way for at least a couple of centuries, and by now it is abundantly clear that despite vast philosophical and other differences, all the major works in this tradition have in common a certain characteristic mathematical form. That form can be taken to define *mathematical astronomy*, and it consists of the following: (1) the systematic recording of astronomical data, where each such datum includes the angular position of some object in the sky as observed at a particular time; (2) the devising of general mathematical rules for computing future from past astronomical data, that is, for making astronomical predictions. An instance of the former of these is the tabulation, in Ptolemy's *Almagest*, of astronomical data for the sun, the moon, the five planets visible to the naked eye, and the fixed stars. An instance of the second is the formulation, in the *Almagest*, of geometrical (epicycle) models for the sun, moon, and planets. (The presence of the tables of data and of the geometrical models can be easily confirmed by even the mathematically unsophisticated reader with a mere glance at the pages of the *Almagest*; any edition in any language will do.)

What, then, of ancient Egyptian astronomy? Let me begin by quoting two summary evaluations, the first by Richard Parker, the second by Otto Neugebauer. (The two are joint editors of the fundamental edition of ancient Egyptian astronomical texts.)

> More than any other ancient people, the Egyptians seem to have occupied themselves with the reckoning of time. They were the first to come to an approximation of the true length of the natural year and to devise a calendar based on it. They were the first to divide the night and day into twelve hours each, and they were the first to make these hours equal. The story of these developments is at the same time the story of the Egyptians' astronomical knowledge, because to a very high degree Egyptian astronomy was the severely practical servant of Egyptian time-reckoning. (R. A. Parker 1978, 706)

> Among the enormous mass of Egyptian inscriptions and papyri from all periods of Egyptian independent history there has not been found a single record of astronomical observations. . . . What is today commonly referred to as "Egyptian astronomy" consists mainly of schematic arrangements for the division of the night into "hours" (accidentally of rather uneven lengths) by means of extremely crude observations of certain stars. (Neugebauer 1975, 2:560)

It is important to understand that despite perceptible differences in tone—Parker's positive, Neugebauer's negative—the two passages are saying substantially the same thing. Neugebauer, in particular, is using something close to the definition of mathematical astronomy that I outlined above. Whether one wants to call Egyptian observations of the stars "astronomy" or not is perhaps a mere matter of terminology. There does seem to be scholarly disagreement, however, on the quality of the observations: Neugebauer characterizes the Egyptian observations as "extremely crude," whereas a more recent historian refers to "the earliest records of this high level of observational astronomy . . . [which] date from about the twenty-first century B.C." (Locher 1983, 141).

More needs to be said about Otto Neugebauer (1899–1980) and his place in the scholarly study of the exact sciences in antiquity. For anyone with even a smattering of knowledge about this area of scholarship there can be no doubt that he is the greatest of all historians of ancient mathematics and astronomy. This presents a formidable intellectual obstacle to any scholar (such as Bernal) who wishes to challenge Neugebauer's view of the scientific achievements of the Egyptians. How such a scholar comes to terms with Neugebauer is a real test of that scholar's integrity and breadth of understanding. How, then, does Bernal cope with this "grand old man of the history of science . . .

whose name has almost tantric power among defenders of the *status quo*" (*BA* 1:276)? Sad to say, mostly by insult, innuendo, and misrepresentation. But of course Bernal's rhetoric is predicated—unwittingly, I am charitable enough to believe—on ignorance and superficial understanding.

To begin with, Bernal mistakenly thinks that "Neugebauer's range is astounding" (*BA* 1:276). The very opposite is the case: Neugebauer's range is very narrow, and he eschews with some disdain all biographical, sociological, and philosophical matters in his consideration of the history of the exact sciences.[7] But there *are* other interesting kinds of historical questions, such as whether mathematical astronomy was developed not by Egyptians but by Mesopotamians because only Mesopotamians, in their insecure geographical position, needed the security afforded by astrology (Hetherington 1987, 22). Bernal then proceeds to declare, perhaps as a sign of his own broad-mindedness, that Neugebauer "has been more broad-minded than most and, just as he has been prepared to concede the Islamic science behind Copernicus, he has demonstrated some significant Mesopotamian influences on Greek mathematics and astronomy" (*BA* 1:276). Apparently, Bernal is assuming that Neugebauer is disposed to be biased against *all* non-Europeans—so that Neugebauer is to be congratulated whenever he manages to "concede" some significant non-European accomplishment. But these insinuations are grotesquely out of place. Consider what Neugebauer says (in a publication known to Bernal; see his bibliography in *BA* 1) following his refutation of a misguided attempt to credit the ancient Babylonians with the discovery of the precession of the equinoxes some two and a half centuries before Hipparchus: "I do not have the slightest interest in questions of personal or national glory and . . . I see no special merit in restoring to Hipparchus the priority which he held before" (1950, 1).

What makes Bernal so sure that Neugebauer is biased is, of course, Neugebauer's evaluation of the astronomy and mathematics of the Egyptians. Specifically, he proceeds to attack Neugebauer for his "condescending and contemptuous attitude towards Egypt and Hermeticism" (*BA* 1:276). As evidence of that contempt Bernal cites only a few pages in Neugebauer's *Exact Sciences in Antiquity*. What do we find on those pages? Neugebauer begins by saying that "of all the civilizations of antiquity, the Egyptian seems to me to have been the most pleasant"; he then defends Egyptian culture against the frequently repeated claim that it was "static"; and finally he draws an analogy with the Middle Ages, when art and architecture flourished even though the sciences were at an "invariably low level" (1957, 71). This does not sound like contempt or condescension to me. Since he cites none of Neugebauer's comments on Hermeticism, one does not know exactly what Bernal has in mind here, but I will say this: it would be quite out of character for Neugebauer to have expressed contempt for *any* of the ancient sources or for *any* civilization as a whole.[8] Neugebauer reserves his contempt for modern commentators who make sweeping judgments about ancient science with no serious attempt to understand what they are talking about.

Bernal makes another charge against Neugebauer, that he "does not take on the Pyramid school. He simply denounces them" (*BA* 1:276). But Neugebauer *does* (without saying so) take on the Pyramid school, namely, in his proposal of an elementary procedure for accurately orienting a pyramid—a procedure that might very well have been used by the Egyptians, as it presupposes no advanced astronomical knowledge (which, of course, Neugebauer believes the Egyptians did not possess). Neugebauer's proposal requires only "the primitive experience of symmetry of shadows in the course of one day" (1980, 1)[9] and is surely more plausible than such extravagant ideas as one leading Afrocentrist's—Cheikh Anta Diop (1991, 282)—that the Egyptians used telescopes for orientation. It is true that Egypt was the preeminent center of glass making from earliest times, but I know of no evidence that lenses were ever ground there, and, in any case, Diop never explains how the telescopes could have been used for orientation purposes. (Further questions about the alleged incorporation of advanced mathematical knowledge in the structure of the pyramids is discussed below, under "Pyramidology.")

Let us return now to the Egyptians or, more precisely, to their knowledge of the heavens. Observational astronomy begins with the stars, for it is against the fixed starry background—especially in the vicinity of the zodiac—that all other heavenly phenomena must be located. But surviving Egyptian star maps cannot even be correlated with the actual constellations as we know them (or, better, as we know they appeared in ancient times). In Neugebauer's words: "The extreme inaccuracy of all aspects of Egyptian astronomy makes it impossible to identify any of its constellations, except for Sirius . . . , for Orion . . . , and for the seven stars of the Great Dipper" (1975, 2:561). There was little quantitative observational astronomy in Egypt; and without quantitative data there can scarcely have been computational schemes to utilize such data; thus it comes as no surprise that no Egyptian texts contain astronomical computations concerning, say, the movements of the planets.[10] In short, *by the two basic criteria outlined above, there simply never was any Egyptian mathematical astronomy*—at least, not prior to the Late Egyptian Period (670–332 B.C.E.), when there was demonstrable influence of Babylonian and Greek mathematical astronomy.[11] And if it be objected that we are inappropriately using criteria from a later astronomical tradition to judge an earlier (Egyptian) astronomical tradition, the reply must be that by the criteria in question there is unmistakable evidence of a quite sophisticated mathematical astronomy in ancient Babylonia (a civilization exactly contemporary with that of ancient Egypt). In particular, Babylonian cuneiform tablets exhibiting tables of astronomical data are known from as early as 700 B.C.E. ("ephemerides texts"), and sets of arithmetical rules—referred to by Neugebauer as "zigzag functions"—for astronomical computations ("procedure texts") are known from as early as 500 B.C.E.[12]

Our initial judgment of Egyptian astronomy must stand. Once again, I quote Neugebauer: "In summary, from the almost three millennia of Egyptian writing, the only texts which have come down to us and deal with a numerical prediction of astronomical phenomena belong to the Hellenistic or Roman period. None of the earlier astronomical documents contains mathematical elements; they are crude observational schemes, partly religious, partly practical in purpose"; or, more succinctly, "Egypt has no place in a work on the history of mathematical astronomy" (1957, 91; 1975, 2:559).

It is interesting to note that in his haste to impugn Neugebauer's objectivity Bernal barely notices Neugebauer's downgrading of the scientific originality of the Greeks. Thus Neugebauer writes that "nowhere within ancient civilizations known to us did the sciences originate independently, neither in pre-Hellenic nor in early Greek civilization, in the ancient Near East, on the Iranian plateau, nor in pre-Arian or Arian India—with the sole exception of Mesopotamia, probably in the early second millennium" (1975, 2:559).[13] He does not mean to deny a very considerable measure of originality to Greek astronomers; he simply means they happened not to have been the first on the scene. But not all non-Greeks are equal: this was true in the 1880s, when, Bernal tells us, the Mesopotamians began to be celebrated as "a new type of less objectionable 'Semite'" (*BA* 1:364), and for some it remains true in the 1980s, when we hear from Diop that "compared to the Egyptians, the Mesopotamians were as mediocre as astronomers as they were as geometers" (1991, 283). Diop's mistake here is easy to diagnose: he simply ignores Babylonian astronomy altogether and restricts his attention to the Babylonian calendar (which, on questionable grounds, he finds far inferior to the Egyptian calendar).

The animus against Mesopotamia goes very deep; thus, in an interview some years ago, Diop had this to say about the origin of civilization: "Egypt was the first to emerge, all ideology put aside [*sic*]. It is not possible—it clashes with chronology—to establish a parallel between Mesopotamia and Egypt, even though the first Mesopotamian civilizations were black" (in Finch 1989, 366). So, not all blacks are equal either! Bernal is clearly uncomfortable with such views: he denies he is an Afrocentrist;[14] he asserts that "few scholars would contest the idea that it was in Mesopotamia that what we call 'civilization' was first assembled" (*BA* 1:12); and he is "very dubious of the utility of the concept 'race' in general because it is impossible to achieve any anatomical precision on the subject" (1:241). He does, however, want to maintain that Egyptian civilization was somehow "fundamentally" or "essentially" African (1:242, 437) and that "many of the most powerful Egyptian dynasties . . . were made up of pharaohs whom one can usefully call black" (1:242).

It is at this point that the implementation of Bernal's political goal (which requires the "useful" image of black, or "essentially" African, Egyptians) conflicts with—and, in my view, undermines—his scholarly goal, "to open up new areas of research" (*BA* 1:73). In the history of science, at least, much of the desiderated research has already been done and by outstanding scholars; but Bernal remains impervious to their findings, which he treats simply as a perpetuation of racist prejudices. In pursuit of political usefulness he sometimes recommends demonstrably incompetent works on the history of ancient science. One such is George G. M. James's *Stolen Legacy* (1954), whose thesis, as suggested by its subtitle, is that all of Greek philosophy and science came from Egypt. Bernal echoes James's thesis in his question as to "why Greek scientists and philosophers should not have learnt much of their science and philosophy in Egypt" (*BA* 1:438). But the most sweeping claims for ancient Egyptian contributions to astronomy, in particular, may be found in an essay by John Pappademos (1984), which it will be useful to examine in some detail.[15]

EGYPTIAN ASTRONOMY AND AFROCENTRISM

Let me begin with a few general remarks about Pappademos's sources (about a dozen in all) for his summary of Egyptian astronomy: all of these are secondary; there is not a single reference to an Egyptian or Greek astronomical text (though the secondary sources occasionally quote primary sources). The sources vary in reliability, and I shall say more about this as we proceed. Neugebauer is quoted twice, first as an example of a racist historian of science,[16] and then for the contrast he draws between the relatively well-preserved cuneiform tablets of Babylonia and the relatively ill-preserved papyri of Egypt (1975, 1:3). Pappademos presumes it is sheer prejudice on Neugebauer's part that prevents him from seeing that his admission of the unsatisfactory state of many Egyptian papyri undercuts his evaluation of Egyptian science, though why it should have been always precisely the *advanced* texts which were damaged or lost is not explained. (Later—see item 5 below—Pappademos introduces the hypothesis of secret, unpublished texts.) Pappademos never refers to any of Neugebauer's interpretations of Egyptian astronomical texts, nor does he mention that Neugebauer is the co-editor of the fundamental edition of those texts.

I now take up Pappademos's points in his order (my numbering):

1. *The Egyptian calendar*. By 3000 B.C.E., the Egyptians had invented "the 365-day calendar, based on astronomical observations," which was "Mankind's first scientific measurement of time" (1984, 96). The question is what

is to be understood by "scientific." Pappademos's single reference explicitly rejects the idea that the Egyptian calendar was based on some sort of advanced astronomy: "The year of 365 days, the best of all ancient calendars, would not then have been the result of Egypt's superiority in astronomy, but of observations of the yearly inundations. Hence the very idea of a precise astronomical science from the third millennium onwards must be rejected" (Vercoutter 1963, 35–36).[17]

One point requires clarification, because it is so frequently misunderstood. What made the Egyptian calendar not only the longest-lasting in human history (astronomers as late as Copernicus in the sixteenth century continued to use it) but also, in Neugebauer's words (1957, 81), "the only intelligent calendar which ever existed in human history"?[18] To begin with, it must be understood that the Egyptian civil calendar had twelve months of thirty days each, with five extra days added at the end of the year. The new year was at first associated with the so-called heliacal rising of the prominent star Sothis (Sirius), a choice apparently suggested by the Egyptians' observation that the Nile began its annual rise on about that date. The actual beginning of the new year, however, came after 365 days had passed regardless of whether Sothis had risen or not. This had the consequence that during the course of many years the seasons would "wander" from month to month because of the one-quarter of a day unaccounted for: the actual length of the tropical year (from, say, one summer solstice to the next) is $365\frac{1}{4}$ days. On the other hand, long-range time keeping was much easier than with a lunar-based calendar (such as the Greek or Babylonian), where it is a real problem to determine the number of days between dates many years apart. So we have the (only apparent) paradox that a calendar which originated from purely practical (probably administrative and financial) considerations turned out to be just what astronomers needed. It should be noted also that the Egyptians supplemented the civil calendar we have been considering with a lunar calendar for agricultural and liturgical purposes.[19]

2. *Instruments for astronomical measurement.* To measure time the Egyptians developed instruments based on the length of shadows cast by the sun, as well as water clocks, and the *merkhet* for nocturnal observation. This last instrument, Pappademos tells us, was used to determine "stellar azimuths" (1984, 96). Once again, his source describes the construction and operation of the *merkhet*:

> The *merkhet* was the rib of a palm leaf, split at its widest point. The slot was held in front of the eye, and the observer looked through it at a lead weight suspended from a straight-edge held horizontally by an assistant. . . . The two observers would face each other along a north-south line, and determine the precise hour from the transit of a given star directly over . . . parts

of the assistant's body. The results were checked against existing diagrams, ruled into squares and depicting a man surrounded by stars. (Vercoutter 1963, 39)

There is no mention of *angle measurement* at all, so stellar azimuths—at least in the usual sense—seem out of the question.[20] About all these instruments Vercoutter remarks on "how poor the Egyptians' standard of accuracy was, and with how little they were satisfied—doubtless one of the reasons why their astronomy made so little progress" (1963, 42).

3. *Precise alignment of temples and pyramids from astronomical observations.* Here (1984, 96) Pappademos refers only to an essay by E. C. Krupp (1977), which opens by referring to "the pyramids [which] have been particularly abused by ranks of enthusiastic interpreters" (203) and goes on to assert that the "very accurate alignments [of the Great Pyramid at Giza, dating from the reign of the Pharaoh Khufu (Cheops)] imply that the Egyptians were able to make precise astronomical measurements and put them to use in the orientation of at least some of their monumental architecture" (Krupp 1977, 233). The trouble is, however, that Krupp has no idea how the alignment of the pyramid was accomplished. As we have already seen, Neugebauer (1980) has proposed a simple method of alignment, requiring no advanced astronomical knowledge, which might have been used by the Egyptians. Krupp, in 1977, could not have known of Neugebauer's proposal but Pappademos should have at least mentioned it.

4. *Knowledge of stellar constellations.* Pappademos says the Egyptians knew "at least 43 constellations" (1984, 96), citing a distinguished historian of Greek mathematics and astronomy, Thomas Heath (1932, xv). But Heath gives no reference, and one must wonder if he had any direct contact with the relevant Egyptian texts, for his expertise was in ancient Greek and he was writing prior to the publication of Neugebauer and Parker's edition of those texts in the 1960s. It is true that stellar constellations were often represented on coffin lids (dating from 2100 to 1800 B.C.E.)—in an entirely nonastronomical context, of course—and, depending upon the strength of one's imagination, one can, no doubt, recognize some familiar constellations.[21] Later on (1500–1000 B.C.E.), there are painted tomb ceilings depicting the sky. Neugebauer, who studied such ceilings, concludes that "artistic principles determined the arrangement of astronomical ceiling decorations. Thus it is a hopeless task to try to find, on the sky, groups of stars whose arrangement might have been the same as the depicted constellations seem to require. Astronomical accuracy was nowhere seriously attempted in these documents" (1957, 89).

5. *The existence of astronomical texts which have not survived.* This is the old story of an alleged body of esoteric lore, deliberately withheld from widespread communication by Egyptian priests and perhaps never even committed to

writing, but containing more advanced astronomical knowledge than anything in surviving texts. But one can only wonder why such astronomical
lore would have been so thoroughly concealed when other forms of esoteric
knowledge, such as Egyptian magic spells for use in the Nether World, were
reproduced over and over again. As Neugebauer puts it: "It would be absurd
to think that secrecy was effective alone for the exact sciences: not a line has
ever been committed to writing and the non-secret sources never contain a
hint which implies underlying secret knowledge. Obviously the assumption
of secret scientific knowledge has no basis whatever" (1975, 2:566).

There are, of course, numerous writers in ancient and later times who
attest to the vast knowledge of the Egyptians in all disciplines, but in astronomy the silence of Ptolemy on significant Egyptian contributions (unlike his
numerous allusions to the Babylonians) has got to be deafening.[22] Among the
ancient writers who refer to Egyptian astronomy is Clement of Alexandria
(second century C.E.), and Pappademos (1984, 97) cites his list of the titles of
four "Hermetic Books" on astronomical phenomena. Pappademos's source
is van der Waerden (1974, 38), who supplies the additional information that
certain Egyptian priests were supposed to have memorized those texts and
recited them during a ritualistic procession. Now, if Pappademos had followed up van der Waerden's source in a monograph by Neugebauer (1942b),
he would have found a subtle analysis of what can be inferred about the dates
of the four books and their likely contents. Neugebauer's conclusion is that
the texts of the books were probably "of old-Egyptian origin" and probably contained "purely mythological" material and no theoretical astronomy
at all (1942b, 239). Somewhat surprisingly, van der Waerden never mentions
Neugebauer's conclusion but instead proceeds, rather tentatively, to identify
three of the books (entitled, respectively, *Syzygies and Phases of the Sun and Moon*,
The Disposition of the Fixed Stars and Stellar Phenomena, and *Risings*) with genuine
Egyptian astronomical texts but of the Hellenistic or Roman period. So, it
turns out, no more than Neugebauer does van der Waerden wish to lend
credence to the idea of a truly indigenous mathematical astronomy in Egypt.

6. *Tables of star culminations and risings*. Pappademos's sources here (1984, 100
nn. 51, 56) are two of those already cited, Sarton (see note 20) and van der
Waerden. One of the four books just discussed above, *Risings*, must have
contained dates, van der Waerden believes, for the annual risings of stars.
Texts of this kind are known from Hellenistic Egypt but also from Greece
and Babylonia, so the question is whether a book like *Risings* might date
from the period *prior* to Alexander's conquest of Egypt. Van der Waerden
quotes the geographer Strabo (first century B.C.E.) to the effect that in the
fifth and fourth centuries B.C.E. the Egyptians taught the Greeks about such
star risings; and, adds van der Waerden, "I feel we can accept this statement,
because it accords well with what we know from other sources" (1974, 39).

Tables of star risings, of course, do not constitute mathematical astronomy in Neugebauer's sense (or in the sense I defined at the outset).

7. *Planetary astronomy.* Pappademos says that the Egyptians knew not only about the five planets but also about the retrograde motion of Mars and the revolution of Mercury and Venus around the sun (1984, 97). As a source he once again cites Thomas Heath, who, once again, himself cites no sources at all. What do the surviving Egyptian sources tell us? According to Richard Parker, although "it is not until the ceiling of Senmut [ca. 1473 B.C.E.] that we have the planets depicted"—with Mars missing for some reason—"the planets were surely recognized and named before we have textual evidence to support such a statement" (1978, 719). As for the description of plane-tary movements by Egyptian astronomers, there are just two relevant texts known, both from Roman times (first and second centuries C.E.),[23] which confirms the absence of serious planetary astronomy in ancient Egypt. As for the famous—or, better, notorious—"Egyptian system," according to which Mercury and Venus revolve about the sun, Pappademos's source here is a popular history of astronomy, which ascribes to Cicero (first century B.C.E.) the attribution of this arrangement of the inner planets to the Egyptians (Abetti 1952, 21). In fact, not Cicero but a commentator on a text by Cicero, Macrobius (fourth century C.E.), makes the attribution in question. Further-more, no other ancient writer makes the same attribution, and Martianus Capella (early fifth century C.E.) refers to the heliocentric motion of the two inner planets without mentioning the Egyptians. Needless to say, there are no known Egyptian texts which set forth the "Egyptian system."

8. *Eclipse prediction.* Pappademos's source (1984, 100 n. 55) is again Thomas Heath, who cites Diodorus Siculus (first century B.C.E.), a historian infamous for his gross chronological errors and uncritical use of sources. It should be emphasized that Ptolemy, who pays particular attention to eclipse determi-nations by his predecessors, records no Egyptian examples; and indeed, as Neugebauer remarks, "ironically the only Egyptian eclipse record ever found concerns a solar eclipse of A.D. 601" (1975, 2:568).[24]

9. *Discovery of occultations of stars and planets by the dark side of the half-moon.* Pappademos's source (1984, 101 n. 58) is Thomas Heath quoting Aristotle, who says that such observations by the Babylonians and Egyptians "go back a great many years" (*De Caelo* 2.12 292a8, cited in Heath 1913, 220). The problem, as always, is the total absence of Egyptian texts containing records of the observations in question.

10. *Discovery of the sphericity of the Earth.* Here (1984, 101 nn. 60–61) Pappa-demos has misread his sources, the two books by Heath already referred to several times. In one of the books Heath says flatly that "there is . . . no evi-dence that [Pythagoras] borrowed the theory [of the sphericity of the Earth] from any non-Greek source" (1913, 48); in the other, he says only that a *different*

Pythagorean doctrine—the possession by the planets of a motion independent of the daily rotation—"was learnt from Babylon or Egypt" (1932, xxvi). Pappademos's allusion to the first measurement of the radius of the Earth by Eratosthenes (1984, 97), in third-century B.C.E. Alexandria, is irrelevant to the character of early Egyptian astronomy before heavy Greek influence.

11. *Discovery of the obliquity of the ecliptic.* Once again, Pappademos cites Heath, who cites the unreliable Diodorus Siculus for the story of how the Egyptian priests, by their own testimony, taught this idea to Oenopides of Chios (fifth century B.C.E.). But Pythagoras (sixth century B.C.E.) made the discovery, according to the historian Aetius (first or second century C.E.) (Heath 1913, 130–31), so Pappademos merely points out that "in view of the fact that both Pythagoras and Oenopides went to Egypt to study astronomy, it would seem only fair to give their Egyptian teachers at least some of the credit" (1984, 97). But why not be fair to the Babylonians? After all, according to another of Pappademos's sources, Pythagoras is likely to have studied in Babylonia as well as Egypt (Sarton 1952, 200). More importantly, we know from thoroughly reliable cuneiform texts that the Babylonians recognized the zodiac, that is, the obliquity of the solar path through the heavens, as early as 700 B.C.E. [25]

12. *Discovery of the precession of the equinoxes.* Pappademos's sole source here (1984, 97) is what I cannot resist calling the fantasies of Norman Lockyer ([1894] 1964), who claimed that the Egyptians realigned the axes of symmetry of their temples in accordance with the shifting positions of the stars due to the precession of the equinoxes (the slight wobbling of the Earth's axis of rotation with a period of about 26,000 years). Even such a sympathetic interpreter of Lockyer's ideas as Krupp concludes:

> Although it is possible that the temples were used as Lockyer described, both observationally and ceremonially, his system of alignments is difficult to confirm in detail. His arguments are incomplete, and until a comprehensive picture of practical Egyptian astronomy is available, in which the decan names can be identified with actual stars and which is fully documented by a consistent interpretation of all pertinent inscriptions, the case will remain unresolved. (1977, 222–23)

But to make such identifications of stars is just what Neugebauer suggests is impossible (see item 4 above).

Bernal takes Lockyer quite seriously, so something more needs to be said. I have no intention of entering into a debate concerning Lockyer's ideas, but I must respond to Bernal's attempt to lend respectability to such astrocosmic speculation by exaggerating the reputation of a historian of science who, in Bernal's words, underwent a "conversion to the belief in a higher ancient wisdom" (*BA* 1:275): Giorgio de Santillana. I apologize in advance for what might seem to some an overly harsh judgment of someone who, I am convinced, was an entirely honorable and generous man and a truly humane scholar.[26] But—Bernal forces me to say it—de Santillana was at best a minor figure, hardly "one of the greatest, if not the greatest, historians of Renaissance science" (*BA* 1:275). His provocative and passionately anticlerical book on Galileo's trial, *The Crime of Galileo* (1955), does not stand up very well in the light of recent research on Galileo's trial and its background, and his revision of a seventeenth-century English version of Galileo's *Dialogue Concerning the Two Chief World Systems* (1953) was already superseded when it appeared by the publication of Stillman Drake's superior translation in the same year. De Santillana spent the last ten years of his life collaborating with Hertha von Dechend, a specialist in comparative mythology, and their book *Hamlet's Mill* was published in 1969. (Bernal makes much of the fact that no university press would publish the work.) Among other things, the authors held that Hipparchus only rediscovered the precession of the equinoxes, which must have been known a thousand years earlier, and they claim that this astronomical phenomenon "was conceived as causing the rise and the cataclysmic fall of ages of the world" (1969, 59). More generally, they propose "a single astronomical origin in the Near East for the entire global corpus of mythologies, including those of the Americas" (L. White 1970, 541).[27]

13. *Proof that the angular diameters of sun and moon are unequal.* The proof was based on an analysis of annular eclipses of the sun, and Pappademos says that the man responsible was "Sosigenes (second century A.D.), the Egyptian astronomer who gave Europe the Julian calendar" (1984, 98). Now, first of all, Pappademos has confused two different individuals: the Sosigenes who was Julius Caesar's contemporary in the first century B.C.E. and who worked on the reform of the Roman civil calendar, and the Sosigenes of the second century C.E. who is supposed to have observed an annular eclipse (the only possible pertinent one occurred in 164 C.E.) (Neugebauer 1975, 1:104 n. 4). There is no reason that I am aware of for holding that *either* of these individuals was an Egyptian. But this question of how to characterize "Egyptians" is one to which we must return.

14. *Use of the clepsydra (water clock) to measure the angular diameter of the sun.* Pappademos's source (1984, 101 n. 67) is Heath (1913, 313), who cites the report of Cleomedes (fourth century C.E.) that the Egyptians had invented a method for measuring the angular diameter of the sun by means of a water clock. Heath does not bother to explain what this method was. Neugebauer does: the idea was to time the rising of the solar disk with a water clock. Neugebauer also explains how this "obviously fictitious story . . . is only a literary cliché" (several ancient authors beside Cleomedes mention this method); for "in order to establish the pretended result it would be necessary, e.g., to guarantee an accuracy of $\frac{1}{1,000}$ in the measurement of the daily outflow" (1975,

2:658). Certainly Egyptian clepsydrae were not up to such accuracy. Occasionally some elementary insight into the physics of a situation helps one to decide whether an alleged technique could ever have actually been used!

15. *Discovery of the conjunction of planets with each other and with the fixed stars.* Pappademos mentions Aristotle's *Meteorology* (fourth century B.C.E.), but his actual citation (1984, 99) is to von der Waerden. Here is what appears on the page he cites:

> As regards Babylonian observations, [Aristotle's] statement is completely borne out by the cuneiform texts. It is from his report that we now learn that the Egyptians too carried out and recorded long-term observations of conjunctions of planets with one another and with the moon and fixed stars. This kind of observational astronomy is quite distinct from the older Egyptian decan astronomy and is quite unintelligible in terms of the Egyptian tradition. We are compelled to assume a Babylonian influence. (van der Waerden 1974, 37)

The last sentence says it all.

16. *The heliocentric theory.* Here, after acknowledging that most historians of science credit Aristarchus of Samos (third century B.C.E.) with the discovery of heliocentricity, Pappademos sets forth a convoluted argument for the priority of the Egyptians. First, he suggests that the passage from Archimedes (ca. 287–212 B.C.E.) which attributes the heliocentric doctrine to Aristarchus does not state explicitly that Aristarchus invented the theory.[28] Also, we know that Aristarchus spent some time in Egypt, where his teacher, Strato of Lampsacus, had worked in the Alexandrian Museum. It is therefore "quite possible, in fact probable" (Pappademos 1984, 98) that Aristarchus first learned about heliocentricity in Egypt. This ignores several pertinent facts: first, that Archimedes was a younger contemporary of Aristarchus and hence would very likely have reliable information about Aristarchus' sources. Furthermore, ancient writers are unanimous in asserting Aristarchus' priority and—for once!—do not mention Egypt. And one of these writers, Plutarch (first–second century C.E.), does tell us of another heliocentrist: the Babylonian Seleucus (second century B.C.E.), who is said to have improved on Aristarchus' theory. (In fact, we have little idea of the details of either Aristarchus' or Seleucus' theory.)[29]

No matter, Pappademos has a clinching argument for Egyptian priority: Isaac Newton traced his heliocentric system (as well as his law of gravitation) back to Egypt, and, Pappademos adds, "we choose to follow Newton" (1984, 98). It is difficult to know how to respond to this final argument, which seems to amount to a mere argument from authority. Now, I myself bow to no one in my admiration for Newton's intellectual stature, but this scarcely means that I feel compelled to ascribe validity or even plausibility to everything he says, particularly on historical matters (not to mention alchemy or theology), where his well-known religious preconceptions and commitments are so strongly at work. Furthermore, by any reasonable historical standards, I find absolutely *nothing* in Newton's adoption of heliocentric astronomy which cannot be fully explained by his success at formulating a widely applicable system of mechanics based on the principle of inertia—and nobody has yet claimed, to my knowledge, that Newtonian mechanics were known to the ancient Egyptians! As for the alleged link between the law of gravitation and ancient Egypt, this will be discussed in the next section.

17. *Ptolemy's Almagest.* According to Pappademos, "the Bible of world astronomy for over a thousand years" was "written in Alexandria about 150 A.D. by an Alexandrian [Ptolemy], in all probability an Egyptian" (1984, 93).[30] He takes for granted that Egyptian means "black," referring at one point to "the Black civilization of the Nile Valley" (93). But Ptolemy is a Greek name, and Ptolemy wrote in Greek—though just what that implied in second-century C.E. Alexandria is not entirely clear. During the Ptolemaic period—which, referring to kings named Ptolemy, and not to our astronomer, had ended some two centuries earlier—there does not seem to have been much mixing of Hellenic and indigenous Egyptian culture, at least not within the elites of Alexandria.[31] To say that Ptolemy was an Egyptian means, I suppose, that he spoke and read Egyptian, which would imply that Egyptian astronomical writings were accessible to him. And Ptolemy does in fact refer to the Egyptian calendar and to Egyptian astrology, *but never to Egyptian astronomical observations or theories.* Whatever Ptolemy's "race," nationality, or ethnic identity, he was working squarely within a Babylonian-Greek astronomical tradition.

NEWTON AND EGYPT

Like Pappademos, Bernal wants to enlist Isaac Newton in the ranks of the Afrocentrists. Specifically, Bernal's claim is that Newton's derivation of the law of gravitation depended on appeals to *prisca sapientia*, "ancient wisdom," going back ultimately to the ancient Egyptians. It is certainly true that in preparation for a second edition of his *Principia* (eventually published in 1713) Newton drew up an extensive set of classical scholia designed to be attached to the succession of propositions (*Principia* book 3, IV–IX) which together formulate his law of gravitation. These scholia, consisting of quotations from more than a dozen authors (mostly ancient), were supposed to show that the Ancients had known the phenomena and laws of universal gravitation. Newton decided (for unknown reasons) not to publish the scholia but gave a copy to David Gregory, who published a summary which became widely available during the course of the eighteenth century. The most reasonable account of the significance of the classical scholia seems to me that of Paolo Casini (1984).[32] He begins by emphasizing how Newton's derivation of his law of gravitation was based squarely on the physics of Galileo, Descartes, and Kepler, and then comments: "It is by no means insignificant that the record of the Ancients and the reinterpretation of their 'fictions' should be super-added to a completed work, with a view to a second edition. The classical Scholia were destined to confer upon a perfectly modern 'reading' of the Book of Nature the anachronistic aura of a truth already inscribed in an ancient palimpsest" (1984, 15). An alternative to Casini's interpretation is that of Betty Jo Dobbs (1991, 193–212), who sees in Newton's appeal to classical authors a record of his (unsuccessful) search for the cause of gravitation. My critique of Bernal does not depend on the validity of either Casini's or Dobbs's interpretation.

Bernal is not satisfied to make the unexceptionable claim that Newton "certainly believed in an Egyptian *prisca sapientia*, which he saw it as his mission to retrieve" (*BA* 1:166) (though this "ancient wisdom" was not, for Newton, exclusively Egyptian). Because Newton was a "pivotal figure" (*BA* 1:169)—this, too, an unexceptionable point—Bernal wants to show that Newton actually *depended* on Egyptian ideas in his scientific work. But in fact Bernal simply repeats the undocumented maundering of Peter Tompkins, whose comprehension of Newton's work on gravitation is virtually nil.[33] Let me document this. What is at issue is an episode during the plague years, 1665–66, when the youthful Newton (he was twenty-three or twenty-four), back home on the family estate, made a calculation to test his theory that the lunar orbit could be explained by the gravitational attraction of the Earth. There are no fewer than three manuscript accounts of this episode, one by Newton himself and two by friends of his, all written many decades after the event. Newton himself says that he found his calculations "answer pretty nearly"; William Whiston's and Henry Pemberton's versions suggest that the result of those calculations was unsatisfactory because Newton's estimate for the radius of the Earth was seriously defective, and he therefore ceased working on the subject.[34] And in fact Newton does not seem to have taken up the subject again until he was compelled to by a dispute with Robert Hooke in 1679 (though an improved calculation based on a better estimate of the radius of the Earth may not have come until after Edmund Halley's famous visit to Cambridge in 1684). Why Newton stopped working on mechanics for so many years remains unclear; his most authoritative biographer thinks that Newton's intense study of alchemy and theology through the 1670s and early 1680s simply left no time for mechanics (Westfall 1982, 131).

All of the above details are unknown to, or at least unmentioned by, Tompkins and, following him, Bernal. What they wish to stress is "the Egyptian connection." So, Bernal tells us, Newton relied, at first, on the "figures of the

Hellenistic mathematician and astronomer Eratosthenes and his followers." When that did not work, Newton's "next assumption was that although Eratosthenes had lived in Egypt he had failed to preserve the ancient measurements accurately. Therefore Newton needed to retrieve the exact length of the original Egyptian cubit . . ." (*BA* 1:166). But all this is sheer invention, a kind of history by free association; there is no evidence that Newton at any time thought he was relying on ancient Egyptian measurements for his theory of gravitation. Newton's source for the radius of the Earth in 1665–66 was almost certainly Galileo's *Dialogue Concerning the Two Chief World Systems* in the English translation of Thomas Salusbury (1661). The evidence for this is to be found in a Newton manuscript of 1665–66 covered with calculations whose original data, including the radius of the Earth, are demonstrably drawn from the Galileo volume (see Herivel 1965, 183–91). *In a totally different context*, Newton became deeply interested in the plan and dimensions of Solomon's temple in Jerusalem, and this led him to study the length units, or cubits, of various ancient peoples, culminating in his composition of a *Dissertation upon the Sacred Cubit of the Jews and the Cubits of the several Nations* (first published in Thomas Birch's edition of *Miscellaneous Works of John Greaves*, in 1737; see Westfall 1980, 348 n. 45). This research on sacred history was carried out, it should be noted, during the 1670s, when Newton was totally unconcerned with physics.

Bernal concludes his discussion of Newton and Egyptian science by commenting that "it is a tragedy that Tompkins's brilliant and scholarly book has been stripped of its scholarly apparatus" (*BA* 1:469 n. 9). Where Bernal sees tragedy I see comedy—or tragicomedy, if I pause to reflect on all Bernal's readers who will be taken in by his confident rhetoric. It seems never to have occurred to Bernal that the absence of scholarly apparatus in Tompkins's account of Newton has a very simple explanation: no scholarly evidence exists to support that account.

ANCIENT MATHEMATICS

Misconceptions concerning ancient Egyptian mathematics abound, not least among specialists on ancient Egypt; here are two instructive examples:

> . . . the few mathematical texts available deal with elementary mathematics. If Egyptian knowledge did not exceed these notions, how could they build a several million ton pyramid with errors of less than an inch and a fraction of a degree. . . . We must, therefore, assume the existence of a science that still escapes us. (Ghalioungui 1973, 51)

> Pyramidiots . . . posit that the ancient Egyptians derived both an exact value for π and could calculate square roots. Recent studies of ancient

Egyptian mathematics have convincingly demonstrated that the ancient Egyptians could do neither. (Bianchi 1991, 84)

As a historian of Egyptian medicine, Ghalioungui really should know that building and orienting pyramids does not require any advanced mathematics;[35] and as the curator in the Egyptian Department of the Brooklyn Museum, Bianchi really should know that the Egyptians estimated π to within 0.6 percent of its actual value and that they could in fact calculate square roots of perfect squares (and possibly even estimate square roots for numbers that are not perfect squares). Let me now cite evaluations of Egyptian mathematics by two specialists in the subject:

> Looking at Egyptian mathematics as a whole, one cannot escape a feeling of disappointment at the general mathematical level, however much one may appreciate particular accomplishments. (van der Waerden 1961, 35)

> It is not proper or fitting that we of the twentieth century should compare too critically [Egyptian] methods with those of the Greeks or any other nation of later emergence, who, as it were, stood on their shoulders. We tend to forget that they were a people who had no plus, minus, multiplication, or division signs, no equals or square-root signs, no zero and no decimal point, no coinage, no indices, and no means of writing even the common fraction p/q; in fact, nothing even approaching a mathematical notation, nothing beyond a very complete knowledge of a twice-times table, and the ability to find two-thirds of any number, whether integral or fractional. With these restrictions they reached a relatively high level of mathematical sophistication. (Gillings 1982, 234)[36]

On the details of Egyptian mathematics, van der Waerden and Gillings do not significantly disagree (especially since, as we shall see later on, Gillings has brought van der Waerden around to his own interpretation of one of the high points of the Egyptian achievement). The difference in tone stems partly from the fact that van der Waerden is looking ahead to Greek mathematics (the quoted remark occurs immediately after a section heading which reads "What could the Greeks learn from the Egyptians?"), whereas Gillings is attempting to evaluate Egyptian mathematics in its own terms. But there is something else: because at about the time that Egyptian mathematics reached its highest level (Middle Kingdom, 2000–1800 B.C.E.), Babylonian mathematics had also reached its highest level (Old Babylonian, 1700 B.C.E.), it seems reasonable—that is, not misleadingly anachronistic—to compare these two mathematical traditions. Van der Waerden draws such comparisons, which are, most of the time but not invariably, in favor of the Babylonians; Gillings never discusses Babylonian mathematics at all. I return to this point later.

Our knowledge of Egyptian mathematics depends on a small number of texts (a dozen or so), all on papyrus except for one leather roll, and numerous ostraca (inscribed fragments of pottery); their present locations now span the globe (Cairo, London, Berlin, Moscow, Boston, Ann Arbor, Manchester). By far the most important texts are the so-called Moscow Mathematical Papyrus (MMP), now located in the Pushkin Museum of Fine Arts, and the so-called Rhind Mathematical Papyrus (RMP), now located in the British Museum.[37] The MMP dates from 1850 B.C.E.; the RMP dates from 1650 B.C.E. but is a copy of a papyrus two hundred years older.

What do these texts tell us about the character of Egyptian mathematics? First of all, there is the question of numerals, or number symbols, for representing numbers. The important point here is what the Egyptians did *not* do: they did not use a so-called place value notation, according to which the value of any number symbol depends on its position in a sequence of number symbols. The great economy of place value notation stems from the fact that a small set of symbols can serve to represent indefinitely large or indefinitely small numbers. (In our own decimal notation the symbol "2," for example, can represent the numbers two, twenty, two hundred, etc., but also two-tenths, two-hundredths, two-thousandths, etc., depending on where the "2" stands in a decimal sequence.) With perhaps a touch of pardonable exaggeration, Neugebauer characterizes place value notation as "undoubtedly one of the most fertile inventions of humanity" and adds that "it can be properly compared with the invention of the alphabet" (1957, 5). (Place value notation was invented by the Babylonians; their number system was sexagesimal—based on the number sixty—rather than, like ours, decimal). Even without place value notation, however, the Egyptians were able to perform on numbers the arithmetical operations of addition, subtraction, multiplication, and division, though this required the use of a host of special tables once fractions came into play. Some of the complications derived from the circumstance that the Egyptians admitted into their number system only unit fractions (except for two-thirds and occasionally three-quarters), that is, fractions with one as the numerator.[38] Thus, much of the material in the surviving sources consists precisely of tables designed to simplify computational techniques involving fractions. For example, the recto of the RMP contains, in addition to sixty mathematical problems, a table of the division of 2 by the odd numbers 3 to 101, the results being expressed as sums of unit fractions. (The verso contains twenty-three more problems.) Gillings goes so far as to say that Egyptian mathematics "was based on two very elementary concepts. The first was their complete knowledge of the *twice-times* table, and the second, their ability to find *two-thirds of any number*, whether integral or fractional. Upon these two very simple foundations the whole structure of Egyptian mathematics was erected" (1982, 3).

Our next question must be: what did the Egyptians compute? They were able to solve linear (first-degree) equations and certain simple quadratic (second-degree) equations; they were able to sum the first n terms of an arithmetic progression, and Gillings (1982, 166–70) finds evidence of the summation of geometric progressions.[39] As I have already mentioned, the Egyptians could calculate square roots of perfect squares: for example, in the Berlin Papyrus 6619 the square root of $1 + \frac{1}{2} + \frac{1}{16}$ is given as $1 + \frac{1}{4}$, and the square root of $6\frac{1}{4}$ is given as $2\frac{1}{2}$ (see Gillings, 216). The trouble is, the scribe does not show us how he obtained his result, which could have been done mentally or read off from a table of squares. Though no such tables have been preserved, Gillings constructs a set of tables which is consistent with all we know of Egyptian arithmetic. Furthermore, the use of such tables "to obtain good approximations to numbers not specifically listed" was also well within the capacities of Egyptian mathematicians, though only one such application is actually known (in a very late Greek papyrus).[40] All this may sound impressive enough for the first mathematicians in history, but, once again, Babylonian mathematicians of about the same period were even more impressive, with their ability to sum not just arithmetic and geometric progressions but also the series of the first ten squares,[41] and with their tables "of cubes and cube roots, of the sums of squares and cubes needed for the numerical solution of special types of cubic equations, of exponential functions, which were used for the computation of compound interest, etc." (Neugebauer 1957, 34).

But the Egyptians also computed areas and volumes, and here they surpassed the Babylonians. Areas of triangles, rectangles, and trapezoids were found by formulas still in use today. The more difficult problem of finding the area of a circle is addressed in RMP Problems 41–43, 48, and 50; in each of the problems the area is computed by the rule "Subtract from the diameter its one-ninth part, and square the remainder. This is its area" (Gillings 1982, 140; 1978, 696). Two questions arise. First, how good is this implicit approximation for π (defined as the ratio of the circumference to the diameter of a circle), which simple calculation shows to be $\frac{256}{81}$, or 3.16? Comparing with the known value of $\pi = 3.14$, the error turns out to be less than 0.6 percent. The Babylonians never obtained as good an approximation for π, usually settling for the value 3 (though there is evidence for $\pi = 3\frac{1}{8}$ in certain texts).[42]

The second question concerns how the Egyptians found their excellent approximation for π. Usually this question is ignored (perhaps because it is considered unanswerable) or answered with vague talk of graphical methods. Gillings, however, following the lead of an earlier scholar, Kurt Vogel, interprets RMP Problem 48 as providing an answer to this question.

Unlike the other four circle-squaring problems in the RMP, Problem 48 contains a diagram which replaces the more usual initial formulation of the problem. This diagram was interpreted by A. B. Chace, in the first English version of the RMP (1927), as a circle inscribed in a square. Gillings points

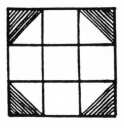

FIGURE I

out that on this assumption, the circle would be very badly drawn compared with the circles in Problems 41 and 50 (and the same scribe drew all three figures).[43] He proposes instead that the diagram in Problem 48 represents a (nonregular) octagon inscribed in a square (of length 9, hence area 81) in such a way that each side of the square is trisected by the vertices of the octagon (see figure 1). This results in four identical triangular corners, whose total area is easily seen to be equivalent to two-ninths of the area of the square, that is, $\frac{2}{9} \times 81 = 18$. Now, subtracting 18 from 81 gives 63 as an approximation for the area of the circle. But 63 is almost 64, which is 8 squared, in agreement with the standard Egyptian formula for the area of a circle.[44]

If Gillings's analysis of RMP Problem 48 is accepted, the Egyptians may be said to have worked out a geometrical argument for their circle-squaring formula. Whether the term "proof" should be used in this context strikes me as at least partly a terminological matter. As Gillings points out, we need not insist on Greek standards of logical rigor in judging Egyptian procedures. (And, I would add, if we insist on modern standards of logical rigor, we might find ourselves forced to deny that the Greeks themselves possessed mathematical proofs—which I consider a *reductio ad absurdum*.) In any case, I think we can conclude that if Gillings is correct, there are depths in Egyptian geometry which have sometimes gone unrecognized. What these depths certainly do *not* include is an understanding of the "irrationality" of the number π. Because this is often misunderstood, some further explanation is necessary.

To speak of the number π in the context of Egyptian mathematics means that Egyptian mathematicians, first of all, recognized the constancy of the ratio of the circumference to the diameter of a circle (independent of the size of the circle). That this recognition was nontrivial is underscored by the fact that we now know geometries in which it does not hold. (In the two varieties of non-Euclidean geometry—hyperbolic and elliptic—the ratio of the circumference to the diameter of a circle *is* a function of the size of the circle.) The Egyptians then proceeded to find a good approximation to the ratio in question, but they never even *approached* the question whether that ratio could be expressed as a ratio of integers, that is, as a rational number.

The first approach to the concept of irrational numbers was in the Pythagorean concept of the incommensurability of certain line segments (the side and the diagonal of a square). But the Greeks did not, of course, show that π is irrational. The irrationality of π was, in fact, only demonstrated in 1767 (by J. H. Lambert) and, more rigorously, in 1794 (by A.-M. Legendre). Mention of the irrationality of π is strictly anachronistic in the Egyptian context.

The Egyptians were also able to calculate volumes of certain solids: rectangular solids (length times width times height), cylinders (height times area of the circular base), and (square) frustums (which are square pyramids truncated by planes parallel to their bases). The (correct) solution to this last problem, which occurs as MMP 14 and is often considered the high point of Egyptian mathematics, is: volume $= h/3\ (a^2 + ab + b^2)$, where h is the height of the pyramid, a is the length of a side of the base, and b is the length of a side of the top. It seems reasonable to assume that the formula for the volume of a (square) pyramid must also have been known (though this is not attested in any known text) and that it was on the basis of the latter formula (volume $= \frac{1}{3}\ ha^2$) that the volume of the frustum was calculated; but we can only guess as to the nature of these calculations. An empirical method could have been used to measure directly the volume of a pyramidal container and of a rectangular box with the same base and height by filling them with sand or water. A more complex (but purely theoretical) method would have been to dissect the pyramid or frustum into component parts and then rearrange those parts into a rectangular solid. But there are many ways in which such a dissection can be effected, and so one can only speculate about the procedure that might have been used. (For some possibilities see Gillings 1982, 189–93).

Did any of the Egyptian results on volumes of solids, or the methods used to obtain such results, influence the Greek geometrical tradition? On the specific matter of the volume of a square pyramid, Archimedes tells us that Eudoxus of Cnidus (first half of the fourth century B.C.E.) was the first to prove the result.[45] Bernal doubts Archimedes' reliability on this point, suggesting that "here, as in some other instances, Archimedes was knowingly or unknowingly mistaken." And Bernal makes much of the time Eudoxus spent in Egypt, where, naturally, Bernal thinks he might have learned of the Egyptian formula for the volume of a pyramid.[46] But Eudoxus was a student of one of the most original Greek mathematicians of his time, Archytas of Tarentum (first half of the fourth century B.C.E.),[47] and twice visited Athens, where he was closely associated with Plato. Eudoxus was thus, it may be assumed, thoroughly steeped in the Greek mathematical and philosophical tradition, and his mathematical proofs must have been of the rigorous axiomatic sort characteristic of that tradition. It is difficult to exaggerate the difference between such proofs and *anything* found in Egyptian mathematics. Bernal reluctantly recognizes this difference but tries to limit its significance with his remark that "it would seem difficult to argue that before the second half of the fourth century B.C. any aspect of Greek 'science'—with the possible exception of axiomatic mathematics—was more advanced than that of Mesopotamia or Egypt" (1992e, 599). Some exception! In any case, given that the *first* half of the fourth century B.C.E. was the age of Archytas and Eudoxus, it would seem that Bernal's chronology is at least several decades off.

More important, Archytas had predecessors, who are usually identified as Pythagoreans. Were the Pythagoreans substantially indebted to the Egyptians? Bernal and most Afrocentrists certainly think so.[48] It is impossible, of course, to deal here in any depth with the vast and unwieldy "Pythagorean problem." One central aspect of that problem, though, is directly relevant to the alleged Pythagorean importation of Egyptian mathematics to Greece: namely, as stressed by Walter Burkert, that "in many cases late tradition gives the name of Pythagoras, where older tradition, dealing with the same topic, does not do so" ([1962] 1972, 10).[49] More specifically, Herodotus (ca. 484–420 B.C.E.) and Isocrates (436–338 B.C.E.) are the earliest writers to connect Pythagoras with Egypt, but neither connects Pythagoras with mathematics; the earliest writers to make the latter connection are the historians Hecataeus of Abdera (ca. 300 B.C.E.) and Anticlides (early third century B.C.E.). This leads Burkert to ask: "Was there a significant change in the image of Pythagoras between Isocrates and the epoch of Hecataeus of Abdera and Anticlides?" and to answer that the tradition of Pythagoras as a mathematician was apparently "manufactured" rather than "transmitted" during that period. (The motive for this manufacturing was, I take it, the intellectual aggrandizement of the semimythical founder of the Pythagorean sect; and this was certainly the motive of later neo-Pythagoreans and neo-Platonists— such as Iamblichus [ca. 250–325 C.E.] in his influential *Life of Pythagoras* and Proclus [410–485 C.E.] in his history of geometry—when they testified to the supreme intellectual prowess of Pythagoras.) Burkert goes on to give persuasive reasons for discounting other ancient testimony for Pythagoras' alleged mathematical interests and discoveries.[50] More positively, Burkert identifies a Greek mathematical tradition independent of Pythagoreanism—including such thinkers (in the sixth and fifth centuries B.C.E.) as Thales, Anaximander, Oenopides, and Hippocrates—and argues that "Greek mathematics did not emerge from the revelation of a Wise Man, and not in the secret precinct of a sect founded for the purpose, but in close connection with, the development of the rational Greek view of the world" ([1962] 1972, 426). Before dismissing Burkert out of hand as an unregenerate Hellenophile, it should be noted that his theme in a more recent book ([1984] 1992) is precisely the influence of Mesopotamian and Phoenician (but not to any great extent Egyptian) culture on Early Archaic Greece (750–650 B.C.E.).[51]

We come, finally, to the controversial MMP Problem 10. The big difficulty

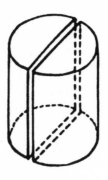

FIGURE 2

here is in reading the text because the scribe's handwriting is baffling at certain crucial points. The problem is clear: to find the area of the surface of a basket; what is unclear is the shape of the basket, and here the authorities disagree. T. E. Peet and van der Waerden (in his earlier interpretation) opt for a semicylinder; W. W. Struve, Gillings, van der Waerden (persuaded by Gillings), and T. G. H. James opt for a hemisphere; Neugebauer at first opted for a different shape and then decided (in a letter to Gillings) that the text was undecipherable (see Gillings 1982, 194). The solution proposed by the scribe is, in effect: area $= \pi/2 \, ab$ (where, in the statement of the problem, $a = b$). If the problem concerns the lateral area of a semicylinder (see figure 2), the formula would be correct, with a corresponding to, say, the diameter of the base and b to the height of the cylinder. But note that this interpretation would seem to presuppose, as Gillings acknowledges, that the formula for the circumference of a circle was known—"a considerable mathematical sophistication for those times [which], if true, would antedate the Greek Dinostratus [fourth century B.C.E.] by more than 1,400 years" (1982, 197–98).[52]

If, on the other hand, we take the basket in Problem 10 to be a hemisphere, (see figure 3), we must read the proposed solution as: area $= \pi/2 \, a^2$, where a is the diameter of the sphere. This would mean that "the scribe who derived the formula anticipated Archimedes by 1,500 years!" (Gillings 1982, 199–200). But Gillings does not wish to exaggerate this possible achievement of Egyptian mathematics, for his overall conclusion is as follows: "Let us, however, be perfectly clear about both the semicylinder and the hemisphere. In neither case has any *proof* . . . been established by the Egyptian scribe that is at all comparable with the clarity of the demonstrations of the Greeks Dinostratus and Archimedes. . . . Whether the scribes stumbled upon a lucky close approximation or whether their methods were the results of considered estimations over centuries of practical applications, we cannot of course tell" (200).

If not in geometry, did Egyptian mathematics significantly influence

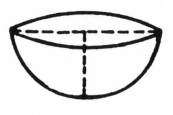

FIGURE 3

Greek achievement in other areas of mathematics? According to Neugebauer, "The role of Egyptian mathematics is probably best described as a retarding force upon numerical procedures" (1957, 80).[53] His point here is that an insistence on the (almost) exclusive use of unit fractions (instead of, say, the elegant sexagesimal fractions of the Babylonians) could only complicate the teaching and practice of arithmetic. And "though experience teaches one very soon to operate within this [Egyptian] framework, one will readily agree that the methods exclude any extensive astronomical computations comparable to the enormous numerical work which one finds incorporated in Greek and late Babylonian astronomy" (78). The *Almagest* is a striking example: Ptolemy does his computations with sexagesimal fractions but expresses his results in unit fractions, so that "sometimes the accuracy of the results is sacrificed in favor of a nicer appearance in the form of unit fractions" (72).

Because Neugebauer has been attacked for his alleged bias against the ancient Egyptians and his preference for the Mesopotamians,[54] his summary evaluation of Babylonian mathematics should be cited by way of comparison:

> one must not overestimate these achievements. . . . the contents of Babylonian mathematics remained profoundly elementary. . . . Babylonian mathematics never transgressed the threshold of pre-scientific thought. It is only in the last three centuries of Babylonian history and in the field of mathematical astronomy that the Babylonian mathematicians or astronomers reached parity with their Greek contemporaries. (1957, 48)

So we are back to comparisons with the Greeks—more specifically, with a definite type of Greek mathematics. If one understands what is involved in this latter type of mathematics, then one knows exactly what Neugebauer is saying, though one might conceivably want to phrase it a little differently (for example, without implying that "pre-scientific" and "scientific" have univocal and unchanging meanings throughout history and across cultures). These issues are worth patient and careful scholarly discussion; accusations of bias can only serve to muddy the waters.

I want now to discuss some of the more extravagant claims which have been made for ancient Egyptian mathematics. In a passing, almost casual remark, Diop attributes the discovery of the regular, or "Platonic," solids

to the Egyptians: "as the documents prove, the Egyptians had already proceeded, two thousand years before [Eudoxus and Plato], with the study [of]
the cube, the pyramid, etc., . . . the basic volumes improperly 'baptized'
Platonic bodies. . ." (1991, 237).[55] That "etc." conceals an allusion to the other
three Platonic solids (octahedron, dodecahedron, and icosahedron) which
even Diop seems unwilling to claim in so many words as discoveries of the
Egyptians of 2400 B.C.E. That the builders of the pyramids knew about the
cube and tetrahedron seems a reasonable supposition; that they also knew
about the octahedron seems a possibility; but that they knew anything about
the two remaining regular solids (dodecahedron and icosahedron) or had any
notion of regular solids in general strains belief. The discovery that there
are only five regular solids and the first studies of their geometrical properties are usually attributed to "the Pythagoreans" and, more particularly, to
Theaetetus (d. 369 B.C.E.). These Greek mathematicians could well have been
stimulated by an acquaintance with Egyptian buildings to study cubical and
pyramidal solids, but it is difficult to imagine them learning anything useful
in their analysis of regular solids from even the most sophisticated Egyptian
geometrical texts known to us (say, the work on truncated pyramids). Anyone
who thinks otherwise ought to try reading book 13 of Euclid's *Elements* (on
the construction of the regular solids).

Another piece of advanced mathematics that has been attributed to the
Egyptians is a knowledge of irrational numbers, or, at least, of one such
number, $\sqrt{2}$. This attribution has been encouraged by the now generally accepted view that the Babylonians knew about $\sqrt{2}$, so why not the Egyptians?
Thus, Bernal writes:

> there is now no doubt that Babylonian scholars were concerned with
> $\sqrt{2}$. . . . The standard [Egyptian] use in land measurement of the diagonal
> of a square of one cubit was the so-called double *remen*, that is to say $\sqrt{2}$
> times the cubit. Thus the irrational number par excellence was employed
> in Egypt from the beginning of the second millennium B.C. at the latest;
> whether or not its irrationality was proved in Euclidean fashion, its use
> provides circumstantial evidence that Egyptian scribes were aware of the
> incommensurability of the side and the diagonal. (1992e, 598–99)

But these confident proclamations betray deep misunderstanding. To begin
with the Babylonians, it is no accident that in Neugebauer's explanation of
the Babylonian concern with $\sqrt{2}$ no mention of irrationality or incommensurability occurs. Indeed he explicitly *denies* (1957, 35, 48) that the Babylonians
were capable of fully understanding the irrationality of $\sqrt{2}$, that is, the im-
possibility of expressing the quantity in question as a ratio of integers.[56] To
find an approximation for $\sqrt{2}$—which is all the Babylonians were doing—
is not necessarily to recognize its irrationality (any more than finding an ap-

proximation for π was to recognize its irrationality; see discussion above). The Babylonian approximation—which is actually written along one of the diagonals of a square depicted on a cuneiform tablet from the Old Babylonian period (ca. 1700 B.C.E.) in the Yale collection—is indeed very good: in decimal terms, 1.414213 (compared with the true value, to six places, of 1.414214) (Neugebauer 1957, 35).

To appreciate more fully the Babylonian approximation for $\sqrt{2}$, it may be seen as just one instance of a general interest in the problem of approximating certain recalcitrant numbers. Specifically, what we find in some Babylonian mathematical tables of reciprocals are expressions such as "7 does not divide," "11 does not divide," etc. The difficulty clearly arises in that division into 1 for the numbers in question leads to a nonterminating recurrent sexagesimal fraction. (Exactly the same thing occurs in the decimal system with such numbers as 3, 7, 9, and 11.) Neugebauer (1957, 33–34) calls this category of numbers—which was obviously recognized by the Babylonians—"irregular," and he explains how a certain Old Babylonian cuneiform tablet deals with approximations for such numbers.[57] Irregular numbers—which were conceptually accessible to Babylonian mathematicians—are, of course, utterly different from irrational numbers, which were not.

As for the Egyptians, their concern with $\sqrt{2}$ had nothing to do with the irrationality of numbers or the incommensurability of line segments. Bernal does not seem to understand that it is not so much a question of whether one can *prove* irrationality of numbers or incommensurability of line segments as of whether one has the conceptual means for *formulating* these concepts. All Bernal—and the scholars he follows—have to rely on is the fact that two prominent Egyptian length units were the cubit and the double *remen*, the latter being defined as the length of the diagonal in a one-cubit square. (The cubit was equal to about 20.6 inches, which made the double *remen* $\sqrt{2} \times 20.6 = 29.132$ inches). Gillings (1982, 208) thinks the double *remen* may (merely *may*) have been used in measuring land, as it provided a means for halving or doubling areas of the same shape. On this rather flimsy basis Lumpkin (1980, 187) has argued that the Egyptians knew that the sum of the squares of the sides of an isosceles right triangle was equal to the square of the hypotenuse.[58] What are far less probable, though, are Lumpkin's further suggestions that the Egyptians "knew other specific cases of the Pythagorean theorem" (1980, 186) and even "contributed to the development of this theorem" (1984, 109). This question of Pythagorean triangles, however, requires separate discussion.

It seems that the first definite association of the ancient Egyptians with Pythagorean triangles was made by the nineteenth-century historian of mathematics Moritz Cantor, as a way of explaining the Egyptians' ability to construct right angles in laying the foundations for temples. Knowing that these procedures were carried out by "rope-stretchers" using knotted ropes, Cantor asks us to "imagine" (the German verb is *sich denken*) the use of ropes with lengths respectively of 3, 4, and 5 units, which, of course, would form a right triangle (Cantor 1880, 1:56). But modern scholars have nearly unanimously rejected what was, after all, only a conjecture on Cantor's part (see, e.g. Gillings 1982, appendix 5).

There is still no definite understanding of just how Egyptian builders did construct right angles; the latest authoritative discussion of Egyptian building methods (D. Arnold 1991, 14–15) suggests two elementary techniques which would have been well within the geometrical capacities of the ancient Egyptians. One of the techniques (first proposed by Reginald Engelbach in 1930) employs a set square which is approximately rectangular. By aligning one leg of the set square along a straight line and then rotating the other leg through one hundred and eighty degrees, one can easily determine how far from true rectangularity the set square is and make the necessary correction. Arnold concludes that "we are not sure, however, if this method is accurate enough for the determination of the right angle of larger structures, such as pyramids, temples, and towns." The other technique employs measuring cords to draw arcs, but "modern surveyors even doubt that measuring cords could have been used for drawing an arc because of the elasticity of the ropes" (1991, 15).

On the question of how to achieve rectangularity by elementary means I have a small suggestion. Builders—at least in the United States, and I suspect elsewhere—regularly employ lengths of string in 3:4:5 ratios to construct right angles. (I rely on discussions with a few experienced builders and architects for this information.) This practice appears to be a matter of (probably oral) tradition rather than being based on, say, recollections of the Pythagorean theorem from high school geometry. Perhaps ancient Egyptian builders had determined by trial and error what they took to be a fixed relation between 3:4:5 triangles and right angles; they need not have known the Pythagorean theorem or any other set of integers satisfying the theorem. The difference, of course, between the contemporary and ancient cases is that the Pythagorean theorem *is* known to many people in present-day societies, and that this knowledge is presumably the proximate source for the builders' practice. (We take up 3:4:5 triangles again below, in connection with the dimensions of Egyptian pyramids.)

To return to the Babylonians for a moment: perhaps their greatest mathematical achievement was their discovery (ca. 1700 B.C.E.) not just of the Pythagorean theorem, but of a general procedure for finding so-called Pythagorean triples, that is, sets of integers such that the sum of the squares of two of them is equal to the square of the third. The now famous cuneiform tablet Plimpton 322, at Columbia University, in Neugebauer's interpretation, contains a list of no fewer than fifteen such triples—ranging in magnitude from {3, 4, 5} to {12,709, 13,500, 18,541}—together with "a strong indication that the fundamental formula for the construction of triples of Pythagorean numbers was known" (1957, 40). A late Egyptian papyrus, by the way, from around 300 B.C.E., contains three Pythagorean triples—{3, 4, 5} {5, 12, 13} {20, 21, 29}—showing, therefore, obvious Babylonian or Greek influence (see Gillings 1982, 690).

EUCLID, ARCHIMEDES, AND EGYPTIAN MATHEMATICS

It may be of some interest to compare the Egyptian procedure hypothesized by Gillings (see above) for finding the area of a circle (RMP 48) with the procedure of Euclid, in his *Elements* (12.2), for finding the area of a circle, and more especially with Archimedes' procedure, in his *On the Measurement of the Circle*, for estimating π. Euclid's proof that the area of a circle is proportional to the square of the diameter uses the so-called method of exhaustion (which probably goes back to Eudoxus).[59] Because the proof involves inscribing regular polygons within a circle, one might be tempted to see the influence of the octagon within a square as featured in RMP 48. Such an influence, I suppose, cannot be absolutely excluded but it should be noted that in the Egyptian problem the octagon is neither regular nor inscribed in the circle. If something like the geometrical procedure of RMP 48 was known to Euclid—or, better, to Eudoxus—that knowledge was utterly transformed in the formulation of the method of exhaustion.

In Archimedes' *On the Measurement of a Circle* we find first a proof that the area of a circle is equal to the area of a right triangle whose two sides enclosing the right angle are equal respectively to the radius and the circumference of the circle (Proposition 1). Then, in an elaborate proof involving an inscribed and a circumscribed polygon, each of 96 sides, Archimedes shows that "the ratio of the circumference of any circle to its diameter is less than $3\frac{1}{7}$ but greater than $3\frac{10}{71}$" (Proposition 3) (Heath 1912, 93)—which, in effect, says that π lies between 3.143 and 3.141 (within 0.06 percent of the true value). (Note that an immediate corollary of Propositions 1 and 3 is that the area of a circle = $\pi/4\,d^2$, where d is the diameter of the circle.)

It is interesting to observe that Archimedes' proof depends crucially on an approximation for $\sqrt{3}$ (already mentioned above), which is nowhere justified in the treatise itself. Archimedes obviously had worked out this approximation by a calculation which has not survived, and much scholarly effort has been expended in trying to find an approximational procedure which Archimedes could conceivably have used. We see that, just as in RMP Problem 48, Archimedes' proof is not fully rigorous and self-contained. It might even be said that the two "proofs" are located at different positions—though surely *widely* different positions — on a dimension of logical rigor. Did Archimedes know of the Problem 48 procedure? He is supposed to have spent some time in Alexandria, and he addressed some of his writings to friends in that city, so it is conceivable that he learned about the procedure from Alexandrian sources. But of what possible use could the procedure have been to him? It must be remembered that by Archimedes' time the method of exhaustion for finding areas and volumes of given figures had evolved into a powerful geometrical technique. (An elementary application by Euclid was mentioned above.) Archimedes used the method of exhaustion to prove Proposition 1 in *On the Measurement of a Circle*, and he most likely derived the critical approximation for $\sqrt{3}$ (required in the proof of Proposition 3) by the method of analysis and synthesis (Heath 1912, lxxx–lxxxiv).

Diop treats Archimedes especially harshly, accusing him, the greatest of Greek mathematicians, of deliberately and dishonestly concealing his borrowings from Egyptian predecessors. Of course, the charge would hardly have any force if Egyptian mathematics contained nothing worth borrowing! In his specific complaints against Archimedes, Diop often seems not to have fully understood what Archimedes was doing. Thus he says that Archimedes' treatise *On the Equilibrium of Planes or the Centres of Gravity of Planes* deals with the equilibrium of the lever, and he points out that Egyptians must have known the principle of the lever by 2600 B.C.E., when the earliest pyramids were being built (Diop 1991, 243). Even if it is granted that applying the principle of the lever in construction is the same as "knowing" that principle, it must be emphasized that Archimedes proves the principle of the lever in Propositions 6–7 of book 1 of his treatise; there follow the eight additional propositions of book 1 and the ten propositions of book 2. These later (and increasingly complex) propositions concern the center of gravity of a parabolic segment and are clearly of purely theoretical interest, remote indeed from the workings of mechanical levers.

In another instance of apparent misunderstanding, Diop states that in Archimedes' *Method*—an extraordinary account of a method of mathematical discovery, long thought lost and rediscovered only in 1905—the method "proceeds by weighing, first empirically . . . before undertaking a demonstration of a theoretical character" (1991, 231). There is, in fact, nothing in any sense "empirical" about Archimedes' procedure; rather, Archimedes uses results from his work on centers of gravity to "balance," in an entirely theoretical way, various well-defined geometrical segments or volumes. Diop's interpretation of Archimedes' method is perhaps designed to show that even such a great mathematician as Archimedes did sometimes appeal to empirical considerations, thereby deflecting to a certain extent the standard criticism of Egyptian science that it was merely empirical (a criticism which Diop hotly denies on numerous occasions).

Finally Archimedes is berated for not acknowledging that his favorite discovery (which he arranged to have carved on his tombstone) had already been discovered by Egyptian predecessors (Diop 1991, 237–42). Rather curiously, Diop does not actually state just what that momentous discovery was: the result (*On the Sphere and Cylinder* book 1, Proposition 14, Corollary) which states that, given a sphere inscribed in a cylinder, first, the volume of the cylinder is $\frac{3}{2}$ the volume of the sphere, and, second, the surface of the cylinder together with its bases is $\frac{3}{2}$ the surface of the sphere (see Heath 1912, 43). (There is, needless to say, nothing even remotely comparable in Egyptian mathematics.) Diop for some reason chooses to conflate the two main disputed interpretations of MMP 10 (discussed above) by pointing out that the formulas for the respective surfaces of a semicylinder on the one hand and of a hemisphere on the other become identical when the height of the cylinder is equal to the diameter of the sphere (1991, 242).[60] Now, the Egyptians had a formula for the volume of a cylinder but not, to our knowledge, for that of a sphere, so they could not, in any case, have known the first part of Archimedes' result (concerning volumes); as for the surfaces, although the Egyptians might (possibly) have had a formula *either* for the surface of a sphere *or* for that of a cylinder, there is surely no reason to assume they had *both* formulas. Furthermore, the formula for the surface of a cylinder which *may* be the proper interpretation of MMP 10 refers only to the curved surface of the cylinder exclusive of the bases, whereas Archimedes' result requires the areas of the bases to be added to that of the curved surface of the cylinder.

All this, of course, is to ignore the critical issue: *Archimedes' proof by the axiomatic method*, which makes this result—and indeed the entire corpus of his work—transcend virtually all previous mathematics. Diop's allegations about Archimedes' dishonesty (1991, 242) are, then, totally unjustified. For the record, I add that Diop at one point grudgingly concedes that "far be it from us to say that Archimedes or the Greeks in general, who came three thousand years after the Egyptians, did not go further than they in the different domains of knowledge" (246). He does not, however, bother to cite a single instance in which he thinks the Greeks did advance beyond the Egyptians.

PYRAMIDOLOGY

Some traditional and still cited arguments for the surpassing quality of Egyptian mathematics depend on evidence derived not from mathematical texts but from measurements of Egyptian buildings, especially temples and pyramids. The most common claims are for the incorporation of π and the "golden section" (or ϕ proportion), as well as Pythagorean triangles, in the external and internal structures of those buildings. Thus Bernal cites the measurements of the archaeologist J. P. Lauer as demonstrating that "one can find such relations as π, ϕ, the 'golden number' and Pythagoras' triangle from them" (*BA* 1:277).[61]

Let us first consider 3:4:5 triangles. G. Robins and C. C. D. Shute have recently proposed that the builders of the pyramids might very well have known the 3:4:5 triangle, which "may even have formed a convenient basis for set squares used by the stonemasons" (1985, 112).[62] Let me briefly outline their argument, leaving out some of the inessential details. They begin by emphasizing the modern researcher's difficulties in making measurements on pyramids, which have lost all or most of their original outer casing, leaving the surviving surfaces extremely rough. Hence to make any measurement requires resorting to "some form of averaging procedure . . . , involving the placing of markers at different levels on the pyramidal face" (108).[63] The particular parameter which concerns them is the inclination of the face of a pyramid—which we normally measure today by the ratio of vertical to horizontal distance in the appropriate right triangle, or, as we would say, by the tangent of the angle with the horizontal.[64] Among the pyramids they studied (some thirteen in all) the inclinations are found to cluster about two principal values: $\frac{14}{11}$ (for earlier pyramids of the Third, Fourth, and Fifth dynasties) and $\frac{4}{3}$ (for later pyramids of the Fourth, Fifth, and Sixth dynasties). Why did the slightly steeper inclination come to be the norm? Not for aesthetic reasons, say Robins and Shute, because the difference is barely perceptible. The explanation is that a pyramid with a $\frac{4}{3}$ inclination "could have been modeled on a 3:4:5 right-angled triangle" (112), which presumably would have simplified the construction process. This seems precisely in line with my own suggestion above. The important thing to note is that Robins and Shute (like me) see no reason to attribute any knowledge of other Pythagorean triples or of the Pythagorean theorem to the Egyptian builders.

We come now to the golden section (symbolized by the Greek letter ϕ) and π. The pyramidological claims here are usually focused on one particular pyramid: the Great Pyramid of the Pharaoh Khufu (Cheops) at Giza. The entire arcane subject seems to begin with a passage describing this pyramid in Herodotus (2.124), where, among other things, we learn the dimensions of the pyramid, which is said to be "square, each side of it eight hundred feet long, and the same in height" (trans. Grene 1987, 186). Herodotus' meaning seems perfectly straightforward, though the dimensions he gives are clearly mistaken. (The average length of the sides of the not-perfectly-square base is 755.79 feet; the height, which must be estimated because the capstone is missing, is somewhere around 481.4 feet.)[65] Pyramidologists, starting with John Taylor (1781–1864) and Edmé-François Jomard (1777–1862), have claimed that the passage in Herodotus must be emended so that it means something like the following: the square of the vertical height of the pyramid is equal to the area of a side.[66] With *s* standing for slant height, *h* for vertical height, and

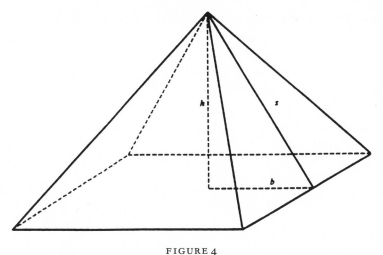

FIGURE 4

$2b$ for the base, one obtains the equation: $b^2 = s \times b$ (see figure 4). Now, using this equation together with the Pythagorean theorem for the triangle defined by slant height, vertical height, and base ($s^2 = b^2 + h^2$), one easily obtains the following quadratic equation for the ratio $r = s/b$: $r^2 - r - 1 = 0$. The positive solution is the golden ratio: $r = (1 + \sqrt{5})/2$, which is approximately 1.618. ϕ is defined as 1.618 . . . , or, sometimes, as 0.618. . . .

A further computation from the dimensions of the Great Pyramid yields a result involving π. One simply takes the ratio of the perimeter of the pyramid to its height: $4 \times \frac{755.79}{481.4} = 6.2799$, or 2π.

That both ϕ and π were intentionally realized in the construction of the Great Pyramid seems to be an article of faith for all pyramidologists.[67] Suppose we thus assume, for the moment, that the dimensions of the Great Pyramid do indeed bear out the above calculations for ϕ and π.[68] There is still a powerful general argument against the likelihood that the calculated relationships were deliberately introduced in the construction. (It must be emphasized that there are no texts which reveal the pyramid builders' intentions or which even suggest that such intentions ever entered an Egyptian builder's mind.) The point is that with no prior constraints on just what is to constitute a fit, almost any large set of measurements can be shown to contain "interesting" numerical relationships. Thus Gillings writes that "the dimensions of the Eiffel Tower or Boulder Dam could be made to produce equally vague and pretentious expressions of a mathematical connotation" (1982, 238). Along these lines, Martin Gardner has actually discovered a plethora of allusions to the number five in the dimensions of the Washington Monument. ("Fiveness" is critical in the speculations of many pyramidologists.) Citing the *World Almanac* as his source, he has come up with the following:

Its height is 555 feet and 5 inches. The base is 55 feet square, and the windows are set at 500 feet from the base. If the base is multiplied by 60 (or five times the number of months in a year) it gives 3,300, which is the exact weight of the capstone in pounds. Also, the word "Washington" has exactly ten letters (two times five). And if the weight of the capstone is multiplied by the base, the result is 181,500 — a fairly close approximation to the speed of light in miles per second. (1957, 179)

That ϕ—the golden section—is especially remarkable is often supposed to be demonstrated by its recurrence in a variety of contexts, particularly in the works and writings of Renaissance artists. Thus, writing about the Renaissance, Erwin Panofsky refers to "the 'golden section,' to which this period of Plato worship attached a quite extravagant importance" (1955, 91). In fact, Panofsky cites just two Renaissance treatises which discuss the golden section, and these, as James Elkins has pointed out (1991, 143), seem to be the only two. As for the presence of the golden section in the composition of Renaissance paintings, there is apparently not a single Renaissance treatise which refers to such a procedure, which implies, Elkins argues, that "whatever harmonious relations we discern in the works . . . is our own discovery" (143).

Elkins in fact has attempted to formulate general criteria for affirming the existence of "harmonious" geometrical relationships in any painted surface, and though his formulations are certainly not the last word on the subject, he has at least made a beginning. His criteria for a plausible fit between measured distances in a painting and some set of hypothesized numerical relations are of three kinds: (1) practical, (2) historical, and (3) probabilistic. The practical criterion refers to the artistic likelihood of the fit, that is, whether it corresponds to "a reasonable working procedure." The historical criterion refers to the historical likelihood of the fit, that is, whether it has historical parallels (which may be taken to include contemporary theoretical texts). The probabilistic criterion refers to the likelihood that the fit is merely fortuitous. Using these criteria, Elkins argues effectively that several of the most famous instances of "surface geometry" in Renaissance painting are based on nothing more than what may be termed a purely subjective will to believe. The whole of his analysis may usefully be applied to the case of the pyramids. And his final word is especially worth remembering in the ancient historical context: "we need to recall that precision in analysis is a modern trait. The Renaissance attitude was less precise, less formal and more flexible" (1991, 154).

Several historians of ancient medicine have made strong claims, first, for the impressive techniques and resources of ancient Egyptian medicine and, second, for its powerful influence on ancient Greek medicine.[69] As already emphasized in my opening remarks, the two types of claims are logically distinct, and evidence for the truth of the first claim is not automatically evidence for the truth of the second. Because it is often difficult to identify "scientific" elements in ancient medicine, we shall be largely concerned with the second claim. Also, it seems obvious that the very posing of the question of influence presupposes a *differentiation* between an indigenous Egyptian medical tradition and an indigenous Greek medical tradition. If (as some Afrocentrists sometimes seem to suggest) early Greek (Hippocratic) medicine is simply Egyptian medicine translated into Greek, then there is no point in even raising questions of influence.

Among the most significant claims for Egyptian medicine are the following. The Egyptians had separate hieroglyphic signs for—and hence recognized as separate parts of the body—"the pupil of the eye, the cornea, the heart, the trachea, the lungs, the vertebral column, the long bones, the brain, the meninges, the spinal cord, the ribs, the intestines, the spleen, the male and female genitals, the uterus, and, possibly, the kidney" (Newsome 1983, 128).[70] The central position of the heart in the cardiovascular system was understood, the pulse was used for diagnostic purposes, and symptoms of various heart ailments (such as angina pectoris, arrhythmia, and palpitations) were identified. Broken bones were set, dislocated jaws and shoulders reduced, tumors excised, abscesses drained, fresh meat applied to stop bleeding, and moldy bread used to prevent infection. As many as a thousand animal, plant, and mineral substances were prescribed as drugs. Tests for fertility and pregnancy in women were performed.[71] Finally, the Hippocratic doctrine of the four bodily humors (black bile, yellow bile, phlegm, and blood) is supposed to have originated in Egypt, with Pythagoras "a major link through which blacks influenced Hippocrates and Greek medicine" (Newsome 1983, 135).

For Greek medicine, things are much more complicated; no mere list of outstanding achievements could even begin to suffice for characterizing ancient Greek medicine. (For one thing, there are so many more medical texts which have survived.) How then shall we proceed? One possibility would be to try to do for medicine what was done earlier for astronomy: formulate a general characterization of the medical tradition. The trouble is, it is perfectly clear that no single, homogeneous medical tradition exists; and if, for example, a tradition of "scientific" or "rational" medicine could somehow be identified, it would quite arbitrarily exclude many nosological, diagnostic, and therapeutic considerations of central importance in the ancient historical context just because they involve folklorical, magical, or religious elements. Nor, in the nature of the case, could there be a single text (like Ptolemy's *Almagest*) which would satisfactorily define a medical tradition. Mention of Ptolemy, though, may remind one of his exact contemporary, Galen (129– ca. 210 C.E.): could not the writings of Galen, immensely voluminous as they are—and especially in view of their numerous citations of, and polemics against, other physicians—perhaps serve to define at least one meaning of "medicine" in the ancient period? But Galen defines his own medical approach and even many of his specific doctrines in terms of a Hippocratic tradition which he more or less reconstructs to his own image.[72] This throws us back on the "Hippocratic question": how to identify authentic works of Hippocrates (if any) and what criteria to use in identifying and dating works in the Hippocratic tradition (roughly, of the late fifth and early fourth centuries B.C.E.).

I shall attempt something far simpler: the location of some prominent areas of medical practice and its underlying theory in which it seems fruitful to inquire about the influence of Egyptian medicine on Greek medicine. And here we are in the fortunate position of possessing as a guide Heinrich von Staden's recent (1989) systematic and balanced analysis of the extent and nature of this influence during the Hellenistic period.[73] It is true, of course, that von Staden is concerned with the relationship between Egyptian and Alexandrian—rather than earlier—Greek medicine. From the Egyptian side this chronological discrepancy makes little difference because, as von Staden tells us, there is "a modern conjectural consensus that native Egyptian medical theory and practice did not change significantly between 1085 B.C. and 300 B.C. . . . or even the second century A.D." (1989, 4). Greek medicine, on the other hand, evolved in very significant ways; as an example, consider Greek medical knowledge of the liver. Von Staden explains how Hippocratic medicine had a clinical rather than an anatomical interest in the liver and even conceived of it as five-lobed (suggesting an observational reliance on the livers of animals). Herophilus gave the first accurate anatomical description of the organ; his contemporary Erasistratus was responsible for advances in knowledge of the physiology and pathology of the liver (1989, 162–64).

Let me begin with a few comments on the literature of ancient Egyptian and Greek medicine. For secondary sources on those topics the bibliography in von Staden's *Herophilus* is comprehensive and up to date. As for primary sources, six volumes of Hippocratic medical texts and one of Galen's medical texts are presently available in the Loeb Classical Library series (in the original Greek with parallel English translations); there is a convenient Pelican volume of Hippocratic writings in English, edited by Geoffrey Lloyd; and several additional medical treatises by Galen have recently been translated into English.[74] Egyptian medical texts are not so readily accessible. To begin with, it must be understood that we are restricting consideration to texts likely to be records of indigenous medicine (and therefore dating from prior to the great influx of Greek culture after Alexander's conquest). These are called "pharaonic" texts, and there are very few of them, just seven or eight principal papyri: Kahun (ca. 1900 B.C.E.); Edwin Smith (ca. 1650 B.C.E., but probably a copy of a text of ca. 2600); Ebers (1550 B.C.E.); Hearst (ca. 1550 B.C.E.); London (ca. 1350 B.C.E.); Carlsberg VIII (ca. 1314–1085 B.C.E.); Berlin (ca. 1250 B.C.E.); and Chester Beatty VI (ca. 1200 B.C.E.). All of these have been published in modern editions usually accompanied by translation into a modern European language; for those who can read German, as Guido Majno wittily remarks, "all Egyptian medicine comes incredibly packaged in the ten volumes of a German *Handbuch*, [Hermann] Grapow's *Grundriss der Medizin der alten Ägypter*, in which every single word is spelled out, catalogued, analyzed, and cross-filed in every possible way as the philologist sees it. This magnificent opus is, in a sense, the gravestone of Egyptian medicine: it implies that the sources are drying up" (1975, 73).[75]

Majno characterizes the formal aspects of Egyptian medical papyri as follows:

> Translated and printed, they would amount to less than 200 pages. Their text . . . consists of short paragraphs that are either prescriptions, spells against a given disease, or diagnoses, that is, short descriptions of a disease. There are roughly 1,200 such paragraphs, of which 900 are pre-scriptions—which amounts to saying that the Egyptian papyri read on the whole like catalogs. (1975, 73)

As for content, the three most important papyri are probably the Ebers, the Edwin Smith, and the Chester Beatty VI. Of these, the Ebers papyrus is the longest, and it seems to reflect accurately the overall nature of Egyptian medicine, namely, "a contradictory mixture of magic and of quite important elements of anatomy, pharmacology, and pathology" (Ghalioungui 1973, 38). The Edwin Smith papyrus consists of several unrelated sections, of which the most important deals with surgery in general and with a variety of specific surgical procedures; another lengthy section consists mostly of incantations. The Chester Beatty VI papyrus contains no fewer than forty-one remedies for diseases of the anus and a few for those of the breast, heart, and bladder, as well as many incantations.

From the standpoint of modern medicine, the surgical portion of the Edwin Smith papyrus is perhaps the most impressive of all the texts. In Sigerist's characterization, "in all probability [it] is a textbook, a manual of surgery written for the instruction of other surgeons" ([1951] 1967, 307), and it consists of forty-nine cases of injuries, wounds, fractures, dislocations, and tumors, described in a systematic order starting with the head and moving through the throat and neck, the clavicle, humerus, sternum and ribs, shoulders, and spinal column. (Sadly, the text breaks off, far from complete, in the middle of a sentence.) Each case has a title, a list of symptoms, an examination report, a diagnosis, a verdict (favorable, uncertain, unfavorable), and a course of treatment. Here is case 10 in its entirety:

Instructions concerning a wound in the top of his eyebrow.

If thou examinest a man having a wound in the top of his eyebrow, penetrating to the bone, thou shouldst palpate his wound, and draw together for him his gash with stitching.

Thou shouldst say concerning him: "One having a wound in his eyebrow. An ailment which I will treat."

Now after thou hast stitched it, thou shouldst bind fresh meat upon it the first day. If thou findst that the stitching of this wound is loose, thou shouldst draw it together for him with two *awy*-strips [of cloth], and thou shouldst treat it with grease and honey every day until he recovers.[76] (Majno 1975, 92)

And here, to illustrate the other side of Egyptian medicine, from the London Papyrus 37, is a spell "against blood" (bleeding? redness?):

Retreat, creature of Horus!
Retreat, creature of Seth!
Dispelled be the blood that cometh by Wnw [a city]
Dispelled be the red blood that cometh by *wnw* [= "by the hour"]
You know not the dam; retreat before Thoth!

This Charm will be Recited over a Red Pearl of Cornelian
Placed in the Anus of the Man or Woman
THIS IS TO DISPEL THE BLOOD.

(Majno 1975, 128)

Let us now turn to a slightly more detailed account of what the Greeks learned, and did not learn, from Egyptian medicine. We shall follow the lead of von Staden, who compares Egyptian and Alexandrian medicine on some seven different critical medical conceptions: the role of magic and religion; the vascular system; pathophysiology; wound care; pharmacology; ophthalmology; fertility and birth prognoses. Instead of attempting to summarize his already highly compressed discussion, I focus attention on issues where there appears to be serious disagreement among historians of ancient Egyptian medicine.

1. Was Egyptian medicine more magico-religious than Greek medicine? Von Staden's answer is cautiously affirmative, but he explicitly asserts that each of the two medical traditions in certain respects acknowledged the sig-

nificance of *both* empirico-rational and magico-religious elements. It is all a question of where and how the magico-religious elements were permitted to intervene, and here von Staden's judgment is that "Alexandrian and Hippocratic medicine appear to eschew the spells, incantations, and charms which dominate many—and intrude upon all—Pharaonic medical papyri" (1989, 8). The big exception would seem to be the Edwin Smith papyrus, which for one historian of Egyptian medicine "proved the existence of an objective and scientific medicine, devoid of theories and of magic, except in one case [S.9]" (Ghalioungui 1973, 38). But while there is just a single magico-religious "intrusion" in the surgical portion of the Edwin Smith papyrus, that portion is immediately followed by a long list of incantations.

The important point here, I believe, is that there is no reason to think that the ancient Egyptian physician saw any essential difference between these two types of medical treatment. In the case of Hippocratic and Alexandrian medicine, on the other hand, there are numerous texts in which the physician is admonished to eschew supernatural or magical explanations or cures for disease: for example, the Hippocratic treatise on epilepsy entitled *The Sacred Disease* opens with the words "I do not believe that the 'Sacred Disease' is any more divine or sacred than any other disease but, on the contrary, has specific characteristics and a definite cause" and goes on to denounce "those who first called this disease 'sacred' . . . [as] witch-doctors, faith-healers, quacks and charlatans" (ed. G. E. R. Lloyd 1978, 237). Von Staden also finds important support for his view in the fact that "in Greek society, priest and physician exercised their distinct functions in sharply different ways, even if they shared the same god; in Egypt many medical practitioners were also priests of the goddess Sekhmet, and all of them engaged in practices which Greek physicians would have thought fit, at best, for priests and 'enchanters' alone" (1989, 8–9). His conclusion is that "in this central respect there can, therefore, be no question of 'Egyptian influence' on Alexandrian medicine" (7).

2. It is generally accepted that "the *metw* dominated Ancient Egyptian medical thought" (Ghalioungui 1973, 57). The *metw*, or *mtw*, are vessels connecting the various organs and other parts of the body.[77] Emanating from the heart and reuniting at, or in the vicinity of, the anus, these vessels carry blood but also air, water, tears, urine, semen, and feces.[78] The fecal material, or something in it—the *whdw* ("rot")—could be absorbed by any of the vessels and thereby cause a great variety of diseases. In his monograph on the *whdw* Steuer writes: "According to my findings *whdw* is the technical expression adopted by a medical school of priest-physicians from a previously existing demoniac conception of *whdw* . . . in order to express the pyogenic activity of faeces within the blood-conveying *mtw*" (1948, 11). It seems not too extreme to say that the central pathological agent for Egyptian medicine is the *whdw*, and this is confirmed by the Egyptians' nearly obsessive concern with the

hygiene of the anus and the bowels.[79] The relevant medical material has been summarized as follows:

> The anus (and rectum) was given great importance in Egyptian physiology. . . . Some physicians, like Iri, specialised in it; the Chester Beatty VI papyrus is entirely devoted to its diseases, the Ebers papyrus contains 33 paragraphs dealing with it, and there are others in the Berlin . . . and Hearst papyri. . . . The descriptions concern piles, prolapse, pruritus, heaviness, heat and unidentified *benou*. Treatment consisted in oral medicaments, suppositories, retention enemata, medicated plugs and bandages, hot dressings. Drugs included carob, ricinus leaves, pine nuts; suppositories contained water melon, honey, white gum, rush nut, celery.[80] (Ghalioungui 1973, 124)

It should be noted, however, that this passage is relegated to a relatively inconspicuous paragraph in the ninth chapter of Ghalioungui's book, entitled simply "Special Subjects III. Varia." (Perhaps this explains why the summaries of Egyptian medicine by Newsome and Finch, cited above, never so much as mention the *whdw* or the vital importance of the anus, even though their authors rely heavily on Ghalioungui's book.)

According to von Staden, nothing like the pervasive Egyptian conception of the *whdw* (or the corresponding wide range of therapies) can be found in Greek medicine. This is flatly denied by J. B. Saunders in the course of defending a general thesis on the profound indebtedness of Greek to Egyptian medicine. Thus, concerning the *whdw*, Saunders holds that "the Ancient Egyptian hypothesis that most internal, suppurative, and infectious diseases were related to the universal observation of the corruptibility of organic matter was brilliant in the extreme and won wide acceptance in the medicine and biological science of classical Greece" (1963, 31). Some of the evidence Saunders presents to support his case is merely negative, such as the (accidental?) survival of so many formulations of the alternative and competing humoral theory in large numbers of Hippocratic and Galenic texts.[81] Moreover, the quotation from Galen that Saunders cites, to the effect that in curing fevers one must prevent "putrefaction," hardly suggests the sweeping character of the Egyptian doctrine of *whdw*. As to therapy, Saunders simply asserts, with no supporting evidence, that "Greek physicians, like their Egyptian colleagues, were so given to the use of the clyster in their therapy that they were frequently referred to as *iatroklystēs* or clyster-physicians" (1963, 25).[82] Ghalioungui (1973, 75) also notes the possible identity of the Greek *iatroklystis* (clyster-physician) with the Egyptian "shepherd of the anus."

Far from being frequently used, however, the term *iatroklystis* has been found just once in the entire corpus of ancient Greek texts (see the entry in Liddell, Scott, and Jones's *Greek–English Lexicon*), and even that one instance is uncertain. The text in question is on papyrus, dates from the second century B.C.E., and takes the form of a letter, perhaps from a mother to her son. Unfortunately, the crucial word (*iatro-?*) is difficult to read, and at least three different renderings have been proposed: *iatroklítis* (Kenyon), *iatrokáystis* (Wilcken), and *iatroklystis* (Witkowski, Sudhoff).[83] Of the three renderings, Kenyon's makes no sense at all, Wilcken's translates as "cautery-doctor," and Witkowski's (which Sudhoff adopts) translates as "enema-doctor." Adopting Sudhoff's rendering, Majno has translated the letter as follows: "I heard that you are learning Egyptian, and I was very happy, for you as well as myself; because now, arriving in the city, you will tutor the sons of Phal . . . the enema-doctor, and make money towards old age" (1975, 317). The enema-doctor here must be an Egyptian (his sons know no Greek), but obviously little can be inferred from such a slender text about the currency of the term *iatroklystis* (which might even have been coined by the letter-writer) or about the prevalence of Greek clyster-physicians. Finally, it might be noted that in a passage in the Hippocratic treatise *Diseases* (4.41), the anus is mentioned as only one of four orifices suitable for purging (the others being the mouth, the nostrils, and the urethra).[84]

Saunders's reference to the Greek humoral theory may serve to remind us that some Afrocentrists have seen that theory also as originating in Egypt, with Pythagoras as the agent of transmission (see above). That Pythagoras was a physician, or even interested in medicine, is far less well attested—and not before the first century C.E.—than that he was a mathematician (Burkert [1962] 1972, 293). Once again, I believe, we must take very seriously Burkert's point that "to a later age it seemed natural to retroject their own notion of 'wisdom' upon the great figures of the past and to impute to them that which from a modern point of view is 'science'" ([1962] 1972, 217). It would be best, then, to forget about Pythagoras and simply ask whether any significant details of the humoral theory seem to echo ideas in Egyptian medical texts. On this question, Steuer concludes that "there is no evidence thus far for [Hippocratic humoral theory's] origin from ancient Egyptian sources" (1948, 31).

On another important medical matter—Herophilus' use of the pulse for diagnostic purposes (what came to be called "sphygmology")—von Staden finds it quite conceivable that he was influenced by the technology of his Egyptian environment (even if not by indigenous Egyptian medicine). Herophilus is said to have measured the pulse rates of his patients with a portable water clock, or clepsydra, which allowed him to adjust for their ages. Such time-measuring devices are supposed to have been common in Egypt. Also, some Egyptian medical texts recognize the importance of the pulse and even, somewhat obscurely, suggest measuring it. The vascular system of Egyptian medicine, on the other hand, failing as it did to distinguish veins from arteries and with its other peculiarities, could hardly have been of much help to Herophilus. Von Staden's conclusion is that "the Alexandrian development of vascular theory and, more specifically, of sphygmology received much greater impetus from the speculation and observation of Greeks such as Aristotle and Herophilus' teacher, Praxagoras of Cos, who was the first to make a firm distinction between arteries and veins, than from Egyptian medicine" (1989, 13).

3. In caring for wounds the most common methods of the Egyptian physician were a slab of fresh meat, a salve composed of honey with animal fat or aromatic resins, and adhesive linen tape. None of these methods was favored by Greek physicians, who preferred washing the wound with wine or vinegar or sprinkling it with an antiseptic styptic liquid or powder composed usually of some metallic compound (such as alum or copper sulphate).[85] Once again, with no textual citations, Saunders refers to "the use of fresh meat as a poultice in both Egyptian and Greek therapy" (1963, 28).[86] In fact, fresh meat seems to be recommended in Greek medicine for only a single condition: an ulcer of the matrix (womb) (Majno 1975, 192).

4. According to von Staden—citing the authoritative Grapow–von Deines–Westendorf edition of Egyptian medical texts—roughly eight hundred drug recipes have been identified in pharaonic Egyptian medical papyri. By contrast, according to one scholar who specializes in ancient drugs, "the entire Hippocratic corpus listed only about 130 medicinal substances" (Riddle 1985, xviii). From Homer on, the idea of Egypt as a fertile source of drugs is a constant refrain among Greek authors, so that "an influx of Egyptian ingredients into pre-Alexandrian Greek pharmacology is . . . solidly attested. It probably reflects an interest in exotica whose use would enhance the physician's prestige" (von Staden 1989, 17). Herophilean pharmacology was further enriched by Egyptian drugs, especially vegetable substances, such as castor-oil leaves, plantain juice, rhubarb, ginger, and tragacanth; and, again following the Egyptians, the Herophileans begin to quantify their prescriptions— though von Staden has his doubts (1989, 19) as to whether this could have really improved the curative powers of the drugs. One precaution is in order, however, as Ann Hanson explains: "The fact that broadly similar drugs, techniques and recipes can be documented widely among societies at similar stages of development, makes arguments for a direct line less convincing" (Hanson 1985, 27).

5. Ophthalmology is a concern of several of the pharaonic medical papyri, especially Ebers, which provides no fewer than one hundred drug prescriptions to remedy blindness. Among the remedies is crocodile dung and liver (the latter, a good source of vitamin A, might have been effective); both of these recur in Herophilus' treatise *On Eyes*. But Herophilus' ophthalmology

far surpasses the Egyptians' in other respects: "The Egyptians might have had a fairly good idea of the external anatomy of the eye, but Herophilus became the first to distinguish carefully between four coats of the eye and to introduce an influential nomenclature for them" (von Staden 1989, 21).

6. Among the examples often cited to demonstrate the indebtedness of Greek to Egyptian medicine are certain prognoses for fertility and pregnancy, which occur in both traditions. Thus, according to the Carlsberg VIII papyrus, by placing an onion on a woman's vulva for a whole night one can determine if she is fertile: if the smell appears in her mouth, she is fertile; if not, she is not. A virtually identical text is found in a Hippocratic document, except that the onion is replaced by a clove of garlic. Ghalioungui thinks this parallel exemplifies "what Greek and later medicine owe to Egyptian science" (1968, 105). He says that the onion test is still used in Anatolia, and—seemingly on the basis of this convergence between Egyptian "science" and modern Anatolian folk medicine—he rather strangely claims that the test "is based on the partly correct assumption of the existence of a patent passage between the vagina and the rest of the body in fertile women" (1968, 101). Later he even refers to what he considers a parallel modern test for fertility which involves injecting a substance into a woman's uterus and then testing for it in her urine (1973, 112). One thing Ghalioungui does not tell us is that, as von Staden explains, "there is no evidence that these popular, durable birth prognoses became part of the Herophilean tradition." And, von Staden continues, "It is conceivable that Herophilus' careful study of reproductive anatomy and physiology and of obstetrics . . . convinced him of the absurdity and uselessness of these Egyptian intrusions into Greek medicine, and that he therefore abandoned what has been hailed as the most significant Egyptian element in Greek medicine" (1989, 22).

Why didn't Egyptian medicine influence Greek medicine more than it seems to have done, especially during the Alexandrian period when contacts between the two medical traditions might have been expected to increase? Von Staden suggests some possible institutional reasons (1989, 22–26). First of all, the organization of the medical profession was traditionally quite different among the Egyptians and Greeks: Egyptian physicians were public officials, working for the state and providing free care to their patients, whereas Greek physicians were, so to speak, in private practice collecting fees from both their patients and apprentices; and Egyptian physicians tended to be specialists, Greek physicians general practitioners. These differences perhaps reduced the likelihood of social and professional contacts between the two groups of physicians. Also, Egyptians seem not to have participated in the work of the Museum and the Library at Alexandria; the first native Egyptian who wrote in Greek was Manetho of Sebennytus (ca. 280 B.C.E.). More generally, the Greek community in Alexandria, like similar colonial out-posts elsewhere, tended to be quite isolated from the surrounding Egyptian population.

One specific cultural practice of the Egyptians, which may have had some influence on the character of Alexandrian medicine, was the procedure of embalming called mummification. It is not so much that the procedure presupposes, or could have yielded, any significant anatomical knowledge. For one thing, embalmers and physicians belonged to two entirely separate priestly castes. Perhaps, however, as von Staden explains, "the existence in Egypt of a priestly caste whose main task involved opening human corpses might have facilitated justifying a temporary breach of the Greek taboo by Hellenistic king and Hellenistic physician, and this in turn made possible the emergence of human dissection as almost synonymous with early Alex-andrian medicine" (1989, 30). On the other hand, he believes that Egyptian physicians never "misinterpreted the religious and legal sanction of mummi-fication as licence to practise dissection, let alone vivisection" (30). This is not necessarily incompatible with Ghalioungui's remark about "the possibility of clandestine autopsies and dissections, which the author of the Edwin Smith papyrus seems to have practised" (1973, 46).

I conclude by mentioning two uniquely Greek cultural practices, which Geoffrey Lloyd has recently proposed as clues (among numerous others) to the causes and character of the Greek "revolution of wisdom with regard to the understanding of nature" (1987, 3). The two practices are public competi-tions between wise men, and open acknowledgment of uncertainty and error by wise men. Each of these practices has its exemplification in the field of medicine. Thus "Galen several times refers to competitive public anatomical dissections in front of an audience quick to ridicule failure," and "[I]n some Hippocratic texts . . . the author explicitly acknowledges that he was himself mistaken" (1987, 89 n. 143, 124). Either of these practices would have been un-thinkable to Egyptian physicians; this is borne out not only by the contents of the medical papyri but also by reports in antiquity concerning the conser-vative and unadventurous character of Egyptian physicians (who "ran a risk of legal sanctions—the death penalty, no less—if they deviated from what the sacred medical books laid down") (55). It is hardly an adequate answer to Lloyd's contentions to cite, as Bernal does, the Middle Kingdom text *Dispute between a Man and His "Ba,"* which takes the form of a debate between a man and his "soul" on the wisdom of dying to end too painful a life.[87] Superb literature though this text may be, and even, in some sense, full of "quite pro-found philosophy" (Bernal's 1992e, 597), its debate is in a double sense private and personal: first, the argument takes place entirely within the mind of one individual (there is no audience); second, the topic of the debate is not some aspect of nature but rather a moral and psychological dilemma. In short, Bernal's argument serves, if anything, to strengthen the case for recognizing a revolutionary approach to the study of nature in classical Greece. Whether, in this connection, one wishes to talk about a "Greek miracle" is perhaps just a matter of taste. (I myself abhor the phrase and would be quite pleased never to hear it again.)[88]

Summary

It may be helpful to add a summary of my main claims in this essay:

The Egyptians never invented a mathematical astronomy in the sense that the Babylonians and the Greeks did. Such an astronomy must include *both* (1) some form of systematic—though not necessarily very precise—observation of sun, moon, and planets, and (2) some observationally based procedures for computing new celestial observations from known ones. Whether the Egyptians ever made *any* celestial observations on which computations *could* have been based may be open to dispute; but it should be noted that mere recognition of particular stars or constellations is hardly enough. There is, however, *no* evidence that the Egyptians developed, on their own, the requisite computational procedures—though, of course, by Hellenistic times Egyptian astronomers were using easily identifiable Babylonian and Greek procedures. Was Greek astronomy, then, entirely uninfluenced by Egyptian ideas? Well, almost entirely, the exception being the adoption of the Egyptian calendar by later Greek astronomers, including Ptolemy.

Egyptian mathematics never approached the depth of understanding revealed in the most advanced Babylonian mathematics, which was in turn far surpassed by the Greeks, so that it is difficult to see how the peak Egyptian achievements—even generously extrapolated to hypothetical results now lost to us—could ever have led to Greek mathematics with its clear conception of rigorous demonstration and its characteristic methods of formulating and solving problems. Specifically, the remarkable Babylonian result on Pythagorean triples implies a deeper understanding of number-theoretical properties (such as the property of being what Neugebauer calls a "regular" number, that is, a number whose reciprocal is expressible as a finite sexagesimal fraction) than anything implicit in the Egyptians' numerical formulas for volumes, areas, or π; yet the failure of the Babylonians to grasp the irrationality of $\sqrt{2}$ (for which they had worked out a good approximation) indicates how far they fell short of the Greeks. But the surpassing Greek achievements in mathematics stemmed from the development of logical procedures for mathematical proofs (such as indirect or *reductio ad absurdum* proof) and the formulation of powerful general principles (such as a general theory of proportion and a general technique for finding areas and volumes by the method of exhaustion). In what ways, then, *could* the Greeks have been stimulated by Egyptian mathematics? Perhaps—and this is only speculation—as a challenge to generalize and derive rigorously the Egyptian geometrical formulas, or as a curiosity about the properties of regular geometrical solids like cubes and pyramids, or as an interest in an arithmetic based on the twice-times multiplication table and the manipulation of unit fractions.

Although there seems little doubt that Greek doctors enlarged their pharmacopoeia with Egyptian drugs, other types of influence of Egyptian medicine on Greek medicine are more difficult to document; and certain radical differences between the two medical traditions are very striking. Specifically, the Greeks never adopted the central and dominating Egyptian anatomical-physiological theory of the *mtw* (a network of vessels emanating from the heart and reuniting near the anus) and its associated therapeutic procedure of frequent purgations via clyster; and the Greeks used wine or vinegar in treating wounds instead of the Egyptians' honey and animal fat or slabs of fresh meat.

NOTES

Reprinted (with minor revisions) by permission from *History of Science* 31 (1993): 227–87. Martin Bernal has responded to this essay, and I have commented on his response: *History of Science* 32 (1994): 445–68; a part of those comments has been included in the present essay as a concluding summary.

My thanks for helpful discussions to Gary Reger, History Department, Trinity College, Hartford, Connecticut; Martha Risser, Classics Department, also of Trinity College, Hartford; and Howard Stein, Philosophy Department, University of Chicago.

1. For a very full listing of writings about the first two volumes of *Black Athena* see Levine 1992b.

2. Bernal 1992e. I shall be responding to specific claims made by Bernal in this essay as the occasion arises.

3. Clagett 1989. The next two promised volumes will deal, respectively, with astronomy and mathematics and with medicine and biology.

4. See also Neugebauer 1989, where he pursues this particular parameter into the Renaissance.

5. See Sigerist [1951] 1967, 357–58. Sigerist, by the way, believes that "there can be no doubt whatsoever that the Greeks learned a great deal [in medicine] from Egypt" (357). A leading historian of Egyptian medicine accepts the Egyptian-Greek connection in this case (Ghalioungui 1968, 99).

6. For an authoritative annotated English translation see Toomer 1984; also Pedersen 1974. On all aspects of ancient mathematical astronomy the definitive work is Neugebauer 1975.

7. Note the amusing opening sentences of Neugebauer 1975 (1:1): "Many things are omitted here. The reader who wants to hear about Archimedes taking a bath or about the silver nose of Tycho Brahe can find innumerable books which dwell on these important biographical matters. Nor do I enumerate the pros and cons concerning the place or movement of the earth and the substance of the spheres."

Earlier, in his preface, he had written: "I have tried to come as close as possible to the astronomical problems themselves without hiding my ignorantia behind the smoke-screen of sociological, biographical and bibliographical irrelevancies" (vii).

8. See Neugebauer 1951 ("The Study of Wretched Subjects"), 111: "the very foundations of our studies [are] the recovery and study of the texts as they are, regardless of our own tastes and prejudices." (Incidentally, the term "wretched," in the title, is not his.)

9. Bernal (1992e, 601) finds Neugebauer's proposal plausible but criticizes him for using the term "primitive" in characterizing the remarkably accurate alignment of the Great Pyramid. It is, however, not the *alignment* which Neugebauer characterizes as primitive but a certain kind of visual *experience*.

10. The distinguished historian of early astronomy Willy Hartner is willing to speculate that Egyptian astronomers probably observed—without, for some reason, recording—lunar eclipses, constellations of stars, and planetary motions as early as the second millennium B.C.E. His really quite moderate claims are stimulating but ultimately unconvincing; see his comments on Giorgio de Santillana's "On Forgotten Sources in the History of Science" (Hartner 1963).

11. For an excellent brief introduction to Egyptian astronomy see R. A. Parker 1978; for a fuller account see van der Waerden 1974, chapter 1. For a compilation of Egyptian astronomical texts see Neugebauer and Parker 1969. This latter corpus of texts excludes "cosmogonic mythology, calendaric problems and time reckoning as well as astrology" (Neugebauer 1975, 2:566–67).

12. For a useful brief introduction to Babylonian astronomy, with full references, see van der Waerden 1978.

13. Elsewhere Neugebauer points out that mathematical astronomy had two more independent origins: in the Chinese and Mayan civilizations.

14. See Dyson 1992, interview with Bernal: "I have . . . sympathy for Afrocentricity, though I'm not an Afrocentrist myself."

15. I discovered this publication in Bernal's bibliography (in *BA* 1). I am uncertain whether Bernal accepts all its claims. According to a biographical note in Van Sertima 1983 (301), Pappademos was at that time a nuclear physicist teaching at the University of Illinois, Chicago Circle, whose "research interests have shifted to the social aspects of physics, including its philosophy and history."

16. Or do I misread Pappademos? I will quote: "Since the rise of slavery with its offspring the doctrine and practice of racism, the Black civilization of the Nile Valley has had its detractors. As recently as 1975, Otto Neugebauer, the well-known historian of ancient science, had this to say: 'Egypt provides us with the exceptional case of a highly sophisticated civilization which flourished for many centuries without making a single contribution to the development of the exact sciences'" (Pappademos 1984, 95). Pappademos seems to have overlooked Neugebauer's phrase "highly sophisticated"—hardly an expression of detraction—and perhaps never even asked what Neugebauer meant by "the exact sciences." Much worse, though, he overlooks Neugebauer's very next sentence: "In fact, however, this is not the exception but the rule" (Neugebauer 1975, 2:559). Even more explicitly, Neugebauer holds that, apart from ancient Babylonia and ancient Greece, "none of the other civilizations

of antiquity, which have otherwise contributed so much to the material and artistic culture of the world, have ever reached an independent level of scientific thought" (1:6).

17. Vercoutter is here following Neugebauer 1942a.

18. Even Diop quotes approvingly this remark by Neugebauer (whom he elsewhere abuses for his alleged anti-Egyptian prejudice). Diop's own preconceptions are perhaps reflected in his erroneous remark that the Egyptian calendar is "the very one which, barely changed, regulates our life today" (1991, 279). He refers in a note to our present (Gregorian) calendar but omits to mention its methods for dealing with leap years, which make it vastly different from the Egyptian calendar—but not, of course, well adapted for astronomical purposes (1991, 401–2 n. 63).

19. For a succinct account of Egyptian calendars, see R. A. Parker 1978, 706–10. Bernal argues that "the Greeks adopted an Egyptian rather than a Mesopotamian calendar" and that "this adoption is indicative of what seems to have been a wider Greek tendency to draw from nearby Egypt rather than more distant Mesopotamia" (1992e, 606). This is wrong on several counts. In the first place, there was never any single civil calendar adopted by the various Greek city-states (which led to the calendaric chaos that classical scholars are still trying to dispel). There is evidence, however, of a "universal" Greek astronomical calendar based on the so-called Metonic cycle, that is, on the assumption that 19 years contain 7 intercalary months (and therefore a total of $19 \times 12 + 7 = 235$ months). Such a cycle was known to the Babylonians from the early fifth century B.C.E., and there is some reason to believe that this was Meton's source. In any case, a calendar based on the Metonic cycle and improved by Callippus was used by Greek astronomers as late as Hipparchus (128 B.C.E.). Later Greek astronomers, including Ptolemy, preferred the Egyptian calendar for reasons already explained. (For details see Toomer 1974.)

20. I suspect Pappademos picked up this allusion to stellar azimuths from one of his other sources; see Sarton 1952, 30: "the combination of a plumb line with a forked rod . . . enabled [the Egyptians] to determine the azimuth of a start [sic]." But no records of such azimuth measurements have been found. On this question of angle measurement Neugebauer remarks: "The coverage of the sky with picturesque configurations of stars"—which the Egyptians certainly accomplished—"is not the equivalent of the use of mathematically defined spherical coordinates" (1975, 2:577).

21. Thus Vercoutter writes that "representations of the sky on certain tombs have enabled scholars to identify some of the constellations known to Egyptians—for example, the Great Bear . . . , Boötes . . . , Cygnus . . . , Orion . . . , Cassiopeia . . . , and Draco, the Pleiades, Scorpio and Aries, each represented by characteristic figures" (1963, 37). Vercoutter gives no specific reference, but his opinion here is an exception to his usual reliance on Neugebauer for the details of Egyptian astronomy.

22. "Ptolemy refers nowhere to Egyptians for astronomical observations or theories . . . , only to calendaric concepts and to some astrological doctrines. . . ." (Neugebauer 1975, 2:562 n. 14).

23. For translation and analysis of these two texts see Neugebauer 1942b.

24. Earlier he had recognized "one doubtful [Egyptian] reference to a partial eclipse of 610 B.C." (1957, 95).

25. Van der Waerden 1974, 83. Cf. Neugebauer 1975, 2:593: "The Almagest and all ancient and medieval mathematical astronomy uses orthogonal ecliptic coordinates for its coordinate system. . . . this system is of Babylonian origin." It is uncertain, however, whether these ecliptic coordinates were ever used much beyond the zone of the ecliptic and the "Normal Stars" (a set of thirty-one reference stars in the vicinity of the ecliptic).

26. See the sensitive "Eloge" by Sivin (1976).

27. White is not unsympathetic to *Hamlet's Mill*; he attributes to von Dechend the book's more farfetched notions, which he characterizes as "arrogant oversimplification" (541).

28. The version of the passage from Archimedes used by Pappademos is in Heath 1913, 302.

29. It is arguable that heliocentricity is of no great significance in the history of mathematical astronomy until Copernicus. As Neugebauer puts it: "Without the accumulation of a vast store of empirical data and without a serious methodology for their analysis the idea of heliocentricity was only a useless play on words" (Neugebauer 1975, 2:698).

30. Bernal (1992e, 606) adds that Ptolemy was called "the Upper Egyptian" in early Arabic writings.

31. One indication of this is that the last of the Ptolemaic rulers (Cleopatra) was the first to speak Egyptian. As a recent study of the two cultures puts it: "Ptolemaic Egypt . . . remained throughout its history a land of two cultures which did coexist but, for the most part, did not coalesce or blend. . . . We . . . discern the manifestations of the two discrete cultures in every aspect of their coexistence. . . . It would be difficult . . . to exaggerate the significance of the fact that, except for some local designations of places, measures, and so on, no native Egyptian word made its way into Greek usage in the thousand years that Greek endured as the language of Ptolemaic, Roman, and Byzantine Egypt" (N. Lewis 1986, 154–55; see also Goudriaan 1988).

32. This is the first full publication of the scholia, occupying some some fourteen pages.

33. Tompkins 1971, 30–33. Tompkins seems to think that once Newton had the correct value for the Earth's radius his task was effectively completed (that is, the law of gravitation had been discovered)—a travesty of Newton's actual route to the law. But then Tompkins also believes that "whoever built the Great Pyramid . . . knew the precise circumference of the planet, and the length of the year to several decimals . . . [and] may well have known the mean length of the earth's orbit round the sun, the specific density of the planet, the 26,000-year cycle of the equinoxes, the acceleration of gravity and the speed of light" (xiv–xv). For a recent account of Newton's "moon test" of the theory of gravitation see A. R. Hall 1992, 59–64.

34. For a transcription of the three accounts, with detailed analysis, see Herivel 1965, 65–76.

35. Bernal too thinks that the existence of advanced (but as yet unrevealed) Egyptian mathematics follows from the fact that Greek and Roman building techniques required such mathematics and the fact that Egyptian architecture was not technically inferior to Greek and Roman architecture (see 1992e, 605). He should ask workers in

the building trades (or even architects) how much advanced mathematics they know! (By advanced mathematics I mean anything in Archimedes or the later books of Euclid's *Elements*.) On Egyptian building techniques see S. Clarke and R. Engelbach [1930] 1990; on Greek building techniques see Coulton 1977. Coulton is properly skeptical about the idea that the Parthenon architects deliberately used conic-section curves (parabolas and hyperbolas) in their design; among his reasons are that the first geometrical analysis of such curves (by Menaichmos) was not formulated until a century later (107–8, 175 n. 22).

36. Gillings's book is the fullest and most up-to-date account in English; he has also written a briefer but still fairly detailed account (1978). With reference to the quoted passage from Gillings, Frank J. Yurco, of the University of Chicago, has explained (personal communication) how the Egyptians actually applied a concept of zero, using a special hieroglyph, to symbolize a zero balance in an accounting text of around 1740 B.C.E. (Papyrus Boulaq no. 18). The Babylonians, on the other hand, implicitly introduced a zero sign in the form of a blank space between numerals; but they were not consistent in this practice and never used it at the end of a number. A special sign for zero may have been introduced by the Babylonians as early as 700 B.C.E. and was in full use by 300 B.C.E. (Neugebauer 1957, 20, 27).

37. Gillings (1982, 704–5) provides a list of all of these texts, with approximate dates and other useful details. One recent publication on Egyptian mathematics should be singled out: a new English version of the RMP including beautiful color facsimiles of the original papyrus; see G. Robins and C. C. D. Shute 1987.

38. The manipulation of unit fractions gives rise to interesting and difficult problems in number theory, which have attracted the attention of modern mathematicians; see M. Gardner 1992. There is, of course, no reason to believe the Egyptians were even capable of formulating such problems. Mott Greene (1992, chapter 2) has recently suggested that the unit fraction notion originated in the unit weights of Egyptian pan balances.

39. Van der Waerden does not mention summation of progressions in his exposition of Egyptian mathematics (1961, chapter 1).

40. Gillings 1982, 214, 217. Diop is, then, clearly mistaken when he says (referring only to the Berlin Papyrus) that "the Egyptians knew how to rigorously extract the square root, even of the most complicated whole or fractional numbers" (1991, 258). It is interesting to note that calculations of square roots by Greek mathematicians are also only imperfectly understood by modern scholars, and here too, plausible guesses have been made as to just how certain approximations, say, to $\sqrt{3}$, were calculated. Greek computational techniques must have been highly sophisticated; Archimedes, for instance, assumes (without explanation) that $\sqrt{3}$ lies between $\frac{265}{153}$ and $\frac{1,351}{780}$, that is, between 1.7320261 and 1.7320512. (The correct value, to seven decimal places, is 1.7320508.) See Heath [1931] 1963, 309–10.

41. See van der Waerden 1961, 77; or 1978, 670.

42. Neugebauer 1957, 47. The value 3 for π is also found, in effect, in the Old Testament (1 Kings 7:23, 2 Chronicles 4:2).

43. Gillings reproduces what seem to be redrawn sketches of the three diagrams

(1982, 139–40), but one can examine photographs of the originals in G. Robins and C. C. D. Shute 1987, plates 14–16.

44. G. Robins and C. C. D. Shute (1987, 44–45) unfortunately provide no interpretation of Problem 48, and their own hypothesis as to how the circle area formula was derived appeals to the Pythagorean theorem, which, as we shall see, the Egyptians almost certainly did not know.

45. Archimedes, trans. Heath 1912, 2. Archimedes repeats this claim, and adds that Democritus was the first to state the result, in the preface to his "Method"; see Heath 1912, supplement, "The Method of Archimedes," 13.

46. Bernal 1992e, 603. Bernal's "many years" for the length of Eudoxus' stay in Egypt is perhaps exaggerated; G. L. Huxley (1971, 466) writes "more than a year." Bernal also follows de Santillana in assuming that Eudoxus could only have visited Egypt in order to improve his mathematical and astronomical knowledge and that Eudoxus' translation of texts from the Egyptian *Book of the Dead* suggests that "Egyptian religious and mystical writings and drawings may well contain esoteric mathematical and astronomical wisdom" (Bernal 1992e, 603). This ignores the fact that Eudoxus had many scholarly interests beyond mathematics and astronomy—and hence other possible motives for visiting Egypt—as shown by the remaining fragments of his geographical treatise, in which "beginning with remote Asia, Eudoxus dealt systematically with each part of the known world in turn, adding political, historical, and ethnographic detail and making use of Greek mythology" (G. L. Huxley 1971, 467).

47. On Archytas, only fragments of whose writings have survived, see the enthusiastic but critical assessment of van der Waerden (1961, 149–59).

48. See, e.g., the entry on Pythagoras in the Glossary at the end of the first volume of Bernal's *Black Athena*: "Greek philosopher and mathematician, c. 582–500 B.C. He studied in Egypt and brought back Egyptian mathematical and religious principles, and founded the Pythagorean brotherhood" (1:521).

49. Bernal ignores Burkert but accuses of "Aryanist ingenuity" (*BA* 1:105) a Belgian scholar (writing in 1922), who was skeptical about the Pythagorean tradition.

50. Burkert [1962] 1972, 408–15. English translations of many of the ancient references to Pythagoras (including those in Herodotus and Isocrates) are conveniently assembled in Barnes 1987, chapter 5.

51. In his introduction Burkert explains the role of anti-Semitism in delaying the acceptance by certain scholars of massive Near Eastern influence on the Greeks, and in this connection he refers to Bernal's work as "provocative" ([1984] 1992, 154 n. 5).

52. Gillings presumes that Dinostratus—about whom we actually know very little—was the first Greek mathematician to find the circumference of a circle.

53. Beatrice Lumpkin objects to what she calls Neugebauer's "highly prejudiced statement" as "an unhistoric judgment . . . much like faulting the inventor of the crystal radio for not inventing solid state television first"; she also asserts that "these same Egyptian fractions were used by scientists for thousands of years after their invention, right on up to the modern period" (1984, 103, 106). But, in the first place, because Neugebauer has in mind a comparison with contemporary Babylonian nu-

merical procedures, there is nothing "unhistoric" about his judgment; secondly, it is a historical fact that although Egyptian arithmetic "probably influenced the Hellenistic and Roman administrative offices and thus spread further into other regions of the Roman empire" (Neugebauer 1957, 72), complicated computations (such as those in mathematical astronomy) have never been carried out, to my knowledge, using the Egyptian technique of unit fractions. Indeed, according to Karl Menninger, even in practical affairs, the Romans and medievals only "now and then . . . expressed a fraction in the Egyptian fashion, as the sum of certain standard fractions" ([1958] 1969, 158).

54. According to Bernal (1992e, 600), Neugebauer had an "early passion for ancient Egypt," which he presumably lost by the time he rejected the hemisphere interpretation of MMP 10 in favor of "a much more primitive interpretation which is preferable" (Neugebauer 1957, 78). Unfortunately for Bernal's (undocumented) interpretation of Neugebauer's changing attitudes toward ancient Egypt, the comment he cites (disapproving its use of the term "primitive") occurs in the same book in which Neugebauer says such glowing things about ancient Egypt (see Neugebauer 1957, 11).

55. The translation must be faulty here, but Diop's meaning seems clear enough: in the quoted text "Platonic bodies" is followed by the phrase "of work," which makes no sense.

56. The Babylonian way of putting it would have been (as Neugebauer suggests, 1957, 48): the irrationality of $\sqrt{2}$ means that $p^2 = 2q^2$ has no integral solutions in p and q.

57. As Neugebauer explains, irregular numbers are those containing prime numbers not contained in 60 (that is, prime numbers different from 2, 3, and 5).

58. On the same evidence, Diop concludes that "the Egyptians knew the theorem attributed to Pythagoras perfectly well" (1991, 260).

59. For an account of the method and its history see van der Waerden 1961, 184–87, 216–25.

60. Later, when he comes to discuss MMP 10, Diop insists that the problem is about the surface of a hemisphere (251).

61. Exactly the same discussion of Lauer appears in Bernal 1992e, 600. The golden section and Pythagorean triangles are usually defined geometrically, but it is the numerical expression of the geometrical relationships which has to be compared with the results of length measurements. The golden section refers to a ratio of two line segments, say, in a rectangle, of $1:(\sqrt{5} - 1)/2$, which is approximately 0.618. (For a discussion of the golden section in the context of ancient Greek mathematics see Cohen and Drabkin 1958, 50–51). Pythagorean triangles, as we have already seen, are right triangles whose sides can be expressed numerically by triples of integers, such that the sum of the squares of two of them is equal to the square of the third, e.g., {3, 4, 5}, {5, 12, 13}, {8, 15, 17}. (For a discussion of Pythagorean triangles in the context of ancient Greek mathematics see Cohen and Drabkin, 21–23.)

62. The authors, as already noted, are the editors of the recent edition of the Rhind Mathematical Papyrus (Robins and Shute 1987); Robins is an Egyptologist in

the Department of Art History at Emory University, and Shute formerly held a chair in medical biology at Cambridge University.

63. They have invented what seems to be a reliable photographic procedure which obviates the need for directly measuring the pyramids themselves (Robins and Shute 1985, 108–9).

64. Robins and Shute make much of the fact that the Egyptian measure of inclination of a pyramid face, the *seked*, was defined in terms of the horizontal displacement in "palms" per vertical drop in "royal cubits" (where a royal cubit was equal to seven palms) (1985, 108). They remind us that the *seked*, unlike our own measure of inclination, is a function of the cotangent of the angle of inclination. (For discussion here, however, the distinction is irrelevant.)

65. I am following the figures in Markowsky 1992, 6. Markowsky's essay contains a valuable bibliography as well as excellent mathematical and critical discussions of various applications of the golden section in art and literature, from the Parthenon to Vergil's *Aeneid* to the United Nations Building in New York City. A very full historical account of the golden section may be found in Herz-Fischler 1987.

66. Gillings (1982, 238–39) rejects the emendation, and following him, so does Markowsky (1992, 17), who gives the original Greek as well as a word-by-word literal translation.

67. For an elaboration of this idea to truly bizarre lengths see Stecchini 1971. Bernal finds "some plausibility" in Stecchini's work (*BA* 1:275).

68. To illustrate the uncertainty of pyramidal measurements I cite those of a contemporary pyramidologist, who recently published "the result of a 15-year study involving, among other research, three trips to Egypt, where I resided for nearly one year, investigating these monuments firsthand on a daily basis" (Lepre 1990, vii). Lepre gives 762.24 feet for the base and 485.5 feet for the height of the Great Pyramid; these figures differ from our previous ones by almost 1 percent. Lepre's compendium of basic information on some one hundred pyramids, as well as his bibliography of some two hundred items, may be useful as a guide for anyone wishing to study pyramidology more deeply. For a recent brief and reliable account of the pyramids by the Director General of the Giza Pyramids and Saqqara see Hawass 1990. It is worth noting that even such a sober student of the pyramids as Hawass feels called upon to begin his essay with the "spiritual aspect" of the pyramids and the claim that they "have made a mockery of death; they cannot be killed. Their physical presence defies the limitations of time" (1). In the very next paragraph, however, we learn that some of the pyramids "are now barely distinguishable from the sand and rubble that surround them"!

69. Bernal is deliberately following these scholars when he remarks that "I should like to take it as given that R. O. Steuer, J. B. de C. M. Saunders, and Paul Ghalioungui have established not merely that Egyptian medicine contained considerable 'scientific' elements long before the emergence of Greek medicine, but that Egyptian medicine played a central role in the development of Greek medicine" (1992e, 599).

70. The liver is notably missing from the list, but this seems to be a simple oversight, for Newsome's source, Gardiner's *Egyptian Grammar* (1957), does in fact

list signs for the liver. (I owe this information to my colleague Martha Risser.) It might be noted that unlike the Mesopotamians, Etruscans, Greeks, and Romans, the Egyptians did not practice hepatoscopy (divination through examination of the livers of animals). Burkert sees "the spread of hepatoscopy [as] one of the clearest examples of cultural contact in the orientalizing period [750–650 B.C.E.]" ([1984] 1992, 51). It is interesting that Cicero (*De Divinatione* 2.12.28)—whom Burkert cites in this connection—seems to attribute hepatoscopy also to the Egyptians (Falconer 1929, 402–3).

71. For all of this information see Finch 1983.

72. See W. D. Smith 1979, chapter 2, "Galen's Hippocratism." As Smith puts it: "Galen's version of Hippocratic science and its tradition is in large part his own, a projection of his concerns onto history. While his medical system was put together out of Hellenistic medical developments, his peculiar Hippocratism was fashioned largely as rhetorical and ideological patina for it. His claims about Hippocrates' original philosophical and scientific system were put forth for the circle of intellectuals in Rome, phrased in terms relevant to them" (175). For an introduction to the problem of identifying the genuine writings of Hippocrates see G. E. R. Lloyd 1978. The only "complete" edition of Hippocrates (Littré 1839–61, Greek texts with facing French translations) was published more than a century and a half ago but remains useful, some would even say indispensable, today. For a discussion of Littré and his edition of Hippocrates see Smith 1979, 31–36.

73. Von Staden's analysis takes the form of an introduction to his edition of all the texts bearing on the medical ideas of the great Alexandrian physician Herophilus (330/320–260/250 B.C.E.), and of his followers. Since none of Herophilus' writings has survived, what von Staden's edition amounts to is a compilation of several hundred passages (in Greek or Latin, with English translations) from more than fifty later medical writers (more from Galen than from anyone else) who mention Herophilus or cite his writings.

74. See May 1968; Furley and Wilkie 1984; Brain 1986; Hankinson 1991.

75. The Grapow volumes—there are actually nine, not ten—were published between 1954 and 1962 in Berlin; Hildegard von Deines and Wolfhart Westendorf were Grapow's co-editors. Von Staden (1989, 6 n. 15) tells us that he has based his English versions of Egyptian medical texts on the German of the Grapow edition.

76. Given the known chemical composition and bactericidal action of honey, Majno explains that in recommending it to dress the wound (which was standard practice) Egyptian physicians "*happened to choose an ingredient that was practically harmless to the tissues, aseptic, antiseptic, and antibiotic. I should say the ingredient*: nothing else, in ancient Egypt, could have begun to match these properties of honey" (1975, 118, emphasis in original). As for grease, Majno's experiments showed that beef fat, vaseline, and butter were either benign or actually favored the healing of wounds. Without benefit of modern experimental method, though, the Egyptians probably selected the honey-grease mixture simply because it prevented bandages from sticking, possessed a soothing consistency, and did not readily spoil (118–20).

77. As there is only scanty evidence for vowels in the Egyptian language, most authors write *mtw*.

78. For a color illustration of the routes of the *mtw* see Majno 1975, plate 3.8. This wildly wrong anatomy makes no appearance in Greek medicine.

79. Herodotus (2.77) writes of the Egyptians: "for three days in succession in each month they physic themselves, hunting health with emetics and purges, because they think that from the food that nourishes mankind come all their diseases" (trans. Grene 1987, 163).

80. On the "enormous pharmacopoeia" of the Egyptians, Majno comments that "if there was one effect it could definitely induce, that was probably diarrhea" (Majno 1975, 129).

81. It may be worth quoting here a formulation of the humoral theory (from the Hippocratic *Nature of Man*): "The body of man has in itself blood, phlegm, yellow bile and black bile; these make up the nature of his body, and through these he feels pain or enjoys health. Now he enjoys the most perfect health when these elements are duly proportioned to one another in respect of compounding, power and bulk, and when they are perfectly mingled." (trans. W. H. S. Jones 1931, 11).

82. Steuer, on the other hand, in his monograph on *whdw*, refers to "views in the Corpus Hippocraticum and in the writings of Aristotle, which appear similar in some respects although not in *the fundamental approach* to the aetiology of suppurative conditions in particular" (1948, 30–31, emphasis in original). Ten years later Steuer discovered in the Cnidian school of medicine (fifth–fourth centuries B.C.E.) an aetiological theory intermediate between Egyptian *mtw* theory and Hippocratic humoral theory. This Cnidian theory identified the causes of disease as putrefaction of phlegm and bile rather than imbalance of the (Hippocratic) humors; see Saunders and Steuer 1959, 35–36. Using as evidence their interpretation of selected texts from the Papyrus Anonymus Londinensis (an Egyptian papyrus of the second century C.E. containing excerpts from a lost history of medicine by Aristotle's pupil, Menon) and from the Hippocratic Collection, Steuer and Saunders conclude that "the most immediate connecting link between Ancient Egyptian and Cnidian aetiology is the belief in the rising of fecal excrements in the body as the primary cause of disease" (1959, 54). Suffice it to say that I find their argument labored and unconvincing. Also, it is curious that Saunders himself does not even cite this work in support of his claims for Egyptian medicine (Saunders 1963).

83. See Kenyon 1893, 1:48; Sudhoff 1909, 260–61; for a photograph of the papyrus, Scott 1893, no. XLIII.

84. See Littré 1839–61 7:562–63. (I owe this reference to Lesley Jones of the Classics Department, University of Texas at Austin.)

85. Wine (both red and white) and vinegar do, in fact, possess germicidal properties. The efficacious agent in the wine is not, however, as one might suppose, the alcohol (which is too dilute to kill germs), but rather a certain organic compound (chemically, a polyphenol) present in all wines. See Majno 1975, 186–88.

86. Von Staden (1989, 14 n. 46) cites four different Hippocratic treatises as evidence for Greek treatment of wounds.

87. Bernal 1992e, 597. Bernal refers only to a very early work by Lloyd, with no mention of *The Revolutions of Wisdom* (1987).

88. Referring to the (eventually successful) Greek struggle to develop a concept

of rigorous proof by deduction from clearly identified premises, G. E. R. Lloyd comments: "There is . . . no call whatsoever in this respect (or indeed in any other) to speak of the Greeks as endowed with some special natural characteristic, some distinctive mental ability, as those who fantasised about the 'Greek miracle' liked to do" (1987, 75). On the other hand, Jonathan Barnes, in an enthusiastic review of Lloyd's book, writes: "It is unfashionable to speak of a Greek 'miracle' . . . But let the pendulum of fashion swing as it may, the Greeks invented science and philosophy" (1988, 1392).

GREECE

THE WORLD TURNED UPSIDE DOWN

Emily T. Vermeule

Martin Bernal's first volume of *Black Athena*, published in 1987, brought him instant fame as a defender of Semitic peoples and cultures against German Aryan propagandists and other anti-Semites of the nineteenth and twentieth centuries. At the same time Bernal became, as he apparently hoped, the chief intellectual antagonist of those who have over the centuries refused to acknowledge the contributions that black Africa has made to the development of ancient Greek and Roman civilizations and therefore to European civilization and to the Eurocentric education of Americans. Egypt, as a geographical mediator between Africa and the Mediterranean, was said by Bernal to be both black and Semitic.

That first volume of *Black Athena* contained some excellent, if brief, nineteenth-century historiography, especially of anti-Semitic German and French scholarship, and sketched the intellectual climate of the several generations between about 1780 and 1940. Bernal was able to select a number of striking quotations from scholars of classical antiquity which might now seem prejudiced, tasteless, laughable, or simply misinformed.

Yet even for eager readers of the first volume of *Black Athena* it was not always easy to understand the nature of the anti-Semitism that so angered Bernal. Friedrich August Wolf, in his *Prolegomena to Homer*, was charged with representing the *Iliad* and the *Odyssey* as oral poetry, a "Romantic" sin in Bernal's view (*BA* 1:283–85). George Grote influenced the teaching of history unfairly by beginning with the first Olympic Games in 776 B.C.E. and thereby excluding the Egyptian and Phoenician contributions to Greek culture in the Bronze Age (1:326–30)—though the Bronze Age was not known yet in 1846 (see Rogers, this volume). Thomas and Matthew Arnold were wrong to admire the classics, and German education, and ought not to have promoted "Victorian Hellenism" (1:347–48). J. B. Bury was at fault when he described the Spartans as refusing to intermarry with their helots, thus keeping their blood "pure" (1:293). Carl Blegen was wrong to suggest that Greece and Asia Minor may have shared common place names like Parnassus; he should have looked first to Egypt and Phoenicia (1:391–92). Rhys Carpenter was wrong— and had "sinister" motives—when he suggested that the Greeks did not adopt the Phoenician alphabet before the eighth century B.C.E. (1:395–97).

Still, even when they were puzzled, many scholars were attracted to the apparently evenhanded and refreshing survey in *BA* 1, with its often justifiable condemnation of the narrow-minded teaching of the classics that assumed the cultural superiority of the Greeks without reference to Egypt and the East. They waited with anticipation for the second volume, which was to offer the archaeological documentation for the belief that Egypt and the Levant inspired the culture of the Greeks.

Greek culture has often been perceived as "special," and this has caused resentment in regions of the world whose art and literature and philosophy have not been so acclaimed. The first volume of *Black Athena* was a thoughtful exposé of how eminent German scholars like Wilhelm von Humboldt felt that "the Greeks" were superior: "Knowledge of the Greeks is not merely pleasant, useful or necessary to us—no, in the Greeks alone we find the ideal of that which we should like to be and produce" (1:287). The "special relationship" between Germany and Greece led some scholars to hope and to believe that the Aryan ancestors of the Greeks had arrived there from the northwest ("somewhere in Germany"), and some to feel that Greek history should be purged of those "darker elements" which might be traced back to the "Orient," the Phoenicians or Egyptians, and so might stain the purity of the Aryan or Indo-European heritage (1:295, 306, 324–25). That process of historical revision was also matched in the treatment of historic sites. On the Acropolis of Athens, for example, buildings from periods of Slavic, Arabic, Crusader, Venetian, and Ottoman rule, or influence, intervening between the ancient Greeks and the modern Germans, were systematically eradicated— so that contact between the intellectual present and the fifth-century Greek past should find no barrier (McNeal 1991, 49).

The archaeological and philological scholars who specialize in ancient Greece made Bernal welcome among them, and debated his theories openly. It is with a slight sense of surprise, then, that we learn in the second volume of *Black Athena* that the entire profession of Bronze Age Aegean and Classical archaeologists is condemned as ignorant, prejudiced, and racist. "Modern archaeologists have been led astray for reasons that can be relatively easily explained in terms of the sociology of knowledge . . . the desire of the new professionals to appear sober and responsible and not indulge in the spectacular theories to which amateurs are so attracted" (2:523). All of us before Bernal have failed to understand the true course of ancient history. At the end of his very long book, he declares, without noticeable modesty, "If a significant quantity of what I claim in this volume is correct, much of contemporary work on the archaeology and ancient history of the East Mediterranean will have to be rethought" (2:527).

But is it correct? Or is it, as with Milton's Belial,

> But all was false and hollow, though his tongue
> Dropp'd manna, and could make the worst appear
> The better reason, to perplex and dash
> Maturest counsels . . .
>
> (*Paradise Lost* 2.112)

A great deal is perplexing about this second volume, which claims to offer "the archaeological evidence." Bernal has done an enormous amount of reading—there are eighty pages of bibliography—but he in fact includes very little standard archaeology, in the sense of reference to excavated evidence, stratification of different civilizations, social organization, or cultural artifacts. There is far more about legends, and linguistics, and revised chronologies. Unfortunately, Bernal handles most of his archaeological discussion by simple assertion.

Bernal, Professor of Government at Cornell, here claims his own authoritative dominance of the Ancient Near Eastern, Egyptian, and Aegean world. That world consists, in archaeological or modern territorial terms, of Egypt, Nubia, the Sudan, the coasts of the Red Sea, Cyrenaica (in modern Libya) and other parts of coastal North Africa, Palestine (Israel and Jordan), Lebanon, Syria, Mesopotamia, Turkey, Cyprus, Crete, Greece, southern Italy, Sicily, and at times also of Malta, Sardinia, and coastal Spain. The period covered is broadly from the Late Stone Age, about 8000 B.C.E. (or 10,000 B.P., before present), to the decline of the ancient Bronze Age empires of Egypt, Hittite Anatolia, and Mycenaean Greece between 1200 and 1100 B.C.E.

One might well ask, and many have, what a modern Chinese specialist of great repute is doing in these old Mediterranean civilizations. An answer might be that none of us can afford in these international times to be ignorant or restricted specialists working in such limited cultural spheres as Bronze Age Greece and Crete, or Greece, or Rome. Another, more personal, reason might be that the author's grandfather was Sir Alan Gardiner, the renowned specialist in the Egyptian scripts and languages, whose Egyptian grammar is still in current use.

Bernal, in order to explore the relationships of cultures in the Mediterranean Bronze Age, has concentrated on a largely artificial "conflict" between East and West, and has claimed that those who believed in some kind of natural intellectual and artistic superiority of the Greeks did so because they were racist, probably anti-Semitic. Yet it was the Greeks themselves who first drew a sharp contrast between Asia and Europe, between "Us" in the democratic West and the "Barbarians" in the royal, imperial East. This distinction is clear both in the case of the national poetic myth of the Trojan War, and in the exhilarating climate of the unexpected Greek victories over the invading Persian armies and navies at the battles of Marathon, Salamis, and Plataea, from 490 to 479 B.C.E.

At first the Greeks—or the southern cities, as opposed to the northern tribes—were simply relieved that they were not to be a part of the Persian Empire after all; then the Athenians began to dream of an empire for themselves, and to act imperially by using their fleet and exacting tribute from others. Then, when that dream turned into a nightmare, by the end of the fifth century, at the end of the Peloponnesian Wars, and Persian gold became a constant "corrupting" element in Greek politics, a new attitude began to coalesce around the theme, perhaps first voiced by Aeschylus in his *Persians*, that Greeks were naturally superior to Persians because they were intelligent and free and subject only to law, whereas Persians were enslaved to the Great King, who was unaccountable for his actions and could kill or mutilate by whim. It should be noted that this familiar conflict between East and West had nothing at all to do with Semites or blacks; Greeks and Persians were both Indo-European in their speech, like the Bronze Age Greeks and Trojans who were their original poetic and mythic models.

Bernal began his quest for a "new" interpretation of history by claiming that the East was largely "Semite" and Egypt largely black, whereas Greece was the land colonized by both. Scholars who did not accept the important contributions made by Egypt and the East to Greek culture were to be castigated. But scholars have at least two reasons to be indignant about Bernal's claims. First, no one has ever doubted the Greek debt to Egypt and the East. Schliemann thought he had found a Chinese pot at Troy, and was delighted; Sir Arthur Evans was equally pleased to see "the Libyan codpiece" turn up in Crete, and confidently derived Cretan *tholos* tombs from stone circles found in modern Libya. (That Libyans build overnight stone circles to restrain their horses even now, and that one of Evans's Libyan circles is in fact an Italian gun emplacement of World War I, does not erase the open-mindedness of the intellect behind the idea.) Why on earth does Bernal claim that he is the first ever to look to Egypt and the East, when virtually all contemporary scholars have welcomed every new sign of contact, and tried to trace, as the the late Egyptologist William Stevenson Smith stated in the title of one of his books (1965), "Interconnections in the Ancient Near East"? The other reason for indignation is the constant perversion of facts in Bernal's second volume, a sad matter from a serious historian.

Bernal believes, or seems to believe, that there is no essential difference between Egyptian culture and language, written in hieroglyphs, and the languages of the ancient Near East, written in cuneiform. Large sections of his book consist of claims that words from one language derive from another. When it is convenient for him, he will also include the language of the Hurrian people in this linguistic melting pot (*BA* 2:40, 45, 119). In the wake of Bernal's imagined Egyptian conquest of central Greece in the third millennium B.C.E., Thisbe in Greek Boeotia is named for Teshub, the Hurrian storm god (2:119–20). It is not clear how the Hurrian storm god is connected to the invading Egyptians, but there is a great deal that is not clear in Bernal's second volume; confusion is the cost of reading it.

Bernal adds Berber as an influential ancient language too; he claims a Berber linguistic root for "Atlas, Atlantic"—the word *adrar*, mountain, which was not attested before the nineteenth century C.E., "but there is no reason to suppose that it is not an ancient word" (2:299). (By the way, Bernal adds [2:301–2], the Atlantic was also named from the Egyptian *itrw*, Nile, perhaps used for any large body of water: "Atlantis as a sea could well be the setting of Thera in the Mediterranean, though it is possible that this combined with a vague sense of America beyond the Atlantic Ocean . . . I see no reason why educated Egyptians should not have known of America at the time of Plato in the early 4th century." The stressed, repeated use of "I" is characteristic of many sentences in this book.)

This indiscriminate use of ancient languages offers to Bernal multiple sources for the etymology of words we used to think of as being Greek. So the psyche, the Greek "breath" or "spirit," is said to come from the Egyptian *sw*, a parasol or shelter (2:264). The magical winged horse Pegasus is derived from the Egyptian *pgw*, a jug for washing (2:95). This is a sad reduction for those of us who imagined Pegasus pawing in the spring Hippocrene; could he fit his hoof into a washing jug? The Greek god Pan is named for a Nile fish, *p3 ỉn* (2:271). It must be said that many of Bernal's linguistic claims are no more than assertive guesses.

In much the same way, Bernal believes there is no essential difference between Egypt and the kingdoms and city-states of the Near East. This premise would have astonished those Egyptian pharaohs who used to lead their armies against the "wicked Asiatics" across the eastern border. Bernal also believes that Egypt was essentially African, and therefore black. But he does not say what we are to make of the historical accounts of Egyptian pharaohs campaigning against black neighbors to the south, in the Land of Kush, as when Tuthmosis I of Egypt, around 1510 B.C.E., annihilated a black Kushite army at the Third Cataract and came home with the body of a black Kushite prince hanging upside down from the prow of his ship (Kendall 1982, 8; Breasted 1906, 34). Perhaps Bernal thinks of this as African tribal warfare.

Of course there were always Nubians, Sudanese, Kushites traveling in and out of Egypt, serving in the army, occasionally taking power as ruling dynasties; but these men of the Upper Nile were normally held to be quite distinct in ethnic background from the Egyptians themselves. Bernal bypasses these facts because he wants Egyptian culture to be an undifferentiated part of African culture. He is well aware—but does not adequately recognize—that the Egyptians regarded their land as being bordered by four neighboring regions: Kush or Nubia to the south, Libya to the west, the Asiatic kingdoms on the east, and the peoples of the isles of the great green, Cretans, other islanders and people of the Greek mainland, as their northern neighbors. These peoples are all painted in Egyptian tombs as being anthropologically distinct and as occupying lands with different natural resources. As Bernal also knows, the different neighbors are often contrasted with one another in the tombs of the fifteenth century B.C.E., to give a sense of how the peoples on the distant edges of the known world loved to bring different kinds of gifts to a dominant Egypt. The best known pictures are in the tomb of Rekhmire, where the men of Kush from the south, wearing animal-skin loincloths, with short woolly hair, bring as tribute longhorned cattle, hunting dogs, a hobbled giraffe, a leashed baboon and green monkeys or vervets on leading reins, logs of ebony, a cheetah, ostrich eggs in a basket, tusks of elephant ivory, cheetah hides, and gold rings. These men are balanced against the Keftiu men of Crete in the north, in their brilliantly patterned kilts and high boots, long black wavy hair combed in three long strands over each shoulder, who bring gold and silver vases of special ceremonial Cretan shapes, textiles, a sword in its scabbard, and an ingot of copper. The Kushites and the Keftiu represent the south and north poles of the Egyptian world, and are distinguished physically both from each other and from the Egyptians.

Sometimes the men of the Upper Nile beyond Egypt's borders are paired with Asiatics, as on the famous finials of King Tutankhamun's footstool, or in the tomb of Sobkhote where Semitic envoys bring gold, silver, and blue vases, the gold ones with fantastic wrought flowers above the rims, an eagle's-head rhyton, even a girl-child. These men are a yellow color and wear long white linen or flax robes with diagonal hems. They are bearded, alternately bald or with long dark hair tied back and pressed down by fillets. They are set off against the men of black Africa, who are painted like to alternate patches of color. They wear giraffe-skinned loincloths, have short black wiry hair, and bring gold rings, ebony logs, a bunch of giraffe tails to use as fly whisks, a basket of fruit, a leopard skin, a green monkey, and a baboon. In this case the polar contrasts are between the lands to the south and east, not to the south and north.

Bernal conceals such polar pairings; and when he does mention the Keftiu scenes in Egypt he omits the Nubians or men of Kush. He would like the Cretans to be "Syro-Palestinians" (2:45, 184, 432). At the same time he leaves out other contacts among the Aegean, Egypt, and black Africa. What about ostrich eggs and ivory, whether African or Syrian, so beloved in the Aegean world? What about the black-painted tribute bearers on the walls of the Mycenaean palace at Pylos, or the "Libyan"-faced warrior on the Silver War Krater from the shaft graves at Mycenae? What about the lion, borrowed from the Egyptian word for a lion-statue, *rw* (as opposed to a living lion, *ma*), vocalized as *rewo*, already attested as a man's name in the Linear B tablets of Knossos in Crete, our first "European" Leon? Bernal dismisses the lion in passing (2:386). Since he devotes so much space to deriving Greek words from the Egyptian language, how can he largely ignore the role of the heroic lion who fills the Homeric epics, as though Homeric poetry might itself be contaminating to the pure vision of Egyptian influence? I cannot even find a passage of interpretation about the constant visits of the Homeric Greek gods to banquet with the Ethiopians.

The archaeological points that are stressed in his book are hard to assess as pure archaeology. Bernal believes, for example, that Egyptians conquered the Greek region of Boeotia in the third millennium B.C.E. Is this claim based on the appearance of Egyptian cultural objects in Greek soil? Apparently not; but who needs objects? Instead Bernal mentions the coincidence of names between Egyptian and Boeotian Thebes and cites a flat-topped tumulus at Boeotian Thebes that he believes to derive from stepped pyramids in Egypt, in the Third Dynasty of the Old Kingdom, so that the conquest of central Greece must date to that period (2:128–31). It also reminds him of Silbury Hill near Avebury in England: "The builders of Silbury were aware of the contemporary Egyptian pyramids" (2:131). The clinching fact is that Lake Kopais in Boeotia was drained in the Bronze Age, and the Egyptians knew all about drainage and irrigation (2:135, 145). The complete lack of archaeological evidence for Egyptians having been in Boeotia does not disturb Bernal, because he is dealing only in "competitive plausibility" (1:8) and is not deterred by the absence of archaeological artifacts.

The same approach is apparent in his sections on Crete. Once Greece is safely Egyptian, Crete must be Egyptian, too, in Bernal's view, because Crete had palaces and Egypt had palaces as well (2:158–62). The two sets of palaces are hard to link archaeologically or architecturally (and the Malkata and Amarna Egyptian palaces are not even in Bernal's index), so it would seem that the Platonic idea of a palace is enough to prove Egyptian conquest. But why is Egypt the model for Crete, and not the Near East, which also had multiple palaces? Because Crete and Egypt shared a special reverence for the sun, for bull cults and bull fights, and King Minos of Crete must be named for the first Egyptian pharaoh, Mn or Menes. Or perhaps he is named for the lecherous Egyptian bull *Min* (2:166–77). This creation of fact by assertion will, I hope, be treated skeptically by students.

I am truly sorry that the second volume of *Black Athena* got into print before the news in the summer of 1992 that the Austrian excavators of Avaris in the Nile Delta, the capital town established by the Hyksos invaders of Egypt, found a thousand fragments of Minoan Cretan painted frescoes there (*Art Journal* 1991, 60; Keys 1991, 4). And in 1991 the archaeologist W. Niemeier reported the discovery of a painted Minoan floor with flowers, from the sixteenth century B.C.E., at Tell Kabri in Israel. What if the influence should, from Bernal's point of view, be flowing the wrong way, out of the Aegean world into Egypt? What if Cretan painters were so renowned that Egyptian princes invited them to show them new aspects of palace decoration? It would not be surprising, considering the respect the East and South had for the craftsmen of Crete in a continually interconnected world.

After Crete, the volcanic island of Thera, the southernmost island of the Cyclades, must be drawn into the Egyptian sphere too. Bernal apparently continues to believe that the Bronze Age eruption of Thera—whenever that was, between 1628 and 1500 B.C.E.—was a "gigantic event" with repercussions around the world (2:275, 281). The eruption of Thera caused dry fog, dimmed sun, cold weather, and failed harvests in China and so, in Bernal's opinion, precipitated the change from the Xia to the Shang Dynasty.

Perhaps the memory of Exodus was connected too. Bernal writes that scholars disbelieved Leon Pomerance's idea that this was so only because he was a Jew. Bernal wants to revive the vivid association between the Thera eruption and the biblical "pillar of cloud . . . by night a pillar of fire" (Exodus 13:21) (*BA* 2:276–77). Now that he has become a high priest of chronology, and can raise dates at will, he reasserts that the link exists and that the eruption must have taken place, in 1628. Still, the biblical account "must have been written many centuries after the event, as it refers to Philistia . . . at the end of the thirteenth century B.C.E." (2:293). Once one starts mingling events in this fashion, in the sphere of oral poetry, why try to claim that one is using archaeological documentation at all? Bernal has indeed blurred the borders of many hard-won distinctions.

Bernal's argument in the second volume of *Black Athena* reminds one of a gigantic chess game without an opponent; the author places his pieces on the world board where he wishes, not constrained by any rules. Would you like an Egyptian conquest of Anatolia around 1900 B.C.E., and especially of the epic town of Troy? "An Egyptian army, many of whom were Black and led by a prince who was Black—the Deep Southern origin of many pharaohs has been noted—had marched through Anatolia from east to west" (2:239, 245, 253, 256–57, 268). Would you like the Scythians and South Russians to be black? Colchis in the modern Russian Caucasus is the same as Kush south of Egypt, and "there is the tantalizing possibility that the long-standing Black population in the area arose, in part, from [Sesostris'] army" (2:271).

Bernal's second volume is a whirling confusion of half-digested reading, bold linguistic supposition, and preconceived dogma. Did you ever wonder why there is so much gold and silver in the shaft graves at Mycenae? The reason is that the royal persons buried in the shaft graves are the refugee "foreign princes" whom the Egyptians called the Hyksos, after the Egyptians threw them out of their foothold in the Nile Delta, from their capital town of Avaris (2:379, 397, 406, 408). Evidently they failed to bring a single Egyptian thing with them north to Greece, or at least they dropped their possessions overboard—all but a single scarab in a later tomb—before they got to Greece. As they came, they shifted from being Egyptian *Hyksos* ("foreign princes") to being Greek *hiketai* ("suppliants") (2:364)—although that word has a well-attested Greek root, *hikneomai, hiko*, "I arrive as a suppliant after exile or murder."

How do we know that the royal skeletons in the shaft graves at Mycenae are the same as the Hyksos? Bernal denies that archaeological, forensic, or osteological findings would supply the answer; archaeologists are not to get in the way either of legend or of imperial fantasy-chess.

> The royalty buried in the Shaft Graves and the other early Mycenaean tombs were Hyksos invaders from Syria, who probably spoke Hurrian and possibly even Indo-Iranian. However, the majority of the ruling class were Levantine Semitic-speakers together with significant numbers of Egyptians and Cretans, most of whom probably spoke a Semitic language themselves. . . . There were foreign conquerors from Egypt and the Levant ruling parts or all of Greece up to the arrival of the Pelopids from Anatolia . . . in the case of Thebes the original Phoenician Dynasty survived until the fall of that city in the 13th century. (2:45)

We are left to conclude that if there are no demonstrably Hyksos objects in the shaft grave burials, there should have been. Bernal writes that some of the pieces seem to share the same international language of art that Hyksos art would have had if we knew more about it. How strange it is that these eastern rulers quite forgot their cuneiform or hieroglyphic scripts when they arrived in Greece, and so could no longer communicate with their original lands. Well, almost certainly they used the written alphabet instead; between 1800 and 1400 B.C.E., although no examples of its use would be found for another thousand years. For Bernal to need examples, or physical objects, to support a hypothesis is to commit the archaeological sin known as "positivism"; it must be resisted (2:66, 133, 135, 522).

It seems to me to be a shame that a friend of mine so intelligent, sophisticated, cultured, and widely read as Martin Bernal should have been driven, for personal or political reasons, to blame the entire world of classical archaeology for having failed to see that Greek culture was in debt to the older civilizations of Egypt and the East. According to him, "the great Bronze Age cultures of Asia and Africa, upon which not only the techniques but the spirit and reason of Classical civilization depended, were, and had to be, denied" (2:38). No serious scholars of antiquity I know of have ever doubted the debt, or the fascination, the Greeks always felt for Egypt and the East. Minoan and Mycenaean painters used Egypt's palm trees and papyrus plants as a kind of shorthand expression for "exotic paradise overseas." Classical Greek mercenary soldiers working in Egypt literally belittled what they saw in order to feel more at home with the monumental scale of the land and its buildings; so those huge stone pointed pillars became "obelisks"—"little spits for roasting"—and large angry crocodiles became "scared yellow lizards," and the ostrich became a sparrow, *strouthos.*

Back in the Bronze Age there were no national borders, no passports, no strange currencies, no obstacles to unlimited travel and the acquisition of new cultural and artistic experiences, except what lack of language skills or local wars might pose. It was natural for Greeks, like Canaanites, Anatolians, Syrians, Egyptians, Nubians, and Libyans, to sail around one another's shores, exchanging goods and learning new things, marrying one another, telling tales of "multicultural diversity" to the children. The wonderful Kaş (Ulu Burun) shipwreck recently found off the Lycian shore of Turkey, with luxuries and medicines and metals from seven cultures aboard, only confirms what we have been teaching for years about the kinds of exchange that took place among Bronze Age peoples. (Bernal treats George Bass's discovery of the wreck patronizingly, as coming from "an unimpeachably gentile source" [2:466], which seems to mean that Bass is not Jewish; is racist language making an unfortunate comeback through such expressions? See Tritle, this volume.)

Bernal has expended enormous energy on *Black Athena,* but he is absolutely wrong to say in conclusion, as he does, that he has rewritten the history of the eastern Mediterranean. His blurring of true distinctions, his claims to superior interpretation,[1] his painfully jumbled exposition of ideas, his naive belief that every person inside a defined space belonged to a single race or ethnic group, his endearingly childlike faith in the absolute historical value of Greek myths (when the Greeks routinely and sometimes with ironic wit liked to refer to the Egyptians as being older, wiser, more scientific, more medical, more cultivated than themselves and therefore as being "our ancestors, our teacher") come as a disappointment from such a quick-minded scholar whose "evidence" was so eagerly awaited.

NOTE

1. Bernal (2:54, 477–79) faults the excavators of Mycenae for failing to discover the temple of the Egyptian pharaoh Amenophis III on that site, for, in Egypt, the finding of faience plaques with the royal name would lead scholars to look for a temple or a shrine. But perhaps, he speculates, the temple did not last long, or was never built. The building, the substantial institution, and the many priests in complex hierarchies may have moved to Eleusis and become the cult of Demeter there. Wait for *Black Athena*, volume 4.

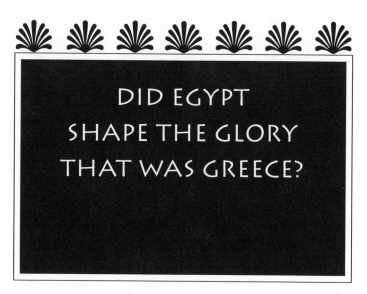

DID EGYPT SHAPE THE GLORY THAT WAS GREECE?

John E. Coleman

> By many other statements like these [about similarities between Egyptian
> and Athenian practices], spoken more out of a love for glory than with
> regard for the truth, as I see the matter, [the Egyptians] claim Athens as a
> colony of theirs because of the fame of that city. In general, the Egyptians
> say that their ancestors sent forth numerous colonies to many parts
> of the inhabited world, by reason of the pre-eminence of their former
> kings and their excessive population; but since they offer no precise proof
> whatsoever for these statements, and since no historian worthy
> of credence testifies in their support, we have not thought
> that their accounts merited recording.
> —Diodorus Siculus 1.29 (1st cent. B.C.E.; trans. Oldfather 1933, 97)

Two of the four projected volumes of *Black Athena*, Martin Bernal's sweeping study of Greek civilization and prehistory, have appeared. The work is
receiving wide media attention for its message that "Afroasiatic roots" were
basic in the formation of classical Greek culture and that these roots have
been ignored because of a prevailing racist vision of an ancient Greece un-
blemished by African and Semitic cultural debts. But is Bernal's picture of
Greek history accurate, and are his accusations of racist distortions true?

At the outset, let me note that nobody would now maintain that Greece developed in a vacuum. Influences and borrowing have long been recognized.
That the Greeks derived their alphabet, for instance, from the Phoenicians
was acknowledged by some classical Greeks[1] and has always been accepted

by modern scholars. Greek writers sometimes also credited the Egyptians and Babylonians with inventing mathematics and astronomy respectively, thereby providing a solid basis for Greek advances in those fields.[2] It has been a commonplace from the later nineteenth century on for archaeologists to refer to the formative period of Greek art (roughly the seventh century B.C.E.) as the "Graeco-Phoenician," "Graeco-Oriental," or "Orientalizing" period because of the wealth of influences from the Eastern Mediterranean.[3] And archaeology is continuously adding new evidence for intercultural contacts, as witnessed, for instance, by the recently discovered Bronze Age shipwreck off the southwestern coast of Turkey at Ulu Burun.[4]

Recognizing that Greek civilization was influenced from abroad and made use of previous advances in mathematics and science, however, is a far cry from asserting that it had "Afroasiatic roots." Claims of massive Eastern influences, as opposed to many cultural exchanges, face major obstacles. There are basic differences between the Greek language, which belongs to the Indo-European family of languages, and Canaanite and Egyptian, which belong to the Afro-Asiatic family. Greek has much more in common in its structure and vocabulary with Hindi or Russian than it does with Egyptian or Canaanite; and as we shall see below, obvious loan words in Greek from the eastern Mediterranean are few. The differences between the religion of classical Greece and those of Egypt and the eastern Mediterranean are much more obvious than the similarities; compare in your mind's eye, for instance, the thoroughly anthropomorphic gods of Greece, like Zeus and Apollo, with the hawk-headed, cow-headed and jackal-headed gods of Egypt.

In order to convince us of Greece's putative debt to Egypt, Bernal and others with similar views must demonstrate the existence of great similarities not now readily apparent and explain how these similar traits are likely to have come from the East, rather than being the result of coincidence, or even of western influence on the eastern world.

Bernal's argument rests on claims that Greece was invaded or colonized in the eighteenth and seventeenth centuries B.C.E. (the Early Mycenaean period) by the Hyksos, a Semitic-speaking Canaanite people from southern Syria-Palestine; that it underwent massive cultural changes as a result of this invasion and subsequent contact; and that the classical Greeks of the first millennium B.C.E. (the Iron Age) knew of these invasions and resultant changes. This is what Bernal calls the "Ancient Model" of the development of Greek civilization.

THE HYKSOS INVASION OF GREECE

Scholars agree that the Hyksos infiltrated and later came to rule Egypt during the Second Intermediate Period (generally dated ca. 1660–1550 B.C.E.).

They were eventually expelled from Egypt by Ahmose, the first pharaoh of the Eighteenth Dynasty (1550–1525 B.C.E.), and he and his immediate successors subsequently campaigned in southern Syria-Palestine and established their hegemony over it. Bernal claims that the Hyksos also invaded Greece, although historical sources do not support this.

The extensive historical records maintained by the peoples of Egypt and the Near East in the Bronze Age make no mention of a conquest of Greece, either by the Hyksos or by any other people. Nor are Hyksos invasions of Greece mentioned by Manetho, an important later source on the Hyksos.[5] On the rare occasions when Egyptian and Canaanite second-millennium documents mention the Aegean, they suggest that the peoples of Egypt and Canaan (i.e., Syria-Palestine) were familiar with Aegean peoples only as traders[6] and, occasionally, as raiders. Mycenaean Linear B documents from the second half of the second millennium B.C.E. also provide no evidence for Hyksos invasions; although they occasionally list people with foreign or possibly foreign names, such as Ai-ku-pi-ti-jo (the "Egyptian"), the rarity of clearly recognizable Egyptian or Semitic names suggests that Egyptian and eastern Mediterranean presence in the Bronze Age Aegean was very slight.

There is also a serious chronological problem with Bernal's proposed date for a Hyksos invasion at the beginning of the Aegean Late Bronze Age. The recent redating of the volcanic eruption of Thera to 1628 B.C.E. indicates that the Late Bronze Age began no later than 1700 B.C.E. The possibility of Hyksos activity in the Aegean at this early date is unlikely, for it would predate the Hyksos rise to power in Egypt. Bernal's thesis that the Hyksos were responsible for Egyptian influences on Greece presupposes that they adopted Egyptian culture before they invaded Greece.[7]

Furthermore, Egyptian or Canaanite objects, although more frequent later, are rarely found in Greece in contexts dating from the time of the supposed invasions. Although Bernal claims that the shaft graves at the Late Bronze Age citadel of Mycenae in southern Greece contained Egyptian objects and were therefore those of Hyksos princes (*BA* 2:395), he fails to mention that the Egyptian attributions are doubtful. Not a single object bears the distinctive marks of Egyptian or eastern Mediterranean origin, except possibly for one scarab and two ostrich eggs (which may have come from Libya via Crete rather than from Egypt).[8] Emily Vermeule concludes in *The Art of the Shaft Graves at Mycenae* that "there is nothing truly Egyptian in the Shaft Graves" (1975, 18).

Bernal's arguments for a foreign origin or connection of the people buried in the shaft graves at Mycenae is only the latest in a long series of such proposals, several of which have already made a connection with the Hyksos or with Egypt. Persson argued that the graves contained Mycenaeans who had served as mercenaries for the Egyptians during the expulsion of the Hyksos;

Marinatos maintained that they contained princes who "entered Greece from Syria or at least via Syria"; Stubbings and Best actually anticipated Bernal in maintaining that the burials were those of the Hyksos themselves.[9] Many others whom Bernal himself discusses[10] have argued that the graves contained the first Indo-European speakers to arrive in Greece, whether from the Balkans to the north (Buck, Nilsson) or from eastern Anatolia and the Caucasus (Muhly, Drews); still others (Hooker, Dickinson), in what I think is the correct view, have emphasized the continuity between the shaft graves and the preceding Middle Helladic culture in Greece. As this wide divergence of opinion demonstrates, the evidence of the shaft graves is at best inconclusive and cannot in itself support the claim for a Hyksos invasion of Greece.

In fact, all scholars agree that the strongest outside influence on the shaft graves comes not from the east but from Minoan Crete. Since at that time the Minoans were culturally more advanced than the Greek mainland and had closer interconnections with the eastern Mediterranean, possible reflections of Egyptian or Levantine customs in the shaft graves are best explained as having come indirectly through Minoan Crete.

Bernal is on safe ground when he emphasizes extensive interconnections between the Aegean and the eastern Mediterranean from the sixteenth century B.C.E. onward. The Aegean is generally recognized as being part of a well-developed network of trade and perhaps even diplomacy. As the Late Bronze Age shipwrecks at Cape Gelidonya and Ulu Burun attest, copper and tin were brought to the Aegean from the eastern Mediterranean or further east. However, although such contacts may have influenced cultural developments in the Aegean, the evidence does not support Bernal's claims of massive borrowing. Greece is, after all, many hundreds of miles from the cultures which are claimed to have influenced it so deeply, and communications were exclusively by sea. Although such conditions were little obstacle to marine trade, they did not favor casual immigration or a gradual mixing of cultures.

It is central to Bernal's thesis that Egypt and Canaan exerted massive influence on Greek religion. Yet not a single recognizably Egyptian or Canaanite god is mentioned in Mycenaean Linear B Greek documents. Instead the names are those of the divinities known from later times, such as Zeus, Poseidon, and Hera.[11] That these divine names are themselves derived from Egyptian and Canaanite ones is also highly doubtful (see below).

Bernal cites no unequivocal instance of cultural borrowing significant enough to be considered basic to Aegean civilization in the Late Bronze Age. Minoan society, for instance, has many unique features, and although some artistic techniques and subjects come from the eastern Mediterranean, many are distinctively Aegean (for example, bare-breasted females with flounced skirts, and bull leaping).[12] Some alleged borrowing may actually have been

Aegean exports to Egypt and Syria-Palestine rather than the reverse. For instance, the "flying gallop," a pose in which animals are depicted with front legs stretched forward and rear legs backward, occurs earlier in the Aegean and probably spread from there to Egypt and the eastern Mediterranean. And there is no prototype in Egypt and Syria-Palestine for the palatial *megaron* (hall), the focus of Mycenaean society. The frescoes with Minoan subjects from Tell el-Dabʿa (Avaris) in Egypt (Bietak 1992), Tell Kabri in Palestine, and Alalakh in north Syria (Niemeier 1991) are far more plausibly explained as due to Cretan artisans traveling eastward than to Hyksos invaders going westward.

A further argument against Hyksos invasions is that Aegean peoples continued to use their local syllabic scripts, Linear A and Linear B, whereas they never used Egyptian hieroglyphics or Near Eastern cuneiform (the few instances of hieroglyphics in the Aegean occur on objects imported from Egypt and Syria-Palestine).[13] Except for dubious arguments about letter forms, there is also no evidence for Bernal's claim (e.g., *BA* 1:432) that the Semitic alphabet was introduced to Greece in the fifteenth or fourteenth century B.C.E. On the contrary, because the alphabet is first attested in Greece no earlier than about 750 B.C.E., it is improbable that it was used there for six hundred years or more previously and left no trace in the archaeological record. Furthermore, neither Linear A nor Linear B shows signs that alphabetic writing was in simultaneous use in the Aegean.

Bernal also supports his thesis of massive cultural borrowing by citing Egyptian and Semitic loan words in classical Greek. He states in the preface of his first volume that "up to a quarter" of Greek vocabulary has Semitic origins and that "one could find plausible etymologies for a further 20–25 per cent of the Greek vocabulary from Egyptian, as well as the names for most Greek gods and many place names" (*BA* 1:xiv). However, he has yet to document in detail such an enormous component of foreign vocabulary in Greek, and many of the putative examples of foreign borrowing he has so far suggested seem little short of fantastic (see below). Obvious and generally recognized Semitic and Egyptian loan words in Greek are relatively few. A compilation in *The Cambridge Ancient History* (T. Braun 1982, 24–29), for instance, lists only thirty-seven Semitic loan words attested earlier than the fourth century B.C.E. Almost all the generally recognized loan words in Greek from eastern Mediterranean sources designate foreign commodities (such as papyrus, linen, ebony, natron, and sesame) and are best explained as resulting from trade contacts. Many others Bernal cites are dubious, especially the personal and place names. After all, proper nouns often lack demonstrable etymologies, and inasmuch as those Bernal cites are truly foreign to Greek and the Indo-European family of languages to which Greek belongs, other source languages more plausible than Egyptian may be suggested. We know, for instance, that the Greeks borrowed some place names from the pre-Greek inhabitants of the Aegean, and other loans from that source may go un-recognized.[14] Words also surely came into Greek from the language of the Minoans. Although Minoan Linear A is undeciphered, good evidence exists that it was neither an Indo-European nor a Semitic language.[15] When items of trade and doubtful names are removed from Bernal's lists, few words remain to support his views of foreign conquest and influence.

In short, there are good reasons for denying such strong cultural influences on the Aegean in the second millennium as Bernal postulates. Mycenaean civilization, as revealed by archaeological and documentary evidence, differs significantly from that of Egypt and Syria-Palestine. There is no evidence that Egyptian or Canaanite scripts or languages were used in the Aegean in the Bronze Age or that Egyptian or Canaanite gods were worshiped there. The available Bronze Age evidence, rather than supporting Bernal's thesis, is strongly opposed to it.

THE ANCIENT GREEK BELIEF IN INVASIONS FROM EGYPT OR SYRIA-PALESTINE

The picture here is far from straightforward. The Homeric and Hesiodic poems, which codified Greek views about the past in the eighth and seventh centuries B.C.E. after the "Dark Ages" (several centuries of cultural isolation and recession following the fall of Bronze Age civilization), are the earliest sources for Greek beliefs about their past. They contradict the view that there was a general Greek belief in such invasions (Bernal's "Ancient Model"), for they make no mention of invasions or immigration from Egypt or Syria-Palestine and generally show only a limited awareness of the Eastern Mediterranean. Because Bernal claims especially strong Near Eastern and Egyptian influence on Greek religion, let us consider Hesiod's *Theogony*, a sort of charter for the origin of the world and human institutions. Among the many generations of gods in the *Theogony* there are more than 120 individually named divinities and characters, almost all explicitly connected with Greek lands. Zeus and the other Olympian gods, for instance, had their abode on Mount Olympus. Other figures include personifications such as Night, Sleep, Death, Strife, and Judgment, all standard Greek words. Also mentioned are at least ten groups of beings, such as the Muses, the nymphs, the rivers, and the stars. I challenge Bernal and other champions of overwhelming Eastern influence to identify any of these 130 or more names in Near Eastern or Egyptian sources.[16] No Egyptian or Near Eastern divinities occur, not even the most common ones, such as Amun, Osiris, Ba'al, Seth, or Astarte.

Most Greeks in all periods accepted without question that most of their gods were indigenous and that their own rituals and cultural practices had been established by those indigenous gods themselves, often with the help of various Greek mythical and semimythical figures like the Muses, Prometheus, Daedalus, Orpheus, Musaeus, and Lycurgus.[17] Bernal's claim that the ancient Greeks believed in massive foreign influences on Greek culture is therefore highly misleading from the outset, as it fails to acknowledge the Greeks' general belief in the overwhelmingly indigenous nature of their own institutions.

When later classical Greek writers mention early Eastern influences on, and/or invasions of Greece, they connect them to mythical characters and events, particularly the coming to Greece of Danaus and of Cadmus. Bernal's insistence that the myths of Danaus and Cadmus reflect historical events ignores the function of myth, whose purpose is to provide explanations and social precedents rather than historical information. The coming of Danaus and the Danaids to Greece from Egypt (pursued by Aegyptus and his sons) is doubtful evidence for a belief in actual invasions. The main characters served to explain the ethnic names of the various peoples of the earth rather than as history. Danaus, for instance, is the eponym of the Greeks themselves (*Danaoi* in the Homeric poems); Aegyptus is the eponym for the Egyptians (*Aigyptioi*). Cadmus' brother Phoenix is the eponym of the Phoenicians (*Phoinices*). Even if Homer and Hesiod believed that Danaus and Cadmus were real people who came to Greece from the Near East, a doubtful proposition,[18] there is no evidence that they regarded them as leading invasions rather than acting as heroic individuals. It was only later, when the myths had been rationalized, that they were interpreted as referring to invasions. Because all these characters were in any case regarded as descendants of Zeus and the Greek princess Io, they could equally as well be taken to refer to Greek penetration of the East as the reverse (T. Braun 1982; Hall, this volume).

The legends about Cadmus' bringing writing and other civilized arts to Greece from Egypt or Phoenicia are confused and inconsistent, differing even over whether Cadmus was an Egyptian or a Phoenician; although he was believed to have founded Greek Thebes during the age of the heroes (that is, the Bronze Age), he was also credited with introducing the alphabet from Phoenicia. As already mentioned, the alphabet is not attested in Greece before about 750 B.C.E. These inconsistencies are, in my view, a strong indication that it is wrong to regard the myth of the coming of Cadmus as a real historical event.

The Greek historian Herodotus (mid–fifth century B.C.E.), despite his belief in the coming of Danaus and Cadmus to Greece, provides equivocal evidence at best for Bernal's position. Herodotus' knowledge of the Bronze Age is sketchy and inaccurate. For instance, the Hyksos were apparently unknown to him: they are not even mentioned for their role in Egyptian history, let alone as invaders of Greece. Among Herodotus' errors are the insertion of the Greek mythological character Proteus into the sequence of pharaohs and the dating of the builders of the Great Pyramids near the end rather than the beginning of Egyptian history.

Thucydides, who knew of Herodotus' histories, makes no mention of invasions or influence from Egypt or Syria-Palestine. Furthermore, Plutarch explicitly disagrees with many of Herodotus' claims of Egyptian influence on Greece and accuses him of "using worthless Egyptian stories to overthrow the most solemn and sacred truths of Greek religion" (*On the Malice of Herodotus* 14). Even Diodorus Siculus, whose account of Egypt resembles that of Herodotus, is highly skeptical about claims of Egyptian invasions, as the passage quoted at the opening of this essay shows. That passage alone casts great doubts on Bernal's alleged "Ancient Model," and his attempts to explain it as meaning something other than it appears to mean are simply in error.[19]

Bernal's position that Greek religious practices had Egyptian roots depends to a large extent on his claims that the actual names of Greek gods were derived from those of Egyptian ones, such as Athena from Nēit (*BA* 1:51–52). Quite apart from the doubts of modern linguists,[20] there is no ancient authority for the particular derivations he asserts. No ancient Greek author mentions them, despite the ancient love of "etymologizing." Not even Herodotus makes specific equations between Egyptian and Greek names for the gods,[21] and a passage in Diodorus Siculus shows that the ancient sources were greatly confused on this point.[22] In fact, rather than resting on detailed similarities between Greece and Egypt, Herodotus' assertions of Egyptian origins for the Greek gods seem to depend primarily on the fact that Egypt was an older civilization, an argument that depends on the fallacy that later phenomena are necessarily the result of earlier ones.[23]

In short, there were various contradictory beliefs about the relationships between Greece on the one hand and Egypt and Syria-Palestine on the other, rather than the single "Ancient Model" postulated by Bernal.

The vagueness of classical Greeks like Herodotus is understandable, given their very limited sources of information. The Bronze Age had ended some seven hundred years earlier, and the "Dark Ages," a period of at least three hundred years in which writing was unknown and cultural memories were orally transmitted, had intervened between the Bronze Age and the time of Homer and Hesiod.[24] The Homeric poems, the principal source on the "heroic age" for later Greeks, present an anachronistic and distorted picture of the Mycenaean period, showing, for instance, that the former existence of Linear B writing had been completely forgotten. Furthermore, although some classical Greeks were familiar with Egypt, there is no evidence that they ever had access to accurate historical records from there. By the time of Herodotus and other Greek visitors, Egypt had long since ceased to be a leading center of civilization—in his day it was a part of the Persian Empire—and priests, a primary source of historical information for the Greeks, were not likely to have been well informed. The ancient "tour guides" who escorted Greeks and others around Egyptian monuments were likely illiterate and even less informed than the priests. Egyptian civilization seemed to Greeks demonstrably older, as indeed it was, and the temptation to ascribe the origins of civilized customs to the older civilization was irresistible in view of the scarcity of precedents in what the Greeks knew of their own past. That the Greeks embroidered their accounts of Egypt and the eastern Mediterranean with mythical characters of their own invention, such as Proteus, Danaus, and Cadmus, demonstrates how ignorant they were of Bronze Age events. Furthermore, classical Greeks were totally unaware that families of languages exist and that their own language belonged to a family (Indo-European) different from that to which the Egyptian and Semitic languages belong. In sum, even if the Greeks had unanimously believed in invasions from the East, we would have reason to be skeptical in the absence of independent evidence.

RACISM IN CLASSICAL SCHOLARSHIP

Racism has been an undeniable factor in classical scholarship and it is much to be deplored and condemned. Bernal has done a great service in charting the course of racism in the nineteenth and earlier twentieth century and in drawing attention to contemporary racist attitudes. However, one is not entitled to conclude without further evidence that racism was the *predominant reason* for widely accepted scholarly views. Surely all scholarship should be judged primarily on the basis of the evidence and arguments it presents. After all, as Bernal himself acknowledges (*BA* 2:10), even racist scholars may reach correct conclusions.

In fact, part of Bernal's reconstruction of the development of nineteenth- and twentieth-century scholarship is erroneous. Scholarly recognition in the nineteenth century of an Orientalizing period of Greek art, as mentioned above, contradicts his view that scholars were increasingly blinded by racism to influences from the East. Nor, so far as I can tell, do archaeological publications in the late nineteenth century and in the first half of the twentieth show any reluctance to suggest eastern and African influences on Bronze Age Greece. W. E. Gladstone, in a preface to Schliemann's 1878 volume on Mycenae, enumerated many foreign traits in the Homeric poems and in the finds from the shaft graves and wrote: "Heroic Greece is full of the marks of what I may term Phoenicianism, most of which passed into the usages of the country, and contributed to form the base of Hellenic life" (xxxvi). In the 1920s Sir Arthur Evans proposed that one branch of the Minoan people of Crete were Libyans from the Nile Delta.[25] In an excavation report on tombs at Midea near Mycenae published in 1942 Persson devoted a whole chapter to

"Mycenae and Egypt" in which he posited great Egyptian influence on the Aegean.[26] Bernal fails adequately to acknowledge such counterexamples to his thesis of the all-pervasiveness of racism in classical scholarship.

Many of Bernal's charges that racism was decisive in scholarship are based on the gradual rejection of the ancient belief that Phoenicians actually settled in Greece.[27] Yet the reasons for this rejection were not solely "external," as Bernal claims. Over the nineteenth and twentieth centuries evidence has steadily accumulated to show that the Phoenicians were not an important presence in the Aegean. The dozens of ancient Greek cities, towns, and sanctuaries and the thousands of tombs that were investigated from 1870 onward showed no traces of the presence of Phoenicians other than as traders. To this day almost no significant traces of Phoenician activity have been found on Greek soil, not even at Thera or Thasus, which are explicitly said by Herodotus (4.146, 6.48) to have been colonized by Phoenicians. Although Bernal assails the argument *ex silentio* ("from silence") as a weak form of argument, it is, in fact, as strong as the amount of evidence on which it is based. In this case, the absence of evidence for Phoenician settlers in Greece became ever more conclusive as more sites were investigated.

Racism was not necessarily decisive in the increasing skepticism in the eighteenth and nineteenth centuries about the influence of Egypt on Greece. Other, more plausible reasons can be given for the change in attitudes. The greater accessibility of Greece and Egypt and the higher standards of rational analysis during the eighteenth-century Enlightenment were surely important factors. Greece was again beginning to be visited and its ancient remains studied by educated Europeans, after a long period of decline and isolation during the later Byzantine Empire and the Turkish occupation. Stuart and Revett, for instance, were in Athens in the 1750s, and their four-volume *Antiquities of Athens* (published between 1762 and 1816) had a tremendous public impact; the detailed drawings of the Parthenon and other classical monuments inspired many an example of Greek Revival architecture in Europe and America. Classical Greek civilization could now be seen as manifestly different from that of Egypt, which was also becoming better known as a result of Napoleon's expedition there (1798–1801) and the reports and artifact collections that soon followed, both on the Continent and in Britain (see Yurco, this volume).

Enormous increases in knowledge occurred simultaneously with the worst of racist preconceptions. Two nineteenth century advances not sufficiently emphasized by Bernal were central to the changes in attitude toward Greece and Egypt: the discovery that Greek was a member of an Indo-European family of languages; and the decipherment of Egyptian hieroglyphics, which made it possible to study Egyptian testimony directly. Comparison of Egyptian and Greek texts soon showed that Egypt, for all its impressive achievements, had not reached the level of Greece in philosophy, history, and science. Cuneiform was also deciphered in the mid–nineteenth century, and the reading of ever-increasing numbers of texts in Sumerian and the Semitic languages of the Near East revolutionized our knowledge of the ancient world.

The Bronze Age in the Aegean was hardly known before 1870, when Schliemann began digging at Troy. The rediscovery of Minoan Crete began only with the excavations of Sir Arthur Evans at Knossos in 1900. Linear B was deciphered only in 1952. Such developments provided us with far more information about the Bronze Age than was available either to ancient Greeks or to earlier scholars. The availability of so much new evidence, coupled with scholarly analysis, has surely been the major driving force behind the changes in our historical interpretations.

Instead of recognizing that these increases in knowledge have had a decisive effect on the evolution of historical interpretation, Bernal would have us believe that the only factors that count are the prejudices and preconceptions of the leading scholars. In his world view, increase and refinement in knowledge apparently count for little in comparison to the waxing and waning of irrational and all-dominating prejudice.

One of the most striking features of Bernal's work is his characterization of sources, both ancient and modern, as following one of three "models," which he calls the Ancient Model, the Aryan Model, and the Revised Ancient Model. My doubts about the Ancient Model and about the predominant role of racism in modern scholarship (which Bernal labels the Aryan Model) have already been expressed. A further question remains, however: What purpose is served by lumping almost all nineteenth- and twentieth-century scholarship together and describing it as "Aryanist," as Bernal does? There have in fact been a great multiplicity of approaches which can be categorized by less emotionally laden terms—positivism, diffusionism, functionalism, etc. So far as I can tell, the only common feature in the views of scholars categorized by Bernal as "Aryanist" is that they subscribe to the view that Greek is an Indo-European language introduced by people coming from somewhere to the north or east of Greece. Yet this view is almost universally accepted. Bernal himself accepts it (e.g., *BA* 1:20).

Scholars today would not call themselves Aryanists, given the connection of the term with the horrors of Nazi Germany. Although "Indo-Aryan" was formerly used as a general term for the family of Indo-European languages, it was already giving way to "Indo-European" *before* the rise of the Nazis, and the terms "Aryan" or "Indo-Aryan" are now restricted in scholarly use to a group of languages spoken in India. Greek was in any case never considered a member of this Indo-Aryan group of languages. Terms such as "Indo-European model" and "Indo-Europeanist" would therefore have been far more accurate and logical for Bernal to use (even if, in my view, an unjustifiable oversimplification) and far less inflammatory. It is difficult to escape the conclusion that he has adopted "Aryan Model," "Aryanist," "extreme Aryanist," etc., in an unfair attempt to stigmatize scholarly opponents.[28]

Contemporary classical scholarship cannot be shoehorned into any single framework or model, let alone an "Aryan" one. Bernal's statements about scholarly conservatism continue to carry the insulting connotation that anyone who disagrees with him has accepted a racist position, whether consciously or not.[29] Not only is that attitude contrary to the principles of open inquiry, but it is especially unfair to those of African or Jewish descent who (not infrequently) express doubts about his claims.

Bernal also often implies that his work, like that of Cyrus Gordon, Michael Astour, and other scholars with similar views, has been ignored or rejected primarily because of racism (including anti-Semitism), or because of a scholarly conservatism that masks racist attitudes. For example, he writes as follows in the preface his second volume about the lack of a review of the first volume of *Black Athena* in the *New York Times*:

> What are the forces blocking any discussion of the ideas behind the book in this crucial newspaper? I suspect that it was [the] following sequence: initially my work was thought to be absurd; then, when it was believed to be worth refuting, there was difficulty in finding experts who were willing or able to do this. As time went on, it became increasingly embarrassing to admit the slowness of their response. Finally, a new factor entered, the fear that, even if they were able to do an effective hatchet job on *Black Athena*, there would be a barrage of letters from my Black supporters. Underlying this sequence, I suspect that there is a fundamental discomfort with the ideas that a respectable academic discipline could have racist roots and that racism has permeated liberal thought as well as that of obvious bigots.
> (2:xxi)

While Bernal's claim of prejudice may be true, or partly true, in a few instances, there are other plausible reasons for most of the negative reactions, including doubts about his scholarly methods (see below). Furthermore, his claims of victimization act as a sort of preemptive strike against potential criticism; readers who even mildly disagree with some points may be reluctant to risk possible charges of racism for speaking out. In any case, as he now acknowledges (e.g., 1992c, 86), *Black Athena* has been more widely discussed in both scholarly and general forums than most books and can hardly be said to have been ignored.

Bernal's claim to be putting forward radically new proposals must be taken with a grain of salt. Almost all of his views have been expressed by one or another earlier scholar, with the exception of some of his linguistic proposals.[30] What is new about Bernal's work, besides his emphasis on Egypt rather than the eastern Mediterranean as a source of Greek roots, is his structuring the argument in terms of competing paradigms.

What then about the plausibility of Bernal's paradigm, his "Revised Ancient Model" (which holds that classical Greek civilization was the product of African and Asian invasions of, and influences on, a Bronze Age Aegean previously peopled in part by speakers of Greek) as a general proposition? First, given the variety of current scholarly views that his "Aryan Model" represents, his claim that his "Revised Ancient Model" should be considered an alternative and competing explanation (e.g., *BA* 2:2–3) creates, to my mind, a false dichotomy. Existing views and theories simply do not form the monolithic whole that he postulates. Hence it is invalid for him to put his claims in terms of "competitive plausibility" as if there were a single opposing position. Second, the model Bernal advocates must stand or fall on the plausibility of the specific claims he makes, whether in the areas of political and military history, or archaeology, or cultural and religious history, or linguistics, or mythology. A case that is implausible but that cannot be ruled out as impossible, as so often happens with archaeology, is not a strong one; and implausible claims in several areas of study do not strengthen the overall proposition.

To his discredit, Bernal generally offers his readers what he calls "thick description," instead of detailed scholarly analysis. As he says in the preface to his second volume, "my intention to keep the different kinds of evidence neatly apart has broken down completely as I have found it impossible to indicate the significance of one type without reference to others. . . . Thus, I abandoned the attempt to apply disciplinary rigour to the material in favour of 'thick description' involving many different types of information simultaneously" (*BA* 2:2). His "thick description" seems in fact to be a rambling combination of description and opinion without regard for the generally accepted tenets of rational analysis.

The lack of scholarly method, of "disciplinary rigour," is everywhere apparent. As a consequence, Bernal's work has been almost universally rejected by Egyptologists, archaeologists, linguists, historians, and other scholars best acquainted with the material evidence. Most regard it as beyond the boundaries of legitimate scientific inquiry. The popular media, on the other hand, have given it a much more favorable reception. Fortunately, however, uninformed readers need not be completely at the mercy of media hype, for many of the scholarly criteria by which claims about antiquity may be assessed are quite accessible to the nonspecialist and to the wider public.

As an aid to the curious but uninformed reader, here are some leading questions to ask about sweeping new historical interpretations, along with some answers provided by Bernal's work. Does the argument presuppose the historical accuracy of myths? (Bernal's work relies heavily on such myths as the coming of Danaus and Cadmus to Greece.) Is the argument coherent and clearly spelled out? Or are terms and concepts so vague that falsification is impossible? (Bernal defines the Hyksos in such a vague and all-encompassing way that they might have been responsible for any conceivable eastern feature found in Greece.)[31] Does the author equivocate? (Bernal's and others' arguments about the "blackness" of the ancient Egyptians often rest on equivocal usage of "black," sometimes referring to a skin color and sometimes to a *group* of physical traits, including skin color, distinctive of Black Africans.)[32] Does the author move from statements of possibility to statements of probability by mere assertion (for example, "it is not unlikely that . . .")? (Bernal does this frequently—as, for instance, in his claims about the conquests of the Hyksos.) Is counterevidence cited and explained? (Bernal frequently ignores or glosses over counterevidence, such as the lack of unequivocal Egyptian or Near Eastern objects in the shaft graves at Mycenae.) Are words said to have been derived from other words that do not sound very similar? Derivatives should generally sound similar *and* have similar meanings. (Most of Bernal's derivations are highly implausible at first glance, for example, that *Athena* is from Egyptian *Nēit*.)[33] Are the reasons given for the rejection of existing methodologies, paradigms, or the like based on sweeping reductionist claims? (Bernal's "Ancient Model" and "Aryan Model" are suspect at the outset because they lump together a great diversity of views.) Does the author claim that his or her views have been suppressed or ignored because the experts are biased? (Bernal claims that classicists are working within a "racist paradigm" which prevents them from accepting his conclusions.) Finally, does the main thesis seem plausible? (Bernal's claims of massive Egyptian influence fly in the face of common sense about distant cultural influences.)[34] A good approach here for the uninformed is to check an encyclopedia for some of the terms and concepts used. Articles in encyclopedias are often written by experts and can give a useful perspective on sweeping new interpretations.

Bernal's general aim, to provide an alternative to the view that what we call the "western tradition" was predominantly a European creation, has been embraced by some supporters of multiculturalism. I myself support multiculturalism, particularly as it implies the expansion and mainstreaming of teaching about African civilizations. I doubt, however, that *Black Athena* will ultimately have a positive influence on current debates. The cultures of Africa and western Asia are worthy of study for their own merits. Exaggerated claims for Afro-Asiatic influences on ancient Greece may provoke a reaction against studying such non-European cultures on the grounds that they did not make such contributions as are claimed. Remember also that not all characteristics of Greek and Western civilization are necessarily creditable. The Greek tendency to regard all non-Greeks as "barbarians" (Coleman, n.d.), for instance, provided precedents for later European racism. The Greeks also shared some deplorable practices with their Eastern neighbors, such as the use of slaves and the subordination of women. In any case, Eurocentrism and racism are best countered by looking at the evidence cited to support them, piece by piece, and analyzing arguments pro and con, rather than dismissing any statement out of hand because of the attitudes of its author. Accuracy and truth above all else should continue to be our guiding principles.

A HISTORICAL SCENARIO

There is a positive side to Bernal's work, despite his many errors, the flaws in his methods, and the failure of his arguments to convince. The long-established disciplines of classics, archaeology, Egyptology, Near Eastern studies, and linguistics are indeed often "set in their ways." And racism has undoubtedly been a factor in the formation of some of the current attitudes towards ancient Greece — even if not, as I have argued, the predominant one. Bernal has been untiring in his challenges to conventional wisdom, both in his books and in lectures. The extraordinary breadth and wealth of detail in his work are further challenges; in cutting across the boundaries of the usual scholarly disciplines, he forces would-be critics to expand their horizons far beyond their areas of expertise.

In the case of archaeology, my own particular specialty, Bernal's work has been stimulating a wide public interest in Bronze Age interrelations in the eastern Mediterranean. In closing, therefore, and in acceptance of the challenge posed by Bernal's work, I here offer my own brief scenario of the relevant parts of Bronze Age and later history.

During the Aegean Early Bronze Age, which I would date ca. 3700–2100 B.C.E. (Coleman 1992c), contacts began between the Aegean and Egypt and the Levant (see Yurco, this volume). Indo-European speakers gradually entered mainland Greece, mingling with or displacing the earlier, pre-Greek inhabitants, but Crete was unaffected by their arrival. The Minoans (Bronze Age Cretans) were descendants of the earlier, Neolithic settlers of Crete, and the non-Indo-European, non-Afro-Asiatic language they spoke throughout the Bronze Age is represented in the undeciphered Linear A script. A major impetus for foreign contacts then and later was trade in metals, both as artifacts and perhaps even as raw material. Tin, an ingredient of bronze, was an essential import, because it was lacking in the Aegean world; wherever the ultimate source was, the eastern Mediterranean was at all times a major intermediary for the supply of tin to the Aegean. The Minoans were the most important Aegean participants in foreign trade in the Early Bronze Age.

In the Middle Bronze Age, which lasted from ca. 2100 to ca. 1725 or 1700 B.C.E., Greek became the predominant language on the Greek mainland, if it was not already so, and towns became increasingly prosperous. In Minoan Crete palaces were built, and rebuilt, without significant interruption from abroad. The Minoans increasingly participated in eastern Mediterranean trade (their pottery is found in Cyprus, at Ugarit in the northeastern corner of the Mediterranean, and in Egypt). Trading contacts with Egypt, which at this time were probably direct rather than through intermediaries, may have led to some sort of official recognition of Crete by Egypt and perhaps even to the sending of Egyptian representatives to Crete.

In the earlier part of the Late Bronze Age, from ca. 1725 or 1700 to ca. 1550 B.C.E., Cretan foreign contacts continued, and the Bronze Age Greeks of the mainland, who we may now appropriately call Mycenaeans because of the importance of Mycenae, also began to participate in foreign activities, which may have included raiding as well as trading. Minoan art and culture exerted a powerful influence on the Mycenaeans, and many of the non-Aegean goods that came to the Greek mainland passed through the hands of the Minoans. The kings buried in the shaft graves at Mycenae early in this phase were Greeks who had obtained their wealth through raids and trade, especially with the Minoans. Minoan and Mycenaean art was influenced by that of Syria-Palestine and Egypt, especially during the time of the Hyksos period in Egypt, when Syria-Palestine was largely independent. Aegean art also influenced that of the eastern Mediterranean, and one can usefully speak of international artistic trends. Damage from the eruption of Thera about 1628 B.C.E. was only a temporary setback to the course of Aegean civilization.

During the latter part of the Late Bronze Age, from ca. 1550 to ca. 1220 B.C.E., the Mycenaeans gradually took over the political and commercial lead from the Minoans. Many Minoan palaces and villas were destroyed and deserted near the beginning of this time, and Knossos, which served for a time thereafter as a Mycenaean center in Crete, was also eventually destroyed. The Egyptians called Crete *Keftiu* in the fifteenth century B.C.E., but it is not clear whether they ever had a general name for the Mycenaeans. From about 1400 to 1200 B.C.E. Mycenaean activities were extensive in the eastern Mediterranean, particular in Cyprus, which was an intermediary in Mycenaean trade with the east. Mycenaeans may even have served on occasion as mercenaries in the eastern Mediterranean. Some Egyptian and Semitic words will have passed into Greek during the Late Bronze Age, chiefly names of artifacts and commodities and vocabulary for seafaring, war, and trade.

Bronze Age civilizations all around the eastern Mediterranean collapsed or declined during a few decades around 1200 B.C.E. The causes of the collapse are debated, but raids on the eastern Mediterranean and Egypt by the "sea peoples" were a factor; the Mycenaeans may have participated in these. Climatic changes may also have played a part. Mycenaean palace society disappeared and, along with it, the use of Linear B writing. Economic decline continued until ca. 1100 B.C.E., by which time there was little left in Greece of a "higher" civilization.

Depressed conditions continued in Greece for centuries (the "Dark Ages"), and contacts with the eastern Mediterranean were few until about 750 B.C.E., at which time the Greeks began to renew their foreign trade and send out colonies to the West, the North and, to a lesser extent, the East. Greek commerce and interest in the eastern Mediterranean was stimulated by contacts with Phoenicians, from whom the Greeks adopted the alphabet and who may even have established trading posts in the Aegean. The Homeric poems were written down soon after 750 B.C.E., and Hesiod may have lived then, or not much later.

During what archaeologists designate the Greek "Orientalizing period" (725–600 B.C.E.) contacts were intensified. Greeks visited and served as mercenaries in Egypt, and there was a flood of influences on all Greek arts and crafts from Egypt and the Levant. At this time many of the foreign words attested in classical times may have passed into Greek. The Orientalizing period was followed by the Archaic (from 600 B.C.E. to the time of the Persian invasions of Greece in the early fifth century B.C.E.), and Classical (480–338 B.C.E.) periods. Greek sages like Solon are said to have visited Egypt in the Archaic period, and Herodotus wrote his history of the Persian Wars in the mid–fifth century B.C.E. At the beginning of the Hellenistic period (338–31 B.C.E.), which followed the Classical period, the conquests of Alexander the Great led to the formation of Greek empires in Syria and Egypt and revolutionized Greek and foreign attitudes toward one another.

Accurate and detailed knowledge of the Bronze Age was lost in Greece because of the discontinuity in Greek civilization during the "Dark Ages," ca. 1200–800 B.C.E. What knowledge survived by means of an oral poetic tradition such as is attested in the Homeric poems was grossly inaccurate and had become overlaid with fable. My view is that the "Dark Ages" were of benefit to the Greek achievement during the Classical period, in that, lacking an accurate memory of the past, the Greeks were stimulated to create an enormously rich and elaborate mythology in its stead. Although the myths paid tribute to tradition in the sense that they took the Bronze Age as a dramatic setting, they also provided an extraordinarily flexible vehicle for the expression of the new insights that arose in Archaic and Classical times.

NOTES

This essay is based on Coleman 1992a and 1992b. I thank William M. Gaugler, Laura M. Purdy, Barry S. Strauss, Stuart Swiny, and James M. Weinstein for reading and making helpful comments on drafts of it. Martin Bernal also read an early draft of Coleman 1992a and made written comments, some of which I have responded to there.

1. E.g., Herodotus 5.58. The connection he makes between "Phoenician letters" (by which he surely meant the alphabet) and "Kadmeian" letters (5.59) shows that he was confused about the date of transmission of the alphabet. As discussed below, the alphabet was not likely to have been introduced before the ninth or eighth century B.C.E., whereas the coming of Cadmus was believed to have taken place long before the Trojan War, which Herodotus dated to the thirteenth century B.C.E. An alternative Greek tradition held that writing was an indigenous development, for its invention is sometimes attributed to Prometheus (e.g., Stesichorus; Aeschylus *Prometheus Bound*, 460), to Palamedes (Euripides), or to Hermes (Mnaseas); for full references see T. Braun 1982, 29.

The Greek alphabet represented an advance over earlier writing systems in that vowels were represented by their own symbols and consonants were regarded as separable sounds; hence a consonant could be combined with any vowel. Earlier alphabets lacked symbols to represent vowels, and all of the other earlier nonalphabetic writing systems, such as cuneiform and hieroglyphics, were syllabaries (that is, each symbol represented a consonant plus a particular vowel).

2. For example, in Plato's *Phaedrus* (274c) Socrates tells a playful story about the invention by the Egyptian god Theuth (Thoth) of "number and calculation, geometry and astronomy . . . drafts and dice, and above all writing." Aristotle wrote in his *Metaphysics* (1.1 981b) about the Egyptian foundation of the mathematical arts and in *De Caelo* (2.12 292a) about the astronomical observations of the Egyptians and Babylonians, "who have watched the stars from the remotest past, and to whom we owe many incontrovertible facts about each of them." There were, of course, alternative traditions that these innovations/inventions were made by Greek gods and sages; see, e.g., below, note 17.

Greek contributions took mathematics and astronomy to a much higher plane than they had been in earlier times. Euclid, for instance, is credited with establishing the need for proofs in mathematics, and by the end of the sixth century B.C.E. Presocratic philosophers like Parmenides and Pythagoras (and/or his followers) are credited with being the first thinkers to recognize that the earth is a sphere.

3. E.g., Schliemann 1878 ("Graeco-Phoenician period"); Collignon 1884, chapter 3, entitled "Période gréco-orientale." Influence from the eastern Mediterranean on Greek vase painting of the seventh century B.C.E. was recognized as early as the 1860s, by Conze (1862, vii).

4. Bass 1987 is an excellent illustrated account. Since its publication there have been several more seasons of excavation on the wreck. For recent preliminary results see Pulak 1992, 1994.

5. Although the work of Manetho is known only from fragments preserved in

other writers, enough is extant to show that he did not record Hyksos invasions of any other country than Egypt. The text of Manetho also mentions the coming of the mythical character Danaus to Greece (see below) but does not connect him with the Hyksos, as Bernal sometimes seems to suggest (e.g., 1992c, 53); on the contrary, Manetho equated Danaus with Harmais or Hermaius, a brother of the nineteenth dynasty pharaoh "Sethos," who is to be dated several centuries after the Hyksos invasions. Waddell 1940 is a convenient collection and translation of the fragments of Manetho; see especially in the index under Hyksos and Danaus.

6. Bernal tends to regard the goods shown being brought to the pharaoh in Egyptian paintings by people of Crete (Keftiu or Kaftu) as tribute, indicating that Crete was somehow subordinate to, and had perhaps even been conquered by Egypt (e.g., *BA* 2:46, 426–28, 432). A recent study of *inw*, the word taken to mean "tribute" in the paintings shows, however, that *inw* meant gifts rather than tribute; the author concludes that the king "is not . . . claiming that he rules an area just because he says that he receives *inw* from its prince" (Bleiberg 1984, 167).

7. The period of Hyksos rule in Egypt is commonly dated to ca. 1660–1550 B.C.E. The recent dating of the volcanic eruption of the Aegean island of Thera to 1628 B.C.E. (see contributions on chronology in Hardy and Renfrew 1990) necessitates the redating of the beginning of Late Helladic I, the period of the royal shaft graves at Mycenae, to no later than ca. 1700 B.C.E. Because Bernal accepts this revision of Aegean chronology (*BA* 2: chapter 7), his theory that the burials in the shaft graves are of Hyksos invaders to Greece compels him to argue that some Hyksos pharaohs, such as Khyan, could "well have reigned in the early seventeenth century B.C.E. or even at the end of the eighteenth" (2: chapter 8, 335). Although it is generally accepted that Asiatic infiltration into the northern Delta of Egypt was a gradual process culminating in seizure of power, few if any Egyptologists would accept such an early dating for the first Hyksos pharaohs. The Turin Canon, a king list dating to the thirteenth century B.C.E., assigns a total of only 108 years to Hyksos rule, and the latest Hyksos pharaoh can be dated no earlier than 1575 B.C.E. at the very earliest. For detailed discussion see Yurco, this volume.

8. Although the scarab was not found in situ in a grave, it may have come from Grave *rho* of Grave Circle B, which was later looted; see Mylonas 1966, 107. Because only the design on the face was published and the object is now lost, doubts exist even as to its date. It is dated to either 1700–1600 B.C.E. or 1450–1200 B.C.E. by Lambrou-Phillipson (1990, 342–43).

9. Persson 1942, chapter 7, "Mycenae and Egypt"; Marinatos 1968, 266; Stubbings 1973, 627–28; Best 1973.

10. For references see the indexes and bibliographies in *BA* 1 and *BA* 2.

11. See, e.g., Chadwick 1973, chapter 9, 275–312.

12. Bernal's attempts to derive the ritual use of the bull in Crete from Egypt (e.g., *BA* 2:22–25, 171–77), which rest primarily on the superficial similarity of the names of the mythical king Minos of Crete and the Egyptian god Min, seem to me highly doubtful. Bulls, after all, are an important element in ritual in all eras throughout the Mediterranean area, and the Cretan practices (bull leaping, sacrifice) do not seem especially close to those of Egypt.

13. It is possible that Mycenaean Greek kings corresponded in cuneiform with Hittite kings in Anatolia, to judge from copies of correspondence between the Hittite kings and kings of "Ahhiyawa" (probably all or part of Mycenaean Greece) found at the Hittite capital of Bogasköy. If so, the use of cuneiform was likely to have been limited in Greece to such occasional royal correspondence, and it would mean no more than that the Mycenaeans were part of the international diplomatic network of the eastern Mediterranean. Akkadian cuneiform was generally used for such diplomacy, even by non-Semitic speakers such as the Egyptians and Hittites.

14. Although Bernal doubts the existence of a pre-Greek substrate (*BA* 1:48–49; 1992c, 54), his arguments are vague and circular. The ending *-ssos*, for instance, which is generally held to be one of the most significant elements of the substrate, is inadequately dismissed as follows: "*-(i)ssos* would seem to be a characteristic Aegean ending, but one that continued to be used at least until the end of the Bronze Age" (*BA* 1:49).

15. Most attempts to decipher Linear A have started with the reasonable assumption that the signs shared by Linear A and B had the same phonetic value in Linear A as they do in Linear B. Even though, on this assumption, the values of roughly one half of the signs in any particular Linear A text are known, no scholar has yet come up with convincing readings of the bulk of the Linear A texts. Such continuous readings are the proof that a decipherment is sound. If the Minoan language had belonged to either the Semitic or the Indo-European language family, one or another of the attempts at decipherment would have been likely to produce continuous readings of the texts, given how much could be extrapolated from other, well-attested members of these language families. The failure of the attempts at decipherment therefore suggests that Minoan, like Etruscan, belonged to an otherwise unattested language group.

16. The only two names which to my mind might be non-Aegean are the Sphinx (Hesiod *Theogony* 326), a word that Bernal suggests (*BA* 2:374) may have been derived from Egyptian, and Hecate (*Theogony* 411–52), which may be Anatolian. The Sphinx is problematic. The word, if from an Egyptian root, might have been imported into Greece along with the representation of the Sphinx as a lion-bodied, human-headed monster. On the other hand, the Greek legend of the sphinx was localized in Boeotia (she terrorized Boeotian Thebes), and the Boeotian version of *sphinx* is *phix*, which is related to and is possibly to be derived from Mount Phikion in Boeotia. Perhaps, therefore, legends of a local monster living on Mount Phikion were combined with Egyptian and eastern Mediterranean iconographical representations of a human-headed lion. The process would have been similar to that by which several other local Greek legends, particularly in Boeotia, were transferred to foreign places after Greek colonization of the Mediterranean in the eighth to sixth centuries B.C.E.; see E. Hall, this volume, and 1992.

The name *Hekatē* probably has an Indo-European root ("she who acts from afar"), and the goddess is usually taken to have originated in Anatolia; see Johnston 1990, 21–22. Hence Hecate does not support Bernal's case, for she does not represent influence from speakers of Semitic or Egyptian.

17. Any good encyclopedia can provide details. In Aeschylus, Prometheus gives

both numbers and letters to humankind (*Prometheus Bound* 459–60). Daedalus invented many of the arts and crafts, especially sculpture. Orpheus contributed many religious customs, Musaeus oracles and cures for diseases, Lycurgus the military/social system of Sparta.

18. Many scholars believe that the Greeks did not originally associate Danaus and Cadmus with the Near East and that they came to do so only after the expansion of Greek activities in the Eastern Mediterranean in the seventh century B.C.E.: e.g., T. Braun 1982, 30, and others cited in Hall, this volume.

19. Bernal (1992c, 55) interprets the latter part of this same passage as not including claims of invasions of Greece. But contrary to his interpretation, Diodorus does indeed intend to express doubts about Egyptian colonies in Greece, as is proven by the first sentence of the passage as quoted above. As the language of the latter part of the passage indicates, Diodorus was summing up his view about Egyptian claims of colonization in general, including those he had just mentioned.

That Diodorus did not regard Herodotus as a "historian worthy of credence," despite Bernal's claims, is also clear. At Diodorus 1.69.7 we read: "Now as for the stories invented by Herodotus and certain writers on Egyptian affairs, who deliberately preferred to the truth the telling of marvellous tales and the invention of myths for the delectation of their readers, these we shall omit . . ." (trans. Oldfather 1933, 241). A sentence in Diodorus 1.37.4, sometimes partially quoted by Bernal (1992f, 2, 13) as if it supported his views, reads in full: "Herodotus, who was a curious enquirer if ever a man was, and widely acquainted with history, undertook, it is true, to give an explanation of [the nature of the Nile], *but is now found to have followed contradictory guesses*" (trans. Oldfather 1933, 127, emphasis mine).

20. See Jasanoff and Nussbaum, this volume. Bernal's derivation of Athena from Nēit is in my view especially unlikely, as it rests on much special pleading for sound changes and the like. At the outset, because the Egyptian word for Nēit is simply *Nt* (vowels were not written in Egyptian hieroglyphics), Bernal is compelled to suppose that the Greeks took their name for the goddess from the expression "temple of Nēit" (Ḥt Nt, a name for Sais, where there was a great temple to Nēit). He must then postulate the addition of an *a* sound at the beginning and the loss of the *t* sound at the end. His view also presupposes that the Greeks were inconsistent in the way that they heard *Ḥt*, as in the generally accepted derivation of the Greek *aigyptos* from *Ḥt Ka Pth* (the temple of the spirit of Ptah; a name for the city of Memphis) they took *Ḥt* as the sound *ai*.

21. Herodotus' views are problematic because, although he states his general belief that "the names (*ounomata*) of almost all the Greek gods come from Egypt" (2.50), he does not in fact make specific equations of divine names, as opposed to characters, between Egypt and Greece. When he does equate divinities (for instance, Osiris and Dionysus), he does not claim that the names sound alike or that the Greek version was derived from the Egyptian. Probably, as A. B. Lloyd suggests (1975–88, 2:203–5), Herodotus mistakenly thought that the Greek names for the gods were the original ones and that the Egyptian names were merely alternatives or had supplanted the original Greek names in Egypt. Or perhaps Herodotus used *ounoma* here in a spe-

cial way to mean "character" or "nature," as some scholars have suggested; see the discussion by Lloyd just cited.

It may be further noted that Bernal's derivation (*BA* 1:67, 2:97) of Poseidon from the "Egypto-Semitic hybrid" *Pr Sidôn* (meaning "he of" or "house of Sidon") is explicitly contradicted by Herodotus, who says that the Greeks "learned about [Poseidon] from the Libyans" (2.50).

22. The passage in question is Diodorus 1.25.1–2: "In general, there is great disagreement over these gods. For the same goddess is called by some Isis, by others Demeter, by others Thesmophorus, by others Selene, by others Hera, while still others apply to her all these names. Osiris has been given the name Sarapis by some, Dionysus by others, Pluto by others, Ammon by others, Zeus by some, and many have considered Pan to be the same god; and some say that Sarapis is the god whom the Greeks call Pluto" (trans. Oldfather 1933, 79).

23. This fallacy, which is known as *post hoc ergo propter hoc*, is frequent in Herodotus; for further discussion see A. B. Lloyd 1975–88, 1:147–49.

24. Bernal's attempts to redate Homer and Hesiod so that they would fall early in the "Dark Ages" are unconvincing. Herodotus himself, whom Bernal so often uses as a credible witness, wrote that he believed the time of Homer and Hesiod to be "not more than four hundred years before my own" (2.53)—no earlier than about 850 B.C.E. Most scholars put them a century or so later. See, e.g., Kirk 1985, 1–16; Lamberton 1988, 14–15.

25. E.g., Evans 1921–35, esp. 2 (1927):22–59. He even suggests (2:45) the possible existence of "negroized elements" in Minoan Crete coming from this source.

26. Persson 1942, chapter 6, 176–96. This work, which is not discussed by Bernal, is a significant counterexample to his thesis about racism, for it was published at a time when racism was at its height.

27. See *BA* 1: chapters 8 ("The Rise and Fall of the Phoenicians, 1830–1885") and 9 ("The Final Solution of the Phoenician Problem, 1985–1945").

28. See also Jasanoff and Nussbaum, this volume. Bernal has attempted to defend his use of the term "Aryan" in response to my criticisms (in Coleman 1992a) on the grounds that "historians and linguists were substantially affected by the intense racism and anti-Semitism of the nineteenth and early twentieth centuries" (1992c, 82). Whomever he judges to be affected by racism, it seems, is deserving of the epithet "Aryanist," regardless of the details of their work.

29. Bernal has modified his stance somewhat since these criticisms were first advanced. He writes, for example, that "Coleman states that I see 'scholarly conservatism' as a 'mask for racist attitudes.' In fact, while I believe that this is sometimes the case, I go to considerable pains to emphasize that many, if not most, of the scholars working within the Aryan Model are not themselves racist, merely that their intellectual framework was founded by men who were proud to be so" (1992c, 86). This statement still suggests, erroneously in my view, that the work of scholars is necessarily restricted by some previous "intellectual framework."

30. Earlier views that the shaft graves at Mycenae contained Hyksos, for example, have already been mentioned. That there were massive eastern Mediterranean

influences on Greek civilization was put forward by C. H. Gordon (1965) and As-tour (1967).

31. Although Bernal usually regards the Hyksos as predominantly Semitic-speaking (e.g., *BA* 2:40–41, "There is absolutely no doubt that these conquerors of Egypt were overwhelmingly Semitic-speaking"), he also describes them in the following terms: "The hypothesis proposed here is that the royalty buried in the Shaft Graves and the other early Mycenaean tombs were Hyksos invaders from Syria, who probably spoke Hurrian and possibly even Indo-Iranian. However, the majority of the ruling class were Levantine Semitic-speakers together with significant numbers of Egyptians and Cretans, most of whom probably spoke a Semitic language themselves" (2:45). Bernal's Hyksos, it seems, were such a mixed group that almost any non-Mycenaean trait may be claimed for them. For the unlikelihood that the Cretans spoke a Semitic language see note 15 above.

32. Although the Egyptians may have been darker-skinned than most people living on the shores of the Mediterranean, they did not generally depict themselves as having other physical characteristics common among people living farther south in Africa, such as woolly hair, broader noses and lips, etc. For excellent illustrations and discussions of Egyptian attitudes toward their neighbors to the south see Vercoutter et al. 1976. (See also Brace et al., this volume.)

33. Among the many other equally doubtful derivations, in my view, are those of *Aphrodite* from Egyptian *Pr W3dyt* (House of W3dyt) (*BA* 1:65–66), *Apollo* from Egyptian *Ḥprr* ("the young sun in the morning" (1:67–68), and *Mycenae* from West Semitic *Maḥăneh* or *Maḥănayim* ("camp" or "two camps") (1:51). (See also Jasanoff and Nussbaum, this volume.)

34. Comparisons with other historical situations are helpful. For example, scholars do not generally consider Canaanite culture to have had Egyptian "roots." How could it be that the Bronze Age Canaanites of Palestine, whose territory bordered that of Egypt, who controlled Egypt for a century or so, and who subsequently underwent centuries of Egyptian military occupation, were less influenced by Egypt than the distant Greeks?

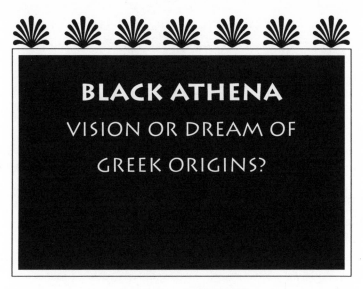

BLACK ATHENA
VISION OR DREAM OF
GREEK ORIGINS?

Lawrence A. Tritle

"Contrariwise," continued Tweedledee, "if it was so, it might be; and if it
were so, it would be: but as it isn't, it ain't. That's logic."
—Lewis Carroll, *Through the Looking Glass*

The second volume of Martin Bernal's projected tetralogy *Black Athena*, since
its appearance in summer 1991, has continued the storm of controversy ig-
nited by the first volume in 1987.[1] It has, however, aroused a far greater
tempest in the United States than in Britain or continental Europe, as various
commentators have noted. The grounds for conflict actually lie outside the
discipline, namely, in the political debates currently taking place on American university campuses. As E. K. Coughlin notes (1991), *Black Athena* now
plays an important role in the multicultural controversy, and Afrocentric
scholars have eagerly appropriated the work in their debate with classicists
and those labeled (or tarred) as Eurocentric. Although Levine denies (1992a,
215) that Bernal's views have exerted any impact on the classics or on the ideas
mentioned above, the video *Black Athena* (late 1991) and numerous articles
in the popular press (e.g., *Newsweek, Ebony, New Republic*), not to mention
scholarly publications, clearly attest the role of Bernal's ideas in shaping these
current intellectual debates.

The evidence is not holy; it is itself a social construct and so should not be taken
at face value any more than one should take *The Times* or a contemporary
academic political scientist as necessarily right.
—K. Hopkins (1978, 183)

Politics, then, has provided *Black Athena* with a receptive audience that finds
Bernal's polemical style of writing history congenial. Such a style and technique applied to the study of history is fraught with methodological and
historiographical pitfalls into which Bernal stumbles repeatedly because he
is a political scientist rather than a historian. Bernal, to be sure, sees this
as a strength rather than as a weakness. In fact it appears that he disavows
twentieth-century historical scholarship, its methodology and historiography. Such hostility cannot be simply accepted or overlooked. Would the
scientific community fail to respond to a critic who rejected Einstein and
relativity in favor of a return to Newtonian absolutes? Historians and classicists should act no differently. Such criticisms have in fact already been raised,
first by Frank Turner (1989) and more recently by Sturt Manning (1990), but I
now propose some additional objections.

Bernal attacks a number of scholars (usually German) throughout both
volumes of *Black Athena* for committing the sin of *Besserwissen*, that is, of
thinking that modern scholars are in a better position to know the past than
their sources (see *BA* 2:9, 237, passim). His relentless onslaught on these
scholars strikes me as hypercritical. But more to the point, his attitude also
reveals a fundamental ignorance of the underlying methodological and historiographical concepts behind the *Besserwissen*. These are rooted in Italian
(rather than in German) thought, especially in Giambattista Vico's philosophy of history. It was Vico who argued that the ancients were rather poorly
informed of their own history and that we moderns were actually in a better
position to know the past (Vico [1744] 1968, 29–32, 58–59; see also Collingwood 1946, 69; Caponigri 1953, 184). Thus, for example, scholars today have
a better understanding of the nature of Athenian democracy in the fifth and
fourth centuries B.C.E. than did Plutarch, who lived only some four hundred
years after the times he describes for us so vividly in his many Athenian
Lives. An accurate and reliable assessment of this view is provided by A. W.
Gomme (in Gomme, Andrewes, and Dover 1945–81, 1:59), who observes that
Plutarch's political temper was that of the Age of Trajan, which limited his
comprehension of Athens and its democracy. As a result of modern archaeological finds and an appreciation of Aristophanic comedy that would have
been lost on Plutarch, we today are in a better position to understand the
subtleties and intricacies of Athenian politics than one of our ancient authori-

ties. This view I would maintain despite Bernal's recent claim to the contrary (1992a, 209–10).

At times, however, Bernal also seems to know better than the ancients he cites so reverently but offers no explanation for his change of heart or method. For example, he suggests in his introduction to the second volume of *Black Athena* (2:5) that Egyptologists today have better information available to them than what Herodotus could find. Yet he repeatedly defends Herodotus' account of Egypt and the veracity of Egyptian influences upon the Greeks. But then in other instances he rejects Herodotus' reports without comment. For example, he ignores Herodotus' statement (2.53.2, ca. 440 B.C.E.) that Homer and Hesiod preceded him by about four hundred years, so that he can shift the date for the two poets to the tenth/ninth centuries B.C.E. (*BA* 2:475). Elsewhere he rejects Herodotus' claim (2.2; cf. *BA* 2:244) that the Phrygians were older than the Egyptians, yet he accepts without question (or discussion) that Herodotus saw alphabetic "Cadmean script" of the thirteenth century B.C.E. in Thebes (5.59.1; cf. *BA* 2:500). He explains Herodotus' error about the antiquity of Egyptian civilization by invoking modern linguistics, and Herodotus' mistake about the writing in Thebes simply by omitting Herodotus' follow-up observation that the letters resembled the Ionic script.

Near the end of the second volume of *Black Athena* (2:502) Bernal asserts that Herodotus was "well-informed" on the foundation of Tyre ca. 2750 B.C.E. (*BA* 2:502) and was able to check on other equally remote matters (*BA* 2:237). Herodotus' confidence in his sources serves as an interesting contrast to Thucydides' (1.1.3), who complained that it was difficult to learn anything substantial regarding the era before his own. For Bernal, however, Thucydides is a *critical* historian, a "nationalist," and a hate-mongering foe of all non-Greek peoples (see *BA* 1:101–3 for the preceding labels); yet Thucydides' own Thracian connection (4.105.1) could well undo all of Bernal's opinions.

Another example of Bernal's *Besserwissen* is his handling of the Egyptian historian Manetho's account of the king Sesostris; he rejects and revises it in the best tradition of Germanic *Quellenkritik*, which elsewhere he so derides (*BA* 1:196–97; see also O'Connor, Yurco, this volume). Finally Bernal makes a rather farfetched claim that historians in antiquity, just like their modern counterparts, systematically engaged in understatement to appear "sober and reasonable" to their readers, while at the same time wishing "to astound their audiences with spectacularly high dates" (*BA* 2:364). Those who remember Ptolemy's talking snakes leading Alexander to Siwah (Arrian 3.3.5) will surely wonder at Bernal's own version of *Besserwissen*.

In addition to these self-contradictory charges and criticisms, Bernal's own approach to the handling of evidence seems curiously antiquarian. In his view—or so it appears—what an ancient author states can only mean what he says, whereas modern authors with their hidden agendas, usually racist or anti-Semitic (or both) never mean what they say. His attitude toward evidence seems not far from that stated by E. H. Carr: "No document can tell us more than what the author of the document thought—what he thought had happened, what he thought ought to happen or would happen, or perhaps only what he wanted others to think he thought, or even only what he himself thought he thought" (1961, 16). This clever-sounding statement, as Arthur Marwick has argued, omits any consideration of unspoken assumption and shared values, not to mention the particular nature of the document or evidence in question.[2] Indeed, Bernal appears to think that evidence exists in some sort of vacuum—pure and simple—and unaffected by the questions asked by the historian and the context in which he asks them. Hence again his criticism of *Besserwissen* and those who question the ancients.[3]

The authors and passages which could be cited in this context include Odysseus' tales of raids upon Egypt (Homer *Odyssey* 14.246–72, 17.425–44). Bernal takes these references as evidence of Greek, that is, Achaian, participation in the attacks of the Sea Peoples on Egypt in the twelfth century B.C.E. (*BA* 2:457–58, 496). Thus he reads Homer as a history book rather than as poetry and does not consider the potential criticisms of this view: that even if Homer preserves a Mycenaean Greek memory of such raids (which is not at all certain), the circumstances have altered considerably, as here Odysseus acts as an individual pirate chieftain or mercenary rather than as a member of a much larger force (so Heubeck and Hoekstra, 1988–91, 2 [1988]:210, not cited by Bernal). But it is more likely, as A. B. Lloyd has argued (1975–88, 1:11–12) that the context reflects the eighth century B.C.E.: references to the Phoenician trader in *Odyssey* 14.288 suggest the Phoenician maritime expansion into northern Africa after 1000 B.C.E., and the Homeric picture of Egypt itself reflects the era following the Twentieth Dynasty (post 1085 B.C.E.). Finally, since the two passages about Egypt closely resemble one another (as Bernal notes, *BA* 2:622, 59), they may represent timeless ("formulaic") episodes based on any number of similar incidents.

There is evidence of similar gullibility and of procrustean methods in Bernal's interpretation of Plutarch's *On the Sign of Socrates* (*Moralia* 575A–598F; cf. *BA* 2:124–28). In this account Plutarch reports the excavation in Boeotia of the tomb of Alcmene at the order of the Spartan king Agesilaus. On the basis of a reported find of a bronze bracelet and two pottery urns, Bernal assigns the tomb to the Bronze Age. On the basis of Plutarch's report that the tomb's inscription could only be read by the Egyptian priest Chonuphis after three days' work, Bernal concludes that the inscription was "Linear B, or possibly Linear A or cuneiform" (*BA* 2:127). He rejects the possibility that Chonuphis might have had any difficulty, like modern day scholars, in making out an obscure but known text; nor does he ask how an Egyptian might have known any of these languages. Thus Bernal accepts the substance of this account as literally true and from it argues (1) that Chonuphis was well informed on Boeotia and "the centrality of the cult of the Muses in the region of Haliartos," (2) that Agesilaus was clever to use a bit of Boeotian folklore to make Boeotia Spartan (or attempt so), and (3) that Egypt was urging Greek unity against Persia in the early fourth century B.C.E.

It is a pity that a text and its author have been so abused. Bernal does not mention in his discussion (only in his notes, *BA* 2:562 n. 1) that the work he uses here is Plutarch's *De Genio Socratis*; nowhere does he inform his reader that the work in question belongs to the most complex form of Greek literature, the philosophical dialogue, or that Plutarch is a master of that literary genre, which unites a factual historical account (the liberation of Thebes in 379 B.C.E.) with a contemplative essay on the simplicity of life and the power of divination (see Russell 1973, 34–41). Bernal has in fact wrenched from its context the purported discovery of Alcmene's tomb so as to support his argument for an Egyptian influence in Thebes and Boeotia during the Bronze Age. Plutarch's account, however, warrants no such claim. As indicated above, Bernal does not even consider that Plutarch's report might be literary creation and influenced by reports of ancient tombs and monuments (both elsewhere in Plutarch, e.g., *Romulus* 28.7, *Lysander* 28.8, and in other authors, e.g., Pausanias 1.41.1, 9.16.7). Moreover, he attempts to make concrete Plutarch's statement that Chonuphis' translation of the mysterious text actually urged the Greeks to enjoy the life of leisure, to seek peace, and to lay aside the weapons of war; as argued above, Bernal simply jumps to conclusions by reading into this "translation" Spartan foreign policy decisions and Egyptian pleas for Greek unity against Persia.

This discussion reveals not only Bernal's simplistic attitude toward evidence but also his lack of concern about citing an author from the second century C.E. as an authority for events in the fourth century B.C.E. and even earlier. The example of Alcmene's tomb is not an exception, and numerous other examples could be cited. One such case is his discussion of the cults of Athena and Alalcomene, where Bernal mixes references from Lactantius in the third century C.E. (citing Bacchylides, from the fifth century B.C.E.), Apollonius of Rhodes (third century B.C.E.), and other sources to establish a link between those two figures, with traces of snakelike creatures from some Boeotian cults and the Egyptian goddess Neit thrown in for good measure (*BA* 2:85–87). This sort of discussion is by no means uncommon, but the factor common to them all is the lack of any kind of evaluation or analysis of the source's origin.

The lack of a methodologically consistent treatment of the evidence will surely provide many critics with opportunities to attack Bernal's thesis and discussion. But he commits other methodological errors which also require mention. Among these is a continual reliance upon the argument from analogy. One example of this is the discussion of the development of Greek syllabary by recourse to an "analogy of the Xixia script in western Xinjiang" (*BA* 2:162–63; for other examples of such rationale see 2:93, 252, 378, 449, 464, passim). Leaving aside the validity of this argument, reliance upon such a method is simply unsound. Analogy is not a substitute for evidence, and Bernal seems not to realize the inherent weakness of such an argument, or that analogies can distort rather than illuminate the past (see the discussion by Oakeshott, 1983, 92). Another problem is Bernal's anachronistic use of language, the most notable example of which is the indiscriminate use of *pharaoh* throughout both volumes. Even first-year university textbooks note that *pharaoh* is a New Kingdom term, one inappropriate to earlier periods of Egyptian history (see, e.g., Chambers 1991, 22; cf. J. A. Wilson 1951, 102–3, the latter not cited by Bernal). Attention must be paid to the proper use of language so as not to distort the true texture of the past. This is an elementary lesson in the writing of history. Its absence in a work that proclaims its own originality and innovative contribution to rewriting that past stands out as a telling comment on the reliability of that portrait.

Equally disconcerting is Bernal's assertion (*BA* 2:282) that natural scientists are more trustworthy than archaeologists and historians, because they follow, presumably, scientific methods whereas the latter are encumbered with scholarly traditions and bias. Such a claim in a day and age when newspapers and news magazines routinely cite the latest conflicting medical and scientific discoveries is simply astounding. Since Einstein's Relativity Revolution and the overthrow of Newtonian absolutes, science has ceased to deal in certainties and looks now to probabilities.[4]

An even more disturbing dimension of Bernal's methodology is his tendency to form rhetorical arguments and statements so as to support his case (see Palter's second contribution, this volume, on the eighteenth century, Appendix 2). One such example of this is his unsupported claim, noted above, that Homer and Hesiod belong to the tenth/ninth centuries B.C.E., although Herodotus dated them to the ninth. Another example is the discussion of the Cape Gelidonya shipwreck explored by G. Bass in the 1960s. Bernal states that "Bass's work was considered very startling and generally unwelcome" (*BA* 2:467) and cites as evidence two reviews, one by G. Cadogan. What did Cadogan in fact say? In response to Bass's argument that the ship in question was Phoenician, Cadogan remarked, "a startling conclusion, but possible." What follows in the review is a discussion of the objects recovered from the wreck; though it is clear that Cadogan interprets Bass's finds in a number of different ways, he concludes: "*Cape Gelidonya* [Bass 1967] is well worth buying and contains plenty to think over. It is a great achievement. Let us hope that the Pennsylvania University Museum will include more Bronze Age wrecks in its underwater programme" (1969, 189). This certainly does not seem like an unfavorable review. Yet Bernal would allow a reader who does not take the time to read Cadogan's original remarks to imagine that some sort of an injustice has been done. In fact, the review, though critical, is a positive one congratulating the author and his team for a job well done. Bernal would like his readers to conceive a conspiracy where in reality none exists (see Lefkowtitz, Vermeule, Coleman, this volume).

One final example of this sort of manipulation of evidence involves the so-called *Rundbauten* discovered in the Peloponnese. Bernal argues (*BA* 2:135–37) that the *Rundbauten* were indeed granaries dating from the Early Bronze Age (ca. 3300–2400 B.C.E.). He attacks Renfrew (1972, 288), whose view on the buildings in question is that they were probably dwellings, or perhaps granaries. Bernal then concludes: "Nevertheless, he [Renfrew] still refuses to see this as damaging to his scheme according to which Greek agriculture in the 3rd millennium was based on a 'subsistence system' " (*BA* 2:136). As in the case of Cadogan above, we must examine what exactly Renfrew says. Readers might be surprised to learn that Renfrew's actual remarks are not nearly as equivocal as Bernal's. Renfrew states that the *Rundbau* at Tiryns "may have been a grain store" and, a few sentences later, concludes that together with the House of Tiles, the *Rundbau* gives "a picture of a subsistence economy expanding, not only in terms of the range of cultivars, but in the organization of their exploitation" (1972, 288). This is rather different from what Bernal would like us to think; the discrepancy reflects yet again the polemical and slanted approach with which he attempts to engage his reader. *Caveat lector!*

GREECE OUT OF EGYPT?

For historical thinking means nothing else than interpreting all the available
evidence with the maximum degree of critical skill.
—R. G. Collingwood (1963, 99)

Bernal's handling of sources, his attitude toward the record of the past, is especially problematic and will undoubtedly provide much grist for his critics' mills. In his second volume he presents the so-called archaeological and documentary evidence meant to substantiate his vision of an Egypto-Levantine influence upon Greece in the Middle and Late Bronze Age. Between the first and second volumes he also has already revised his positions, most notably perhaps that regarding the "Revised Ancient Model." He adds two qualifications: (1) that Greek is essentially an Indo-European language (which requires at some stage northern invasions); and (2) that Egypto-Levantine colonization occurred in the late eighteenth century B.C.E. with the arrival of the Hyksos, rather than in the early sixteenth century (*BA* 2:41,

363–64). In making these claims he admits that he must "part company with the ancient historians." He can provide only the unconvincing justification that ancient writers, like their modern counterparts, in order to be seen as rational and sober, simply lowered their chronologies. Moreover, he claims that the Greeks themselves wanted to be seen as hosts to exiles rather than as victims of conquest, and this too led them to distort the past. This is evident, he asserts, in the similarity of Greek *hikes(ios)*, to "Hyksos," which Aeschylus punned in his play of that name, *Suppliants* (*Hiketes* or *Hiketides*) (*BA* 1:22, 2:364; cf. 1:97, and Hall, this volume). Leaving linguistic objections aside (as well as the question of whether Aeschylus would even have known about the Hyksos), it is evident here that Bernal can be as arbitrary and as biased as any of the scholars he attacks for *Besserwissen*.

Again in volume 2 Bernal sets out his position as a "modified diffusionist" (2:64–67), but one can only wonder what he means by "modified," in view of some of his claims for Egyptian influence. For example, he insists on an Egyptian origin for the so-called Tomb of Amphion and Zethos at Thebes (2:128–33), and also for the "pyramid" at Silbury Hill near Avebury in Wessex. In the case of Silbury his language is especially perplexing: ". . . there is no doubt in my mind that the builders of Silbury were aware of the contemporary Egyptian pyramids. On the other hand, it is extremely unlikely— to say the least—that Wessex was colonized by Egyptians of the 3rd or 4th Dynasties" (2:131). Beneath the rhetoric we can discern the traces of staunch diffusionism.[5]

A major theme common to both volumes of *Black Athena* is the Egyptian influence upon Greek culture and the "blackness" of this influence, particularly that of the Middle Kingdom and its most spectacular figure, Sesostris. This topic was introduced in the first volume (*BA* 1:18–19, 329) but receives far greater treatment in the second, constituting two full chapters (5 and 6, on Sesostris I and II). In these Bernal argues for an early second-millennium B.C.E. Egyptian conquest of the eastern Mediterranean world, stretching as far north as the Danube and as far east as Colchis. Oddly enough Greece was spared from this great Egyptian conquest, whereas Thrace, Macedonia, and probably Troy all felt the wrath of Egyptian arms (2:201–4). The historical reality of Sesostris and these victories, however, cannot be sustained with the evidence that Bernal presents.

The Greek historians Herodotus and Diodorus, and to a lesser extent the Egyptian Manetho, provide Bernal with the bulk of his narrative evidence. But their testimony, as noted above, is taken literally and is not subjected to any sort of questioning or analysis. Again Bernal seems to think that a text can only mean what it states and nothing more. Such credulity leads him seriously astray.

In his discussion of Herodotus and Diodorus, Bernal resists (aside from the observation at *BA* 2:200 that such interpretations smack of *Besserwissen*) the parallels between the conquests and achievements or failures of Sesostris and those of the Persian kings Darius and Cambyses; like Darius, Sesostris has difficulties in Thrace (as reported by Diodorus) and unlike Cambyses, Sesostris has no difficulties in subduing Ethiopia (as reported by both Herodotus and Diodorus). Bernal essentially ignores the historiographical traditions which provide the context for these accounts, namely, the assimilation of generations of Greek and Egyptian traditions into the Herodotean account (as argued by A. B. Lloyd 1975–88, 3:16–17) and the Hellenistic traditions of deified conquerors such as Alexander the Great, Ninis, and Semiramis, which influenced the narrative of Diodorus (so Sacks 1990, 75–76).

One can further object to Bernal's use of Herodotus. According to Herodotus (2.102.4), Sesostris treated with honor those enemies who resisted bravely and fought for freedom (*tēs eleutheriēs*), while he denigrated those who did not by calling them women (cf. *BA* 2:197). The reference in this instance to *eleutheria* is important, but Bernal ignores it. Freedom is perhaps the most powerful word in the Greek political vocabulary, from Herodotus through Aristotle (see Sinclair 1988, 21) and on into the nineteenth- and twentieth-century struggles for Greek independence (even today, if the graffiti visible in Cyprus are any indication). But Bernal ignores this reference, which would have alerted him to the very real existence of fifth-century Greek concepts shaping Herodotus' account of Sesostris, which lack an Egyptian context in the early second millennium B.C.E. Again his uncritical, antiquated attitude toward the evidence leads him to ignore important testimony which might enable him to understand ancient authors on their own terms.

Literary accounts of the great conquests of Sesostris can not be relied upon as they reflect the mixing of Egypto-Greek traditions of a later time, ranging over hundreds of years. Moreover, it is plainly evident that Herodotus' account is colored by the emerging political consciousness of the Greeks in the fifth century B.C.E. Bernal attempts to bolster these accounts by referring to a Middle Kingdom text, the Mit Rahina inscription, which he claims supports his view of a massive Egyptian conquest from Thrace to Colchis (*BA* 2:188–94, 230–34). Like so much else in *Black Athena*, this too proves illusory.

Bernal would lead the unsuspecting reader to think that this inscription is trouble-free, its translation and interpretation only challenged by those scholars who think that they "know better." In fact, as he himself notes, the text is fragmentary, and Egyptologists are still unable to agree not only on an accurate translation but also on the places mentioned in the document. It is clear that the inscription refers to military campaigns and to the taking of prisoners and booty, but, it seems most likely, instead from Syria-Palestine, as the inscription's editor suggests (see Farag 1980, 75). Bernal claims that one word in the text, *Stt*, refers to Asia, which would support his view of

Sesostris' great campaign into the east and north. This assertion, however, has been discounted by Egyptologists, who argue that the name refers to Syria-Palestine and nowhere else. The Mit Rahina inscription thus does not provide the corroborative evidence which Bernal claims. Moreover, the areas of destruction in Anatolia which Bernal attributes to Sesostris' great campaign (*BA* 2:216–23) cannot be precisely dated to his reign, despite Bernal's efforts to the contrary. The campaigns of Sesostris, then, at least those in Europe and Anatolia, are best left to the realm of legend and ancient nationalist propaganda. (For comprehensive discussion of the Sesostris legend see A. B. Lloyd 1975–88, 3:16–37, and Eddy 1961, 280–85, the latter apparently unknown to Bernal.)

In his discussion of Sesostris' presumed conquests Bernal renews the topic of the king's "blackness" (*BA* 2:245–57, esp. 251–57). Perhaps nowhere else is his equivocal language more in evidence than in these discussions. He admits that the ancient Egyptians came in all colors, from white to brown and black, but then asserts that the Old and Middle Kingdoms were fundamentally African, or black.[6] This statement ignores much pictorial evidence to the contrary from the Old and Middle Kingdoms, which depicts Egyptian men as brownish-red in color and women in lighter hues (e.g., the well-known statues, from the Fourth Dynasty, of Prince Rahotep and Princess Nofret in the Egyptian Museum in Cairo, and nonroyal figures such as the "Kneeling Scribe" and various other servants from the Fifth Dynasty in the same collection; see also Bard, this volume). Bernal's intended assault on racism is laudable, but in the process he only succeeds in imposing nineteenth- and twentieth-century perceptions of race on the society of ancient Egypt. Thus he not only distorts the texture of the past but also subjects the ancient Egyptians to the indignity of racial stereotypes and attitudes spawned by the misguided modern age.[7]

According to Herodotus, Sesostris left behind a colony of soldiers in Colchis, as the descendants of these men reportedly believed in Herodotus' time. Herodotus describes the Colchians as black-skinned with woolly hair, just like the Egyptians (2.104.1–2, *melauchroes eisi kai oulotriches*). Bernal believes that this evidence should be taken "at face value," that is, "that the African army (i.e., Sesostris') did reach the Eastern Black Sea in the 20th century B.C.E." (*BA* 2:257). However, the evidence which he adduces for this view is hardly compelling and in fact has been soundly rejected by Snowden (1989). (See Bernal 1989c for a response which does not satisfactorily address Snowden's points.) Snowden argues that when Herodotus wants to refer to "blacks" (in the twentieth-century sense of the term), he uses the term "Ethiopian." What this suggests, then, is that the Herodotean description of the Colchians as black-skinned and woolly-haired like the Egyptians points away from the Colchians as "black" or "African." A. B. Lloyd, who also rejects the "Africanness" of the Colchians, suggests that Herodotus may have generalized from a section of the Colchian population which possessed certain physical resemblances to Egyptians. Also interesting in this light are the traditions found in Hecataeus (*FGrH* 1 F18a) that the Argonauts returned from Colchis by way of the Nile, and a mention in the Elder Pliny (*Historia Naturalis* 33.52) that Sesostris had been conquered by the Colchian king Saulaces (Lloyd 1975–88, 3:22). The ancient traditions concerning Egypt and Colchis are considerably more complicated than Bernal would have his readers believe.

Also disquieting is Bernal's use of Apollonius of Rhodes and the *Argonautica* (third century B.C.E.) as an authority for Bronze Age geographical knowledge (e.g., *BA* 2:30–31, 250–51). Here he simply ignores the whole tradition of Hellenistic geography and discoveries of the fourth and third centuries B.C.E. which had provided Apollonius with much of the information in the *Argonautica*—another instance of Bernal's insensitivity to the ancient evidence he claims to respect.

Herodotus provides Bernal not only with the substance of his account of Sesostris but also with a great deal of information about Greek religion. In particular, Bernal relies on Herodotus' statement that the Greeks acquired the names of the twelve gods from the Egyptians (2.4.2; cf. *BA* 2:109–10), as well as such divine figures as Dionysus and Heracles. That discussion, and Bernal's treatment of many other aspects of Greek religion, must be carefully examined for the forced conclusions to which his diffusionist-inspired treatment often leads.

Even Herodotus appears to be slightly more cautious, more circumspect than Bernal in accepting the testimony of the Egyptians. In prefacing his remarks on Egyptian religion, Herodotus states that in his opinion all men are equally knowledgeable about the gods—that is, they do not know much (2.3.2). This remark, as Burkert has acutely noted ([1977] 1985, 313), places Herodotus squarely in the intellectual milieu of the fifth century B.C.E. Greek "Enlightenment" and reveals the skepticism which he would have shared with contemporary intellectuals, such as Protagoras. Again, as observed above concerning *eleutheria*, Bernal seems not to be aware of the influence of contemporary ideas and movements on Herodotus' work.

In the case of Dionysus, Bernal's treatment is unpersuasive and superficial (*BA* 2:79–80, 116, 238–39, 244). An easy identification of Dionysus with Osiris is made without any discussion of Dionysus' attributes and powers— for example, intoxication, joy, and the orgiastic rituals and festivals—or of his Anatolian and Thracian connections (see, e.g., Burkert [1977] 1985, 161–67). Bernal is content to see only an Egyptian influence (which does exist, but not as early as he imagines) emanating from the cult of Osiris in the Eighteenth Dynasty, if not earlier; oddly enough, however, most of the evidence cited—from Diodorus and Plutarch—reflects the Hellenistic fusion of the two cults. Finally, it might be asked to what extent the cult of Osiris influenced the essence of that of Dionysus. Burkert refers to the arrival of Osirian ship processions in the sixth century B.C.E. ([1977] 1985, 163), and there are probably some similarities regarding the connection of both deities to life and death. Yet Dionysus does not appear to share Osiris' symbolic quality of resurrection, whereas the liquid essence of life, wild ritualistic dancing, and divine epiphany associated with Dionysus seem absent from the religion of Osiris (see, e.g., Dodds 1960, xii–xvi). The references, then, to Osiris and the various attributes of Dionysian cult (such as cultivation of the vine, music) are best explained by the conscious reform of the latter in Egypt by Ptolemy Philopator, ca. 200 B.C.E. (see Eddy 1961, 283, in contrast to Bernal, *BA* 2:238–40).

An Egyptian origin is postulated for another putative son of Zeus, the hero Heracles (*BA* 2:106–22). Bernal rejects the Semitic traces and background of Heracles—for example, the use of clubs by both Heracles and Gilgamesh, and Heracles' similarity to the Phoenician god Melqart—and proposes that the Egyptian origin of the demigod detailed by Herodotus be accepted. Herodotus, however, distinguished between the divine Heracles, son of Zeus, and the heroic one, the son of Amphitryon (2.43.2, 2.44.5; cf. 6.53.2), which points to a rationalizing of the mythology—and again the influence of the "Enlightenment"—as multiple explanations were devised in order to explain the different legends of a particular god. (See A. B. Lloyd 1975–88, 2:201–4, and How and Wells 1912, 2:187, the latter not cited by Bernal.) Bernal insists on the Egyptian origins, and this leads him to argue that Heracles "should be considered . . . as the Greek image of a Middle Kingdom pharaoh" (*BA* 2:115). On the face of it, it is difficult to see how the Greeks could make such distinctions (Old Kingdom, Middle Kingdom, etc.). Bernal claims that the purported conquests of Sesostris would have inspired the pharaonic image of Heracles. But as argued above, these conquests are essentially ahistorical, if not wholly imaginary, and it seems doubtful that many Greeks beyond Herodotus (and possibly a few other intellectuals) would have known of such traditions to be so inspired. Thus the conquests of Sesostris are unlikely to have provided the sort of stimulus that Bernal suggests.

The pharaonic imagery of Heracles that Bernal postulates extends to many of the feats and roles played by Heracles in myth. For example, Heracles typically acts alone or perhaps with a single companion, just like Egyptian kings who conquer mighty hordes "with little if any support from [their] armies" (*BA* 2:116). Also, like both Old and Middle Kingdom kings, Heracles acts as a sort of "hydraulic engineer" (digging canals and tunnels), which Bernal claims is unusual. Finally he asserts that Heracles was a "Middle Kingdom pharaoh in Boeotia" and "essentially a Theban hero. Thebes was his birthplace and the scene of many of his earlier heroic deeds. There were also a number of sites in Boiotia where he was worshipped" (2:119). But this account is misleading. A. R. Schulman (1982) has discussed battle scenes of the Middle Kingdom which illustrate Nubian archers and Egyptian infantry attacking an Asiatic city (interestingly enough, these are distinguished from one another by the usual skin tones, and officers are identified by symbols of rank), without any indication of the king's role. Similar iconography is visible on the monument of Merneptah at Karnak, which records the Egyptian attack on Ashkelon ca. 1211–1209 B.C.E.; it too shows Egyptian infantry pressing its attack as the pharaoh, inscribed in a larger scale, casts his shadow over the whole scene.[8]

What illustrations like these suggest, contrary to Bernal, is that Egyptian kings were not depicted as solitary heroes striking down their foes, but rather as victorious commanders. Again contrary to Bernal, there were other figures from the ancient world who were also famous for their construction projects. One of the most interesting of these was the Babylonian queen Semiramis, whom he scarcely mentions (cf. *BA* 2:583, n. 16). Yet as an anti-Persian (then anti-Greek) heroine, Semiramis in part won eternal fame from the great canals and temples she built (see, e.g., Eddy 1961, 121–25). Lastly, the identification of Heracles with Thebes that Bernal posits (2:119) cannot be embraced uncritically. Other traditions record Heracles' birth in Argos, in the vicinity of which his Labors occurred, and from there his cult spread to Thebes and throughout Greece (Burkert 1985, 198, 205, 208–11). Heracles' Argive connection and the "pan-Hellenic" nature of the cult thus mitigates the special link between Heracles and Thebes that Bernal seeks to establish.

The Egyptian origins hypothesized by Bernal for Heracles and Dionysus are also advanced for other aspects of Greek religion, namely the Minoan bull cult and two dimensions of Greek belief, "fate" (*kēr*) and "soul" (*psychē*). Generally, these views are unpersuasive. In regard to the Minoan bull cult, Bernal rejects the Anatolian origins advanced by Burkert ([1977] 1985, 37–40) and instead argues that the Egyptian bull cult associated with Mn or Mēnēs, the first king of Egypt, and the fighting bulls of Apis and Ptah in Memphis were carried to Crete by the Egyptians (*BA* 2:165–77). Evidence from Crete, however, especially the famous frescoes of young men and women running with the bulls so to speak (jumping over them, actually) suggests an altogether different ritual, one involving human worshipers and not simply fighting animals. Perhaps Bernal thinks this is only a Minoan variation on an Egyptian theme, though he makes no reference to this essential difference between the two cults. It would seem more reasonable, however, to infer from these discrepancies two different cults, both with their own origins, rituals, and meanings.

Similar problems afflict Bernal's attempt to connect several key aspects of the Greek soul to origins in the Egyptian (see Jasanoff and Nussbaum, this volume). This is evident first in his attempt to link Greek *kēr* ("fate," "doom") to Egyptian *ka* (*k3*), which represented that dimension of the soul that guided and protected—that is, not simply "soul" (cf. J. A. Wilson 1951, 86). The desire to find a connection here must be resisted on two grounds: (1) the nature of *ka* and the unity of body and soul in Egyptian belief (leading to mummification) that is so foreign to the Greek, and (2) the linguistic argument.

Bernal suggests that in the Old Kingdom the *ka* acquired the meaning of a "spiritual companion" (afterwards "ghost") that one met at death, and it was this that inspired the Greek concept of *kēr* or "fate" (*BA* 2:264). Yet the Greek appears more ambiguous, less specific in meaning than Bernal allows. Sometimes *kēr* is "fate" but at other times "death" (e.g., Homer *Odyssey* 11.171), and in still other situations it refers to the souls of the dead and even ghosts (cf. LSJ s.v. *kēr*). Bernal's interpretation would appear to suggest that by the Old Kingdom *ka* had become "fate," but two millennia later it seems that the meaning of its offspring *kēr* remained quite flexible. This inconsistency suggests that the rather specific definition he assigns to *kēr* is unwarranted and determined by his linguistic analysis (see Jasanoff and Nussbaum, this volume). Bernal claims that the semantic fit between *k3* and *kēr*, although not matched phonetically, remains good. He attempts to explain how *kēr* originated from *ka* by recourse to late Greek and Coptic transcriptions of the latter (e.g., *ke, ki, choi*). But how can any of these produce *kēr*? In fact in late Egyptian the *r* sound has broken down and disappeared, though in actuality it was not quite an *r* sound, but more like the "Boston *r*" (as in President Kennedy's "Cuber" in the 1960s). It dropped out first in speech and then in writing. Even if it had ever been attached to *k3*, by the time the Greeks came along it would not even have been present. How then could they have acquired it?

The etymology suggested by Bernal for *psychē* is even less justified linguistically. He attempts to establish a link between the Egyptian root *šw*, which denotes "dry, sun-baked," etc., with *psychē* by tying the Egyptian *šw* to the masculine definite article *p3*, which he claims (without supplying evidence) was replacing its feminine equivalent (*t3*) in the late second millennium (*BA* 2:264–65). The attempt to derive *psychē* from the Egyptian *šw* does not succeed. The view, then, that the Greeks borrowed these terms and concepts is no more convincing than the argument that Osiris is Dionysus.[9]

A peripheral debate over etymological and linguistic arguments such as these has now been joined, with Bernal's partisans and his critics ranged on opposing sides (cf. Rendsburg, 1989, 67–82; Ray, 1990, 77–81; Jasanoff and Nussbaum, this volume). To date, most of the controversy has focused on etymologies, but this seems to be the least satisfactory level of linguistic analysis. To establish evidence of linguistic influence, it is first of all necessary to show that 20 to 30 percent of words in one language derive from another. The next step is to demonstrate phonetic similarity; but in the adaption of the Greek alphabet to the Coptic, the Egyptians had to take seven letters from the earlier Demotic script to represent sounds that the Greek could not supply; moreover, Greek sounds are used differently in Coptic. Finally, the best method of revealing linguistic borrowing is to demonstrate parallelisms in the grammatic structures—and in this it would appear that there are none between Greek and Egyptian. Bernal, then, is working from the least satisfactory level of linguistic analysis, which should be sufficient cause to consider his linguistic arguments as at most tentative, at worst tendentious.

THE AEGEAN BRONZE AGE WORLD

But we are historians, seeking to restore past reality. Historical work must always be judged on that basis, not on the intellectual skill and rhetorical dexterity with which an author may manipulate and combine miscellaneous, inadequately criticized bits into a towering edifice of gossamer.
—C. G. Starr (1965, 272)

As the Middle Kingdom conquests of Sesostris had, in Bernal's eyes, made the Mediterranean world Egyptian, the eruption of Thera had wiped it all away, leaving Egypt as the preserver of civilization. The impact of Thera (and another volcanic blast in Iceland, Hekla, late in the Bronze Age) was worldwide, reaching even to China, and Bernal insists that such legends as Atlantis record its memory. These views, comprising the essence of the seventh chapter of Bernal's second volume ("The Thera Eruption: From the Aegean to China"), are interesting perhaps, but in the end remain just that.

There can be no question that the Greek island of Santorini or Thera is an ancient caldera. The problem comes in trying to determine the date of the devastating blast that tore the island apart. Most would agree today with Bernal that the date initially advanced by Marinatos a half-century ago is too late and should be raised. But how much? Bernal renews his argument for a date in the late seventeenth century B.C.E., specifically 1628 (cf. *BA* 1:42 and 2:285). The rationale for this date is unconvincing despite his effort to invest the argument with an impressive cloak of scientific terms, such as radiocarbon and dendrochronological (tree-ring) evidence. But these techniques (and other, newer types of studies such as ice cores) to which Bernal appeals for certainty here do not succeed.

In a discussion of such methods as applied to the Thera eruption, Pyle (1989, not cited by Bernal) concludes that the chronology may never be resolved. Though radiocarbon has yielded a wide range of dates, these can be "interpreted according to one's prejudice" (1989, 91), whereas acidity peaks and tree rings are at once *potentially* more precise yet also highly ambiguous. The certainty, then, of Bernal's date for the Thera eruption can be no more secure than any other.

Thera did blow up, but was it Atlantis? Few stories or legends have excited the human imagination more than this one, about an advanced and powerful civilization that in an instant ceased to exist. Bernal refers to a German writer (*BA* 2:297) who has estimated that more than seven thousand books and twenty thousand articles and other items have been written on that vanished world. But what is the justification for the existence of the lost continent? Much of Bernal's discussion (2:295–98, 302–4) hinges on Plato's *Timaeus*, which in part relates a dialogue between Solon and an Egyptian priest. The latter first chides Solon and all the Greeks for their childishness, and then outlines Atlantis' story while praising Egyptian cultural preeminence.

Plato's account of Atlantis is rather more complex than Bernal recognizes. He ignores the likelihood that it is influenced by events more recent to the author than the twelfth-century B.C.E. invasion of the Sea Peoples or the even more remote arrival of the Hyksos in Greece (*BA* 2:302, 304). Bernal first confuses the familial relationship in *Timaeus* (not that it is clear), stating that the "Kritias . . . of that name in Plato's dialogues, was the philosopher's great grandfather" (2:297). In *Timaeus*, however, the interlocutor is instead most likely the tyrant Kritias, one of the Thirty Tyrants, who in the course of the dialogue refers to *his* grandfather Kritias. Most likely Plato has telescoped the generations here so as to enhance the plausibility of the story/myth that Solon relates (for discussion see J. K. Davies 1971, 324–26). This would indicate that Plato drew his information from a more immediate context than what Bernal suggests. It seems much more probable that the mighty conflict alluded to in *Timaeus* emerged from the traditions and accounts of the Persian Wars. This great conflict left an indelible mark on the citizens of Athens (cf. the "Marathon fighters" of Aristophanes) and all Greece—the sort of thing Plato as a boy would have heard much of as he grew up—and much more so than distant invasions of bygone times, ostensibly kept alive by the etymological origins of various words in Greek, such as Atlantis, "Atlantic," and Okeanos (*BA* 2:298–302).[10]

As mentioned above, Bernal suggests that Plato's account of Atlantis embodies a folk memory of sorts of a Hyksos invasion of Greece. In two chapters of his second volume (8, "The Hyksos," and 9, "Crete, Thera, and the Birth of Mycenaean Culture in the Eighteenth and Seventeenth Centuries B.C.E.") Bernal discusses the Hyksos' origins and background, their occupation of Egypt, and their expulsion and flight to Greece. "Chieftains of the hill country" (the meaning he attaches to *Hyksos*) swept into Egypt in the course of the eighteenth century B.C.E. Pushing aside the Thirteenth and Fourteenth Dynasties, these foreign princes, characterized as a "multinational corporation" (*BA* 2:345–46), ruled into the mid–sixteenth century before their expulsion by the Egyptians. Bernal accepts that there may well have been Indo-European and Hurrian elements among the Hyksos, arguing successfully against those who would describe the Hyksos as merely Asiatic invaders from Syria-Palestine (2:338–45, 406). (His ideas are not as novel as he would suppose; cf. J. A. Wilson 1951, 161–62.) Also attractive in this context is his discussion of the Egyptian etymologies of horses and chariots, for instance that Egyptian *ssmt* derives from Hebrew *sûs* and Akkadian *sîsû* (2:346–52).

Though Bernal's discussion of the Hyksos in Egypt at first is generally persuasive, it soon breaks down as he argues (after Stubbings 1973, 2.1:629–35) for a Hyksos invasion of Greece beginning in the late eighteenth century B.C.E. (*BA* 2:363). He further argues that at this time some Egyptian religious institutions were established and that most of the Egypto-Levantine objects found in Greece in Bronze Age contexts date from this era. In all of this, perhaps the most explosive claim is that made for Mycenae as a Hyksos camp, on his etymology of Mycenae from the Ugaritic toponym *mḫnt*, meaning "camp," or *mḫnm*, meaning "two camps," (*BA* 1:51, 2:389–91). Schliemann's famous finds, then, in the shaft graves at Mycenae are Hyksos, not Greek, and the famous gold death mask of Agamemnon (in the National Archaeological Museum in Athens) might be in reality that of a Hyksos warlord (2:391–97).

Objections to the proposed origin of Mycenae can be made on two grounds. First, it takes no account of the Greek origin of *Mycenae*, "mushroom," which reflects similar names of other Greek places—for example, *Sicyon*, "pumpkin," or *Phlius*, "spinach." Secondly, the etymology that Bernal proposes can be challenged on the basis of the harsh *ḫ* (*kh*) in (e.g.) *mḫnt*, which is not related phonetically to Greek kappa. In fact it seems that the Greeks were confused by the Semitic *ḫ* and sometimes dropped it or used chi instead. What all this suggests is that the Greek etymology of Mycenae should be retained.

That the treasures of Mycenae must demonstrate Egyptian or Semitic origins also seems unnecessary. Studies of gold objects, for example, from the Egyptian Eighteenth Dynasty reveal a silver content of 11 to 17 percent, whereas "Mycenaean" gold objects have a silver content of about 8 percent (A. B. Lloyd 1975–88, 1:5, with bibliography). While these figures are not conclusive, the discrepancy suggests that one should look closer to home, say, to Crete, to account for the rich gold objects in the Mycenaean graves. Similarly the *tholos* tombs in Mycenae and elsewhere in Greece may be explained without recourse to Egyptian pyramids and other Eastern explanations (cf. *BA* 2:391–93). Round underground tombs are the easiest type to build (Vermeule 1964, 121) and are known in Middle Minoan Crete at Mesara and elsewhere (see, e.g., Renfrew 1972, 82). The appearance, then, of *tholoi* in Greece can be readily explained without recourse to Hyksos invaders or other Egyptian and Eastern sources.

In conclusion, Bernal's theory that Hyksos invaders arrived in Greece (and also touched on Crete and Thera along the way; see *BA* 2:377–83) and so launched Mycenaean Greek culture (esp. 2:406–8) breaks down when some of the major points are scrutinized, such as the meaning of *Mycenae*, analysis of tomb objects from the shaft graves, and the origin of the *tholos*. Moreover, recent discoveries of the Austrian Archaeological Institute (Cairo) at Tell el-Dabʿa (Avaris) in the Egyptian Delta have revealed a volcanic layer— surely that from the great Thera eruption—*covering* the Hyksos site (see Yurco, Morris, Vermeule, Coleman, this volume). One wonders how the Hyksos, surely devastated by such a disaster, would be in a position or condition to embark on new conquests.[11] The greater objection, however, to Bernal's view of a Hyksos conquest of Greece is the relentless nature of the diffusionist onslaught here, "modified" or not, which perceives all the major movements, influences, etc., as proceeding from Egypt to the north. The grudging admission (*BA* 2:363) that "Greeks" ("pre-" or otherwise) were now arriving in their future homeland really counts for little, as it is clear that Bernal imagines them to be just sitting around waiting to learn how to build, how to write, and how to make war. The implausibility of this hypothesis is readily apparent (see *BA* 2:449 for a good example).

In Bernal's reconstruction, however, the Hyksos "invasion" was actually the second time that Greece had been occupied by colonizers from Egypt. In his view, the first invasion occurred in the third millennium B.C.E., when Egyptian colonizers arrived in Greece bringing with them their advanced building skills and their cults and religion. This discussion takes up two chapters (2 and 3, "Egypt's Influence on Boiotia and the Peloponnese in the 3rd Millennium," parts 1 and 2) sandwiched between two others dealing with Crete (1, "Crete before the Palaces, 7000–2100 B.C.E.") and its relations with Egypt (4, "The Old Palace Period in Crete and the Egyptian Middle Kingdom, 2100 to 1730 B.C.E."). Yet in making this claim, Bernal never pauses to consider the essentially isolationist nature of the ancient Egyptians, their opinion that all other peoples—Asiatic, Libyan, Nubian—were barbarians (and note too Herodotus 2.39.2, 2.41.3, which suggest the survival of that attitude into later times), or that the thought of living anywhere other than in Egypt was repugnant. Such isolationism can be seen in the *Story of Sinuhe*, the memoir of a Twelfth Dynasty courtier who was so very unhappy as a prosperous exile somewhere in Lebanon (cf. *BA* 2:190, 191, 193, 225, 411). Sinuhe's complaints, as J. A. Wilson puts it, show that "there was but one land which was the center and summit of the universe, and no other home was satisfactory" (1951, 135, passim). Why, then, would the Egyptians travel to Greece, hardly at their doorstep and not an easy journey, for purposes of settlement? This issue begs for discussion, but Bernal does not recognize it.[12]

Evidence for this third-millennium Egyptian presence in Greece postulated by Bernal appears ostensibly in the personages of various cults and on monuments, especially tombs, that have been found both in antiquity and in modern times. Analysis of the various cults and figures from myth discussed here (for example, Neit and Athena, and Heracles) suggests that Bernal's case for Egyptian influence at this time is rather weak (*BA* 2:79–90). For example, J. D. Ray (1990, 80) has shown the difficulties in Bernal's identification and etymology of Neit and Athena (*BA* 1:51–52; cf. also Bernal 1990b, 120–21, in response to Ray, a view continued in 1992a, 211), particularly that the long vowel in the middle of the Greek equivalent has no counterpart in the Egyptian form. (See also Jasanoff and Nussbaum, this volume.) I have already suggested, in a prior section of this essay, various weaknesses in Bernal's recognition of Heracles as a "Middle Kingdom pharaoh." Again problematic in this discussion is the way that he mixes his sources; for example, in treating the figures of Semele and Alcmene, he introduces Pausanias and Pindar, as if they could provide independent corroborating testimony to third-millennium events (*BA* 2:80).

Similarly, Bernal's discussion of building techniques and the construction of tombs in Boeotia and elsewhere in Greece seems to derive from his diffusionist concepts. The purported discovery of the tomb of Alcmene near Thebes (cf. *BA* 2:124–28) is, as argued above, ahistorical and unable to withstand the criticism that it is essentially a literary fiction of Plutarch's. No stronger is the argument (2:128–33) that the tomb of Amphion and Zethus at Thebes is an Egyptian step-pyramid.

In the summer of 1993 I visited Thebes and surveyed closely the hilltop tomb of Amphion and Zethus. From the base of the hill, the ground slopes gradually upward (about sixty degrees; see figure 1) and so forms a part of the ridges and ravines surrounding Thebes, which sits atop them all on the site of the ancient Cadmea.[13] The road that rings the hill also tends to obscure the true lay of the land (see figure 2), as the lower slopes have been cut away to make room for the roadbed.[14] As a result, the hill's steepness is exaggerated, particularly on the southwest side of the hill below the school that shares the hilltop with the tomb.

Here the cut of the road is particularly deep and effectively interrupts the hill's gradual ascent. With its (at most) moderately rising slopes, the idea that this site could be a "step-pyramid" is little more than a flight of fantasy.[15] What has to be seen then is that the hill of Amphion and Zethus is simply a tumulus-style mound found elsewhere in Greece. The hilltop had once a large mound covering the grave, which has since been removed, exposing

FIGURE I. *Amphion and Zethus from the northwest, from near the bottom of the hill*

FIGURE 2. *The road ringing Amphion and Zethus from the summits*

FIGURE 3. *Excavated mound, showing the remains of the tomb and Mycenaean aqueduct*

the tomb (see figure 3). Neither the mound nor the grave was especially large, particularly in comparison with those, say, at Cerveteri in Italy. The actual tomb, moreover, does not suggest any parallels to an Egyptian burial.[16]

Arguments that these various monuments were the product of Egyptian engineering or know-how seem driven by the view that the indigenous craftsmen and artisans were incapable of working with stone, or of conceiving such projects. Thus, for example, Bernal criticizes Renfrew for arguing that the bow drill (used to make bowls, etc., from stone) could have been a local development and was not brought to Crete from Egypt in later Neolithic or early Predynastic times (*BA* 2:68). Yet he is silent regarding contemporaneous use of bow drills on the mainland (in present-day Bulgaria and Romania). Their existence there suggests that there were corresponding developments in both the northern Balkans and the Mediterranean (see Renfrew 1972, 347). Or maybe Egyptian colonists had already arrived on the scene? What this points to is the absence of any compelling reason to suppose that the construction of granaries in Early Bronze Age Greece was, as Bernal would maintain (*BA* 2:135–37), the work of Egyptian engineers, or that the same technicians were again responsible for the draining of Lake Kopais (2:133–35). As similar techniques of working stone can be found in contemporaneous contexts from Bulgaria and Egypt, it would certainly seem possible that the early inhabitants of the Balkan peninsula possessed the skills essential to building and irrigation.

One last objection to this hypothesis of third-millennium Egyptian colonization and suzerainty in Greece follows from Bernal's own appraisal of what might have taken place (*BA* 2:152). He notes that it is unlikely that what occurred was "direct colonization." He offers no clues as to the identity of the mystery colonists, which makes one wonder how then they can be construed as Egyptian. Additionally, he admits that Egyptian objects from this era have not been found in Greece and that there is no Egyptian attestation of such colonies; one might add to these points the absence of any Egyptian inscriptions or other documentary evidence that would support his arguments. The absence of such evidence undercuts his thesis significantly. When these considerations are added to the isolationist inclinations of the ancient Egyptians, one is forced to conclude that this Egyptian colonization of Greece is a theoretical construct rather than historical reality.

In the later Bronze Age, however, there were many contacts between the Aegean and Egypto-Levantine regions; this Bernal explores in two of the final three chapters in his second volume (10, "Egyptian, Mesopotamian and Levantine Contacts with the Aegean: The Documentary Evidence," and 11, "Egyptian and Levantine Contacts with the Aegean, 1550–1250 B.C.E.: The Archaeological Evidence"). The ground here is a bit less slippery, and some of the points that Bernal raises are attractive, though not particularly surprising. For instance, he argues for a strong Egypto-Levantine presence in the eastern Mediterranean, extending to Crete and the Aegean (*BA* 2:432, 434–35, 450–52), which the Cape Gelidonya and Kaş shipwrecks (and their excavations) would seem to confirm (2:465–74, 492). Though the destinations of these ships, the "nationality" of their crews, and the exact nature of their cargoes is a subject of much debate and disagreement, I do not think many would challenge the view that in the later Bronze Age substantial trade was being conducted in the area. (Indeed some of Bernal's critics have complained in this instance that he ignores the Levant in preference to Egypt; see e.g., S. P. Morris 1990, 57–66; Bikai 1990).

Even in these contexts, however, racism again rears its ugly head. Bernal suggests (*BA* 2:443–44) that in this Bronze Age commercial boom, "African Blacks" participated, only to be subjected to modern forms of racial prejudice. Such prejudice is evident, he claims, in the appearance of Mycenaean Greek names like Sima, Simos (= Simōn, Simmos), and references to Ethiopians as *simoi* ("the snub-nosed ones"), since the Indo-European root *sim-* in Latin *simia* connotes "monkey." It is truly alarming that a view that misrepresents the actual situation so completely could find its way into print. The Romans called monkeys *simiae* because they were snub-nosed. The Greeks applied the term to people as well as to animals, including fish. Bernal ignores references (see LSJ s.v. *simos*) to Scythians—usually regarded as the opposite to the Ethiopians in physical attributes—as *simoi* too. Additionally, Dover

(1993, 46) has noted that *simos* can mean both "flat-nosed" and "snub-nosed," and that Socrates, according to Xenophon (*Symposium* 5.6), described himself as *simotēs*. Bernal apparently has not reflected that non-African people, from Socrates in antiquity to my sister today, can have flat, snub, or pug noses. That such a distortion of the linguistic evidence (however well-intentioned) could find its way into print in a historical study in the late twentieth century strikes me as a retrograde step in historiography.

By contrast, one solid indication of wide-ranging Bronze Age economic activity lies in the vocabulary of trade that Bernal discusses (*BA* 2:482–89). He proposes, for example, that Greek *sitos* may be influenced by a group of Egypto-Levantine terms (e.g., Assyrian *šeu*) that likewise mean "grain." Such borrowing reflects the widespread practice in the Near East of the adoption of words commonly used in trade and commerce. Less persuasive, however, is his attempt to make the Danaans and the Ahhiyawa of Hittite annals identical with the Egyptian Dene/Denyan (*Dn[n]*) and Ekwesh (*ikwš*) respectively, and so participants in the famous invasions of the Sea Peoples of the thirteenth century B.C.E. (2:418–23, 456–60). Equally plausible arguments establish the Danaans as a Cilician or Syro-Palestinian people known as well to the Hittites as to the Egyptians. It might well be that the similarity between Homer's Danaoi and the *Dn(n)* or Danaans is merely coincidental (see A. B. Lloyd 1975–88, 1:8, 125). As for the identification of the Ekwesh as the Ahhiyawa (= Achaians), the Egyptian sources record that the former were circumcised; it is widely believed that the Mycenaean Greeks were not. This should weaken the identification of the Ahhiyawa/Ekwesh with the Achaians that D. L. Page (1972, 21–23, not cited by Bernal) observed had become an article of faith for many scholars, including now Bernal. This is not, however, to discount entirely a Mycenaean element among the Sea Peoples. Some time ago Desborough (1964, 209–14) identified Mycenaean-style pottery among the Philistines (= Peleset), which may point to a Mycenaean presence there. Yet it remains unclear just how the Egyptians would have known what their enemies termed themselves in their own languages, and whether the Egyptians might not have just given to those peoples names that described them in some fashion or were borrowed from their Syrian and Hittite neighbors. It would not be the first or the last time that an ethnic "identity" was incorrectly ascribed. Convenient assumptions in the place of evidence should be avoided. Though it probably would satisfy an innate instinct to establish connections in such events as these, the search for such certainty becomes too frequently a chimerical pursuit.

This discussion of the Aegean and Mediterranean world leads Bernal to conclude (*BA* 2:494) that the origins of Greek culture must be pushed back to the eighteenth and seventeenth centuries B.C.E., "in Hyksos times," when "local Indo-European with Egyptian and Levantine influences that we call Greek civilization was first and lastingly formed." Yet the evidence that Bernal advances for this view, as reviewed above, does not justify his conclusion.

The end to the Greek Bronze Age and the Aegean world order constitutes the final chapter to Bernal's discussion in the second volume of *Black Athena*: "The Heroic End to the Heroic Age: The Fall of Thebes, Troy, and Mycenae, 1250–1150 B.C.E." He accepts the idea of a Phoenician or Cadmean settlement of Thebes in Boeotia ca. 1470 B.C.E. and sees evidence of this in the Parian Marble, which recorded Cadmus' arrival in Thebes in 1518/17 B.C.E., and Herodotus' (5.59.1) report of seeing "Cadmean letters" in Thebes. From this he argues that Linear B was used contemporaneously with an alphabetic script (2:497–501).

Unfortunately, the Parian Marble can not be cited so easily. Dating from the third century B.C.E., it clearly reflects the conscious systemizing of the Greeks of later times, the desire to assign dates and chronologies to all events. As such dates were usually computed in a rather arbitrary manner — for example, the average length of generations — there would seem to be little justification for accepting its dating of Cadmus' arrival in Thebes (cf. the other dates mentioned by Bernal, *BA* 2:501, for the same event). Herodotus' report that he saw "Cadmean letters" in Thebes is simply accepted by Bernal without reservation. Moreover, he does not note that Herodotus goes on to say that these Cadmean letters were shaped like Ionian. No consideration is given to the possibility that Herodotus may have come upon a forgery here. Nor does Bernal assess the implications of the translations that Herodotus provides. Is it really likely that a language would have remained static over eight hundred years, that Herodotus in the fifth century B.C.E. could translate a text from the thirteenth? The inherent difficulties to this reinforce the opinion that what Herodotus reported seeing in Thebes was a seventh-century B.C.E. inscription (and forgery), not an original from a thirteenth (see How and Wells 1912, 2:27, Vermeule 1964, 239).

All the same, Bernal argues that Cadmean Thebes represents a Hyksos occupation (as does that of Danaus), at which time Bernal places the introduction of the alphabet in Greece. Yet in making this claim he does not stop to consider his own argument that "written evidence indicates that in every region the Hyksos ruled the native script remained in use" (*BA* 2:407). Where is the evidence? Is there anything to show that the Hyksos continued to use their cuneiform and hieroglyphics, presumably acquired in their many travels? Why would they suddenly stop writing in one of several (supposedly) familiar scripts and adopt another? Bernal offers not a clue to solving his own Theban riddle.

The Cadmean alphabet's introduction leads Bernal to reject (*BA* 2:500–504) the position maintained by most classicists since the 1930s that the alphabet was not introduced into Greece until the eighth century B.C.E. This revisionist view requires the coexistence of the alphabet with the Linear B script, which is itself not a major obstacle, as it is known that in Bronze Age Crete and Cyprus, for example, several different languages or dialects of the same were written in various scripts (see Davies 1986, 98–99) at the same time. A far greater problem to Bernal's theory is simply the lack of evidence for an alphabetic script in Greece before the eighth century B.C.E. The elimination of the Herodotean passage discussed above makes this even more crucial. This problem is not adequately addressed by Bernal, and while Semiticists would argue for an earlier date for the alphabet than many classicists seem to realize, the absence of any evidence makes it difficult to sustain the case for a mid–second millennium introduction of the alphabet into Greece.[17]

Bernal closes his second volume with the destruction of Bronze Age Thebes, ca. 1250 B.C.E., which he attributes to the "Seven Heroes" of Greek legend and drama; a discussion of Troy and its history, outlined within a context of Hittite and Homeric accounts (including also a survey of Troy's chronology), ending with its destruction ca. 1210 B.C.E.; and an account of the collapse of Mycenaean civilization, ca. 1150 B.C.E., which he attributes to the arrival of northern Greek tribes—Dorians, Boeotians, and Thessalians (BA 2:511–21). Much of his discussion here depends on the Homeric poems, which he reads, as in earlier places, as if they were factual history. Thus the raid into Egypt ostensibly conducted by Odysseus and the description of the power and wealth of Idomeneus in Crete acquire an objective reality of their own (2:429–30, 457). Similarly, Diomedes and Sthenelus become lucky survivors of the destructions of Thebes and Troy (2:518), and Homer's silence over the Hittites is ascribed to an Anatolian famine that weakened Hittite control over western Asia Minor (2:514–15).

The era of the Trojan War and the Greek and Trojan heroes who fought so valiantly, as Homer so eloquently relates, is a fascinating story and one in which Bernal has great faith. Homer, however, is not a historian. To read him as one is to distort his essential quality; he is a poet, who seeks eternal truths, whatever they may be. Thus it requires faith to believe in the historicity of a Trojan War (and here it will be clear that I am in league with M. I. Finley (1960) and others whom Bernal would label skeptics), and faith, as D. Easton has remarked (1985, 195), is a theological rather than a historical virtue.

It has recently been remarked (cf. Hall, Liverani, this volume) that *Black Athena* has generated more excitement than any other book (now, with the second volume, books) dealing with classical antiquity published in the last half of this century. That may be true, though we might well differ on the causes behind this fame. Bernal's work has certainly called attention to the Bronze Age, Greek or other, and this is a good thing, especially for scholars like myself who occupy themselves with the "Classical age" of the fifth and fourth centuries B.C.E. At the same time, the excitement frequently outweighs the substance, as one must spend an inordinate amount of time and effort sorting the plausible from the merely fanciful. The greater defect of Bernal's endeavor is that its polemical undercurrents and antiquarian-style pursuit of the past not only distort the true texture of that past but negate the manner in which historians strive to understand it.

NOTES

Reprinted, with minor revisions, by permission from *Liverpool Classical Monthly* 17.6 (June 1992): 85–96. My thanks to my colleague Matthew Dillon and to the late Dr. John Pinsent, founding editor of *Liverpool Classical Monthly*, for their criticisms and suggestions concerning earlier drafts of this essay, and to W. J. Fulco, S.J., and F. Yurco for sharing their linguistic expertise with me.

1. Branham 1989 was one of the few reviews of *BA* 1 to appear in any classics journal.

2. See Marwick 1984, 14, for forceful but cogent criticisms of this statement.

3. For a clear and concise discussion of this issue see Marwick 1971, 170–86, esp. 173.

4. See Marwick 1971, 125–26, for discussion. This is not to equate historians with scientists, for there are important differences: for example, the historian cannot recreate an event in the same way that a scientist can repeat an experiment.

5. Bernal's claim that he is a "modified diffusionist" should be accepted cautiously. For example, in *BA* 1:198–201 he attributes the origins of the modern idea of "progress" to Turgot and the French Enlightenment without a single word of reference to Adam Smith and the "Scottish Enlightenment," which developed the idea of progress independently and at the same time. See Gay 1966, 108–12, 360–62, and Forbes 1953–54, 643–45, 661, for discussion (not cited by Bernal). Admitting that something like this could happen, however, would seriously undermine the whole concept of diffusionism.

6. On this question see Yurco 1989 for a full discussion of the subject based on physical remains (i.e., mummies) and pictorial evidence. Also of some concern is the easy equation of "African" with "black" that Bernal makes in reference to the Egyptians (see *BA* 1:242, 2:257), who would no doubt have been puzzled by the term "Africa" and the significance of "black." See Snowden, and Brace et al., this volume.

7. At *BA* 2:203 he again accuses scholars of racist attitudes which have inspired them to distort and ignore the accomplishments of Egypt through the ages (cf. *BA* 1:201–4). This has led him, for example, to claim that nineteenth-century historians simply ignored the successes of Muhammed Ali and Ibrahim Pasha in Greece during the Greek War of Independence (1:246–50, at 250). Yet he fails to cite the standard account of that war (Finlay 1877), which is remarkably free of the sort of racism that Bernal presumes. See, for example, Finlay's description of events at Navarino in 1825, where Ibrahim prevented a group of Turks from avenging earlier Greek massacres: "But Ibrahim was a man of firmer character and more enlarged political views than

the primates and chieftains of Greece" (1877, 6:364). More troubling are Bernal's more recent opinions on racism (in Coughlin 1991, A6, and in the video discussion *Black Athena*) where he claims to hate "racism of any kind" but thinks that white racism is more frightening (this in response to an inquiry regarding the more extreme causes which his work has been used to support). The claim that (any) one form of racism is less objectionable or contemptible than another is astounding, especially from one who preaches otherwise. Bernal appears to conceive of race in the standard and now obsolete terms of the Enlightenment (see Palter's second contribution, this volume, on the eighteenth century). What does it mean, and how does it help to use such labels as "Negroid," "Caucasian," etc., when there are individuals today (and more than a few!) who can claim (for example) African-American and Scotch-Irish grandmothers, Cherokee and Puerto Rican grandfathers? Those broader racial definitions are definitions and models created in the eighteenth-century pursuit of knowledge that have simply outlived their usefulness—that is, if they were ever useful in the first place; so too, by extension, such terms as German-American, Arab-American, or African-American. For discussion see Hannaford 1994 (thanks to my colleague Thomas Buckley, S.J., for this reference).

8. Schulman 1982, 168–70, and Yurco 1990, 29 (for illustration of the Merneptah monument at Karnak).

9. Another view regarding Greek and Egyptian religion that Bernal will find difficult to sustain is the notion that the Athenian "families of priests—the Eumolpids and Kerykes—resemble the two ranks of Egyptian priests" (*BA* 2:478). First, there was little similarity between Greek and Egyptian priests: the former were "democratic" (see Burkert [1977] 1985, 95–98, for a good discussion), whereas the Greek families that Bernal names included generals, treasurers, politicians, and expounders of law, as well as religious officials—a range of duties unmatched by Egyptian priests (see, e.g., MacKendrick 1969, 99–103, for a convenient list of *gennetai* belonging to these two clans).

10. Some points that cannot be covered here include the traditions of famous Greeks such as Solon visiting Egypt, which Bernal, for example, accepts (e.g., *BA* 2:297–98). For an opposing view see A. B. Lloyd 1975–88, 1:49–60. See also Hartmann (1987), who argues for a Platonic fabrication while allowing for a folk memory of the eruption. Bernal's discussion of Thera's impact on China also requires cautious handling. My former colleague Professor Xin Zhang (now of Indiana University) characterizes it as "old-timer's stuff" (in a personal communication). He notes that the attention to oracle bones (cf. *BA* 2:313) is exaggerated (other sources of evidence are studied today), that the idea of shamanism (cf. *BA* 2:312) is inappropriate to Chinese culture, and that rebellions did occur without a "sign from heaven," which could easily be invented for the occasion (cf. *BA* 2:313–16). Finally, he suggests that many of Bernal's ideas on China would be criticized today by Sinologists for their Western orientation.

11. Reported (with slide illustrations) by the Institute's director M. Bietak, "Recent Finds at Tel El-Dab'a, the Hyksos Capital in the Egyptian Nile Delta," 10 February 1993, at the University of California, Los Angeles.

12. I thank W. J. Fulco, S.J., for reminding me of this.

13. See Symeonoglou 1985, 9–10 and plates 9–10 at end, which show the topography of Thebes from ground level. The ravines around the city were created by Thebes' three rivers, the Agianni (ancient Ismenos), Plakiotissa (Dirke), and Chrysorroas (Strophia); these created the irregular terrain about the site, with "long, conical ridges" and "countless sloping depressions" that made building difficult (p. 10).

14. Thebes is usually bypassed by tourists today despite its attractive little museum. (Mention to Greeks that you plan a visit there, and watch the look of surprise you will get!) A sketch of the hill drawn early in the present century (Keramopoullos 1917, 384) shows the road cutting into the hillside as argued here, but it does not give a clear impression of the hill's height.

15. Bernal claims (*BA* 2:130–33) that he is only following the argument of the excavator (see Spyropoulos 1973, 248–50). But the notion that the hill of Amphion and Zethus is a step-pyramid is rejected both by Symeonoglou (1985, 143) and by other archaeologists with whom I spoke in Thebes.

16. See Symeonoglou (1985, 25, 143), who notes that the site was part of the Mycenaean aqueduct.

17. See, e.g., references cited at *BA* 1:3–4; cf., however, Powell 1991, 19–20, who mentions the rarity and variety of early Phoenician writing before 500 B.C.E.

HISTORIOGRAPHY

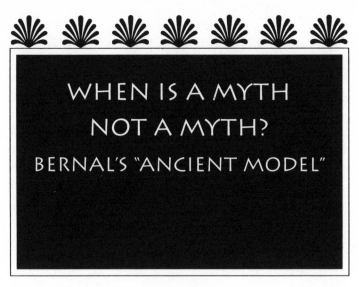

WHEN IS A MYTH NOT A MYTH?
BERNAL'S "ANCIENT MODEL"

Edith Hall

Martin Bernal's *The Fabrication of Ancient Greece 1785–1985*, the first volume of his *Black Athena: The Afroasiatic Roots of Classical Civilization*, has excited more controversy than almost any other book dealing with Greco-Roman antiquity to have been published in the second half of the twentieth century. Its importance was reflected in the decision of the American Philological Association to make it the subject of an interdisciplinary dialogue constituting the presidential panel of their 120th meeting in Baltimore in 1989; the papers there delivered, with additions, have been published as a special issue of *Arethusa* (Levine and Peradotto 1989). It is my present aim, while using arguments similar to those put forward by Tamara Green in that volume, to supplement the existing published comments on Bernal's work with some thoughts on the ancient Greeks' construction of their ethnicity. This paper was first presented in one of a series of other interdisciplinary seminars on Bernal's book, organized by Amélie Kuhrt and John North, and held at the Institute of Classical Studies in London, January–March 1990, under the title *The Origins of Graeco-Roman Culture: Around Black Athena*.

THE ANCIENT MODEL

The argument of Bernal's *Black Athena* sets up two rival models of Greek prehistory. The one, which he terms "the Ancient Model," was, he claims, the conventional view held by most Greeks in the classical and Hellenistic eras; according to this model, Greek culture had arisen as a result of colonization, around 1500 B.C.E., by Egyptians and Phoenicians who civilized the native inhabitants of (what was later called) Hellas. This model therefore sees ancient Greece as essentially a Levantine culture, on the periphery of the Egyptian and Semitic spheres of influence. The rival model, on the other hand, which he chooses to term "the extreme Aryan Model," was invented, he argues, in the early nineteenth century. It saw the Greeks as Indo-European-speaking invaders from the north, who had overwhelmed the indigenous pre-Hellenic culture; sometimes the myth of the return of the Heraclidae was interpreted as holding a kernel of the historical "truth" of these invasions from the north. Ancient Hellas, according to this model, is thus viewed as European, the pure Aryan *Ursprung* of modern Europe. Bernal argues from a historically relativist standpoint that the original "Ancient Model," though surviving until fairly recently, was overthrown by the "Aryan Model" as a result of the contingent ideological requirements of the late eighteenth and nineteenth centuries. The theory of the biologically distinct races of humankind and their congenital inequalities in terms of intelligence and so on, which was to develop so disastrously into the practical policies of National Socialism, was first promulgated in print by Blumenbach in 1775; it was a product of the racist tendencies of European artists, intellectuals, and academics, and it was fed by their romanticism. They found it intolerable to admit any Semitic or African influence on the "pure childhood" of Europe. The "Ancient Model" was officially overthrown by Karl Otfried Müller in 1820.

Modern classicists may have *adapted* the "Aryan Model" to accommodate the discovery of Levantine objects on Late Bronze Age and Early Iron Age sites in the Aegean, and would now mostly admit to the possibility of Bronze Age western Semitic settlements on islands and even at Thebes, as well as to Phoenician influence on Iron Age Greece dating back as far as the tenth century B.C.E. But they are still working, Bernal argues, within what he calls the "Broad Aryan Model." He urges that we must now decide whether we are to retain any respect at all for the "Aryan Model," and continue to work within it, or whether we are to discard it altogether and get back to the "Ancient Model." That is, are we to believe the ancient Greeks themselves, or the northern European thinkers of the eighteenth and nineteenth centuries? Bernal admits that there is no possibility that either model can be proven (*BA* 1:8) but submits that each of the two models must be assessed according to its "competitive plausibility."

The challenge the book presents is an important one; academic discourse is as ideologically laden as political discourse, journalism, art, and literature, and we must constantly review the assumptions we are bringing to bear on the ancient world, constantly try to understand ourselves, as academics, as part of our own ideology and culture, indeed as some of the most influential makers or reproducers of ideology *for* our culture. Every era of classical scholarship looks into the ancient world and finds in it reflected its own contingent sociopolitical preoccupations. The clearest example from recent years of the way in which academic attitudes have altered as a result of political shifts has been the development of feminist theory and women's studies in all disciplines: this can in no way be separated from the rise and success of the women's movement in the political arena. Increasing political sensitivity in certain quarters to the problematic legacy of European imperialism, racism, and chauvinism has also at long last begun to produce academic work which admits to a latent ethnocentrism in almost all European historiography ancient and modern; such works as Preiswerk and Perrot's *Ethnocentrism and History* (1978), Diamond's *In Search of the Primitive* (1974), Said's *Orientalism* (1978), Hay's *Europe: The Emergence of an Idea* (1968), Barker's edition of a collection of essays entitled *Europe and Its Others* (1985), Kabbani's *Europe's Myths of Orient* (1986), and now some works by classicists are beginning to impinge on the comfortable ethnocentric and racist assumptions of many establishment academics (Snowden 1983; Hall 1989). We therefore cannot dismiss Bernal's book out of hand.

Bernal's argument rests on many different kinds of evidence, but the three kinds of testimony on which his thesis ultimately depends are literary, archaeological, and linguistic. Others have done much better than I can at sorting out the archaeological and linguistic evidence. My remarks here are confined to what is the first, and really the most vital, plank in Bernal's argument, which itself breaks down into two separate subtheses: first, he asks us to accept that the Greeks themselves genuinely believed that they were descended from Egyptians or Phoenicians; secondly, he asks us to believe that they were right. This basic thesis is set out in chapter 1, of the first volume of *Black Athena*, "The Ancient Model in Antiquity." In that chapter Bernal also adduces testimony to the influence which the arts, crafts, religions, and technologies of Africa and the Levant continued to exert on Hellenic culture long after his proposed colonial invasions; we are not concerned here with that aspect of his argument, although I myself take a sympathetic view of academic works arguing that the amount of interchange between Hellenophone and other communities, whether commercial or cultural, was considerably larger than has generally been assumed (see, e.g., Burkert 1984). There is, moreover, little doubt that Bernal is correct in arguing that modern racial prejudice has been one of the reasons why cultural contact between ancient Hellenophone communities and ancient Semitic and black peoples has been and is still being played down.[1]

Bernal himself unfortunately often conflates his "cultural borrowing" arguments and his arguments for the return to the "Ancient Model"; attention here is primarily addressed to the latter. Did the Greeks think that they had come from Egypt and Phoenicia? Did they *all* think this, *all* the time? And is there any reason why their theories about their original ethnic derivation and provenance should be any more accurate or valid than our own?

Bernal's entire thesis rests ultimately on his argument that the versions of certain myths preserved in some ancient literary sources contain kernels of that nebulous entity "historical truth" and ought therefore to be believed. Most of these sources involve the mythical pattern by which someone from outside of Hellas proper—Cadmus, Danaus—came to the Greek mainland, to Thebes or Argos, and settled there.[2] Bernal believes these myths, rather than the myth invented by nineteenth-century classical scholarship, that the Greeks were all Aryans coming down from the north. He thinks that the Greeks' myths actually crystallize a kernel of fact. This is, of course, an old-fashioned view of the generation, function, and nature of the truth expressed by myth, and I shall have more to say about it later.

SUBJECTIVE AND OBJECTIVE ETHNICITY

Bernal's work fails to take adequately into account the important distinction, first proposed by Max Weber (1921) and since used by social anthropologists, between objective and subjective ethnicity. Objective ethnicity is a biological category which defines groups of human beings in terms of their shared physical characteristics resulting from a common gene pool. Subjective ethnicity, however, describes the *ideology* of an ethnic group by defining as shared its ancestors, history, language, mode of production, religion, customs, culture, etc., and is therefore a social construct, not a fact of nature (see esp. Isajiw 1974). Objective and subjective ethnicity may and often do overlap, and the subjective, ideological boundaries between ethnic groups may be commensurate with objective ethnic boundaries (Barth 1969), especially where an ethnic group has been isolated or has rigorously avoided intermarriage. But there is a world of difference between saying that the Greeks *were* the descendants of Egyptians and Phoenicians, and saying that the Greeks *thought* that they were descended from Egyptians and Phoenicians. The first statement tries to define the ancient Greeks' ethnicity objectively, the second subjectively. When Bernal discusses "colonization myths" such as those of Cadmus and Danaus, he uses myths defining ethnicity subjectively as proof of the objective ethnic origins of the Greeks, which is a logical non sequitur and a methodological flaw. This will be discussed further later. But first it is important to state some simple empirical objections to Bernal's uses of literary sources.

The cornerstone of Bernal's argument is the tradition that Thebes was founded by Cadmus the Phoenician. In Homeric epic the only tradition mentioned is the original foundation of Thebes by Amphion and Zethus (*Odyssey* 11.262). Yet Bernal implies (*BA* 1:19) that the story of Cadmus arriving from the east to *re*found the Thebes of Amphion and Zethus is likewise to be found already there.

Bernal (1:85–86) attacks Gomme's theory, put forward in an article in 1913, that Cadmus had only been Orientalized in the fifth century. Gomme pointed out that the word *phoinix* had many meanings other than "Phoenician" and that references in *Archaic* poetry to Europa as the daughter of Phoinix need not be understood as meaning the daughter of an ethnic Phoenician. To my knowledge Gomme's argument has not yet been rendered untenable, though R. Edwards has tried hard to make the ethnic significance of Phoinix's name an Archaic, even Mycenaean, rather than Classical-period tradition (1979, 65–87). Bernal makes much of the papyrus fragment of the pseudo-Hesiodic *Ehoiai* or *Catalogue of Women* (ca. 600 B.C.E.) referring to Europa (Merkelbach and West fragment 141). This, however, can still be interpreted as calling her "daughter of the noble Phoinix" rather than "daughter of the noble Phoenician" (*kou]r[e]i Phoinikos agauou*, line 7).

Lest anyone think that by arguing that Gomme may have been right I am here working only within the "Aryan Model" and failing to take a simple, sensible view of the ancient evidence, it is necessary to point out that several proper names occurring in early literature do not necessarily bear the same specific ethnic significance that they come to bear later. Homer's *Aithiopes*, for example, are not even described as dark of skin. Now although certain dark-skinned peoples were by the fifth century being described as *Aithiopes*, and their name interpreted as meaning "of heavily tanned complexion," the name *Aithiops* really is of perfectly good Greek etymology (*aitho*, "blaze, burn," + *ops*, "face"). It is, furthermore, just as plausible to argue that a fabulous people of Archaic epic, who lived in the furthest East or West and whose name indicated a brilliance in the eyes or face of reflected light from the rising or setting sun, were identified during the period of the rise of ethnography in the sixth century B.C.E. with real, outlying dark-skinned peoples, and that the name was reinterpreted accordingly (Forsdyke 1956, 97; Dihle 1965, 67–69). Can we discount the possibility that similar things may have happened to the word *phoinix*? Given that an unquestionably Greek hero on the Achaean side in the *Iliad* is called Phoinix, and that the word *phoinix* really can and often does mean "purple," "red," "pertaining to the date palm," or a kind of musical instrument as well as to a Phoenician, and that it is cognate with such words as *phoineeis* and *phoinios*, "bloody, blood-colored," is anyone justified in insisting on the antiquity of the tradition that Europa was a daughter not of a hero called Phoinix, but of a Phoenician?[3]

DANAUS

The argument is just as difficult for Bernal when it comes to Danaus and the Archaic sources. He somehow overlooks two Hesiodic fragments of relevance: Merkelbach and West fragment 296, from a poem entitled the *Aegimius*, connecting Io's impregnation by Zeus not with the mouth of the Nile but with Euboea; and Merkelbach and West fragment 124 = [Apollodorus] *Bibl.* 2.1.3, which makes Io a daughter not of Inachus but of Pieren. These fragments are important because they show (1) that the mythical tradition about the ethnicity of a particular character or family which succeeded in becoming the most widespread may not be the most ancient and (2) that there may have existed a whole alternative tradition about Io's descendants through Epaphus to the Danaids, and of course also to Heracles, which had a local mainland Greek color and very little to do with Egypt. Neither Bernal nor anyone else has to my knowledge *dis*proved that there was a process by which the story of Io and her descendants became Egyptianized, perhaps in the seventh century B.C.E. under Psamthek, when identification of the cow-maiden with the Egyptian horned goddess Isis would have been one of the more natural religious syncretisms made by the Greeks abroad (A. B. Lloyd 1975–88, 1:125). The mostly lost epic poem called the *Danais* or *Danaides* of which Bernal is forced to make so much is usually dated to the sixth century B.C.E.; anyway, by that time the story of Io's descendants had certainly brought them into connection with Egypt, for there was an important process, of which Bernal seems unaware, by which many traditional mythical figures were brought into connection with foreign peoples and places. This process was associated with *Greek* colonization, as the poetgenealogists sought to provide their Hellenophone public, now spread over all corners of the Mediterranean, with mythical progenitors and founders who had prefigured their own activities in foreign parts.

It is possible to argue, for example, that it is the widening horizons of the *Greeks* which are reflected both by the appropriation of oriental gods to Hellenic family trees in the *Catalogue of Women* (Adonis does indeed become a son of Phoinix, Merkelbach and West fragment 139; but then there is evidence that the Adonis cult had been adopted by Hellenophone communities by the time of Sappho [fragment 140.1, 211b ii Lobel-Page 1955], ca. 600 B.C.E.) and by its genealogical explanations of numerous foreign ethnic groups.[4] The *Catalogue of Women* traces most of its Greeks back to the founding father Deucalion, including their eponymous ancestor Hellen. In its second and third books, however, it focuses on the descendants of the Argive Inachus.

It was from one of them, Io (the Argive princess who, I would argue, is only now being diverted in myth to Egypt), that the largest group of non-Greek peoples was thought to have sprung. Argos became the center of a vast international genealogy, and Io's family the ancestors and descendants of the Egyptians, Arabs, Phoenicians, and Libyans. Belus (probably a Hellenization of the oriental cult title Baʿal) heads the family of Aegyptus and Danaus; Agenor's descendants include Cadmus. These genealogies are, however, actually profoundly ethnocentric from a *Hellenic* point of view, for they seek to trace the origin of all peoples of the world back to Greek gods and heroes (Bickerman 1952)—thus, it could be argued, legitimizing and mythically prefiguring the existence of Greeks in far-flung Greek colonies. It is significant that Danaus and Cadmus, though in family trees leading to foreign peoples such as the Egyptians and Phoenicians, are ultimately traced back to Hellas and Inachus; Bernal consistently forgets this in his interpretation of the narratives which recount their stories, and sees them purely as aliens coming in from outside.

The reason for focusing on this sparse Archaic literary evidence is that it is of the greatest possible importance to Bernal's argument: he wants the Greek myths to contain historical truth, and he would be most likely to convince us of the plausibility of this thesis if he could prove that Cadmus and Danaus had been Phoenician and Egyptian in the earliest extant testimony to the mythopoeic tradition. I hope to have shown by this time that even this step in his argument is susceptible to doubt. By the fifth century B.C.E., of course, myth was being reinterpreted, ornamented, manipulated, and transformed for many different purposes; using it now in any way as a factual historical record is methodologically even more dubious. And when Bernal resorts to such late sources as writers from the first century C.E. (Strabo) or the second (Pausanias) (*BA* 1:79), credulity is stretched to the limit. Whether Plutarch regarded Greek religion as a borrowing from Egypt or not is irrelevant to the "truth"; at the time he was writing (second century C.E.), he was plugging into a centuries-old stream of discourse, a debate with its own goalposts and primary texts (such as Herodotus). He was in little better position to judge than we are.

COMPETITIVE GENEALOGIES

Subjective definitions of ethnicity, by their very nature as social constructs, are open to challenge. Different people can define a particular ethnic group's genealogy in different ways according to their contingent purposes at the time. A good illustration from ancient history is the argument waged over the provenance of the Romans. Once the Julio-Claudian family (especially Julius Caesar and Augustus) had taken it upon themselves to prove that they were descended from the gods via Aeneas, the hero of Troy, the problem of the Trojans' own ethnic origins wagged its head.[5] Poets were suborned to the cause of defining the Romans' ethnicity; Propertius, defending his practice of writing love poetry, complains to Maecenas that he has not the heart to trace the line of Caesar to his Phrygian forefathers (II.41–2). Virgil, of course, made Dardanus, the ancestor of the Trojans, into an Italian, thus presenting Aeneas' colonization of Italy less as an external imperial invasion than as a *nostos*, or homecoming, a reclaiming of what was rightfully his: the Trojans' return to their own autochthonous origins. On the other hand, the whole of the first book of Dionysius of Halicarnassus, who was writing for a different readership and with different aims, is concerned to demonstrate that all the tribes from which Rome sprang—Aborigines, Pelasgians, Arcadians, the followers of Heracles and Aeneas' Trojans—were more ancient and more *Greek* than any others (*toutōn gar an ouden heuroi tōn ethnōn oute archaioteron oute Hellē- / nikōteron*, 1.89.1–2).[6] Until the eighteenth century, however, numerous European royal families insisted, like the Julio-Claudians, on their derivation from Trojan exiles: to question their Trojan ancestry was to contest the legitimacy of the *ancien régime* (Vickers 1987, 481). In modern times our myths of ethnic provenance may seem no less incredible (see A. D. Smith 1986); the Mormons, for example, claim descent from the lost tribes of Israel.

Did the Greeks *all* believe that they were descended from Egyptians and Phoenicians, *all* the time? The simple answer to this is no. Rival traditions were propounded, along with competitive subjective ethnicities. A striking example is the "Pelasgian" theory. This may have been invented by Hecataeus (*FGrHist* 1 F119), but it is Herodotus who gives it its fullest exegesis. Greece, says Herodotus, had been in early times populated by the Pelasgians, a prehistoric, indigenous Mediterranean people, speakers of a non-Greek language (1.57). The Pelasgians had been supplanted in some areas, especially Sparta, by incursive Dorians, who were the original Hellenes (1.56). (The theory can thus be viewed as an ancient "Aryan Model.") Thereafter the Hellenic tongue had spread even to the autochthonous Pelasgians in Hellas, but not to the "barbarian" Pelasgians that Herodotus maintains were still to be found elsewhere in the Mediterranean—in the Hellespont, Thrace, Samothrace, Lemnos, Imbros, and the Troad (2.51, 4.145, 5.26, 7.42). Characters in both Sophocles (fr. 270.4, Radt 1977) and Hellanicus (*FGrHist* 4 F4) identify the barbarian Pelasgians also with the "Tyrseni" or Etruscans.

But Thucydides has a different argument: indigenous Pelasgians had been "Hellenized" by the Hellenes, the "sons of Hellen," who had of course originated in Phthiotis (1.3.2)—Hellas in the *Iliad* (9.395) is just one district in Thessaly. The early Argive historian Acusilaus offered yet another explanation, for he ratified Pelasgus' place in his own city's mythology by making him a brother of Argos and a son of Zeus (*FGrHist* 2 F25a). Hence Argos in tragedy is frequently described as "Pelasgia," for those peoples who made a claim to autochthony, like the Arcadians or the Athenians, tried to trace themselves back to a Pelasgian origin (Herodotus 1.56–57, 8.44). Argos indeed, said by many authors to have been founded for the second time by the barbarian Egyptian Danaus, was in fact thought to have had a particular claim to autochthony because of its Homeric epithet "Pelasgian." The whole Pelasgian/Hellene theory is therefore in a terrible state of confusion in the ancient writers, from the fifth century onwards,[7] reflecting the attempts of a disparate people, spread around numerous autonomous city-states, with very little "national" Hellenic ethnic identity, to create for themselves an intelligible mytho-historical tradition of their ethnic provenance.

ATHENIAN SOURCES

A central problem with Bernal's argument, indeed, is that he believes in a homogeneous entity called Greek Myth; he is constantly talking about What the Greeks Themselves Believed or the Greek Patriotic Tendency. What he fails to account for is that the ruling families in every polis defined their subjective ethnicity by tracing their forefathers' genealogies in different ways: one only has to look at the contradictory and confusing family trees that Pindar so ingeniously devised for his parvenu tyrants around the edges of the Greek-speaking world. And the fact is that nearly every one of Bernal's sources for the barbarian provenance of Danaus and Cadmus is either actually Athenian, or has an Athenocentric interest (Herodotus), or is plugging into a narrative tradition probably ultimately deriving from Athenian sources. And what was the distinguishing feature of the Athenians' own view of their provenance and ethnic identity? Of course, that they were autochthonous.[8]

Athenian propagandists constantly sought to contrast their own compatriots' allegedly autochthonous ancestors with Cadmus, Danaus, and Pelops, the barbarian progenitors of the Thebans and Peloponnesians; this was to become one of the standard clichéd topoi of the Athenian funeral orations and of patriotic purple passages in other forms of oratory (see, e.g., Isocrates 10.68; Plato *Menexenus* 245c–d). It is interesting that Thucydides does not use these myths, although I do not think that that was because of "motives of national prejudice," as Bernal alleges (*BA* 1:102): perhaps it was because he (as we should) saw through their polis-propagandist origins. Bernal, of course, does use such sources without pointing out the significance of their Athenian provenance. I am not altogether sure whether he is aware of the problem with which this presents him. On the one hand, he constantly talks about "Hellenic nationalism" and "national pride" in the fifth century, as if he did not know about the Peloponnesian War or the almost incessant enmity between Athens and Thebes. But, on the other, we do get a brief hint that he may after all be aware of the problem presented by the myth of Athenian autochthony, for he feels the need to place the rare, late, alternative, Egyptian foundation myth as early as the fifth century B.C.E.: he claims in an aside, without any textual references, that the tradition that Kekrops (founder of Athens) was Egyptian, was "probably current in Herodotus' day" (*BA* 1:79). I would like to hear of a text which can support this claim.

Bernal uses an Athenian text, Aeschylus' *Suppliants*, a play about the arrival of Danaus and his fifty daughters from Egypt to Argos, as one of the linchpins of his argument. In this play a decidedly Egyptianized and black Danaus and his fifty daughters arrive at Argos to claim asylum from the indigenous Pelasgians, ruled by King Pelasgus but also described repeatedly as "Hellenes." Danaus and the Danaids are in flight from Aegyptus and his fifty sons: their claim for asylum is based on the blood tie that binds them to the Argives through their joint ancestress Io, and here Aeschylus uses something similar to the genealogy presented in the *Catalogue of Women*. It is fairly certain that in the rest of the trilogy, now lost, Danaus acceded to the throne of Argos and that the tragic myth presented an explanation of the doubleness of the traditions surrounding the foundation of the city. But what Bernal forgets is that this is an *Athenian* interpretation of the Argive foundation myths, and that this casts doubt on his entire argument that Aeschylus would have wanted to diminish the Egyptian element in the Argive tradition because of current "national" chauvinism. He goes through the play looking for references to Egyptian religion, equating Zeus Chthonios with Osiris and so on (*BA* 1:91–97); and indeed Aeschylus is undoubtedly exploiting all the new literary potential which had been opened up by the invention of ethnography, the idea of the barbarian, and the *logoi* which had sprung up during and in response to the Persian Wars. But the Egyptianness of the Athenian Aeschylus' Danaus and Danaids, though indisputable, cannot be taken as historical evidence for a "real" Egyptian colonization: Aeschylus, writing from an Athenian perspective, is attempting to make sense of the Argive foundation myths, and, as we have seen, the Egyptian element in them may not be much more than a century and a half older than Aeschylus' text itself. Bernal is skating not on thin ice but on water when he claims (1:97) that Aeschylus' sources were from the seventh century; the most plausible candidate for the poet's information about Egypt is undoubtedly the early fifth-century Ionian historian Hecataeus (E. Hall 1989, 133). In this same context (*BA* 1:97), we may pass over Bernal's observation that the title *Suppliants* (*Hiketes* or *Hiketides* in Greek), or rather *hikesios* ("pertaining to supplication"), its parallel form, "strikingly resembles the Egyptian Ḥḳȝ ḥȝst)"—which, even if it were rendered in a later century into Greek as *Hyksos* (Bernal neglects to cite his source) strikes me as one of the most implausible etymological suggestions in the book. (Cf. Vermeule, Tritle, this volume.)

When Bernal starts to use later tragedy, such as Euripides' *Phoenissae*, in which the Phoenician connection of the Thebans is elaborated poetically and exploited in the use of the popular female barbarian chorus, he makes the same mistakes. Athenians liked to emphasize the tradition of the Thebans' barbarian origins and, moreover, in tragedy displaced their own stasis and internal strife to other, historically hostile, Greek cities: the tragic Thebes is a counterculture, a mirror opposite of the tragic Athens (Zeitlin 1986). Thebes houses tyrants, incest, stasis, and sexual deviationists, whereas the Athens of tragedy is nearly always presented as an idealized polis, free from internal conflict and led by democratically minded kings almost indistinguishable from democratically elected *stratēgoi*.

As we have seen, Bernal similarly misuses the works of such Athenian propagandists as Isocrates and the writers of *epitaphioi logoi* when they are cataloguing the barbarian roots of non-Athenian Greek city-states. In later writers the tenacity of the fifth- and fourth-century Athenian versions of the Cadmus and Danaus myths is surely not to be explained, as Bernal would have it, as evidence of the historical truth of those particular versions of the myths—but rather as evidence of the greater amount of Athenian literature produced in comparison with that from other cities, and the Athenocentrism of those who used and transmitted the texts in the ancient intellectual world.

FLUIDITY OF ETHNICITY IN MYTH

Another problem which needs to be isolated is that subjective ethnicity is an extremely fluid social construct which can change remarkably quickly (Banton 1981, Keyes 1981a, 14–28). In myth the ethnicity of heroic figures is remarkably mutable. Heroes can change their ethnicity altogether according to the ideologial requirements of the imaginations interpreting their stories. We often have a diachronic perspective on the volatility of particular heroes' and dynasties' ethnicities, and so the subtleties and complexities of the ideas proposed and the changes involved can actually be illustrated.

Ethnicity could be proved or challenged by inventing genealogies and mythical precedents.[9] Euripides wrote propagandist plays for such peoples as the Macedonians (*Archelaus*) and probably the Molossians (*Andromache*), trying to prove by claims of mythical origins and genealogical manipulation that these peoples had a claim to Hellenicity, when their detractors in the Greek world insisted that they were barbarians. In Athenian hands Tantalus, Niobe, and Pelops are sometimes Lydian, sometimes Phrygian, but from their earliest appearance in literature in Greek they may also be of indeterminate provenance.

A change in ethnicity may take the form of a renaming process. It was only in the fifth century B.C.E., for example, that the Trojans become identified with Phrygia and called *Phruges*, as the Trojan myth was rehandled to provide a mythical precursor of the Persian Wars, a previous defeat inflicted by Hellenic conquerors on an eastern empire (E. Hall 1988). Alteration in ethnicity, on the other hand, may be a matter of localizing a hero whose ethnicity is indeterminate: Lycurgus, for example, the mythical king who (like Pentheus) was punished for rejecting Dionysus, is of indeterminate ethnicity in Archaic poetry but in fifth-century works becomes stabilized in Thrace, as Dionysiac themes are attracted to that country (E. Hall 1989, 107). But many mythical figures can be seen changing their ethnicity altogether. It is not just that the family of Atreus is derived variously from Mycenae, Argos, or Sparta, according to the political purposes of different literary presentations of the myth, for at least all three of these locations are within the Peloponnese: heroes and heroines can actually be transformed from Greeks into barbarians and vice versa.

Medea, for example, almost certainly began as the northern Peloponnesian Agamede of the *Iliad*, a sorceress and granddaughter of the Sun (11.740–41). In Eumelus' epic, where myth was manipulated in order to justify Corinthian claims to territory in the Black Sea (Drews 1976, 24–29), she was presented as the Corinthian daughter of King Aeëtes, who emigrated to the Pontus (Pausanias 2.3.10). Her name, by being confused with the ethnic Medes, may have suggested her mother's name, Perse, in the *Odyssey* (10.138–39), but there is no other evidence for a truly barbarian, Colchian Medea until Euripides' play of 431 B.C.E. (D. Page 1938, lxii n. 1). Tereus, again, began as a Megarian hero, but by the time of Sophocles' famous tragedy had been transformed into a Thracian, probably an Odrysian Thracian, simply because his name was similar to that of the fifth-century Odrysian king Teres (E. Hall 1989, 104–5). Similarly in the *Odyssey* the Cimmerians may once have been the Cheimerians, inhabitants of Cheimerion on the River Acheron, near the Thesprotian *nekyomanteion* (oracle of the dead), and were only assimilated to the "Cimmerians" when the Greeks heard of the strange tribes who inhabited the "Crimea," the Tauric Chersonese (G. L. Huxley 1958; J. H. Finley 1978, 58 and n. 3). Ritual names also became confused with ethnic terms: Artemis' cultic title Tauropolos ("Bull-hunting") almost certainly became confused with the tribe known as the Taurians in the Tauric Chersonese (Lloyd-Jones 1983, 96), giving rise to the myth represented in Euripides' *Iphigeneia in Tauris*.

ETHNICITY AS AN ARTICULATOR OF ABSTRACTIONS

It is also necessary to point out that ethnicity can be used to express real truths in terms of the Greeks' conceptualizations of different abstractions, without being *literally* true. The Greeks' picture of their own past, in particular, overlapped with their picture of the elsewhere—a pattern seen in

Thucydides' drawing of parallels between what the barbarians still practice and obsolete Greek customs (1.5). The Protagorean vision of the linear progression up through technological inventions to the Greek democratic polis relied on a concept of a less civilized past, and this past was often identified with the elsewhere. But a contradiction lay at the heart of the Greeks' view of the non-Greek world, for the rise, paradoxically, could also be defined as a fall (witness the complexities of Hesiod's myth of the cycle of generations). The retrospective vision expressed the ideas both of primitive chaos and of a more virtuous era when men were nearer to the gods. Because the past and the elsewhere often merged and overlapped, the notion of the special spirituality of the golden age, before humanity was estranged by technological progress, could also be reproduced in narratives about known, contemporary barbarian communities.

This schizophrenic vision of the ethnically other expressed a contradictory conceptualization of non-Greek lands. Tyrants and savages lurked in the barbarian world, but it also supported idealized peoples and harmonious relations with heaven. The countries believed to be older than Hellas, especially Egypt, thus became the sources in ethnography of numerous gods and rituals (witness Herodotus) and in Platonic philosophy of original wisdom. In this conceptual system, therefore, anarchy and tyranny and cruelty all belonged to the non-Greek world, but so did mystics like Orpheus, sages like Anacharsis, and the kinds of religious practices and intellectual skills that the Greeks believed were derived from the Egyptians. And a grammar of associations was built up connecting different abstractions with specific areas of the world. The West was often the home of post-mortem havens and of utopias; the North, of shamanistic practices, nomads, and primitivism both savage and utopian; the East, of sex, decadence, and tyranny; the South, especially Egypt, of cults, medicine, and primeval wisdom.

A telling example is the figure of Dionysus. Nearly everyone[10] used to believe narratives (such as Euripides' *Bacchae*) which tell of the bringing of Dionysiac religion from Asia or Thrace to Hellas, and so placed the introduction of this new religion at some time in the eighth century. But the almost certain appearance of the name Dionysus in Linear B (Burkert 1985, 162) has shown that the idea of a late-arriving eastern god appearing in Greece after the "Dark Ages" is an academic fiction derived from an overly literal reading of myth; indeed, Dionysus does not seem to have become Orientalized in the Greek imagination until the sixth century (T. H. Carpenter 1986, 74–75, 124). This process was no doubt partly a result of syncretism with genuine eastern divinities such as Sabazius, but what is important is that calling Dionysus Phrygian or Thracian expressed something other than historical ethnic derivation: these lands were from the sixth century onward always associated with mystery cults, with liberation from self-control and the constraints of civic existence, and with dangerous release of the emotions and physical passions. Dionysus is also the god of epiphany who arrives from the sea: this finds mythical expression in the narratives of his introduction. The same associations of Thrace led to Orpheus' being located there. The definition of that perfectly good Greek religious figure, The Mother, was the result of a similar process. Epic already expresses the association of specific concepts with the Egyptians and the Phoenicians, but without any of Bernal's colonization narratives. Egypt in the *Odyssey* is the land of wise doctors and great riches; from Phoenicia derive wily merchants and slave dealers. The ancient wisdom of Egypt and the cunning of the Phoenicians were to remain elements in the Greco-Roman stereotypes of these countries throughout antiquity.

CONCLUSION: MYTH AND HISTORY

Ultimately the decision whether to accept or reject Bernal's advocacy of the "ancient model" depends on whether we can accept his handling of ancient Greek myth. This would mean that we must accept that certain myths do contain unmediated literal, historical truths. *Black Athena* seems to present an unsophisticated view of myth in general, and Greek myth in particular (T. Green 1989). Of course in the nineteenth and early twentieth centuries myth used regularly to be treated as history, as if its value existed in the information it bore about the past, rather than the present, the "here and now" of the culture producing the myth. It used to be argued that the myth of the Olympian victory over the Titans and Giants held a folk memory of *Homo sapiens'* victory over *Homo neanderthalensis*; many once saw the myths of the successions of the ages of gold, iron, and bronze as holding an orally transmitted memory of technological innovations.

A prime example is the myth of the Amazons, which clearly used to be taken as near-literal historical truth. This is the story of the matriarchal tribe subordinated by Greek male heroes, which itself underwent transmutations as the conquering hero changed from Heracles to Theseus in Athenian sources, and as the Amazons took on features borrowed from the *logos* of the Persian Wars. Bachofen (1861), in his work on matriarchy in prehistoric cultures, used the Amazon myth to show that matriarchy had preceded patriarchy. He pointed to Herodotus' discernment of a matrilineal system of inheritance in Lycia (1.173) and argued that this was a vestigial matriarchy. He saw the Amazon myth as recording man's usurpation of power from woman. But few would now see the truth of the Amazon myth as residing in its historicity: since the work of Pembroke (1967) and others,[11] it has been taken rather to express the Greek male's own self-definition of himself as patriarchal, by the construction of an "other," a matriarchal society embodying the exact opposite of his gender hierarchy. The myth of the conquest of the Amazons by Greek males defined by ahistorical aetiology the contemporary social structure.

Are we to abandon the sophisticated theories of the twentieth century which have helped us to understand how mythology works? Are we going to return to a simple nineteenth-century model which ignores all the post-Malinowskian, post-Freudian, and post-Lévi-Straussian work on myths as ideological charters for social institutions, as expressions of subconscious desires, or as mediators of abstractors of concern to the contemporary world? Are we to ignore all the work done by social scientists in recent decades, since Weber's pioneering labors, on the way subjective ethnicity is constituted? Accepting Bernal's "Revised Ancient Model" requires us to do all this.

What he has done for us is to make us reject forever the "Aryan Model" and leave the question of who the Greeks actually were, biologically at least, buried with a proper degree of contempt. But in altogether abandoning the "Aryan Model," the nineteenth century's Myth of the Northern Origin of the Greeks, we ought not simply substitute another myth, the Myth of the Egyptian and Phoenician Takeover of Pre-Greece. What we must do is reject the historical validity of both myths and turn ourselves to the three really important questions which do need to be asked in greater detail, and with more sensitivity than hitherto, in regards to ethnicity as a social, subjective construct which signifies abstractions having little to do with ethnicity: who on earth did the Greeks *think* they were? Why did they think it? And what is it about the late twentieth century which renders the issue so important to *us*?

NOTES

Reprinted, with revisions, by permission of the author and The Johns Hopkins University Press from *Arethusa* 25 (1992): 181–201. I thank the editor of *Arethusa* and the anonymous readers for helpful comments on a previous draft.

1. See esp. S. P. Morris 1989, arguing that Greek contact with Levantine culture was even greater than Bernal supposes.

2. The third familiar myth following this pattern, often mentioned by ancient writers in conjunction with those of Cadmus and Danaus, is that of Pelops the Lydian or Phrygian, who colonized the Peloponnese. Bernal singularly overlooks Pelops, perhaps because the idea that Greece was colonized from the northwest corner of the Asiatic seaboard does not fit the argument of his book.

3. See also Vian 1963, 52–75.

4. See Merkelbach 1968; Drews 1973, 7–9; West 1985, 149–50; E. Hall 1989, 35–37, 48.

5. Tiberius was supposedly so concerned about the Trojans' genealogy that he wrote a dissertation entitled *Quae Mater Hecubae Fuerit*; see Leaf 1902, comment on *Iliad* 16.717.

6. See further H. Hill 1961, 88–89 and nn. 7–8.

7. The ancient testimony to the "Pelasgian" theory is assembled in Lochner von Hüttenbach 1960.

8. Bernal tries without success (1989a, 22) to counter the argument from the Athenians' myth of autochthony, which was apparently raised by S. P. Morris during discussion at the American Philological Association panel in 1989.

9. The following owes much to E. Hall 1989.

10. Otto (1965, 52–64) was a conspicuous exception.

11. See also Bamberger 1974, Tyrrell 1984, 23–25.

EIGHTEENTH-CENTURY HISTORIOGRAPHY IN **BLACK ATHENA**

Robert Palter

According to Martin Bernal, the political purpose of his Black Athena project is "to lessen European cultural arrogance" (*BA* 1:73). In pursuit of this eminently worthy goal—and recognizing the exalted status of science and technology in the contemporary world—I myself often appeal to the following: the impressive achievements of the ancient Babylonians (located in what is roughly present-day Iraq) in mathematics and astronomy, and their significant influence on the ancient Greeks; the striking technological inventions of the early Chinese and Arabs, some of which reached Europe in its early Middle Ages; and the technical mastery of Benin "bronzes" (which are generally made of brass) from Nigeria in West Africa, dating to as early as the fourteenth century C.E.[1] (I should add that I prefer to avoid alluding to ancient Egypt because far too many people already possess exaggerated, when not fantastic, ideas of the scientific and technological achievements of that great civilization.)[2] My own efforts on behalf of reducing cultural provincialism are, however, admittedly quite modest compared with those of Bernal.

Bernal's goal is nothing less than to rewrite the early history of "Western Civilization." Specifically, he wants to replace what he calls the "Aryan Model" of ancient Greek history with what he calls the Ancient—or, better, the Revised Ancient—Model. According to the Aryan Model (which he sees as originating in the first part of the nineteenth century), ancient Greece was essentially Aryan—or at least European; according to the Ancient Model (which he sees as representing a scholarly consensus from ancient Greek times

349

until the nineteenth century), ancient Greece was Levantine with a strong admixture of Egyptian and Semitic (Phoenician and Syro-Mesopotamian) elements. The Revised Ancient Model—which he favors—is recent: it supplements the Ancient Model with a hypothesis which is a feature of the Aryan Model, namely, presumed invasions of mainland Greece by Indo-European-speaking northerners during the fourth or third millennium B.C.E. It is primarily in the second volume of *Black Athena* that Bernal presents his evidence for the Revised Ancient Model: archaeological evidence (for example, the discovery of artifacts suggesting the occurrence of several Egyptian invasions of mainland Greece in the second millennium B.C.E.) and documentary evidence (for example, allusions in ancient Greek writings to invasions of mainland Greece by Egyptians; but see esp. Coleman, Tritle, Hall, this volume). In the first volume he is occupied with the explanation and history of these two (or three) models and, more generally, with the historiography of ancient Egypt and ancient Greece during the past two and a half millennia.

Most criticisms to date of *Black Athena* have been concerned with the ancient archaeological and documentary evidence, while many otherwise critical readers have accepted (without much question) the account in volume 1 of how ethnic and racial biases, especially during the nineteenth and twentieth centuries, have distorted scholarly accounts of the ancient world. As Bernal mentions in the preface to his second volume, "The mixed reviews usually accepted the historiographical portion of my work" (*BA* 2:xvi). One reason for the uncritical acceptance of his historiographical thesis is, one may suspect, that so few historians of modern Europe have read and evaluated his work.[3] Consider by way of illustration the response to that first volume by a black feminist classicist: "only recently has the impact of the Anglo-Germanic construction of the discipline of classics upon the evidence of the ancient world been fully investigated. . . . Martin Bernal shows the impact of black slavery, racial science, and Romanticism upon the reading of ancient evidence" (Haley 1993, 37).[4]

Now, whatever Bernal has done, he has certainly *not* "fully investigated" the relevant history of classical historiography; and, indeed, what contributions he has made to such a history are vitiated by fundamental errors in his understanding of eighteenth-century political, social, and cultural history. It must be emphasized that the eighteenth century is crucial to his thesis—"the nub of this volume" (*BA* 1:189)—because that was the period during which there allegedly occurred the decisive shift, among European thinkers, from pervasive Egyptophilia to pervasive Egyptophobia. But as we shall see, the evidence for such a shift is anything but convincing, which tends to undermine his account of an alleged turn toward racist scholarship among influential eighteenth- and nineteenth-century classicists. It follows that those today who are seriously concerned with formulating a radical political critique of contemporary scholarship—and, in particular, of contemporary classical scholarship—might wish to think twice before associating themselves with the methods and claims of Bernal's work;[5] for his lapses in the most rudimentary requirements of sound historical study—traditional, critical, *any* kind of historical study—should make one wary of his grandiose historiographical pronouncements. In any case, our immediate concern here is less with those pronouncements than with the weaknesses in his fundamental historical data, constructs, and inferences. In the absence of adequate controls on evidence and argument, the view of history presented in *Black Athena* is continually on the verge of collapsing into sheer ideology. Let me illustrate with a small twentieth-century example.

Bernal thinks he sees the influence of the Aryan Model in a recent study of some Egyptian scarabs associated with the tomb of Childeric (d. 481), father of Clovis, the first Christian king of France (*BA* 1:151, 466–67 n. 88). The tomb was discovered in 1653, and shortly thereafter its contents were published in an illustrated account by Jean-Jacques Chiflet. In analyzing the coins in the tomb, Chiflet adduced, among other comparative illustrations, some of Egyptian scarabs; then, in the eighteenth century—according to the conservator of the collection presently containing the tomb's contents (Dumas 1976, 6)—a distinguished archaeologist, Bernard de Montfaucon (1655–1741),[6] mistakenly identified the scarabs as among the original tomb contents— to the confusion of many people ever since. Bernal's response is only too characteristic:

> Why should [Dumas] see her forerunners as having made a chain of such improbable errors? There are, in fact, powerful ideological reasons why 19th- and 20th-century scholars should have wanted to remove the scarabs. The Germanic Frankish kings who founded the French monarchy are very dear to the heart of the French Right, and to those believing in collaboration between France and Germany. It is no coincidence that the symbol of Vichy France was the *francisque*, the Frankish double-headed axe—a splendid example of which was found in Childeric's tomb. Thus the presence of Egyptian scarabs in such a shrine to Aryan, northern barbarian vigour was intolerable. (*BA* 1:467 n. 88)

This is intolerably ideological: Bernal presents no evidence at all that Dumas was influenced by Aryan prejudice in general or by the French political right wing in particular; and, I would add, to drag in the Vichy regime (1940–44)—Dumas was writing in 1976—is not only farfetched but approaches defamation.

From now on, our main focus will be on chapters 3 and 4 and parts of chapter 6 in the first volume of *Black Athena*, entitled, respectively, "The Triumph of Egypt in the 17th and 18th Centuries," "Hostilities to Egypt in the

18th Century," and "Hellenomania, I: The Fall of the Ancient Model, 1790–1830." (Parallel to the shift in attitudes toward Egypt Bernal also perceives a shift involving Phoenicia, but that did not occur until the later nineteenth century; see chapter 8, "The Rise and Fall of the Phoenicians, 1830–85.") It should be understood that Bernal is to be challenged in his own terms and on his own ground, mostly the rather straightforward explication and comparison of texts. He does appeal to something like a social history of ideas when he comes to discuss the emergence of the modern discipline of classical studies in late eighteenth-century Germany; but, once again, his arguments there are weakened by dubious textual interpretations.

The possibility of a more cogent reworking of Bernal's project, utilizing some of the newer cultural and historical methodologies, remains open. Thus the classicist already quoted, Shelley Haley, argues that the "symbolic construction" of Black Cleopatra can be validated by seeing it as part of an oral tradition among African-Americans, which serves to "re-empower" African-American women (an eminently worthy political goal which is in part complementary to Bernal's goal of lessening European cultural arrogance). But it should be understood that any attempt to secure either of these political goals with the help of weak or tendentious scholarship is doomed to be, even in the short run, both futile and counterproductive. Haley herself thinks Black Cleopatra can be validated, once racist blinders have been removed, by the ordinary procedures of classical scholarship, thus apparently accepting the conventional scholarly standards of her discipline.[7]

EIGHTEENTH-CENTURY FRENCH THOUGHT

Bernal's chronology for the alleged shift from Egyptophilia to Egyptophobia is not entirely clear, for on successive pages we read that "this enthusiasm [for ancient Egypt] soared in the century from 1680 to 1780" (*BA* 1:169), and that "the middle of the 18th century was a high point of Egyptophilia" (1:170). Later on he asserts that "the status of Egypt fell with the rise of racism in the 1820s" (1:442). One can hardly resist asking: did Egyptophilia culminate in mid-century? or in 1780? or did it continue unabated until the 1820s? In fact Bernal's presentation is entirely lacking in a satisfactory chronological framework, and he mentions dates only sporadically and casually. (We are told at one point that "by 1767 Britons were even beginning to assert Greek superiority over the Egyptians" [1:211].) Moreover, he never clearly identifies just who was subscribing to these shifting attitudes toward ancient Egypt and ancient Greece. At first he restricts his consideration to the French and English—as in his remark that "the mainstream of fashionable opinion in England and France seems to have been . . . unequivocally enthusiastic about Egypt" (1:170)—and, as for Egyptophilia in German-culture areas, he refers only to Mozart's *Magic Flute*, while discussing the influential Winckelmann at some length as an Egyptophobe. It emerges finally that principled opposition to the Ancient Model seems to have come largely from German scholars (though we do hear about the French linguist and novelist J.-J. Barthélémey and the English classical scholar Samuel Musgrave, each of whom, in the 1780s, disputed the Ancient Model). There is a serious inconsistency here: in describing eighteenth-century attitudes Bernal both invokes and ignores national boundaries, sometimes referring to specific countries and sometimes to just an undifferentiated "Europe" or "the Enlightenment," as in his remark that "most of the figures of the Enlightenment had a great admiration for Egypt and appear to have had no problem with the Ancient Model" (1992c, 82).

Bernal's evidence for Egyptophilic attitudes consists of a small sample of citations, based on no discernible principle of selection, from a dozen or so French and British authors. Furthermore, he sometimes egregiously misconstrues the meaning of his own citations and almost always ignores crucial contextual details. The French authors include Montesquieu, Antoine Banier, Charles Dupuis, Jean-Baptiste le Mascrier, and Jean Terrasson; discussion below considers each of these along with Rousseau, Diderot, Voltaire, and the Abbé Grégoire. To begin with, Montesquieu is enlisted—on four separate occasions (*BA* 1:170, 172, 198, 216)—in support of Bernal's claims on the basis of a single remark in *The Spirit of the Laws* (1748): " 'the Egyptians were the best philosophers in the world' " (1:170). In characterizing Montesquieu as "Eurocentric" (1:172) and in saying that Montesquieu "was forced to concede" (1:170) the truth about Egyptian philosophers, Bernal apparently recognizes that the quoted remark is by no means an instance of unequivocally enthusiastic Egyptophilia. But what he perhaps misses or ignores is the context of Montesquieu's remark, which is a discussion (book 15, chapter 5) containing a bitterly ironic denunciation of Negro slavery; the relevant paragraph reads in its entirety: "The color of a man's skin may be determined by his hair. So important was this to the Egyptians, the world's best philosophers, that they put to death all red-haired persons falling into their hands" ([1748], trans. Richter 1977, 267). Montesquieu's gibe at the Egyptian distaste for red hair is surely meant to be extended to the Egyptian capacity for philosophy. His irony here has often been misunderstood, not least in his own time (see Richter 1977, 339 n. 12; Davis 1966, 403).

Bernal dismisses another great figure of the French Enlightenment, Rousseau, as a Eurocentric thinker with little interest in Egypt. He thus seems to have missed some evidence for his Egyptophilia thesis—in Rousseau's remark, in his youthful *Discourse on the Sciences and the Arts* (1750), that Egypt was "the first school of the universe," the "mother of philosophy and the fine arts."[8] Perhaps, though, Bernal was well advised not to have enlisted Rousseau among the Egyptophiles, because the point of Rousseau's remark was to serve as historical evidence for his provocative thesis that "our souls have become corrupted in proportion as our Sciences and Arts have advanced toward perfection" ([1750] 1986, 7).

As for two other outstanding figures of the Enlightenment, Voltaire and Diderot, Bernal almost completely ignores them and, in particular, *never discloses their strong anti-Egyptian stance*. Diderot published a substantial essay (some five thousand words) on "the philosophy of the Egyptians" in the *Encyclopédie*—"the biggest bestseller of the century" (Darnton 1979, 6)—but there seems not to be a single reference to him in the first volume of *Black Athena*. In that essay (relevant portions are translated below, in Appendix 1) Diderot takes the opportunity to attack the clergy in contemporary France, under the guise of an attack on the Egyptian priesthood, but, of course, our concerns here are less with Diderot's motivation than with his expressed attitude toward ancient Egypt, which is quite negative.[9] Although Bernal mentions Voltaire in passing several times, he never reports Voltaire's strong Egyptophobia, as evidenced, for example, by the following remark from his *Philosophical Dictionary*: "Great things have been said about the Egyptians. I know of no more contemptible people" ([1764] 1972, 43). Also, like Diderot, Voltaire downgraded the scientific skills of the Egyptians, as in this comment from his *Essay on the Customs and the Spirit of the Nations*: "Vitruvius, in his ninth Book, in which he talks of sundials, of the height of the sun and the length of shadows, and of light reflected from the moon, always quotes the ancient Chaldeans and not the Egyptians. This seems to me a fairly strong proof that it was Chaldea and not Egypt that was regarded as the cradle of this science" ([1756] 1963, 273)—though he does add that "nothing is truer than the old Latin proverb: 'The Egyptians learned from the Babylonians, and the Greeks from the Egyptians'" (273).

Let us turn next to the Abbé Antoine Banier (1675–1741), the author in 1738–40 of *La mythologie et les fables expliquées par l'histoire*, which Bernal refers to as "the standard 18th-century work on ancient mythology," and which "continued the Classical and Renaissance traditions of deriving the Greek and Roman gods from those of the Egyptians" (*BA* 1:171). (Banier's work on mythology was also extensively drawn on by Diderot for the *Encyclopédie*.) Considering Banier's obvious importance as evidence for Bernal's thesis—indeed, he is the best evidence—he is given surprisingly short shrift: only two brief mentions (*BA* 1:171, 181) and a reference (1:472 n. 73) to chapter 3 ("The Euhemerists and Isaac Newton") of Frank Manuel's *The Eighteenth Century Confronts the Gods* (1959). It is thus worth spending some time clarifying exactly what Banier's views were on Egypt and Greece. Banier was broad-minded and eclectic in his explanations of ancient myths, at one point in *La mythologie* expounding no fewer than sixteen alternative origins of myth; his favorite explanation, however, was the Euhemerist idea that myths recount the main events of a society's political history (with, for example, the gods representing kings or other heroic figures; see Manuel [1959] 1967, 104–7; Feldman and Richardson 1972, 86–87). As for Egypt, Banier did subscribe to an old tradition, much heralded by Bernal, that things Egyptian had a powerful impact on things Greek, stemming initially from actual colonization of Greece by Egyptians:

> The Greeks are far from being so ancient as the other People of the East; Arts and Politeness were reigning in Egypt, when the Western Nations were still living in a brutish Rusticity; 'twas from Colonies that came from the East, that they learnt to build Cities, to live in Society, and to wear Clothes. From them they had the Ceremonies of Religion, the Worship of the Gods, and Sacrifices. This is a thing not to be called in question, after the plainest Testimony of the most ancient Authors. (Banier [1740] 1976, 1:69)

As for mythology and fables, Banier says that "we may look upon Phenicia and Egypt as the first Theater of Fable, whence they passed with the Colonies to the West, and to Greece especially, where they incredibly multiplied, the Greeks having a powerful Byass towards Fictions" ([1740] 1976, 1:72). In accordance with this allusion early in Banier's work to the power of the Greek mythopoeic imagination, it is no surprise when we realize later on that he has no intention of attempting to explain all Greek myths and fables solely in terms of Egyptian antecedents; and, indeed, his references to Egypt are mostly confined to the first volume of his work, in particular to book 1 (on general issues in the study of mythology) and to book 6 (on the gods of the Eastern countries). (I have relied here on the excellent index, no less than 148 pages in length, in the (anonymous) English translation.) Even more significantly, Banier traces his crucial category of heroes or demigods exclusively to the Greeks: "the Egyptians, according to Herodotus, knew neither Heroes nor Demi-Gods, and consequently had no Worship that referred to them, Heroism having properly taken its Rise in Greece" (3:336).

Banier accepts the idea that all ancient myths and fables are postdiluvian idolatries to be contrasted with "the Knowledge and Worship of the true God [which] were again united in the Family of Noah" ([1740] 1976, 1:167). Though he is not much concerned with religious polemics, he feels compelled to respond to Moses' allusion to "the Abominations of Egypt" (1:487), which he takes to be a reference to Egyptian animal-worship. Several ancient authors, including Herodotus, Cicero, and Diodorus Siculus, see this Egyptian religious practice as having originated in the utility of certain animals for human life, but Banier rejects that hypothesis with a counterexample, namely, the numerous Egyptian divinities that take the form of (useless) "Monsters and

Insects." Besides, he adds, "Let us not rely too much upon Greek and Latin Authors, who were not always well instructed in the Egyptian Mysteries, which the Priests concealed from them as from profane Persons" (1:548). Banier's caution here is surely commendable. He does accept without question Herodotus' ascription (2.123) to the Egyptians of "the Doctrine of the Metempsychosis, which taught that the Soul passed after Death into the Body of Animals" (1:492); we now know that ancient Egyptian religious beliefs did not include transmigration of souls—hardly compatible, after all, with the elaborate domestic surroundings they provided for the deceased in tombs— and that we have here one of Herodotus' most notorious errors.[10] But perhaps Banier may be excused, for he did not, in his day, have any access to the primary sources for ancient Egyptian religion.

There is less excuse for a modern scholar like Bernal to be uncritical about such a secondary source as Herodotus (by far his favorite ancient author, with more than two dozen entries in the index to the first volume of *Black Athena*). It is thus disconcerting to find that when he discusses metempsychosis (as an example of an influential Egyptian doctrine transmitted to the Renaissance in the form of Neoplatonic and Hermetic texts in Greek and Latin) he ignores the fact that the doctrine is not to be found in ancient Egypt at all. Instead he points to the link between metempsychosis and vegetarianism and specu- lates, about the latter, that it "could well date back to the Old Kingdom" (*BA* 1:72); and, again, in another place, he characterizes metempsychosis as "very Egyptian and non-Christian" (1:133) without mentioning that we have no evi- dence of the doctrine in question from Egypt before the Hellenistic period. Such critical historical facts cannot be simply swept under the rug. (For an example on a larger scale of this habit of *suppressio veri* see Appendix 2, below.) Or is it simply more "useful" to ignore Herodotus' error, just as Bernal says it is "more useful to see the denial of Egyptian monotheism" by twentieth- century scholars as a consequence of "racism and Romantic Hellenism" than as a consequence of "increased knowledge of Ancient Egypt" (1:259)—even though presumably he would admit that this increased knowledge in fact rules out Egyptian monotheism?[11] And it is no adequate response to assert that "we are not concerned here with the rightness or wrongness of [Herodo- tus'] conclusions . . . but merely with the facts that he himself believed in them and that he was being relatively conventional in doing so" (1:100).

To sum up this discussion of Banier, I would say that he can hardly be described as unequivocally enthusiastic about Egypt; indeed, the sober abbé is rarely enthusiastic about anything, and certainly not about the Egyptian religion.

By contrast with Banier, Charles François Dupuis (1742–1809) was gen- uinely enthusiastic about ancient Egypt, viewing Greece, in Bernal's words, "as an appendage of Egypt" (*BA* 1:183) and arguing that "all mythologies and religions could be traced back to one source, Egypt" (1:182). Dupuis was no dispassionate scholar; his concern as a mythographer was to refute the claims of Christianity to a privileged position among world religions. For this reason his magnum opus, *Origine de tous les cultes* (1795), was highly controversial, attracting passionate disciples and critics in his lifetime and later (the book was reissued in 1835). For many scholars today his sweeping claims will immediately discredit his enterprise, and their skepticism may be intensified when they learn of his explanatory scheme for demonstrating the unity of all mythology. Dupuis really has two schemes—astronomical (the Sun represents Hercules, who is equated with the Egyptian Serapis) and sexual (centered on phallus worship)—but he insists they are actually one.[12] For Bernal, Dupuis is a greatly underrated figure of positively heroic intellectual stature. But, then, Bernal is impressed by such details as "a series of astounding correspondences, or coincidences, between such myths as the twelve labours of Herakles and the annual stellar movements through the twelve houses of the zodiac" (*BA* 1:183).[13] He should not be impressed. Even the most cursory perusal of Dupuis's text discloses the suspicious fact that in only three of the twelve cases (Leo the lion, Aries the ram, and Taurus the bull) does the object represented by the zodiacal sign actually occur in the narrative of the corresponding Herculean labor. To take advantage, in this way, of three successful correspondences while silently ignoring nine failures is to violate the most elementary rules of sound inductive reasoning.

In conclusion, it may be said that Dupuis's views were certainly widely read, pondered, and debated, but frequently by people, such as President John Adams (see Manuel 1959, 271–80), who were much more interested in returning to a pure, aboriginal Christianity than in studying the relations between ancient Egypt and ancient Greece.

Another French source cited in the first volume of *Black Athena* consists of a short paragraph, dating from around 1740, by an obscure French antiquarian (never named by Bernal), the Abbé Jean-Baptiste le Mascrier (1697–1760). The gist of the paragraph (see Charles-Roux 1929, 14), of which Bernal quotes the first three sentences in English translation (*BA* 1:170), is that mummies, pyramids, and the Nile are all the rage in France. It is clear that the author is exaggerating when he writes that the "only" (*ne . . . que*) things talked about are Egyptian; but it is not clear just *how much* he is exaggerating. (Bernal apparently never bothered to wonder.) To set this historical situation in perspective, it is worth mentioning that Turkey was much in vogue in Paris at about the same time. Thus in a recent exhibition catalogue of eighteenth-century French painting we learn that a "vogue for *les Turqueries* . . . swept Parisian society in the 1720's. . . . Montesquieu's *Lettres Persanes* was published in 1721, the Ottoman ambassador, Mehmet Affendi, visited Paris in March of that year, and thereafter an enormous number of novels and plays would treat Turkish themes. . . . It was principally in decorative painting that *les Tur-queries* dominated."[14] Various exoticisms were apparently eagerly embraced by elite circles in Paris (and elsewhere),[15] but whether Egypt or Turkey (or some other country) generated the most enthusiasm I find it difficult to make out. Obviously, at the very least, French Egyptophilia ought to be considered against the background of a pervasive eighteenth-century interest in exotic cultures.[16]

Another example is provided by the Abbé Terrasson (1670–1750), author of the popular novel *Séthos* (1731; English and German translations appeared in 1732). Bernal says that "using Classical quotations, [Terrasson] demonstrated that the founders of Greek politics, astronomy, engineering and mathematics had all studied in Egypt. Further, he also maintained that there were close parallels between Greek and Egyptian mythology and ritual and that the Greeks had derived their forms from Egypt" (*BA* 1:180). But whether Terrasson really thought he had "demonstrated" anything by his numerous footnoted citations of ancient authors seems doubtful, and surely few of his readers took at face value his literary conceit of having translated the novel from an anonymous Greek manuscript written during the reign of Marcus Aurelius.[17]

Let us consider one final French figure (I am surprised that Bernal has missed him): the revolutionary Abbé Henri Grégoire, who was one of the leading opponents of racism and slavery in Europe during the late eighteenth century. In the very first chapter of his book detailing significant Negro cultural achievements Grégoire takes up the question of the Egyptians: what was their race, and what were their accomplishments? He describes first a dispute as to whether the Sphinx exhibits Negroid features and concludes that it does, from which he tells us, "Volney concludes, that to the black race, now slaves, we are indebted for the arts, sciences, and even for speech" ([1808] 1810, 23). He goes on:

[George] Gregory [1754–1808] in his *Historical and Moral Essays*, refers us to remote ages, to shew in like manner, that the negroes are our masters in science; for the Egyptians, among whom Pythagoras and other Greeks travelled, to learn philosophy, were in the opinion of many writers, no other than negroes. . . .

Meiners . . . support[s] . . . the opinion, that we owe little to the Egyptians, and a man of letters at Caen [Cailly], has published a dissertation to develope this position. Already it had for its defender, Edward Long, the anonymous author of the History of *Jamaica*; who, in giving to negroes, a character very analagous [*sic*] to that of the ancient Egyptians, charges the latter with bad qualities, refuses them genius and taste, disputes their talent for music, painting, eloquence and poetry, and grants them only mediocrity in architecture. ([1808] 1810, 23–24)

Grégoire's own conclusion is that "without ascribing to Egypt the greatest degree of human knowledge, all antiquity decides in favour of those who consider it as a celebrated school, from which proceeded many of the venerable and learned men of Greece" (25).

We have seen that French thinkers from the eighteenth century display a wide range of attitudes toward ancient Egypt and ancient Greece—attitudes often correlated, but not always in simple ways, with their ideological commitments. And we shall see a similar variety repeated in eighteenth-century English and German thinkers. A main weakness in Bernal's discussion of these matters is his failure to recognize this variety.

EIGHTEENTH-CENTURY BRITISH THOUGHT

Bernal's British thinkers include Edward Young, Jacob Bryant, Edward Gibbon, and William Mitford. Young (1683–1765) may be disposed of fairly quickly. Bernal says Young wrote a "series of Egyptian plays" and was "one of the best-known English playwrights of the mid-18th century" (*BA* 1:170). In fact, of Young's total dramatic output—three tragedies—only one has an Egyptian setting; this was *Busiris*, which ran for nine nights in 1719 and then effectively disappeared from the London stage.[18] His two other plays, *The Revenge* (1722) and *The Brothers* (1726, not produced until 1753) have, respectively, Spanish and ancient Greek settings (see Bliss 1969, 51–56, 133–36). What about Young's contemporaries in the theater? The eighteenth century was not, by and large, a period of high creativity for the English stage, but at the time when Young's first two plays were being produced—the early (not, as Bernal would have it, the mid-) eighteenth century—there were popular theatrical successes by such skillful playwrights as Nicholas Rowe, Joseph Addison, and John Gay. Though they composed plays about Cato, Ulysses, Tamerlane, and Achilles, none of them, to my knowledge, ever set a play in ancient Egypt.[19] There may be evidence of pervasive Egyptophilia in British plays of the eighteenth century, but Bernal has not found it.

We come next to Jacob Bryant (1715–1804), whose vast work *A New System, or, An Analysis of Ancient Mythology* was widely read; the first edition of 1774 was amplified for new editions in 1775–76 and 1807. According to Bernal, Bryant "tried to explain [the] origins [of Greek and Roman mythology] in terms of an 'Amonian' culture that contained both Egyptian and Phoenician elements," and, in his view, "despite the many fantastic aspects of [Bryant's] work . . . his approach was fundamentally the right one" (*BA* 1:171). What

Bernal neglects to tell us is that Bryant's (wholly imaginary) sun-worshiping Amonian culture—which dated to postdiluvian times—was also supposed to contain elements of all other antediluvian cultures (Babylonian, Chaldean, Canaanite, Dorian, Scythian, etc.), such that the Egyptian and Phoenician elements were not privileged.[20]

Bernal finds further evidence for eighteenth-century enthusiasm for ancient Egypt in the fifteen-year-old Edward Gibbon's choice of a topic for his first attempt at historical research, an essay (1752) entitled "The Age of Sesostris" (see *BA* 1:170). But here once again he has ignored the interesting—and pertinent—details. As Gibbon himself explains in a passage of his memoirs (composed toward the end of his life), his sole concern in that essay was with the purely chronological problem of the date of Sesostris, and his argument, he tells us, revolved about his guess that the Egyptian high priest Manetho *had deliberately lied* in writing a history of Egypt in order to flatter his patron, Ptolemy Philadelphus, by identifying Ptolemy's ancestor, Sesostris, with the elder brother of Danaus, the legendary immigrant to Argos in mainland Greece. (Bernal makes much of the legendary Danaus; see the index to *BA 1*.) "At a riper age," Gibbon continues, "I no longer presume to connect the Greek, the Jewish and the Egyptian antiquities which are lost in a distant cloud; nor is this the only instance, in which the belief and knowledge of the child are superseded by the more rational ignorance of the man" ([1792–93] 1984, 83). Bernal quotes this passage (omitting the last clause), but he misses the fact that by the time Gibbon was twenty-seven, in 1764, he was already no longer interested in Egypt, as being "too far away, too obscure, and too enigmatic to interest me greatly" (as quoted in Craddock 1982, 202).[21]

As an aging scholar myself, I find quite admirable Gibbon's mature stance of "rational ignorance," but I suspect that Bernal would not agree; his own explanation of the alleged late eighteenth-century shift from Egyptophilia, to indifference to Egypt or even to Egyptophobia, depends upon an appeal to the intensification of nationalist and ethnocentric trends in Europe. From this perspective Gibbon would have to be viewed as a (presumably unconscious) victim of the trends of his age. It might be noted, however, that Frank Turner, in his book on the Greeks and the Victorians, holds that "Greek antiquity began to absorb the interest of Europeans in the second half of the eighteenth century when the values, ideas, and institutions inherited from the Roman and Christian past became problematical . . . in the wake of the Enlightenment and of revolution. In some cases the appeal to Greece served to foster further change, in others to combat the forces of disruption" (1981, 2). Bernal acknowledges an indebtedness to Turner's book, especially for "the crucial insight that inordinate respect for Greece was a new phenomenon in the early nineteenth century" (1989b, 26). But he carelessly fails to note that this insight of Turner's is restricted to Britain (which is, after all, the subject of Turner's book); as we have seen, other Europeans—Turner mentions the Germans, and perhaps one should add the French (see above, note 8)—were half a century ahead of the British. (Even from a self-professed methodological "lumper" like Bernal [1989b, 26] one should expect some serious attention to national differences on critical issues.) In Turner's view, late eighteenth- and early nineteenth-century Hellenism was, at least in part, a positive and creative response to radical political and social change; for Bernal, fixated on the fortunes of the Ancient Model, such Hellenism can only be seen as politically retrograde.

Bernal's only real evidence of Egyptophilia in the British context is the work of the English historian William Mitford (1744–1810), whose influential *History of Greece* (8 vols., 1784–1810) proclaimed the superiority of Egypt to Greece and accepted the tradition of Egyptian colonization of Greece. Mitford was a good scholar, but it must not be forgotten that his passionate antidemocratic beliefs fostered an intense animus against ancient Athens;[22] his Egyptophilia was a reflex of his Hellenophobia. Bernal barely acknowledges this when he characterizes Mitford as "a consistent conservative [who] rejected the idea of 'progress'" (*BA* 1:187). Arnaldo Momigliano, more forthrightly, refers to Mitford as "a determined supporter of the rights of kings . . . respectfully hated by Byron and by the young Macaulay" (1966, 59–60).

That Bernal has failed to produce much evidence of British Egyptophilia in the eighteenth century is, of course, not a decisive reason for thinking no such evidence exists. Indeed, there *is* such evidence—but its interpretation is not entirely straightforward and hardly supports any simpleminded thesis concerning the gradual rise in the reputation of ancient Greece at the expense of ancient Egypt during the late eighteenth century. The fact is that the people compared, and contrasted, with the Egyptians during the seventeenth and eighteenth centuries were often the Jews rather than the Greeks. As John Gascoigne puts it, "a widespread belief in the significance of Egyptian culture . . . by the late eighteenth century, was beginning to supplant the traditional biblically-based view that the central focus of ancient history was the civilisation of the Jews. . . . Such an interest and admiration for Egyptian civilisation was, in part, an indication of the secularising trend of the Enlightenment" (1994, 175–76).[23] We cannot pause to consider the details of this controversy among British scholars in the eighteenth century over the historical significance of Egyptians versus Jews, but I summarize here in tabular form Gascoigne's citations (1991 and 1994) of those scholars—reserving Newton for later discussion—with the publication dates of their main writings:[24]

Focus on Jews	*Focus on Egyptians*
Theophilus Gale (1669–77)	John Marsham (1672)

John Woodward (1690s; 1777)   John Spencer (1685)
John Edwards (1699)   Thomas Burnet (1692)
Daniel Waterland (1731)   John Toland (1704)
                                  Matthew Tindal (1730)
                                  Conyers Middleton (1731)
                                  William Warburton (1741)
                                  Joseph Banks (1768–71; 1962)
                                  James Burnett, Lord Monboddo (1773–92)

If these thirteen scholars can be taken to constitute a representative sampling of opinion on the question at issue, Gascoigne's thesis seems plausible: there does seem to have been a growing tendency in Britain during the eighteenth century to focus on the Egyptians at the expense of the Jews (though it should be noted that only a couple of Gascoigne's examples come from the latter half of that century).

Gascoigne also points, however, to a "long-engrained tendency to down-play the importance of Egyptian culture" (1991, 195), citing *BA* 1:191 as corroboration. It should be clear that in the case of Egyptians versus Jews the variety and inconsistency of the intellectual traditions, together with the inherent malleability of an ill-defined historical subject matter, left ample room for individual, even idiosyncratic, choices. Furthermore, a preference for the Egyptians over the Jews left open the question of the Greeks. Monboddo, for instance, argues that Egyptian was the world's first language, from which all other languages derive, yet at the same time he holds that Greek is the most perfect language.[25] Again, Warburton, as Bernal notes (1:197), was ambivalent in his attitude toward the Egyptians, emphasizing their influence on the Jews but also their inferiority to the Greeks.

Not everyone took these learned controversies seriously. Consider the satirical essay by Alexander Pope, Thomas Parnell, and Dr. John Arbuthnot, written probably in 1714 (but not published until 1732), "An Essay of the Learned Martinus Scriblerus, Concerning the Origine of Sciences." The satire is directed against Dr. John Woodward (see the list above), a favorite target of Pope and his friends. The second paragraph begins with the assertion that "it is universally agreed, that Arts and sciences were deriv'd to us from the Ægyptians and Indians; but from whom they first receiv'd them, is yet a secret" (ed. Cowler 1986, 286). Though the authors might somehow have learned of his attack against the claims made on behalf of the Egyptians in his unpublished essay (1690s, in the list above), it is Woodward's unimaginative methodology which is being satirized here. The "satire" in the Scriblerian essay consists in a demonstration that the Egyptians derived their arts and sciences from the monkeys in Ethiopia. Woodward, incidentally, was directing his anti-Egyptian thrusts against such writings as the essay "On Ancient and Modern Learning" (1690), by William Temple, which asserts: "There is nothing more agreed than, That all the Learning of the *Greeks* was deduced Originally from *Egypt* or *Pheonicia* [*sic*]" (as quoted in Cowler 1986, 296).

Newton took the Egyptians versus Jews controversy very seriously indeed, to the extent of composing well over a million words about it and related theologico-historical matters, such as his conviction that Christ, though the Son of God, was not himself God (the theological doctrine known as Arianism). With such a surviving mass of writings on these topics—none of them in finished form, and virtually none published in his lifetime—Newton's ideas are not always easy to make out. Thus he could reasonably be positioned on either or both sides of the list above; sometimes he twists biblical chronology to make the Egyptians responsible for the corruption of the original, true Noachic religion (whose theology was monotheistic, whose cosmology was heliocentric, and whose defining ritual was worship of a perpetual fire in a sacred place); other times he refers to Egypt as the oldest of kingdoms and as the inventor of the arts and sciences.[26]

Bernal, for whom Newton is a "pivotal figure" (*BA* 1:169), attempts to account for these inconsistencies in Newton's stance toward Egypt by hypothesizing a shift from youthful Egyptophilia (presumably in the 1670s and 1680s) to something close to Egyptophobia later on (presumably in the 1710s and 1720s). That hypothesis would require us to believe that toward the end of his life, as his theological and historical beliefs became more radical (from Arianism to deism), Newton felt an increasing need to distance himself from contemporary pantheist, even atheist, ideas supposedly associated with certain ancient Egyptian traditions. But according to Westfall (1982, 30), Newton in his later years was countenancing such extreme theological beliefs as the denial of the Fall and of any special truths revealed by Christ. This sounds very different from Bernal's view that "Newton's later work . . . should be seen as a 'respectable' deist and Christian defence against the Radical Enlightenment" (*BA* 1:192). As for Egypt and Greece, Newton always seems to have understood the latter as indebted to the former—but sometimes for deeply erroneous ideas. It should not be forgotten that Newton regarded two of his favorite *bêtes noires*, Ptolemy and Athanasius, as Egyptians rather than Greeks.

I believe the only safe conclusion to draw concerning eighteenth-century attitudes towards Greece and Egypt is that they were varied, often ambivalent, and frequently in the service of one ideology or another. Such mixed attitudes are familiar enough to classicists.[27] Bernal, on the other hand, thinks differently: "no one," he says, "before 1600 seriously questioned either the belief that Greek civilization and philosophy derived from Egypt, or that the

chief ways in which they had been transmitted were through Egyptian colonizations of Greece and later Greek study in Egypt" (*BA* 1:121). And, as we
have seen, according to Bernal, it was only during the late eighteenth century
that real animosity against Egypt began to emerge.[28] But many ancient Greek
thinkers claimed that civilization itself began in Greece, which certainly constitutes "implicit dissent from the Ancient Model" (P. Gordon 1993, 72).[29]
And there is also the long Greco-Roman tradition of vehement objections to
Egyptian superstition, Egyptian magic, and Egyptian materialism—not to
mention Egyptian cannibalism (the controlling theme of the fifteenth satire
of Juvenal [ca. 55–130 C.E.]),[30] Egyptian prostitution, Egyptian tattooing, and
Egyptian incest (these three latter practices referred to by Sextus Empiricus
[ca. 200 C.E.]).[31]

If, by the way, we turn to nineteenth century Britain, we find that the
prevalence of contradictory attitudes toward classical antiquity seems to constitute the moral, if there is any moral, of Turner's book (1981), and also of
Jenkyns's book (1980) about the presence of ancient Greece in Victorian Britain. (Jenkyns nicely complements Turner by dealing primarily with novelists,
poets, artists, and critics rather than Turner's classical scholars and educators.)
The episodes recounted by Turner and by Jenkyns are alternately, sometimes
simultaneously, hilarious and depressing, and may even induce despair about
the ability of contemporary classical scholars to surpass their Victorian predecessors. I want, however, at least to record what is for me a sustaining
conviction: as scholars, and as consumers of scholarship, we have no choice
but to assume that verisimilitude in our picture of the classical world, or of
any other historical period, is a matter of degree; that habitual practice of the
traditional scholarly virtues (respect for the evidence, uneasiness with inconsistency, disciplined imagination) can lead, under favorable circumstances,
to a heightening of that verisimilitude.

RACISM AND ANTIRACISM IN
EIGHTEENTH-CENTURY THOUGHT

We turn now to the causes for the decline of the Ancient Model and its
replacement by the Aryan Model. In this connection Bernal discusses four
interrelated factors—and one specific event in the year 1821: "the Greek War
of Independence broke out and Western Europe was swept by Philhellen-
ism" (*BA* 1:282). The four factors are (1) racism, that is, the "opinions that
dark skin colour was linked to moral and mental inferiority" (1:203),[32] (2) the
defensiveness of an embattled Christianity, (3) the rise of the paradigm of
historical progress, and (4) the growth of Romantic Hellenism. Racism must
be discussed in some detail, for it seems to be, for Bernal, the most impor-

tant of the factors. We had best begin, however, by briefly characterizing the other three factors. (2) In response to the religious and political challenges of the late seventeenth-century Radical Enlightenment (a heady mixture of materialism, pantheism, Hermeticism, and republicanism), eighteenth-century politico-religious establishments (in Britain, led by Isaac Newton) became more critical of the supposed source of these dangerous ideas: ancient Egypt. (We have already discussed Newton in this connection.) (3) The eighteenth-century paradigm of temporal progress, applied to the ancient world, led to a demotion of earlier civilizations (like Egypt) and a corresponding promotion of later civilizations (like Greece and Rome). (4) On the Romantic Hellenism of the eighteenth century, it is best to quote Bernal himself:

> Romantics longed for small, virtuous and "pure" communities in remote and cold places: Switzerland, North Germany and Scotland. When considering the past, their natural choice was Greece. . . . In many ways the destruction of the Ancient Model and the establishment of the Aryan one can best be seen as attempts to impose these Romantic ideals of remoteness, cold and purity on this most unsuitable candidate. (*BA* 1:209)

One way of expressing Bernal's historiographical thesis is to say that a specific alliance of religious zeal, historical speculation, and spiritual yearnings began to challenge the Ancient Model during the late eighteenth century, so that by the early decades of the nineteenth century that model was ripe for demolition by the potent force of racism; at least, that is how I interpret Bernal's remark (already quoted above) that "the status of Egypt fell with the rise of racism in the 1820s" (*BA* 1:442). (It should be noted that this last claim presupposes that the Egyptians were seen as black, or, at least, nonwhite.)[33] Much could be said about the three other factors—capacious conceptions each of them, to which Bernal can scarcely do justice in his few impressionistic pages. (But one of Bernal's claims must be summarily dismissed: that Newton, in an early, Egyptophilic phase of his career, hoped to rely on ancient Egyptian measurements of the circumference of the Earth in deriving his law of gravitation [*BA* 1:166].)[34] Let us turn, rather, to the apparently decisive factor: racism.

Bernal begins with a generalization which he must take to be so obvious that it requires no supporting argument or evidence: "the intensity and pervasiveness of Northern European, American and other colonial racism since the 17th century have been . . . much greater than the norm" (*BA* 1:201). (What norm? That of all earlier European history? Of all previously recorded history?) How is the degree of racism in a society to be estimated? Bernal then goes on to formulate what he terms the "generally accepted" claim that racism was intensified after 1650 as a result of "the increased colonization of

North America, with its twin policies of extermination of the Native Americans and enslavement of Africans," which "presented moral problems" that "could be eased only by strong racism" (*BA* 1:201–2). Here he takes a stand—apparently without realizing it—on a hotly debated issue in the historiography of American slavery, namely, whether slavery led to racism or racism to slavery. According to one recent study, "the most convincing explanation, offered by Winthrop Jordan and others, is that the institution of chattel slavery and the clear belief in the racial inferiority of the African marched hand in hand, with each supporting and reinforcing the other" (Parish 1989, 13).[35] In any case, in the interests of conceptual clarity it is important to distinguish racism and slavery, both institutionally and in the mind-sets of individual thinkers; one must be prepared to find belief in the inferiority of blacks combined with opposition to slavery, and, conversely, antiracism combined with acceptance of slavery. Finally, it is worth noting that recent historical research has demonstrated the existence of widespread and large-scale slavery *within Africa*, where, of course, there was no underlying racist ideology at all.[36]

But let us look at what Bernal provides in the way of evidence for European racism directed against blacks. He begins by citing a few allegedly influential racist texts by Aristotle, Locke, Hume, and Montesquieu; these can at best serve as *illustrations* of racist ideas among a small and select group of European thinkers and provide only limited evidence for the pervasiveness of racism throughout European society. Bernal then turns to Germany, where the founding of the University of Göttingen in 1737 by the British monarch George II supposedly established a connection with British philosophical and political ideas, including the racist ideas of Locke and Hume. In the course of his argument, Bernal provides brief and fragmentary surveys of the scholarly work of numerous Göttingen professors (including Heumann, Gatterer, Spittler, Meiners, Blumenbach, Schlözer, Heeren, and Heyne), especially anthropological studies by certain of these scholars on the classification of human races, and historical studies by certain others on the ancient world. He concludes that formulations of "scientific" racism in Göttingen helped bring about the glorification of ancient Greece at the expense of ancient Egypt.

Bernal's argument is rambling and vague on crucial matters, making it difficult to evaluate in all its detail. Some of its main weaknesses, however, are easy to identify. First of all, as has been amply demonstrated above, he is not always careful in his choice and reading of texts. Thus the connection between racism and slavery in late seventeenth- and eighteenth-century thought is said to derive from Aristotle, specifically from a passage in his *Politics* (7.7) in which " 'the Hellenic race,' " owing to the bracing moral effects of its geographical position midway between the races of Asia and northern Europe, is said to be especially " 'capable of ruling others' " (*BA* 1:202). Now, in fact, this passage is not about slavery, which Aristotle discusses at the very beginning of his *Politics* in connection with the structure of the household (1.4–7). It is true that in the passage quoted by Bernal, Aristotle speaks of Asians as having "remained both enslaved and subject," but this is an allusion to the political tyranny of Asian states, not to the slave–master relationship (Davis 1966, 71). Eighteenth-century thinkers may, of course, have interpreted the passage in Bernal's sense, but he provides no evidence of this. (The subtleties of Aristotle's conception of slavery—which, for example, distinguishes slavery by law from slavery by nature—are perhaps not to the point here.) Worse errors mar Bernal's references to Locke and Hume: for example, he makes much of Locke's approval of slavery but fails to inform us that Hume was opposed to slavery.[37]

Let us turn now to the important historical questions (1) whether what Bernal calls "the centrality of racism to European society after 1700" (*BA* 1:204) is, without serious qualification and supplementation, a viable historical construct, and (2) whether such a construct can help account for the decline in Egyptophilia and the downfall of the Ancient Model. As to the first question, although Bernal, not surprisingly, includes America in his historical thesis concerning European racism, he has his doubts about France: "Racism was not so clear-cut," he writes, "in 18th-century France" (1:204). He has thus, in one sentence, asserted a generalization about Europe and then, in the very next sentence, asserted a large exception to that generalization (France). The problem here is not merely that he has contradicted himself but also that he makes no effort to resolve, or even to recognize, the contradiction. In fact, recent historical scholarship suggests that in eighteenth-century France racism was at least as virulent as anywhere else in Europe, and furthermore that certain French thinkers led the way in formulating theories of "scientific" racism.[38] Nevertheless, I follow Bernal below, concentrating on Britain, America, and Germany.

I begin by suggesting that *if racist beliefs and practices were centrally important in eighteenth-century British and American society, so was the opposition to such beliefs and practices.* (Which is not to say that racism and antiracism were "equally" strong or entrenched in those societies.) To support this claim we might first note that slavery—the institution whose legitimation, according to Bernal, required the production of racist ideologies—was, after all, eventually abolished throughout Europe and the Americas during the nineteenth century, and we know that many of the most effective abolitionists drew on the antiracist arguments of their eighteenth-century (black and white) predecessors.[39] It might, of course, be argued that eighteenth-century antiracism was a superficial epiphenomenon, especially considering that theories of "scientific" racism emerged precisely during the period when, first, the slave trade and, then, slavery were being abolished. As Drescher puts it:

> If racial attitudes were altered temporarily by the ending of the [slave] trade, we must still deal with the contention that the entire abolitionist process altered the path of racism very little. For those who see late nineteenth-century racism largely as the continuation and intensification of earlier xenophobia and arrogance, toward blacks in particular, abolition was hardly more than a dramatic, quite anomalous interlude in a pattern of general hostility. (1992, 388)

Drescher himself does not accept that point of view, for he insists that "the great novelty of this process [of abolition] lay in the fact that for the first time in history the non-slave masses, including working men and women, played a direct and decisive role in bringing chattel slavery to an end" (1987, 166).

Though Drescher is writing only about abolition in Britain, it happens that the latest large-scale interpretation of abolition and its consequences in the United States (during the Reconstruction period) also emphasizes the role of the working masses—only in this case it was the black workers (slave and free). The author of this interpretation, Eric Foner, puts it as follows:

> Rather than passive victims of the actions of others or simply a "problem" confronting white society, blacks were active agents in the making of Reconstruction. During the Civil War, their actions helped force the nation down the road to emancipation, and in the aftermath of that conflict, their quest for individual and community autonomy did much to establish Reconstruction's political and economic agenda. . . . Black participation in Southern public life after 1867 was the most radical development of the Reconstruction years, a massive experiment in interracial democracy without precedent in the history of this or any other country that abolished slavery in the nineteenth century. (1988, xxiv–xxv)

It would seem hard to deny that antiracist beliefs and practices must have played a vital role in activating the abolitionist workers of both Britain and the United States, and that such activation almost certainly drew upon historical traditions of antiracism going back to the eighteenth century.

In saying this, I do not intend to be offering an answer to another vexed question, namely, which factors contributed most to the eventual abolition of slavery: material factors (associated with the rise of industrial capitalism), ideological factors (associated with particular religious and moral doctrines),[40] or political factors (conflicts between slaves and masters).[41] What I am proposing is that *opposition* to racism and slavery was a significant part of eighteenth-century society, and hence that to ignore such opposition is to abandon any serious attempt to understand racism or slavery in that society. The point is nicely put by an art historian concerned with Hogarth's depictions of blacks:

The early 1730s, the period when Hogarth was launched into popular notoriety and when he began to use Blacks in his pictures, was a critical moment with respect to the slavery issue, colonization and the condition of Blacks in England. . . . It was probably dialectical: things got both worse and better, and opinion polarized. There was certainly an increase in humanitarian consciousness and activism in some quarters of the ruling classes, in which Hogarth shared. . . . (D. Kunzle 1987, 397, reviewing Dabydeen 1987)

To repeat: that racist ideologies did not go unchallenged in eighteenth-century Britain and America is clear from the mere existence of abolitionist movements, in whose propaganda antiracist arguments figured prominently (though not all antiracists were abolitionists, nor were all abolitionists anti-racists). But even apart from such movements there were eminent individuals who opposed both racism and slavery by word and action. For example, it is perhaps not widely enough known that the greatest English literary figure of the eighteenth century, Samuel Johnson, once proposed a toast "when in company with some very grave men at Oxford . . . 'to the next insurrection of the negroes in the West Indies'" (Boswell [1791] 1965, 876). Johnson also adopted a twelve-year-old Negro orphan boy from Jamaica named Francis Barber, secured him an education, and made him principal beneficiary in his will.[42]

Long before Dr. Johnson's toast, however, a figure in a novel issued what has been described as "the first call for a slave revolt in modern literature" (Davis 1966, 476). This was the eponymous hero of Aphra Behn's novel *Oroonoko, or, The Royal Slave* (1688). The ambiguous and limited character of the antiracist attitudes represented by Behn's story emerges right at the beginning, in her description of the idealized physical characteristics of her hero, with his "polished Jett" complexion, "Roman" nose, and "the finest shaped" mouth.[43] In any case, through translations into French and adaptations for the stage, "the tale of Oroonoko became one of the most internationally popular stories of the eighteenth century, and served as the prototype for a vast literature depicting noble African slaves" (Davis 1966, 473). Thus, Thomas Southerne's theatrical version—which, however, differed radically from Behn's novel, most blatantly in changing Oroonoko's beloved from a Negro into a white woman—was performed in London in 1695 and then at least once a year until as late as 1829. (It should be noted that there are today considerable differences of opinion as to the exact attitudes toward slavery, racism, and colonialism to be found in Behn's novel and Southerne's play.)[44]

Bernal never so much as mentions either the abolitionist movements or individual opponents of racism. To deal with eighteenth-century racism adequately would certainly have complicated his task—but it might also have helped him to take better account of the concrete political and intellectual issues faced by his historical agents, instead of merely alluding vaguely to the dire effects on each of them of a presumed set of (undifferentiated and unmediated) racist attitudes. Again, the example of Hogarth is to the point, for in his satirical works Hogarth sometimes "consciously employs current myths and stereotypes about blacks, relating to their sexuality, paganism, primitivism and simian ancestry, so as to comment on the morality of the English aristocratic class. The black is used as a yardstick, as well as a stick to beat the whites" (Dabydeen 1987, 130). Furthermore, Hogarth's own personal situation as an artist may have influenced his antislavery attitudes; as Dabydeen explains, "it is significant that Hogarth uses the metaphor of slavery in describing his own condition as an artist" when he refers to "the way artists are 'oppress'd by the Tyranny of the Rich,' meaning the wealthy businessmen who dominated the printselling trade" (132).

Further illustration of the complexity of eighteenth-century attitudes toward blacks appears in the following passage by Adam Smith:[45]

> There is not a negro from the coast of Africa who does not, in this respect, possess a degree of magnanimity which the soul of his sordid master is scarce capable of conceiving. Fortune never exerted more cruelly her empire over mankind, than when she subjected those nations of heroes to the refuse of the jails of Europe, to wretches who possess the virtues neither of the countries which they came from, nor of those which they go to, and whose levity, brutality and baseness, so justly expose them to the contempt of the vanquished. ([1759] 1971, 5.2, p. 402)

Out of context, this may appear to be remarkably sweeping praise of Negroes; the restrictive phrase, "in this respect," however, refers back to the immediately previous sentence, where Smith attributes to Negroes "the same contempt of death and torture [which] prevails among all other savage nations" (402). Nevertheless, Smith's remark, limited as it is in its attribution of admirable traits to Negroes, may be seen, at the very least, as paving the way for the attribution of further human feelings and impulses to them, thereby helping to remove the moral stigma inherent in many eighteenth-century images of the Negro. (And it must be remembered that Adam Smith's was no obscure treatise: after its initial publication in 1759 it had gone through no fewer than six editions by 1790.)

On the issue of Negro intelligence, some of the best evidence for the attitudes of American thinkers is summarized in one of Bernal's own sources, Winthrop Jordan's *White Over Black* (1969). But Bernal's casual characterization of Benjamin Franklin as a "racist" (*BA* 1:203),[46] contrasts sharply with Jordan's assertion that "by the 1770s outright denials of Negro mental inferiority had become common. Benjamin Franklin thought Negroes 'not deficient in natural Understanding'" (1969, 282).[47] Much more influential than Franklin on the question of Negro mental capacities was Thomas Jefferson, who affirmed a fully developed moral sense in the Negro while denying the existence of an intelligence equal to that of whites. It must be emphasized, though, that Jefferson's publication of these views, in his *Notes on Virginia* (1785–89), led almost immediately to numerous published refutations (see Jordan, 441–45). Jefferson also, much later in life, wrote of his wish "to see a complete refutation of the doubts I have myself entertained and expressed on the grade of understanding allotted to [Negroes] by nature, and to find that in this respect they are on a par with ourselves" (letter to Henri Grégoire, 25 February 1809; see Koch and Peden 1944, 594–95; or Peterson 1977, 517). There is, however, some doubt as to the sincerity of that letter, for Jefferson told another correspondent that "he had given Grégoire 'a very soft answer'" (as quoted by Jordan, 454), and in any case, "in old age, Jefferson could not endorse emancipation, even as he repeated the tired litany of his theoretical support for abolition sometime in the future" (Finkelman 1993, 210).[48]

I have no statistical evidence on whether, as Bernal would have it, "most 18th-century English-speaking thinkers . . . were racist" (*BA* 1:203), but so far as I can see, neither does he; and there certainly were many prominent and outspoken antiracists in Britain and America.[49]

EIGHTEENTH-CENTURY GERMAN THOUGHT

We come now to Germany. Bernal's thesis, it will be recalled, is that certain German thinkers were the first to formulate a new scholarly-cum-ideological framework for studying the ancient world, one of whose most momentous consequences was the replacement of the Ancient by the Aryan Model. To support this thesis he tries to show two things: first, that eighteenth-century German society was as deeply racist as the societies of Britain, France, and America and, second, that German thinkers possessed the dubious distinction of formulating the earliest "scientific" theories justifying racism. Let us begin by examining what he describes as the "ethnicity and racism" characterizing "prevailing opinion in German cultivated society as a whole" (*BA* 1:215) during the eighteenth century.

His sole reference here is to a short book by Sander Gilman (1982, chapters 2–5, on the eighteenth century). First of all, as there were virtually no blacks in Germany in the eighteenth century (nor, for that matter, later on right up through the twentieth century), Gilman's history naturally restricts itself to high culture (what Bernal calls "cultivated society"). (Somewhat surprisingly, Gilman almost entirely ignores German universities, a topic addressed below.) Gilman's four eighteenth-century case studies deal with the image of the black in aesthetics (chapter 2), on the German and Austrian stage (chapters 3 and 5), and in the physiognomic theories of Lavater and Lichtenberg (chapter 4). Contrary to Bernal's unqualified assertion concerning the pervasive racism of eighteenth-century German society, we find that Gilman traces in each of his case studies *an evolution during the eighteenth century toward a more positive image of blackness and toward an increasing sensitivity to the horrors of black slavery*. (See the summary concluding paragraphs of chapters 2–5 in Gilman 1982). For further evidence along these lines, let us consider the exemplary cases of Kant and Herder.

In his early thought on the nature of human races Immanuel Kant (1724–1804) was influenced by a remark of David Hume, who wrote in a footnote to his essay "Of National Characters" that "I am apt to suspect the negroes to be naturally inferior to the whites" ([1777] 1987, 208 n. 10).[50] This remark was cited with some frequency especially by writers engaged in pro- and antislavery polemics in the late eighteenth and early nineteenth centuries; Kant was not among them, but he did paraphrase Hume's remark in an early essay on aesthetics, as follows: "The Negroes of Africa have by nature no feeling that rises above the trifling. Mr. Hume challenges anyone to cite a single example in which a Negro has shown talents. . . . So fundamental is the difference between these two races of man [white and Negro], and it appears to be as great in regard to mental capacities as in color" ([1764] 1991, 111). A couple of pages later he remarks—gratuitously and (for me) puzzlingly—of a certain Negro carpenter (the subject of an incident which he has just recounted) that "this fellow was quite black from head to foot, a clear proof that what he said was stupid" (113).

Understandably, today, at a time of heightened consciousness about racist tendencies in traditional Western philosophy, Kant's remarks have provoked some strong critical responses, of which this by Henry Louis Gates, Jr. is one of the more restrained: "Kant . . . is one of the earliest major European philosophers to conflate color with intelligence, a determining relation he posits with dictatorial surety" (1987, 18). Less understandable perhaps is the fixation of too many recent critics of Kant's racist remarks on an early work, to the complete exclusion of the quite different attitudes and opinions Kant expressed in his more mature works. Specifically, in later writings on race Kant avoided any denigration of blacks; as Gilman explains: "In [Kant's] second essay on race, 'Die Bestimmung des Begriffs einer Menschenrasse' [Definition of the Concept of a Race] (1785), . . . all negative value judgments concerning the nature of the Black have been eliminated" (1982, 33).[51] And in a still later remark about blacks, this time in one of his most important critical writings, the *Critique of Judgment* (1790), Kant insisted on the relativity of ideals of beauty, arguing that "a negro must necessarily . . . have a different normal idea of the beauty of forms from what a white man has, and the Chinaman one different from the European" ([1790] 1911, 78).[52] Admittedly, Kant is here writing in a specialized aesthetic context, but Gilman's explication of the passage—with an emphasis precisely on the close connection of the aesthetic and the political—should be congenial enough in many intellectual quarters today:

> With the ever greater awareness of the political exploitation of the Black through the institution of slavery . . . [M]ore and more, aestheticians asked whether the Black perceived reality in the same manner as the European. Racism gave way to the question of cultural relativism. The Black attained, by the end of the [eighteenth] century, the position of an observer rather than an object perceived. The anthropomorphism of darkness was completed and the Black stood as an individual, perceiving reality, rather than as the embodiment of a natural force. (1982, 34)

Turning to Johann Gottfried von Herder (1744–1803), we may note first that he had strong antiracist views. Consider, for example, what he says about blacks vis-à-vis whites in his *Philosophie der Geschichte der Menschheit* (1784):[53]

> Since whiteness is a mark of degeneracy in many animals near the pole, the negro has as much right to term his savage robbers albinoes and white devils, degenerated through the weakness of nature, as we have to deem him the emblem of evil, and a descendant of Ham, branded by his father's curse. I, might he say, I, the black, am the original man. I have taken the deepest draughts from the source of life, the Sun. . . . ([1783–91] 1966, 146]

In a later work, the tenth of his *Briefe zu Beförderung der Humanität* (Letters on the Advancement of Humanity) (1797), Herder expresses the same view in slightly different terms:[54]

> The naturalist does not postulate an order of merit among the creatures which he observes; all are of equal value and concern. Thus also the human naturalist. The Black has as much right to consider the white a mutant, a born vermin, as the white has to consider him a beast, a black animal. (as quoted in Gilman 1982, 31)

Another of the letters in that collection contains five poems, "Negro-Idylls," which one recent critic describes as "the most coherent body of information on Negro slavery assembled by Herder, and the most compelling attack on the institution" (Feuser 1978, 118). Furthermore, Herder was an ardent opponent of colonialism in all of its guises, as we learn from the following passage:

"Can you name a land," [Herder] asks in his *Letters on the Advancement of Mankind* (1793–97), "where Europeans have entered without defiling themselves forever before defenceless, trusting mankind, by the unjust word, greedy deceit, crushing oppression, diseases, fatal gifts they have brought? Our part of the earth should be called not the wisest, but the most arrogant, aggressive, money-minded: what it has given these peoples is not civilization but the destruction of the rudiments of their own cultures wherever they could achieve this." (as quoted in Berlin 1976, 160–61)

One final point about Herder: he was no uncritical Egyptophile, and, in particular, he was skeptical about Egyptian intellectual achievements— though *not* because he considered them members of an inferior race. Here, for example, are some excerpts from his account of the Egyptians in his *Philosophy of the History of Man* ([1783–91] 1966, 345–47; 1968, 156–58):

Secrets are in vain sought within the pyramids, or concealed wisdom from the obelisks.

Their road to science was obstructed by hieroglyphics, and thus their attention was the more turned towards objects of sense. The fertile valley of the Nile rendered their agriculture easy: they learned to measure and calculate those periodic inundations, on which their welfare depended. A people, whose life and comforts were connected with one single natural change, which, annually recurring, formed an eternal national calendar must ultimately become expert in the measure of the year and the seasons.

Egypt has always remained a child in knowledge, because it always expressed its knowledge as a child, and its infantile ideas are probably for ever lost to us.

Egypt would not easily have attained the high reputation it enjoys for wisdom, but for its less remote situation, the ruins of its antiquities, and above all the tales of the Greeks.

It is worth adding that at about the same time, Kant was contrasting Egyptian and Greek mathematics as follows:

In the earliest times to which the history of human reason extends, *mathematics*, among that wonderful people, the Greeks, had already entered upon the sure path of science. . . . I believe that it [mathematics] long remained, especially among the Egyptians, in the groping stage . . . ([1787] 1965, 19)

Bernal does not mention Herder's antiracist, antislavery, anticolonialist views, nor Herder's opinion of ancient Egypt; he prefers to see in Herder's "concern with history and local particularity, and the disdain for rationality or 'pure reason' . . . a firm basis for the chauvinism and racism of the following two centuries" (*BA* 1:206). Herder's complex and not always consistent views can be—and at the hands of his nineteenth-century followers certainly were—interpreted (and misinterpreted) in various ways. Nevertheless, Bernal's claim strikes me as (at the very least) drastically oversimplified. (See also Norton, this volume.)

GÖTTINGEN AND THE ENLIGHTENMENT

We must now consider what Bernal has to say about the eighteenth-century German university; and here we find him at least occasionally adumbrating that social history of ideas so conspicuously absent in his treatment of British and American racism. Unfortunately, as before, there are serious deficiencies in textual interpretation and too many inadequately supported assertions of causal nexus.

Generally speaking, German universities (with the important exception of Göttingen) were not thriving institutions during the eighteenth century. Enrollments were dropping, funds were scarce, the "philosophical" (liberal arts) faculties were in decay. There was, however, "a malaise much deeper and more chronic. All during the eighteenth century the immense prestige of the universities, the very ideal of university education, had been slipping perceptibly away. One unmistakable sign of this loss lay in the growing number of attacks upon the universities" (R. S. Turner 1974, 500). A full discussion of German universities and their changing character during the eighteenth century would have to deal with the Prussian universities and especially Halle, the (mostly southern) Catholic universities, and such competing institutions as the Berlin Academy, but I here follow Bernal in concentrating on the University of Göttingen. (He considers other German universities, of course, when he comes to discuss the educational reforms of Wilhelm von Humboldt in the early nineteenth century.) Göttingen was a place where "advanced study and research in history and law, as well as in the mathematical sciences and medicine, were actively encouraged . . . by the endowment of the only really satisfactory university library in Germany, together with scientific and medical laboratories and museums" (Bruford 1968, 245). It is also worth noting that the exceptional character of Göttingen University was widely recognized at the time; in 1784, for example, when the Prussian ministry of education sent Friedrich Gedicke to investigate German universities outside Prussia, it received from him a highly favorable report about Göttingen.[55]

Bernal believes that Göttingen University was the cradle of the modern discipline of classics (in German, *Philologie* or *Altertumswissenschaft*)—tainted from birth, so he maintains, with the racism, chauvinism, and political conservatism of its professorial progenitors. Here is how he characterizes "Göttingen scholarship":

> while exclusive professionalism was [its] distinctive form . . . , the chief unifying principle of its content was ethnicity and racism . . . the result . . . of prevailing opinion in German cultivated society as a whole. Despite the Göttingen professors' insistence on their academic high standards and detachment, they were inevitably influenced by such 'popular' writers as Winckelmann, Goethe and Lessing. (*BA* 1:215)

The close juxtaposition of these last three names with "ethnicity and racism" is perhaps fortuitous; one certainly hopes so, for whatever one may think of Winckelmann's peculiar brand of Hellenophilia, to deliberately associate Goethe and Lessing with ethnicity and racism would suggest a deep ignorance of German cultural history. (On Lessing in particular, see below, note 65.)

It must be said at the outset that a full and proper evaluation of Bernal's claims would require a major effort of historical analysis and would necessarily extend well into the nineteenth century. My much more modest aim is to raise some questions about what he says and to introduce some considerations which he has overlooked. As will become apparent, I see certain historical situations rather differently than he does, even when we are appealing to the same sources.[56] A good introductory example is our respective views on one of the earliest Göttingen professors, Christoph August Heumann (1681–1764).

Heumann became a professor at the University upon its founding in 1737. His main scholarly interests were in philology, philosophy, and theology, on which he published many books (in Latin) between 1711 and 1763.[57] Bernal (following L. Braun 1973, 101–115) is concerned with a particular set of Heumann's writings on the history of philosophy, which were published in the journal he started in 1715 (and continued to edit until it ceased publication in 1723). Despite its Latin title, *Acta Philosophorum*, the journal was published in German, unusual at a time when Latin was still the main language of scholarship in Germany. In his discussion of the history of philosophy Heumann asserts as a fact that philosophy began in ancient Greece, and then attempts to explain this fact by the principle that philosophy can only flourish in temperate climates (thereby ruling out Egypt). For Bernal, the following inferences then seem obvious: that Heumann was very daring, first, in choosing to write about philosophy in German, and, second, "in impugning the massive ancient and modern tradition which saw Egypt and the Orient as the seats of wisdom and philosophy" (in both of these activities he was "more than fifty years ahead of his time"); his motivation was "his German nationalism and his Europocentricism" (*BA* 1:216). None of this is very convincing.

For consider: it was Christian Wolff (1679–1754) who first created a definitive language for philosophy in German, beginning as early as 1710 (so much for Heumann's being fifty years ahead of his time). Wolff's self-professed motivation was, first of all, "to provide his students with suitable manuals," but also to "be intelligible to a wider public than that which attended his lectures" (Blackall 1978, 37). (Wolff, like Heumann, continued to compose philosophical treatises in Latin throughout his life.) Are we to assume that Heumann was more nationalistic than Wolff? Of course, it might be said that Wolff's nationalistic feelings were ultimately what moved him to be concerned about his pedagogy, but that would have to be argued in detail to be persuasive. In fact it is more plausible to assume that Heumann's writing in German was part of his attempt to stimulate, in Braun's words, "a lasting dialogue among scholars interested in the history of philosophy" (1973, 103). As for Heumann's conception of ancient Egypt, it suffices to say that "the massive ancient and modern tradition" to which Bernal refers is a figment of his imagination: we should not expect to find in *any* period of European history a uniform set of attitudes toward Egypt and Greece. Rather, for many people, not excepting classical scholars, "Egypt" and "Greece" have come to resemble Rorschach tests, where what individual subjects claim to see is importantly influenced by reflections or projections of their own inner lives. An excellent set of examples of this interaction between objective and subjective elements in individual perceptions of classical antiquity is provided by the corpus of modern literature on travel to Greece. Thus, in her recent book about French travelers to Greece, Olga Augustinos stresses "the interplay between objective reality and subjective perception in this type of writing" (1994, xii) and finds that "the shifting balance between the subjective and the objective in favor of the former" achieves some sort of culmination in the travel writings of Chateaubriand (1767–1848).[58] I would continue to insist, of course, that to make sense of the scholarly enterprise of doing history, we must attach varying degrees of reliability—depending somehow on the critical use of sources—to competing claims about the ancient world.

I now offer some additional evidence that during the late eighteenth and early nineteenth centuries there were *significant antiracist and universalistic (antichauvinistic) elements in German culture as a whole, and in Göttingen higher education in particular.* Let us consider first the views of Göttingen's leading theorist of race, Johann Friedrich Blumenbach (1752–1840). He was a professor of medicine, and, starting in 1776, a dominating intellectual presence at Göttingen for more than half a century.[59] Pretty much all that Bernal tells us about Blumenbach is that his "was the first attempt at a 'scientific' study of human races of the type Linnaeus had written for natural history a few decades earlier"; that according to Blumenbach "the white or Caucasian was the first and most beautiful and talented race, from which all the others had degenerated to become Chinese, Negroes, etc."; and that "Blumenbach was conventional for his period in that he included 'Semites' and 'Egyptians' among his Caucasians" (*BA* 1:219–20).

Bernal has left out a lot, and a lot of what he has left out is important. Although he realizes that Blumenbach was a key figure in academic Göttingen in the late eighteenth and early nineteenth centuries, he makes little effort to grapple with the complexities and tensions in Blumenbach's thought. He does, to be sure, contrast Blumenbach's theory of human races with the egregiously racist theory of Blumenbach's colleague, the professor of philosophy Christoph Meiners (1747–1810), who was "later to be honoured by the Nazis as a founder of racial theory" (*BA* 1:217):[60] compared with Meiners, "a more cautious and systematic racial hierarchy was established by J. F. Blumenbach" (1:219). Blumenbach is in fact (as I hope to have shown in Appendix 3, below) a much more interesting thinker than Bernal makes him out to be—but for that very reason, perhaps, less available as evidence for Bernal's claims.[61] Meiners, on the other hand, wrote primarily about the history of ancient cultures, and Bernal takes his historiographical innovations to have been decisive in the formation of the new discipline of classics. Let us proceed to further details.

Blumenbach was the first true physical anthropologist, with a deep commitment to empirical research and an aversion to overspeculative ideas (such as vitalism in biology). His dissertation for his medical degree, *De Generis Humani Varietate Nativa* (1775), attempted to explain the origin of the various human races; twice revised (1781, 1795) and translated into German, it is his fullest statement of his theory of human races. Among his research tools were extensive natural history collections, including a famous assortment of human skulls from around the world (eventually numbering some 245), which were critical in his classification of human races (see Appendix 3, below). His conclusion was that there are three main human races (the pristine Caucasian and the derivative Mongolian and Ethiopian), and two secondary races (the American, intermediate between the Caucasian and Mongolian; and the Malay, intermediate between the Caucasian and the Ethiopian). His prime criterion was an aesthetic one, and it is not true (as Bernal says) that he supposed the Caucasians to be "more talented," either morally or intellectually, than the other races.

But why, it may be asked, does any of this matter? Blumenbach did, after all, place Caucasians on top and Ethiopians together with Mongolians at the bottom (there being no strict hierarchy of races, since, for Blumenbach, Mongolians and Ethiopians seem to be equally distant from the Caucasian norm), and the subtle details of his theory would hardly have mattered to those of his readers looking for "scientific" justifications of their own racist opinions. In other words, ought not political ideology in this case to override intellectual hairsplitting? One response might be to suggest that intellectual distinctions are at the heart of intellectual history; without them, the discipline becomes a mere game in which one searches for heroic or villainous precursors. I would defend that response, but in Blumenbach's case a further reply may be made. Suppose we look at one of his more popular writings on race, a short tract which eschews technical detail.

The twelfth section of Blumenbach's *Beyträge zur Naturgeschichte* (Contributions to Natural History) (1806) describes the five principal races of mankind; then comes a section, "Of the Negro in Particular," which begins as follows:

> . . . it has been asserted that the negroes are specifically different in their bodily structure from other men, and must also be placed considerably in the rear, from the condition of their obtuse mental capacities. Personal observation, combined with the accounts of trustworthy and unprejudiced witnesses, has, however, long since convinced me of the want of foundation in both these assertions. ([1806] 1865, 305)

Blumenbach proceeds to praise unstintingly both the moral qualities of "our black brethren" and the outstanding talents of individual Negroes in the arts and sciences, mentioning such names as that of the concert violinist Freidig; the astronomer Benjamin Banneker; the writers Ignatius Sancho, Gustavus Vaso (Olaudah Equians), and Phillis Wheatley; the philosopher Anthony William Amo; and the theologian Jacobus Eliza Capitein (whose portrait, by the way, Blumenbach uses as his type specimen of the Ethiopian race; see Appendix 3, below). (Indeed, we are told by his French biographer [in Blumenbach 1865, 57] that he "collected everything in [the African race's] favour" and "had a library entirely composed of books written by negroes.") The chapter concludes with this ringing affirmation:

> Finally, I am of opinion that after all these numerous instances I have brought together of negroes of capacity, it would not be difficult to mention entire well-known provinces of Europe, from out of which you would not easily expect to obtain off-hand such good authors, poets, philosophers, and correspondents of the Paris Academy; and on the other hand, there is no so-called savage nation known under the sun which has so much distinguished itself by such examples of perfectibility and original capacity for scientific culture, and thereby attached itself so closely to the most civilized nations of the earth, *as the Negro.* ([1806] 1865, 312)

This is as far as Enlightenment universalism can take Blumenbach (or perhaps any eighteenth-century thinker): "civilization" is still measured by European achievement. Blumenbach did not, to my knowledge, call for the abolition of slavery (though he was certainly sensitive to the evils of the slave trade and of slavery itself). Nevertheless, enough has been said, I hope, to suggest that Blumenbach's Göttingen was perhaps not quite the hotbed of racism and chauvinism required to sustain Bernal's account of the rise of a new "Aryan" historical paradigm destined to lead to the downfall of the Ancient Model. Further evidence at odds with Bernal's account may be found in the *reception* of Meiners's blatantly racist and proslavery opinions in Göttingen.

As we have already noted, Blumenbach hardly seems to have taken Meiners's racist theories as serious contributions to anthropology (see note 60). The distinguished classical scholar and university librarian Christian Gottlob Heyne (1729–1812)—in Bernal's words, "the central figure in both the town and the university" (*BA* 1:221)—strenuously rejected Meiners's ideas on race. Though Heyne did not openly challenge Meiners owing to the demands of collegiality (he even delivered the eulogy when Meiners died), he worked hard surreptitiously to keep Meiners from publishing his views on race. (For example, as editor of *Göttingischen Anzeigen* (Göttingen Proceedings) Heyne tried to assign books on race to reviewers other than Meiners (see Horst Fiedler's remarks in Forster 1958–85, 11:419). One such reviewer was his son-in-law, Georg Forster (1754–94),[62] who had no qualms about disagreeing with Meiners. Forster was not an academic (though he had many academic acquaintances, including Blumenbach and Meiners); rather, he was a man of letters, his meager income derived mostly from translating and book-reviewing. Brash, impulsive, with a wide-ranging and acute intellect, Forster is an appealing figure despite a quixotic streak which tended (as we shall see) to warp his practical political judgment.

Forster's culminating attack on Meiners's racist ideology was a long (anonymous) article filling two successive issues of *Allgemeine Literatur-Zeitung* in January 1791 (for the text see Forster 1958–85, 11:236–52). This was not the first critique of Meiners's racism in that newspaper, for an earlier (also anonymous) article, appearing in four issues in May 1789, had criticized Meiners for his methodology and for the offensiveness of his views while emphasizing the "novelty" of his "hypothesis."[63] In his own critique, Forster stressed the unity of the human species, welcomed the rich diversity of human cultures, and insisted that for cultures, there is no "rank ordering with respect to absolute worth" (11:245)[64]—all the time drawing on historical evidence as well as on his own personal experiences as a world traveler. (He knew at first hand something of the wide range of human diversity; he and his father, Reinhold, had served as the official naturalists on Captain Cook's second voyage, 1772–75, to the South Pacific.)

Forster's article was enthusiastically received by his friends, including

Heyne, the philosopher F. H. Jacobi, and the diplomat and politician C. W. von Dohm.[65] (Meiners guessed the author's identity and eventually, in 1792, published a reply to Forster.) More generally, it seems that Forster's friends were members of a community of like-minded people, sharing certain humane and humanistic attitudes about human diversity. That they were not accustomed to encountering theoretical expressions of racial prejudice would seem to be the point of Fiedler's remark that Meiners's racism was "still an isolated phenomenon" at that time (in Forster 1958–85, 11:415). On the other hand, we may properly wonder how many members of that community were capable of appreciating Forster's ironic comment in a letter to his father-in-law (Mainz, 5–6 November 1789): "The black wet-nurse truly represents a victory over prejudice in dear enlightened Göttingen!"[66]

One must not exaggerate what might be called Forster's "Enlightenment universalism": he did, after all, subscribe to a qualified Eurocentrism in his attitudes toward world cultures, with "no qualms about asking the white race to assist the black race in attaining to the European's level of development and thus joining, and taking part in, the universal progress of mankind" (Saine 1972, 48). And, Saine explains, for Forster, among historical cultures, the ancient Greeks had a privileged place; "Greek art," for example, "is not the only one, only the highest, the most splendid, and the nearest to the European in space and time" (90). Forster was also deeply interested in Indian culture, but his German version of the *Sakontala* (1791), from the English translation of Sir William Jones, was thought of as a contribution to his "program of collecting and propagating the art of lesser developed peoples as a means of restoring the European taste" (Saine, 91).

Bernal tells us nothing of Forster's views on the classification of human races or what he thought of the ancient world; rather, he cites Forster's political views, especially his enthusiastic support for the French Revolution and his visit to Paris in March 1793. But even here he omits crucial facts (cf. Saine 1972, chapter 5), most notably that a French army had occupied Mainz (where Forster was then head librarian of the university) and that the object of the trip to Paris was to present to the French National Convention a petition for the incorporation of Mainz and its surrounding territories into the French Republic. (It required strongarm tactics, engineered by Forster, to get the petition approved by the citizens of Mainz, who were experiencing harsh conditions from the occupation.) The petition became a dead letter when German armies retook Mainz—which meant, of course, that Forster could no longer return home. Meanwhile one of the two other members of Forster's delegation was guillotined for publishing a laudatory account of Charlotte Corday's demeanor at her execution. Forster's ardor for the Revolution cooled somewhat, but, says Saine, he maintained a "belief in the historical necessity of the whole process, and [a] belief that all humanity will rise to a higher level of perfection as a result" (1972, 153). In October 1793, with some difficulty, he slipped into Switzerland and spent three days with his wife, Therese, and their children, who were now living there together with her lover, Ludwig Huber, an erstwhile protégé of Forster's. (The affair between Therese and Huber had started in 1790, while Forster was away in England.) Returning to Paris, Forster contracted pneumonia and died of a stroke on 10 January 1794.

Bernal's main concern with Forster's personal life involves Forster's break with Heyne, his father-in-law, over the French Revolution. Bernal wishes to depict Heyne as exemplifying the prevailing political attitudes of Göttingen academics: in their own eyes they were occupying a middle ground between reaction and revolution, but in actuality they were "shor[ing] up the *status quo*" (*BA* 1:282). Apparently uncertain that Heyne's anger with Forster can be fully accounted for by their political differences, Bernal suggests that "Forster had not merely gone to Paris to take part in the Revolution but had left his wife — Heyne's daughter — for the love of her best friend Caroline [Böhmer], the daughter of the Semitist Michaelis" (1:222).[67] In fact it is not at all certain that there was a liaison between Caroline Böhmer and Forster, but if there was, it occurred well after Therese had become involved with Huber. (She later married Huber; Caroline married, successively, A. W. Schlegel and F. W. Schelling.) To make sense of Heyne's break with Forster thus requires not an appeal to some personal peeve on Heyne's part, but merely a clear understanding of what Forster supported — not just the French Revolution, but the annexation of German territory by a French nation in the throes of the Terror. To oppose Forster vehemently on this matter hardly required much antirevolutionary fervor on Heyne's part (or on the part of Forster's other friends, who also broke with him).

GÖTTINGEN AND THE NEW HISTORY

As mentioned earlier, Meiners figures in another way in Bernal's characterization of the intellectual climate of late eighteenth-century Göttingen: Bernal singles him out as a great innovator in historical method, in particular as the inventor of "source criticism" (*BA* 1:217). This conception of Meiners's role is perhaps exaggerated, for many of his colleagues at Göttingen were using and advocating pretty much the same methods. And, indeed, elsewhere Bernal refers to Heyne as the scholar who "promoted the new technique of 'source criticism'" (1989c, 7). Herbert Butterfield (1960) never even mentions Meiners, yet holds that "the university of Göttingen prepared the way for what was to be the Scientific Revolution in historical study. In the closing decades of the eighteenth century it built itself up as the leading German historical school, seeking to give the subject a scientific character, and making itself the centre for the study of method" (42).[68]

Recent writers have tended to agree with Butterfield about the innovative character of Göttingen historical writing, but these historiographical issues themselves should be put in historical perspective by recalling that the current consensus represents a revisionist rejection of the thesis of Friedrich Meinecke's powerful *Entstehung des Historismus* (1936), in which the Göttingen historians are disposed of in a few lines in favor of their three great nonacademic contemporaries Justus Möser, Herder, and Goethe.[69] Without actually mentioning Meinecke, Butterfield does seem to be directly challenging him when he comments that "the dynamic ideas which helped to transform historical study may have arisen outside the universities; but in Göttingen we see them critically considered and carefully combined so as to form a system of historical scholarship" (1960, 61).

What, then, were the new methods of the Göttingen historians? To begin with, they systematized, in Butterfield's words, "the collation of manuscripts; the recovery of a purified text; the diagnosis of interpolations and corruptions; the discovery of the earlier sources which the writer has used" (1960, 58). The master of this treatment of sources, according to Butterfield, was August Ludwig Schlözer (1735–1809), whose greatest work was a critical edition of *Nestor* (a medieval Russsian chronicle), "one of the remarkable documents in the history of historiography" (Butterfield, 56). (Bernal refers to Schlözer only for his establishment of a "Semitic" family of languages [*BA* 1:220].) All Bernal tells us about "source criticism" (*Quellenkritik*) is that it is a technique which enables the historian to choose among a set of competing sources those which are especially revealing of the *Zeitgeist*, or "spirit of the age." For a fuller account we can turn to one of Bernal's own sources, Lucien Braun.

As Braun explains, according to this "new" way of treating sources, "It is not the quantity of citations which enables one to corroborate a thesis, but their quality. And this depends on the man who is speaking. . . . Meiners . . . asks what sort of man is the author [of his sources] and in what context were they produced" (1973, 176). Meiners applied this procedure in his study of ancient Pythagoreanism and was led to a rehabilitation of Aristotle as not only among the earliest but also among the most reliable of the extant sources concerning Pythagorean philosophy:[70]

Meiners confirms this opinion of Aristotle by psychological considerations: Aristotle was well informed because of his curiosity about the thought of others; he was well acquainted with the writings of his time because in this regard he had excellent facilities; he understood what he read because he was intelligent. Moreover, why would he seek to distort the thought of Pythagoras? That would be consistent with neither his prudence nor his wisdom, and would add nothing to his own fame, since his contemporaries were informed about the ideas he might have thus claimed for himself. Besides, one knows of no forgery attributed to Aristotle. (176)

Despite his reliance on Braun in his discussion of Meiners, Bernal never mentions Braun's discussion of this supposedly exemplary application of source criticism by Meiners. Elsewhere, to be sure, Bernal is quite concerned about the pernicious effects of "Aryan" influence on the interpretation of Pythagoras, as when he remarks that "it takes the greatest Aryanist ingenuity to deny the strong ancient traditions—referred to by Herodotos and given in detail by later writers—that there was such a person as Pythagoras and that his school was established on the basis of his long studies in Egypt" (*BA* 1:105). This remark is directed against a book published in 1922; Bernal never engages with Walter Burkert's major study of Pythagoreanism, published nearly half a century later.

In any case, Meiners's procedures—which privilege Aristotle as a source over a host of later, sometimes much more detailed, sources—yield exactly the sort of result that bothers Bernal. He is willing to grant that "Meiners' procedures . . . do seem essential to a historian as opposed to a chronicler: it is inevitable that one should give different weight to different sources." The trouble comes when certain sources are neglected or rejected as being inconsistent with what is taken to be the spirit of the age; in this manner, "the historian can impose almost any pattern he chooses" (*BA* 1:218). One may agree with Bernal that the introduction of a subjectively defined or intuitively grasped "spirit of the age" is open to abuse.[71] But perhaps it is not expecting too much for source criticism to have evolved its own specialized and relatively objective canons. A good example would be the principle that one should be suspicious of an "expanding" tradition of texts in which the later ones claim to know more about a certain event or individual than the earlier ones: for example, "in many cases late tradition gives the name of Pythagoras, where older tradition, dealing with the same topic, does not do so" (Burkert [1962] 1972, 10). It is on the basis of that principle that Burkert questions the reliability of late sources which identify Pythagoras as a mathematician, when the earliest sources, such as Herodotus, say nothing about this.

Meiners himself was hardly consistent in his use of source criticism; at least, so some of his critics believed. Thus in a letter of 21 January 1787 to Herder, Forster criticized one of Meiners's recently published books for its lapses in the treatment of sources:[72]

I also have Mr. Meiners's work. It is Göttingen-ish erudition in support of an untenable hypothesis. . . . Dearest heaven! for him every travel writer and every compiler is on the same level, one entitled to as much confidence as the other! . . . The best I can say for his work is that he has prepared the way for others, who possess enough ingenuity to use his accumulations with discrimination. (1958–85, 14:621–22)

Clearly, source criticism can be, and is, used by scholars across the political spectrum. Nevertheless, Meiners and Forster were members of the same socio-intellectual community characterized by many shared presuppositions and values, and it is interesting to raise the question why it was appropriate—if not even *necessary*—for a new form of scholarship (including source criticism) to be urgently sought in that community. An answer is provided by R. Steven Turner's analysis of the Prussian intelligentsia, or *Gelehrtenstand*, in the period 1790 to 1840. These were individuals—jurists, government officials, school teachers, professors, churchmen, doctors—who had received a higher education in Latin: an *Allgemeines Gelehrtentum*, as it has been called, "a social group defined around an intellectual style; and that style was not one of expertise or subtlety or piety, but one of eloquence and erudition" (R. S. Turner 1983, 452). (The group in question existed, of course, also outside Prussia, for instance in the state of Hanover, where Göttingen University was located.)[73]

By the third quarter of the eighteenth century, the integrity of this group was being threatened by various forms of modernism, including, for example, an increasing use in German society of the vernacular at the expense of Latin. For obvious reasons, the professors ultimately responsible for the Latin core of the traditional university curriculum felt especially threatened and responded defensively by making themselves over into thoroughgoing professionals, with a specialized discipline of their own, which "rapidly became the 'cult of method'" (Turner 1983, 460). And at Göttingen, as we already know, the method came to feature source criticism. (Turner does not provide any details of the method, and so never mentions source criticism.)

Perhaps, however, this is not the whole story; perhaps what we have here is a case of *overdetermination*: that is, a dynamic internal to the traditional discipline of classics was operating concomitantly with, but independently of, the need to relieve status anxieties among the classical scholars. That dynamic could have been a function of the unresolved problems faced by classical scholars—problems which perhaps began to look more and more unresolvable within the traditional methodological framework for studying the ancient world. And, after all, other historians' disciplines likewise faced internal crisis: we have noted how Schlözer radically revised the history of medieval Russia with his new methods for editing texts. Schlözer's questions—"Where does our knowledge come from, and how has it reached us?"—could obviously be raised also in the ancient context; indeed, he fully expected that "ancient world-history would require complete revision if the sources for the history of Egypt, Persia, etc., were completed, assembled and subjected to critical treatment" (Butterfield 1960, 58 n. 5).

We have already mentioned that Bernal charges the new discipline of classics with having been politically conservative: "its effect was to shore up the *status quo*. The educational institutions and the Classical *Bildung* that infused them became pillars of 19th-century Prussian and German social order" (*BA* 1:282). But the gap here between the educational curriculum on the one hand and the social order on the other would have to be bridged with some persuasive mediating hypotheses before Bernal's claim could be evaluated, much less accepted—unless, of course, it is taken as axiomatic that education *always* tends to support the regnant social order (which would reduce Bernal's claim to an unexciting tautology). In any case, the narrow and fixed ideological focus in *Black Athena* may tend to obscure more subtle—but still, broadly, political—effects of the struggle to achieve a new professional identity on the part of eighteenth-century German academics; and, given the sorry state of most German universities throughout the eighteenth century, it *was* a struggle.

At this point we may recall Butterfield's emphasis on the revolutionary character of the new history. Without getting hung up on the vague notion of an intellectual revolution, we may be tempted to speculate about the possible political effects of this renovated discipline on the various people who conceived, taught, learned, and financed it. It is of considerable interest, then, that a recent study by Konrad Jarausch concludes that the new history was actually disruptive (if hardly revolutionary) in various ways:[74]

> Some of the critical and emancipatory thrust of *Aufklärung* history derived from the professional frustrations of historians trying to escape the tutelage of clerics or lawyers. As part of the rising *Bildungsbürgertum* professors challenged the birth prerogatives of the nobility with a new code, based on personal merit. Much of the encyclopedic breadth of cultural, social and economic history stemmed from a bourgeois rejection of the court or diplomacy and from the ill-defined boundaries of a potentially all-encompassing discipline. (1986, 47)

As I see it, three different species of emancipation—or empowerment—of the history professoriate are being alluded to here: professional (enhanced status vis-à-vis the law and theological faculties), social (increased independence vis-à-vis the upper-class student body), and disciplinary (freedom to ignore the political and diplomatic framework of traditional history with its frequent church and state patronage).

Looking ahead into nineteenth-century Germany, we find that academic historians solidified their position; there was a "gradual reversal of roles from history as handmaiden of theology and law to historical thinking as a dominant form of humanistic and legal scholarship" (Jarausch 1986, 48). Also, during the nineteenth century the role of academic historians was no longer defined solely in terms of their mission of educating an elite student body—quite different from the past, when, "attracting a noble and wealthy clientele, the universities were still primarily centers of professional training for officials and of liberal education for the *Gebildete* rather than generators of original research" (46). Finally, however, as far as the scope of academic history was concerned, the nineteenth century witnessed a retreat to narrowly political subject matter, albeit using the new Rankean historicist approach; and this, for Jarausch, raises the question of "the connection between the triumph of historicism and the loss of the emancipatory, comprehensive (i.e. cultural, social and economic) as well as statistical thrust of history" (48). This leads him to warn that "should the institutionalization of the discipline inevitably require such a deepening but narrowing of method, methodology and ideology, it might be too high a price to pay" (48). Here one may even venture a generalization to the effect that emancipation considered as a historical process is sometimes a mixed blessing—which is never a sufficient reason to oppose emancipation, but only a reason to think harder about its historical character. We need more case studies like Jarausch's modest yet illuminating effort, to help us deal in intellectually—and also politically—satisfying ways with the place of historical disciplines such as classics in Western and in world history.

APPENDIX 1: DIDEROT'S "PHILOSOPHY OF THE EGYPTIANS"

"Generally speaking," Diderot begins, "the history of Egypt is a chaos in which chronology, religion, and philosophy are especially fraught with obscurity and confusion."[75] For our purposes, what needs emphasis is Diderot's open denigration of the wisdom of the Egyptian priests (and hence of the cultural achievements of the Egyptians). Right at the start, he remarks that "the reputation of [the priests'] so-called wisdom became all the greater the more it was seasoned with mystery," and he contends that "trickery was the origin of their ancient fame." Indeed, "people came to Egypt from all over the world to seek wisdom," including "Moses, Orpheus, Linus, Plato, Pythagoras, Democritus, Thales, in short, all the Greek philosophers." But far from learning from the priests, it was the priests who learned from the philosophers: "These philosophers depended on the authority of the hierophants to legitimate their own systems. As for the hierophants, they claimed for themselves the discoveries of the philosophers. That is how those doctrines which divided the different Greek sects came to find their places successively in Egyptian schools."

Later in his essay Diderot tells us that the priests "spent their leisure in the study of arithmetic, geometry, and experimental physics"; but he seems uncertain as to just how far they had progressed in those subjects. Thus, for example, in astronomy he leaves it open whether Thales invented his method for predicting eclipses or learned it in Egypt, and he comments that the celestial observations of the Egyptians "owed their reputation only to the inaccuracy of those made everywhere else." Furthermore, "Pythagoras had long since ceased being [the priests'] disciple by the time he was engaged in investigating the relations between tonal intervals." As for Egyptian medicine, it was "a bundle of superstitious practices, highly convenient for mitigating the ineffectiveness of the remedies and the ignorance of the physicians. If the patient did not recover, it was because he had a bad conscience." What is reported about Egyptian chemistry is "scholarly nonsense; it has been proven that the issue of transmutation of metals was not raised before the reign of Constantine." Finally, "it cannot be denied that [the Egyptians] practiced judicial astrology for many years; but shall we respect them any the more for that?"

We are not, of course, concerned here with the accuracy of any of Diderot's observations. His chronology is a jumble throughout, and he had no access to genuine ancient Egyptian texts—which he must have fully realized, for he tells us that most writings on Egyptian antiquities perished in the burning of the Alexandrian library and that "what is left is apocryphal, with the exception of a few fragments quoted in other works." His *attitude*, however, is clear enough: he is skeptical of Egyptian intellectual achievements and utterly contemptuous of the Egyptian religion, which he deems saddled with a great mass of imported superstitions: "there was no persecuted god on the face of the earth who would not find a refuge in an Egyptian temple." Diderot was no Egyptophile.

APPENDIX 2: TWO NOTES ON BERNAL'S METHODOLOGY

Ideology and Scholarship: Some Pictures on a Greek Vase

It is a most unfortunate characteristic of Bernal's approach to scholarly debate that he sees disagreement so frequently as *blatantly* driven by political ideology. It is not the claim of a pervasive role of such ideology in scholarship that I deplore (that is something I am quite prepared to entertain); it is rather the way in which he seemingly always hits on the most obvious, least subtle, ideological—usually racist—interpretations of his opponent's views. Consider his objection to descriptions by John Boardman (1980, 149–51, 205) and Frank Snowden, Jr. (1976, 139–40) of one of the paintings on a remarkable black figure Greek vase (of the type called a hydria) from Caere in

Etruria, dating from 510–500 B.C.E., now in the Kunsthistorisches Museum in Vienna.[76] There are three scenes painted on the vase, two relating to the legend of Heracles and the Egyptian king Busiris. On one side of the vase we see Busiris' bodyguard; on the other, Heracles routing Busiris and his retainers. The five members of the bodyguard are obviously black, and both Boardman and Snowden mention this. Where Bernal faults Boardman and Snowden is in their failure to "mention the fact that the 'Greek hero Herakles' is depicted as a curly-haired African Black!" He adds, "This is something that the Aryan Model is completely unable to handle. For reasons Herakles should have been seen in this way, see vol. 3" (*BA* 1:477 n. 81). (*BA* 3 has not yet been published, as of this writing.) He is clearly implying that Boardman and Snowden have been influenced, wittingly or not, by the (racist) Aryan Model. Such a charge should never be lightly made, particularly by someone who lacks expertise in the subject matter under consideration. But, as usual, Bernal has no qualms about taxing those whom he takes to be establishment scholars with inadvertent, if not deliberate, prejudice.

His criticism of Boardman and Snowden is in fact totally misconceived. Indeed, owing perhaps to his own ideological preoccupations, he has seriously misinterpreted the image of Heracles on the Vienna Busiris vase. To begin with, it must be noted that the vase painting is polychromatic, with red, yellow, and white over the usual black glaze. Most importantly, Heracles' skin was originally painted red, although the paint has flaked off in places, showing patches of background black. (The flaking is apparent in Snowden's and Hemelrijk's illustrations but not in Boardman's; illustrations in all three books are in black and white.)[77] As for Heracles' curly hair (which, together with his beard, is black), it is not an unusual style for Greeks on Attic vases of the period (Hemelrijk 1984, text p. 214 n. 280), which means that any similarity between the hairstyle of Heracles and that of the five bodyguards need not imply that Heracles is an African black. It is also of interest that another depiction of Heracles on a Caeretan hydria of the same period (Louvre Nessus; Hemelrijk's no. 17) shows the hero with black skin and curly—but red!—hair. The painter of no. 17—the so-called Eagle Painter—is believed to have been a close colleague of the Busiris painter; they shared a workshop, and a certain quirkiness is evident in their work (as in the whimsical coloring of Heracles).

I trust we shall hear no more of the Vienna Busiris Heracles in subsequent volumes of Bernal's *Black Athena* (except, one hopes, for an apology to Boardman and Snowden).

Suppressio Veri: Egyptology in the Early Nineteenth Century

One of the more disturbing features of Bernal's historical studies is his all too frequent failure to mention crucial facts whose existence would be embarrassing or inconvenient for him to acknowledge. Here are some examples from his version of the history of Egyptology in the first half of the nineteenth century.

Whatever might have been the case in the first half of the eighteenth century, there is clear evidence of an infatuation with Egypt in Paris during the first few decades of the nineteenth century. This occurred, of course, in the wake of Napoleon's expedition of 1798, which led to (among other things) two important French publications: the popular travel book of Vivant Denon (who had been a member of Napoleon's expedition) and the scholarly presentation of Egyptian antiquities commissioned by Napoleon himself. Denon's *Travels in Upper and Lower Egypt* was first published in 1802, reprinted many times, and translated into English and German. The collectively authored *Description of Egypt* was published between 1809 and 1822 in nine text volumes and eleven volumes of illustrations. (The illustrations—some three thousand in all—have recently been published in a single massive volume [Néret 1994] with a high standard of reproduction despite the vast reduction in size from the original folio.) A recent account of the influence of these two publications runs as follows:

> It is hard to imagine today the feverish excitement prompted by the dual publication of Denon's work and . . . the *Description of Egypt*. . . . Egypt became fashionable literally overnight. Between 1802 and 1830 a dozen travelers of note came from France, England, Germany, and Switzerland to see for themselves the wonders revealed by the *Journey* and the *Description*, and the accounts and drawings they brought back from their travels . . . helped to maintain the momentum of Egypt's growing popularity. (Vercoutter 1992, 54)

Bernal ignores both of these landmark publications in his study of the development of Egyptology in the early nineteenth century. He chooses instead to dwell on the figure of Jean-François Champollion—one of Bernal's heroes because of his "championing of Egypt over Greece" (*BA* 1:225) and because he argued, to the dismay of "the Christians and the Hellenists," that "the Egyptian calendar, and hence Egyptian civilization, went back to 3285 B.C." (1:253). Champollion, most famous today as the first really successful decipherer of Egyptian hieroglyphics, died in 1832 (at the early age of forty-one); Bernal believes that, as a result, "Egyptology went into recession for a quarter of a century, while his Hellenist and Orientalist enemies went on to dominate the French Academic Establishment" (1:253). Furthermore, "this absence of any serious consideration of Egyptology between 1831 and 1860" was accompanied by the decline of the Ancient Model and the triumph of the Aryan Model (1:253).

Here Bernal assumes that serious Egyptology requires a comprehension

of hieroglyphics. It is certainly true that without the ability to interpret written texts Egyptology was severely impoverished. Nevertheless, on the one
hand, by any reasonable criterion, Egyptology was *flourishing* in France—as
well as in England and Germany—during the period in question; and, on the
other hand, there were some valid scholarly—rather than, as Bernal would
have it, merely ideological—reasons for the initial neglect of Champollion's
great achievement. Some of the evidence for these two propositions can be
sketched as follows.

After twelve years of exploration in Egypt and making hardly any use
of Champollion's decipherment of Egyptian hieroglyphics, John Gardner
Wilkinson (1797–1875)—usually regarded as the founder of Egyptology in
England—"through his reproductions of many Egyptian paintings . . .
succeeded in presenting a huge amount of detailed information about the
civilization, culture, and religion of the ancient Egyptians . . . his *Manners
and Customs of the Ancient Egyptians* [1837] remained the best account of Egyptian civilization until late in the nineteenth century" (Wortham 1971, 64–65).
Consider next the German Egyptologist Karl Richard Lepsius (1810–84),
who studied in Paris in 1833, attending lectures by Jean-Antoine Letronne—
one of Bernal's "Hellenist" villains (*BA* 1:253)—and learning to decipher
hieroglyphics from Champollion's posthumous writings. (Bernal might have
mentioned that Champollion's greatest work, *Monuments of Egypt and Nubia*,
was only published in 1845.) In 1842–45 Lepsius led an expedition to Egypt,
the fruits of which were published in the twelve volumes of his *Discoveries
in Egypt and Ethiopia* (1849–59), which "continues to be a standard reference
work for Egyptologists today" (Vercoutter 1992, 96). And, in 1851, just two
decades after Champollion's death, the French Egyptologist Auguste Mariette (1821–81) excavated the underground burial chambers of the Apis bulls,
the so-called Memphis Serapeum; this "remains one of the great discoveries
of Egyptology" (Vercoutter, 104). Mariette was also responsible for establishing the Egyptian Antiquities Service and he was its director from 1858
until 1881. Through this agency the Egyptian government was able to begin
exercising control over commercial exploitation (and, only too often, con-
comitant destruction) of Egyptian antiquities. (Bernal refers to Mariette only
as the author of the plot of Verdi's *Aida* [*BA* 1:269].)

As for the reception of Champollion's work on hieroglyphics, it must be
understood that decipherment of an entire writing system is never an all-or-
nothing affair (like decoding a single message); other linguists had to correct
and supplement Champollion's findings. One of his major mistakes was to
assume that every phonetic hieroglyph was uniconsonantal, that is, that it
represented just a single consonantal sound, such as *m* or *t*. (There are no
vowel sounds in early Egyptian written languages.) As a result, the number
of homophones (different signs with the same sound) that Champollion dis-

covered multiplied alarmingly.[78] This mistake, incidentally, was corrected by the aforementioned Karl Lepsius, thereby removing "the principal stumbling block which prevented the general acceptance and propagation of [Champollion's] system" (Iversen 1993, 144). Also, Champollion mistakenly assumed that the language of the inscriptions was essentially identical with Coptic, the latest form of the Egyptian language (Iversen, 144). Finally, the immediate fruits of hieroglyphic decipherment in terms of enlarged understanding of Egyptian civilization were not very great, and this too discouraged some Egyptologists.[79]

Bernal may not like the direction Egyptology was taking or the ideological convictions of some of its practitioners during the second third of the nineteenth century. But he is not entitled to distort the history of a scholarly discipline for his own political purposes.

APPENDIX 3: BLUMENBACH ON RACE

Blumenbach recognized that, before unfolding his classificatory racial scheme, he must first prove that all human beings belong to the same species. Having rejected the criterion of hybrid fertility (which others, including Kant, had used) for defining species, he proposed to rely on morphological and physiological attributes. But this would only work when the attributes with respect to which the putative members of a species differ from one another could be shown to possess a genealogical connection. This connection he designated "degeneration" (*Entartung*), a process whereby an attribute can change in degree and in response to changes in the surrounding physical and cultural environment (including changes in climate, diet, and mode of life). What degeneration amounts to is an alteration in the unique "formative force" (*Bildungstrieb*) characteristic of each species. Blumenbach thought that these formative forces were analogous to Newtonian forces, and he believed that like the latter, they did not violate the tenets of empiricism. In the first instance, at least, degeneration would seem to possess no necessarily moral or psychological overtones. Using the notion of degeneration, then, Blumenbach formulated his criterion for species-membership:

> We say that animals belong to one and the same species, if they agree so well in form and constitution, that those things in which they do [essentially?] differ may have arisen from degeneration [*Entartung*]. We say that those, on the other hand, are of different species, whose essential difference is such as cannot be explained by the known sources of degeneration, if I may be allowed to use such a word. (*De Generis Humani Varietate Nativa*, [1795] 1865, 188)

But the criterion, as stated, seems—illegitimately—to presuppose a grasp of "essential [= specific] differences," which, if already known, would obviate any need for the criterion. In any case, his real proof for the unity of the human species is that practically any attribute of a group of putative human beings can always be found, in varying degrees, in all other such groups. In his own words, "no variety [of mankind] exists, whether of colour, countenance, or stature, &c., so singular as not to be connected with others of the same kind by such an imperceptible transition, that it is very clear they are all related, or only differ from each other in degree" (264). But this more or less continuous distribution of human attributes seems to have as a consequence that racial classifications cannot really capture anything essential about human beings (though, of course, Blumenbach does not draw this conclusion).[80] Indeed he tries hard to persuade us (and, one suspects, himself) that his racial criteria are objective, by the following argument:

> As, however, even among these arbitrary kinds of divisions, one is said to be better and preferable to another; after a long and attentive consideration, all mankind, as far as it is at present known to us, seems to me as if it may best, according to natural truth, be divided into the five following varieties. . . . (264)

Blumenbach's language (here, admittedly, in English translation) seems to betray the underlying ambivalence in his thinking about race: what the surfeit of qualifications and the tortuous syntax unwittingly convey is the embarrassing subjectivity of his chosen criteria. Let us consider his line of thought.

First, he cites what he calls "a cloud of eyewitnesses" who unanimously testify to the surpassing "beauty" of the inhabitants of the southern slopes of Mount Caucasus in Georgia. This leads him to single out the skull configuration of those people as superlatively beautiful and to classify all other human skulls in terms of how far they depart from the norm so defined. (But just five years before, it will be recalled—from discussion in the main part of this essay, above—Kant, in his *Critique of Judgment* [1790], had pointed to the subjectivity of ideals of beauty; and Blumenbach must have known the passage, for he cites the book in other contexts [see Lenoir 1980, 89].) Next Blumenbach selects two other skull configurations, which "diverge by most easy gradations on both sides to the two ultimate extremes (that is, on one side the Mongolian, on the other the Ethiopian)" (269).[81] For no very compelling reason (as he recognizes), he adds two more skull configurations to mediate, so to speak, between the Caucasian and Mongolian on one side (the American) and the Caucasian and Ethiopian on the other (the Malay). Finally, he addresses the question how these different skull configurations are related genealogically—that is, by the process of degeneration—and here he argues that "it is very easy for [white] to degenerate into brown, but very much more difficult for dark to become white, when the secretion and precipitation of this carbonaceous pigment has once deeply struck root" (269).

It follows from Blumenbach's theory that Mongolians and Ethiopians have degenerated farthest from the human norm. The norm itself sometimes seems to be simply a matter of temporal priority; at other times the priority is aesthetic, but never moral or intellectual. Blumenbach's attitude toward the five races is reflected in his choices of exemplary individual portraits: each of the five faces—all are male—positively glows with vigor and intelligence.[82]

NOTES

1. On Babylonian mathematics and astronomy see Neugebauer 1957. On Chinese technology see Needham, Ling, et al. 1965, 4, part 2: "Mechanical Engineering." On Arabic technology see al-Hassan and Hill 1986; Hill 1991. For Chinese and Arabic influence on Western technology see L. White 1962. On Benin art see Dark 1973, as well as Ezra 1992, the catalogue of a major exhibition of Benin art at the Metropolitan Museum of Art in New York City. On Benin technology see Garrard 1983. The high status of Benin art has been validated not only by the application to it of traditional art-historical methods but also by the crucial test of auction prices: according to a story in the *New York Times* (26 January 1992, 2:33) a sixteenth-century Benin brass head of a king was sold at auction at Christie's in London for $2.08 million.

2. For my attempt to formulate a balanced assessment of ancient Egyptian science, see my essay "*Black Athena*, Afrocentrism, and the History of Science," also in this volume.

3. One notable exception is Frank M. Turner's (1989) critique of Bernal's treatment of the nineteenth-century historiography of classical scholarship; see also Bernal's response (1989b).

4. Haley finds congenial Bernal's challenge to what she takes to be the very foundations of her discipline, but apparently she has no doubts about his competence as a historian of modern Europe.

5. One writer (see Stevens 1993, 14) has even coined a phrase, "the Martin Bernal syndrome," for what he sees as the tendency, in African studies, to privilege ancient Egypt.

6. See Montfaucon 1719–24, his ten-volume archaeological survey of ancient Egypt. According to J. S. Curl, Montfaucon "rejected the far-fetched interpretations of hieroglyphs, despised the admiration of 'Egyptian wisdom,' and denounced Egyptian religion and art as monstrous. Here was the mind of the Enlightenment at work: sober, discriminating, rational, unemotive, and sceptical" (1982, 69). Directly contrary to Bernal's view, we shall encounter, as we proceed, many more examples of this rejection of Egyptophilia by eighteenth-century Enlightenment thinkers. Bernal, incidentally, lists Curl's book in his bibliography (*BA* 1) but never refers to it in his text. A new edition of Curl's book, by the way, contains the same remarks about Montfaucon's attitude toward Egypt, with some small verbal changes (1994, 79).

7. See Haley 1993, 28–30. For a recent account of the oral tradition to which Haley is appealing see P. A. Turner 1993. Mary Hamer's studies of varying interpretations of the Cleopatra myth in Western culture (1993) do not include Black Cleopatra.

8. Cited in Gay 1966, 77 n. 3. Gay, incidentally, holds that "the philosophes paraded their admiration for Greece" in explicit opposition to many seventeenth-century Egyptophiles (78). But this does not mean that the philosophes were Egyptophobes; for they "balanced the cultural and scientific inventions which they ascribed to the Egyptians and Phoenicians against the beliefs, practices, and possibilities of these civilizations as a whole, and these were always markedly inferior to Greek thought and action" (79). As we shall see, however, neither Diderot nor Voltaire was particularly impressed by Egyptian science.

9. See Diderot and D'Alembert 1755, 434–38. On the authorship of the encyclopedia entry see A. M. Wilson 1972, 168.

10. Cf. Kirk, Raven, and Schofield 1983, 220: "metempsychosis, unlike metamorphosis into animal forms, is not attested in Egyptian documents or art: Herodotus frequently posits Egyptian origins for thoroughly Greek ideas and practices."

11. On the question of Egyptian monotheism see a book that Bernal cites, Hornung [1971] 1982: "The attempt to see in Egyptian conceptions of god precursors of monotheistic belief has the character of an apologia and leads us away from [the] reality [of the gods]" (252).

12. In Manuel's words, "Astronomic and sexual symbolism were always supplementary, not contradictory, forms" (1959, 267).

13. This passage from Dupuis's book may be conveniently studied in an English version in Feldman and Richardson 1972, 282–85.

14. Bailey 1985, 82. It may be recalled that Egypt was part of the Ottoman Empire at that time.

15. See Rousseau and Porter 1990, which has essays on India, China, Tahiti, and North America but none on Egypt. For a discussion of the presence of Egyptian elements in eighteenth-century European art, architecture, and design see Curl 1994, chapters 4 and 5.

16. On Egyptian revivals see Carrott 1978; Curl 1982, 1994; Conner 1983; Bloemink 1990; Lant 1992; and, most recently, the catalogue of a monumental exhibition in Paris, Ottawa, and Vienna: Humbert et al. 1994.

17. The relation between Egyptian and Greek astronomy and mathematics (and medicine) I have discussed in "*Black Athena*, Afrocentrism, and the History of Science," this volume. In a personal communication, Mary Lefkowitz writes to me that Terrasson never claimed to be "demonstrating" anything, and, moreover, that "Terrasson noted that certain details in his narrative were drawn from classical sources, but he makes it quite clear that the rest of his narrative is fictional." (See also Lefkowitz 1994.)

18. See Bliss 1969, 51: "*Busiris*, well received on its first appearance, played for nine nights, gave Young three benefits, and was considered a success. It was played once in 1722, and at least once in later years. Its success was more immediate than lasting."

19. For titles of their plays see Dobrée 1959, under Individual Authors in his bibliography.

20. See Feldman and Richardson 1972, 241. It is perhaps worth noting that even such an intrepid intellectual historian as Frank Manuel despairs of comprehending Bryant's "system," which Manuel characterizes as "an eclectic potpourri based on borrowings from French contemporaries, impossible of analysis" (1959, 274–75). Northrop Frye puts it perhaps even more strongly when he refers to Bryant's work as a "mausoleum of misinformation and bad etymology" (1969, 173). Bernal cites Frye in connection with his own claim that Bryant's book "was a major source . . . for the Romantic poets and above all for Blake" (*BA* 1:172), but Frye actually says something rather different, namely, that although Bryant's book "is referred to by Blake as authority for his 'All Religions are One' thesis . . . the present writer has read [Bryant's book] with sufficient care to hazard the guess that Blake had not" (1969, 173). On the other hand, some Blake scholars now believe that Blake may have designed and engraved a vignette in Bryant's book and that, conversely, Blake may have been influenced by other illustrations in Bryant's book; see Damon 1988, 61. About Bryant and Blake, Damon comments: "Blake doubtless liked Bryant's contempt for the Greeks, and would have disliked his ignoring of the Druids. He followed Bryant in a few points" (61).

21. The passage is Craddock's translation from Gibbon's French travel journal; for the French see Craddock 1982, 346 n. 16.

22. Ironically, in David Brion Davis's words, "William Mitford's multivolume *History of Greece* attributed the evils of Athenian slavery to excessive democracy" (1984, 112).

23. A fuller exposition of his ideas is in Gascoigne 1991.

24. Where there are two dates, the first is that of composition and the second that of publication. Of the thirteen names, only two — Burnet and Warburton — appear in *BA* 1.

25. See Monboddo 1774–92, vol. 1, book 4, chapter 13; vol. 4, book 1, chapter 4.

26. See Manuel 1963, 98, quoting Newton's *Chronology of Ancient Kingdoms Amended*, " '. . . the original of letters, agriculture, navigation, music, arts and sciences, metals, smiths, and carpenters, towns and houses, was not older in Europe than the days of Eli, Samuel, and David' "; and 1963, 119, quoting a Newton manuscript, " '. . . the Egyptians were learned before the days of Moses.' "

27. For a recent expression of this view see Cameron and Long 1993, 254: "Greek ambivalence about Egypt stretches back to the classical period."

28. Cf. S. P. Morris 1992, xxii: "this book [*Daidalos and the Origins of Greek Art*] demonstrates how Bernal's 'Aryan model' began in the fifth century [B.C.E.], after the Persian wars, and not in modern Europe."

29. Gordon also notes a specific denial of the Ancient Model by the influential third-century C.E. writer Diogenes Laertius, in his *Lives of the Eminent Philosophers*.

30. Cameron and Long 1993, 255 n. 6, recommend J. E. B. Mayor's commentary on Juvenal 15 (1881, 355–400) for extensive citations of passages from classical authors hostile to Egypt.

31. Sextus Empiricus *Outlines of Pyrrhonism* 3.201, 202, 205. I found this reference in Geffcken 1907, x; Cameron and Long (1993, 255 n. 6) cite Geffcken pp. ix–xi for

a survey of "contradictory Greek and Roman attitudes to Egyptian civilization and religion."

32. Bernal is insufficiently attentive to the growing tendency during the first half of the nineteenth century to single out characteristics other than skin color for the classification of races (and for the corresponding brand of racism). This historical point is discussed for Britain in Curtin 1964 (a book listed in the bibliography of *BA* 1), chapter 15: head shape and language were two of the favorite substitutes for skin color.

33. Bernal remarks that "with the huge increase of pictorial representations of Ancient Egyptians available to Europeans during the first half of the 19th century, which showed them to have been a thoroughly mixed population, the Egyptians tended to be seen as increasingly African and black" (*BA* 1:245). Basil Davidson, on the other hand, in the course of a highly laudatory essay on *BA* 1, seems to contradict Bernal: "That the ancient Egyptians were black (again, in any variant you may prefer)—or, as I myself think it more useful to say, were African—is a belief which has been denied in Europe since about 1830, not before" (1994, 319). Neither Bernal nor Davidson provides any significant documentation for these observations.

34. See Palter, "*Black Athena*, Afrocentrism, and the History of Science," this volume (on Newton and Egypt). Part of Bernal's evidence for Newton's Egyptophilia is a passage in a draft for the *Principia*, which went unpublished until 1728, when it was included in Newton's *System of the World*. Bernal quotes a long excerpt from this passage, including the assertion that " 'the Egyptians were the earliest observers of the heavens and from them, probably, this philosophy was spread abroad' " (*BA* 1:167). It is worth noting that later in the passage Newton remarks that "the Chaldeans [were] the most learned astronomers of their time" (Newton 1947, 550). In his concern with the "ancient wisdom" Newton was never as fixated on Egypt as Bernal would have us believe. For a skeptical—but, I think, persuasive—view of the (thoroughly limited) role of the ancient wisdom in Newton's scientific thought see Casini 1984. Casini's is the first publication to reproduce Newton's fullest set of allusions to the ancient wisdom—the so-called classical scholia—in their entirety.

35. For a recent critique of both sides in the debate, by a self-styled "proletarian intellectual," see Allen 1994, 1: Introduction.

36. One of the leading historians of African slavery, Paul Lovejoy, puts it as follows: "It is perhaps common sense, however often overlooked, that the African slaves who were brought from Africa were slaves before they left Africa. The scholarship of the last twenty years has demonstrated that the variety and intensity of servile relationships and methods of oppression that can be equated with slavery were probably more developed in Africa than anywhere else in the world at any period in history. Furthermore, there were probably more slaves in Africa in the nineteenth century than there were in the Americas at any time" (1991, 7). For a recent summary of research—and of the attendant deep controversies—on the history of African slavery, see Feierman 1993, 187–97.

37. The alleged racism in Locke's *Essay Concerning Human Understanding* occurs in just two places (book 2, chapter 25, section 1, and book 4, chapter 7, section 16),

which, I believe, have been misunderstood by some recent critics; for an effective response to those who find racist attitudes in these two passages see Squadrito 1979. Hume expresses racist beliefs in his essay "Of National Characters" (1748, 1753, 1777) and attacks slavery in his essay "Of the Populousness of Ancient Nations" (1752); for a detailed discussion see Palter 1995.

38. E.g., William B. Cohen writes: "in regard to blacks the tradition of racial inequality was dominant in French history" (1980, x); and Seymour Drescher (1992, 373–88) explains how "scientific" racism was more blatant in France than in Britain during the late eighteenth and early nineteenth centuries and how Britain even imported some of its racist ideas from France.

39. Cf. the concluding chapter in Davis 1966, "The Changing Image of the Negro": "We . . . know . . . that by the 1770s antislavery writers as diverse as Raynal and Wesley were able to exploit a whole range of themes and conventions which portrayed the Negro slave as a man of natural virtue and sensitivity who was at once oppressed by the worst vices of civilization and yet capable of receiving its greatest benefits" (482).

40. On the material and ideological factors, see T. L. Haskell 1985; and the "Forum" in *American Historical Review* 1987, with contributions by David Brion Davis, John Ashworth, and Haskell. The entire symposium, together with two new essays by Ashworth and Davis, is reprinted in Bender 1992.

41. As Robin Blackburn puts it: "socio-economic forces and the discourses of ideology are so inherently antagonistic and contradictory that they open up a space of political choice and action which must also be registered if the dynamic of historical development is to be grasped" (1988, 28–29.)

42. See Bate 1975, 325–27, and (for a picture of Barber) illustration 20; there is also a short biography of Barber in Fryer 1984, 424–26.

43. Behn [1688] 1973, 8. The novel was also reprinted earlier in an Everyman's Library edition: *Shorter Novels*, vol. 2, *Jacobean and Restoration* (London 1930).

44. For one of many recent discussions of this question see Rosenthal 1992. About Behn's novel, Rosenthal concludes that "if we cannot praise *Oroonoko* for being an abolitionist text, we can appreciate its critique of colonialism and resistance to *some* colonialist stereotypes of African sexuality, as well as its representation— however ethnocentric—of an Africa with a culture prior to and independent of the British slave trade" (36); "Southerne's play, on the other hand, indulges the audience's fascination with miscegenation" (46).

45. The passage is quoted by Davis (1966, 440) with a key phrase, "in this respect," elided, thereby seriously altering the meaning.

46. Cf. his unwarranted perception of racist (Aryan Model) failings in two distinguished contemporary scholars, discussed at some length in Appendix 2 below.

47. In his early life Franklin not only owned but even sold slaves; later he acted to free his own and one of his friends' slaves, and he became active in the antislavery movement; see Van Horne 1993, 433–437.

48. Finkelman's hard-hitting indictment of Jefferson (which fails even to mention the letter to Grégoire) should be read along with Gordon S. Wood's balanced assessment, containing these summary words: "The human Jefferson was essentially a

man of the eighteenth century, a very intelligent and bookish slaveholding southern planter, enlightened and progressive no doubt, but possessing as many weaknesses as strengths, as much folly as wisdom, as much blindness as foresight. . . . It is the ultimate irony of Jefferson's life, a life filled with ironies, that he should not have understood the democratic revolution that he himself supremely spoke for" (1993, 401).

49. For a list of some of them in America see Aptheker 1992, 19: "Before the close of the eighteenth century . . . the specific denial of inferiority and denunciation of racial prejudice came from a long list of outstanding figures, among whom may be named the Reverend Samuel Davies (speaking shortly before he became president of the College of New Jersey, that is, Princeton), James Otis, Benjamin Franklin, John Jay, Benjamin Rush, Alexander Hamilton, John Wesley, James McHenry, Samuel Hopkins, Nathaniel Appleton, William Pinkney, Robert Pleasants, Moses Brown, and Jeremy Belknap—hardly obscure or marginal figures in the history of the United States."

50. The essay was originally published in 1748; the sentence quoted here comes from the final version of the essay, published in 1777. An earlier version of the footnote read as follows: "I am apt to suspect the negroes, and in general all the other species of men (for there are four or five different kinds) to be naturally inferior to the whites" (see Hume 1987, 629).

51. For the German text of that essay see Kant [1785] 1912–22, 4:223–40.

52. In his recent book *(Dis)Forming the American Canon: African-Arabic Slave Narratives and the Vernacular* (1993), Ronald A. T. Judy attempts to use the framework of Kant's critical philosophy to analyze the meaning of Kant's remarks about Negroes in his (pre-critical) *Observations of the Feeling of the Beautiful and the Sublime* (1764). Surprisingly, Judy finds no time, during his prolonged analysis (1993, 106–46), to address the remark about the Negro ideal of beauty cited here from Kant's *Critique of Judgment*.

53. The recent abridgement of an English version of this work by Frank Manuel (1968) omits this passage.

54. Gilman further comments that "Herder specifically condemned the destruction of Black society through the slave trade" (1982, 31). On the other hand, Richard Popkin cites a passage in which Herder refers contemptuously to African languages: "the slothful African stammers brokenly and droopingly" (1973, 256 n. 9). The essay from which that comment is drawn was Herder's first published philosophical work, "Über den Fleiss in mehreren gelehrten Sprachen" (1764), translated as "On Diligence in the Study of Several Learned Languages" in Menze and Menges 1992. Herder's tone is rather different twenty years later in his *Philosophy of the History of Man* (book 9, chapter 2): "can men be as distant from one another in the sphere of true and useful ideas, as proud speculation supposes? Both the history of nations, and the nature of reason and language, forbid me to think so. The poor savage, who has seen but very few things, and combined very few ideas, proceeds in combining them after the same manner as the first of philosophers. He has language like them; and by means of it exercises his understanding and memory, his imagination and recollection, a thousand ways. . . . Let us then adore kind Providence, for having rendered men

intrinsically more similar to each other, by the imperfect but general mean of language, than their exteriour indicates" ([1783–91] 1966, 236–37). But he still maintains (book 13, chapter 2) that Greek is "the most refined" language in the world, while German has "degenerated" from its earlier similarity to Greek (1966, 359).

55. For translated excerpts from Gedicke's report on Göttingen, see Forster and Forster 1969, 312–20.

56. In addition to Bernal's sources, I have consulted the following: R. S. Turner 1974; Reill 1975 (usefully reviewed by Liebel 1977); Blanke and Rüsen 1984; Bödeker et al. 1986.

57. For a list of some of the books, see the entry on Heumann in Michaud's *Biographie universelle*, 19:392–93.

58. After seeing Greece for the first time in 1806, Chateaubriand wrote to a friend: "Well, Monsieur, I have seen Greece! I visited Sparta, Argos, Mycenae, Corinth, Athens; beautiful names, alas! nothing more. . . . Never see Greece, Monsieur, except in Homer. It is the best way" (quoted in Augustinos 1994, 178). One thing that is shocking here is the implication that anything after Homer is inferior.

59. Two biographical memoirs of Blumenbach (by K. F. H. Marx and M.-J.-P. Flourens) may be found in the volume containing English versions of several of his writings on the diversity of human races (Blumenbach 1865). Both Marx and Flourens are excessively hagiographical but nevertheless provide some of the essential facts about Blumenbach's life and work. There is also a brief entry in the *Dictionary of Scientific Biography* (Gillispie 1970–), and a much longer one in Michaud's *Biographie universelle*. For an account of some of Blumenbach's main biological ideas see Lenoir 1980.

60. It is difficult to believe that Blumenbach took Meiners's racial theory seriously, for he devotes just three sentences to summarizing it (without comment): "Meiners refers all nations to two stocks: (1) handsome, (2) ugly; the first white, the latter dark. He includes in the handsome stock the Celts, Sarmatians [Poles], and oriental nations. The ugly stock embraces all the rest of mankind" (*De Generis Humani Varietate Nativa*, 3d ed., 1795, in Blumenbach 1865, 268. The entry on Meiners in Michaud (*Biographie universelle*, 27:534) states that Blumenbach "completely refutes" Meiners's theory (presumably by formulating a sounder theory).

61. See esp. two recent discussions of Blumenbach, Schiebinger 1993 and Bertoletti 1994.

62. For a brief introduction to Forster's life and thought see Saine 1972.

63. See Fiedler's commentary in Forster 1958–85 11:415. The author of the anonymous article has not been identified.

64. For a detailed analysis of Forster's problematic conception of human diversity see Barnouw 1993.

65. Dohm was, along with Lessing, among the few German thinkers of the time who attempted to promulgate an enlightened view of Jews, as opposed to the fierce anti-Semitism of orthodox Lutheranism; see Manuel 1992, 251.

66. For the German text see Forster 1958–85, 15:366. I am indebted for this reference to Barnouw 1993, 342 n. 28; she refers, however, to "a black nurse in the Göttingen hospital," whereas Forster mentions no hospital and his term *Amme* means

"wet-nurse." Forster clearly indicates that his wife has just given birth to a daughter (their second).

67. See Saine 1972, 174 n. 20: "There has always been some suspicion of a romantic attachment between Forster and Caroline, and some of the older writers who were partial to Therese even asserted that Caroline was a principal cause of the failure of Forster's marriage. This is hardly the case, whether or not there is anything to the idea that she was his mistress." Bernal's source is Schwab [1950] 1984, 59. Schwab gives no source at all, but he may have been overeager to enlist Caroline and Forster into the ranks of "the extraordinary couples created in Romantic Germany by the encounters between philology, philosophy, poetry, religion itself, and the love of women." Perhaps all that needs to be said here is that Schwab is being much more "Romantic" than Forster ever was.

68. Reill's *German Enlightenment and the Rise of Historicism* (1975) does not even include Meiners in the bibliography.

69. Meinecke [1936] 1972, 236–37. Meinecke's definition of "historism"—usually written "historicism"—is as follows: "the substitution of a process of *individualising* observation for a *generalising* view of human forces in history" (lv). Butterfield's suggestive way of characterizing Meinecke's enterprise is as an investigation of "the way in which the study of the past came to gain in depth through the development of the right imaginative approach—the cultivation of what we call historical-mindedness" (1960, 17).

70. Cf. Walter Burkert: "in default of other sources, there is nothing else to do than—with due caution—to follow Aristotle's hints" (Burkert [1962] 1972, 28).

71. Casini makes a closely related complaint against the claims of certain recent authors concerning Newton's attachment to the *prisca philosophia* (ancient wisdom): ". . . the 'readings' of Newton that do not square with the pre-selected image of the *prisca* are all alike sacrificed"; Casini proposes to base a more correct interpretation "on the letter—rather than the 'spirit'—of the classical Scholia" (1984, 3–4).

72. The passage is discussed by Horst Fiedler (in Forster 1958–85, 11:416) as an example of *Quellenkritik*.

73. Turner says he believes that his conclusions "have validity for Germany as a whole" (1983, 450 n. 1).

74. Jarausch's data includes the social origins of university students, the development of university chairs in history, and the topics of university lectures on history. It is also worth quoting his remark that "since research into the institutionalization of historical scholarship is only beginning, the present conclusions have to remain tentative" (46).

75. Diderot and d'Alembert 1755, 434–38. I am indebted to Marie-Claire Rohinsky (Modern Languages Department, Central Connecticut State University), who prepared a translation of Diderot's essay, from which, with some modification, I have quoted.

76. The standard work on Caeretan hydriae, containing a *catalogue raisonné* of all thirty-nine examples known at the time of publication, is Hemelrijk 1984; the vase in question is no. 34 (Vienna Busiris), text pp. 50–54 with plates 118–25. I am indebted to Martha Risser of the Classics Department, Trinity College, for helpful discussions.

77. See Hemelrijk 1984, text p. 54: "skin red, but the red has flaked off and has taken the underpaint with it (the red being streaky, I believe it to be on thin under-paint). The black of the beard and the moustache (and perhaps also of the hair) was painted over the red!" It has even been suggested that Heracles' red skin was supposed to signify vigor and good blood circulation. (204 n. 47). For a technical description of how red was painted on black-figure vases see Noble 1988, 137; a color reproduction of a Caeretan hydria depicting Heracles by the Eagle painter can be found in Noble's plate III.

78. There are, in fact, some twenty-six uniconsonantal signs, fewer than a hundred biconsonantal signs (e.g., *pr*), and between forty and fifty triconsonantal signs (e.g., *nfr*); see Davies 1989, 31–32.

79. Wortham puts it this way: "Several decades passed before hieroglyphic studies revealed any significant information about the history and literature of Egypt. This slow development proved very disappointing to many scholars" (1971, 55).

80. Bertoletti notes the ambivalence in Blumenbach's ideas on race to which I have referred but draws a different conclusion: "any attempt to define boundaries can only be arbitrary, and . . . he is well aware that this also applies to his own proposals for human racial classification. . . . What cannot be denied, however, is the undeniably nominalist and conventionalist nature of Blumenbach's thought" (1994, 117). It seems to me that Blumenbach does attempt to deny the nominalist and conventionalist character of his thought about race.

81. Schiebinger (1993, 152) suggests that Blumenbach was being unconventional in selecting female skulls for three of his five races (Caucasian, Ethiopian, and Malay) and adds that he mentions only the Caucasian specimen as being female. It is true that in the plate depicting the five skulls only the Caucasian is labeled "feminae," but in the descriptions of the plates the Ethiopian skull is said to be from a female African of Guinea. As for the Malay skull, it is described as an Otaheitan, with no mention of sex. I have not, however, had access to the text of Blumenbach's publication of a complete census of all his skulls, which appeared serially during the years 1790–1828.

82. For reproductions of the portraits see J. C. Greene 1961, 225, or Schiebinger 1993, 154–55.

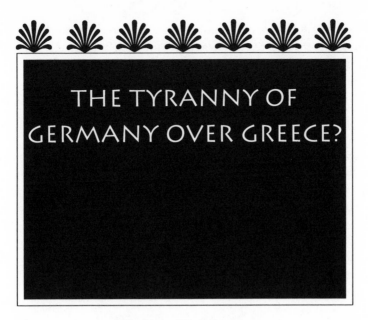

THE TYRANNY OF GERMANY OVER GREECE?

Robert E. Norton

One of the reasons, presumably, that the International Herder Society came into being in 1985 was to celebrate its namesake by promoting the study and serious discussion of Herder's thought and of the context in which he lived and worked. The group of scholars that has devoted itself to this pursuit is diverse, but if there is one shared belief that unites them it is the conviction that Herder was a committed champion of a liberal, pluralistic conception of humanity; that he was an early advocate of the idea that every cultural entity and every historical era possessed its own inviolate dignity and worth; and that he insisted that his readers, as Western-European observers, may try to understand the past sympathetically, but that in the end they cannot— or rather *should* not—judge it at all because they were inevitably biased by their own culturally determined preconceptions. These appear to be laudable, even strikingly modern, principles to which many of us, especially today, would readily subscribe. And indeed they have provided something like the ideological creed that has given the Herder Society its nominal unity.

But outside of the still relatively narrow compass of that organization, Herder often appears in a much less favorable light which shows him to be diametrically opposite to the figure I have just described. A recent example of this kind of perception can be found in a book by Paul Rose, entitled *Revolutionary Antisemitism in Germany from Kant to Wagner* (1990). Rose argues that, contrary to what he calls the "myth of Herder as a liberal pluralist," Herder was in fact one of the main, though previously misapprehended, agents in the formation of the virulent German anti-Semitism that ultimately led to the gas chambers of Auschwitz.[1] Another work that recently appeared leveled a similar accusation at Herder (and other of his contemporaries): the first volume of Martin Bernal's *Black Athena: The Afroasiatic Roots of Classical Civilization* (1987). The title is deliberately provocative, and its subtitle is even more explicit: *The Fabrication of Ancient Greece*.

The book—as this present collection of essays itself attests—caused a sensation: *Black Athena* has attracted an enormous amount of media attention for an academic work. Given the debates about multiculturalism that continue to preoccupy the popular press when it turns to higher education, it is no surprise that *Black Athena* met with such a response. For Bernal's work seemed to be both a poison and a cure—a *pharmakon*, surely, if there ever was one—for many of the self-serving assumptions held about classical antiquity, and more generally about Western European cultural traditions. To put his thesis succinctly, Bernal claims that, as opposed to our accustomed view, the culture of Ancient Greece was not unique or even original to Greece itself but was essentially indebted to Egypt, and only later did these ancient lines of transmission become obscured and finally forgotten. Thus the cradle of Western civilization is to be sought not in Athens, but in Africa.

Now, I am not a trained classicist and I cannot pretend that I have the knowledge to weigh the merits of Bernal's assertions about the origins of Greek culture. But the centerpiece of his argument—or, as he calls it, the "nub of this volume" (*BA* 1:189)—is an issue that very much concerns my own sphere of competence. Bernal asserts that until about the middle of the eighteenth century the contribution of Egypt to Greek thought and society was universally recognized and appreciated; this way of understanding the past is what he calls the "Ancient Model." But around 1750, for a variety of reasons that I will mention in a moment, this older conception gave way to something that Bernal calls the "Aryan Model," whose advocates claimed that Greek culture arose as a wholly indigenous, autochthonous creation. According to the "Aryan Model," Greece was not only the sole and absolute origin for many of the West's most cherished institutions, it also attained a level of perfection that has remained unequaled since. Bernal is very explicit about the causes for the displacement of the "Ancient Model": "For 18th- and 19th-century Romantics and racists it was simply intolerable for Greece, which was seen not merely as the epitome of Europe but also as its pure childhood, to have been the result of the mixture of native Europeans and colonizing Africans and Semites" (*BA* 1:2). And he is no less clear about who these "Romantics and racists" were: "The most powerful figure concerned with this aspect of the Romantic movement," he writes, "was Johann Gottfried Herder" (*BA* 1:206).

Bernal is, of course, well aware that he is at odds with received opinion regarding Herder, and he even makes some allowance for Herder's reputation as a pluralist. But he then turns Herder's advocacy for the value of native or autonomous cultures against itself, so that those very aspects of Herder's thought which have been most admired appear to have been no more than a pretext for his real motives: namely, his opposition to foreign influences—foremost among them the French—in Germany. What Herder promoted as a program of tolerance and independence really amounted therefore to nothing more than hostility and aggressive nationalism in a clever disguise. In Bernal's opinion, then, while Herder himself remains exempt from the most damning criticism, the entire period of German classicism and romanticism that followed him is fully implicated by the consequences of his ideas:

> Herder himself stayed within the universalist bounds of the Enlightenment, maintaining that all peoples, not merely Germans, should be encouraged to discover and develop their own genii. Nevertheless, the concern with history and local particularity, and the disdain for rationality or "pure reason" apparent in his views and those of other late-18th- and early-19th-century German thinkers including Kant, Fichte, Hegel and the Schlegels, provided a firm basis for the chauvinism and racism of the following two centuries. (*BA* 1:206)

Racism, in other words, was the implicit and unavoidable consequence of the kind of historiography that saw Herder as its progenitor, or at least as its patron saint. And the admiration, and even adulation, of Greece that was especially strong in Germany was therefore, Bernal argues, the indirect product of disdain for non-European peoples. By positing Greece as the unsullied source of European civilization and by holding up its achievements as absolute models to which everyone ought to aspire, German philhellenes were not simply engaging in harmless myth-making. They were pursuing by default a policy of cultural exclusion that had specifically racist roots.

This is a serious and potentially devastating charge, particularly as it concerns Herder. It is a charge that, because of its gravity, requires careful examination. To begin with, it must be said that the German relationship to Greece in general has indeed been fraught with troubling ambiguities, not all of which are savory to contemplate. Bernal is certainly correct that toward the end of the eighteenth century and then thereafter, many aspects of the German attitude toward Greece were unquestionably based on nationalistic and chauvinistic prejudice. One of the earliest and clearest examples of the German belief in a special affinity between themselves and the Greeks can be found in Friedrich Schlegel's essay "Über das Studium der Griechischen Poesie," in which he claimed that "an entirely new and incomparably higher stage in the study of Greek things has been introduced by *Germans*, and it will perhaps remain for quite some time to come their sole possession" ([1795–96] 1906, 177). The notion that Germans were somehow constitutionally better equipped to understand the Greeks never really died in the succeeding decades.

The Germans' belief in their special attunement to the Greeks received perhaps its most disturbing expression in the notorious interview that the philosopher Martin Heidegger—then in his late seventies—gave to the news magazine *Der Spiegel* in 1966. Referring to Heidegger's statement that a cultural "conversion" in Western Europe was necessary and that this conversion could be accomplished in dialogue with Hölderlin, the interviewer asked him: "Do you believe that the Germans have specific qualifications for this conversion?" Heidegger responded by saying: "I'm thinking of the special inner relationship between the German language and the language and thinkers of the Greeks. The French confirm this more and more to me now. When they begin to think, they speak German" (Heidegger [1966] 1977, 24). The deadly irony of this apparently ingenuous comment is underscored by the fact that the interview also contains Heidegger's only public discussion of his involvement with National Socialism.

But what of Herder himself? Is the image of Herder that I outlined at the beginning also simply the product of a mythology fueled by nationalistic bias? Elsewhere (Norton 1995), I have examined racist elements regarding blacks in one of Herder's youthful essays. And it is true that the history of Herder scholarship, which has been persuasively critiqued by Claus Träger (1979) and Bernhard Becker (1987a, 1987b), displays a depressing, but probably predictable, conformity to the dominant German ideology. But as these scholars have also admirably shown, what has been said about Herder and what he actually said himself are frequently two very different things. As we shall see, it is important to call attention to this disparity, for Bernal's argument, here as elsewhere, rests virtually exclusively on secondary sources. For this reason, the reliability of those secondary works (which are inevitably driven by their own ideological interests) will obviously have affected his own conclusions.

It is striking that although Bernal lays very sobering accusations at Herder's feet, he never cites Herder's own words to support his claims. One is therefore forced to go to Herder himself to see if Bernal's arguments are borne out by Herder's own texts. Bernal would not have had to go far had he made this effort himself: within the first few pages of Herder's first and probably most influential historical work, *Auch eine Philosophie der Geschichte zur Bildung der Menschheit* (1774), the reader encounters a discussion of Egypt's historical place in the development of humanity as a whole. Yet, contrary to what we may expect after reading Bernal, Herder has nothing but the highest praise for the Egyptians. He writes, for instance, that they were the first to cease nomadic existence and were the first to establish agriculture and for-mulate the idea of property. (It bears reminding ourselves that for Herder—as well as for his contemporaries—primacy always carried a positive flavor; one of the great intellectual tasks the Enlightenment set for itself was the discovery of the "origins" of all natural and cultural phenomena.) Out of these circumstances emerged "security of the land, the cultivation of justice, order, police, all of which had not been possible in the nomadic life of the orient: there arose a new world." Herder goes on to say that "given the spirit of Egyptian precision and agricultural industriousness, these arts could not have done anything else but reach a high degree of mechanical perfection" ([1774] 1891, 487). He also states that because the Egyptians lacked wood, they had to learn to build with stone—and, he exclaims, "how high this art rose! and how much it encouraged the development of other arts!" (489). These are hardly the words of someone who wanted to deny significant cultural achievements to Egypt. (See also Palter's second contribution, this volume, on the eighteenth century.)

But Herder also specifically chastises those who would view Egypt with the eyes of an eighteenth-century European. Alluding to the Earl of Shaftesbury, he writes: "You may pour as much scorn [*Galle*] as you wish over Egyptian superstition and clericalism—as, for example, that amiable Plato of Europe has done, who only too much wants to shape everything according to the Greek model—that's all true, that's fine, if Egypt is supposed to be *your coun-try* and *your time*" ([1774] 1891, 490). He even dares to criticize the high priest of German neo-Hellenism: "The best historian of ancient art, Winckelmann, apparently judged the Egyptians' art works only according to Greek stan-dards, and thus described them *negatively* very well, but so little according to their *own nature and kind* that in almost every one of his sentences in this section of his book his clearly one-sided and squint-eyed perspective shines through" (491). Finally, in his discussion of the Greeks themselves—whom Herder certainly did admire, but not at the expense of other peoples—we read the crucial statements:

> I believe that the light in which I have placed Greece also contributes to resolving somewhat "the eternal dispute about the *originality of the Greeks* or their imitation of foreign nations": agreement could have been reached long ago in this question, too, if people had only understood one another better. It seems to me that it is undeniable that Greece received the seeds of culture, language, arts and sciences from somewhere else, and it can be plainly demonstrated in some of them, as in sculpture, architecture, mythology, and literature. (498)

It is clear from the same page that by "somewhere else" Herder explicitly means Egypt. It is startling not only how much Herder's own words conflict with Bernal's description of him, but also how directly Herder addressed the very issues, almost exactly two centuries ago, that now interest Bernal. How are we to account for this discrepancy?

The answer has to do, I think, with Bernal's larger aims in writing his book. At one point in *Black Athena* he discusses Friedrich August Wolf, the author most famously of the *Prolegomena to Homer* and one of the founding fathers of the modern discipline of classical philology or, as it is more clumsily called in German, *Altertumswissenschaft*. Bernal cites Wolf's scholarly credo, " 'All research is historical and critical not of *things* hoped for but [of] *facts*. Arts should be loved but history revered,' " and responds with the terse comment "This simple-minded approach has dominated the practice of most history and Classics ever since" (*BA* 1:286). The question of what constitutes a "fact," or of whether one can usefully speak of "facts" at all, is a philosophical problem that deserves and has received a great deal of skeptical scrutiny. But Bernal's swift and categorical dismissal of Wolf's scholarly method bespeaks an attitude of indifference toward even basic textual evidence. Such indifference demands equally critical examination.

Much later in his book, while discussing nineteenth-century perceptions of the destruction of Carthage, Bernal writes: "Even in the 18th century, Herder *is reported as having said* that Carthage was so flawed by its abominations that it should be compared to a jackal which the Roman she-wolf should destroy; by the late 19th century the deserved destruction of the city was a platitude" (emphasis mine). Farther down on the same page, he then states: "This principle—of a final solution—was extended in propaganda towards England in the two World Wars, and in actuality towards the Jews in the Holocaust." (*BA* 1:359). The implication of these extremely inflammatory words is clear: that by ostensibly approving of the ruin of Carthage, which lay on the North African coast, Herder obliquely endorsed the destruction of the entire continent's black inhabitants, and, even worse, Herder is by extension made to seem somehow vaguely responsible for the twentieth-century events Bernal mentions.

But when one looks for the source of that peculiar phrase—that "Herder is *reported as having said*" these things—one finds in Bernal's endnotes two citations of scholarly works about the Phoenicians that have nothing to do with Herder at all. But one also finds in the note Bernal's revealing admission about Herder's comment: "While I have no reason to doubt it, I have not been able to find the original" (*BA* 1:499 n. 480).[2] We have already seen his disdain for mere "facts" and the "simple-minded approach" that demands evidence for such assertions. Thus it falls to us to look once more not at what Herder is reported as having said, but at what he actually did say.

Herder's mature work on the philosophy of history, his *Ideen zur Philosophie der Geschichte der Menschheit*, which appeared in four parts between 1783 and

1791, is still widely regarded as his most significant work; and it is, by the way, available in English translation (see Herder 1966, 1968), unlike most of his other writings. In this work Herder at one point turns to the question of Carthage, in a section prominently entitled "Conquests of the Romans":

> When Rome had subjugated Italy, she began with Carthage; and this in a manner at which her most determined friends must blush. Her assisting the Marmertines, in order to gain a footing in Sicily; her seizing upon Corsica and Sardinia, while Carthage was embroiled with her mercenaries; and lastly the deliberating of her grave senators, whether a Carthage should be suffered to exist on this Earth, with as little ceremony as if the debate had been about a weed they had planted themselves; all of this and a hundred other severities render Roman history, despite the valor and address it otherwise displays, a history of demons [*Dämonengeschichte*]. ([1783–91] 1968, 238–39, trans. Manuel [slightly modified])

Herder's moral indignation is unmistakable, and this passage is, moreover, representative of his attitude toward Imperial Rome generally.

Elsewhere in his discussions of Carthage, Herder shows that he tries to take a balanced view, combining historical fidelity with typical eighteenth-century moral evaluation. "Far be it from me," he writes at another point, "to rob one noble Carthaginian of the least of his merits: for even Carthage, though erected on the lowest ground of avaricious conquest, has produced great minds, and nourished a multitude of arts." It is in this context that the reader also finds the "original" of the statement that Bernal was unable to locate:

> In the fertile soil of Africa agriculture was of all arts that which tended most to promote their trade; and into this, as a rich source of gain, the Carthaginians introduced many improvements. But unfortunately the barbarous state of the Romans occasioned the destruction of all the books of the Carthaginians, as well as of their town: we know nothing of the nation, but from its enemies, and a few ruins, which scarcely enable us to guess at the seat of the anciently famed mistress of the sea. It is to be lamented, that the principal figure Carthage makes in history is on the occasion of her contests with Rome: this wolf, that was afterwards to ravage the World, was first to exercise her powers against an African jackal, till he fell beneath her jaws. ([1783–91] 1968, 150–51, trans. Manuel)

The difference in tone and substance between Herder's actual words and what Bernal, in his contempt for mere "facts," wants us to believe on the basis of hearsay or mere gossip, needs no further comment.

The issue here is not simply whether Bernal's scholarly credibility has been seriously compromised—as I believe in this case it has—but what his motives are. About this, too, he is disarmingly frank: he says that his "scholarly purpose" was "to open up new areas of research to women and men with far better qualifications than I have. The political purpose of *Black Athena* is, of course, to lessen European cultural arrogance" (*BA* 1:73). He is undoubtedly right that uninformed prejudice has always had a pernicious influence wherever it has emerged and that such hateful arrogance should be vigorously challenged whenever it arises. But I think it is equally true that, at least so far as Herder is concerned, Bernal has left the domain of "mere" scholarly inquiry and entered the arena of demagoguery.

NOTES

This essay is a revised version of a talk I gave on the panel sponsored by the International Herder Society at the March 1992 (Seattle) meeting of the American Society for Eighteenth-Century Studies. Translations from German are my own unless otherwise noted.

1. Rose 1990, 108. See the chapter "Herder: 'Humanity' and the Jewish Question."

2. The works to which Bernal is referring are Herm 1975, 118, and Kunzl 1976, 15–20.

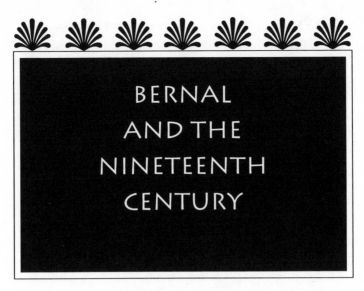

BERNAL
AND THE
NINETEENTH
CENTURY

Richard Jenkyns

"It is absurd to try to summarize this book in a dozen paragraphs": so Martin Bernal, reasonably enough, begins the Conclusion to the first volume of *Black Athena* (1:439). Yet it will be useful here to start with an even briefer summary, however rough and oversimplified. Bernal argues that in the second millennium B.C.E. Greece must have been colonized by Egyptians and Phoenicians. In his view, some 25 percent of Greek vocabulary— that is, virtually everything which is not Indo-European—can be plausibly derived from these sources. Later Greeks acknowledged their debt to these other peoples, and their myths of colonization—Danaus' coming to Greece from Egypt, Cadmus' bringing Phoenicians to found Thebes—are likely to preserve a historical memory.

This picture of the origins of Hellenic civilization, so the argument continues, lasted into the eighteenth century; Bernal calls it the "Ancient Model." It was then abandoned, mainly because of "the two principal paradigms of the nineteenth century—'progress' and racism" (*BA* 1:273). Belief in a progressive or evolutionary model of history meant that the antiquity of the Egyptians, previously admired, now made them inferior to the Greeks; racism made it intolerable that Hellenism could owe anything to Africa.

During the nineteenth century the discovery of a family of Indo-European languages made it possible to create what Bernal calls a "Broad Aryan Model," according to which invasions from the north formed the Greeks' language and the base of their civilization. This Broad Aryan Model tried to do away with the Egyptians; fiercer racism later in the century led to an

"Extreme Aryan Model," which sought to dispose of the Phoenicians as well, because they were Semites. Since the mid-twentieth century, the Holocaust and the foundation of the state of Israel have so far changed European attitudes that the Phoenicians have been allowed back into the picture; but because prejudice against blacks lingers on, the Egyptians are still kept out. However, there is nothing seriously wrong with the "Ancient Model," and Bernal believes that his "Revised Ancient Model," which allows a place in the story to Aryan invasions, will come to be accepted in the early twenty-first century.

There are two principal areas of argument here, the first concerned with the ancient world, the second with the last two centuries — "The Fabrication of Ancient Greece, 1785–1985," as the subtitle of Bernal's first volume has it. (There is also a third area, between the other two, when Bernal takes us through late antique Hermeticism, Renaissance neo-Platonism, and Freemasonry. This part of the book strikes me as more credulous and more confused in argument than the rest; because it does not seem necessary to the overall thesis, it may be set aside for present purposes.) My concern here is mainly with the second area, though as we shall see, Bernal's account of more recent times cannot be considered in isolation from his account of the ancient world.

His Ancient Argument (if one may call it that) needs to be treated somewhat differently from his Modern Argument. Most of the more important claims in his Ancient Argument are over matters of fact, which are in principle capable of proof or disproof (whether in practice they can be proved or disproved is of course another matter). That Egyptians and Phoenicians colonized Greece in the middle of the second millennium B.C.E., that the Phoenician alphabetic system reached Greece in the middle of the second millennium, that there was no later period of nonliteracy in Greece, that such-and-such a Greek word is derived from Egyptian, that Hesiod belongs in the tenth century and Homer at the beginning of the ninth — all these claims are made by Bernal, and they are either right or wrong. But much of his Modern Argument does not admit neatly determinate answers, even in principle. He is in the business of assigning large historical causes to developments in nineteenth-century scholarship, and any talk of such causes is necessarily imprecise. Moreover, he is concerned with attributing motives to nineteenth-century scholars, which may be conscious or unconscious (he usually, and quite reasonably, does not specify which), and in most cases analysis of motive, above all when it is unconscious, must remain to some extent speculative. Most of the claims in the Ancient Argument invite acceptance or rejection; most of the claims in the Modern Argument may expect a response in more shaded terms.

The Modern Argument cannot be assessed in isolation from the Ancient

Argument because Bernal's claim is that the nineteenth century perverted the truth: he needs to insist that the men whom he attacks were not only wrong but culpably wrong. And our judgments on this will depend to some degree on whether we ourselves think that they were right or wrong, and, if the latter, whether we think that they erred on reasonable grounds. Bernal distinguishes between "internalist" and "externalist" influences on scholars, the former being advances within the subject itself, the latter being scholars' own social and moral outlooks. Certainly our views are affected, willy-nilly, by the attitudes and assumptions of our own time; I also agree that in the nineteenth century the externalist pressures upon the study of Greece were abnormally strong: Hellas was admired, even worshiped, as a means of satisfying certain cultural needs. The historian's task is to judge the balance between internal and external forces; Bernal tips it a very long way toward the latter. The only internal force to which he allows any significant strength in the nineteenth century is the discovery of the Indo-European language family; almost everything else is due to racism or various kinds of bad faith.

A problem with any strongly externalist argument is that you have to release a small band of the elect from original sin: if objectivity is a mirage and almost all scholars are distorters, why should Bernal and the few people who have written in similar terms before him be exceptions? The question is the more pressing in his case for two particular reasons. The first is that he has, avowedly, a political purpose (of which more later). Here it may possibly be thought that by being so open about his political aim, he imposes a kind of check upon himself. The second reason is subtler, and more deeply problematic.

He makes a good deal of the notion that professional scholars in any field can get stuck in a rut, unthinkingly taking received opinions as proven truths, so that it may need an outsider to make a fundamental advance in a subject. The implication behind this idea is not modest, but the point is fairly made. And Bernal is indeed voracious in his intellectual curiosity, exhilarating in his range and enthusiasm. Yet there is a hole in the middle of his first volume, and that is where the Greeks themselves should be. Whatever may be thought of his theories about prehistory and comparative philology, there can be no doubt that he has read very widely and thought hard on these topics; he is on the other hand much less interested in the Greeks of the Classical period themselves and has little sense of the material with which scholars of historical Greece must deal. He fancies that Plato's philosophy was "heavily dependent on Egyptian religion and thought" (*BA* 1:145). But we can see for ourselves how it evolved from Presocratic thought, the Sophistic movement and the teaching of Socrates himself; to suppose that Platonism is in some way a development of Egyptian religion and thought is simply to misunderstand what Platonism is.

Underestimating the quantity and force of our evidence, Bernal tends to see classical Greece almost as a free field for the exercise of prejudice. One example will have to suffice—a case where Bernal might well seem to have caught stuffy, conventional scholars on the hop. It used to be thought that *Suppliants* was Aeschylus' oldest surviving play (and thus the oldest European drama extant). But in 1952 there was published a papyrus with a list of dates on it. Though the papyrus is defective, some complicated but secure deductions enable us to date the play confidently to 464–463 B.C.E.; *Suppliants* is therefore a work of Aeschylus' maturity, and considerably later than his *Persians*. Why had scholars been wrong? According to Bernal, "The most plausible reason is that it was considered unworthy of the greatest Greek tragedian in his prime to treat a topic that could be understood to suggest that Egyptians had settled in the Peloponnese" (*BA* 1:89). That surmise is wildly astray: the reason why *Suppliants* had been dated earlier was simple and innocent. We know that Greek drama began as a dialogue between a chorus and a single actor; in due course a second actor was introduced (allegedly by Aeschylus himself), then a third; and the importance of the chorus began to decline. *Suppliants* has an enormous part for the chorus (more than half the play is choral lyric, a larger proportion than in any other extant play), and the second actor is used in a way that suggests that he was an innovation, scarcely developed. Therefore the play was supposed to represent an earlier stage in the evolution of Greek tragedy than any other surviving work. The inference was wrong, but it was reasonable. As a matter of fact, E. C. Yorke, an Oxford scholar of impeccably conventional upbringing, had already (1936) argued for a later dating of the play on technical grounds of meter. It would be a wonder if either he or any of his readers supposed that there was even a hint of a "political" issue at stake.

In a curious way Bernal, so keen to put the Greeks in their place by asserting their dependence on Egypt, seems to underestimate Egypt itself. The modern visitor to that country is moved to awe and admiration; the Greeks too were dazzled by the power, magnificence, stability, and immemorial antiquity of Egyptian civilization. As with Aeschylus' *Suppliants*, Bernal argues that the evidence of Herodotus, who attributes various Greek rites and customs to Egyptian or Phoenician origins, is the more persuasive because his claims were "unpatriotic"; these ideas seem to have been "relatively conventional," Bernal adds, and yet the "passionate Greek chauvinism" of the times hated the idea of cultural inferiority to Phoenicians or Egyptians (*BA* 1:100).

One may feel that this argument comes close to supplying its own refutation: if the Greeks had so abhorred the thought of deriving anything from these other peoples, why did they keep on about it? That apart, Bernal seems to be working with too flat a view of human nature. A very coarse and defensive chauvinism of the "Stalin invented television" kind might deny any outside influence whatever, but even strongly nationalistic societies are seldom quite so crass. Nationalism is more likely to want to annex or to claim a kinship with the great achievements of other peoples. Cicero thought that the business of putting Greek philosophy into Latin dress or writing histories on the Greek pattern was a patriotic task for a Roman. Or to take a case closer to home, the temples of European art erected in every large American city in a way express a feeling of cultural inferiority. But they exemplify the natural response to such a sense of inferiority: to buy up the best European art on the market, and to add on an American wing, implying a descent from the great tradition of the Old World. Struck with the glamour of Egypt, the Greeks would be happy enough to look to it for kinship or origins.

And there is another factor which we should take into account: the syncretist habit among ancient peoples, the Jews excepted, of identifying their own gods with the gods of other nations. Thus Roman Juno was identified with Greek Hera, and Carthaginian Tanit with Roman Juno. The Greeks claimed the Egyptian goddess Neit to be the same as their own Athena (hence Bernal's title). It would be extraordinary if they had not done so: but the claim has in itself no evidential value. In fact, we can sometimes catch the Greeks attributing to Egypt ideas that cannot have come from there: Herodotus (2.123) claims that the Egyptians invented the idea of the transmigration of souls, a doctrine taught by Pythagoras, but that belief is entirely incompatible with Egyptian religion. Certainly the Greeks felt themselves to be superior to the rest of the world, the *barbaroi*; but it was a relaxed and confident feeling. They were, besides, an inquisitive people, curious to know where they and their customs came from, and aware, without resentment, that they had learned from Egypt and the Near East. Greek legend said that the Danaids came from Egypt, medieval English chroniclers told that the British race was descended from Brutus the Trojan; the one myth is no more certain to be the grudging admission of an undeniable truth than the other.

A respect for other cultures need not be in opposition to a pride in one's own: the two things may act as counterpoises to each other (a truth worth remembering when thinking about the nineteenth century), and indeed an admiration for another culture may actually enhance a sense of the distinctive quality of one's own identity. This can be illustrated by a story told in Plato's *Timaeus*. Solon visited Egypt and enquired of the priests about the past. He told them the Greeks' myths of earliest origins, but an aged priest answered, "O Solon, Solon, you Greeks are always children, and there is no Greek who is an old man. . . . You are all young in your souls, and you have in them no old belief handed down by ancient tradition nor any knowledge that is hoary with age" (22b). The significance of the story is that it is of course a Greek story: the Greeks feel conscious of their freshness and dynamism in contrast to the immense and majestic depths of the Egyptian past. Plato's tale will have a moral for us when we come to consider Bernal's "political" aim.

Bernal's method in examining the nineteenth century is to take a large number of individual cases—scholars or writers—and examine them one by one. Judgment is not always easy, partly because most of these cases are dealt with quite briefly, partly because Bernal ranges very widely and one would need to have read as much as he has to assess him with authority: sometimes I believe that he is right, sometimes I believe that he is wrong, and often I am not sure. At times he is fully convincing: he has interesting quotations, for example, to show that there was a comparison in the air between the ancient Phoenicians and the modern British, as maritime, trading peoples, with the consequence that French scholars, such as Michelet, tended to depreciate the Phoenicians whereas English scholars saw them in a kindlier light. On the other hand, we can sometimes catch Bernal whistling to keep his spirits up: his claim that the cranky beliefs of Charles François Dupuis, whose *Origin of All Cults* (1795) traced all mythologies and religions back to Egypt, "had to be buried" (*BA* 1:182)—because they threatened Christianity and the idolization of Greece—is mere assertion, though it is kept up loudly for a page or two. More subtly and more seriously apt to mislead are those places where he underestimates the power of genuine evidence over scholars—in his terms, internalist causes—through not knowing just what that evidence is. For instance, he is very ready to belittle F. A. Wolf's epoch-making *Prolegomena to Homer* (1795) (*BA* 1:283–84). I myself happen to believe that Wolf's theory of how the Homeric epics came into being is wrong, but the fact remains that he had powerful arguments on his side, and the Wolfians may be reckoned to have had the better of the argument up to the end of the nineteenth century. (Nor were they necessarily Christians or romantic reactionaries: the two most prominent Wolfians in Victorian England were George Grote and George Eliot, progressive rationalists both.)

Though I accept that the externalist pressures upon nineteenth-century views of the Greeks were great, and did have a distorting effect, I believe nonetheless that Bernal overestimates them. Some of his claims for externalist forces are very strongly put:

> I am convinced that European politics and society from 1880 to 1939 were so steeped in racism and anti-Semitism, and Classics was so central to the educational and social systems, that—regardless of the historical and archaeological evidence—it would have been impossible to change the image of ancient Greece in the way Bérard wanted to do [i.e., by trying "to stop the steamroller of Extreme Aryanism"]. (*BA* 1:382)

I see this destruction of the Ancient Model as entirely the result of social forces such as these [Christian reaction, racism, etc.], and the requirements put upon the Ancient Greeks by 19th-century Northern Europeans. My belief is that no internalist force—or advance in the knowledge of Ancient Greece—can explain the change. (1:441)

Bernal studies four forces which, in his view, led to "the replacement of Egypt by Greece as the fount of European civilization." These were: "Christian reaction, the rise of the concept of 'progress,' the growth of racism, and Romantic Hellenism" (1:189). With each one of these he has a case but overplays his hand.

There was indeed one respect in which Egypt could threaten traditional Christian belief: a very high (early) dating for the early Egyptian dynasties could cast doubt on the historicity of the Old Testament. Bernal illustrates this most effectively with the example of a pope who was reportedly delighted to learn, as he thought, that the researches of Champollion had "humbled and confounded the pride of this philosophy which claimed to have discovered in the zodiac of Dendera a chronology earlier than that of the Holy Scriptures." The pope asked to be sent an account of the arguments by which it was established that no monument existed earlier than 2200 B.C.E., the supposed date of Abraham, so that "in accordance with our faith, there remain approximately eighteen centuries of darkness through which interpretation of the Holy Scriptures alone can guide us" (*BA* 1:252).

However, it was in the Christian interest to derive Greek mythology from Semitic sources, as Bernal himself wants to do. Gladstone was among those who argued for a large Semitic influence on Greek myth and belief: if this influence were present, above all in Homer, it could be maintained that Greek myths were corruptions of truths originally revealed to man in the Garden of Eden or to the first patriarchs. Turning from life to an accurately observed fiction, we find Mr. Casaubon, in George Eliot's *Middlemarch*, engaged on much the same project. Casaubon is a parson; his views are pooh-poohed by the agnostic Ladislaw. In Bernal's own pages a good number of the dramatis personae turn up on the wrong side. The young Gibbon believed in a connection between Greek, Egyptian, and Jewish antiquities but soon recanted; at the same time, he was turning from Roman Catholicism to skepticism. William Mitford argued for an Egyptian colonization of Greece in terms so close to Bernal's own that Bernal quotes them in bold type: "'Some of the best-supported of Ancient Grecian traditions relate to the establishment of Egyptian colonies in Greece; traditions so little accommodating to national prejudice and so perfectly consonant to all known history, that for their essential circumstances they seem unquestionable'" (*BA* 1:187). But Mitford was an outspoken Tory; his history of Greece was to be opposed, in this and other respects, by Connop Thirlwall, a bishop of Liberal Anglican outlook, and George Grote, who was both a radical and an agnostic. Bernal condemns Hume as a racist and misrepresents him as a Christian (1:203). His prize example of pure Hellenomania is Shelley, a left-wing atheist (*BA* 1:290–91).

Belief in progress is undoubtedly a strong strand in nineteenth-century thought, but it is unlikely that it can explain what Bernal wants it to explain. Here is one of those areas where he seems to be working with too flat a view of human nature. The elites of nations with a strong sense of their own power and progress may like to use the achievements of other times and cultures as a kind of counterweight; they call the old world into existence to redress the balance of the new. The adoration of Hellas found in so many nineteenth-century writers and thinkers seldom comes with the implication that the ancient Greeks had a spiritual kinship with themselves, at least in Britain (the story in Germany is somewhat different); the stress is rather upon the immense difference between Greece and England, ancient and modern, North and South. Some people, to be sure, took refuge in a vision of pure, bright, youthful Hellas because they disliked the effects of modern progress, but for others the contrast itself was a source of fascination. We may recall the story of Solon and the Egyptian priest, and Plato's appreciation both of his own culture and of the different quality of another. In the nineteenth century, belief in progress was one side of a coin, the other side of which was a passion for the past and, sometimes, more specifically, a delight in whatever was early, primitive, nobly savage. Homer was worshiped because he was the first of the Greek poets, not despite that. After all, "Hellenomania" itself—the idea that the highest summit of human achievement was as distant as the fifth century B.C.E.—is a species of primitivism. It is hard to think, therefore, that lovers of Greece would have held the oldness of the Egyptians' civilization against them.

It is axiomatic for Bernal that there was a massive increase of racism in Europe beginning around 1780 and accelerating in the later nineteenth century. I am unsure how solidly this is based. One may learn from John Hale's *The Civilization of Europe in the Renaissance* (1993, esp. 51–66) the extraordinary range and variety of hostile caricatures that the European peoples made of each other in the sixteenth century; contempt for other nations or races was nothing new. The case for an increase in racism in the Romantic age needs to be argued; but it may well be so. It is certainly true that racial explanations of historical processes were pervasive in the nineteenth century. The idealization of the *Volk* was a stress on community, not necessarily on race; however, it easily led to a belief in the immutable character of races, and thence to the notion that some races are permanently superior to others. There was also a good deal of anti-Semitism around, ranging from a distaste for Jewish "upstarts" to a fullblown racial hatred (see also Rogers, this volume). It would be very surprising if this had no effect on the study of the ancient world, and some at least of Bernal's cases are convincing. The effect of racial considerations on the nineteenth-century view of the Egyptians must remain more doubtful.

Modern conditions are far enough from the experience of nineteenth-century European elites for the term "racism" to risk having misleading connotations when applied to them, even where it is strictly correct. (It is in any case a dangerously vague term—but let us sidestep that minefield for now.) Bernal's notion seems to be that nineteenth-century scholars were driven by a kind of terror to keep the Egyptians out of the Greek story as far as they could; but what was there to give rise to terror? He himself points out that "at the end of the 18th century the predominant view was that of Mozart and his librettist Emanuel Schikaneder in *The Magic Flute*: that the Egyptians were neither Negro nor essentially African" (*BA* 1:244)—one might add, in passing, that although the heroine of Verdi's *Aida* is an Ethiopian, the racial difference between her lover Radames and herself is not an issue. Why should the racists of Bernal's hypothesis not stick to this? There would be nothing in the progress of Egyptology to disturb them. We have what are clearly realistic portraits surviving from ancient Egypt, especially from the Old Kingdom; the features are not Negroid. Most tellingly, there are many scenes in their art where the Egyptians distinguish themselves from their southern enemies, who are represented in a conventionalized form as Negro, with snub noses and woolly hair. Nor will color-consciousness come to the rescue of Bernal's argument, for he wants to maintain that in the Romantic period "the passion for India also meant that it replaced Egypt as the exotic ancestor of Europe" (1:224). There might be room for debate about the color of the Egyptians' skin; there could be no doubt that the Indians' skin was dark.

Bernal is frank about his broader intention. "The political purpose of *Black Athena* is, of course, to lessen European cultural arrogance" (*BA* 1:73). But does it succeed? Let us suppose, purely for the sake of argument, that Bernal were wholly right about Greek prehistory. Perhaps the Nazis would have been shocked to think that Greek blood and culture had so much Semitism in them—but who else would be? What scholars have thought worth examining are the achievements of the Greeks as we know them—in historic times. By pushing back Egyptian and Semitic influences on Greece earlier than is usual, Bernal makes the rise of Greek civilization a more purely European phenomenon than do those more conventional scholars who lay weight rather on Greek borrowings at a later date (from Egyptian sculpture and architecture, for instance).

And it is surely his aim also to do what he must know he cannot quite manage: to give African-Americans a share of the credit for Egyptian civilization

(*BA* 1:242). But is this project not Eurocentric? After all, no one cares a straw that Britain's influence on ancient Greece was nil. It is because blacks are, seemingly, outside the traditional European story that Bernal wants to find them a place in that sun; and however well-meaning this aim, it can hardly help being patronizing. And there is another consideration which ought to weigh with Bernal: that he is encouraging blacks to enter an invidious competition. The cultural achievements of different parts of the world vary immensely—that is simply a fact. In terms of "high culture," the achievement of Italy, for example, is far greater than that of North and South America put together. In 2000 B.C.E. the achievement of Africa (that is, Egypt) was incomparably greater than Europe's. In 4000 C.E., who shall say? Meanwhile, if it is to be essential to a people's self-esteem that it should have a high culture on the European model—a long history, great art, and so on—the outlook is bleak for many. But such an expectation is itself Eurocentric; Antiguans and New Zealanders need not despair.

More speculatively, one may wonder if it is not counterproductive to press other peoples to get themselves a culture on the European model. Again, the story from Plato's *Timaeus* comes to mind: the Greeks had the wit to admire and do otherwise. It can be hard to squeeze into patterns invented elsewhere: one may feel that America has underperformed in those areas where the canons had been established in Europe—painting, sculpture, art, music, even (though less markedly) literature—and contrast its vitality in areas which do not fit traditional "Western" categories of culture: popular music (where the African influence on the West has gone deepest), popular film, the skyscraper city. In Europe itself some of the once richest seams appear to be near exhaustion; other peoples may be best placed to find new ones. A great tradition can become a burden as well as a glory—which is no reason, of course, to pretend that it does not exist. Bernal's work has appealed to those who have an animus against Western culture and a desire to belittle it. That is not a mistake which he makes himself; if he is eager, in missionary spirit, to rescue Europeans from the sin of cultural arrogance, we may suspect that it is because he fears that they have all too much to tempt them.

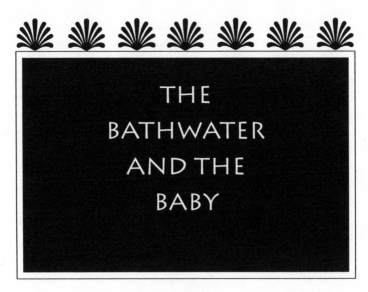

THE
BATHWATER
AND THE
BABY

Mario Liverani

Black Athena must be the most discussed book on the ancient history of the eastern Mediterranean world since the Bible. Nearly a decade after the publication of the first volume (1987), and with the second (1991) now long since in circulation, professional historians are still being asked to evaluate it. I have to confess that my first reaction is annoyance. How many other books much more professional in style, sound in conclusion, and innovative in methodology have been denied comparable attention? However, this reaction is naive: *Black Athena* enjoys such continued attention because it raises important scholarly questions, and because it makes a difficult subject available to a large audience. Professional ancient historians generally avoid the most fundamental questions about their subjects. They know too well how problematic those questions actually are, and do not dare to do without or go beyond the proven methods of classical philology.

Now that the first of the storm over *Black Athena* has dissipated and successive reviews have clarified the factuality and motivations of the book, we can perhaps evaluate its basic meaning and place it in proper cultural and historical context. I take it as given that it is filled with too many logical and methodological inconsistencies, historical and philological mistakes, and documentary and bibliographical omissions to discuss here in detail. It is not with the details of Bernal's work, but with his basic historiographical principles that I propose to disagree.

The logical structure of the first volume of *Black Athena* is built on a syllogism whose accuracy I fully concede. The major premise is that scholarship (historiography in particular) is influenced by the scholar's sociopolitical background. The minor premise is that the ancient history of the eastern Mediterranean world was constructed by European scholars living in imperial times and countries. The conclusion is that their work was biased by imperialism and is now in need of thorough revision. Conservative scholars object to such a syllogism, invoking the alternative major premise of "pure scholarship." However, the syllogism is accepted by most progressive (not necessarily Marxist) scholars and is certainly not Bernal's invention. Conservative classical scholars seem to have been more seriously offended (or simply surprised) by Bernal's presumption of imperial bias than Orientalists were by Edward Said's in *Orientalism* (1978) a few years before.

From the mid–nineteenth century to World War II, Europe controlled or influenced most of the world: by immigration, colonization, conquest, and trade all of the Americas, Australia and Oceania, Africa, and most of Asia were either organized into states of European design or directly ruled by European empires. The Fascist conquest of Ethiopia in 1936 made Europe's hegemony complete in Africa; China remained the only relevant exception in Asia; both Turkey in the West and Japan in the East tried to face Europe and the United States by shaping themselves into European-like states.

The cultural tools and the sublimated characteristics of Western imperialism and colonialization were ethnology and Orientalism. As for Greece, in the early nineteenth century it was rather a Levantine than a European country. It entered Europe only after its war of independence against the Ottoman empire (1821–29), an event which the romantic European intelligentsia viewed and took part in as if on the model of the Greek war against Persia which had occurred more than two thousand years before. The division of Greece from the Near East was partly based on the racial factor distinguishing "Aryans" from "Semites." Although Bernal gives the most emphasis to this factor, it was not the only one. (And Aryan Persia, always considered to be typically "Oriental," is a case worthy of deeper study.) Cultural and political features were perhaps more important in counterpoising Europe and the Orient: rational thought versus magic, freedom versus serfdom, democracy versus despotism, development versus stagnation, individualism versus collectivism, and so on.

Eurocentrism gave rise to a privileged axis in world history: civilization was considered to have been successively displaced in time and space, from the Ancient Near East to Greece, to Rome, to the Christian Middle Ages, to the Western European Renaissance, to the industrial empires. This privileged axis, which clearly explained the late nineteenth-century preeminence of the Western world, existed before the imperial era but was not fully implemented until the discovery of new data on ancient Near Eastern civilizations by nineteenth-century Western archaeologists, who were themselves—although unwittingly—the sublimated representatives of colonial conquest. The shift of cultural primacy from the Near East to Greece (the one dealt with in Bernal's book) was interpreted in line with two slogans: *Ex Oriente Lux* ("Light from the East") (mostly used by Orientalists) and "The Greek Miracle" (mostly used by Classicists). These slogans appeared to represent opposing ideas but in fact were one and the same notion: the Western appropriation of ancient Near Eastern culture for the sake of its own development.

After World War II, the process of decolonization changed the world map: now the Near and Middle East are ruled by local, independent states (even Israel, despite its European origin, is becoming a local state); the rest of Asia and Africa are also largely independent. Because of this marked political change, the most sudden and extensive through all of world history, and the related cultural changes—the progress of mass communications (the "global village"), the growth of Western-style schools of historical research in Asian and African universities, to the very establishment of world cultural organizations (UNESCO)—a new model is now required in the reconstruction of world history: a multicultural model, in which different centers and different political and cultural strategies are all granted equal attention and merits as due, quite apart from their greater or lesser success in the course of events.

The construction of a new multicentered model is a difficult scholarly task. It is the main historiographical challenge of this generation. Scholars from universities and other cultural institutions in Europe and America, Asia and Africa are working on this model, making use of different methodological tools, and, of course, laboring under biases produced by their own cultural backgrounds. On the one hand it is clear that scholars in the new states outside of Europe and North America or in the marginalized ethnic minorities inside the industrialized world often have not yet acquired the necessary technical standards, so that most of the burden of the enterprise still falls on Western scholars. On the other hand it is also obvious that non-Western scholars are distrustful of the West (and rightly so!) and willing to go ahead by themselves, even at the risk of allowing their own simplifications and nationalistic and ethnic biases to interfere with a multicentered global approach. A satisfactory elaboration of the new model will take a long time and must surmount many problems, both historiographical and political.

In building the new model, a critical evaluation of the former, Eurocentered approach is a necessary and very delicate operation. Bernal has contributed to such a revisionary evaluation, together with other scholars before and after him, but there is still a long road ahead. He has been most successful in reaching so large an audience, but the popularity of his project could seriously damage a good cause, because his work contains serious historiographical flaws. His stress on a Western "conspiracy" instead of on inevitable conditioning (for which allowance must always later be made), and on racial rather than political and economic distinctions, is politically disruptive and historically regressive. In fact, as I shall show, Bernal's historiographical method is severely outdated and naive. And instead of offering a new, multicentric model he merely seems to suggest an Afrocentric and Levantine model, reverting to the old-fashioned *Ex Oriente Lux* position.

If we were to apply Bernal's criteria to some of the non-Western historiographical trends of our time with which he is sympathetic, such as Afrocentrism, we should immediately have to dismiss them as grossly biased, as well as lacking in necessary documentation. The so-called scholars of the Afrocentric school along with Bernal himself are guilty (unintentionally or not) of "falsifications" which are even more gross and crude than those of past European scholars. As a result, they do not so much advance a just cause, as discredit it. A truly progressive strategy of research would certainly not be to try to counterpoise a crude and incompetent Afrocentrism to the much more sophisticated Eurocentrism of the past century, but to work without prejudices and hidden agendas, with a self-consciousness derived from a critical appreciation of how sociopolitical conditions influence scholarship. Though Bernal's *pars destruens* (destructive element) is a contribution to multicentered scholarship, his *pars construens* (constructive element) poses an insurmountable obstacle to scholarly progress.

THE NINETEENTH-CENTURY REVOLUTION: HISTORICAL AND PHILOLOGICAL METHOD

In my opinion, Bernal committed the basic error of "throwing out the baby with the bathwater" (cf. S. P. Morris 1989, 51). By dismissing as biased the "racist" approach of the European scholars of past centuries, he also dismisses their achievements in historical methodology and regresses to the pre-paradigmatic lack of methodology of earlier antiquarians.

The scholars of the mid–nineteenth century established the very "rules" of philological method (critical editing of texts, critical textual history), the rules of linguistic method (etymology and comparative linguistics), the rules of historical method (critical analysis of sources and of traditions, and economy of explanation), the rules of the religio-historical method (the nature of myths and legends), and also deontological standards (systematic collection of primary data, systematic reading of secondary bibliography). All these professional rules can of course be improved upon or even replaced by demonstrably better rules; but they cannot simply be dismissed out of hand without providing a substitute. What Bernal does is to go back to a pre-paradigmatic behavior. He does without a methodology: he interprets sources at face value, avoids a critical analysis of traditions, suggests etymologies by simple assonance, confers on myths the value of true history, and limits his primary and secondary sources to those which confirm his own perceptions. His treatments of etymology and mythical tradition are especially incompetent, and unfortunately most of his conclusions are built on them.

Bernal not only dismisses mid–nineteenth century rules of philological method which are still valid, but also ignores changes in historical method which have taken place since the mid–nineteenth century. Like most amateurs, he is able to glean from readings (which in this case are indeed extensive) individual pieces of information, but not a professional historical method. As a result, his historiography is old-fashioned and contradictory. He still attaches paramount importance to the concepts of "race" and "peoples"; he still explains cultural change in terms of migration and conquest; he still ignores socioeconomic factors; he still overlooks the proper use of archaeological data in reconstructing protohistorical societies. All these points could be substantiated with a long citation of examples; but every professional historian who has read the book and its reviews knows that this is no longer necessary. Hardly a single chapter (or even page) of *Black Athena* escapes the blame of ignoring correct methodology, adopting old-fashioned explanations, and omitting relevant data and literature. (See also Tritle, this volume.)

GREECE AND THE ANCIENT NEAR EAST

I now touch briefly on the substantial problem of the relationship between ancient Greece and the Near East. Both models, *Ex Oriente Lux* (adopted by Bernal) and "The Greek Miracle" (refused by Bernal) are Eurocentric: the first model only values Oriental (Near Eastern) cultures for their perceived contribution to Western civilization; the second suggests that civilization began positively to evolve only with the intervention of Western peoples, who either modified and appropriated or dismissed Oriental contributions.

What we need to construct instead is a historical model of the origin and growth of Greek civilization within the framework of eastern Mediterranean cultures; many scholars have been working on this model, quite apart from, and even prior to, Bernal. Archaeological and textual data provide the documentary evidence, while etymology and myth should be relegated to a secondary role. Throughout Bernal's books we find too often an attempt to prove that myths are "true," and too seldom an objective analysis of the relevant archaeological and historical data.

During the Late Bronze Age, the balance between Greece and Near Eastern civilizations seems rather clear. If we were to place on distribution maps features such as towns, palaces, archives, specialized trades and crafts, etc., a consistent pattern would emerge: Greece would be on the westernmost periphery of a large Near Eastern area whose core was Mesopotamia. Most features of so-called "high culture" were established in Greece thanks to Near Eastern suggestions, but these suggestions found the local culture "ready" because of its own inner development, and they received in Greece a distinctive local form, as always happens in such cases. The modes of suggestion were varied: mostly the exchange of goods, ideas, and specialized people, not necessarily conquest, migration, and colonization. The Near Eastern regional system of the Late Bronze Age worked through a complex interplay of diplomats and messengers, scribes and administrative officials, traders and prospectors, in which the Aegean region (the Mycenaean world) held a marginal though not necessarily subordinate position; it could not be considered an adequate *counterpart* to the Oriental world, merely a part of it.

After the Sea Peoples disrupted the eastern Mediterranean, and during the whole of the Iron I–II period (ca. 1150–750 B.C.E.), the situation changed. In Egypt and in Mesopotamia the major Oriental states and cultures survived and continued to develop along the old traditional lines, while the formerly urbanized area west of the Euphrates and north of the Sinai (Palestine, Syria, Cyprus, Anatolia, the Aegean, and Greece) shared an interesting process of innovation at a comparable level and with similar trends in their cultural development. We can cite the following features: alphabetic writing and iron technology, aristocratic governments in the city-states and national feeling in the new states of tribal origin, more equitable relationships between town and countryside, an economy less dependent on palaces, and so on. We can enlarge the notion of the term "Levant" to include the area between the Euphrates and the Ionian Sea, which is differentiated from the truly Oriental world on the one side, and from emerging protohistoric Europe on the other. Within this Levantine world influences traveled in many directions, but especially from the more developed, eastern regions (Syria-Palestine, Cyprus, southeastern Anatolia) to the less developed West (western Anatolia, the Aegean islands, south-central Greece). Egypt and Mesopotamia still served as reservoirs of the old wisdom and scribal sciences, while the West provided resources and possible adepts. Until the mid–eighth century, we cannot yet reasonably balance Greece against the Oriental world.

In the Third Iron Period (from 750 B.C.E.) the situation changed again, because of the growth of empires in Mesopotamia (Assyria, Babylonia), also in Egypt (though less successfully), and finally in Iran (Media and Persia). Over the course of two centuries the Levantine countries were conquered, largely ruined in terms of demography, economy, and culture, and made into provinces of those Eastern empires. Unlike Syria-Palestine and Anatolia, however, Greece was able and lucky enough to resist this annexation because of the great distance separating it from the cores of the empires. It is significant that the two centuries (ca. 750–550 B.C.E.) during which the Levant was under pressure were also the centuries during which Oriental influences on Archaic Greece peaked (the so-called "Orientalizing" period). In the meantime, urbanization and state structures spread toward Europe and the central Mediterranean, so that Greece became part (a preeminent part) of a western world, counterbalanced to the Oriental empires. The budding of Greek civilization is strictly linked to the growth of Eastern empires such as Persia's and to the political collapse of the Levant. At this point, empires and city-states became the counterpoised bases for cultural developments which went in different directions. After ca. 550 B.C.E. this counterpoise did not erase Oriental influences from Greece, but it certainly diminished their importance, except in some specialized fields in which the Oriental tradition kept its primacy and prestige.

It is quite clear to me that the emergence of Greece from the Levantine world, its struggle against the empires, the development of its own cultural features in order to create a definite identity, are issues which cannot be left to the classicists alone. The Orientalists have just as much to say about all that. In any case, the reconstruction of such a complicated set of historical problems is an enormously difficult task, even for professional historians; outsiders do not have the necessary equipment—in methodology, source control, interdisciplinary approach—to tackle it. We duly thank Martin Bernal for his useful insights about the biased approaches of former (and present) classical scholars, but we have to go along on our own way without him. We will keep and we like (at least I like) his baby, but we must throw out all his dirty water.

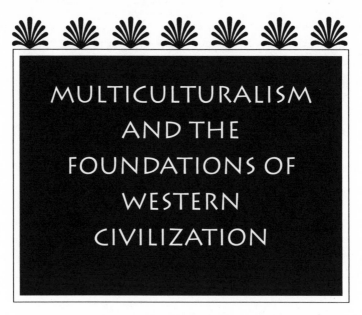

MULTICULTURALISM AND THE FOUNDATIONS OF WESTERN CIVILIZATION

Guy MacLean Rogers

In a recent essay entitled "The Question of Orientalism" (Lewis 1993) the distinguished historian Bernard Lewis has attempted to explain how the terms "Orientalism" and "Orientalist" have been emptied of their previous meanings and endowed with new ones for the sake of contemporary creeds or causes. According to Lewis, the term "Orientalist" first was attached to a group of artists, mostly from western Europe, who visited the Middle East and North Africa and portrayed what they saw or imagined. The term "Orientalism" was also used to describe an academic discipline, which originally focused upon the study of Hebrew; later the boundaries of the discipline were expanded to include other eastern languages.

In the later twentieth century, mostly for reasons of nationalism and ideology, some scholars have used the term "Orientalism" to condemn a tradition of scholarship which is allegedly hostile to or unsympathetic with the peoples of the East that it studies. To explain how such a shift in the meaning of the term has come about, Lewis invites his readers to indulge in a kind of scholarly fantasy, imagining a situation in which a group of "patriots and radicals from Greece have decided that the profession of classical studies is insulting to the great heritage of Hellas and that those engaged in these studies, known as classicists, are the latest manifestation of a deep and evil conspiracy, incubated for centuries, hatched in Western Europe, fledged in America, the purpose of which is to denigrate the Greek achievement and subjugate the

Greek lands and peoples" (1993, 99). After he has constructed this fantasy, Lewis comments that the fantasy, stated in terms of classics and the modern Greeks, is absurd. Yet a similar fantasy about the ancient Greeks and classical scholarship now has been fledged. For Martin Bernal, in successive volumes of *Black Athena*, has constructed such a fantasy about Hellas and classical scholarship.

Specifically, Bernal has argued that for reasons of racism and anti-Semitism, classicists and ancient historians in the West have hidden or lied about the contributions made by the ancient Phoenicians and the ancient Egyptians to early Greek culture. Thus classicists, the leaders of a grand conspiracy directed against the Middle East and Africa, have systematically distorted or falsified the story of the origins of classical civilization and the West. Far from being treated as absurd, this conspiracy theory has become very popular. Indeed, few books published about the ancient world since World War II have provoked as much interest both inside and outside the discipline of classics as has *Black Athena*.

Since *The Guardian* in England devoted a double-page feature to the first volume shortly after its publication in March 1987, journalists as well as scholars from many different disciplines have appropriated Bernal's central hypothesis, that the ancient Egyptians and Phoenicians fundamentally influenced the formation of early Greek civilization. Indeed, some scholars now regard the "Afroasiatic Roots of Classical Civilization"—the subtitle of *Black Athena*—as gospel. According to John Henrik Clarke, for example, "They have to admit that the foundations of what you call Western civilization was laid by non-Europeans" (quoted in Marriott 1991, 18).

What is the explanation for this phenomenon of rapid social diffusion? From the comments of Clarke and others, it seems that many people believe that *Black Athena* constitutes the first cohesive and well-documented argument for the non-European or multicultural foundations of Western civilization.

Now if the foundations of Western civilization were multicultural (in the quite specific sense of deriving from many cultures), it would be important, not only to scholars concerned with the question of what we should teach students about what happened in the ancient world. It would also be important to all of us who (living in the West) consider ourselves to be heirs of Western civilization. For we all understand that the foundation myth of Western civilization helps to define who we think we are, or would like to think we are. Thus, if the tree of our civilization were shown to have roots in the soils of many different lands, a vision of ourselves as a pluralistic, diverse, multiethnic, and multiracial society might be legitimated.

As we shall see, however, *Black Athena* does *not* provide an argument for the multicultural foundations of classical or Western civilization; rather, Bernal has created a selective myth of the foundations of classical civilization. This selective myth might be called the Afro-Asiatic myth. In that myth, Egyptians and Phoenicians are revealed as the true and sole founders of classical and Western civilization: they taught the early Greeks religion, philosophy, literature, in fact, civilization itself. And they alone were the teachers of the early Greeks. No other peoples of the ancient Near East taught the early Greeks anything significant about civilization.

Thus Bernal has not argued for a multicultural foundation myth of the West at all, and his Afro-Asiatic myth cannot be used to legitimate a multicultural vision of ourselves. The irony (and indeed the tragedy) about the impact that *Black Athena* has made upon the general public is that considerable ancient evidence supports exactly the multicultural foundation story of classical civilization which Bernal's supporters have mistakenly attributed to him. The ancient evidence shows that many different peoples made diverse and complex contributions to the birth of Western civilization over a long period of time.

THE HISTORIOGRAPHICAL ARGUMENT

To demonstrate first that *Black Athena* does not furnish an argument for the multicultural foundations of Western civilization, it will be useful to separate the historiographical contentions of *Black Athena* about the "fabrication" of ancient Greece from 1785 to 1985 from Bernal's historical assertions about Egyptian and Phoenician colonization of Greece during the second millennium B.C.E.

The core historiographical argument of *Black Athena* is that racist and anti-Semitic scholars in nineteenth- and twentieth-century Europe systematically purged all traces of the Egyptian and Phoenician contributions to early Greek civilization from the scholarly record. According to Bernal, the ancient Egyptians and Phoenicians suffered this cultural *damnatio memoriae* as a direct result of the imperialism and colonialism practiced by the major European powers against the peoples of the Near East and Africa, especially after the expedition of Napoleon to Egypt in 1798.

Furthermore, Bernal maintains, there were assertions of what he calls the "Ancient Model" right to the end of the nineteenth century. Scholars such as Victor Bérard argued for fundamental Egyptian and/or Phoenician contributions to early Greek civilization at exactly the time when "Aryanist" scholars denied the truth of the Egyptian and Phoenician colonizations, and promoted what Bernal terms the "Aryan model." The essence of this Aryan model was the idea that the Greek language and civilization developed in a state of cultural isolation.

Anyone who believes that Bernal has exaggerated at least one part of the historiographical record has only to read through a few pages of the rogues' gallery of racists and anti-Semites assembled in the first volume of *Black Athena* to recognize the justice of his historiographical claims about some lines of historiography during the nineteenth century. One example he cites (*BA* 1:342) from the works of Émile Burnouf embodies both the racism and anti-Semitism which pervaded some of European classical historiography during the late nineteenth century.

> A real Semite has smooth hair with curly ends, a strongly hooked nose, fleshy projecting lips, massive extremities, thin calves, and flat feet. And what is more, he belongs to the occipital races: that is to say, those whose hinder part of the head is more developed than the front. His growth is very rapid, and at fifteen or sixteen it is over. At that age, the divisions of the skull which contain the organs of intelligence are already joined, and in some cases even welded together. From that period the growth of the brain is arrested. In the Aryan races this phenomenon, or anything like it, never occurs, at any time of life. . . . (Burnouf 1872, 318–19)

Notwithstanding the learned and eloquent dissent of F. M. Turner (1989), Bernal's reconstruction of how some European scholars, in an atmosphere of racism and anti-Semitism (especially during the nineteenth century), attempted to root out the contributions of the ancient Egyptians and Phoenicians to early Greek civilization seems to me to be beyond dispute. Racism and anti-Semitism pervaded *some* lines of European historical inquiry about the ancient world. Some nineteenth-century scholars of antiquity did understand what we might today call cultural differences in terms of "race." But not all nineteenth-century scholars of the ancient world were racists or anti-Semites.

Bernal's attempt, for instance, to link the career and ideas of George Grote, one of the most famous liberal scholars in nineteenth-century Europe, to the views of Niebuhr, Thirlwall, and Curtius, is not borne out by the evidence he cites. As is well known, Grote had been the youngest member of the original Council which established the University of London in 1826. According to Negley Harte and John North (who published a fine pictorial history of University College, London, in 1979 to help celebrate the sesquicentennial anniversary of the founding of the University of London), at a time when membership in the Church of England was necessary for admission to Oxford and for graduation from Cambridge, the main appeal of the new university was to those excluded from the established system of higher education, especially Nonconformists, Catholics, and Jews. Indeed, in keeping with one of the goals of the new institution—to provide a secular higher education for those to whom it had been denied—Grote himself severed his relationship to the College on 1 February 1830 over the appointment of an

Independent minister of religion, the Reverend John Hoppus, to a chair of Logic and the Philosophy of Mind. Grote eventually was reelected to the Council in 1849, and went on to serve as vice-chancellor of the University and president of the College in 1868. But his position on the necessary separation of religious and scientific instruction never changed: near the end of his life (1871), he endowed a professorship of Mind and Logic at the College, on the following conditions:

> If therefore any such Minister should at any time or times be appointed by the Council to the Professorship of Mind and Logic, or if any Professor of Philosophy of Mind and Logic, having been appointed a layman, shall subsequently take Orders or become a Minister of any such creed or doctrines as aforesaid, I direct that no payment should be made to him out of the present endowments, but that the annual Income when received shall, so far as the law admits, be reinvested and added to the principal, until the time when said Professorship shall be occupied by a Layman. (as quoted in M. L. Clarke 1962, 159)

Thus Grote can be reasonably accused of an anticlerical bias. (He was officially an "unbeliever" in religion, despite the fact that "his father had been a conventional churchman, and his mother a pious evangelical"; Clarke, 1962, 4, 21).

But was Grote guilty of anti-Semitism, racism, and romanticism, as Bernal implies? In what sense does helping to establish the first modern university in Britain which was open to Jews and dissenters—an institution "born in liberty for liberty" (Momigliano 1966), as the greatest historiographer of this century put it—qualify Grote as an anti-Semite or racist? Nor is it easy to detect racism in Grote's writings. As Bernal himself admits (*BA* 1:318), Grote, whose twelve-volume *History of Greece* appeared between 1846 and 1856, simply refused to speculate about the veracity of the Greeks' legends about their past, including the stories of Egyptian and Phoenician colonization. Why?

Grote refused to speculate about these stories because the evidence available to him—decades before the excavations of Schliemann at Troy (1870), Mycenae (1874), Orchomenus (1880), and Tiryns (1885) and of Evans at Knossos (1899) began to reveal contacts between the first Greek speakers and the cultures of the eastern Mediterranean—was insufficient or could not be verified. According to Bernal, Grote's refusal to speculate about Greek legends helped to discredit the stories of Egyptian and Phoenician colonization: in Grote's wake, subsequent scholars also wanted proof that colonization had taken place. Thus because Grote refused to speculate about stories of colonization before 1000 B.C.E. which he could not possibly have confirmed or invalidated, Bernal has accused him of romanticism and possible racism

(*BA* 1:336). So Grote is a romantic or a possible racist because he could not anticipate the results of future archaeological excavations!

Such accusations are not merely unfair because they require Grote to have been a kind of archaeological prophet. They are also unfair because, as any reader of Grote's work knows, Grote was essentially interested in the later classical period. Indeed, as Arnaldo Momigliano pointed out in his famous Inaugural Lecture delivered at University College London in 1952, "George Grote and the Study of Greek History" (1955, 1966), in his Greek history Grote was only marginally concerned with early Greece. Rather, he had begun to contemplate Greek history, as early as 1815, at least in partial response to Mitford's *History of Greece* (1784–1804), which had portrayed the Athenian *dēmos* (popular assembly) as capricious, ungrateful, and tyrannical — and as the ancient counterpart of the French revolutionary mob (Clarke 1962, 103). He was thus centrally interested in the origins of democratic government at Athens and the principles of freedom of thought and rational inquiry (Momigliano 1966, 62). He argued especially for a dynamic relationship between the growth of democracy and the production of great art at Athens in the period just before the Peloponnesian War which was of extraordinary importance in Greek history.

> It is not, of course, to Perikles that the renown of these splendid productions of art belongs: but the great sculptors and architects by whom they were conceived and executed, belonged to that same period of expanding and stimulating Athenian democracy which called forth a similar creative genius in oratory, in dramatic poetry, and in philosophical speculation. (Grote 1900, 22)

Grote was fundamentally concerned with the culture of Athens between the battle of Salamis and the outbreak of the Peloponnesian War — a fifty-year period which occurred approximately one millennium after the events Bernal focuses upon. Thus far Bernal has not been disposed to contest Grote's idea that at Athens during the fifth century, democracy stimulated artistic creativity (and vice versa) in a way which profoundly impressed not only contemporaries but subsequent generations.

It is hard to see how Grote's focus upon the fifth century and passionate case for the interplay between democracy and art at Athens during the fifth century makes him into a racist, fit for the company of Niebuhr, Thirlwall, and Curtius. Above all, Grote loved Athens because it was the place where — on the evidence available to him — liberty had been born, a liberty which he was fighting to establish in his own day against racists and anti-Semites. Grote may have confused the ancient and modern concepts of liberty. Does that confusion make him a racist? This is certainly not the impression one gets from reading contemporary assessments.

In 1863 the young Viennese Hellenist Theodor Gomperz went to London to meet the great liberal scholar, who in his sixty-ninth year was still hard at work on Plato. Gompérz left the following description of his first meeting with Grote in a letter to his sister:

> Seriously, I expected a great deal of this distinguished man, but I have found far more than I expected;—above all, a mind completely open and free from all prejudice—"open-minded," as a very clever woman recently described him, in the highest degree, not a narrow great man, but as far from it as I could have believed possible. . . . With light goes warmth, and I have already today had several refreshing glimpses into the heartfelt, overflowing goodwill, the ungrudging recognition of others, that all embracing patience of this fine spirit. Grote is certainly much more even than his great History shows on the surface, more than he has ever shown even to the most sympathetic reader, who, like me, knows how to interpret the hidden clues. I knew Grote's philosophic point of view very well, all the better in that it is also mine, but I did not know that the philosophic feeling and spirit works in him in so strong and lively a fashion, and that dull learning has seldom hidden and never blocked up this spring of life in him. The mere man of learning, whose ideal is a library that has acquired self-consciousness, is completely subordinate, as should be the case, to the thinker, and indeed the universal thinker, a relationship which looks perfectly straightforward, very clear and simple as a prescription, but is one that very few chemists know how to make up. (quoted in Clarke 1962, 90)

This letter and the rest of the evidence we have for Grote's ideas and work suggest that Bernal's summary judgment of Grote is fundamentally misleading. Only by omitting vital evidence about Grote's commitment to higher education for Jews, dissidents, and Nonconformists, and his principled stand on the separation of religious doctrine and scientific knowledge, has Bernal managed to fit him into a neat category of romantics, racists, and anti-Semites.

The problem with such neat categories is that they tend to collapse under closer scrutiny. In the case of Grote (and, one wonders, of how many other scholars thus summarily condemned?) the reality is far more complex. When we take into account what the evidence available to Grote actually was, his views about early Greek civilization become perfectly explicable. As a general rule of scholarly inquiry, we must take into account all of the evidence; we must also see previous scholars within their own complex historical contexts. Too often in *Black Athena* Bernal treats scholars (such as Grote) as decontextualized or selectively contextualized straw men: they are put up to be connected with other straw men of alleged racist and anti-Semitic views. But Grote and other scholars of the nineteenth century were real, complex individuals, influenced by their times and influencing their times in turn. Any reconstruction of nineteenth-century European classical historiography which presents a monolithic picture of racism and anti-Semitism is over-simplified. Not all nineteenth-century European historians were racists or anti-Semites.

THE HISTORICAL ARGUMENT

The historical argument of *Black Athena* turns on the credibility of various stories about the Egyptian and Phoenician colonization of later Greek lands found particularly in the *Histories* of Herodotus (2.49–52, 2.171, 2.182, 4.147, 5.58, 6.55). No doubt scholars now will argue about the reliability of those stories for years; in fact, spirited discussions of the literary and archaeological evidence for such colonization have already recommenced (see Coleman, Morris, this volume). I do not propose to enter into these disputes about colonization here. I should mention, however, that I doubt that those who have recently argued against significant colonization have done so out of a desire to exclude Africans or Phoenicians from the foundation story of the West (as Bernal implies). Nor do I think that the cultural achievements of later Greeks would be changed or diminished in any way, even if scholars decided that there had been massive African and Asian colonization during the second millennium of what would later become Greek lands.

In what sense could we say, for example, that Sophocles' *Antigone* owes anything substantial to Egypt, simply because the action of the tragedy is set in Thebes, which Bernal claims was colonized by Egyptians more than a thousand years earlier? If we applied Bernal's linear notion of cultural inheritance to other historical contexts, absurd conclusions would ensue. Do we believe, for instance, that because Constantine, who refounded Byzantium as a specifically Christian city called Constantinople on 11 May 330 c.e., was born at Naissus in the Danubian region, the present-day inhabitants of Istanbul owe their religious belief system to Naissus? We should remember that the modern citizens of Istanbul live almost exactly as far away from the time when Istanbul was refounded as a Christian city as the fifth-century Greeks lived from the time of the alleged Egyptian colonization!

It is not specifically on the historicity of Egyptian and Phoenician colonization, however, that Bernal seriously leads astray those less familiar with the Near Eastern world. No scholar doubts that Near Eastern cultures influenced the early Greeks. But was that cultural influence as restricted to Egypt and Phoenicia as Bernal insists in *Black Athena*? (And it is to his positions as stated in *Black Athena* and not to subsequent private qualifications that he, just as any other scholar, must be held.)

According to Bernal, it was *only* the Egyptians and Phoenicians who significantly influenced early Greek civilization. This reconstruction is directly and unequivocally contradicted by evidence that is widely known among Near Eastern historians. In fact, the evidence is so well known, and is presented so consistently, even in generalist books on the ancient Near East, that the absence or dismissal of this evidence in *Black Athena* calls for an explanation, which Bernal has not yet offered. (My own summary presentation of some of that evidence here can hardly be seen as a *cri de coeur* from the Sumero-Babylonian scholarly establishment: my research interests lie within the chronological time parameters and physical borders of the eastern provinces of the Roman empire).

Why, then, has Bernal ignored or dismissed the evidence for contacts with or contributions to early Greek civilization other than by two cultures of the ancient Near East? I shall argue shortly that the absence or dismissal of evidence in *Black Athena* for widespread Near Eastern influence upon and contacts with early Greek civilization exposes both the explicit and implicit contemporary political agenda of *Black Athena*.

THE CULTURAL LANDSCAPE OF THE ANCIENT NEAR EAST

Bernal's cultural landscape of the Near East in the second millennium B.C.E. is missing some players whom Near Eastern scholars have argued directly influenced, prefigured, or paralleled Greek achievements in precisely those areas of political institutions, science, and philosophy or religion which Bernal maintains the ancient Greeks derived entirely "from Egypt in particular" (*BA* 1:120). Although it would be easy to offer many examples drawn from a thousand-year period of interaction, I restrict myself here to one from each of the areas Bernal cites, to illustrate how Near Eastern cultures outside of Egypt or Phoenicia anticipated the achievements or directly influenced the early Greeks.

Sumerian "Democracy"

A particularly revealing example comes from Sumer at the earliest stages of development of the Sumerian city-states. Thorkild Jacobsen (1943; 1970) has argued that Sumerian myths and epics indicate that an assembly of all adult free men originally constituted the sovereign government within Sumerian cities, although elders handled the normal run of public affairs (see also Postgate 1992, 80–81). Indeed Jacobsen and others have spoken of the Sumerian city-states as primitive democracies, in precisely the later Greek sense that the Sumerian citizen-bodies held political power. (In fact at least one classical historian has hinted at a correlation not only between Sumerian and Greek political institutions but also between Sumerian and Phoenician institutions; see Snodgrass 1980, 31–32).

It should be noted here that Semiticists do not claim that Athenians of the fifth century B.C.E. learned democracy from their Near Eastern predecessors; rather, they reason that prior or parallel developments were possible under similar demographic and geographic conditions (Saggs 1989, 34–35). For our purposes, the important point is that the evidence for Sumerian democracy would seem to present Bernal with some excellent ammunition to attack one of the last bastions of Greek cultural "uniqueness," namely, the invention of the world's first real democracy. What could "lessen" European cultural arrogance more than the revelation that the Sumerians established the world's first popular government along the banks of the lower Euphrates *at the beginning of the second millennium B.C.E.!*

Why has Bernal completely ignored this politically explosive piece of evidence and generally discussed Sumerian and Mesopotamian civilization only in terms of the external social and political forces that shaped the study of Mesopotamian history and culture during the nineteenth century of the present era? Certainly not because the Sumerians influenced Western civilization any less than the Phoenicians. Rather, the Sumerians have been unlucky in their alleged heirs; most recently, an unpopular dictator named Saddam Hussein has claimed to have been descended from the Sumerians. He has used sixty million bricks (many bearing his name) in rebuilding the walls, towers, streets, and palaces of Nebuchadnezzar's Babylon (*Times Saturday Review* 1991).

Mesopotamian Science

The case that Near Eastern cultures outside Egypt influenced, prefigured, and even surpassed later Greek scientific achievements is even stronger than the case for political institutions. (For a detailed analysis of the relationship between Egyptian and Greek astronomy, mathematics, and medicine see Palter, this volume, on the history of science.)

In Mesopotamia by around 1800 B.C.E. the Babylonians had calculated the square root of two correctly to one in two million. Furthermore, twelve centuries before the birth of the Greek Pythagoras, the same Babylonians had already figured out that in any right-angled triangle, the square of the hypotenuse is equal to the sum of the squares of the other two sides. In other words, some Babylonians of the early second millennium B.C.E. had discovered the theorem the Greeks attributed to Pythagoras more than a thousand years later. During the same period the Babylonians developed algebraic processes to solve various mathematical problems and eventually learned how to calculate cube roots. These accomplishments have led Near Eastern historians to conclude that the expertise of the Babylonian mathematicians in

1800 B.C.E. exceeded that of the majority of people today other than those who hold a college degree in mathematics (Saggs 1989, 225). And, in the field of mathematical astronomy, the Greek geographer and traveler Strabo (17.1.29) informs us that Greco-Roman astrologers during the first century C.E. still learned their arts from the Chaldaeans.

How could Bernal overlook such remarkable achievements in scientific fields such as mathematics and astronomy, especially since Western scholars have often claimed that those fields are areas of unique Western origin and prowess? In *Black Athena* the scientific achievements of the Babylonians and Chaldaeans are passed over in near silence—perhaps because "German Orientalists" took up the case of their contributions to Greek and other European cultures (1:365).

Bernard Lewis thought he had constructed an instructive fantasy about another scholarly discipline, classics; Bernal's treatment of Mesopotamian science shows us that one man's fantasy is another's conspiracy. According to Bernal, classicists left the Egyptians and the Phoenicians out of the foundation story of the West; Orientalists substituted the Babylonians and the Chaldaeans. Classicists and Orientalists thus have conspired to deny our Afro-Asiatic roots. Classicism and Orientalism are part of the same Western scholarly conspiracy against the East.

Mesopotamian, Hurrian, and Hittite Myth

In the area of philosophy or religion the evidence is also abundant and clear. For example, the theme of the son who castrates his own father to gain power which we find in the Greek Kronos and Ouranos myth actually originated in the Babylonian myth of Harab (Jacobsen 1984). From Babylon the myth probably was spread to the the Hurrian kingdom of Mittanni, which was centered on the Habur Valley but extended from Lake Van and the Zagros to the Mediterranean coast. The Hurrians, in turn, passed along the Harab myth to their neighbors, the Hittites in central Anatolia, where it is found in Hittite texts as the Kumarbi myth. It was from Hittite sources that the myth entered the canon of early Greek cosmologies.

In this case, we have an excellent example, not just of one Near Eastern culture anticipating Greek thought or practice, but of several cultures directly and indirectly influencing the formation of Greek mythology. Furthermore, there is no controversy about Hittite colonization of later Greek lands: many later Greek sites in Anatolia, right down to the western coast, such as Ephesos, were indeed Hittite settlements or were in contact with the Hittites, as the extensive archaeological excavations at Ephesos and elsewhere have revealed. Why, then, has Bernal ignored or summarily dismissed the direct and long-lasting contributions to early Greek civilization of the Babylonians, the Hurrians, the Hittites, the Luwians, and all Near Eastern cultures other than those made by the Egyptians and the Phoenicians?

All other Near Eastern cultures have been excluded from Bernal's foundation myth of Western civilization because the scholars who have argued for their contributions have (to his mind) worked from within the conceptual framework of the "Aryan Model" he proposes, which would deny a fundamental Egyptian and Phoenician contribution to early Greek civilization. And all scholars who either have denied the fundamental Egyptian and Phoenician contribution to early Greek civilization or argued for contributions of non-blacks or Semites have done so (in his view) for reasons of racism and anti-Semitism. In other words, the Hittites have lost their place at the birth of the West solely because they spoke an Indo-European language—and thus were favored by German Orientalists!

But what was the "sin" of the Babylonians? Some spoke the Semitic language Akkadian during the later period, but Sumerian was the language of the people who first sparked the Mesopotamian urban revolution around 3000 B.C.E. Why should the record of *their* influence upon and interaction with later Mediterranean cultures be ignored?

The answer to this crucial question lies not in the evidence of the ancient Near East in 2000 B.C.E., but in the later twentieth century.

THE AFRO-ASIATIC ORIGINS OF CLASSICAL CIVILIZATION

To show that the Afro-Asiatic origins of classical civilization is foremost a myth of the twentieth century, we need first to look more closely at exactly who (according to Bernal) were the ancient Egyptians and Phoenicians. On this point he is very clear—and controversial: Egyptian civilization was fundamentally African, and many of the most powerful dynasties of Upper Egypt could "usefully" be termed black (*BA* 1:242); as for the Phoenicians, they were culturally related to the Jews (1:337, 344). Let us ignore for the moment that no Egyptian of the early second millennium would have understood what it meant to be African in any possible modern sense, for the modern concept of Africa had not been invented at the time. Nor is it critical that experts have responded that the equation of Egyptian with "black" is a "chimera, cultural baggage from our own society that can only be imposed artificially on ancient Egyptian society" (Yurco 1989, 24; see also Snowden 1983, esp. 5–17). (For further viewpoints on the issue of "race" in ancient Egypt see Bard, Snowden, Brace et al., Yurco, all in this volume). For our purposes, in fact, it does not matter whether the ancient Egyptians were black, white, or mixed, or whether the ancient Phoenicians were culturally related to the ancient Jews. What does matter, and crucially, is to recognize what kind of identification Bernal makes in both cases: he defines the ancient Egyptians as a people in racial terms; the Phoenicians, on the other hand, he defines ethnically.

Thus we have returned to a reconstruction of the past based upon essentializing principles of race and ethnic origins; race, ethnicity, and culture have been conflated. We have returned, in other words, to the nineteenth-century style of "race"-bound and ethnocentric historiography that Bernal himself (among many of his contemporaries) has so rightly questioned — except that in the later twentieth century Bernal would now replace white Indo-Europeans as the founders of Western civilization with black Africans and Semites.

THE MYTH OF MARTIN BERNAL

Why has the "true" identity of the founders of classical and Western civilization been reasserted at the present time? Bernal himself has provided the explicit answer to this question.

Trained in Chinese studies, and a teacher and researcher of intellectual relations between China and the West at the turn of the twentieth century, according to his own public revelations, Bernal became concerned after 1962 with the war in Indochina. He studied Vietnam both to contribute to the movement against American military involvement there and for its own sake (*BA* 1:xii). In 1975 he rediscovered his own Jewish roots:

> In 1975 I came to a mid-life crisis. The personal reasons for this are not particularly interesting. Politically, however, it was related to the end of the American intervention in Indo-China and the awareness that the Maoist era in China was coming to an end. It now seemed to me that the central focus of danger and interest in the world was no longer East Asia but the Eastern Mediterranean. This shift led me to a concern for Jewish history. (*BA* 1:xii–xiii)

He also tells us that it was specifically the exploration of his Jewish roots that led him to look at Jewish history in relation to Canaanite and Phoenician history. His subsequent "discovery" of a large number of loan words from Canaanite/Phoenician into Greek led him, in turn, to the stories of the Phoenician colonization of Greece. The search for the quarter to the third proportion of Greek vocabulary which could not be attributed to Indo-European or Phoenician/Canaanite sources brought him to late ancient Egyptian, and the stories of the Egyptian colonization of Greece (1:xiv–xv).

Thus a specific social and personal context gave birth to the new foundation myth of the West: it was conceived in Bernal's mind during the years of the Vietnam War and the civil rights movement in America; it developed as he rediscovered his own Jewish roots only two years after the victory of Israel in the Yom Kippur War, and less than a decade after the dramatic triumph of the Six Day War, at a time when many Jews living in the Diaspora reassessed their relationships to Judaism and Israel.

It was therefore no accident at all, or the result of an impersonal scientific inquiry, that when the new foundation myth first saw the light of day, its identity was Afro-Asiatic. The social and personal context in which it was conceived by Bernal ensured that the new founders of classical civilization should only be Egyptians (some of whose most powerful dynasties could "usefully" be called black) and Phoenicians (who were culturally related to the Jews). That context also explains why people who spoke Indo-European languages, such as the Hittites, had to be left out of the new foundation myth of the West. It was not simply because "Aryanist" scholars of the nineteenth century, hunting around for Indo-European language speakers to fit their racist theories, had championed the contributions made by the Hittites and others to Greek civilization. The Hittites and others were also excluded because Bernal could not trace his own personal roots or changing intellectual interests to the Hittites, the Hurrians, or the Babylonians.

Such a reconstruction of Bernal's enterprise as the above is inevitable; he himself has anticipated such a reconstruction, possibly because he has applied precisely such a method of historiographical analysis to countless scholars in *Black Athena*. Indeed, he has tried to mitigate the implications of such a reconstruction of his endeavor. He has taken care to insist that even where scholars have worked within the Aryan model, the origins of their projects do not necessarily invalidate their results (*BA* 1:442).

The origins of a scientific project may well be divorced from initial consideration of its results (and it is perhaps to Bernal's credit that he has openly laid out what he wants the world to believe about the story behind *Black Athena*). But if, after due consideration, the results of a project appear to be closely linked to its origins, scholars are obligated—as Bernal himself has felt obligated—to examine the relationship between the two. Given the stated social and personal contexts from which *Black Athena* evolved, it is hard in retrospect not to see the entire enterprise of *Black Athena* as a massive, fundamentally misguided projection upon the second millennium B.C.E. of Martin Bernal's personal struggle to establish an identity during the later twentieth century.

The outcome of that struggle has been the creation of a highly selective myth of influences on early Greek civilization. As we have seen (and much more evidence could easily be produced), the selectivity of Bernal's foundation myth cannot be explained on the basis of the ancient evidence; the reasons for that selectivity lie inescapably in the personal odyssey of Martin Bernal.

BLACK ATHENA, MULTICULTURALISM, AND THE FOUNDATIONS OF WESTERN CIVILIZATION

Worse still from the point of view of those individuals or communities who have seen *Black Athena* as an argument for the first multicultural foundations of Western civilization, in its structure and conception of cultural heritage, the foundation myth of *Black Athena* implicitly accepts, indeed depends vitally upon, an acceptance of the cultural primacy of the West. (See also Baines, this volume.) The cultures which Bernal argues laid the foundations of Western civilization are valued primarily for laying the foundations of the West. They are not studied on their own terms, or for their own cultural achievements. Late ancient Egyptian and Canaanite/Phoenician languages are evaluated for what they contributed to Greek. Archaeological evidence is only significant if it proves contacts between Egyptians and Phoenicians, and Greeks.

As others also have noticed, *Black Athena* therefore remains inescapably Eurocentric in its approach and method. What has not been noticed before is the extent to which Bernal's Eurocentricity fundamentally undermines the explicit political purpose of *Black Athena*. Readers should ask: Will a four-volume enterprise dedicated to showing how two cultures of the ancient Near East influenced early Greek civilization make Europe less or more culturally arrogant?

It is sad and ironic that such a Eurocentric view of Africa should be advanced and become popular at a time when systematic archaeological investigations and major museum exhibitions, such as the Nubia exhibit at the Museum of Fine Arts in Boston organized by Rita Freed, are dramatically changing both scholarly and public perception of the indigenous cultures of Africa and their achievements (see esp. Phillipson 1993). The ancient cultures of Africa and the Near East do not need to be the founders of the West to be worthy of global interest and study; they are intrinsically interesting. It is simply another form of colonialism to insist that the Egyptians and Phoenicians have value only if they taught the Greeks "civilization."

Furthermore, we might well inquire whether the alleged descendants of those two Near Eastern cultures wish to have their contributions to the human experiment on Earth measured by their comparative contributions to classical and Western civilization. Do their histories deserve attention only if their stories form part of the foundation story of the West?

Did the new founders only teach the ancient Greeks religion, philosophy, and literature? From whom did the Greeks learn how to fight wars or enslave their neighbors? We should also remember that in the present century alone, scientists living in Western countries have, to be sure, produced vaccinations for diphtheria, typhoid fever, cholera, and plague. Elected leaders of Western nations have also initiated the Holocaust. How much of the long and complex Western legacy would the new founders of Western civilization wish to claim?

Whatever these alleged descendants decide about the desirability of being identified as the founders of Western civilization, the editors of this volume have tried to show that *Black Athena* is not the bible of the multicultural foundations of the West, nor is Bernal its author. Rather, he is (sadly) only a false prophet along the road to that multicultural foundation story of Western civilization which, I have suggested, best suits *all* of the ancient evidence. As it stands, the true gospel of the multicultural foundations of the West awaits its Messiah.

Nevertheless, to his credit, Professor Bernal has reminded the general public that the Greeks were not born, like Athena, fully formed from the brow of Zeus. Greek civilization indeed grew out of a wider Mediterranean context. Furthermore, Bernal has exposed how some of the actors in that wider Mediterranean context were written out of the story of early Western civilization during the nineteenth century by some scholars for reasons of racism and anti-Semitism. The West must be constantly on guard against its oldest internal enemies, anti-Semitism and racism.

Finally, Bernal has done for classicists, ancient historians, and classical archaeologists what they have done less well recently for themselves: he has made their fields and them important, relevant, even critical to a national, some would even say global debate about who we are (or rather who we would like to think we are), and what we should tell our children about the past we have claimed. The role of *Black Athena* in that debate will be to remind future generations—if I may slightly paraphrase the wise words of Arnaldo Momigliano—that all historiography, if not history, is contemporary.

CONCLUSION

QUO VADIS?

Guy MacLean Rogers

As the bibliography at the end of this book reveals, since the first review of the first volume of *Black Athena* appeared in *The Guardian* in 1987, at least sixty-eight reviews, articles, and films have appeared about Martin Bernal's hypotheses, argumentation, and conclusions in that volume and in his second one, which appeared in 1991. No one can maintain plausibly that *Black Athena* has been ignored either by scholars or by the general public.

In these discussions about *Black Athena* reviewers have concentrated on a series of questions implicitly or explicitly raised by Bernal in his work. Among the most frequently recurring questions are these:

- Who were the ancient Egyptians?
- Were the ancient Egyptians "black"?
- Was Egypt African?
- Did the ancient Egyptians or Hyksos colonize Greece?
- Did the ancient Egyptians and/or Phoenicians massively influence the early Greeks in the areas of language, religion, science and/or philosophy?
- Did the Greeks believe that they were descended from the Egyptians and Phoenicians?
- Did eighteenth- and nineteenth-century scholars obscure the Afro-Asiatic roots of classical civilization for reasons of racism and anti-Semitism?
- Are the scholarly methods of *Black Athena* credible?

The editors of this volume present here some preliminary answers to these questions. These preliminary answers are based upon summaries of the articles edited for this volume (although there obviously are some differences among the contributors about details). In setting out these preliminary answers, we hope to provide scholars and the general public with a handy reference to the state of expert judgment on some difficult scholarly questions.

We recognize that Bernal (and other scholars) may well disagree with our answers to these questions. We welcome his response. At the end of this conclusion, we make some suggestions about how the debate about the roots of classical civilization might be framed most productively in the future. We look forward to the next round in the debate.

Who were the ancient Egyptians? Although the population of ancient Egypt had ties to the north and to the south, and was also intermediate between populations to the east and west, the population of ancient Egypt was distinct and basically Egyptian from the Neolithic period right up to historic times.

Were the ancient Egyptians "black"? Many of the scholars who contributed to this volume found this question to be disturbing, at least as it was formulated in *Black Athena*. Several contributors specifically have been concerned that ancient evidence and archaeological remains have been identified with concepts of race and racial issues which belong to the modern world. Such issues appear to have been absent in the conceptual world of ancient Egyptians and Greeks. Indeed, in the ancient Mediterranean world in general, color terms did not carry the stigma of inferiority similar to that associated with color terms in postclassical societies, which have subjected darker skinned peoples to terrible forms of discrimination on the basis of the color of their skin.

But since Bernal himself has raised this question, both in *Black Athena* and in subsequent public comments, scholars have felt obliged to set the record straight for the sake of their peers as well as the general public.

We believe that the attempt to assign the people of the Nile valley to "Caucasoid" or "Negroid" categories is an arbitrary act and wholly devoid of historical or biological significance. It would be inaccurate to describe the ancient Egyptians as either black or white; the population of ancient Egypt was one of mixed pigmentation. Essentially, the Egyptians were the Egyptians. To describe them otherwise promotes a misconception about the ancient Egyptians, with racist undertones, that reveals much more about those who wish to make such attempts than about the ancient Egyptians themselves.

Was Egypt African? Although Egypt lies geographically on the continent of Africa, in anthropological terms the categorical labeling of the civilization of ancient Egypt as "fundamentally African" is misleadingly simplistic. In fact the archaeological evidence of African kingdoms south of Egypt suggests distinctly different cultures that were often in conflict with ancient Egypt. *Black Athena* hardly treats these relations—and still less so the widespread evidence in other parts of the continent for the independent evolution of civilizations. In tracing the alleged Afro-Asiatic roots of classical civilization, Bernal has almost nothing to say about the entire continent of Africa and its many and diverse ancient civilizations. In short, *Black Athena* is not about ancient Africa at all.

Did the ancient Egyptians or Hyksos colonize Greece? In *Black Athena* Bernal claims that Greece was colonized from Egypt not once, but twice: first during the third millennium B.C.E., when Egyptian colonists arrived in Greece, bringing advanced building skills, their cults and religion; and second, during the eighteenth/seventeenth centuries B.C.E., when the Hyksos, having been driven out of Egypt, invaded the Argolid and ruled there.

Unambiguous archaeological evidence in support of an Egyptian colonization of Greece is absent from the Aegean area, despite decades of field research. Nor do the historical records of Egypt or any other Near Eastern culture support the idea of a Hyksos invasion and colonization of the Argolid.

Did the ancient Egyptians and/or the Phoenicians massively influence the early Greeks in the areas of language, religion, science, and/or philosophy? No expert in the field doubts that there was a Greek cultural debt to the ancient Near East. The real questions are: How large was the debt? Was it massive, as Bernal claims? Was it limited to the Egyptians and the Phoenicians?

The consensus of the contributors to this volume is that the debt cannot be described as massive; nor was the debt limited to Egypt and Phoenicia.

Certainly the evidence shows that the Eighteenth Dynasty and the Aegean world were in close contact at certain levels; but such contacts are not equivalent to "suzerainty" and do not imply the substantial cultural impact upon the Aegean that is required by Bernal's claims.

All of the contributors agree that the early Greeks got their alphabet from the Phoenicians; but little else. Indeed, in terms of language, the evidence that Bernal has presented thus far for the influence of Egyptian or Phoenician on ancient Greek has failed to meet any of the standard tests which are required for the proof of extensive influence, including a large percentage of undisputed vocabulary borrowings, phonetic similarity, and parallelisms in grammar. Overall, the fact remains that Egyptian and Canaanite scripts were never used widely in historical Greece.

Similarly, in the area of religion, Egyptian and Canaanite deities were never worshiped on Greek soil in their indigenous forms. Nor does the abundant archaeological evidence support claims of deep and pervasive influence in the area of cult.

The case for Egyptian influence on Greek mathematical astronomy, mathematics, and medicine is only somewhat stronger. In these areas the Egyptians definitely influenced the Greeks; but Greek achievements, especially in the fields of mathematics and medicine, became quite distinct and original.

Several contributors, while convinced of the influence of the Mediterranean cultures of the ancient Near East on early Greek civilization, especially through the medium of trade, nevertheless could not agree that Egypt or Phoenicia was the principal axis of that influence. Instead they point to relations that were probably more critical to long-term developments in Greece, including (especially) relations with the northern Levant, Anatolia, and, ultimately, Babylonia, which was much more influential culturally than Egypt generally in the Near East. Furthermore, there were more geographical routes available by which that Babylonian influence could travel.

Finally, several contributors have drawn attention to a different model of interaction between the ancient Near East and early Greece. Instead of Bernal's model of colonization and/or massive influence moving from Egypt and Phoenicia to Greece, Near Eastern specialists suggest a model of regular, widespread, and mutually profitable contacts between many different Near Eastern cultures and the early Greeks over a much greater time span. Several scholars emphasized that there is, in fact, increasing evidence of Minoan and early Greek influence on the culture not only of Egypt, but of Palestine as well. The cultural road to early Greece apparently was not a one-way street; rather there were many two-lane highways of cultural exchange, connecting many different Near Eastern cultures not only with the early Greeks but also with each other.

Did the Greeks believe that they were descended from the Egyptians and the Phoenicians? There were rival traditions propounded about the origins of the Greeks, at different times and for different reasons. We might call such rival traditions competitive subjective ethnicities. The Cadmus and Danaus myths, for instance, upon which Bernal places such weight, were created or revised (in the forms which we now have them) by Athenian poets and historians who wished to emphasize the autochthony of Athens by contrast with the alleged foreign origins of rival city states. Greek myths of ethnic origins, in other words, do not bear unmediated, literal truths about the origins of the Greeks.

Did eighteenth- and nineteenth-century scholars obscure the Afro-Asiatic roots of classical civilization for reasons of racism and anti-Semitism? Some eighteenth- and nineteenth-century scholars who wrote about the question of Greece's cultural debt to Egypt or Phoenicia did so from a point of view that today would be considered racist or anti-Semitic. Some of those scholars denied or underemphasized that debt for the sake of maintaining the uniqueness and originality of European culture in their own day.

But not all or even the majority of eighteenth- and nineteenth-century classical scholars who downplayed Greece's debt to Egypt or Phoenicia were racists or anti-Semites. Rather, the majority of those scholars downplayed that debt because they saw little evidence for the kind of massive influence that Bernal has argued for. Nor has he been able to produce new evidence or a new interpretation of old evidence which might convince the majority of scholars today that the majority of eighteenth- and nineteenth-century scholars were essentially wrong.

Furthermore, as the essays collected in this volume have shown, Professor Bernal's attempt to portray figures such as Herder and Grote as racists or romantics is not supported by a careful, contextualized study of all of the evidence. Too often in *Black Athena* he has selected only a few sentences from the works of earlier scholars and has decontextualized those sentences in order to build up a picture of undifferentiated racism and anti-Semitism—but only on the part of those previous scholars who have questioned the depth of Greece's debt to Egypt or Phoenicia.

The scholarly record is, in fact, far more complex and contradictory than Bernal allows. The picture of attitudes toward blacks in Britain and America, for instance, is far more complicated than he makes it out to be. There certainly were many prominent and outspoken intellectual antiracists in Britain and America, a fact readers would never discover from reading *Black Athena*.

More to the point, many scholars in the eighteenth and nineteenth centuries questioned the depth of Greece's debt to Egypt and Phoenicia, not for reasons of racism and anti-Semitism, as Bernal would insist, but because evidence leading to that conclusion was lacking; or, more importantly, because the discovery of new evidence led in the opposite direction. In particular, the discovery of the Indo-European language group, of which Greek was proved to be a member, encouraged nineteenth-century scholars especially to think of Greek civilization as being fundamentally different from the civilizations of Egypt and Phoenicia.

In sum, Bernal's presentation of European classical historiography of the eighteenth and nineteenth centuries as pervaded by racism and anti-Semitism that prevented scholars from accurately assessing the Afro-Asiatic roots of classical civilization, is oversimplified and unconvincing.

Are the scholarly methods of Black Athena *credible?* Archaeologists, linguists, historians, and literary critics have the gravest reservations about the scholarly methods used in *Black Athena*. Archaeologists cite a constant misconstruing of facts and conclusions and misinterpretation of such archaeological evidence as there is. Still more pernicious is the assumption that archaeological objects can be identified with race and questions of racial origins. Linguists see Bernal's methods as little more than a series of assertive guesses, often bordering on the fantastic. Historians and literary critics find his treatment of Greek myth and literature naive, old-fashioned, and curiously conservative.

Finally, few scholars would care to adopt Bernal's principle of "competitive plausibility" as a guiding methodology for reconstructing the ancient past. What may have happened in the past is certainly not the same thing as what probably happened, as best we can reconstruct it, based upon a careful, thorough, contextualized evaluation of *all* the evidence.

Many contributors think it unwise to abandon the present century's hard-won methodological gains in analyzing complex societies and categories of evidence for the sake of a new methodological paradigm based on competitive plausibility, the explicit goal of which is to advance a particular anti-European cultural agenda. In short, as an advertisement for the application and results of his new methodology, *Black Athena* represents a stunningly effective demonstration of the virtues of the old methodology of careful, contextualized scholarship.

QUO VADIS?

Nothing is healthier for an academic discipline than to have intelligent, interested outsiders bring questions to familiar material. Certainly, the fundamental question raised by *Black Athena*—that of the relationship between early Greek civilization and the ancient Near East—is a legitimate, interesting, and important one. It is also one that ancient historians, archaeologists, and classicists have been laboring over for at least two hundred years. Bernal's main strategy for exploring this important question—treating Egyptian and Phoenician cultures through their influence on early classical civilization—has invited, and perhaps even insures, however, the opposite of his intended effect of lessening European cultural arrogance. He pays attention and gives stature to Egypt and Phoenicia only in relation to a later and different Western culture. Thus *Black Athena* succumbs to exactly the Eurocentrism it was written to combat.

In addition, by linking his interpretation of the ancient evidence to an anachronistic conception of race, Bernal has reinforced some destructive popular misconceptions, not only about the ancient world but also about modern scholarship. Insofar as he has helped to establish that linkage, he is responsible for those misconceptions. *Black Athena* has in various respects bolstered the agenda of some Afrocentrists, whose racial theories would return many important debates about the past to the rightly abandoned premises of some of the worst examples of the racist historiography of the nineteenth century. In particular, we deplore the attempt to revivify the discredited premise that cultural achievements can be explained in terms of alleged "racial" origins. To reduce human beings to physical characteristics over which they have no control—such as the color of their skin—is both an error and a human sin.

For these reasons, the editors of this volume call upon Bernal to reject publicly, explicitly, and unambiguously any theories of history which conflate race and culture. Not to do so would be a signal that he supports a view of the past which has in fact been one of the causes of racism and anti-Semitism in the modern world.

We believe that the study of the cultures of Africa and the Near East will prosper more in a truly pluralistic scholarship that encompasses civilizations of the whole world without necessarily seeking a single line of cultural evolution, than in a scholarship which focuses upon or requires a single (or selective) tradition or cultural style. In this book we have attempted to set out a historical model of the origins and development of Greek civilization within a truly pluralistic framework of ancient cultures which are studied simultaneously, not just for what those cultures contributed to the Greeks, or to any society since, but for their own sakes. We owe the ancient civilizations of Greece, Africa, the Near East—and ourselves—no less.

BIBLIOGRAPHY

Asterisks indicate reviews or critiques of *Black Athena*; daggers indicate recommended further reading.

Abetti, G. 1952. *The History of Astronomy*. New York: H. Schuman.

Adams, B. 1984. *Egyptian Mummies*. Princes Risborough, Aylesbury: Shire Publications.

Adams, W. Y. 1967. "Continuity and Change in Nubian Culture History." *Sudan Notes and Records* 48:1–32.

———. 1977. *Nubia: Corridor to Africa*. Princeton: Princeton University Press.

———. 1979. "Kush and the Peoples of Northeast Africa." In *Africa in Antiquity: The Arts of Ancient Nubia and the Sudan*, edited by F. Hintze, 9–13. Berlin: Akademie-Verlag.

†———. 1984. *Nubia: Corridor to Africa*. 2d edition. Princeton: Allen Lane.

Addison, F. 1949. *The Wellcome Excavations in the Sudan*. London: Oxford University Press.

Aldred, C. 1970. "Some Royal Portraits of the Middle Kingdom in Ancient Egypt." *Metropolitan Museum of Art Journal* 3:27–50.

†———. 1984. *The Egyptians*. Rev. ed. London: Thames & Hudson.

Al-Hassan, A. Y., and D. R. Hill. 1986. *Islamic Technology: An Illustrated History*. Cambridge: Cambridge University Press.

*Allen, N. 1990. "*Black Athena*: An Interview with Martin Bernal." *Free Inquiry* 10:18–22.

*Allen, P. S. 1992. "*Black Athena*." *American Anthropologist* 94, no. 4:1024–26. (Film review)

Allen, T. W. 1994. *The Invention of the White Race*. Vol. 1, *Racial Oppression and Social Control*. London: Verso.

Allport, G. W. 1964. *The Nature of Prejudice*. Reading, Mass.: Addison-Wesley.

†*American Historical Review. 1987. "Forum." 92, no. 4:797–878.

Ammerman, A., and L. L. Cavalli-Sforza. 1973. "A Population Model for the Diffusion of Early Farming in Europe." In *The Explanation of Culture Change*, edited by C. Renfrew, 343–57. London: Duckworth.

———. 1979. "The Wave of Advance Model for the Spread of Agriculture in Europe." In *Transformations: Mathematical Approaches to Culture Change*, edited by C. Renfrew and K. L. Cooke, 270–93. New York: Academic Press.

Anderson, J. E. 1968. "Late Paleolithic Skeletal Remains from Nubia." In *The Prehistory of Nubia*, vol. 2, edited by F. Wendorf, 996–1040. Dallas: Southern Methodist University Press.

*Anderson, P. 1987. "The Myth of Hellenism." *The Guardian* (Manchester), 13 March, 14. (Review of *BA* 1)

†Andrewes, A. 1967. *The Greeks*. London: Hutchinson.

Andrews, C. 1981. *The Rosetta Stone*. New ed. London: British Museum Publications.

————. 1984. *Egyptian Mummies*. Cambridge: Harvard University Press.

†Appiah, K. A. 1992. *In My Father's House: Africa in the Philosophy of Culture*. New York: Oxford University Press.

————. 1993. "Europe Upside Down: Fallacies of the New Afrocentrism." *Times Literary Supplement* (London), 12 February, 24–25.

Aptheker, H. 1992. *Anti-Racism in U.S. History: The First Two Hundred Years*. New York: Greenwood Press.

Arambourg, C., M. Boule, and R. Verneau. 1934. *Les grottes paléolithiques des Beni Segoual, Algérie*. Archives de l'Institut de Paléontologie Humaine, Mémoire 13. Paris: Masson.

Archimedes. 1912. *On the Sphere and Cylinder*. In *The Works of Archimedes*, translated by M. L. Heath. New York: Dover.

Arlotto, A. 1971. *Introduction to Historical Linguistics*. New York: Houghton Mifflin.

Arnett, W. 1982. *The Predynastic Origin of Egyptian Hieroglyphs*. Washington, D.C.: University Press of America.

Arnold, D. 1991. *Building in Egypt: Pharonic Stone Masonry*. New York: Oxford University Press.

Arnold, D., and A. Oppenheim. 1995. "Reexcavating the Senwosret III Pyramid Complex at Dâshur." *KMT* 6, no. 2:44–46.

Arnold, F. 1992. "New Evidence for the Length of the Reign of Senwosret III?" *Göttinger Miszellen* 129:27–29.

The Art Journal. 1991. [On Minoan frescoes at Avaris.] September. Page 60.

Asante, M. K. 1990. *Kemet, Afrocentricity, and Knowledge*. Trenton, N.J.: Africa World Press.

————. 1991a. "Multiculturalism: An Exchange." *American Scholar* 60, no. 2:267–72. (Critique of Ravitch 1990)

*————. 1991b. Response. *Challenging Tradition: Cultural Interaction in Antiquity and Bernal's Black Athena*, tape 5B.

————. 1993a. "On the Wings of Nonsense: The Attack on Afrocentricity." *Black Books Bulletin: Wordswork* 16:38–41.

————. 1993b. "Social Studies." *African–Puerto-Rican Centric Curriculum Guide*, vol. 1 (grades 1 and 2). Camden, N.J.: Camden City Public Schools.

Assmann, J. 1969. *Liturgische Lieder an den Sonnengott: Studien zur altägyptischen Hymnik*. Vol. 1. Münchner Ägyptologische Studien 19. Berlin: Bruno Hessling.

————. 1983. *Re und Amun: Die Krise des polytheistischen Weltbilds im Ägypten der 18.–20. Dynastie*. Orbis Biblicus et Orientalis 51. Fribourg: Universitätsverlag; Göttingen: Vandenhoeck & Ruprecht.

————. 1992. *Das kulturelle Gedächtnis: Schrift, Erinnerung und politische Identität in frühen Hochkulturen*. Munich: C. H. Beck.

Associated Press. 1989. "Egypt Says Ramses II Wasn't Black." *Washington Post*, 23 March, D8.

Astour, M. C. 1967. *Hellenosemitica: An Ethnic and Cultural Study in West Semitic Impact on Mycenean Greece*. 2d ed., with additions and corrections. Leiden: Brill.

————. 1973. "Ugarit and the Aegean." In *Orient and Occident: Essays Presented to*

Cyrus H. Gordon on the Occasion of His Sixty-Fifty Birthday, edited by H. Hoffner, 17–27. Alter Orient und Altes Testament 22. Neukirchen-Vluyn: Butzon & Bercker Kevelaer.

Augustinos, O. 1994. *French Odysseys: Greece in French Travel Literature from the Renaissance to the Romantic Era*. Baltimore: The Johns Hopkins University Press.

*Aune, J. 1993. Review of *BA* 2. *Quarterly Journal of Speech* 79:119–22.

BA 1 = Bernal 1987a.

BA 2 = Bernal 1991a.

Bachofen, J. J. 1861. *Das Mutterrecht: Eine Untersuchung über die Gynokratie der alten Welt nach ihrer religiösen und rechtlichen Natur*. Stuttgart: Krais & Hoffman.

Baer, K. 1979. Unpublished notes. Oriental Institute Museum Archives, Chicago.

†Bagnall, R. 1993. *Egypt in Late Antiquity*. Princeton: Princeton University Press.

Bailey, C. B. 1985. *The First Painters of the King: French Royal Taste from Louis XIV to the Revolution*. New York: Stair Sainty Matthiesen.

Baines, J. 1983. "Literacy and Ancient Egyptian Society." *Man*, n.s. 18:572–99.

———. 1989. "Ancient Egyptian Concepts and Uses of the Past: 3rd to 2nd Millennium B.C. Evidence." In *Who Needs the Past? Indigenous Values and Archaeology*, edited by R. Layton, 131–49. London: Unwin Hyman.

———. 1990. "Restricted Knowledge, Hierarchy, and Decorum: Modern Perceptions and Ancient Institutions." *Journal of the American Research Center in Egypt* 27:1–23.

*———. 1991. "Was Civilization Made in Africa?" *New York Times Book Reviews*, 11 August, 12–13. (Review of *BA* 2 and Diop 1991).

Baines, J., and N. Yoffee. In press. "Order, Legitimacy, and Wealth in Ancient Egypt and Mesopotamia." In *The Archaic State: a Comparative Approach*, edited by J. Marcus and G. M. Feinstein.

Baker, J. R. 1974. *Race*. London and New York: Oxford University Press.

Baldry, H. C. 1965. *The Unity of Mankind in Greek Thought*. Cambridge: Cambridge University Press.

Bamberger, J. 1974. "The Myth of Matriarchy: Why Men Rule in Primitive Societies." In *Woman, Culture, and Society*, edited by M. Z. Rosaldo and L. Lamphere, 263–80. Palo Alto: Stanford University Press.

Banier, A. [1740] 1976. *The Mythology and Fables of the Ancients Explain'd from History*. 4 vols. London and New York: Garland.

Banton, M. 1981. "The Direction and Speech of Ethnic Change." In *Ethnic Change*, edited by C. F. Keyes, 32–52. London and Seattle: University of Washington Press.

Bard, K. 1992. "Ancient Egyptians and the Issue of Race." *Bostonia* 2:41–43, 69. (= Bard, this volume)

Barker, F., ed. 1985. *Europe and Its Others*. Proceedings of the Essex Conference on the Sociology of Literature. Colchester: University of Essex.

*BARlines. 1993. *Biblical Archaeology Review* 19, no. 4:16.

†Barnes, J. 1987. *Early Greek Philosophy*. Harmondsworth, Middlesex: Penguin.

———. 1988. Review of G. E. R. Lloyd 1987. *Times Literary Supplement* (London), 16–22 December, 1392.

Barnett, R. D. 1982. *Ancient Ivories in the Middle East*. Qedem: Monographs of the Institute of Archaeology, 14. Jerusalem: Hebrew University.

Barnouw, D. 1993. "Eräugnis: Georg Forster on the Difficulties of Diversity." In *Impure Reason: Dialectic of Enlightenment in Germany*, edited by W. D. Wilson and R. C. Holub, 322–43. Detroit: Wayne State University Press.

Barringer, F. 1990. "Africa's Claim to Egypt's History Grows More Insistent." *New York Times*, 4 February, E6.

Barta, W. 1981. "Der Dekankalendar des Nutbildes und das Sothisdatum aus dem 7. Regierungsjahr Sesostris' III." *Studien zur altägyptischen Kultur* 9:85–103.

Barth, F., ed. 1969. *Ethnic Groups and Boundaries*. Results of a Symposium held at the University of Bergen. Boston: Little, Brown.

Bass, G. 1967. *Cape Gelidonya: A Bronze Age Shipwreck*. Transactions of the American Philosophical Society 57, part 8. Philadelphia: American Philosophical Society.

———. 1986. "A Bronze Age Shipwreck at Ulu Burun (Kaş)." *American Journal of Archaeology* 90, no. 3:269–96.

———. 1987. "Oldest Known Shipwreck Reveals Splendors of the Bronze Age." *National Geographic* 172:692–733.

Bass, G., et al. 1988. "The Bronze Age Shipwreck at Ulu Burun: 1986 Campaign." *American Journal of Archaeology* 93:1–29.

Bate, W. J. 1977. *Samuel Johnson*. New York: Harcourt Brace Jovanovich.

Batrawi, A. D. El-. 1935. "Report on the Human Remains, Part II: The Racial Problem." In *Mission archéologique de Nubie 1929–1934*, 160–77. Cairo: Government Press.

———. 1945. "The Racial History of Egypt and Nubia, Part I." *Journal of the Royal Anthropological Society of Great Britain and Ireland* 75:81–101.

———. 1946. "The Racial History of Egypt and Nubia, Part II: The Racial Relationships of the Ancient and Modern Populations of Egypt and Nubia." *Journal of the Royal Anthropological Institute of Great Britain and Ireland* 76:131–56.

Becker, B. 1987a. *Herder-Rezeption in Deutschland: Eine Ideologiekritische Untersuchung*. St. Ingbert: Werner Röhrig.

———. 1987b. "Phasen der Herder-Rezeption von 1871–1945." In *Johann Gottfried Herder, 1744–1803*, edited by Gerhard Sauder, 423–36. Hamburg: Felix Meiner.

Begley, S., F. Chideya, and L. Wilson. 1991. "Out of Egypt, Greece." *Newsweek*, 23 September, 49–50.

Behn, A. [1688] 1973. *Oroonoko, or The Royal Slave*. New York: Norton.

Bender, T., ed. 1992. *The Antislavery Debate: Capitalism and Abolitionism as a Problem in Historical Interpretation*. Berkeley and Los Angeles: University of California Press.

ben-Jochanan, Y. A. A. 1970. *Black Man of the Nile*. New York: Alkebu-lan Books.

———. [1971] 1988. *Africa, Mother of Western Civilization*. Baltimore: Alkebu-lan Books/Black Classic Press.

———. 1989. *Black Man of the Nile and His Family*. Baltimore: Alkebu-lan Books.

Ben-Tor, A. 1991. "More Light on the Relations between Egypt and Southern Palestine during the Early Bronze Age." *Bulletin of the American Schools of Oriental Research* 281:3–10.

†Berlin, I. 1976. *Vico and Herder: Two Studies in the History of Ideas*. London and New
York: Viking.

Bernal, M. 1985. "Black Athena: The African and Levantine Roots of Greece." In
African Presence in Early Europe, edited by I. Van Sertima, 66–82. New Brunswick,
N.J.: Transaction Books.

———. 1987a. *Black Athena: The Afroasiatic Roots of Classical Civilization*. Vol. 1, *The
Fabrication of Ancient Greece 1785–1985*. London: Free Association Books; New
Brunswick: Rutgers University Press.

———. 1987b. "On the Transmission of the Alphabet into the Aegean before
1400 B.C." *Bulletin of the American School of Oriental Research* 267:1–19.

———. 1989a. "*Black Athena* and the APA." In Levine and Peradotto 1989 =
Arethusa 22:17–38.

———. 1989b. "Response to Professor Turner." In Levine and Peradotto 1989 =
Arethusa 22:26–30.

———. 1989c. "Response to Professor Snowden." *Arethusa* 22:30–32.

———. 1989d. "First by Land, Then by Sea: Thoughts about the Social Formation
of the Mediterranean and Greece." In *Geography in Historical Perspective*, edited by
E. Genovese and L. Hochberg, 3–33. Oxford: Blackwell.

———. 1990a. *Cadmean Letters: The Transmission of the Alphabet to the Aegean and Further
West before 1400 B.C.* Winona Lake, Ind.: Eisenbrauns.

———. 1990b. "Responses to Critical Reviews of *Black Athena*, Volume 1." *Journal of
Mediterranean Archaeology* 3, no. 1:111–37.

———. 1991a. *Black Athena: The Afro-Asiatic Roots of Classical Civilization*. Vol. 2, *The
Archaeological and Documentary Evidence*. London: Free Association Books; New
Brunswick, N.J.: Rutgers University Press.

———. 1991b. Response. *Challenging Tradition: Cultural Interaction in Antiquity and
Bernal's Black Athena*, tape 7A.

———. 1992a. "Response to Edith Hall." *Arethusa* 25:203–14.

———. 1992b. "Response to Mary Lefkowitz, 'Not Out of Africa.'" *New Republic*,
9 March, 4–5.

———. 1992c. "The Case for Massive Egyptian Influence in the Aegean."
Archaeology 45, no. 5:53–55, 82–86.

———. 1992d. "Bernal Replies to *New York Review* Attack." *Bookpress* (April): 2, 4, 9,
13–14.

———. 1992e. "Animadversions on the Origins of Western Science." In special
section, "The Cultures of Ancient Science." *Isis* 83, no. 4 (December): 596–607.

———. 1992f. "A Response to John Coleman (Part II)." *The Bookpress* 2, no. 2:2, 13.

———. 1993a. "Response to S. O. Y. Keita." *Arethusa* 26:315–19.

———. 1993b. "Response, The Debate over *Black Athena*." *Journal of Women's History*
4, no. 3:119–35.

———. 1993c. "Phoenician Politics and Egyptian Justice in Ancient Greece." In
Anfänge politischen Denkens in der Antike: Die nah-östlichen Kulturen und die Griechen,
edited by K. Raaflaub, 241–61. Munich: R. Oldenbourg.

———. 1994. "Response to Robert Palter." *History of Science* 32, no. 4:445–64.

————. 1995. Review of Morris 1992. *Arethusa* 28, no. 1:113–35.

Berry, A. C., and R. J. Berry. 1973. "Origins and Relationships of the Ancient Egyptians, Based on a Study of Non-metrical Variations in the Skull." In *Population Biology of the Ancient Egyptians*, edited by D. R. Brothwell and B. A. Chiarelli, 199–208. London: Academic Press.

Berry, A. C., R. J. Berry, and P. J. Ucko. 1967. "Genetical Change in Ancient Egypt." *Man*, n.s. 2:551–68.

Bertoletti, S. F. 1994. "The Anthropological Theory of Johann Friedrich Blumenbach." In *Romanticism in Science: Science in Europe, 1790–1840*, edited by S. Poggi and M. Bossi, 103–25. Dordrecht: Kluwer Academie.

Best, J. 1973. *The Arrival of the Greeks*. Amsterdam: Adolf M. Hakkert.

Bianchi, R. S. 1991. "Pyramidiots." *Archaeology* 44, no. 6:84.

Bickerman, E. J. 1952. "Origines Gentium." *Classical Philology* 47:65–81.

Bietak, M. 1979. *Avaris and Piramesse*. Proceedings of the British Academy (London), 65. Oxford: Oxford University Press.

————. 1992. "Minoan Wall-Paintings Unearthed at Ancient Avaris." *Egyptian Archaeology: Bulletin of the Egyptian Archaeological Society* 2:26–28.

Bikai, P. 1990. "Black Athena and the Phoenicians." *Journal of Mediterranean Archaeology* 3, no. 1:67–75.

Bilfinger, G. 1888. *Der bürgerliche Tag*. Stuttgart: W. Kohlhammer.

Birdsell, J. B. 1966. Comment on W. W. Howells, "Population Distances: Biological, Linguistic, Geographical, and Environments." *Current Anthropology* 7:536–37.

Blackall, E. A. 1978. *The Emergence of German as a Literary Language*. 2d ed. Ithaca: Cornell University Press.

Black Athena. 1991. Videotape produced by Tariq Ali and directed by Christopher Spencer for the Bandung File. London: Bandung Ltd.; San Francisco: California Newsreel.

Blackburn, R. 1988. *The Overthrow of Colonial Slavery*. London and New York: Verso.

Blanke, H. W., and J. Rüsen, eds. 1984. *Von der Aufklärung zum Historismus*. Paderborn: Schöningh.

Bleiberg, E. 1984. "The King's Privy Purse during the New Kingdom: An Examination of INW." *Journal of the American Research Center in Egypt* 31:155–67.

Blench, R. 1993. "Recent Developments in African Language Classification and Their Implications for Prehistory." In *The Archaeology of Africa*, edited by T. Shaw et al., 126–38. London: Routledge.

Bliss, I. S. 1969. *Edward Young*. New York: Twayne.

Bloch, M. 1986. *From Blessing to Violence: History and Ideology in the Circumcision Ritual of the Merina of Madagascar*. Cambridge Studies in Social Anthropology 61. Cambridge: Cambridge University Press.

Bloemink, B. 1990. Introduction to *The Sphinx and the Lotus: The Egyptian Movement in American Decorative Arts 1865–1935; Essays by Kevin Stayton and Bernadette M. Sigler*. Yonkers, N.Y.: The Museum.

Blumenbach, J. F. 1794. "Observations on Some Egyptian Mummies Opened in London." Addressed to Sir Joseph Banks, Bart., P.R.S. *Philosophical Transactions of the Royal Society of London*, part 1:177–95.

———. 1795. *De Generis Humani Varietate Nativa*. Göttingen: Vandenhoeck & Ruprecht.

———. 1865. *The Anthropological Treatises of Johann Friedrich Blumenbach*. Translated and edited by T. Bendyshe. London: Longman, Green, Longman, Roberts & Green.

†Boardman, J. 1980. *The Greeks Overseas: Their Early Colonies and Trade*. New ed. London: Thames & Hudson.

Bödeker, H. E., et al., eds. 1986. *Deutsche Geschichtswissenschaft im Zeitalter der Aufklärung*. Göttingen: Vandenhoeck & Ruprecht.

Bonnet, C. 1978. "Fouilles archéologiques à Kerma (Soudan): Rapport préliminaire de la Campagne 1977–78." *Genava*, n.s. 26:107–34.

———. 1979. "Remarques sur la ville de Kerma." In *Hommage à la mémoire de Serge Sauneron 1927–1976*, vol. 1, *Egypte pharaonique*, 3–10. Cairo: Institut Français d'Archéologie Orientale.

———. 1980. "Les fouilles archéologiques de Kerma (Soudan)." *Genava*, n.s. 28:31–64.

———. 1982. "Les fouilles archéologiques de Kerma (Soudan)." *Genava*, n.s. 30:29–53.

———. 1986a. "Kerma 1984–85, 1985–86." *Genava*, n.s. 34:5–20. English suppl., i–xxii.

———. 1986b. *Kerma: territoire et metropole*. Bibliothèque d'Étude, 9. Cairo: Institut Français d'Archéologie Orientale.

———. 1987a. "Travaux de la Mission de l'Université de Genève sur le site de Kerma (Soudan, Province du Nord)." *Bulletin de la Société Française d'Egyptologie* 109:8–23.

———. 1987b. "The Archaeological Mission of Geneva University at Kerma (Sudan): 1984–1985 and 1985–1986 Campaigns." *Nyame Akuma* 28:38–40.

———. 1987c. "Mission of the University of Geneva to the Sudan." *Nyame Akuma* 29:52–53.

———. 1988. "Archaeological Mission of the University of Geneva to Kerma (Sudan): Final Report, 1987–88 Season." *Nyame Akuma* 30:32–33.

———. 1989. "The Archaeological Mission of the University of Geneva to Kerma (Sudan), Season 1988–89." *Nyame Akuma* 31:35–37.

———. 1992. "Excavations at the Nubian Royal Town of Kerma: 1975–91." *Antiquity* 66:611–25.

Bonnet, H. 1952. *Reallexikon der Ägyptischen Religionsgeschichte*. Berlin: Walter de Gruyter.

Boswell, J. [1791] 1965. *Life of Johnson*. London: Oxford University Press.

Bourriau, J. 1988. *Pharaohs and Mortals: Egyptian Art in the Middle Kingdom*. Cambridge and New York: Cambridge University Press.

Bower, B. 1991. "Race Falls from Grace: Report from the Annual Meeting of the American Anthropological Association." *Science News* 140:380.

*Bowersock, G. 1989. Review of *BA* 1. *Journal of Interdisciplinary History* 19:490–91.

†Bowman, A. K. 1986. *Egypt after the Pharaohs, 332 B.C.–A.D. 642: From Alexander to the Arab Conquest*. Berkeley and Los Angeles: Unversity of California Press.

Brace, C. L. 1967. *The Stages of Human Evolution: Human and Cultural Origins.*
Englewood Cliffs, N.J.: Prentice-Hall.

―――. 1979. "Krapina, 'Classic' Neanderthals, and the Evolution of the European
Face." *Journal of Human Evolution* 8:527–50.

―――. 1981. "Tales of the Phylogenetic Woods: The Evolution and Significance of
Phylogenetic Trees." *American Journal of Physical Anthropology* 56:411–29.

―――. 1982. "The Roots of the Race Concept in American Physical
Anthropology." In *A History of American Physical Anthropology 1930–1980*, edited by
F. Spencer, 11–29. New York: Academic Press.

―――. 1988. "Punctuationism, Cladistics and the Legacy of Medieval
Neoplatonism." *Human Evolution* 3:121–38.

―――. 1989. "Medieval Thinking and the Paradigms of Paleoanthropology."
American Anthropologist 91:442–46.

―――. 1990. *Race Is a Four-Letter Word: Clines, Clusters, and the Biology of Human
Variation.* Typescript in author's possession.

―――. 1991. *The Stages of Human Evolution.* 4th ed. Englewood Cliffs, N.J.:
Prentice-Hall.

―――. 1993a [in press]. "A Four-Letter Word Called 'Race.' " In *Race and Other
Miscalculations and Mismeasures: Papers in Honor of Ashley Montagu*, edited by L. J.
Reynolds and L. Lieberman. Dix Hills, N.Y.: General Hall.

―――. 1993b. "The Creation of Specific Hominid Names: *Gloria in Excelsis Deo?* or
Ego? or Praxis?" *Human Evolution* 8, no. 3:151–66.

―――. 1993c [in press]. "Modern Human Origins and the Dynamics of Regional
Continuity." In *Prehistoric Mongoloid Dispersals* (Symposium 1992), ed. T. Akazawa.
New York: Oxford University Press.

―――. 1994. "Trends in the Evolution of Human Tooth Size." In *Aspects of Dental
Biology; Palaeontology, Anthropology, and Evolution*, edited by J. Moggi-Cecchi, 6–14.
Florence: Angelo Pontecorboli.

Brace, C. L., and K. D. Hunt. 1990. "A Non-Racial Craniofacial Perspective on
Human Variation: A(ustralia) to Z(uni)." *American Journal of Physical Anthropology*
82:341–60.

Brace, C. L., and D. P. Tracer. 1992. "Craniofacial Continuity and Change: A
Comparison of Late Pleistocene and Recent Europe and Asia." In *The Evolution
and Dispersal of Modern Humans in Asia*, edited by T. Akazawa, K. Aoki, and
T. Kimura, 439–71. Tokyo: Hokusen-Sha.

Brace, C. L., M. L. Brace, and W. R. Leonard. 1989. "Reflections on the Face of
Japan." *American Journal of Physical Anthropology* 78:93–113.

Brace, C. L., K. R. Rosenberg, and K. D. Hunt. 1987. "Gradual Change in Human
Tooth Size in the Late Pleistocene and Post-Pleistocene." *Evolution* 41:705–20.

Brace, C. L., S. L. Smith, and K. D. Hunt. 1991. "What Big Teeth You Had,
Grandma! Human Tooth Size, Past and Present." In *Advances in Dental
Anthropology*, edited by M. A. Kelley and C. S. Larson, 33–57. New York:
Wiley-Liss.

Brace, C. L., D. P. Tracer, and K. D. Hunt. 1992. "Human Craniofacial Form and the Evidence for the Peopling of the Pacific." *Bulletin of the Indo-Pacific Prehistory Association* 11 = *Indo-Pacific Prehistory* 2 (1990), edited by P. Bellwood, 247–69.

Brace, C. L., M. L. Brace, Y. Dodo, W. R. Leonard, Y. Li, S. Sangvichen, X. Shao, and Z. Zhang. 1990. "Micronesians, Asians, Thais and Relations: Craniofacial and Odontometric Perspective." *Micronesica*, suppl. 2:323–48.

Brace, C. L., D. P. Tracer, L. A. Yaroch, J. Robb, K. Brandt, and A. R. Nelson. 1993. "Clines and Clusters versus 'Race': A Test in Ancient Egypt and the Case of a Death on the Nile." *Yearbook of Physical Anthropology* 36:1–31. (= Brace, this volume)

Brain, P. 1986. *Galen on Bloodletting: A Study of the Origins, Development and Validity of His Opinions, with a Translation of the Three Works.* Cambridge: Cambridge University Press.

*Branham, B. 1989. "Hellenomania." *Liverpool Classical Monthly* 14:56–60. (Review of *BA* 1.)

Braun, L. 1973. *Histoire de l'histoire de la philosophie.* Paris: Editions Ophrys.

†Braun, T. F. R. G. 1982. "The Greeks in the Near East." *The Cambridge Ancient History*, III.3:1–31. Cambridge: Cambridge University Press.

Breasted, J. H. 1906. *Ancient Records of Egypt.* Vol. 2. Chicago: University of Chicago Press.

———. 1909. *A History of Egypt from the Earliest Times to the Persian Conquest.* New ed. New York: Charles Scribner's Sons.

Brigham, C. C. 1923. *A Study of American Intelligence.* Princeton: Princeton University Press.

Brilliant, R. 1979. "Africa and the Arts of Greece and Rome." In *Africa in Antiquity: The Arts of Ancient Nubia and the Sudan*, edited by F. Hintze, 55–64. Berlin: Akademie-Verlag.

Brown, K. S. 1994. "Seeing Stars: Character and Identity in the Landscapes of Modern Macedonia." *Antiquity* 68:784–96.

Bruford, W. H. 1968. *Germany in the Eighteenth Century: The Social Background of the Literary Revival.* Cambridge: Cambridge University Press.

Brunton, G. 1937. *Mostagedda and the Tasian Culture.* British Museum Expedition to Middle Egypt, 1928–29. London: Bernard Quaritch.

Brunton, G., and G. Thompson 1928. *Badarian Civilisation and Predynastic Remains near Badari.* British School of Archaeology, vol. 46. London.

Budge, E. A. W. 1925. *The Mummy: A Handbook of Egyptian Funerary Archaeology.* 2d ed. Cambridge: Cambridge University Press.

Buitron-Oliver, D., guest curator. 1988. *The Human Figure in Early Greek Art.* Athens: Greek Ministry of Culture; Washington, D.C.: National Gallery of Art.

———, ed. 1991. *New Perspectives in Early Greek Art.* Studies in the History of Art 32. Center for Advanced Study in the Visual Arts: Symposium Papers 16. Washington, D.C.: National Gallery of Art, with University Press of New England.

Burkert, W. [1962] 1972. *Lore and Science in Ancient Pythagoreanism.* Cambridge: Harvard University Press.

†————. [1977] 1985. *Greek Religion: Archaic and Classical*. English translation of *Griechische Religion der archaischen und klassischen Epoche*. Oxford: Blackwell; Cambridge: Harvard University Press.

————. 1984. *Die orientalisierende Epoche in der griechischen Religion und Literatur*. Sitzungsberichte der Heidelberger Akademie der Wissenschaften, philosophisch-historischer Klasse, 1. Heidelberg: Winter.

†————. [1984] 1992. *The Orientalizing Revolution: Near Eastern Influence on Greek Culture in the Early Archaic Age*. Translated by M. E. Pinder and W. Burkert. Cambridge: Harvard University Press.

Burnor, D. R., and J. E. Harris. 1968. "Racial Continuity in Lower Nubia: 12,000 to the Present." *Proceedings of the Indiana Academy of Science* 77:113–21.

Burnouf, E. 1872. *La science des religions*. Paris: Maisonneuve.

*Burstein, S. 1993. "Review of *Black Athena*, Volume II." *Classical Philology* 88, no. 2:157–62.

Butterfield, F. 1992. "Afro-American Studies Get New Life at Harvard." *New York Times*, 3 June, B7.

Butterfield, H. 1960. *Man on His Past: The Study of the History of Historical Scholarship*. New ed. Boston: Beacon.

Butzer, K. W. 1976. *Early Hydraulic Civilization in Egypt*. Chicago: University of Chicago Press.

Cadogan, G. 1969. Review of *Cape Gelidonya: A Bronze Age Shipwreck*, by G. Bass. *Journal of Hellenic Studies* 89:187–89.

Cameron, A., and J. Long. 1993. *Barbarians and Politics at the Court of Arcadius*. Berkeley and Los Angeles: University of California Press.

Caminos, R. A. 1977. *A Tale of Woe, from a Hieratic Papyrus in the A. S. Pushkin Museum of Fine Arts in Moscow*. Oxford: Griffith Institute.

Cann, R. L. 1988. "DNA and Human Origins." *Annual Review of Anthropology* 17:127–43.

Cann, R. L., M. Stoneking, and A. C. Wilson. 1987. "Mitochondrial DNA and Human Evolution." *Nature* 325:31–36.

Cantor, M. 1880. *Vorlesungen über Geschichte der Mathematik*, vol. 1. Leipzig: B. G. Teubner.

Caponigri, A. R. 1953. *Time and Idea: The Theory of History in G. Vico*. Notre Dame: Notre Dame University Press.

Carlson, D. S., and D. P. Van Gerven. 1977. "Masticatory Function and Post-Pleistocene Evolution in Nubia." *American Journal of Physical Anthropology* 46:495–506.

————. 1979. "Diffusion, Biological Determinism, and Biocultural Adaptation in the Nubian Corridor." *American Anthropologist* 81:561–80.

Carpenter, R. 1966. *Discontinuity in Greek Civilization*. Cambridge: Cambridge University Press.

Carpenter, T. H. 1986. *Dionysian Imagery in Archaic Greek Art*. Oxford: Clarendon Press.

Carr, E. H. 1961. *What Is History?* New York: Random House.

Carrott, R. G. 1978. *The Egyptian Revival: Its Sources, Monuments, and Meaning 1808–1858*. Berkeley and Los Angeles: University of California Press.

*Carruthers, J. 1992. "Outside of Academia: Bernal's Critique of the Black Champions of Ancient Egypt." *Journal of Black Studies* 22, no. 4:459–76. (First presented as *Challenging Tradition: Cultural Interaction in Antiquity and Bernal's Black Athena*, tape 1B.)

Casini, P., ed. 1984. "Newton: The Classical Scholia." *History of Science* 22, no. 1 (March): 1–58.

Castillos, J. J. 1981. "An Analysis of the Tombs in the Predynastic Cemeteries at Naqada." *Journal of the Society for the Study of Egyptian Antiquities* 11:97–106.

Cavalli-Sforza, L. L., P. Menozzi, and A. Piazza. 1993. "Demic Expansions and Human Evolution." *Science* 259:639–46.

CCL = *Corpus Christianorum*. Series Latina. Turnhout and Paris, 1953–.

Černý, J. 1954. "Consanguineous Marriages in Pharonic Egypt." *Journal of Egyptian Archaeology* 40:23–29.

Černý, J., and T. E. Peet. 1927. "A Marriage Settlement of the Twentieth Dynasty: An Unpublished Document from Turin." *Journal of Egyptian Archaeology* 13:32.

†Chadwick, J. 1973. *Documents in Mycenaean Greek*. Cambridge: Cambridge University Press.

†———. 1976. *The Mycenaean World*. Cambridge: Cambridge University Press.

Challenging Tradition: Cultural Interaction in Antiquity and Bernal's Black Athena. 1991. Proceedings of a conference held at Temple University, 19–20 October. Audio and videotape. Temple University Classics Department, Philadelphia.

Chambers, M., et al. 1991. *The Western Experience*. 5th ed. New York: McGraw-Hill.

Chantraine, P. 1961. *Morphologie historique du grec*. Paris: Klincksieck.

———. 1968–75. *Dictionnaire étymologique de la langue grecque*. 4 vols. Paris: Klincksieck.

Charles-Roux, F. 1929. *Le projet français de conquête de l'Egypte sous le règne de Louis XVI: Mémoires présentés à l'Institut d'Egypte*. Cairo.

Chinnock, E. J. 1884. *The Anabasis of Alexander, or The History of the Wars and Conquests of Alexander the Great, Literally Translated, with a Commentary, from the Greek of Arrian the Nicomedian*. London: Hodder & Stoughton.

Christie, A. 1937. *Death on the Nile*. In *Perilous Journeys of Hercule Poirot* [collected novels]. New York: Dodd, Mead.

Clagett, M., ed. 1989. *Ancient Egyptian Science: A Source Book*. Vol. 1 (in two parts), *Knowledge and Order*. Philadelphia: American Philosophical Society.

Clarke, J. H. 1984. "African Warrior Queens." In *Black Women in Antiquity*, edited by I. Van Sertima, 126–27. New Brunswick, N.J.: Transaction Books.

Clarke, M. L. 1962. *George Grote: A Biography*. London: Athlone.

Clarke, S., and R. Engelbach. [1930] 1990. *Ancient Egyptian Construction and Architecture*. New York: Dover.

Cline, E. 1987. "Amenhotep III and the Aegean: A Reassessment of Egypt-Cretan Relations in the 14th Century B.C." *Orientalia* 56:1–36.

———. 1990. "An Unpublished Amenhotep Faience Plaque from Mycenae." *Journal of the American Oriental Society* 110:200–212.

Close, A. 1990. "Living on the Edge: Neolithic Herders in the Eastern Sahara."
  Antiquity 64:79–96.
Cogan, M. 1974. *Imperialism and Religion: Assyria, Judah, and Israel in the Eighth and
  Seventh Centuries B.C.E.* Missoula: Society for Biblical Literature and Scholars Press.
Cohen, M. R., and I. E. Drabkin, eds. 1958. *A Source Book in Greek Science*. Vol. 1 (in
  two parts), *Knowledge and Order*. Cambridge: Harvard University Press.
Cohen, W. B. 1980. *The French Encounter with Africans: White Responses to Blacks,
  1530–1880*. Bloomington: Indiana University Press.
Coleman, J. E. 1992a. "Did Egypt Shape the Glory That Was Greece? The Case
  against Martin Bernal's *Black Athena*." *Archaeology* 45, no. 5:48–52, 77–81.
———. 1992b. "Greece and the Eastern Mediterranean." *Bostonia* (Summer): 44–46.
———. 1992c. "Greece, the Aegean and Cyprus." In *Chronologies in Old World
  Archaeology*, edited by R. W. Ehrich, 1:247–88, 2:203–29. Chicago and London:
  University of Chicago Press.
———. n.d. "Ancient Greek Ethnocentrism." Typescript in possession of the
  author.
Colfax, R. H. 1833. *Evidence against the Views of the Abolitionists, Consisting of Physical and
  Moral Proofs of the Natural Inferiority of the Negroes*. New York: J. R. M. Bleakley.
Collignon, M. 1884. *Manuel d'archéologie grecque*. Paris: A. Quantin.
Collingwood, R. G. 1946. *The Idea of History*. Oxford: Oxford University Press.
———. 1963. "The Limits of Historical Knowledge." In *Essays in the Philosophy of
  History*, edited by W. Dobbins, 90–103. Austin: University of Texas Press.
Comstock, M., and C. C. Vermeule. 1971. *Greek, Etruscan, and Roman Bronzes in the
  Museum of Fine Arts, Boston*. Greenwich, Conn. (distributed by The New York
  Graphic Society).
†Connah, G. 1987. *African Civilizations: Precolonial Cities and States in Tropical Africa: An
  Archaeological Perspective*. Cambridge: Cambridge University Press.
Conner, P. 1983. *The Inspiration of Egypt: Its Influence on British Artists, Travellers, and
  Designers 1700–1900*. Brighton: Brighton Borough Council.
Connor, W. R. 1970a. Review of *Blacks in Antiquity: Ethiopians in the Greco-Roman
  Experience*, by F. M. Snowden, Jr. *Good Reading: Review of Books Recommended by the
  Princeton Faculty* 21, no. 3:3–4.
———. 1970b. "Theseus in Classical Athens." In *The Quest for Theseus*, edited by
  A. G. Ward, 143–74. New York: Praeger.
Conze, A. C. L. 1862. *Melische Thongefässe*. Leipzig: Teubner.
†Copenhaver, B. 1992. *Hermetica*. Cambridge: Cambridge University Press.
*Coughlin, E. K. 1991. "In Multiculturalism Debate, Scholarly Book on Ancient
  Greece Plays Controversial Part: Afrocentric Scholars and Classicists at Odds
  over *Black Athena*." *Chronicle of Higher Education*, 31 July, A5–A6.
†Coulton, J. J. 1977. *Ancient Greek Architects at Work*. Ithaca: Cornell University Press.
Cowler, R., ed. 1986. *The Prose Works of Alexander Pope*. Vol. 2, *The Major Works,
  1725–1744*. Hamden, Conn.: Archon.
Craddock, P. B. 1982. *Young Edward Gibbon: Gentleman of Letters*. Baltimore: The
  Johns Hopkins University Press.
Crewdson-Benington, R. 1911. "Cranial Type-Contours." *Biometrika* 8:139–201.

Crichton, J. M. 1966. "A Multiple Discriminant Analysis of Egyptian and African Negro Crania." In *Craniometry and Multivariate Analysis*, edited by William White Howells, 46–67. Papers of the Peabody Museum of Archaeology and Ethnology 57. Cambridge: Peabody Museum, Harvard University.

Cruz-Uribe, E. 1987. "The Fall of the Middle Kingdom." *Varia Aegyptica* 3:107–11.

Cuny, A. 1910. "Les mots du fonds préhellénique en grec, latin et sémitique occidental." *Revue des Etudes Anciennes* 12:154–64.

Curl, J. S. 1982. *The Egyptian Revival: An Introductory Study of a Recurring Theme in the History of Taste*. London and Boston: G. Allen & Unwin.

———. 1994. *Egyptomania, the Egyptian Revival: A Recurring Theme in the History of Taste*. Manchester: Manchester University Press.

Currid, J. 1991. "An Examination of the Egyptian Background of the Genesis Cosmology." *Biblische Zeitschrift* 35:18–40.

Curtin, P. D. 1964. *The Image of Africa: British Ideas and Action, 1780–1850*. Madison: University of Wisconsin Press.

Cuvier, G. 1817. "Extrait d'observations faites sur le cadavre d'une femme connue à Paris et à Londres sous le nom de Vénus Hottentotte." *Mémoires du Muséum d'Histoire Naturelle* 3:259–74.

Dabydeen, D. 1987. *Hogarth's Blacks: Images of Blacks in Eighteenth Century Art*. Athens: University of Georgia Press.

Dalven, R. 1990. *The Jews of Ioannina*. Athens: Lycabettus Press.

Damon, S. F. 1988. *A Blake Dictionary*. Rev. ed. Hanover, N.H.: University Press of New England.

Dark, P. J. C. 1973. *An Introduction to Benin Art and Technology*. Oxford: Clarendon Press.

Darnton, R. 1971. "The Social History of Ideas." *Journal of Modern History* 43:113–32. Reprinted in R. Darnton, *The Kiss of Lamourette: Reflections in Cultural History*. New York: Norton, 1990.

———. 1979. *The Business of Enlightenment: A Publishing History of the Encyclopédie, 1775–1800*. Cambridge: Harvard University Press.

Darwin, C. R. 1859. *On the Origin of Species by Means of Natural Science, or The Preservation of the Favoured Races in the Struggle for Life*. London: John Murray.

Davidson, B. 1994a. "The Ancient World and Africa: Whose Roots?" In *The Search for Africa: History, Culture, Politics*. New York: Times Books.

†———. 1994b. *The Search for Africa*. London: James Currey.

Davies, A. M. 1986. "The Linguistic Evidence: Is There Any?" In *The End of the Early Bronze Age in the Aegean*, edited by G. Cadogan, 93–123. Leiden: E. J. Brill.

Davies, J. K. 1971. *Athenian Propertied Classes, 600–300 B.C.* Oxford: Clarendon Press.

Davies, W. H. 1989. *Egyptian Hieroglyphs*. Berkeley and Los Angeles: University of California Press.

Davies, W. V., and L. Schofield. 1995. *Egypt, the Aegean and the Levant: Interconnections in the Second Millennium B.C.* London: British Museum Press.

Davis, D. B. 1966. *The Problem of Slavery in Western Culture*. Ithaca: Cornell University Press.

———. 1984. *Slavery and Human Progress*. New York: Oxford University Press.

Denon, V. [1802] 1986. *Travels in Upper and Lower Egypt*. London: Darf.

Derchain, P. 1962. "L'authenticité de l'inspiration égyptienne dans le 'Corpus Hermeticum.'" *Revue de l'histoire des religions* 161:175–98.

Derry, D. E. 1956. "The Dynastic Race in Egypt." *Journal of Egyptian Archaeology* 42:80–85.

Desborough, V. R. d'A. 1964. *The Last Mycenaeans and Their Successors*. Oxford: Clarendon Press.

Diamond, S. 1974. *In Search of the Primitive: A Critique of Civilization*. New Brunswick, N.J.: Transaction Books.

Diderot, D., and J. D'Alembert. 1755. *L'encyclopédie*. Paris.

Dihle, A. 1965. "Zur Geschichte des Aithiopennamens." In *Umstrittene Daten: Untersuchungen zum Auftreten der Griechen am roten Meer*, 65–79. Cologne: Westdeutscher Verlag.

Diodorus of Sicily. 1933. *The Library of History*. Vol. 1, translated by C. H. Oldfather. London and New York: Loeb Classical Library.

Diop, C. A. 1955. *Nations nègres et culture de l'antiquité nègre-égyptienne aux problèmes culturels de l'Afrique noire d'aujourd'hui*. 2d ed. Paris: Présence Africaine.

———. 1968. "Preface to Negro Nations and Culture." In *Problems in African History*, edited by R. O. Collins, 23–24. Englewood Cliffs, N.J.: Prentice-Hall.

———. 1974. *The African Origin of Civilization: Myth or Reality?* Translated by Mercer Cook. Westport, Conn.: Lawrence Hill.

———. 1978. *The Cultural Unity of Black Africa: The Domains of Patriarchy and Matriarchy in Classical Antiquity*. Chicago: Third World Press.

———. 1981. "Origin of the Ancient Egyptians." In *General History of Africa*, vol. 2, *Ancient Civilizations of Africa*, edited by G. Mokhtar, 27–51. Berkeley and Los Angeles: UNESCO and University of California Press.

———. [1981] 1991. *Civilization or Barbarism: An Authentic Anthropology*. Translated by Y-L. M. Ngemi and edited by H. J. Salemson and M. de Jager. Brooklyn, N.Y.: Lawrence Hill/Chicago Review Press.

———. 1987. *Precolonial Black Africa: A Comparative Study of the Political and Social Systems of Europe and Black Africa, from Antiquity to the Formation of Modern States*. Translated by H. J. Salemson. Westport, Conn.: Lawrence Hill.

Dobbs, B. J. T. 1991. *The Janus Faces of Genius: The Role of Alchemy in Newton's Thought*. Cambridge and New York: Cambridge University Press.

Dobrée, B. 1959. *English Literature in the Early Eighteenth Century, 1700–1740*. Oxford: Clarendon Press.

Dodds, E. R., ed. 1960. *Euripides' Bacchae*. 2d ed. Oxford: Clarendon Press.

Dothan, T., and M. Dothan 1992. *People of the Sea*. New York: Macmillan.

Dover, K. J. 1993. "Simia." *Liverpool Classical Monthly* 18, no. 3:46.

Drescher, S. 1987. *Capitalism and Antislavery: British Mobilization in Comparative Perspective*. New York: Oxford University Press.

———. 1992. "The Ending of the Slave Trade and the Evolution of European Scientific Racism." In *The Atlantic Slave Trade: Effects on Economies, Societies, and Peoples in Africa, the Americas, and Europe*, edited by J. E. Inikori and S. L. Engerman. Durham: Duke University Press.

Drews, R. 1973. *The Greek Accounts of Eastern History*. Cambridge: Harvard University Press.

———. 1976. "The Earliest Greek Settlements on the Black Sea." *Journal of Hellenic Studies* 96:18–31.

†———. 1993. *The End of the Bronze Age*. Princeton: Princeton University Press.

Dreyer, G. 1992. "Recent Discoveries in the U-Cemetery at Abydos." In *The Nile Delta in Transition: 4th–3rd Millennium B.C.*, 293–300. Tel Aviv: Van den Brink.

Drower, M. 1973. "Syria c. 1550–1400 B.C." *The Cambridge Ancient History*, 2d ed., II.1:417–525. Cambridge: Cambridge University Press.

———. 1985. *Flinders Petrie: A Life in Archaeology*. London: Gollancz.

Dumas, F. 1976. *Le tombeau de Childeric*. Paris: Le Cabinet.

Dunham, D. 1950. *The Royal Cemeteries of Kush*. Vol. 1, *El Kurru*. Cambridge: Harvard University Press.

Dupuis, C. [1795] 1984. *Origin of All Religious Worship*. English trans. of *Origine de tous les cultes*, introduction by R. Richardson. New York: Garland.

During-Caspers, E. 1965. "Further Evidence for Cultural Relations between India, Baluchistan, and Iran and Mesopotamia in Early Dynastic Times." *Journal of Near Eastern Studies* 24:53–56.

———. 1970–71. "Some Motifs as Evidence for Maritime Contact between Sumer and the Indus Valley." *Persica* 5:107–18.

———. 1971. "New Archaeological Evidence for Maritime Trade in the Persian Gulf during the Late Protoliterate Period." *East and West* 21:21–44.

*Dyson, M. E. 1992. Interview with Martin Bernal, "On Black Athena." *Z* 5, no. 1:56.

Easton, D. 1985. "Has the Trojan War Been Found?" *Antiquity* 59:188–96.

Eddy, S. K. 1961. *The King Is Dead: Studies in the Near Eastern Resistance to Hellenism, 334–31 B.C.* Lincoln: University of Nebraska Press.

Edel, E. 1964. "Zu den Inschriften auf den Jahreszeitenreliefs der 'Weltkammer' aus dem Sonnenheiligtum des Niuserre II." *Nachrichten der Akademie der Wissenschaften in Göttingen* 4–5 (Philologisch-historische Klasse, 1963). Göttingen: Vandenhoeck & Ruprecht.

———. 1966. *Die Ortsnamenlisten aus dem Totentempel Amenhopis III*. Bonn: Hanstein.

Edgerton, W. F. 1937. "On the Chronology of the Early Eighteenth Dynasty (Amenhotep I–Thutmose III)." *American Journal of Semitic Languages and Literature* 53, no. 4:188–97.

———. 1951. "The Strikes in Ramses III's Twenty-Ninth Year." *Journal of Near Eastern Studies* 10, no. 3:137–45.

Edwards, I. E. S. 1985. *The Pyramids of Egypt*. Rev. ed. New York: Penguin/Viking.

†Edwards, R. 1979. *Kadmos the Phoenician: A Study in Greek Legend and the Mycenaean Age*. Amsterdam: Adolf M. Hakkert.

Egberts, A. 1991. "The Chronology of The Report of Wenamun." *Journal of Egyptian Archaeology* 77:57–67.

Einarson, B. 1967. "Notes on the Development of the Greek Alphabet." *Classical Philology* 62:1–24.

Elkins, J. 1991. "The Case against Surface Geometry." *Art History* 14, no. 2:143–74.

Emery, W. B. 1961. *Archaic Egypt*. Harmondsworth and Baltimore: Penguin.

———. 1967. *Archaic Egypt*. Baltimore: Penguin.

Engelbach, R. 1943. "On the Advent of the Dynastic Race in Egypt and Its Consequences." *Annales du service des antiquités égyptiennes* 42:193–209.

Epigraphic Survey. 1930. *Medinet Habu*. Vol. 1, *Earlier Historical Records of Ramses III*. Oriental Institute Publication no. 8. Chicago: University of Chicago Press.

Epigraphic Survey. 1932. *Medinet Habu*. Vol. 2, *Later Historical Records of Ramses III*. Oriental Institute Publication no. 9. Chicago: University of Chicago Press.

Ernout, A., and A. Meillet. 1985. *Dictionnaire étymologique de la langue latine*. 4th ed., by Jacques André. Paris: C. Klincksieck.

Evans, A. E. 1921–35. *The Palace of Minos at Knossos*. London: Macmillan.

Ezra, K. 1992. *Royal Art of Benin: The Perls Collection*. New York: Metropolitan Museum of Art (distributed by H. N. Abrams).

Falconer, W. A., trans. 1929. Cicero. *De Divinatione*. In *Selections*. Loeb Classical Library. Cambridge: Harvard University Press.

Farag, S. 1980. "Une inscription memphite de la XIIe dynastie." *Revue d'égyptologie* 32:75–82.

Fawcett, C. D., and A. Lee. 1901. "A Second Study of the Variation and Correlation of the Human Skull, with Special Reference in the Naqada Crania." *Biometrika* 1:408–67.

Fecht, G. 1965. *Literarische Zeugnisse zur "persönlichen Frömmigkeit" in Ägypten: Analyse der Beispiele aus den ramessidischen Schulpapyri*. Abhandlungen der Heidelberger Akademie der Wissenschaften 1965, 1. Heidelberg: Carl Winter Universitätsverlag.

Feder, K. L. 1990. *Frauds, Myths, and Mysteries*. Mountainview, Calif.: Mayfield Press.

Feierman, S. 1993. "African Histories and the Dissolution of World History." In *Africa and the Disciplines*, edited by Robert H. Bates et al., 167–212. Chicago: University of Chicago Press.

Feldman, B., and R. D. Richardson. 1972. *The Rise of Modern Mythology, 1680–1860*. Bloomington: Indiana University Press.

Fell, B. 1976. *America B.C.: Ancient Settlers in the New World*. New York: Quadrangle/New York Times Book Company.

Feuser, W. F. 1978. "The Image of the Black in the Writings of Johann Gottfried Herder." *Journal of European Studies* 7:109–28.

FGrHist = F. Jacoby. *Die Fragmente der griechischen Historiker*. Leiden: Brill, 1923–57.

Finch, C. S. 1983. "The African Background of Medical Science." In *Blacks in Science: Ancient and Modern*, edited by I. Van Sertima, 140–56. New Brunswick, N.J.: Transaction Books.

———. 1985. "Race and Evolution in Prehistory." In *African Presence in Early Europe*, edited by I. Van Sertima, 288–312. New Brunswick, N.J.: Transaction Books.

———. 1989. "Interview with Cheikh Anta Diop." *Présence africaine*, no. 149–50 (June): 366.

Finkelman, P. 1993. "Jefferson and Slavery: Treason against the Hopes of the World." In *Jeffersonian Legacies*, edited by P. S. Onuf, 181–221. Charlottesville: University Press of Virginia.

Finlay, G. 1877. *A History of Greece*. Rev. ed. by F. Tozer. 7 vols. Oxford: Clarendon Press.

Finley, J. H. 1978. *Homer's Odyssey*. London and Cambridge: Harvard University Press.

Finley, M. I. 1960. "Lost: The Trojan War." In *Aspects of Antiquity*, 24–37. New York: Viking Press.

†————. 1975. *The Use and Abuse of History*. New York: Viking. Reprinted, New York: Penguin, 1987.

Fischer, H. G. 1961. "The Nubian Mercenaries of Gebelein during the First Intermediate Period." *Kush: Journal of the Sudan Antiquities Service* 9:56–80.

Fisher, R. A. 1936a. " 'The Coefficient of Racial Likeness' and the Future of Craniometry." *Journal of the Royal Anthropological Institute of Great Britain and Ireland* 66:57–63.

————. 1936b. "The use of Multiple Measurements in Taxonomic Problems." *Annals of Eugenics* 7:179–88.

————. 1938. "The Statistical Utilization of Multiple Measurements." *Annals of Eugenics* 8:376–86.

Flower, W. H. 1885. "On the Size of Teeth as a Character of Race." *Journal of the Royal Anthropological Institute of Great Britain and Ireland* 14:183–87.

Foner, E. 1988. *Reconstruction: America's Unfinished Revolution, 1863–1877*. New York: Harper & Row.

Forbes, D. 1953–54. " 'Scientific' Whiggism: Adam Smith and John Millar." *Cambridge Journal* 7:643–70.

Forsdyke, J. 1956. *Greece before Homer*. London: Max Parrish.

Forster, G. 1958–85. *Georg Forsters Werke*. Various editors. Vols. 1–5, 7–9, 11–18 to date. Berlin: Akademie-Verlag.

Forster, R., and E. Forster, eds. 1969. *European Society in the Eighteenth Century*. New York: Harper & Row.

Foster, J. L. 1981. "The Conclusion to the Testament of Amenemmes, King of Egypt." *Journal of Egyptian Archaeology* 67:36–47.

Fournet, J.-L. 1989. "Les emprunts du grec a l'égyptien." *Bulletin de la Société de Linguistique de Paris* 84:55–80.

†Fowden, G. 1986. *The Egyptian Hermes: A Historical Approach to the Late Antique Pagan Mind*. Cambridge: Cambridge University Press.

Fox, D. J., and K. E. Guire. 1976. *Documentation for MIDAS*. 3d edition. Ann Arbor: Statistical Research Laboratory, University of Michigan.

Frandsen, P. J. 1979. "Egyptian Imperialism." in *Power and Propaganda*, edited by M. T. Larsen, 167–90. Mesopotamia 7. Copenhagen: Akademisk Forlag.

Franke, D. 1988. "Zur Chronologie des Mittleren Reiches (12.–18. Dynastie)." *Orientalia* 57:113–38, 245–74.

Frankfort, H. 1951. *The Birth of Civilization in the Near East*. Bloomington: Indiana University Press.

Frey, H. 1892. *L'annamite, mère des langues: communauté d'origine des races celtiques, sémitiques, soudanaises et de l'Indochine*. Paris: Hachette.

—. 1905. *Les Egyptiens préhistoriques identifiés avec les Annamites d'après les inscriptions hiéroglyphiques*. Paris: Hachette.

Friedman, J. 1992. "The Past in the Future: History and the Politics of Identity." *American Anthropologist* 94, no. 4:837–59.

Frisk, H. 1955–72. *Griechisches etymologisches Wörterbuch*. Heidelberg: Carl Winter.

Frye, N. 1969. *Fearful Symmetry: A Study of William Blake*. Princeton: Princeton University Press.

Fryer, P. 1984. *Staying Power: The History of Black People in Britain*. London: Pluto Press; Atlantic Highlands, N.J.: Humanities Press.

Fulco, W. J. 1981. Review of *The Classification of Chadic within Afro-Asiatic*, by P. Newman. *Orientalia*, n.s. 50, no. 4:472–74.

Furley, D. J., and J. S. Wilkie. 1984. *Galen: On Respiration and the Arteries*. Princeton: Princeton University Press.

GCS = Die griechischen christlichen Schriftsteller der ersten drei Jahrhunderte. Leipzig: J. C. Hinrichs, 1897–.

Gardiner, A. H. 1941. "Writing and Literature." In *The Legacy of Egypt*, 53–79. Oxford: Clarendon Press.

—. 1947. *Ancient Egyptian Onomastica*. Vol. 1. Oxford: Oxford University Press.

—. 1957. *Egyptian Grammar*. 3d ed. Oxford: Oxford University Press.

—. 1959. *The Royal Canon of Turin*. Oxford: Oxford University Press.

—. 1961. *Egypt of the Pharaohs*. Oxford: Oxford University Press.

*Gardner, J. F. 1991. "The Debate on Black Athena." *Classical Review* 41, no. 1:167. (Review of Levine and Peradotto 1989 = *Arethusa* 22, no. 1.)

Gardner, M. 1957. *Fads and Fallacies in the Name of Science*. New York: Dover.

—. 1992. "Egyptian Fractions." In *Fractal Music, Hypercards, and More . . . : Mathematical Recreations from "Scientific American,"* comp. M. Gardner, 100–109. San Francisco and New York: W. H. Freeman.

Garrard, T. F. 1983. "Benin Metal-Casting Technology." In *The Art of Power, the Power of Art: Studies in Benin Iconography*, edited by P. Ben-Amos and A. Rubin, 17–20. Los Angeles: Museum of Cultural History, UCLA.

Garrett, H. E. 1962. "Racial Differences and Witch Hunting." *Science* 135:982–84.

Garvey, M. [1925] 1986. *The Philosophy and Opinions of Marcus Garvey*. Edited by A. Jacques-Garvey. 2 vols. Dover, Mass.: Majority Press.

Gascoigne, J. 1991. " 'The Wisdom of the Egyptians' and the Secularisation of History in the Age of Newton." In *The Uses of Antiquity: The Scientific Revolution and the Classical Tradition*, edited by Stephen Gaukroger, 171–212. Dordrecht: Kluwer Academie.

—. 1994. *Joseph Banks and the English Enlightenment: Useful Knowledge and Polite Culture*. Cambridge: Cambridge University Press.

Gates, H. L. 1987. *Figures in Black: Words, Signs, and the "Racial" Self*. New York: Oxford University Press.

—. 1991. "Beware of the New Pharaohs." *Newsweek*, 23 September, 47.

Gates, M. H. 1994. "Archaeology in Turkey." *American Journal of Archaeology* 98:249–78.

Gay, P. 1966. *The Enlightenment: An Interpretation*. New York: Knopf.

Geffcken, J. 1907. *Zwei griechische Apologeten*. Leipzig: B. G. Teubner.

*Georgakas, D. 1993. "*Black Athena*: Aryans, Semites, Egyptians, and Hellenes."
  Cineaste 19, no. 2–3:55–56.

———. 1994. "Defending Greek Athena." *Odyssey* (Summer): 34–38.

Ghalioungui, P. 1968. "The Relation of Pharaonic to Greek and Later Medicine."
  Bulletin of the Cleveland Medical Library 15, no. 3:96–107.

———. 1973. *The House of Life: Per Ankh; Magic and Medical Science in Ancient Egypt*.
  2d ed. Amsterdam: B. M. Israel.

*Giannaris, C. 1987. "Rocking the Cradle." *New Statesman*, 10 July, 31. (Review of
  BA 1)

Gibbon, E. 1984. *Memoirs of My Life*. Edited by B. Radice. New York: Penguin.

Gillings, R. J. [1972] 1982. *Mathematics in the Time of the Pharaohs*. New York: Dover.
  (First published by MIT Press)

———. 1978. "The Mathematics of Ancient Egypt." In *Dictionary of Scientific
  Biography*, edited by C. C. Gillispie, 15 (= Supplement 1): 696. New York: Scribner.

Gillispie, C. C., ed. 1970–. *Dictionary of Scientific Biography*. Vols. 2 (1970), 4 (1971), 9
  (1974), 15 = Supplement 1 (1978). New York: Scribner.

Gilman, S. L. 1982. *On Blackness without Blacks: Essays on the Image of the Black in
  Germany*. Boston: G. K. Hall.

Ginzburg, C. 1989. *Clues, Myths and the Historical Method*. Baltimore: The Johns
  Hopkins University Press.

Giveon, R. 1974. "Hyksos Scarabs with Names of Kings and Officials from
  Canaan." *Chronique d'Egypte* 49/98:222–33.

Glanville, E. V. 1969. "Nasal Shape, Prognathism and Adaptation in Man." *American
  Journal of Physical Anthropology* 30:29–38.

Goedicke, H. 1985. "The End of the Hyksos in Egypt." In *Egyptological Studies in
  Honor of Richard J. Parker*, edited by L. Lesko, 37–47. Hanover, N.H.: University
  Press of New England for Brown University.

Gomme, A. W. 1913. "The Legend of Cadmus and the Logographoi." *Journal of
  Hellenic Studies* 33:53–72, 223–45.

Gomme, A. W., A. Andrewes, and K. J. Dover. 1945–81. *A Historical Commentary on
  Thucydides*. 5 vols. Oxford: Clarendon Press.

Goonatilake, S. 1989. "The Son, the Father, and the Holy Ghosts." *Economic and
  Political Weekly*, 5 August, 1768–69.

Gophna, R. 1990. "The Egyptian Pottery of 'En Besor." *Tel Aviv* 17:144–62.

Gordon, C. 1962a. *Before the Bible: The Common Background of Greek and Hebrew
  Civilizations*. New York: Harper & Row.

———. 1962b. "Eteocretan." *Journal of Near Eastern Studies* 21:211–14.

———. 1965. *The Common Background of Greek and Hebrew Civilizations*. New York:
  Norton.

———. 1966. *Evidence for the Minoan Language*. Ventnor, N.J.: Ventnor Publishers.

———. 1982. *Forgotten Scripts: Their Ongoing Discovery and Decipherment*. New York:
  Basic Books.

*Gordon, P. 1993. "On *Black Athena*: Ancient Critiques of the 'Ancient Model' of
  Greek History." *Classical World* 87.1:71–2.

Goudriaan, K. 1988. *Ethnicity in Ptolemaic Egypt*. Amsterdam: Gieben.

Graindor, P. 1930. *Un milliardaire antique: Hérode Atticus et sa famille*. Université Egyptienne, Recueil de travaux publiés par la Faculté des Lettres, fasc. 5. Cairo.

Grant, M. 1918. *The Passing of the Great Race, or The Racial Basis of European History*. 2d ed. New York: Charles Scribner's Sons.

Gratien, B. 1978. *Les cultures Kerma: essai de classification*. Lille: Université de Lille.

Graves, R. 1948. *The White Goddess*. New York: Creative Age Press.

Green, P. 1994. "'By klepht and Styx': The Glory That Was Greece." *Times Literary Supplement* (London), 29 July, 3.

*Green, T. 1989. "Black Athena and Classical Historiography: Other Approaches, Other Views." In Levine and Peradotto 1989 = *Arethusa* 22:55–65.

Greenberg, J. H. 1955. *Studies in African Linguistic Classification*. New Haven, Conn.: Compass.

Greene, D. L. 1966. "Dentition and the Biological Relationships of Some Meroitic, X-Group and Christian Populations from Wadi Halfa, Sudan." *Kush* 14:285–88.

———. 1972. "Dental Anthropology of Early Egypt and Nubia." *Journal of Human Evolution* 1:315–24.

Greene, D. L., and G. J. Armelagos. 1972. *The Wadi Halfa Mesolithic Population*. Department of Anthropology Research Report no. 11. Amherst: University of Massachusetts.

Greene J. C. 1961. *The Death of Adam*. New York: American Library.

Greene, M. 1992. *Natural Knowledge in Preclassical Antiquity*. Baltimore: The Johns Hopkins University Press.

Gregerson, E. A. 1977. *Language in Africa: An Introductory Survey*. New York: Gordon & Breach.

Grégoire, H. [1808] 1810. *An Enquiry Concerning the Intellectual and Moral Faculties, and Literature of Negroes*. Translated by D. B. Warden. Brooklyn: Thomas Kirk.

Grene, D., trans. 1987. *Herotodus: The History*. Chicago: University of Chicago Press.

*Gress, D. 1989. "The Case against Martin Bernal." *New Criterion* 8, no. 4:36–43.

*Griffin, J. 1989. "Who Are These Coming to the Sacrifice?" *New York Review of Books*, 15 June, 25–27. (Review of *BA* 1)

†Grimal, N. 1992. *A History of Ancient Egypt*. Oxford: Blackwell.

Grote, G. 1900. *Greece*. Vol. 6. Reprinted from the 2d London ed. New York: Peter Fenelon Collier & Son.

Gruen, E. S. 1993. "Cultural Fictions and Cultural Identity." Presidential Address, 1992. *Transactions of the American Philological Association* 123:1–14.

Gsell, S. 1921–. *Histoire ancienne de l'Afrique du Nord*. Vols. 2 (1921), 5 (1927), 7 (1930). Paris: Hachette.

Gutbub, A. 1984. "Rait" and "Rat-taui." *Lexikon der Ägyptologie*, 4:87–90, 151–55. Wiesbaden: Otto Harrassowitz.

Haaland, R. 1992. "Fish, Pots, and Grain: Early Mid-Holocene Adaptations in the Central Sudan." *African Archaeological Review* 10:43–64.

Habachi, L. 1972. *The Second Stela of Kamose and His Struggle against the Hyksos Ruler and His Capital*. Gluckstadt: J. J. Augustin.

Hale, J. 1993. *The Civilization of Europe in the Renaissance*. London: Harper Collins.

Haley, S. P. 1993. "Black Feminist Thought and Classics: Re-membering, Re-claiming, Re-empowering." In *Feminist Theory and the Classics*, edited by N. S. Rabinowitz and A. Richlin, 23–43. New York: Routledge.

Hall, A. R. 1992. *Isaac Newton: Adventurer in Thought*. Oxford: Blackwell.

Hall, E. 1988. "When Did the Trojans Turn into Phrygians? Alcaeus 42.15." *Zeitschrift für Papyrologie und Epigraphik* 73:15–18.

———. 1989. *Inventing the Barbarian*. Oxford: Clarendon Press.

*———. 1991. "Myths Missing That Black Magic." *Times Higher Education Supplement* (London), 13 September, 15, 18.

*———. 1992. "When Is a Myth Not a Myth?" *Arethusa* 25:181–201. (= Hall, this volume)

*Hall, J. 1990. "*Black Athena*: A Sheep in Wolf's Clothing?" *Journal of Mediterranean Archaeology* 3, no. 2:247–54.

Hallet, J.-P., and A. Pelle. 1973. *Pygmy Kitabu*. New York: Random House.

Hamer, M. 1993. *Signs of Cleopatra: History, Politics, Representation*. London: Routledge.

Hamilton, E., and H. Cairns, eds. 1961. *The Collected Dialogues of Plato*. Bollingen Series 71. Princeton: Princeton University Press.

Hampe, R., and E. Simon. 1981. *The Birth of Greek Art from the Mycenaean to Archaic Period*. New York: Oxford University Press.

Hankey, V. 1970. "Mycenaean Trade with the Southeastern Mediterranean." *Mélanges de l'Université St. Joseph* 46:11–30.

Hankinson, R. J. 1991. *Galen: On the Therapeutic Method, Books I and II*. Oxford: Clarendon Press.

Hannaford, I. 1994. "The Idiocy of Race." *Wilson Quarterly* 18:8–35.

Hanson, A. E. 1985. "Papyri of Medical Content." *Yale Classical Studies* 28 (special issue, Papyrology, edited by N. Lewis): 25–47.

Hardy, D. A., and A. C. Renfrew, eds. 1990. *Thera and the Aegean World*. Vol. 3, *Chronology*. London: The Thera Foundation.

Harlan, J. 1969. "Ethiopia: A Center of Diversity." *Economic Botany* 3:309–14.

———. 1971. "Agricultural Origins: Centers and Noncenters." *Science* 174:468–74.

Harlan, J. R., J. M. J. De Wet, and A. B. L. Stemler, eds. 1976. *Origins of African Plant Domestication*. The Hague: Mouton.

Harte, N., and J. North. 1979. *The World of University College London, 1828–1978*. London: University College London Press.

Hartmann, N. 1987. "Atlantis Lost and Found: The Ancient Aegean from Politics to Volcanoes." *Expedition* 29:19–26.

Hartner, W. 1963. Discussion of G. de Santillana's "On Forgotten Sources in the History of Science." In *Scientific Change*, edited by A. C. Crombie, 868–75. New York: Basic Books.

Haskell, F. 1993. *History and its Images: Art and the Interpretation of the Past*. New Haven: Yale University Press.

Haskell, T. L. 1985. "Capitalism and the Origins of the Humanitarian Sensibility." Part 1, *American Historical Review* 90, no. 2:339–61; Part 2, 90, no. 3:547–66.

Hassan, F. A. 1983. "The Roots of Egyptian Writing." *Quarterly Review of Archaeology* 4, no. 3:1–8.

———. 1985. "Radiocarbon Chronology of Neolithic and Predynastic Sites in Upper Egypt and the Delta." *African Archaeological Review* 3:95–116.

———. 1986. "Chronology of the Khartoum 'Mesolithic' and 'Neolithic,' and related Sites in the Sudan." *African Archaeology Review* 4:83–101.

———. 1988. "The Predynastic of Egypt." *Journal of World Prehistory* 2:135–85.

Hawass, Z. A. 1990. *The Pyramids of Ancient Egypt.* Pittsburgh: Carnegie Museum of Natural History.

Hay, D. 1968. *Europe: The Emergence of an Idea.* 2d ed. Edinburgh: Edinburgh University Press.

Hayes, W. C. 1953a. "Notes on the Government of Egypt in the Late Middle Kingdom." *Journal of Near Eastern Studies* 12:31–39.

———. 1953b. *The Scepter of Egypt.* Vol. 1. New York: Metropolitan Museum of Art.

———. 1955. *A Papyrus of the Late Middle Kingdom in the Brooklyn Museum: Papyrus Brooklyn 35.1446.* Brooklyn: Brooklyn Museum.

†Haynes, J. L. 1992. *Nubia: Ancient Kingdoms of Africa.* Boston: Museum of Fine Arts.

†Healey, J. F. 1990. *Reading the Past: The Early Alphabet.* Berkeley and Los Angeles: University of California Press and the British Museum.

Heath, T. L., trans. 1912. *The Works of Archimedes.* New York: Dover.

———. 1913. *Aristarchus of Samos: The Ancient Copernicus.* Oxford: Clarendon Press.

———. [1931] 1963. *A Manual of Greek Mathematics.* New York: Dover.

———. 1932. *Greek Astronomy.* New York: E. P. Dutton.

Heidegger, M. [1966] 1977. "Only a God Can Save Us Now: An Interview with Martin Heidegger in *Der Spiegel*." Translated by David Schendler. *Graduate Faculty Philosophy Journal* (New School for Social Research) 6:5–27.

Helck, W. 1971. *Die Beziehungen Ägyptens zu Vorderasiens im 3. und 2. Jahrtausend v. Chr.* Wiesbaden: Otto Harrassowitz.

———. 1976. "Ägyptische Statuen im Ausland—ein Chronologisches Problem." *Ugarit Forschung* 8:101–15.

———. 1979. *Die Beziehungen Ägyptens und Vorderasiens zur Agais bis in 7. Jahrhunderts v. Chr.* Darmstadt: Wissenschaftliche Buchgesellschaft.

Hemelrijk, J. M. 1984. *Caeretan Hydriae.* 2 vols. Mainz am Rhein: P. von Zabern.

Herder, J. G. [1774] 1891. *Auch eine Philosophie der Geschichte zur Bildung der Menschheit.* In *Sämmtliche Werke*, edited by Bernhard Suphan, 5:475–586. Berlin: Weidmannsche Buchhandlung.

———. [1783–91] 1966. *Outlines of a Philosophy of the History of Man.* Translated by T. Churchill. New York: Bergman Publishers. (German title *Ideen zur Philosophie der Geschichte der Menschheit.*)

———. [1783–91] 1968. *Reflections on the Philosophy of the History of Mankind.* Translated by F. Manuel. Chicago: University of Chicago Press. (German title *Ideen zur Philosophie der Geschichte der Menschheit.*)

Herford, T. 1962. *The Ethics of the Talmud: Sayings of the Fathers.* New York: Schocken.

Herivel, J. 1965. *The Background to Newton's Principia.* Oxford: Clarendon Press.

Herm, G. 1975. *The Phoenicians: The Purple Empire of the Ancient World.* Translated by
C. Hillier. New York: Morrow.

Herodotus. 1924. *The Egypt of Herodotus: Being the Second Book, Entitled Euterpe, of the
History.* Translated by G. Rawlinson, preface and notes E. H. Blakeney. London:
Martin Hopkinson & Co.

———. 1985. *The History.* Translated by David Grene. Chicago: University of
Chicago Press.

Herz-Fischler, R. 1987. *A Mathematical History of Division in Extreme and Mean Ratio.*
Waterloo, Ont.: Wilfrid Laurier University Press.

Hetherington, N. S. 1987. *Ancient Astronomy and Civilization.* Tucson, Ariz.: Pachart.

Heubeck, A., and A. Hoekstra. 1988–91. *A Commentary on Homer's Odyssey.* 3 vols.
Oxford: Clarendon Press.

Hexter, J. H. 1979. *On Historians: Reappraisals of Some of the Makers of Modern History.*
Cambridge and London: Harvard University Press.

Hill, D. R. 1991. "Mechanical Engineering in the Medieval Near East." *Scientific
American* 261, no. 5:100–105.

Hill, H. 1961. "Dionysius of Halicarnassus and the Origins of Rome." *Journal of
Roman Studies* 51:88–93.

Hippocrates. 1839–61. *Oeuvres complètes.* Translated by E. Littré. 10 vols. Paris: J. B.
Baillière.

Hobsbawm, E., and T. Rangers, eds. 1983. *The Invention of Tradition.* Cambridge:
Cambridge University Press.

Hoch, J. 1994. *Semitic Words in Egyptian Texts of the New Kingdom and Third Intermediate
Period.* Princeton: Princeton University Press.

Hock, H. 1991. *Principles of Historical Linguistics.* 2d ed. Berlin and New York: Mouton
de Gruyter.

Hodge, C. T., ed. 1971. *Afroasiatic: A Survey.* The Hague: Mouton.

Hoetink, H. 1967. *The Two Variants in Caribbean Race Relations: A Contribution to the
Sociology of Segmented Societies.* Translated by E. M. Hookykaas. London, New York,
and Toronto: Oxford University Press.

†Hoffman, M. A. 1988. "Before the Pharaohs: How Egypt Became the World's First
Nation-State." *The Sciences* (January–February): 40–47.

———. 1991. *Egypt before the Pharaohs.* Rev. and updated ed. Austin: University of
Texas Press.

Hopkins, K. 1978. "Rules of Evidence." *Journal of Roman Studies* 68:178–86.

Horn, J. 1972. "Ägyptologie als Wissenschaft in der Gesellschaft." *Göttinger Miszellen*
1:42–48.

Hornung, E. [1971] 1982. *Conceptions of God in Ancient Egypt: The One and the Many.*
Translated by John Baines. Ithaca: Cornell University Press.

———. 1984. *Ägyptische Unterweltsbücher.* Die Bibliothek der Alten Welt: Der Alte
Orient. Zurich and Munich: Artemis.

Horton, M. 1987. "The Swahili Corridor." *Scientific American* 257, no. 3:86–93.

How, W. W., and J. Wells. 1912. *A Commentary on Herodotus.* 2 vols. Oxford:
Clarendon Press.

Howells, W. W. 1966. "Population Distances: Biological, Linguistic, Geographical, and Environmental." *Current Anthropology* 7:531–40.

———. 1973. *Cranial Variation in Man: A Study by Multivariate Analysis of Patterns of Difference among Recent Human Populations*. Papers of the Peabody Museum of Archaeology and Ethnology, 67. Cambridge: Peabody Museum, Harvard University.

———. 1986. "Physical Anthropology of the Prehistoric Japanese." In *Windows on the Japanese Past: Studies in Archaeology and Prehistory*, edited by E. W. Pearson, G. L. Barnes, and K. L. Hutterer, 85–90. Ann Arbor: University of Michigan Center for Japanese Studies.

———. 1989. *Skull Shapes and the Map: Craniometric Analyses in the Dispersion of Modern Homo*. Papers of the Peabody Museum of Archaeology and Ethnology, 79. Cambridge: Peabody Museum, Harvard University.

Humbert, J.-M., et al. 1994. *Egyptomania: Egypt in Western Art, 1730–1930*. Ottawa: National Gallery of Canada.

Hume, D. [1777] 1987. "Of the Populousness of Ancient Nations." In *Essays: Moral, Political, and Literary*. Edited by E. F. Miller. Rev. ed. Indianapolis: Liberty Classics.

Huxley, G. L. 1958. "Odysseus and the Thesprotian Oracle of the Dead." *La parola del passato* 13:145–58.

———. 1971. "Eudoxus of Cnidus." In *Dictionary of Scientific Biography*, edited by C. C. Gillispie, 4:465–67. New York: Scribner.

Huxley, J. S. 1938. "Clines: An Auxiliary Taxonomic Principle." *Nature* 142:219–20.

Isajiw, W. 1974. "Definitions of Ethnicity." *Ethnicity* 1:111–24.

†Iversen, E. 1993. *The Myth of Egypt and Its Hieroglyphs in European Tradition*. New ed. Princeton: Princeton University Press.

Jackson, J. G. [1970] 1990. *Introduction to African Civilizations*. New York: Carol Publishing Co.

Jacobsen, T. 1943. "Primitive Democracy in Ancient Mesopotamia." *Journal of Near Eastern Studies* 2:159–72.

———. 1970. "Primitive Democracy in Ancient Mesopotamia." In *Towards the Images of Tammuz*, edited by W. L. Moran, 157–70. Cambridge: Havard University Press.

———. 1984. "The Harab Myth." In *Sources from the Ancient Near East*, 2:6–26. Malibu: Undena Publications.

James, G. G. M. [1954] 1973. *Stolen Legacy: The Greeks Were Not the Authors of Greek Philosophy, but the People of North Africa, Commonly Called the Egyptians*. New York: Philosophical Library. Reprinted, San Francisco: Julian Richardson Associates.

———. [1954] 1989. *Stolen Legacy*. Reprinted, New York: African Islamic Mission Publications.

James, T. G. H. 1973. "Egypt from the Expulsion of the Hyksos to Amenophis I." *The Cambridge Ancient History*, 2d ed., II.2:289–312. Cambridge: Cambridge University Press.

———. 1984. *Pharaoh's People*. Chicago: University of Chicago Press.

———. 1988. *Ancient Egypt: The Land and Its Legacy*. Austin: The University of Texas Press.

Janssen, J. J. 1975. *Commodity Prices from the Ramesside Period*. Leiden: E. J. Brill.

Jarausch, K. H. 1986. "The Institutionalization of History in 18th-Century Germany." In *Aufklärung und Geschichte: Studien zur deutschen Geschichtswissenschaft im 18. Jahrhundert*, edited by H. E. Bödeker et al., 25–48. Göttingen: Vandenhoeck & Ruprecht.

†Jenkyns, R. 1980. *The Victorians and Ancient Greece*. Cambridge: Harvard University Press.

Jensen, A. R. 1969. Edited reply to a letter by D. N. Robinson. *New York Times Magazine*, 21 September, 14.

Johnson, A. L., and N. C. Lovell. 1994. "Biological Differentiation at Predynastic Naqada, Egypt: An Analysis of Dental Morphological Traits." *American Journal of Physical Anthropology* 93:427–33.

Johnson, E. M. 1978. "Who Homer Really Was." *College Language Association Journal* 22:54–62.

*Johnson-Odim, C. 1993. "Comment: The Debate over *Black Athena*." *Journal of Women's History* 4, no. 3:84–89.

Johnston, S. 1990. *Hecate Soteira*. Atlanta: Scholars Press.

Jones, E. L. 1972. *Profiles in African Heritage: Black Studies Series (in Classical History)*. Seattle, Wash.: Frayn.

Jones, W. H. S., trans. 1931. *Hippocrates*. Vol. 4. Loeb Classical Library. Cambridge: Harvard University Press.

Jordan, W. D. 1969. *White over Black: American Attitudes toward the Negro, 1550–1812*. Baltimore: Penguin.

*Journal of Mediterranean Archaeology. 1990. "Discussion and Debate: Special Review Section on M. Bernal, *Black Athena: The Afroasiatic Roots of Classical Civilization*, Vol. I." Vol. 3, no. 1:53–137; 3, no. 2:247–74.

*Journal of Women's History. 1993. "Dialogue: Martin Bernal's *Black Athena*." Vol. 4, no. 3:6–8, 84–135.

Judt, T. 1994. "The New Old Nationalism." *New York Review of Books*, 26 May, 44–51.

Judy, R. A. T. 1993. *(Dis)Forming the American Canon: African-Arabic Slave Narratives and the Vernacular*. Minneapolis: University of Minnesota Press.

Kabbani, R. 1986. *Europe's Myths of Orient: Devise and Rule*. Bloomington: Indiana University Press.

Kadish, G. 1973. "British Museum Writing Board 5645: The Complaints of Kha-Kheper-reʿsenebu." *Journal of Egyptian Archaeology* 59:77–90.

Kaiser, W. 1957. "Zur Inneren Chronologie der Naqada Kultur." *Archaeologica Graphica* 6:69–77.

———. 1959–64. "Einige Bemerkungen zur ägyptischen Frühzeit." 3 parts in 4. *Zeitschrift für Ägyptische Sprache und Altertumskunde* 84:119–32, 85:119–37, 86:39–61, 91:86–125.

Kamp, K. A., and N. Yoffee. 1980. "Ethnicity in Ancient Western Asia during the Early Second Millennium B.C.: Archaeological Assessments and Ethnoarchaeological Prospectives." *Bulletin of the American Schools of Oriental Research* 237:85–104.

Kant, I. [1764] 1991. *Observations of the Feeling of the Beautiful and Sublime*. Translated by J. T. Goldthwait. Berkeley and Los Angeles: University of California Press.

———. [1787] 1965. *Critique of Pure Reason*. Translated by N. K. Smith. New York: St. Martin's Press.

———. [1790] 1911. *Critique of Aesthetic Judgement*. Translated by J. C. Meredith. Reprinted, Oxford: Clarendon Press, 1986.

———. 1912–22. *Immanuel Kants Werke*. Vol. 4, edited by E. Cassirer. Berlin: B. Cassirer.

Kantor, H. J. 1944. "The Final Phase of Predynastic Culture: Gerzean or Semainean?" *Journal of Near Eastern Studies* 3:110–36.

———. 1965. "The Relative Chronology of Egypt and Its Foreign Corelations before the Late Bronze Age." In *Chronologies in Old World Archaeology*, edited by R. Ehrich, 19–22. Chicago: University of Chicago Press.

*Karenga, M. 1991. "The Contested Terrain of Ancient Egypt: Diop, Bernal and Paradigms in Africana Studies." *Challenging Tradition: Cultural Interaction in Antiquity and Bernal's Black Athena*, tape 5A.

†Keita, S. O. Y. 1990. "Studies of Ancient Crania from Northern Africa." *American Journal of Physical Anthropology* 85:35–48.

†———. 1992. "Further Studies of Ancient Northern African Crania." *American Journal of Physical Anthropology* 87:445–54.

*———. 1993a. "*Black Athena*: 'Race,' Bernal, and Snowden." *Arethusa* 26:295–314.

*———. 1993b. "Response to Bernal and Snowden." *Arethusa* 26:329–34.

†Kelly, D. H. 1991. "Egyptians and Ethiopians: Color, Race, and Racism." *Classical Outlook* 68:77–82.

Kemp, B. J. 1978. "Imperialism and Empire in New Kingdom Egypt (c. 1575–1087 B.C.)." In *Imperialism in the Ancient World*, 7–57, 284–97, 368–73. Cambridge University Research Seminar in Ancient History. Cambridge: Cambridge University Press.

———. 1980. "Egyptian Radiocarbon Dating: A Reply to James Mellaart." *Antiquity* 54:25–28.

†Kendall, T. 1991a. *Kush, Lost Kingdom of the Nile*. Brockton, Mass.: Brockton Art Museum/Fuller Memorial.

———. 1991b. In J. N. Wilford, "Nubian Treasures Reflect Black Influence on Egypt." *New York Times*, 11 February, C1, C10.

Kenyon, F. G., ed. 1893. *Greek Papyri in the British Museum*. 5 vols. London: British Museum.

Keramopoullos, A. 1917. "Thēbaika." *Deltion* 3:1–503.

Keyes, C. F. 1981a. "The Dialectics of Ethnic Change." In *Ethnic Change* (Keyes 1981b), 3–30.

———, ed. 1981b. *Ethnic Change*. London and Seattle; University of Washington Press.

Keys, D. 1991. [On Minoan frescoes at Avaris.] *Minerva* 2, no. 5 (September/October): 4.

King, R. 1990. *The African Origin of Biological Psychiatry*. Germantown, Tenn.: Seymour Smith.

Kipling, R. 1912. *Just So Stories*. Garden City, N.Y.: Country Life Press.

Kirk, G. S. 1985. *The Iliad: A Commentary.* Vol. 1. Cambridge: Cambridge University Press.

†Kirk, G. S., J. E. Raven, and M. Schofield, eds. 1983. *The Presocratic Philosophers.* 2d ed. Cambridge: Cambridge University Press.

Kitchen, K. 1968. *Ramesside Inscriptions, Historical and Biographical.* Vol. 4. Oxford: Blackwell.

———. 1977. *The Bible in Its World.* Exeter: Paternoster Press.

———. 1982. *Pharaoh Triumphant.* Mississauga, Ont.: Benben Press.

———. 1986. *The Third Intermediate Period in Egypt.* 2d ed. Warminster: Aris & Phillips.

———. 1992. "The Exodus." In *The Anchor Bible Dictionary,* edited by O. Freedman et al., 2:700–708. New York: Doubleday.

———. 1993. "The Land of Punt." In *The Archaeology of Africa: Food, Metals and Towns,* edited by T. Shaw et al., 587–608. London: Routledge.

Kluckhohn, C. 1961. *Anthropology and the Classics.* Providence: Brown University Press.

Koch, A., and W. Peden, eds. 1944. *The Life and Selected Writings of Thomas Jefferson.* New York: The Modern Library.

Kokhavi, M. 1990. *Aphek in Canaan: The Egyptian Governor's Residence and Its Finds.* Jerusalem: Israel Museum.

†Kopcke, G., and I. Tokumaru, eds. 1992. *Greece between East and West: 10th–8th Centuries B.C.* Mainz: Philipp von Zabern.

Krauss, R. 1981. "Sothis, Elephantine und die altägyptische Chronologie." *Göttinger Miszellen* 50:71–80.

———. 1985. *Sothis- und Monddaten: Studien zur astronomischen und technischen Chronologie Altägyptens.* Hildesheimer Ägyptologische Beiträge 20. Hildesheim: Gerstenberg.

Kristeller, P. 1995. Comment on *Black Athena. Journal of the History of Ideas* 56, no. 1:125–27.

Krupp, E. C. 1977. "Astronomers, Pyramids, and Priests." In *In Search of Ancient Astronomies,* edited by E. C. Krupp, 186–218. New York: Doubleday.

†Kuhn, T. S. 1970. *The Structure of Scientific Revolutions.* 2d ed. Chicago: University of Chicago Press.

Kunzl, A. 1976. *Der Gegensatz Rom-Kartago im Spiegel historisch-politischer Äusserungen der Zeit um den Ersten Weltkrieg.* Dissertation. University of Erlangen.

Kunzle, D. 1987. "Hogarth's Suppressed Blacks." *Art History* 10, no. 3:396–401.

Lamberton, R. 1988. *Hesiod.* New Haven: Yale University Press.

Lambrou-Phillipson, C. 1990. *Hellenorientalia.* Studies in Mediterranean Archaeology, Pocket-book 95. Göteborg: Paul Åströms Förlag.

Langdon, S. 1989. "The Return of the Horse-Leader." *American Journal of Archaeology* 93:185–201.

———. 1990. "From Monkey to Man: The Evolution of a Geometric Sculptural Type." *American Journal of Archaeology* 94:407–24.

———, ed. 1993. *From Pasture to Polis: Art in the Age of Homer.* Columbia: University of Missouri, Museum of Art and Archaeology; University of Missouri Press.

Lant, A. 1992. "The Curse of the Pharaoh, or How Cinema Contracted Egyptomania." *October*, no. 59 (Winter): 86–112.

Lauer, P. 1976. *Saqqara*. New York: Charles Scribner's Sons.

Lawrence, W. 1819. *Lectures on Physiology, Zoology, and the Natural History of Man.* London: J. Callow.

Leach, E. 1987. "Aryan Warlords in Their Chariots." *London Review of Books*, 2 April, 11.

Leaf, W., ed. 1902. *The Iliad*. Vol. 2. 2d ed. London and New York: Macmillan.

Leca, A.-P. 1981. *The Egyptian Way of Death: Mummies and the Cult of the Immortal.* Garden City, N.Y.: Doubleday.

Lee, D. 1960. "Homeric *kér* and Others." *Glotta* 39:191–207.

Lefkowitz, M. R. 1992a. "Afrocentrism Poses a Threat to the Rationalist Tradition." *Chronicle of Higher Education*, 6 May, A52.

*———. 1992b. "Not Out of Africa." *New Republic*, 10 February, 29–36. (= Lefkowitz, this volume)

*———. 1992c. "Reply to Martin Bernal." *New Republic*, 9 March, 5.

———. 1992d. "Point of View." *Chronicle of Higher Education*, 6 May, A52.

———. 1993a. "Afrocentrists Wage War on Ancient Greeks." *Wall Street Journal*, 7 April, A14.

*———. 1993b. "Ethnocentric History from Aristobulus to Bernal." *Academic Questions* 62:12–20.

†———. 1994. "The Myth of a 'Stolen Legacy,' " *Society* 31, no. 3:27–33. (Abridged version in *Alternatives to Afrocentrism*, 27–31. Washington, D.C.: The Manhattan Institute.)

Lemay, J. A. L., ed. 1993. *Reappraising Benjamin Franklin: A Bicentennial Perspective.* Newark, Del.: University of Delaware Press.

Lenoir, T. 1980. "Kant, Blumenbach, and Vital Materialism in German Biology." *Isis* 71:77–108.

Lepre, J. P. 1990. *The Egyptian Pyramids: A Comprehensive Illustrated Reference.* Jefferson, N.C.: McFarland.

*Lerner, G. 1993. "Comment: The Debate over Black Athena." *Journal of Women's History* 4, no. 3:90–94.

Lesky, A. 1972. *Die tragische Dichtung der Hellenen*. Göttingen: Vandenhoeck & Ruprecht.

*Levine, M. M. 1989. "The Challenge of Black Athena to Classics Today." In Levine and Peradotto 1989 = *Arethusa* 22:7–15.

———. 1990. "Classical Scholarship — Anti-Black and Anti-Semitic?" *Bible Review* 6, no. 3:32–36, 40–41.

———. 1992a. "Multiculturalism and the Classics." *Arethusa* 25:215–20.

†*———. 1992b. "The Use and Abuse of *Black Athena*." *American Historical Review* 97, no. 2:440–64.

†*Levine, M. M., and J. Peradotto, eds. 1989. *The Challenge of Black Athena*. Special issue, *Arethusa* 22 no. 1 (Fall).

†Lewis, B. 1993. "The Question of Orientalism." In *Islam and the West*, 99–118. New York: Oxford University Press.

Lewis, N. 1986. *Greeks in Ptolemaic Egypt: Case Studies in the Social History of the Hellenic World*. Oxford: Clarendon Press.

Lhote, H. 1959. *The Search for the Tassili Frescoes*. New York: E. P. Dutton.

Li, Y., C. L. Brace, J. Gao, and D. P. Tracer. 1991. "Dimensions of Face in Asia in the Perspective of Geography and Prehistory." *American Journal of Physical Anthropology* 85:269–79.

Lichtheim, M. 1973, 1976. *Ancient Egyptian Literature*. Vols. 1–2. Berkeley and Los Angeles: University of California Press.

Liebel, H. 1977. Review of *The German Enlightenment and the Rise of Historicism*, by P. H. Reill. *History and Theory* 16:204–17.

Littré, E. 1839–61. *Oeuvres complètes d'Hippocrate*. 10 vols. Paris: J. B. Baillière.

†Liverani, M. 1990. *Prestige and Interest: International Relations in the Near East ca. 1600–1100 B.C.* History of the Ancient Near East/Studies 1. Padua: Sargon.

Livingstone, F. B. 1958. "Anthropological Implications of Sickle Cell Gene Distribution in West Africa." *American Anthropologist* 60:533–62.

———. 1962. "On the Non-Existence of Human Races." *Current Anthropology* 3:279.

———. 1989a. "Simulation of the Diffusion of the B-Globin Variants in the Old World." *Human Biology* 5:297–309.

———. 1989b. "Who Gave Whom Hemoglobin S.: The Use of Restriction Site Haplotype Variation for the Interpretation of the Evolution of the B^s-globin Gene." *American Journal of Human Biology* 1:289–302.

Lloyd, A. B. 1975–88. *Herodotus Book II*. 3 vols. Leiden: E. J. Brill.

———. 1982. "Nationalist Propaganda in Ptolemaic Egypt." *Historia* 31:33–55.

Lloyd, G. E. R. 1975. "The Hippocratic Question." *Classical Quarterly*, n.s. 25:171–92.

———. 1987. *The Revolutions of Wisdom: Studies in the Claims and Practices of Ancient Greek Science*. Berkeley and Los Angeles: University of California Press.

———. 1992. "Methods and Problems in the History of Ancient Science." *Isis* 83, no.4 (special section, "The Cultures of Ancient Science"): 564–77.

———, ed. 1978. *Hippocratic Writings*. Harmondsworth, Middlesex: Penguin.

*Lloyd, R. B. 1988. "Review of *Black Athena*, Vol. I." *Choice* 25:1547.

Lloyd-Jones, H. 1983. "Artemis and Iphigeneia." *Journal of Hellenic Studies* 103:87–102.

———. 1992. "Becoming Homer." *New York Review of Books*, 5 March, 52–7.

Lobel, E., and D. Page. 1955. *Poetarum Lesbiorum Fragmenta*. Oxford: Clarendon Press.

Locher, K. 1983. "A Further Coffin-Lid with a Diagonal Star-Clock from the Egyptian Middle Kingdom." *Journal for the History of Astronomy* 14:141–44.

Lochner von Hüttenbach, F. 1960. *Die Pelasger*. Vienna: Gerold.

Lockyer, J. N. [1894] 1964. *The Dawn of Astronomy*. Reprinted, Cambridge: MIT Press. (First published, London: Macmillan)

Loprieno, A. 1988. *Topos und Mimesis: Zum Auslander in der Ägyptischen Literatur*. Ägyptologische Handlungen 48. Wiesbaden: Otto Harrassowitz.

———. In press. "Defining Egyptian Literature: Ancient Texts and Modern Literary Theory." In *The Study of the Ancient Near East in the 21st Century: The William Foxwell Albright Centennial Conference*. Winona Lake, Ind.: Eisenbrauns.

Loraux, N. 1986. *The Invention of Athens: The Funeral Oration in the Classical City*. Translated by Allan Sheridan. Cambridge: Harvard University Press.

Lovejoy, P. 1991. Foreword. In *The Anthropology of Slavery: The Womb of Iron and Gold*, by Claude Meillassoux, 7–8. Chicago: University of Chicago Press.

LSJ = Liddell, H. G., and R. Scott. 1925–40. *A Greek-English Lexicon*. 9th ed., rev. by H. Stuart Jones and R. McKenzie. Oxford: Clarendon Press.

Luft, U. 1982. "Illahunstudien I: Zur den Chronologie und den Beamten in den Schreiben aus Illahun." *Oikumene* 3:101–56.

———. 1992. *Chronologische Fixierung des altägyptischen Mittleren Reiches nach dem Tempelarchiv von Illahun*. Österreichische Akademie der Wissenschaften, Philosophisch Historische Klasse. Sitzungsberichte 598. Vienna.

Lumpkin, B. 1980. "The Egyptians and Pythagorean Triples." *Historia Mathematica* 7:186.

———. 1984. "Mathematics and Engineering in the Nile Valley." *Journal of African Civilizations* 6, no. 2:102–19.

McCann, A. M. 1968. *The Portraits of Septimius Severus (A.D. 193–211)*. Memoirs of the American Academy in Rome 30. Rome: American Academy.

McCrindle, J. W., trans. and ed. 1896. *The Invasion of India by Alexander the Great, as Described by Arrian, Q. Curtius, Diodorus, Plutarch and Justin*. Westminster: C. Constable.

MacGaffey, W. 1966. "Concepts of Race in the Historiography of Northeast Africa." *Journal of African History* 7:1–17.

MacIver, D. 1900. "Recent Anthropometrical Work in Egypt." *Journal of the Royal Anthropological Institute of Great Britain and Ireland* 30:95–103.

MacKendrick, P. 1969. *The Athenian Aristocracy, 399 to 31 B.C.* Cambridge: Harvard University Press.

McNeal, R. A. 1991. "Archaeology and the Destruction of the Later Athenian Acropolis." *Antiquity* 65 (March): 49–63.

*———. 1992. "Review Essay, *Black Athena*, Vol. I." *History and Theory* 31:47–55.

Mahalanobis, P. C. 1930. "On Tests and Measures of Group Divergence." *Journal of the Asiatic Society of Bengal* 26:541–88.

———. 1936. "On the Generalised Distance in Statistics." *Proceedings of the National Institute of Science in India*, Part A2:49–55.

———. 1949. "Appendix 1: Historical Note on the D2 Statistic." In "Anthropometric Survey of the United Provinces 1941: A Statistical Study." edited by P. C. Mahalanobis, C. N. Majumdar, and C. R. Rao. *Journal of Statistics* 9:237–40.

Majno, G. 1975. *The Healing Hand: Man and Wound in the Ancient World*. Cambridge: Harvard University Press.

*Malamud, M. A. 1989. "Review of *Black Athena*, Vol. I." *Criticism* 31, no. 3:317–22.

Malik, A. D. 1976. *Alexander the Great: A Military Study*. New Delhi: Light and Life Publishers.

Mallory, J. P. 1989. *In Search of the Indo-Europeans: Language, Archaeology and Myth*. London: Thames & Hudson.

Manning, S. 1990. "Frames of Reference for the Past: Some Thoughts on Bernal, Truth, and Reality." *Journal of Mediterranean Archaeology* 3, no. 2:255–74.

Manuel, F. E. [1959] 1967. *The Eighteenth Century Confronts the Gods*. Cambridge: Harvard University Press.

———. 1963. *Isaac Newton, Historian*. Cambridge: Harvard University Press.

———, ed. 1968. J. G. von Herder, *Reflections of the Philosophy of the History of Mankind*. Translated by T. Churchill. Chicago: University of Chicago Press.

†———. 1992. *The Broken Staff*. Cambridge: Harvard University Press.

Marinatos, S. 1968. "Mycenaean Culture within the Frame of Mediterranean Anthropology and Archaeology." In *Atti e memorie del 1° Congresso Internazionale di Micenologia*, 259–76. Rome: Edizioni dell'Ateno.

Markowsky, G. 1992. "Misconceptions about the Golden Ratio." *College Mathematics Journal* 23, no. 1:2–19.

Marriott, M. 1991. "As a Discipline Advances: A Debate on Scholarship." *New York Times*, 11 August, 18.

Marshall, E. 1990. "Paleoanthropology Gets Physical." *Science* 247:798–801.

Marsot, A. L. al-S. 1988. *Egypt in the Reign of Muhammad Ali*. Cambridge: Cambridge University Press.

Martin, R. 1928. *Lehrbuch der Anthropologie in Systematischer Darstellung*. Vol. 2, *Kraniologie, Osteologie*. Jena: Gustav Fischer.

Martin, T. [1976] 1986. *Race First*. Dover, Mass.: Majority Press.

———. 1993. *The Jewish Onslaught: Despatches from the Wellesley Battlefront*. Dover, Mass.: Majority Press.

Marwick, A. 1971. *The Nature of History*. New York: Knopf.

———. 1984. "In Pursuit of the Past." *Times Higher Education Supplement*, 16 November, 14.

Masson, E. 1967. *Recherches sur les plus anciens emprunts sémitiques en grec*. Paris: Klincksieck.

May, M. T. 1968. *Galen: On the Usefulness of the Parts of the Body*. Ithaca: Cornell University Press.

Mayor, J. E. B. 1881. *Thirteen Satires of Juvenal*. London: Macmillan.

Meinecke, F. [1936] 1972. *Historism: The Rise of a New Historical Outlook*. Translated by J. E. Anderson. New York: Herder & Herder.

Mellaart, J. 1979. "Egyptian and Near Eastern Chronology: A Dilemma?" *Antiquity* 53:6–18.

Menninger, K. [1958] 1969. *Number Words and Number Symbols: A Cultural History of Numbers*. Cambridge: MIT Press. (First published in German)

Menze, E. A., and K. Menges, eds. 1992. *Johann Gottfried Herder: Selected Early Works, 1764–1767*. University Park: Pennsylvania State University Press.

Merkelbach, R. 1968. "Les papyrus d'Hésiode et la géographie mythologique de la Grèce." *Chronique d'Egypte* 43:133–55.

Merritt, G. 1993. "Was Nefertiti Black?" *Archaeology* 46, no. 1:12. (A letter to the editor)

Michaud. 1811–62. *Biographie universelle*. Paris: Michaud Frères.

*Michelini, A. N. 1993. "Comment: The Debate over *Black Athena*." *Journal of Women's History* 4, no. 3:95–105.

Miller, E. 1991. "Viewpoints II." *Washington View*, March/April.

Mokhtar, G., and J. Vercoutter. 1981. Introduction. In *General History of Africa*, vol. 2, *Ancient Civilizations of Africa*, edited by G. Mokhtar, 1–25. Berkeley and Los Angeles: University of California Press.

Momigliano, A. 1955. *Contributo alla storia degli studi classici*. Rome: Edizioni di Storia e Letteratura.

———. 1966. "George Grote and the Study of Greek History." In *Studies in Historiography*, 56–74. New York: Harper & Row.

†———. 1990. *The Classical Foundations of Modern Historiography*. Berkeley and Los Angeles: University of California Press.

Monboddo, [James Burnett, Lord]. 1774–92. *Of the Origin and Progress of Language*. 6 vols. Edinburgh: J. Balfour.

Mond, R., and O. H. Mond. 1937. *Cemeteries of Armant*. 2 vols. London: Egypt Exploration Society and Oxford University Press.

Montfaucon, B. 1719–24. *L'antiquité expliquée et representée en figures*. 10 vols. Paris.

Moorey, P. R. S. 1990. "From Gulf to Delta in the Fourth Millennium B.C.E." In *Eretz Israel*, vol. 21 (Ruth Amiran volume), *Archaeological, Historical, and Geographical Studies*, edited by A. Eitan, R. Gophna, and M. Kochavi, 62–69. Jerusalem: Israel Exploration Society.

Morant, G. M. 1925. "A Study of Egyptian Craniology from Prehistoric to Roman Times." *Biometrika* 17:1–52.

———. 1935. "A Study of Pre-Dynastic Egyptian Skulls from Badari Based on Measurements Taken by Miss B. N. Stoessiger and Professor D. E. Derry." *Biometrika* 27:293–309.

———. 1937. "The Predynastic Egyptian Skulls from Badari and Their Racial Affinities." In *Mostagedda and the Tasian Culture*, edited by G. Brunton, 63–66. London: Bernard Quaritch.

Morris, I. 1987. *Burial and Ancient Society: The Rise of the Greek City-State*. New Studies in Archaeology. Cambridge: Cambridge University Press.

Morris, S. P. 1989. "Daidalos and Kadmos: Classicism and 'Orientalism.'" In Levine and Peradotto 1989 = *Arethusa* 22:39–54.

†———. 1990. "Greece and the Levant." *Journal of Mediterranean Archaeology* 3, no. 1:57–66.

†———. 1992. *Daidalos and the Origins of Greek Art*. Princeton: Princeton University Press.

Morton, S. G. 1844. *Crania Aegyptica, or Observations on Egyptian Ethnography, Derived from Anatomy, History and the Monuments*. Philadelphia: John Penington.

*Muhly, J. D. 1990a. Preface. *Journal of Mediterranean Archaeology* 3, no. 1:53–55.

†*———. 1990b. "Black Athena versus Traditional Scholarship." *Journal of Mediterranean Archaeology* 3, no. 1:83–110.

*———. 1991a. "Where the Greeks Got Their Gifts." *Washington Post Book World*, 21 July, 3.

*———. 1991b. "Is There Evidence of Egyptian Colonization in Central Greece?"

Challenging Tradition: Cultural Interaction in Antiquity and Bernal's Black Athena,
tape 4B.

———. 1993. "Early Bronze Age Tin and the Taurus." *American Journal of Archaeology*
97, no. 2:239–53.

*———, ed. 1990c. "Discussion and Debate: Special Review Section." *Journal of
Mediterranean Archaeology* 3:51–137.

Müller, K. O. [1820] 1844. *Orchomenos und die Minyer* (= *Geschichten hellenischer Stämme
und Städte*, vol. 1). 2d ed. Breslau: Josef Max.

Myers, C. S. 1905. "Contributions to Egyptian Anthropometry, II: The
Comparative Anthropometry of the Most Ancient and Modern Inhabitants."
Journal of the Royal Anthropological Institute of Great Britain and Ireland 35:80–91.

Mylonas, G. E. 1966. *Mycenae and the Mycenaean World*. Princeton: Princeton
University Press.

Na'aman, N. 1991. "The Kingdom of Judah under Josiah." *Tel Aviv* 18:3–71.

Nagy, G. 1979. *The Best of the Achaeans: Concepts of the Hero in Archaic Greek Poetry*.
Baltimore and London: The Johns Hopkins University Press.

Needham, J., W. Ling, et al. 1954–94. *Science and Civilisation in China*. 6 vols.
Cambridge: Cambridge University Press.

Néret, G. 1994. *Description de l'Egypte*. Cologne: Benedikt Taschen.

Neugebauer, O. 1942a. "The Origin of the Egyptian Calendar." *Journal of Near
Eastern Studies* 1:397–403. Reprinted in Neugebauer 1983.

———. 1942b. *Egyptian Planetary Texts*. Transactions of the American Philosophical
Society, n.s. 32. Philadelphia.

———. 1950. "The Alleged Babylonian Discovery of the Precession of the
Equinoxes." *Journal of the American Oriental Society* 70, no. 1:1–8. Reprinted in
Neugebauer 1983.

———. 1951. "The Study of Wretched Subjects." *Isis* 42:111. Reprinted in
Neugebauer 1983.

†———. 1957. *The Exact Sciences in Antiquity*, 2d ed. Providence: Brown University
Press.

†———. 1975. *A History of Ancient Mathematical Astronomy*. 3 vols. New York:
Springer-Verlag.

———. 1980. "On the Orientation of Pyramids." *Centaurus* 24:1–3. Reprinted in
Neugebauer 1983.

†———. 1983. *Astronomy and History: Selected Essays*. New York: Springer-Verlag.

———. 1988. "A Babylonian Lunar Ephemeris from Roman Egypt." In *A Scientific
Humanist: Studies in Memory of Abraham Sachs*, edited by E. Leichty et al., 301–4.
Philadelphia: Samuel Noah Kramer Fund, The University Museum.

———. 1989. "From Assyriology to Renaissance Art." *Proceedings of the American
Philosophical Society* 133, no. 3:391–403.

Neugebauer, O., and R. A. Parker. 1960, 1964, 1969. *Egyptian Astronomical Texts*.
3 vols. Providence: Brown University Press.

Newsome, F. 1983. "Black Contributions to the Early History of Western Medicine."
In *Blacks in Science: Ancient and Modern*, edited by I. Van Sertima, 127–39. New
Brunswick, N.J.: Transaction Books.

Newton, I. 1947. [*Principia Mathematica.*] *Sir Isaac Newton's Mathematical Principles of Natural Philosophy and His System of the World*]. Translated by F. Cajori. Berkeley and Los Angeles: University of California Press.

Niemeier, W.-D. 1991. "Minoan Artists Travelling Overseas: The Alalakh Frescoes and the Painted Plaster Floor at Tel Kabri (Western Galilee)." In *Thalassa: l'Egée préhistorique et la mer; Actes de la troisième Rencontre Egéenne Internationale de l'Université de Liège*, 189–201. Aegaeum 7. Liège: Université de Liège, Histoire de l'Art et Archéologie de la Grèce Antique.

Nilsson, M. P. [1932] 1972. *The Mycenean Origin of Greek Mythology*. Berkeley and Los Angeles: University of California Press.

Nims, C. F. 1968. "Second Tenses in Wenamun." *Journal of Egyptian Archaeology* 54:161–64.

Noble, J. V. 1988. *The Techniques of Painted Attic Pottery*. Rev. ed. London: Thames & Hudson.

Noel, P. 1991. "Black Heart, White Hunter." *Village Voice*, 27 August, 40.

Norton, R. E. 1995. "Racism, History, and Physiognomy: Herder and the Tradition of Moral Beauty in the Eighteenth Century." In *Werke und Werte, Ethik und Aesthetik in der Literatur des 18.–20. Jahrhunderts: Festschrift für Wolfgang Wittkowski*, edited by Richard Fisher and Helmut Kreuzer, 43–54. Frankfurt: Lang.

Nott, J. C. 1844. *Two Lectures on the Natural History of the Caucasian and Negro Races*. Mobile, Ala.: Dade & Thompson.

Oakeshott, M. 1983. *On History*. Oxford: Blackwell.

Obsomer, C. 1989. *Les campagnes de Sésostris dans Hérodote*. Brussels: Connaisance de l'Egypte Ancienne.

Ockinga, B. G. 1983. "The Burden of Kha-Kheperre'sonbu." *Journal of Egyptian Archaeology* 69:88–95.

O'Connor, D. 1971. "Ancient Egypt and Black Africa—Early Contacts." *Expedition: The Magazine of Archaeology/Anthropology* 14, no. 1:2–9.

———. 1984. "Kerma and Egypt: The Significance of the Monumental Buildings Kerma I, II, and XI." *Journal of the American Research Center in Egypt* 21:65–108.

———. 1987a. "The Location of Irem." *Journal of Egyptian Archaeology* 73:99–136.

———. 1987b. "The Locations of Yam and Kush and Their Historical Implications." *Journal of the American Research Center in Egypt* 23:27–50.

———. 1993. "Chiefs or Kings?" *Expedition* 35, no. 2:4–15.

†———. 1994. *Ancient Nubia: Egypt's Rival in Africa*. Philadephia: University Museum of Archeology and Anthropology.

Oppenheim, A. L. 1954. "Sea-Faring Merchants of Ur." *Journal of the American Oriental Society* 74:6–17.

†———. 1977. *Mesopotamia: Portrait of a Dead Civilization*, Rev. ed., by Erica Reiner. Chicago: University of Chicago Press.

Ortiz de Montellano, B. 1991. "Multicultural Pseudoscience: Spreading Scientific Illiteracy among Minorities—Part 1." *Sceptical Inquirer* 16, no. 1:46–50.

———. 1992. "Avoiding Egyptocentric Pseudoscience: Colleges Must Help Set Standards for Schools." *Chronicle of Higher Education*, 25 March, B1–B2.

Osing, J. 1976. *Die Nominalbildung des Ägyptischen.* 2 vols. Mainz: Verlag Philipp von Zabern.

———. 1992. *Aspects de la culture pharaonique.* Mémoires de l'Académie des Inscriptions et Belles Lettres, n.s. 12. Paris: Diffusion de Boccard.

Otto, W. F. 1965. *Dionysos: Myth and Cult.* Translated by R. B. Palmer. Bloomington: Indiana University Press.

Page, A. 1976. *Egyptian Sculpture: Archaic to Saite from the Petrie Collection.* Edited by H. S. Smith. Warminster: Aris & Phillips.

Page, D. 1972. *History and the Homeric Iliad.* Berkeley and Los Angeles: University of California Press.

———, ed. 1938. *Euripides' Medea.* Oxford: Clarendon Press.

*Palter, R. 1993. "Black Athena, Afro-Centrism, and the History of Science." *History of Science* 31, no. 3:227–87. (= Palter, this volume)

*———. 1994. Comment on Bernal 1994 [Response to Palter 1993]. *History of Science* 32, no. 4:464–68.

———. 1995. "Hume and Prejudice." *Hume Studies* 21, no. 1:3–23.

Panofsky, E. 1955. "The History of the Theory of Human Proportions as a Reflection of the History of Styles." In *Meaning in the Visual Arts,* 55–107. New York: Doubleday.

Pappademos, J. 1984. "The Newtonian Synthesis in Physical Science and Its Roots in the Nile Valley." *Journal of African Civilizations* 6, no. 2:84–101.

Pardoe, C. 1991. "Evolution and Isolation in Tasmania." *Current Anthropology* 32:1–21.

Parish, P. J. 1989. *Slavery: History and Historians.* New York: Harper & Row.

Parker, R. 1986. "Myths of Early Athens." In *Interpretations of Greek Mythology,* edited by J. Bremmer, 187–214. Totowa, N.J.: Barnes & Noble.

Parker, R. A. 1950. *The Calendars of Ancient Egypt.* The Oriental Institute of the University of Chicago, Studies in Ancient Oriental Civilization 26. Chicago: University of Chicago Press.

———. 1971. "The Calendars and Chronology." In *The Legacy of Egypt,* 2d ed., edited by J. R. Harris, 15–20. Oxford: Clarendon Press.

———. 1976. "The Sothic Dating of the Twelfth and Eighteenth Dynasties." In *Studies in Honor of George R. Hughes,* edited by Edward F. Wente and Janet Johnson, 177–89. Studies in Ancient Oriental Civlizations 39. Chicago: Oriental Institute.

———. 1978. "Egyptian Astronomy, Astrology, and Calendrical Reckoning." In *Dictionary of Scientific Biography,* edited by C. C. Gillispie, 15 (= Supplement 1): 706–27. New York: Scribner.

Parrish, J. A., R. R. Anderson, F. Urbach, and D. Pitts. 1978. *UV-A: Biological Effects of Ultraviolet Radiation with Emphasis on Human Responses to Longwave Ultraviolet.* New York: Plenum.

†Patterson, O. 1971. "Rethinking Black History." *Harvard Educational Review* 41, no. 3:297–315.

*Patterson, T. C. 1988. "Another Blow to Eurocentrism." *Monthly Review: An Independent Socialist Magazine* 40 (December): 42–45.

Pearson, K. 1896. "Mathematic Contributions to the Theory of Evolution, III:

Regression, Heredity and Panmixia." *Philological Transactions of the Royal Society of London* (A) 187:253–318.

Pearson, K., and A. G. Davin. 1924. "On the Biometric Constants of the Human Skull." *Biometrika* 16:328–63.

†Pedersen, H. [1924] 1965. *The Discovery of Language: Linguistic Science in the Nineteenth Century*. Translated by J. W. Spargo. Bloomington: Indiana University Press by arrangement with Harvard University Press. (First published in Danish)

———. 1931. *Linguistic Science in the Nineteenth Century*. Cambridge: Harvard University Press.

Pedersen, O. 1974. *A Survey of the Almagest*. Odense: Odense Universitetsforlag.

Pembroke, S. 1967. "Women in Charge: The Function of Alternatives in Early Greek Tradition and the Ancient Idea of Matriarchy." *Journal of the Warburg and Courtauld Institutes* 30:1–35.

Peradotto, J. 1991. Letter to the editor. *Chronicle of Higher Education*, 4 September, B5.

Persson, A. 1942. *New Tombs at Dendra Near Midea*. Lund: Gleerup.

Peters, M. 1980. *Untersuchungen zur Vertretung der indogermanischen Laryngale im Griechischen*. Vienna: Verlag der Österreichischen Akadamie der Wissenschaften.

Peterson, M., ed. 1977. *The Portable Thomas Jefferson*. New York: Penguin Books.

Petrie, W. M. F. 1899. *A History of Egypt*. New York: Charles Scribner's Sons.

———. 1901. "The Races of Early Egypt." *Journal of the Royal Anthropological Society of Great Britain and Ireland* 31:248–55.

———. 1907. *Gizeh and Rifeh*. London: Bernard Quaritch.

———. 1911. *Roman Portraits and Memphis*. Vol. 4. London: Bernard Quaritch.

———. 1920. *Prehistoric Egypt*. London: British School of Archaeology in Egypt.

———. 1931. "Peoples of Egypt." *Ancient Egypt* 16:77–85.

———. 1937. "Dynastic Invasion of Egypt." *Syro-Egypt* 2:6–8.

———. 1939. *The Making of Egypt*. London: Sheldon Press.

Petrie, W. M. F., and J. E. Quibell. 1896. *Naqada and Ballas*. London: Bernard Quaritch.

Pettinato, G. 1981. *The Archives of Ebla*. Garden City, N.Y.: Doubleday.

Phillip, M. 1995. "Secrets from the Sepulcher." *Black Issues in Higher Education* 12:12–17.

†Phillipson, D. W. 1993. *African Archaeology*. Cambridge: Cambridge University Press.

Pierce, R. 1971. "Egyptian Loan Words in Ancient Greek?" *Symbolae Osloenses* 46:96–107.

Pietrusewsky, M. 1984. *Metric and Non-Metric Cranial Variation in Australian Aboriginal Populations Compared with Populations from the Pacific and Asia*. Occasional Papers in Human Biology, 3; Australian Institute of Aboriginal Studies, 49. Canberra.

———. 1990. "Craniofacial Variation in Australasian and Pacific Populations." *American Journal of Physical Anthropology* 82:319–40.

Pietrusewsky, M., Y. Li, X. Shao, and N. Q. Quyen. 1992. "Modern and Near Modern Populations of Asia and the Pacific: A Multivariate Craniometric Interpretation." In *The Evolution and Dispersal of Modern Humans in Asia*, edited by T. Akazawa, K. Aoki, and T. Kimura, 531–58. Tokyo: Hokusen-Sha.

Plato. 1919. *The Dialogues of Plato*. Vol. 2, *The Republic*. Translated by B. Jowett. New
York: Bigelow, Brown.

*Poliakoff, M. 1991. "Roll over, Aristotle: Martin Bernal and His Critics." *Academic
Questions* 4, no. 3:12–28.

Poliakov, L. 1974. *The Aryan Myth: A History of Racist and Nationalistic Ideas in Europe*.
Translated by E. Howard. London: Chatto & Windus and Heinemann for Sussex
University Press.

Popkin, R. 1973. "The Philosophical Basis of Eighteenth-Century Racism." In
Studies in Eighteenth-Century Culture: Racism in the Eighteenth Century, edited by H. E.
Pagliaro, 245–62. Cleveland: Press of Case Western Reserve University.

Popper, K. R. [1947] 1966. *The Open Society and Its Enemies*. Vol. 1, *The Spell of Plato*.
London: Routledge & Kegan Paul.

Posener, G. 1956. *Littérature et politique dans l'Egypte de la XIIe dynastie*. Bibliothèque de
l'Ecole des Hautes Etudes, no. 307. Paris: Honoré Champion.

———. 1971. "Literature." In *The Legacy of Egypt*, 2d ed., edited by J. R. Harris,
220–56. Oxford: Clarendon Press.

———. 1982. "A New Royal Inscription of the XIIth Dynasty." *Journal of the Society
for the Study of Egyptian Antiquities* 12:7–8.

†Postgate, J. N. 1992. *Early Mesopotamia: Society and Economy at the Dawn of History*.
London: Routledge.

*Pounder, R. 1992. "*Black Athena* II: History without Rules." *American Historical
Review* 97:461–64.

†Powell, B. B. 1991. *Homer and the Origins of the Greek Alphabet*. Cambridge:
Cambridge University Press.

Preiswerk, R., and Perrot, D. 1978. *Ethnocentrism and History*. New York: NOK
Publishers International.

Prichard, J. C. 1851. *Researches into the Physical History of Mankind*. Vol. 2, *Researches into
the Physical Ethnography of the African Races*. 4th ed. London: Houlston &
Stoneman.

Pritchard, J. B., ed. 1969a. *Ancient Near Eastern Texts Relating to the Old Testament*.
Princeton: Princeton University Press.

———. 1969b. *The Ancient Near East in Pictures Relating to the Old Testament*. 3d ed.
Princeton: Princeton University Press.

Pritchett, K. 1993. *The Liar School of Herodotos*. Amsterdam: Gieben.

Pruner-Bey, F. 1863. "Recherches sur l'origine de l'ancienne race égyptienne."
Mémoires de la Société d'Anthropologie de Paris 1:399–433.

Puhvel, J. 1984–. *Hittite Etymological Dictionary*. Berlin and New York: de Gruyter.

Pulak, C. 1992. "The Shipwreck at Uluburun, Turkey: 1992 Excavation Campaign."
Institute of Nautical Archaeology Quarterly 19, no. 4:4–11, 21.

———. 1994. "1994 Excavation at Uluburun: The Final Campaign." *Institute of
Nautical Archaeology Quarterly* 21, no. 4:8–16.

Pyle, D. M. 1989. "Ice-Core Acidity Peaks, Retarded Tree Growth and Putative
Eruptions." *Archaeometry* 31:88–91.

Rabel, G. 1963. *Kant*. Oxford: Clarendon Press.

Rabinowitz, N. S. 1993. Introduction. In *Feminist Theory and the Classics*, edited by
N. S. Rabinowitz and A. Richlin, 1–20. London: Routledge.

Radt, S. 1977. *Tragicorum Graecorum Fragmenta*. Vol. 4, *Sophocles*. Göttingen:
Vandenhoeck & Ruprecht.

Rampino, M., and S. Self 1982. "Historic Eruption of Tambora 1815, Krakatoa 1883,
and Agung 1963, Their Stratospheric Aerosols and Climate Impact." *Quaternary
Research* 18:127–43.

Randall-MacIver, D., and C. L. Woolley. 1909. *Areika*. Publications of the Egyptian
Department of the University Museum. Philadelphia: University of
Pennsylvania.

Rao, C. R. 1973. *Linear Statistical Inference and Its Applications*. 2d ed. New York: John
Wiley & Sons.

Ratnagar, S. 1981. *Encounters: The Westerly Trade of the Harappa Civilisation*. Delhi:
Oxford University Press.

Ravitch, D. 1990. "Multiculturalism: E Pluribus Plures." *American Scholar* 59,
no. 3:337–54.

———. 1991. "Multiculturalism: An Exchange." *American Scholar* 60, no. 2:272–76.
(Reply to Asante 1991a)

Ray, J. D. 1986. "The Emergence of Writing in Egypt." *World Archaeology* 17:307–16.

———. 1990. "An Egyptian Perspective." *Journal of Mediterranean Archaeology* 3,
no. 1:77–81.

*———. 1991a. "Levant Ascendant: The Invasion Theory of the Origins of
European Civilization." *Times Literary Supplement*, 18 October, 3–4. (Review of *BA*
2 and Diop 1991)

*———. 1991b. Review of *BA* 2. *Times Literary Supplement*, 18 October, 4.

Raubitschek, A. 1989. "What the Greeks Thought of Their Early History." *Ancient
World* 20:39–45.

Redford, D. B. 1970. "The Hyksos Invasion in History and Tradition." *Orientalia*,
n.s. 39, no. 1:1–51.

———. 1982. "A Bronze Age Itinerary in Transjordan." *Journal of the Society for the
Study of Egyptian Antiquities* 12:55–74. (Nos. 89–101 of Thutmose III's list of
Asiatic toponyms)

———. 1984. *Akhenaten: The Heretic King*. Princeton: Princeton University Press.

†———. 1992. *Egypt, Canaan, and Israel in Ancient Times*. Princeton: Princeton
University Press.

Reeves, N. 1990. *The Complete Tutankhamun*. London: Thames & Hudson.

Reill, P. H. 1975. *The German Enlightenment and the Rise of Historicism*. Berkeley and Los
Angeles: University of California Press.

Reisner, G. A. 1909. "The Archaeological Survey of Nubia." *Archaeological Survey of
Nubia*, Bulletin no. 3:520. Cairo: National Printing Department.

———. 1923a. *Excavations at Kerma, I–III*. Harvard African Series, vol. 5.
Cambridge: Harvard University Press; Peabody Museum of Harvard University.

———. 1923b. *Excavations at Kerma, VI*. Harvard African Series, vol. 6. Cambridge:
Harvard University Press.

*Reiss, T. J. 1992. Review of *BA* 2. *Canadian Review of Comparative Literature* 19, no. 3:429–35.

*Rendsburg, G. A. 1989. "*Black Athena*: An Etymological Response." In Levine and Peradotto 1989 = *Arethusa* 22:67–82.

Renfrew, C. 1972. *The Emergence of Civilisation: The Cyclades and the Aegean in the Third Millennium B.C.* London: Methuen & Co.

†————. 1987. *Archaeology and Language: The Puzzle of Indo-European Origins.* New York: Cambridge University Press.

†Rice, M. 1990. *Egypt's Making: The Origins of Ancient Egypt, 5000–2000 B.C.* London and New York: Routledge.

Richter, M. 1977. *The Political Theory of Montesquieu.* Cambridge: Cambridge University Press.

Riddle, J. M. 1985. *Dioscorides on Pharmacy and Medicine.* Austin: University of Texas Press.

Ripley, W. Z. 1899. *The Races of Europe: A Sociological Study.* New York: D. Appleton.

Robins, A. H. 1991. *Biological Perspectives on Human Pigmentation.* New York: Cambridge University Press.

Robins, G., and C. C. D. Shute. 1985. "Mathematical Bases of Ancient Egyptian Architecture and Graphic Art." *Historia Mathematica* 12, 107–22.

————. 1986. "Predynastic Egyptian Stature and Physical Proportions." *Human Evolution* 1:313–24.

————, eds. 1987. *The Rhind Mathematical Papyrus: An Ancient Egyptian Text.* New York and London: British Museum Publications.

Rogers, J. A. 1946. *World's Great Men of Color.* Vol. 1. New York: J. A. Rogers.

————. 1967. *Sex and Race: Negro-Caucasian Mixing in All Ages and All Lands.* New York: Helga M. Rogers.

Romesburg, H. C. 1984. *Cluster Analysis for Researchers.* Belmont, Calif.: Lifetime Learning Publications.

Rose, P. L. 1990. *Revolutionary Anti-Semitism in Germany from Kant to Wagner.* Princeton: Princeton University Press.

Rosenthal, L. J. 1992. "Owning Oroonoko: Behn, Southerne, and the Contingencies of Property." In *Renaissance Drama in an Age of Colonization*, edited by M. B. Rose, 25–58. Evanston, Ill.: Northwestern University Press.

Rousseau, G. S., and R. Porter, eds. 1990. *Exoticism and the Enlightenment.* Manchester: Manchester University Press.

Rousseau, J.-J. 1986. *First and Second Discourses* and *Essay on the Origin of Languages.* Translated by V. Gourevitch. New York: Perennial Library.

†Roux, G. 1964. *Ancient Iraq.* New York and Cleveland: World.

Rushton, J. P. 1989. "Interview on Quirks and Quarks." Toronto *CBC*, 18 February.

Russell, D. A. 1973. *Plutarch.* New York: Charles Scribner's Sons.

Sacks, K. 1990. *Diodorus Siculus and the First Century.* Princeton: Princeton University Press.

†Saggs, H. W. F. 1984. *The Might that was Assyria.* London: Sidgwick & Jackson.

————. 1989. *Civilization before Greece and Rome.* New Haven: Yale University Press.

†Said, E. W. 1978. *Orientalism*. London: Routledge & Kegan Paul.

Saine, T. P. 1972. *Georg Forster*. New York: Twayne.

Salerno, L. 1965. *Palazzo Rondinini*. Rome: De Luca.

†Sandars, N. K. 1987. *The Sea Peoples*. 2d ed. London: Thames & Hudson.

Sandford, K. S., and W. J. Arkell. 1928. *First Report of the Prehistoric Survey*. Oriental Institute Report, no. 3. Chicago: University of Chicago Press.

———. 1929. *Prehistoric Survey of Egypt and Western Asia*. Vol. 1, *Palaeolithic Man and the Nile–Fayum Divide*. Oriental Institute Publication 10. Chicago: University of Chicago Press.

———. 1933. *Prehistoric Survey of Egypt and Western Asia*. Vol. 2, *Palaeolithic Man and the Nile Valley in Nubia and Upper Egypt*. Oriental Institute Publication 17. Chicago: University of Chicago Press.

———. 1939. *Prehistoric Survey of Egypt and Western Asia*. Vol. 3, *Lower Egypt*. Oriental Institute Publication 46. Chicago: University of Chicago Press.

de Santillana, G., and H. von Dechend. 1969. *Hamlet's Mill: An Essay on Myth and the Frame of Time*. Boston: Gambit.

Sarton, G. 1952. *A History of Science: Ancient Science through the Golden Age of Greece*. Cambridge: Harvard University Press.

Sartre, J.-P. 1948. "Orphée Noir." In *Anthologie de la nouvelle poésie nègre et malagache de langue française*, edited by L. S. Senghor, ix–xliv. Paris: Presses Universitaires de France.

Saunders, J. B. de C. M. 1963. *The Transitions from Ancient Egyptian to Greek Medicine*. Lawrence, Kansas: University of Kansas Press.

Saunders, J. B. de C. M., and R. O. Steuer. 1959. *Ancient Egyptian and Cnidian Medicine*. Berkeley and Los Angeles: University of California Press.

Saussure, F. de. 1879. *Mémoire sur le système primitif des voyelles dans les langues indo-européennes*. Leipzig: B. G. Teubner.

———. 1916. *Cours de linguistique générale*. Lausanne: Payot.

Säve-Söderbergh, T. 1941. *Aegypten und Nubien*. Lund: H. Ohlssons Boktryckeri.

———. 1946. *The Navy of the Eighteenth Egyptian Dynasty*. Uppsala: Lundequistska Bokhandeln.

Sayce, A. H. 1896. *The Egypt of the Hebrews and Herodotos*. 2d ed. London: Rivington, Percival.

Schachemeyr, F. 1969. "Hornehelme und Federkronen als Kopfbedeckungen bei den Seevolkern der Ägyptischen Reliefs." *Ugaritica* 6:451–60.

Schaeffer, C. 1953. "Les fouilles de Ras Shamra-Ugarit." *Annales Archéologiques de Syrie* 3:117–44.

Schiebinger, L. 1993. *Nature's Body: Gender in the Making of Modern Science*. Boston: Beacon Press.

Schlegel, F. [1795–96] 1906. "Über das Studium der Griechischen Poesie." In *Prosaische Jugendschriften, 1794–1802*, edited by J. Minor, 1:85–178. Vienna: Carl Konegen.

Schlesinger, A., Jr. 1991. *The Disuniting of America*. Knoxville, Tenn.: Whittle Direct Books. Reprinted, New York: Norton, 1992.

Schliemann, H. 1878. *Mycenae*. London: John Murray.

Schmandt-Besserat, D. 1992. *Before Writing: From Counting to Cuneiform*. Vol. 1. Austin: University of Texas Press.

Schott, R. 1982. "Nith." In *Lexikon der Ägyptologie*, edited by W. Helck and W. Westendorf, 4:392–94. Wiesbaden: Otto Harrassowitz.

Schulman, A. R. 1982. "The Battle Scenes of the Middle Kingdom." *Journal of the Society for the Study of Egyptian Antiquities* 12:165–83.

Schwab, R. [1950] 1984. *The Oriental Renaissance: Europe's Rediscovery of India and the East, 1680–1880*. Translated by G. Patterson-Black and V. Reinking. New York: Columbia University Press. (First published in French)

Scott, E. 1893. *Greek Papyri in the British Museum: Facsimiles*. London: British Museum.

Seligman, C. G. 1913. "Some Aspects of the Hamitic Problem in the Anglo-Egyptian Sudan." *Journal of the Royal Anthropological Institute of Great Britian and Ireland* 43:593–706.

———. 1915. "Transactions of Section H." Presidential Address, in *Report of the Eighty-Fifth Meeting of the British Association for the Advancement of Science*, 651–65. London: John Murray.

———. 1930. *Races of Africa*. London: Thornton Butterworth.

———. 1934. *Egypt and Negro Africa: A Study in Divine Kingship*. London: G. Routledge & Sons.

———. 1957. *Races of Africa*. 3d ed. London: Oxford University Press.

Sextus Empiricus. 1933. *Outlines of Pyrrhonism*. Translated by R. G. Bury. 3 vols. Loeb Classical Library. Cambridge: Harvard University Press.

Shaw, I. M. E. 1985. "Egyptian Chronology and the Irish Oak Calibration." *Journal of Near Eastern Studies* 44:295–317.

Sherratt, S. 1993. "Daidalic Inventions: The Hellenization of Art and the Art of Hellenization." *Antiquity* 67:915–18.

†Shinnie, P. L. 1967. *Meroe: A Civilization of the Sudan*. New York and Washington: Frederick A. Praeger.

———. 1971. "The Legacy to Africa." In *The Legacy of Egypt*, 2d ed., edited by J. R. Harris, 434–55. Oxford: Clarendon Press.

†Sigerist, H. E. [1951] 1967. *Primitive and Archaic Medicine*. New York: Oxford University Press.

Sigurdsson, H., S. Carey, and J. D. Devine. 1990. "Thera and the Aegean World." *Proceedings of the Third International Congress*, Santorini, Greece, 3–9 September 1989. Vol. 2, *Earth Sciences*, edited by O. A. Hardy, 100–112. London: Thera Foundation.

Silberman, N. A. 1990. *Between Past and Present: Archaeology, Ideology, and Nationalism in the Modern Middle East*. New York: Henry Holt.

Simkin, T., and R. Fiske. 1983. *Krakatau 1883: The Volcanic Eruption and Its Effects*. Washington, D.C.: Smithsonian Press.

Simpson, W. K. 1972. "A Tomb Chapel Relief of Amunemhat III and Some Observations on the Length of the Reign of Sesostris III." *Chronique d'Egypte* 47, nos. 93–94:45–54.

————. 1973. *The Literature of Ancient Egypt*. New Haven: Yale University Press.

————. 1984. "Sesostris III." In *Lexikon der Ägyptologie*, 5:900–906. Wiesbaden: Otto Harrassowitz.

Sinclair, R. K. 1988. *Democracy and Participation in Athens*. Cambridge: Cambridge University Press.

Sivin, N. 1976. "Eloge Giorgio Diaz de Santillana." *Isis* 67:439–43.

Smith, A. [1759] 1971. *Theory of Moral Sentiments*. London and New York: Garland.

Smith, A. D. 1986. *The Ethnic Origins of Nations*. Oxford: Blackwell.

Smith, G. E. 1909. "Anatomical Report (A)." *Archaeological Survey of Nubia*, Bulletin no. 3:21–27. Cairo: National Printing Department.

————. 1910. "The Racial Problem." In *Report on the Human Remains*, vol. 2, *The Archaeological Survey of Nubia Report for 1907–1908*, edited by G. E. Smith and F. U. T. Jones, 15–36. Cairo: National Printing Department.

————. [1923] 1970. *The Ancient Egyptians and the Origin of Civilization*. Freeport, New York: Books for Libraries Press.

Smith, G. E., and W. R. Dawson. 1924. *Egyptian Mummies*. London: George Allen & Unwin.

Smith, G. E., and D. E. Derry. 1910. "Anatomical Report: Dealing with the Work during the Months of January and February, 1910." *Archaeological Survey of Nubia*, Bulletin no. 6:9–30.

Smith, W. D. 1979. *The Hippocratic Tradition*. Ithaca: Cornell University Press.

Smith, W. S. 1960. *Ancient Egypt as Represented in the Museum of Fine Arts, Boston*. Boston: Museum of Fine Arts.

————. 1965. *Interconnections in the Ancient Near East*. New Haven: Yale University Press.

————. 1981. *The Art and Architecture of Ancient Egypt*. Rev. ed., by W. K. Simpson. Harmondsworth and Baltimore: Penguin.

Smithana, D. 1990. *America—Land of the Rising Sun*. San Diego: Anasazi Publishing Group.

Sneath, P. H. A., and R. R. Sokal. 1973. *Numerical Taxonomy: The Principles and Practices of Numerical Classification*. San Francisco: Freeman.

Snodgrass, A. 1980. *Archaic Greece: The Age of Experiment*. Berkeley and Los Angeles: University of California Press.

†Snowden, F. M., Jr. 1970. *Blacks in Antiquity: Ethiopians in the Greco-Roman Experience*. Cambridge and London: Harvard University Press.

————. 1976. "Iconographical Evidence on the Black Population of Greco-Roman Antiquity." In Vercoutter et al. 1976, 1:133–245, 287–307.

†————. 1983. *Before Color Prejudice: The Ancient View of Blacks*. Cambridge: Harvard University Press.

*————. 1989. "Bernal's 'Blacks,' Herodotus, and Other Classical Evidence." In Levine and Peradotto 1989 = *Arethusa* 22:83–95.

————. 1991. "Asclepiades' Didyme." *Greek, Roman, and Byzantine Studies* 32, no. 3:239–53.

————. 1993. Response [to S. O. Y. Keita]. *Arethusa*, 26:319–27.

Sokal, R. R., N. L. Oden, and C. Wilson. 1991. "Genetic Evidence for the Spread of Agriculture in Europe by Demic Diffusion." *Nature* 351:143–45.

Sollors, W. 1986. *Beyond Ethnicity: Consent and Descent in American Culture*. New York: Oxford University Press.

Specter, M. 1990. "Was Nefertiti Black? Bitter Debate Erupts." *Washington Post*, 26 February, A3.

Spencer, A. J. 1982. *Death in Ancient Egypt*. New York: Penguin.

Spuhler, J. N. 1988. "Evolution of Mitochondrial DNA in Monkeys, Apes, and Humans." *Yearbook of Physical Anthropology* 31:15–48.

———. 1989. "Raymond Pearl Memorial Lecture, 1988: Evolution of Mitochondrial DNA in Human and Other Organisms." *American Journal of Human Biology* 1:509–28.

Spyropoulos, T. 1973. "Archaiotetes kai Mnemeia Boiotias-Phthiotas." *Archaiologikon Deltion* 28, no. 2:247–81.

Squadrito, K. 1979. "Racism and Empiricism." *Behaviorism* 7:105–15.

Stager, L. E., and S. R. Wolff. 1984. "Child Sacrifice at Carthage—Religious Rite or Population Control?" *Biblical Archaeology* 10, no. 1:30–51.

Starr, C. G. 1961. *The Origins of Greek Civilization 1100–650 B.C.* New York: Knopf.

———. 1965. "The Credibility of Early Spartan History." *Historia* 14:257–72.

Stavroulakis, N. 1990. *The Jews of Greece: An Essay*. Athens: Talos Press.

Stecchini, L. C. 1971. "Notes on the Relation of Ancient Measures to the Great Pyramid." In *Secrets of the Great Pyramid*, by P. Tompkins, 287–382. New York: Harper & Row.

Steele, S. 1989. "The Recoloring of Campus Life." *Harper's* (February), 47–55. Reprinted in *The Content of Our Character: A New Vision of Race in America*. New York: St. Martins Press, 1990.

Stieber, M. 1994. Review of Buitron-Oliver 1991. *American Journal of Archaeology* 98:168–69.

Stemler, A. B. L. 1980. "Origins of Domestication in the Sahara and the Nile Valley." In *The Sahara and the Nile: Quaternary Environments and Prehistoric Occupation in Northern Africa*, edited by M. A. J. Williams and H. Faure, 503–26. Rotterdam: Balkema.

Sternberg, R. J. 1985. "Intelligence Reexamined." Review of *Beyond I.Q.*, by R. Glaser. *Science* 230:59–61.

Steuer, R. O. 1948. *The Aetiological Principle of Pyaemia in Ancient Egyptian Medicine*. Bulletin of the History of Medicine, suppl. 10. Baltimore: The Johns Hopkins University Press.

Stevens, P., Jr. 1993. Dialogue: "On 'First Word,' January 1993." *African Arts* 26, no. 4:14.

Stoessiger, B. N. 1927. "A Study of the Badarian Crania Excavated by the British School of Archaeology in Egypt." *Biometrika* 19:110–50.

Stommel, H., and E. Stommel. 1979. "The Year without a Summer." *Scientific American* 240, no. 6:179–86.

Stringer, C. B., and P. Andrews. 1988. "Genetic and Fossil Evidence for the Origin of Modern Humans." *Science* 239:1263–68.

Strouhal, E. 1971. "Evidence of the Early Penetration of Negroes into Prehistoric Egypt." *Journal of African History* 12:1–9.

Stubbings, F. 1973. "The Rise of Mycenaean Civilization." *The Cambridge Ancient History*, 3d ed., II.1:627–58. Cambridge: Cambridge University Press.

Sudhoff, K. 1909. *Ärztliches aus griechischen Papyrus-Urkunden*. Leipzig: J. A. Barth.

Sullivan, A. 1990. "Racism 101: A Crash Course in Afrocentrism." *New Republic*, 26 November, 20–21.

Symeonoglou, S. 1985. *The Topography of Thebes from the Bronze Age to Modern Times*. Princeton: Princeton University Press.

*Tate, G. 1989. "History: The Colorized Version, or Everything You Learned in School Was Wrong." *The Village Voice*, 28 March, 48–50. (Review of *BA* 1, with G. G. M. James's *Stolen Legacy* and I. K. Kush's *What They Never Told You in History Class*)

Taton, R., ed. 1963. *History of Science*. New York: Basic Books.

Teissier, B. In press. *Egyptian Iconography on Syro-Levantine Cylinder Seals of the Middle Bronze Age*. Orbis Biblicus et Orientalis, Series Archaeologica. Fribourg: Universitätsverlag.

Templeton, A. R. 1992. "Human Origins and Analysis of Mitochondrial DNA Sequences." *Science* 256:737.

———. 1993. "The 'Eve' Hypothesis: A Genetic Critique and Reanalysis." *American Anthropologist* 95:51–72.

Times Saturday Review (London). "An Oasis Hanging in the Balance." 3 August 1991.

Tompkins, P. 1971. *Secrets of the Great Pyramid*. New York: Harper & Row.

Toomer, G. J. 1974. "Meton." In *Dictionary of Scientific Biography*, edited by C. C. Gillispie, 9:337–39. New York: Scribner.

———. 1984. *Ptolemy's Almagest*. New York: Springer-Verlag.

Török, L. 1989. "Kush and the External World." In *Studia Meroitica 1984: Proceedings of the Fifth International Conference for Meroitic Studies, Rome 1984*, 47–215. Berlin: Akademie-Verlag.

Toussaint, A. 1966. *History of the Indian Ocean*. Chicago: University of Chicago Press.

Träger, C. 1979. *Die Herder-Legende des deutschen Historismus*. Berlin: Verlag Marxistische Blätter.

Trigger, B. G. 1968. *Beyond History: The Methods of Prehistory*. New York: Holt, Rinehart & Winston.

†———. 1976. *Nubia under the Pharaohs*. London: Thames & Hudson; Boulder, Colo.: Westview Press.

———. 1978. "Nubian, Negro, Black, Nilotic?" In *Africa in Antiquity: The Arts of Nubia and the Sudan*, vol. 1, edited by S. Hochfield and E. Riefstahl, 27–35. New York: The Brooklyn Museum.

*———. 1992. "Brown Athena: A Postprocessual Goddess?" *Current Anthropology* 33, no. 1:121–23. (Review of *BA* 1–2)

†Trigger, B. G., B. J. Kemp, D. O'Connor, and A. B. Lloyd. 1983. *Ancient Egypt: A Social History*. Cambridge: Cambridge University Press.

*Tritle, L. A. 1992. Review discussion of *BA* 2. *Liverpool Classical Monthly* 17, no. 6:82–96. (= Tritle, this volume)

†Turner, F. M. 1981. *The Greek Heritage in Victorian Britain*. New Haven: Yale University Press.

*———. 1989. "Martin Bernal's *Black Athena*: A Dissent." In Levine and Peradotto 1989 = *Arethusa* 22:97–109.

Turner, P. A. 1993. *I Heard It through the Grapevine: Rumor in African-American Culture*. Berkeley and Los Angeles: University of California Press.

Turner, R. S. 1974. "University Reformers and Professorial Scholarship in Germany 1760–1806." In *The University in Society*, vol. 2, edited by L. Stone, 495–531. Princeton: Princeton University Press.

———. 1983. "Historicism, *Kritik*, and the Prussian Professoriate, 1790 to 1840." In *Philologie und Hermeneutik im 19. Jahrhundert*, vol. 2, edited by M. Bollack and H. Wismann, 450–89. Göttingen: Vandenhoeck & Ruprecht.

Tyrrell, W. B. 1984. *Amazons: A Study in Athenian Mythmaking*. Baltimore: The Johns Hopkins University Press.

University of Chicago Magazine. 1993. Vol. 85, no. 3:37.

Urbach, F. 1969. *The Biologic Effects of Ultraviolet Radiation (With Emphasis on the Skin)*. New York: Pergamon.

Urk. 4 = *Urkunden der 18. Dynastie*. Edited by K. Sethe. Leipzig: J. C. Hinrichs, 1906–27.

Vallois, H. V. 1953. "Race." In *Anthropology Today*, edited by A. L. Kroeber, 145–62. Chicago: University of Chicago Press.

Vallois, H. V., and H. L. Movius. 1953. *Catalogue des hommes fossiles*. Macon: Protat Frères.

Van der Berghe, P. L. 1967. *Race and Racism: A Comparative Perspective*. New York: John Wiley & Sons.

Vandersleyen, C. 1971. *Les guerres d'Amosis*. Brussels: Fondation Egyptologique Reine Elisabeth.

———. 1985. "Le dossier égyptien des Philistins." In *The Land of Israel: Crossroads of Civilization*, edited by C. Lipinski, 39–54. Leuven: Uitgeverij Peeters.

†van der Waerden, B. L. 1961. *Science Awakening*. New York: Oxford University Press.

———. 1974. *Science Awakening*. Vol. 2, *The Birth of Astronomy*. Leyden: Noordhoff; New York: Oxford University Press.

———. 1978. "Mathematics and Astronomy in Mesopotamia." In *Dictionary of Scientific Biography*, edited by C. C. Gillispie, 15 (= Supplement 1): 667–80. New York: Scribner.

Van Gerven, D. P. 1982. "The Contribution of Time and Local Geography to Craniofacial Variation in Nubia's Batn el Hajar." *American Journal of Physical Anthropology* 59:307–16.

Van Gerven, D. P., D. S. Carlson, and G. J. Armelagos. 1973. "Racial History and Bio-Cultural Adaptation of Nubian Archaeological Populations." *Journal of African History* 14:555–64.

Van Horne, J. C. 1993. "Collective Benevolence and the Common Good in Franklin's Philanthropy." In *Reappraising Benjamin Franklin: A Bicentennial Perspective*, edited by J. A. L. Lemay, 425–40. Newark, Del.: University of Delaware Press.

Van Sertima, I. 1984. *Black Women in Antiquity*. New Brunswick, N.J.: Transaction Books.

———. 1985a. "The African Presence in Early Europe: The Definitional Problems." In Van Sertima 1985b, 134–43.

———, ed. 1983. *Blacks in Science: Ancient and Modern*. New Brunswick, N.J.: Transaction Books.

———, ed. 1985b. *African Presence in Early Europe*. New Brunswick, N.J.: Transaction Books.

Vavilov, N. I. 1951. *The Origin, Variation, Immunity, and Breeding of Cultivated Plants*. Selected writings translated from the Russian by K. S. Chester. Waltham, Mass.: Chronica Botanica.

Vercoutter, J. 1945. *Les objets égyptiens et égyptisants du mobilier funéraire carthaginois*. Bibliothèque Archéologique et Historique 40. Paris: Paul Geuthner.

———. 1948. "Les Haou Nebout." *Bulletin de l'Institut Français d'Archéologie Orientale* 46:125–48.

———. 1956. *L'Egypte et le monde égéen préhellénique*. Institut Français d'Archéologie Orientale, Bibliothèque d'Etude 22. Cairo: Imprimerie de l'Institut Français d'Archéologie Orientale.

———. 1963. "Egypt: Mathematics and Astronomy." In *History of Science*, edited by R. Taton, 17–44. New York: Basic Books.

———. 1976. "The Iconography of the Black in Ancient Egypt from the Beginnings to the Twenty-Fifth Dynasty." In Vercoutter et al. 1976, 32–88, 291–92.

†———. [1986] 1992. *The Search for Ancient Egypt*. New York; London: Thames & Hudson. (First published in French)

Vercoutter, J., J. Leclant, F. M. Snowden, and J. Desanges. 1976. *The Image of the Black in Western Art*. Vol. 1, *From the Pharaohs to the Fall of the Roman Empire*. New York: William Morrow.

†Vermeule, E. T. 1964. *Greece in the Bronze Age*. Chicago: University of Chicago Press.

———. 1975. *The Art of the Shaft Graves at Mycenae*. Cincinnati: University of Cincinnati.

*———. 1992. "The World Turned Upside Down." *New York Review of Books*, 26 March, 40–43. (Review of *BA* 2 = Vermeule, this volume)

Vian, F. 1963. *Les origines de Thèbes: Cadmos et les Spartes*. Paris: C. Klincksieck.

*Vickers, M. 1987. Review of *BA* 1. *Antiquity* 61:480–81.

Vico, G. [1744] 1968. *The New Science*. Unabridged translation, by T. G. Bergin and M. H. Fisch, of the 3rd ed., with the addition of "Practice of the New Science." Ithaca: Cornell University Press.

Vila, A. 1963. "Un dépôt de textes d'envoutement au Moyen Empire." *Journal des Savants* July–September, 135–60.

Volney, C. F. 1792. *Voyage en Syrie et Egypte pendant les années 1783, 1784 & 1785*. Nouvelle éd. Vol. 1. Paris: Desenne.

———. [1802] 1979. *A New Translation of Volney's Ruins*. Reprinted from the 1802 edition printed for Levrault, New York: Garland.

————. 1823. *The Ruins, or A Survey of the Revolutions of Empires. A new translation from the French*. Exeter: Joseph Mann.

Voltaire. [1756] 1963. "Essay on the Customs and the Spirit of the Nations." in *The Age of Louis XIV and Other Selected Writings*, translated by J. H. Brumfitt. New York: Twayne.

————. [1764] 1972. "Apis." In *Philosophical Dictionary*, translated by T. Besterman. Harmondsworth, Middlesex; and New York: Penguin.

Von Beckerath, J. 1958. "Notes on the Viziers 'Ankhu and Iymeru in the Thirteenth Egyptian Dynasty." *Journal of Near Eastern Studies* 17:263–68.

Von der Way, T. 1988. "Investigations Concerning the Early Periods in the Northern Delta of Egypt." In *The Archaeology of the Nile Delta: Problems and Priorities*, edited by E. C. M. Van den Brink, 245–49. Amsterdam: Netherlands Foundation for Archaeological Research.

†von Staden, H. 1989. *Herophilus: The Art of Medicine in Early Alexandria*. Cambridge: Cambridge University Press.

————. 1992. "Affinities and Elisions: Helen and Hellenocentrism." *Isis* 83:578–95.

Wachsmann, S. 1987. *Aegeans in the Theban Tombs*. Orientalia Lovaniensia Analecta 20. Leuven: Peeters.

Waddell, W. G. 1940. *Manetho, with an English Translation*. Loeb Classical Library. Cambridge: Harvard University Press.

Wainwright, G. A. 1960. "Meneptah's Aid to the Hittites." *Journal of Egyptian Archaeology* 46:24–28.

*Walcot, P. 1992. Review of *BA* 2. *Greece and Rome* 39:78–79.

Walker, C. 1993. "You Can't Go Home Again: The Problem with Afrocentrism." *Prospects* 18:535–44.

Ward, W. A. 1991. "Early Contacts between Egypt, Canaan, and Sinai: Remarks on the Paper by Amnon Ben-Tor." *Bulletin of the American Schools of Oriental Research* 281:11–26.

Warren, E. 1898. "The Investigation on the Variability of the Human Skeleton: With Especial Reference to the Naqada Race Discovered by Professor Flinders Petrie in His Explorations in Egypt." *Philological Transactions of the Royal Society of London* (B) 189:135–227.

*Washington, M. 1993. "Revitalizing the Old Argument: *Black Athena* and Black History." Comment, special section: "The Debate over *Black Athena*." *Journal of Women's History* 4, no. 3:106–13.

Watkins, N. D., R. S. J. Sparks, H. Sigurdsson, T. C. Huang, A. Federman, and S. Carey. 1978. "Volume and Extent of the Minoan Tephra from Santorini Volcano: New Evidence from Deepsea Sediment Cores." *Nature* 271, no. 1:122–26.

Weber, M. 1921. "Ethnische Gemeinschaften." *Wirtschaft und Gesellschaft: Grundriss der Sozialökonomik* Abteilung 3, Teil 2:215–26. Tübingen.

Weinstein, J. 1974. "A Statuette of the Princess Sobeknoferu at Tell Gezer." *Bulletin of the American School of Oriental Research* 213:49–57.

————. 1975. "Egyptian Relations with Palestine during the Middle Kingdom." *Bulletin of the American Schools of Oriental Research* 217:1–16.

———. 1980. "Palestinian Radiocarbon Dating: A Reply to James Mellaart." *Antiquity* 54:21–24.

———. 1981. "The Egyptian Empire in Palestine: A Reassessment." *Bulletin of the American Schools of Oriental Research* 241:1–28.

*———. 1992. Review of *BA* 2. *American Journal of Archaeology* 96, no. 2:381–83.

———. 1993. "Radiocarbon Dating." In *Colloquenda Mediterranea*, 51–55. Bradford, U.K.: Loid Publishing. (Review of Peter James et al., *Centuries of Darkness*)

Wells, R. A. 1985. "Sothis and the Satet Temple on Elephantine." *Studien zur altägyptischen Kultur* 12:255–302.

Wendorf, F. 1968. "Site 117: A Nubian Final Paleolithic Graveyard Near Jebel Sahaba." In *Prehistory of Nubia*, edited by F. Wendorf, 2:954–95. Dallas: Southern Methodist University Press.

Wendorf, F., and R. Schild. 1976. *Prehistory of the Nile Valley*. New York: Academic Press.

Wendorf, F., R. Schild, and A. E. Close. 1984. *Cattle Keepers of the Eastern Sahara: The Neolithic of Bir Kiseiba*. Dallas: Southern Methodist University Press.

Wenke, R. J. 1989. "Egypt: Origins of Complex Societies." *Annual Review of Anthropology* 18:129–55.

Wente, E. F. 1975. "Thutmose III's Accession and the Beginning of the New Kingdom." *Journal of Near Eastern Studies* 34, no. 4:265–72.

———. 1990. *Letters from Ancient Egypt*. Edited by Edmund Meltzer. Atlanta: Scholars Press.

Wente, E. F., and C. C. Van Siclen III. 1976. "A Chronology of the New Kingdom." In *Studies in Honor of George R. Hughes*, edited by Edward F. Wente and Janet H. Johnson, 217–62. Studies in Ancient Oriental Civilizations, no. 39. Chicago: Oriental Institute.

West, M. L. 1985. *The Hesiodic Catalogue of Women*. Oxford: Oxford University Press.

Westfall, R. J. 1980. *Never at Rest: A Biography of Isaac Newton*. Cambridge: Cambridge University Press.

———. 1982. "Newton's Theological Manuscripts." In *Contemporary Newtonian Research*, edited by Zev Bechler, 15–34. Dordrecht and Boston: D. Reidel.

Wetterstrom, W. 1993. "Foraging and Farming in Egypt: The Transition from Hunting and Gathering to Horticulture in the Egyptian Nile Valley." In *The Archaeology of Africa: Food, Metals and Towns*, edited by T. Shaw et al., 165–226. London: Routledge.

White, L. Jr. 1962. *Medieval Technology and Social Change*. Oxford: Clarendon Press.

———. 1970. Review of de Santillana and von Dechend 1969. *Isis* 61: 541.

White, N. 1992. *Hopkins: A Literary Biography*. Oxford: Clarendon Press.

*Whitney, G. 1990. "Is the American Academy Racist?" *The University Bookman* 30, no. 2:4–15. (Review of *BA* 1)

Who Was Cleopatra? 1992. Produced by N. Valcour and T. Naughton, directed by B. Morin for The Learning Channel and the Archaeological Institute of America, Arkios Productions. 23 minutes, color. Distributed by Films for the Humanities (#FFH 3983), Box 2053, Princeton, New Jersey, 08543-2053.

Wilkinson, J. G. 1837. *Manners and Customs of the Ancient Egyptians*. London: J. Murray.

Williams, B. 1986. *The A-Group Royal Cemetery at Qustul: Cemetery b*. Chicago: Oriental Institute.

Williams, B., and T. Logan. 1984. "The Metropolitan Museum Knife Handle and Aspects of Pharaonic Imagery before Narmor." *Journal of Near Eastern Studies* 46:245–85.

Williams, C. [1971] 1987. *The Destruction of Black Civilization: Great Issues of a Race from 4500 B.C. to 2000 A.D.* Dubuque, Iowa: Kendall/Hunt. Reprinted, Chicago: Third World Press.

Wilson, A. C., and R. L. Cann. 1992. "The Recent African Genesis of Humans." *Scientific American* 266:66–73.

Wilson, A. M. 1972. *Diderot*. New York: Oxford University Press.

Wilson, J. A. 1951. *The Culture of Ancient Egypt*. Chicago: University of Chicago Press.

†Wilson, J. A., H. and H. A. Frankfort, T. Jacobsen, and W. A. Irwin. 1950. *The Intellectual Adventure of Ancient Man: An Essay on Speculative Thought in the Ancient Near East*. Chicago: University of Chicago Press.

Winter, I. J. 1973. *North Syria in the Early First Millennium B.C., with Special Reference to Ivory Carving*. Dissertation, Columbia University.

Winter, J. 1972. *Bronze Age Trade between the Aegean and Egypt*. Brooklyn: Brooklyn Museum.

Wolf, F. A. [1795] 1985. *Prolegomena to Homer,* translated with introduction and notes by A. Grafton, G. Most, and J. Zetzel. Princeton: Princeton University Press.

Woo, T. L., and G. M. Morant. 1934. "A Biometric Study of the 'Flatness' of the Facial Skeleton in Man." *Biometrika* 26:196–250.

Wood, B. G. 1991. "The Philistines Enter Canaan." *Biblical Archaeology Review* 17, no. 6:44–52, 89–92.

Wood, G. 1993. "The Trials and Tribulations of Thomas Jefferson." In *Jeffersonian Legacies*, edited by P. S. Onuf, 395–417. Charlottesville: University of Virginia Press.

Wortham, J. D. 1971. *British Egyptology*. Newton Abbot, Devon: David & Charles.

Yener, K. A., and P. B. Vandiver. 1993a. "Tin Processing at Goltepe, an Early Bronze Age Site in Anatolia." *American Journal of Archaeology* 97, no. 2:207–38.

———. 1993b. Reply to Muhly 1993 ["Early Bronze Age Tin and the Taurus"]. *American Journal of Archaeology* 97, no. 2:255–64.

Yoffee, N., and G. L. Cowgill, eds. 1988. *The Collapse of Ancient States and Civilizations*. Tucson: University of Arizona Press.

Yorke, E. C. 1936. "Trisyllabic Feet in the Dialogue of Aeschylus." *Classical Quarterly* 30:116–19.

Young, P. A. 1992. "Was Nefertiti Black?" *Archaeology* 45, no. 5:2.

Young, W. J. 1972. "The Fabulous Gold of the Pactolus Valley." *Boston Museum Bulletin* 70:5–13.

Yurco, F. J. 1986. "Merenptah's Canaanite Campaign." *Journal of the American Research Center in Egypt* 23:189–215.

†———. 1989. "Were the Ancient Egyptians Black or White?" *Biblical Archaeology Review* 15, no. 5:24–29, 58.

———. 1990. "3,200 Year Old Picture of Israelites Found in Egypt." *Biblical Archaeology Review* 16, no. 5:20–38.

———. 1991. Letter to the editor. *Chronicle of Higher Education*, 4 September, B4.

———. 1993. "An Egyptological Response to Centuries of Darkness." *Collequenda Mediterranea*, 8–13. Bradford, U.K.: Loid Publishing. (Review of Peter James et al., *Centuries of Darkness*)

———. In press. "Egypt and Nubia: Old, Middle, and New Kingdom Eras."

Zeitlin, F. 1986, "Thebes: Theater of Self and Society in Athenian Drama." In *Greek Tragedy and Political Theory*, edited by J. P. Euben, 101–41. Berkeley and Los Angeles: University of California Press.

Zeuner, F. E. 1969. *A History of Domesticated Animals*. London: Hutchinson.

*Zilfi, M. C. 1993. "Martin Bernal's *Black Athena*." Comment, special section: "The Debate over *Black Athena*." *Journal of Women's History* 4, no. 3:114–18.

CONTRIBUTORS

John Baines is Professor of Egyptology in the University of Oxford.

Kathryn A. Bard is Assistant Professor of Archaeology at Boston University.

C. Loring Brace is Professor of Anthropology and Curator of Biological Anthropology in the Museum of Anthropology at the University of Michigan. David P. Tracer (University of Washington) and Lucia Allen Yaroch, John Robb, Kari Brandt, and A. Russell Nelson (all at the University of Michigan) also contributed to the chapter presented in this volume.

John E. Coleman is Professor of Classics at Cornell University.

Edith Hall is Lecturer in Classics at the University of Reading, England.

Jay H. Jasanoff is Jacob Gould Schurman Professor of Linguistics at Cornell University.

Richard Jenkyns is a Fellow and Tutor of Lady Margaret Hall, Oxford, and University Lecturer in Classics in the University of Oxford.

Mary R. Lefkowitz is Andrew W. Mellon Professor in the Humanities at Wellesley College.

Mario Liverani is Professor of Ancient Near Eastern History at the Università di Roma, "La Sapienza."

Sarah P. Morris is Professor of Classics at the University of California at Los Angeles.

Robert E. Norton is Associate Professor of German at Vassar College.

Alan Nussbaum is Associate Professor of Classics at Cornell University.

David O'Connor is Professor of Egyptology at the University of Pennsylvania, and Curator in Charge of the Egyptian Section in the University Museum, University of Pennsylvania.

Robert Palter is Dana Professor Emeritus of the History of Science at Trinity College, Connecticut.

Guy MacLean Rogers is Associate Professor of Greek and Latin and History at Wellesley College.

Frank M. Snowden, Jr., is Professor of Classics Emeritus at Howard University.

Lawrence A. Tritle is Associate Professor of History at Loyola Marymount University.

Emily T. Vermeule is Samuel E. Zemurray, Jr., and Doris Zemurray Stone-Radcliffe Professor Emerita at Harvard University.

Frank J. Yurco is an Egyptologist affiliated with both the Field Museum of Natural History and the University of Chicago.

INDEXES

PERSONAL NAMES

Lloyd, G. E. R., 210, 246, 249, 254, 264 (n. 72), 265 (n. 87)

Locke, J., 366–67, 397 (n. 37)

Luxorius, 124

Lycurgus, 286, 300 (n. 17)

Macaulay, T., 361

Majno, G., 247–48, 251–52, 264 (n. 76), 265 (nn. 78, 80, 85)

Mallory, J. P., 180

Manetho, 282, 297 (n. 5), 305, 310, 360

Manilius, 113

Manuel, F., 354–55, 357, 395 (n. 12), 396 (n. 20), 296 (n. 26), 399 (n. 53), 400 (n. 65)

Medea, 344

Meinecke, F., 383, 401 (n. 69)

Meiners, C., 358, 366, 378, 380–85, 400 (n. 60)

Mellaart, J., 29, 36, 71

Memnon, 51 (n. 2), 125

Menander, 123

Menas, St., 127

Menes, 40, 71

Mentuhotep II, 109

Michelet, J., 416

Minos, 29, 298 (n. 12)

Minotaur, 82

Mitford, W., 359, 361, 396 (n. 22), 417, 433

Mithras, 184

Momigliano, A., 22, 361, 432–33, 443

Mont. See Montu

Montesquieu, 353, 357, 366

Montu, 29, 45, 51 (n. 1), 190

Moses, 64, 126, 355, 387, 396 (n. 26); Abba Moses, 127

Mozart, W. A., 353, 419

Musaeus, 286, 300 (n. 17)

Napoleon, 64, 289, 430

Nebhepetre Mentuhotep, 29

Neferhotep, 88

Nefertari, 107

Neferti, 73–74

Neit, 78, 193–94, 287, 293, 300 (n. 20), 307, 321, 415

Neugebauer, O., 211, 213–23, 229–30, 234–38, 255, 256 (n. 4), 257 (nn. 8, 9, 11, 13, 16), 258 (nn. 17, 18, 20, 22), 259 (nn. 25, 29), 260 (nn. 36, 42), 261 (n. 53), 262 (nn. 54, 57)

Newton, I., 224–27, 259 (n. 23), 354, 361, 363, 365, 396 (n. 26), 397 (n. 34), 400 (n. 71)

Niebuhr, C., 431, 433

Niemeier, W., 276

North, J., 333, 431

Nt. See Neit

Odysseus, 94, 306, 327

Orestes, 8

Origen, 126

Orpheus, 286, 299 (n. 17), 387

Osiris, 285, 301 (n. 22), 313–14, 316

Ouranos, 438

Pan, 192, 273

Pappademos, J., 217–25, 257 (n. 16), 258 (n. 20), 259 (n. 28)

Parker, R. A., 69–70, 86–87, 99 (n. 28), 213, 219, 221, 257 (n. 11), 258 (n. 19)

Patterson, O., 117–18

Pausanias, 339, 344

Pegasus, 273

Pelops, 10, 11, 168, 341, 343, 347 (n. 2)

Pepy I, 81

Per-Ramesses, 93

Persia, 64

Persson, A., 282, 288

Petrie, W. M. Flinders, 45, 47, 65–66, 98 (n. 1), 103, 105, 131–32, 134, 140–41, 163 (n. 5)

Philip the Evangelist, 126

Philostratus, 113

Phoinix, 337–38

Pierce, R. H., 199

Pindar, 341

Piye, 110

Plato, 3, 8, 9, 14, 21, 27, 86, 297 (n. 2), 318, 387, 407, 413, 415–16, 418, 420

Plutarch, 177, 287, 304, 306–7, 313, 321, 339

Pomerance, L., 276

Pope, A., 362

Popper, K., 27

Poseidon, 205 (n. 18), 283, 301 (n. 21)

Prometheus, 286, 297 (n. 1), 299 (n. 17)

Propertius, 340

Proteus, 287–88

Psamthek (Psammetichus) I, 338

Psamtik II, 83

Ptolemies, 91

Ptolemy (Claudius Ptolemaeus), 212, 220–21, 225, 235, 246, 255, 363

Ptolemy I Soter, 121

Ptolemy II Philadelphus, 121, 360

Pythagoras, 8, 221–22, 233, 242, 245, 251, 261 (n. 50), 262 (n. 58), 358, 383–84, 387–88, 415, 437

Radames, 419

Ramesses: II, 72, 86, 91–94; III, 84, 94; VI–VIII, 84; IX, 84

Ray, J., 117

Reisner, G., 105, 110

Rekhmire, 90, 274

Renfrew, C., 35, 131

Rhadamanthys, 29, 45, 190, 191, 194

Rhea, 45

Robins, G., 242, 262–63 (nn. 62–64)

Rogers, J. A., 119, 121

Rose, P., 403, 410

Rousseau, G. S., 395

Rousseau, J. -J., 353–54

Sahure, 76, 81

Said, E., 35, 335, 422

Sargon II, 82

Sarton, G., 220, 222

Satan, 194

Saunders, J. B. 250–52, 263 (n. 69), 265 (n. 82)

Schelling, F. W., 382

Schikaneder, E., 419

Schlegel, A. W., 382, 405

Schliemann, H., 272, 288, 290, 297 (n. 3), 432

Schlözer, L., 366, 383, 385

Semiramis, 311, 315

Sennuwy, 81

Senwosret: I, 29, 43, 51–52, 70, 72–74, 78; II, 69, 74, 76; III, 69 (n. 35), 70, 74–76, 86, 99 (n. 9)

Septimius Severus, 119, 120–21, 124

Serapis, 357

Sesostris, 18–19, 21, 51, 72, 75, 167–68, 305, 310–14, 317

Seth, 285

Sextus Empiricus, 364, 396 (n. 31)

Sety (Sethos) I, 93

Shakespeare, W., 120

Shalmanesar V, 82

Shelley, P. B., 418

Shuppululiumas II, 83

Sigerist, H. E., 211, 247, 256 (n. 5)

Sinuhe, 170

Smith, A., 370

Smith, W. S., 272

Snowden, F. M., Jr., 173, 388–89

Sobek, 194

Sobek-noferu, 75

Sobkhote, 274

Socrates, 3–6, 21, 22 (n. 1), 297 (n. 2)

Solon, 8, 318, 329 (n. 10), 415, 418

Sophocles, 12, 340, 344, 435

Steuer, R. O. 249, 251, 263 (n. 69), 265 (n. 82)

Strabo, 114, 122–23, 339, 438

Stubbings, F., 283, 298 (n. 9)

Sudanese, 274

Taharqa, 122

Tanit, 194, 415

Terence, 125

Tereus, 344

Terrasson, J., 15, 353, 358, 395 (n. 17)

Teshub, 273

Thales, 387–88

Theuth, 297 (n. 2)
Thirlwall, C., 418, 431, 433
Thucydides, 287, 305, 340–41, 345
Thutmose III, 72, 87, 90, 93
Tompkins, P. 226–27, 259 (n. 33)
Toomer, G., 256 (n. 6), 258 (n. 19)
Turner, F., 304, 360–61, 364, 394 (n. 3),
    431
Turner, P., 395 (n. 7)
Turner, R., 375, 385, 400
Tutankhamen, 106–9, 274
Tuthmosis: I, 273; III, 52, 107

Ulysses, 359
Urhi-Teshub, 91
Urhiya, 91

Van der Waerden, B. L., 220, 224, 228,
    234, 257 (n. 12), 259 (n. 25), 260
    (n. 39), 261 (n. 47), 262 (n. 59)
Van Sertima, I., 121, 257 (n. 15)
Ventris, M., 201
Vercoutter, J., 218–19, 258 (n. 21), 391
Verdi, G., 419
Vico, G. B., 304

Virgil, 8, 340
Voltaire, 202, 353–54, 395 (n. 8)
Von Staden, H., 210, 246, 248–54, 264
    (nn. 73, 75), 265 (n. 86)

Wagner, R., 403
Weber, M., 336, 347
Wenamun, 170
Westfall, R. J., 226–27, 363
Wilamowitz, U. von, 169
Wilkinson, J. G., 391
Winckelmann, J. J., 353, 376, 407
Wolf, F. A., 269, 408, 416
Wolff, C., 377
Wood, G. S., 398 (n. 48)
Woodward, J., 362

Xenophon, 325

Yorke, E. C., 414
Young, E., 359

Zethus, 337
Zeus, 171, 190, 281, 283, 285–86, 301
    (n. 22), 338, 340, 342

PLACES AND PEOPLES

Achaemaenids, 72. *See also* Persians
Aegean, 39, 41–43, 271, 275–76,
    282–85, 289–90, 292, 294–96, 298
    (n. 7), 299 (nn. 14, 16), 317, 426
Africa, 32, 43, 45, 50, 63, 95–96, 103–6,
    111, 113–14, 117, 122, 124, 133–34,
    136, 141–42, 145–51, 155–57, 159,
    171, 209, 293, 335, 404, 409, 411, 420,
    422–23, 428–30, 439, 442, 448–49,
    453; North, 66, 79, 84, 120, 127–28,
    271; West, 98, 105, 106
African-Americans, and Egypt, 171;
    oral traditions among, 352; vital cul-
    ture of, 420. *See also* "Subjects": Afro-
    centrism
Africans, in antiquity, 103–4, 112–16,

125; modern notions of, 6–9, 111,
    117–21; pigmentation, 32, 65, 81,
    112–15, 118, 120–27, 128 (nn. 1, 3),
    148–49, 274, 394, 448; tropical, 65;
    sub-Saharan, 66, 98; descriptions of,
    112, 114–16, 118, 123, 128 (n. 1),
    134, 148–54, 159, 163 (n. 18); as
    "Negroes," 358, 369–72, 378–79, 399
    (n. 52), 448; in slave trade, 366, 397
    (nn. 33, 36)
Ahhiyawa, 92, 325
Akkadians, 64, 439
Alexandria, 7, 9, 121, 123–24, 127
Algeria, 66, 142, 145, 146
Amarna, 170, 171, 275
Americans, native, 366, 378, 393

Americas, 77, 98, 422–23
Anatolia, 72, 74–76, 84, 92, 100 (n. 31),
    168, 171, 271, 276–77, 283, 299
    (nn. 13, 16), 426, 427, 450
Aramaeans, 84, 169
Argolid, 449
Argos, 204 (n. 15), 336, 339–42, 344
Arzawa, 56, 59
Ashanti, 105
Asia, 73–74, 103, 105–6, 140, 345,
    422–23
Asiatics, 72–73, 76
Assyria, 56, 59, 426
Assyrians, 64, 82, 83, 85
Athens, 8, 16, 20, 74, 97, 193–94, 270,
    280, 289, 341–43, 404; Athenians, 2,
    179, 194–96, 272, 341–43, 346
Aswan, 89, 107
Atlantis, 317–18
Australia, 422
Avaris (Tell el-Dabʻa), 33, 76–77,
    88–89, 93, 169, 171, 276–77, 284,
    320. See also Hyksos

Babylonia, 56, 59, 82, 90, 215, 217, 220,
    222, 426, 450; Babylonians, 222,
    437–39, 441
Badarians, 65–66, 96
Baghdad, 76, 89
Balkans, 152–53, 283
Benin, 349, 394
Berbers, 67, 105, 179, 273
Black Sea, 72, 82, 83
Boeotia, 18, 29, 76–79, 190, 273, 275.
    See also Kopais; Thebes
Buhen, 74, 88
Byblos, 33, 41, 43, 54, 67, 74, 81, 91,
    95–97, 171

Cairo, 131, 153, 229
Canaan, 75; Canaanites, 183, 190, 192,
    194, 195, 278, 440, 442, 449
Cape Gelidonya, 92, 283
Carthage, 13–14, 124–25, 408, 409
Caucasus, 283, 393; Caucasian, 378, 448

Chaldaeans, 360, 438
China, 77, 85, 155, 164 (n. 33), 422, 440;
    history, 98, 440
Christians, 64, 79, 417–18
Cnossus. See Knossos
Colchis, 72, 82–83, 191, 310–13
Congo, 145, 149
Constantinople, 97, 435
Copais. See Kopais
Crete, 51–52, 54–56, 59–60, 74, 76,
    80–82, 85, 89–95, 98, 170, 186, 190,
    271–72, 274–77, 282–83, 288, 290,
    295, 298 (nn. 6, 12). See also Minoans
Cyprus, 91–92, 170, 271, 295, 426
Cyrenaica, 94, 271
Cyrene, 120, 193

Danaoi, 92, 325
Deir el-Bahri, 108, 109
Delta. See Nile
Dorak, 76–77, 81
Dravidians, 83

East Asia, 184
Ebla, 67, 96–97
Egypt: history and myth, 7–21 passim;
    influence in the Aegean, 27–34,
    40–47, 48 (nn. 1, 4); during Bronze
    Age, 49–61 passim; history of, 62–99
    passim; archaic, 68, 71; archaeology
    and anthropology of, 103–17 passim,
    120–30 passim, 140–48, 153–59,
    162, 164 (n. 33); "race" of, 103–119
    passim, 122–25, 127 (n. 3), 130, 132,
    136, 138, 140, 142, 145, 147, 151, 153,
    155–59, 162, 163 (n. 18); and the
    Near East, 168–72; scientific achieve-
    ments of, 212–25 passim, 227–41
    passim, 249, 251–55, 256 (n. 5), 257
    (n. 16), 258 (nn. 19, 20), 260 (n. 40),
    261 (nn. 44, 46), 262 (nn. 54, 58), 263
    (n. 68), 264 (nn. 70, 76), 265 (n. 80);
    Egyptians and Greeks, 269–89 pas-
    sim, 292–96, 297 (n. 2), 298 (nn. 5, 7,
    9, 12), 299 (n. 13), 300 (n. 21), 305–7,

309–10, 312–20, 323–24, 327, 328
(n. 7), 329 (n. 10); historiography of,
334–42, 345–46, 349–61 passim,
363–66, 374, 376–78, 384, 386–88,
390–91, 394 (nn. 5, 6), 395 (nn. 14,
15), 396 (nn. 26, 27), 397 (nn. 33, 34),
402 (n. 76), 406–7, 411–12, 418–19,
429–31, 435–42, 447–52. *See also*
"Subjects": Dynasty I–VIII

Elam, 83
Elephantine, 69, 72–73, 87
El-Kurru, 110–11
England, 25, 70, 99, 142, 145, 162,
183–84, 275, 369, 382, 390–91, 408,
415–16, 418, 429, 431
Ephesos, 438
Ethiopia, 67, 105, 123, 311, 362, 391,
422; Ethiopians, 84, 112–15, 118–19,
121, 123–24, 126, 128 (n. 3)
Etruria, 389
Euphrates, 86, 90, 426, 437
Europe, 63, 84, 129, 136, 140–42,
145–46, 151, 210, 223, 404, 418–20,
422–23, 427

Fayum, 75
France, 184, 351

Gebel Barkal, 110–11
Gelidonya, 283
Germans: universities, 372, 375, 386;
perceived affinity with Greeks,
403–8, 410, 418
Giza, 105, 108, 130–32, 134, 142–43,
145–46, 154
Göttingen, 366, 375–78, 380–85,
400–401 (nn. 55, 66)
Greece (Hellas): ancient, 3–22, 269–330
passim, 413–16; Greco-Egyptian
culture, 17, 311; and Egypt, 49–61
passim, 80–86, 89–97; language of,
78–80, 177–205 passim; Greco-
Roman culture, 79, 118, 123–25, 127;
and blacks, 121–28; modern, 171,
364; history of, 284–86; "invasions"

of, 285–88, 319–26, 337–39; ideas
of, in eighteenth century, 354–57,
359–66, 403–7; ideas of, in nineteenth century, 416–19; and Near
East, 422–27; ideas of, in twentieth
century, 428–29. *See also* "Subjects":
Languages, Coptic

Habur valley, 438
Harappan culture, 63, 80
Haunebut, 55
Hekla, 83–85, 97, 99 (n. 27)
Hittites, 63, 83, 85, 92–95, 97, 179, 185,
203, 438–39, 441
Hurrians, 46, 88, 273, 277, 438, 439, 441
Hyksos, 15–16, 18–19, 23 (n. 7), 30,
33, 46, 51, 54, 60, 63, 76–77, 79–81,
84–90, 95, 98, 167, 169–70, 178,
189–91, 276–77, 281–84, 286, 293,
295, 298 (nn. 5, 7), 301 (n. 30), 302
(n. 31), 309–10, 318–20, 325–26, 329
(n. 11), 449; etymology of, 16, 277,
310, 342

Iceland, 84, 97
India, 63, 65, 77, 91, 136, 140–42, 150,
155, 157, 216, 290
Indo-China, 440
Indus Valley, 63, 77, 80, 91–92, 97–98
Iran, 63, 184, 426
Israel, 136, 169, 171, 271, 276, 340, 423,
441
Istanbul, 435
Italy, 116, 122–23, 126, 271, 340, 409

Jebel Moya, 105, 106
Jerusalem, 227
Jews, 62, 170–71, 173, 174 (n. 5), 441.
See also "Subjects": Anti-Semitism
Jordan, 192, 271

Kabri, Tell, 169, 276, 284
Kaphtor, 170
Karnak, 85
Kassites, 63, 85, 90

Keftiu, 91, 170, 274, 275, 298 (n. 6);
    Kefty, 55. *See also* Crete
Kerma, 41, 73, 75, 81, 88–89, 100
    (n. 35), 110–11
Kmt (Red Land, Egypt), 104
Knossos, 4, 18, 290, 295, 432
Kopais, 76–78, 190, 192, 275, 323
Kush, 41, 47, 53–54, 70, 72–76, 67,
    80–82, 96–97, 110, 124, 273–75, 277;
    Kushites, 73, 75–76, 81, 83, 86–89,
    91, 96, 110–12, 115, 121, 274

Lacedaemon (Laconia), 193, 197
Laris(s)a, 190–91
Lebanon, 53, 56, 97, 271
Levant, 34, 49, 51, 55, 59, 62–63, 76, 80,
    85, 89, 91–95, 98, 99 (n. 13), 169–71,
    177, 183, 270, 277, 294, 296, 324, 335,
    422, 424, 426–27, 450
Libya, 190–91, 271–72, 274, 282;
    Libyans, 94, 272, 278
Luv(w)ians, 179, 439
Luxor, 134. *See also* Thebes

Macedonia, 172, 174 (n. 16), 190
Media, 426. *See also* Persia
Memphis, 69, 87, 125, 170, 300 (n. 20),
    315, 391
Meroë, 111
Mesopotamia, 34, 44, 62–65, 68, 76–77,
    85–86, 96–98, 103, 183, 216, 233, 258
    (n. 19), 271, 426; Mesopotamian cul-
    ture, 34, 62, 65, 67–68, 80, 91–92,
    95–96, 210, 214, 216, 235, 264 (n. 70),
    437
Minoans, 29–30, 33, 90, 93, 169–70,
    276, 278, 283–85, 288, 290, 295, 299,
    300, 315, 319, 450
Mittani, 56, 59
Mycenae, 4, 10, 29–30, 52, 60, 74,
    89–92, 100 (n. 31), 193, 282, 288–89,
    293, 295, 298 (n. 7), 300, 301 (n. 30),
    319–20, 326, 432; Mycenaean culture,
    80, 84, 90–92, 94–95, 168

Nag Hammadi, 104
Naissus, 435
Napata, 83, 122
Naqada, 65–68, 76, 96, 100 (n. 36), 106,
    132, 134, 136, 140, 142–43, 145–46,
    148
Near East, 18, 27–40 passim, 42–47, 48
    (nn. 4, 13), 50, 64, 77, 82, 86, 88–89,
    92, 95, 99 (n. 29), 103–4, 111, 167–
    69, 172–73, 174 (n. 14), 186, 216, 223,
    256, 261 (n. 51), 271–75, 282, 284–
    86, 290, 293–94, 300 (n. 18), 325, 344,
    346, 415, 422–23, 425–26, 430, 435–
    39, 442, 449, 450, 452–53
Nigeria, 349
Nile, 64–67, 73, 84, 96, 103–5, 107,
    110–11, 113–14, 128–32, 134, 136,
    146–47, 149, 152–56, 158–59, 162,
    169–70, 276–77, 448
Nuba Hills, 67
Nubia, 32, 38, 47, 53–54, 59–60, 73–76,
    80, 86–87, 96–97, 107–10, 113, 115,
    117, 121–23, 136, 141, 145–47, 153,
    156, 271, 274, 442; Nubian culture,
    67, 69, 73, 75, 86, 88, 95–97, 100
    (n. 35), 107–8, 111–13, 115–16, 121–
    23, 125, 127, 274–75, 278; A-Group,
    97, 109; C-Group, 110
Nubt, 96, 100 (n. 36)

Orchomenus, 432

Palestine, 53–56, 61, 72–73, 105–6, 271,
    302 (n. 36), 426, 450
Paris, 357–58, 381–82, 390–91, 395
    (n. 16)
Pelasgians, 340–41, 348 (n. 7)
Persia, 64, 386, 422, 426–27
Phoenicia, 10, 11, 270, 286, 335, 346,
    352, 435, 436, 449–52; Phoenicians,
    33, 62, 79, 177, 188, 204 (n. 8), 334–
    36, 339–40, 346, 411–12, 414, 416,
    429–31, 435, 437–42, 447, 449, 450
Punt, 54, 74, 97, 108
Pylos, 275

SUBJECTS

"Revised," 14, 17, 50, 178, 187–89, 193, 201, 350

Anthropology, 131, 138, 149, 155, 158, 292; physical, 131, 138, 162 (n. 1)

Anti-Semitism, 62–63, 269, 272, 280, 404, 422, 429, 431, 432, 435, 439, 443, 447, 450, 451, 453

Arianism, 363

"Arrogance, cultural," 50, 412–13, 419, 420, 452. *See also* Eurocentrism

"Aryan Model," 13, 19, 62, 63, 65, 67, 68, 95, 97, 290, 334, 337, 347, 349, 350, 351, 364, 371, 389, 390, 396 (n. 20), 398 (n. 46), 422, 430, 439, 441. *See also* Language: Indo-European

Astrology, 214, 225, 257, 388

Astronomy, 36, 43, 209–57 passim, 450

Autochthony, 9, 450

Barbarians (foreigners), 7, 10, 12, 76, 80, 91, 94, 95, 96, 100 (n. 34), 343. *See also* Ethnicity

Besserwissen, 304–6, 310–11

Bible, 65, 172; flood in, 64, 86

Biological determinants, 129, 149–54, 159

Blacks. *See* Africans

Book of the Dead, 8, 23 (n. 4)

Bronze Age, 38, 49–56, 55–56, 59–61, 177, 187, 192, 270, 271, 272, 275–76, 278; late, 80, 89, 92, 94, 100 (n. 31)

Bull cult, 51, 82, 275

"Cadmean letters," 326

Calendar, 71, 213, 216–18, 223, 225, 255, 258 (n. 18), 374, 390

Captives, 76, 83, 94

Catalogue of Women, 337–38, 342

Cattle. *See* Domestic animals

Cedar, 67–68, 74, 96–97

Ceramics, 66–67, 81, 90–92

Chariot technology, 63, 76, 88

Chronology, 18, 29, 36, 37, 68–69, 86–88, 97, 99 (n. 28), 167, 189, 216, 233, 276, 287, 298 (n. 7), 317, 326–27,

363, 387–88, 396 (n. 26), 414, 417; and carbon 14, 68–69, 71, 97; Royal canon of Turin, 69, 71, 75–76, 86–87, 99 (n. 31); Sothic, 69, 71, 87; dendro-chronology, 69, 83, 97; low, 72; high, 86; lunar, 87; Greek, 269, 326. *See also* Calendar

Circumcision, 21, 82

Clay tokens, 68, 96. *See also* Literacy

Clepsydra (water-clock), 223, 251

Climate, 12, 66, 67, 84–85, 92, 114, 392. *See also* Volcanoes

Clines, 129, 150, 159, 162 (n. 1)

Clusters, 129, 134, 136, 139, 140–42, 145, 149, 150, 152, 159, 162 (n. 1); regional, 134, 136, 140, 142, 150, 152

Colonization, 44, 49, 50, 53, 55, 60, 79, 91, 95, 422, 426, 430, 432, 435, 438, 440, 449, 450; decolonization, 423

Comparative method, 180, 182, 202, 205 (n. 22)

"Competitive plausibility," 275, 292, 450, 452; and probability, 50, 56

Consonants, 182, 185, 192, 194, 200–202, 205 (n. 23)

Conspiracy theory, 424, 428–29, 438

Craniometry, 63, 105, 131

Creation epics, 64, 86

Cubit, 227, 236–37, 263 (n. 64)

Cultures, comparison of, 11–13, 15, 17, 21–22, 373, 415, 418–20, 425; exchange among, 19

Cuneiform, 64, 96, 177, 273, 277, 284, 290, 297 (n. 1), 299

Dark Ages, 85, 285, 287, 296, 300

Deism, 363

Desert, 66, 84, 96, 97, 100 (n. 36). *See also* "Places and Peoples": Sahara

Determinism, 35, 385

Developmental model, 98

Diffusionism, 41, 68, 97, 98, 310, 328 (n. 5)

Diplomacy, 76, 81, 89–90

Hermeticism, 14, 44, 365

Hero(es), 10, 18, 64, 170, 190, 314, 337, 338, 340, 344, 346, 355, 369–70, 389–90

Hieroglyphics, 64, 130, 155, 177, 202, 273, 394 (n. 6). *See also* Champollion, J. -F.

Hippocratic question, 246

Historical argument, 32, 36, 38, 39, 40–42, 47, 293, 308; objectivity, 5; method, 27, 39, 47, 131, 138–39, 412–13, 421, 424–25, 427; setting, 28; interpretation, 35; hypotheses, 50, 51; "texts," 168–70, 172; grammars, 202; linguistics, 202, 205 (n. 22); progress, 364, 417–19; conditioning, 424

Historiography, 269, 405, 421–25, 431, 435, 440, 443, 451, 453; method, 36, 424; external/internal forces in, 413, 416; principles, 421; classical, 431, 435

History, 61–64, 72, 83, 85, 96–98, 177, 181–82, 196, 200–205, 421–25, 453; politics in, x, 5, 413–14, 416, 419, 422–23, 424, 427; intellectual, 172

Holocaust, the, 22, 408, 412, 443

Homeric Epics, 92, 94; *Iliad*, 269, 337, 340, 344, 347 (n. 5); *Odyssey*, 269, 337, 344, 346, 442. *See also* "Personal Names": Homer

Hydria, 388, 389, 401 (n. 76)

Ideology, 53, 107, 334, 336

Immigration, 18, 20, 422

Imperialism, 35, 335, 422, 430

Inflection, 180, 183, 195

Influence, cultural, 5–6, 8, 15–20, 62, 67–68, 79, 80–82, 91–92, 95, 272, 281, 405, 450

Invasion, 5, 16, 18–20, 23 (n. 7), 53, 281, 281–83

Ionian-Mycenaean population, 92

Iron I-II-III period, 426

Islam, 91

Ka, 316. *See also* Soul

Kingdom: Old, 68–71, 76, 81, 88, 91, 96; Middle, 54, 60, 69–73, 76, 80–83, 88, 91, 97, 168; New, 60, 72, 75, 80, 83, 89–94

Kingship, 63, 95

Knowledge, sociology of, 46, 271

Languages: Linear B, 4, 92, 196, 201, 282–84, 287, 290, 296, 299 (n. 15); Indo-European, 46, 63, 79, 82, 99 (n. 17), 179–80, 183, 185–90, 195–98, 200, 202, 203 (n. 2), 205 (nn. 19, 21), 270, 272, 281, 283–85, 288–90, 294, 299 (nn. 15–16), 411, 413, 439–41, 451; Latin, 63, 179, 180–82, 184–85, 202, 203 (n. 4); Coptic, 64, 67, 78, 79, 392; Akkadian, 64, 177, 179, 183; Persian, 64, 179, 184–85; Demotic, 64–65, 78–79; Tuareg, 67; Afro-Asiatic, 67, 79, 96, 104–5, 179, 191, 195, 449–51; Chadic, 67, 105; Omotic, 67, 105; Egyptian, 78–79, 94, 104–5, 177–205 passim; Semitic, 78–79, 179–203, 281, 284, 290, 295, 299 (nn. 15–16), 417; Hebrew, 91, 179, 202, 204 (n. 14), 428; Linear A, 92, 186, 203 (n. 6), 284–85, 294, 299 (n. 15); Bantu, 105; Galla, 105; Arabic, 105, 170, 179, 183–85, 205 (n. 20); Greek, 177–205 passim; Doric, 179; Hindi, 179; Indo-Afro-Asiatic, 179; Lydian, 179; Russian, 179, 183, 197; Anatolian, 179, 184, 194, 203 (n. 2); Celtic, 179, 184, 202; Sanskrit, 179–83, 185, 196–97, 199; Indo-European (PIE), 180–82, 195–99, 203 (n. 3); Armenian, 182–84, 198; Chinese, 184–85, 188; Eteo-cretan, 186; Hungarian, 202; families of, 202, 381–82; Indo-Hittite, 203

Lapis lazuli, 67, 96, 97

Legacy, 3, 7, 8, 17, 20, 22

Linguistics, 177–203; as history, 4, 6, 10–11, 16–17, 19–22, 49, 362, 376–

Pythagorean problem, 233; theorem, 237–38, 242–43, 261 (n. 44), 437; triples, 238, 239, 242, 255

Quellenkritik (source criticism), 382–85, 400 (n. 72)

Race, 7, 19, 30, 32, 46, 62, 103–64 passim, 448, 452–53; theories of, 380, 386, 392–3, 398 (nn. 38, 39), 399 (nn. 49, 50, 52, 54), 422–26, 452
Racism, 31, 44, 130, 147, 155, 278, 288–91, 294, 300 (n. 8), 349–94 passim, 405, 411, 413–19, 429, 431, 432, 435, 439, 443, 447, 450, 451, 453; in Europe, 62; antiracism, 364, 366, 367, 368; in America, 365–67, 370–71; "scientific," 366–67
Reconstruction, in U.S.A., 368
Rectangles, 238
Religion, 6, 10–12, 14, 18–19, 37, 43, 45, 51–53, 91, 313–15, 320, 329 (n. 9), 345, 387, 415
Renaissance, 64, 423
Rig-Veda, 185
Romantic(ism), 28, 43, 269, 364–65, 396 (n. 20), 401 (nn. 66–67), 404, 416–19, 422, 433, 404–5
Rosetta Stone, 64
Royal Annals, 69, 96

Scenarios, hypothetical, 167–72
Scholarship, 30, 35, 40, 42, 50, 422; classical, 3, 4, 5, 30–31, 44, 92, 95, 413; Near Eastern, 28, 33–39, 42, 45–47, 103; French, 66
Scribes, 68, 70, 96
Second stela, 77, 89
Semantics, 187–99 passim. *See also* Linguistics
Semicylinder, 234, 241
Semiticists, 437
Seqenenre and Apophis, The Story of, 89
Shadow kings, 86, 88

Shaft graves, 29, 30, 51, 275, 277, 282–83, 288, 293, 295, 298 (n. 7), 301 (n. 30), 319–20
Shipwrecks, 33, 92
Silver, 74, 97
Sinuhe, Story of, 73, 80, 91
Six Day War, 441
Slavery, 62, 350, 353, 358, 366–70, 372–73, 380, 396 (n. 22), 397 (nn. 36, 37), 398 (nn. 38, 39), 399 (n. 52). *See also* "Places and Peoples": Africans, in slave trade
Sophists, 413
Sothic. *See* Chronology
Soul, 315–16. *See also* Metempsychosis
Sounds. *See* Linguistics: phonemes
Species, 380, 386, 392, 393, 399 (n. 50)
Statue bases. *See* Evidence
Stone Age, 271
Sun, 212, 218, 220–23, 255, 259 (n. 33); ecliptic of, 222, 259 (n. 25)

Teaching of Amenemhet, 73
Technology, 349, 394 (n. 1)
Ten Lost Tribes, 82
Trade, 11–12, 19–20, 33, 53–54, 60, 67, 74–97 passim, 278; sea, 81, 91, 97; slave, 368, 380, 398 (n. 44), 399 (n. 54)
Transmigration of souls. *See* Metempsychosis
Tribute, 73, 74, 90
Trojan War, 10, 272, 327
Twice-times table, 228

Unit fractions, 229, 235, 256, 260 (n. 33), 262 (n. 53)

Viziers, 70, 75, 86, 90
Volcanoes, 84, 85, 97. *See also* "Places and Peoples": Thera
Vowels, 180–82, 185, 199–200, 202, 204 (nn. 8, 16)

Indexes : 521